BOUNDARIES, POSSESSIONS, AND CONFLICTS
IN SOUTH AMERICA

LONDON : HUMPHREY MILFORD

OXFORD UNIVERSITY PRESS

CHRIST OF THE ANDES

BOUNDARIES, POSSESSIONS, AND CONFLICTS IN SOUTH AMERICA

BY

GORDON IRELAND

Sometime Assistant Professor of Latin-American Law, Harvard Law School
Lately Professor of Civil and Latin-American Law, Louisiana State
University Law School

CAMBRIDGE, MASSACHUSETTS
HARVARD UNIVERSITY PRESS
1938

103682
F
2236
I66

The Bureau of International Research of Harvard University and Radcliffe College has aided the author in carrying on research and in publishing the results, but assumes no responsibility for the views expressed.

PRINTED AT THE HARVARD UNIVERSITY PRESS
CAMBRIDGE, MASS., U.S.A.

PREFACE

THIS book represents an attempt to present in a single volume the factual story of the boundary disputes which have constituted so large a proportion of the international problems of the South American republics for over a hundred years. The material has been built together from sentences, paragraphs, and chapters scattered in hundreds of books and distilled from the bulky reports of a dozen arbitrations, with the constant endeavor to approach the ideal of a compilation at once easy to read and useful to consult. The historical background has been strictly limited to matters that seemed to bear directly upon the boundary problems, excluding almost entirely the incessant internal factional troubles and numerous temporary diplomatic incidents. Pecuniary claims by another nation, whether or not arbitrated, if not resulting in any overt unfriendly act beyond severance of relations, have been uniformly omitted. In no sense a general history, everything not relevant to boundary questions has thus been elided; in no degree a legal treatise, arguments on and generalizations from international law principles have been avoided; and in no way, fashion, or form propaganda for or against any nation or notion, earnest endeavor has been made to present every situation unemotionally and impartially. No two compilers probably would make exactly the same selections or treat them in the same way, but it is hoped that for five or ten who would have left out something that has been put in, there may be but one or two who know of anything omitted that should properly have been included. The profusion of notes arises at least in part from the double purpose they serve of indicating authority for the facts stated and of suggesting starting places for those who may desire to obtain further light on a particular point. The names and spellings used for institutions, men, and places have been chosen with regard for what seemed most likely under actual conditions to impart readiest comprehension and fullest understanding, rather than to be inflexibly consistent with the usage of any single authority. Once chosen, the form is intended to be kept constant with itself throughout the work. Proper names are given in full usually only the first time of mentioning; and places have sometimes been designated too early by the names by which they have come to be generally known, where the anachronism can cause no misapprehension.

Grateful acknowledgment is due to the Bureau of International Research, Harvard University and Radcliffe College, for the ten months' grant which made possible this study. Sincere and enduring gratitude is proffered Professor George Grafton Wilson, the former Chairman of the Bureau, for warm, friendly interest at all stages of the work and sage and inspiring advice on doubtful points, and to Professor Sidney B. Fay, present Chairman, for support, encouragement, and assistance in putting the book through the press. Grateful mention should also be made of several who have assisted in the more mechanical labors incidental to this production: Miss Agnes F. Barclay of the Library Staff of the Harvard Law School, patient, persistent, and successful in locating elusive volumes; Mrs. Margaret Greninger of Cambridge, secretary and expert typist for the creative period, efficient even amid stress and storm; Messrs. Francis J. Sullivan of Erie, Pa., and Richard C. Cox, Jr., of Cambridge for willing, devoted, and skillful preparation of the original maps. Express acknowledgment and thanks are due to Mr. E. Prada, Town Clerk of Port-of-Spain, Trinidad, B.W.I., for efficient and friendly search of and quotation from the records of the municipality; and to the Foreign Ministries of the Republics of Bolivia, Brazil, Chile, Colombia, Ecuador, Mexico, Peru, and Venezuela for prompt and courteous replies to inquiries concerning various treaties.

GORDON IRELAND

Cambridge, Mass.
  October, 1937

CONTENTS

I. DISPUTES AND ADJUSTMENTS

LIST OF MAPS

BOUNDARIES, POSSESSIONS, AND CONFLICTS
IN SOUTH AMERICA

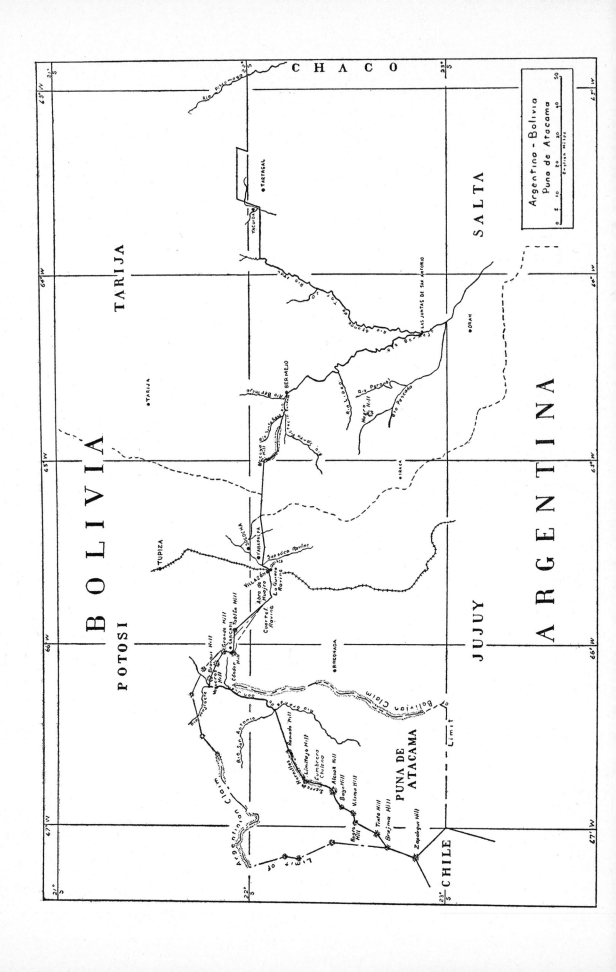

CHAPTER I

DISPUTES AND ADJUSTMENTS

1. Argentina–Bolivia. Puna de Atacama

THE FOUR provinces of Upper Peru which the General Congress of the Provinces of the Plata declared on May 9, 1825, were free to dispose of their own future had with the other eight of the viceroyalty of the Plata been last described in a royal order of Charles III on August 22, 1783. The intendency of Cochabamba was to be composed of the then existing gobiernos of Santa Cruz de la Sierra and of the city of Cochabamba; and the district of Potosí included all the territory belonging to the province of Porco, in which it lay, and those of Atacama, Chayanta, Chichos, Lipes, and Tarija. The gobierno of Santa Cruz de la Sierra was then the bishopric of the same name, exclusive of the missions of Mojos and Chiquitos, which had been separated from that bishopric on August 5, 1777, and put under the viceroy of Buenos Aires and so continued under the Intendents Ordinance of January 28, 1782, and the Royal Cédula of August 5, 1783. Another royal cédula of February 17, 1807, transferred Tarija from the archbishopric of Charcas to the newly created bishopric of Salta, but whether for spiritual purposes only or for temporal government as well was disputed. Atacama formed part of the intendency of Salta, and was defended by it from the Spaniards in Upper Peru in 1816; but in 1825 when Upper Peru had been wholly freed, General Miller, the acting president of the department of Potosí, in whose district it lay, claimed Atacama from General Juan Antonio Alvarez de Arenales, governor of Salta, and without waiting for Arenales' response issued orders to the commander of the district of Atacama. General Arenales on August 6, 1825, protested to General Miller and complained to Bolívar, then commanding in Peru, who ruled on November 17, 1825, that Tarija and Atacama were apparently both included under the law of May 9, 1825, and therefore free to make their own provisions. The councilors of Tarija voted to join Upper Peru, and the Bolivian Congress by a law of October 3, 1826, declined to consider further demands from Salta and declared the matter closed. The sparsely settled Atacama was taken also to be a part of Bolivia without further question.

The treaty of friendship, commerce, and navigation between Argentina and Bolivia signed by Colonel Quintín Quevedo, Bolivian minister, and Dr. Rufino de Elizalde, Argentine minister of foreign relations, at Buenos Aires on July 9, 1868,[1] provided (Article 20) that the boundaries between the two countries should be arranged by a special convention and commissioners appointed by both parties to present the project or projects for the boundary line, and that any points respecting the boundaries on which questions might arise which could not be amicably arranged between the parties should be submitted to the arbitration of a friendly nation; until demarcation was made, possession was to confer no right to territories which did not belong in the first instance to either nation. Bolivia, however, felt that the boundary question should be settled more definitely, and that postponement might be prejudicial to her interests, the more especially as it was recited in Article 16 of the Treaty of May 1, 1865,[2] under which the Triple Alliance was then waging war with Paraguay, that the Gran Chaco and all the west bank of the Paraguay as far as Bahia Negra belonged exclusively to Argentina. The Bolivian Assembly accordingly rejected the Treaty of 1868 until Article 20 should be modified; and, after negotiations, a protocol was signed by Quevedo and Dr. Mariano Varela, Argentine minister of foreign relations, at Buenos Aires on February 27, 1869,[3] which canceled Article 20 and substituted for it a provision that the question of boundaries should be settled by a special convention after the termination of the war with Paraguay, any difficulties which might arise being settled by the arbitration of a friendly nation provided the parties could not arrive at an agreement upon them.

As soon as the war with Paraguay ended, in 1870, Bolivia requested Argentina to dispose of the boundary question, and after some incidents on the Chaco frontier Mariano Reyes Cardona, Bolivian minister, and Carlos Tejedor, Argentine minister of foreign relations, signed at Buenos Aires on August 29, 1872,[4] a preliminary protocol which provided that neither country should advance its lines of actual occupation in the Chaco until a final agreement could be reached, but saying nothing about the rest of the boundary. Negotiations continued, but no further agreement could then be reached.

The 1872 protocol, instead of settling the boundary, gave rise by reason

[1] *Tratados Vigentes, 1825-1925* (Bolivia, 1925), I, 21-35. 72 *British and Foreign State Papers* 601-608. Ratifications exchanged at Buenos Aires, Sept. 24, 1869; promulgated by Bolivia, Dec. 28, 1869.

[2] *U. S. Dipl. Corr.*, 1866-67, Part II, pp. 576-578. 55 *British and Foreign State Papers* 83-87. Martens, *Nouv. Rec. Gén. de Traités*, XX, 601-606. *Arch. Dipl.*, 1868, IV,

1692-1696. Martens et Cussy, *Rec. Man. et Prat. de Traités* (Leipzig, 1885), 2e Sér., I, 325-329.

[3] *Trat. Vig.* (Bolivia, 1925), I, 36-40. 72 *British and Foreign State Papers* 608-611. Approved by Argentine Law #297, July 20, 1869.

[4] Samuel Oropeza, *Límites entre la República de Bolivia y la República Argentina* (Sucre, 1892), pp. 144-145.

of the vagueness of its terms to further claims and discussion. Argentina contended that the territory of the viceroyalty of the Plata ran to meet the grant of Diego Hernández de Zerpa on the upper Amazon, and that the eastern boundary of Upper Peru was then the Parapiti or San Miguel de Chiquitos, leaving Argentina with a right to all of the Mojos and Chiquitos territories and the provinces of Santa Cruz and Tarija; and the dispute raged in articles and pamphlets [5] by Argentine and Bolivian writers from 1872 to 1888. Finally a *modus vivendi* was adopted by a protocol signed by Norberto Quirno Costa, Argentine minister of foreign relations, and Santiago Vaca Guzmán, Bolivian minister, at Buenos Aires on June 5, 1888,[6] which selected the 22° parallel as far as its intersection with the Pilcomayo as a provisional boundary in the Chaco, Bolivia to have jurisdiction to the north and Argentina to the south, Bolivia to come to an understanding with Paraguay in all that related to a determination of their territorial limits; outside the Chaco where Bolivia bordered on Argentina each government was not to advance beyond its actual possessions; the provisional arrangement was to imply no renunciation as to the territory to which either party might lay claim; conferences to determine the boundary definitely were to begin in November, 1888, or before if possible. Continued negotiations at Buenos Aires by the same ministers resulted in the signature by Vaca Guzmán and Costa on May 10, 1889,[7] of a treaty purposing to put an end to the controversy which had lasted so many years. The boundary was fixed in Article 1: in the territory of Atacama, to follow the cordillera of the same name from the head of the Diablo ravine to the northwest by the east branch of the same cordillera to where the Zapalegui ridge begins; from this point the line continues to the Esmoraca ridge along the highest summits until it reaches the western head of La Quiaca ravine, thence descending by this ravine to its opening onto the Yanapalpa, and thence straight from west to east to the peak of the hill of Porongal; thence descending to the western source of the Porongal river and by its waters to its confluence with the Bermejo river opposite Bermejo town; from this point down the Bermejo to its confluence with the Rio Grande de Tarija, or the town of Las Juntas de San Antonio; from Las Juntas up the Tarija to the mouth of the Itaú, and thence by the waters of the Itaú to the 22° parallel and by such parallel to the waters of the Pilcomayo. Demarcation of this

[5] Manuel Ricardo Trelles, *Cuestión de Límites entre la República Argentina y Bolivia* (Buenos Aires, 1872). Julio Méndez, *Límites Argentino-Bolivianos en Tarija* (La Paz, 1888).

[6] Samuel Oropeza, *Límites entre la República de Bolivia y la República Argentina* (Sucre, 1892), pp. 150–151. 79

British and Foreign State Papers 832–833. Approved by president of Argentina, Aug. 1, 1888.

[7] *Tratados de Argentina*, Pub. Ofic. (Buenos Aires, 1901), I, 343–346. *Trat. Vig.* (Bolivia, 1925), I, 52–56, 60. 106 *British and Foreign State Papers* 823–824.

line was to be made as soon as possible by two experts, one named by each party, differences between them to be settled by a third named by agreement of both parties; and any question arising by reason of this agreement or for any other cause to be submitted to the decision of a friendly power, the boundaries fixed by the treaty to be in any case immovable. Argentine public opinion was not satisfied,[8] and Congress on November 12, 1891,[9] approved the treaty only with a modification of the western part of the line as set forth in Article 1, to run: on the west, by the highest peaks of the cordillera of the Andes from the northernmost point of the boundary of Argentina with Chile to the intersection with the 23° parallel, thence along such parallel to its intersection with the highest point of the Zapalegui ridge; and thence as in the treaty. The Bolivian Congress after some delay approved [10] the treaty as thus modified, perhaps as a token of friendship for Argentina, perhaps not valuing the region very highly and not wishing it to fall into the hands of the victor in the War of the Pacific. Following the exchange of ratifications at Buenos Aires on March 10, 1893, arrangements were started by a protocol signed at Buenos Aires, June 26, 1894,[11] for marking the line. By this treaty, and Argentina's success in moving the west line from the ridge of the eastern branch of the cordillera to the highest peaks, which lay in the western branch, Bolivia lost the intermontane plateau of the Puna de Atacama, which became the Argentine territory of Los Andes.[12]

Bolivia made with Argentina on June 30, 1894,[13] an agreement for an extension of the North Central Railroad across the frontier and a connection from La Quiaca through Villazón and Tupiza to Uyuni, Oruro, and La Paz. Argentina was to lend up to 50 per cent of the costs of construction in Bolivian territory, to be secured by receipts of the road, but the financial arrangements were modified several times.[14] The work was carried on from both sides, and through service for the 1,400 miles between La Paz and Buenos Aires began in 1925.

Demarcation of the boundary on paper was completed by an interna-

[8] Samuel Oropeza, *Límites entre la República de Bolivia y la República Argentina* (Sucre, 1892).

[9] Law #2851. Da Rocha, *Col. Com. de Leyes Nac.* (Buenos Aires, 1918), IX, 368–369. *Trat. Vig.* (Bolivia, 1925), I, 56–58. 106 *British and Foreign State Papers* 824–825.

[10] Law of Sept. 15, 1892; Decree of Jan. 2, 1893. *Anuario de Leyes*, 1892 (La Paz, 1893), pp. 342–346. *Trat. Vig.* (Bolivia, 1925), I, 58–59.

[11] *Trat. de Argentina* (Buenos Aires, 1901), I, 392–393.

[12] Law #3906, Jan. 13, 1900. *Reg. Nac. de la Rep. Argentina*, 1900, pp. 17–18. Further cession by the province of Salta, Law #4059, Jan. 18, 1902. Da Rocha, *Col. Comp. de Leyes Nac.* (Buenos Aires, 1918), XII, 602.

[13] *Trat. Vig.* (Bolivia, 1925), I, 61–68. Martens, *Nouv. Rec. Gén. de Traités*, 3e Sér., VI, 293–295. *Arch. Dipl.*, 3e Sér., CXXIV, 51–60. Ratifications exchanged at Sucre, Dec. 14, 1895.

[14] *Trat. Vig.* (Bolivia, 1925), I, 79–89, 93–106; *ibid.*, III, Apen. 3–7. 100 *British and Foreign State Papers* 604–605. *Rev. de Der. Int.* (Havana), IV (1923), 466–470; *ibid.*, V (1924), 175–179. Martens, *Nouv. Rec. Gén. de Traités*, 3e Sér., VI (1913), 296–297, 774–775; *ibid.*, X (1920), 272–273.

tional commission on March 24, 1899, and numerous protocols were signed to remove the difficulties with the actual placing of posts as they arose, but the setting of marks was suspended on October 20, 1902. A protocol signed by Claudio Pinilla, Bolivian minister of foreign relations, and Dr. Dardo Rocha, Argentine minister, at La Paz on September 15, 1911,[15] provided for the appointment by each government within six months of the expert required by the Treaty of 1889, the experts to meet in Salta on May 15, 1912, and proceed to the boundary to renew the demarcation; and it was actually resumed in 1913. On January 4, 1919,[16] there was signed at Buenos Aires a convention as to the frontier in the Chaco, providing for coöperation by the frontier police garrisons to prevent fugitives from justice or armed bands from either side obtaining refuge across the border and permitting hot pursuit except for political crimes, with immediate notice and surrender of the captives to the country in whose territory they were taken, pending extradition.

The line described in 1891 proved very difficult actually to locate on the ground, because of the geographical misconceptions which it perpetuated.[17] The highest point of the Zapalegui ridge proved to lie north of the 23° parallel. From Zapalegui to the Esmoraca ridge along the highest summits to the western head of La Quiaca ravine was thought by the Argentine commissioner to run along a ridge called Azulejos and Rupascayo on the left (north) bank of the San Juan and by the Bolivian commissioner to run along the ridge designated by the name of Esmoraca on the map in the atlas of Dr. V. Martin de Moussy on the right (south) bank of the same river. La Quiaca ravine does not open onto the Yanapalpa, but joins the Toro-Ara and Sansana ravines to become San Mateo ravine, which changes to the Torohuaico ravine and opens onto the Sococha, as the Yanapalpa is called from above its confluence with the Torohuaico. The Argentine commissioner maintained that the line should run down La Quiaca, San Mateo, and Torohuaico ravines to the Sococha and up the Sococha to the Yanapalpa ravine, carrying into Argentina the town of Sococha and the village of Yanapalpa, while the Bolivian commissioner would run the line from the junction of La Quiaca and Toro-Ara ravines to the head of La Raya ravine and down that to the Yanapalpa, leaving the town of Sococha and the village of Yanapalpa to Bolivia. Porongal hill was taken by the Argentine commissioner to mean Mecoya hill at 22°5'11″ S. 64°59'54″ W., and by the Bolivian commissioner to mean

[15] Trat. Vig. (Bolivia, 1925), I, 90–93. Approved by the Bolivian Cabinet, Oct. 12, 1911.
[16] Trat. Vig. (Bolivia, 1925), I, 94–97. Approved by the Bolivian Cabinet, Aug. 3, 1919.
[17] La Cuestión de Límites pendiente con la República Argentina, Min. de Rel. Ext. (La Paz, 1922). Horacio Carrillo, Los Límites con Bolivia (Buenos Aires, 1925).

Negro hill at 22°36′46″ S. 64°44′41″ W. The Porongal does not empty into the Bermejo but into the Pescado, which empties into the Bermejo not above but below Las Juntas de San Antonio and not opposite the town of Bermejo; for the Porongal the Argentine commissioner took the Condado, the Bolivian commissioner the Lipeo (Lipio), both of which empty into the Bermejo above Las Juntas de San Antonio, the Condado one and a quarter miles and the Lipeo twenty-five miles from Bermejo town. Bolivia furthermore wished to keep both the towns of Yacuiba at 22°1′ S. and Tartagal, the latter, however, perhaps only for bargaining purposes, as it lay some distance south and east of the disputed line and the claim to it was not later pressed. Bolivia made with Argentina on January 6, 1922,[18] an agreement for the extension with Argentine funds of the North Central Railroad from Yacuiba, across the boundary from Tartagal in Argentina, north 300 miles along the foot of the mountains near the oil lands to Santa Cruz de la Sierra; but this agreement was modified by the Argentine government and had not been approved by the Bolivian Congress before the outbreak of the war with Paraguay which suspended peace-time plans for the development of this region.

After further discussion of the boundary situation a new treaty was signed by Eduardo Díez de Medina, Bolivian minister of foreign relations, and Dr. Horacio Carrillo, Argentine minister, at La Paz on July 9, 1925.[19] The boundary was fixed in Article 1 to start from Zapaleri or Sapalegui hill and run north-northeast to Brajma hill, then to Tinte, Negro, Vilama, Bayo, Alcoak, and Panizos hills; thence by the Cumbrera Chilena and Sierra de Hornillos to Limitajo hill; thence by the peaks in chain to the north-northeast, passing Cuevas and Panizos hills to the summit of La Ramada; thence by a straight line to the confluence of the San Antonio and the San Juan; thence by the course of the San Juan to its union with the Mojinete; thence by a straight line to the summit of Branqui hill, then to the summit of Vaqueros and from there to the summit of Grande hill; from the south side of that peak by another line to the peak of Condor hill in such manner that Sarcari remained within Bolivian territory; from Condor hill to the east to Tablon hill in the Altos de Piscuno, thence by a straight line to the southeast to Post No. 1 of the Abra de Huajra; thence by the posts already placed in the ravines of Cuartel and La Quiaca, following the latter to the mouth of Sansana ravine; thence by a straight line to the west end of La Raya ravine, and descending by that ravine to its union with the Yanalpa; thence by another straight line from west to east to the summit of Mecoya hill; thence descend-

---

[18] Protocol of Nov. 14, 1923. *Trat. Vig.* (Bolivia, 1925), I, 98–106.

[19] *Ibid.*, III, Apen. 7–11. Approved by the Bolivian Cabinet, July 11, 1925.

ing to the sources of the Mecoyita stream, following its course to the Santa Rosa; thence down to its confluence with the Santa Victoria, forming the Condado, and continuing down the Condado to its point of emptying into the Bermejo, more or less opposite the town of that name; thence descending by the waters of the Bermejo to its confluence with the Rio Grande de Tarija at the town of Las Juntas de San Antonio; from Las Juntas up the Tarija to the mouth of the Itaú, and following its course to the 22° parallel, thence by that parallel to the San Roque stream; thence down that stream and by the Yacuiba stream to its confluence with the Pocitos stream and ascending the course of the last to the 22° parallel so that the settlement of Yacuiba remained within Bolivian sovereignty, in the triangular zone formed by such streams and the 22° parallel; from the point where the Pocitos stream crosses the 22° parallel the line to continue along that parallel, as already traced, to the Pilcomayo, which is the northeast boundary of Argentina in the Chaco. As soon as ratifications of this treaty should be exchanged, a mixed commission of Bolivian and Argentine technicians was to proceed to fix on the land the agreed line and to place permanent demarcation posts. By notes of October 14/16, 1925,[20] Carrillo and Díez de Medina agreed that both nations would respect the titles of private owners of real property which might change sovereignty, if registered in the new country within one year. The Treaty of 1925 was approved at once by Bolivia, but although transmitted by President Marcelo Torcuato de Alvear on July 28, 1925,[21] with a message of approval, it has not yet been acted on by the Argentine Congress.

An English company began in 1925 the construction of a meter-gauge railroad from Potosí northeastward down over the mountains, and in six years had reached Yotala, ninety-eight miles from Potosí and nine from Sucre; but in 1931 the state took over the road, and maintenance each year now falls a little short of repairing the damage done by washouts and landslides of the preceding rainy season. The southeastern departments of Tarija, Chuquisaca, and Santa Cruz lie on the plains east of the mountains, and are more naturally and easily to be connected with the Argentine railroads on a similar level across the Pilcomayo and Bermejo to the south than with the high Bolivian dorsal system. Among the projects for which a large loan was obtained in 1934 was a road to link Sucre with the oil fields of middle and eastern Bolivia.

On September 21, 1935, a deputy in the Argentine Chamber expressed the fear that Bolivia would denounce the 1925 treaty now that it appeared that the oil fields in Tarija might extend across the border into Salta Province. It

[20] *Trat. Vig.* (Bolivia, 1925), III, Apen. 12-15.   [21] *Presidencia Alvear*, 1922-1928 (Buenos Aires, 1928), III, 292-294, 328-331.

was further charged that the proposed law putting under federal control pipe lines which touched on any federal railroad had been drawn up for the benefit of the Standard Oil and other foreign companies.

In the same month Senator Sanchez Zorondo alleged that Bolivian civilians had filtered into an area of 2,700 square miles in the northwest corner of Jujuy province, and that it was being administered by Bolivian military and civilian authorities. Foreign Minister Carlos Saavedra Lamas explained that the occupation had existed and been known to Argentina for several years, and resulted from the fact that the frontier between Argentina and Bolivia had not been definitely fixed. Because the treaty of 1925, although approved by the Bolivian Congress and by the the Argentine Senate, had not been ratified by the Chamber of Deputies, Argentina had not made any formal protest to Bolivia as to the occupation.

In October 1935 Argentina disbanded the special detachment, composed of infantry, cavalry, and aviation units, created in September 1932 to enforce neutrality along the Argentine frontier with Bolivia and Paraguay, but commanders were instructed not to withdraw the troops until their positions had been taken over by gendarmes.

In November 1935 an investigating commission sent by the Argentine government to the Bolivian frontier reported that there was no clandestine pipe line on the Standard Oil Company's property; but that there were pipes under the Bermejo River used for pumping water from the river.

The underlying problem between these nations of how far the viceroyalty of the Plata ran northward into the unreduced swampland of the Chaco was not clarified by the vague language of the first protocols and, with the later issue as to which of two branches of the cordillera of the Andes was in fact intended by a call for the highest peaks, was finally resolved by an opportune agreement not wholly advantageous to the smaller contestant, and the line was described in detail in a pending demarcation treaty. The direct results of the Chaco war between Bolivia and Paraguay do not reach southwest of the Pilcomayo; and when the 1925 treaty is approved by Argentina this boundary may be thought to be definitely settled.

2. ARGENTINA–BRAZIL. MISIONES

Following the Bulls of 1493 and the Treaty of Tordesillas of 1494, the Jesuits in the latter part of the sixteenth century began to explore and settle in the Plata region, and Philip III in 1608 gave them permission to establish

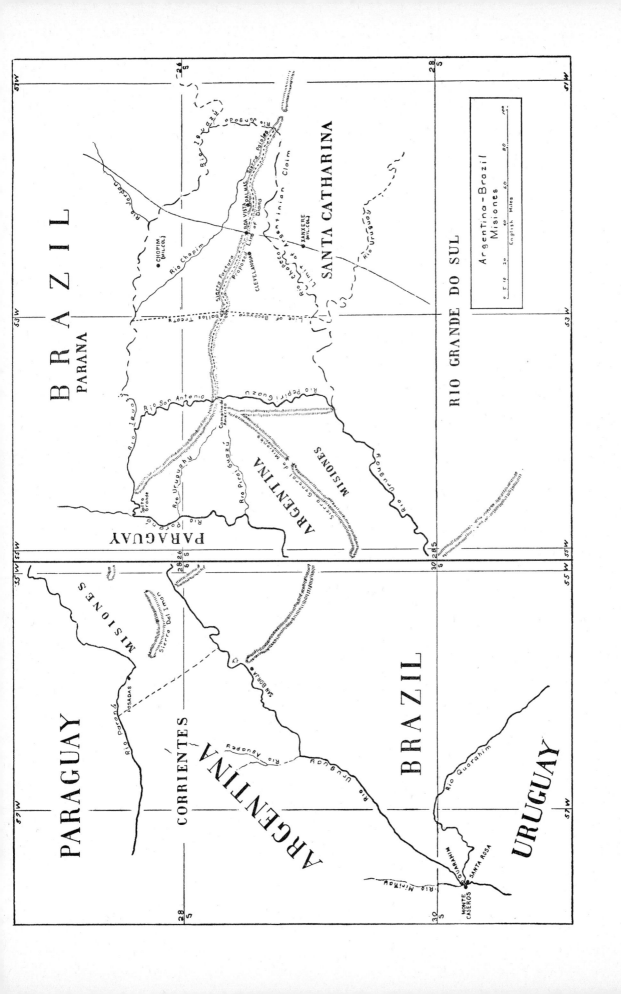

BRAZIL

PARANA

SANTA CATHARINA

RIO GRANDE DO SUL

ARGENTINA

MISIONES

PARAGUAY

Rio Paraná

Rio Iguazú

Rio San Antonio

Rio Chopim

CHOPIM
(MIL.COL.)

BOA VISTA
(MIL.COL.)

CLEVELANDIA

XANXERE
(MIL.COL.)

Rio Uruguay

Rio Pepiriguazú

Rio Piroi Guazú

Rio Paraná

Rio Uruguay

Rio Paraná

Sierra Gen Del Imar

Salto Grande

Santa Fortuna

Line of Proposed
Argentinian Claim

Line of Brazilian Claim

Proposed Treaty

Salto
Grande

Campiña del
Almirón

Sierra
General

Rio Jordão

Rio Uraí

Rio Cavaco

Rio Passo
Fundo

Rio Jacutinga

Rio Chapecó

ARGENTINA

MISIONES

PARAGUAY

CORRIENTES

BRAZIL

URUGUAY

POSADAS

SAN BORJA

Rio Paraná

Rio Aguapey

Rio Uruguay

Rio Guarahim

Rio Miriñay

GUARAHIM

SANTA ROSA

MONTE
CASEROS

Sierra Del Imar

Argentina–Brazil
Misiones

English Miles
0 5 10 20 40 60 80 100

26 S

28 S

30 S

28 S

26 S

28 S

30 S

57 W

55 W

53 W

57 W

55 W

53 W

missions on the Upper Paraná. A royal cédula of 1634 approved the occupation by the Jesuits of the interior provinces, and Reductions became numerous, governed from Candelaria as the capital of the religious empire. The Mamelukes or Paulistas from Sao Paulo and San Vicente overran the missions with continual raids from 1600 to 1650. In 1631 the Jesuits resolved to abandon the province of Guayra, withdrawing to the territory between the Paraná and the Uruguay, and they did not return to the east bank of the Uruguay until 1687. Thirty Reductions were mentioned in the Royal Cédula of December 28, 1743. By the Treaty of Madrid, January 13, 1750, the Portuguese were to give up Colonia and the Spaniards to abandon the Seven Missions in the Ibicuhy region; and though the treaty was annulled by the convention signed at Pardo, February 12, 1761, the Portuguese had already driven out the Jesuits and the converted Indians, and the Reductions were never successfully reëstablished. The Jesuits were expelled from the Plata in 1768, and their territories were taken under the government of Buenos Aires. By the Treaty of San Ildefonso of October 1, 1777,[1] Spain and Portugal agreed that the boundary line between their possessions should be from the Uruguay up the river Piquiry or Pepirí Guazú, across by the highest land and down the San Antonio to the Curityba, but the provisions of this treaty for survey and demarcation on the ground were never carried out by the commissioners. The viceroyalty of Rio de la Plata created on August 1, 1776, purported to include the region of the Misiones, and there were no further changes until 1810, when the independent government at Buenos Aires replaced the royal governor with Colonel Tomás de Rocamora. On December 10, 1814, the National Assembly at Buenos Aires erected the city of Corrientes and the towns of Misiones into the province of Corrientes; and the Misiones were represented in the general constituent congresses of 1816 and 1824. Thereafter the territory of Misiones was continued by Argentina under the government of the province of Corrientes. Palmas, 200 miles inland from Itajahy, and supposed to belong to the Brazilian state of Paraná, was founded by Paulistas in 1838. The preliminary peace convention of August 27, 1828,[2] between Argentina and Brazil recognizing the independence of Uruguay was succeeded by the treaty of peace, friendship, commerce, and navigation signed at Paraná, March 7, 1856,[3] which confirmed (Article 3) the obligation of both to defend the in-

[1] Art. 8. Cantillo, *Tratados de España* (Madrid, 1843), 537–544. Melitón Gonzáles, *El Límite Oriental del Territorio de Misiones* (Montevideo, 1883), I. Ricardo Aranda, *Col. de Trat. del Peru* (Lima, 1890), II, 637–652. Martens, *Recueil de Traités* (2ᵉ ed., Gottingue, 1817), II, 545–558. *Cf.* Report of Theodorick Bland, Nov. 2, 1818; 6 *British and Foreign State Papers* 706. See also App. B, *infra*.

[2] *Trat. de Argentina* (Buenos Aires, 1911), II, 411–420.

[3] *Trat. de Argentina* (Buenos Aires, 1911), II, 426–438. Antonio Pereira Pinto, *Apontamentos para o Direito Int.* (Rio de Janeiro, 1866), III, 494–501. 46 *British and Foreign State Papers* 1310–1315. Ratifications exchanged at Paraná, June 25, 1856.

dependence and integrity of Uruguay, as undertaken in the treaty of August 27, 1828; agreed (Article 14) that the merchant and war ships of both should be free to navigate the Paraná, the Uruguay, and the Paraguay in the parts belonging to either nation; and further (Article 18) promised to oppose by all means that the island of Martín García should cease to belong to one of the states of the Plata interested in its free navigation. An additional convention between the Argentine Confederation and Brazil signed at Paraná, November 20, 1857,[4] agreed to the free navigation by the commerce of all nations of the Uruguay, Paraná, and Paraguay from the Plata to the ports already opened or which should be opened for that purpose, but not to apply to the affluents of those rivers nor between ports of the same nation.

Bernabé López, Argentine minister of foreign relations, Santiago Derqui, Argentine minister of the interior, and José Maria da Silva Paranhos, Brazilian minister to the Argentine Confederation, signed at Paraná on December 14, 1857,[5] a treaty, with a protocol, which provided that (Article 1) the boundary should be the Uruguay, whose right or western bank belonged altogether to the Confederation and left or eastern bank to Brazil, from the mouth of its tributary Quarahim to the mouth of the Pepirí-Guazú, where Brazilian possessions occupied both banks of the Uruguay; thence by the waters of the Pepirí-Guazú to its chief source; thence by the highest land to the principal head of the San Antonio, to its entrance into the Iguazú or the Rio Grande de Curityba and by that river to its confluence with the Paraná. The land divided by the rivers Pepirí-Guazú, San Antonio, and Iguazú should belong on the east to Brazil and on the west to the Argentine Confederation, the waters of the first two rivers for all their length and of the Iguazú from the confluence of the San Antonio to the Paraná only being common to both nations. Article 2 specified that the Pepirí-Guazú and the San Antonio spoken of in Article 1 should be those which were recognized in 1759 by the demarcation under the treaty of January 13, 1750, between Portugal and Spain. Opposition developed in Argentina, and Congress approved the treaty on September 24, 1858,[6] only with an amendment providing that the rivers Pepirí-Guazú and San Antonio were those which were to be found more to the east with these names as appeared in the demarcation referred to in Article 2. On this modification the parties could not agree, and ratifications of the treaty were never exchanged. Brazil on November 16, 1859,[7] ordered

[4] *Col. de Trat. celebrados por la República Argentina* (Buenos Aires, 1884), I, 494-527. Antonio Pereira Pinto, *Apontamentos para o Direito Int.* (Rio de Janeiro, 1869), IV, 40-59. 49 *British and Foreign State Papers* 1306-1315. Ratifications exchanged at Paraná, July 20, 1858.

[5] *Trat. de Argentina* (Buenos Aires, 1911), II, 475-479. 49 *British and Foreign State Papers* 1316-1319.
[6] Law #192. Da Rocha, *Col. Com. Leyes Nac. de Arg.* (Buenos Aires, 1918), I, 356-358.
[7] Decree #2502. *Coll. das Leis do Brazil*, 1859, XX,

two military colonies to be established in the province of Paraná west of the
Chapecó and the Chopim, but it was not until 1880 that the minister of war
took measures to carry this order into effect.

The Constitution of 1864 of the state of Corrientes bounded the state on
the east by the Uruguay, on the north by the Paraná as far as the Pepirí-
Guazú and San Antonio-Guazú. In 1876 Brazil sent Baron Aguíar d'Andrada
to Buenos Aires to reopen negotiations, and there were prolonged discussions.
The federal territory of Misiones was organized into five departments with
the capital at Ciudad de San Martin (formerly Corpus) by an Argentine decree of March 16, 1882,[8] and this apparent abandonment by Argentina of the
existing tacit agreement between the two countries that neither would occupy
or take other steps to disturb the *status quo* of the region aroused public protest in Brazil and sharp responses from Argentina, and there followed a flood
of printed argument in periodicals and books.[9] A treaty for further exploration of the territory was signed by Francisco J. Ortiz, Argentine minister of
foreign relations, and Leonel M. de Alençar, Brazilian minister, at Buenos
Aires on September 28, 1885.[10] This treaty recited that both governments
understood that the common frontier ought to run from the Uruguay to the
Iguazú or Rio Grande de Curityba, and constituted a mixed commission of
two members with substitutes and aides, which, under detailed instructions
annexed to the treaty, should explore and map the rivers Pepirí-Guazú and
San Antonio and the two rivers to the east of these known in Brazil as the
Chapecó and the Chopim and called by the Argentines Pequirí-Guazú and
San Antonio Guazú, as well as the territory between the four rivers. This
commission ended its labors on September 24, 1891.

On September 7, 1889,[11] there was signed by Norberto Quirno Costa,
acting Argentine minister of foreign relations, and the Baron de Alençar,
Brazilian minister, at Buenos Aires a treaty for arbitration of the dispute by
the president of the United States, if ninety days [12] after presentation of

Parte I, 578–580. *Arbitration upon Misiones Arg. Evidence*
(New York, 1893), I, 611–622.

[8] *Reg. Nac. de la Rep. Arg.*, 1882, XXI, 156.

[9] Melitón González, *El Límite Oriental del Territorio
de Misiones* (Montevideo-Buenos Aires, 1883–1886), 3 vols.
J. A. Teixeira de Mello, *Limites do Brasil com a Confe-
deracao Argentina* (Rio de Janeiro, 1883). J. M. N. Azambuja, *Questão Territorial com a Republica Argentina* (Rio de
Janeiro, 1891), vol. I. *U. S. For. Rel.*, 1882, pp. 25–28.

[10] *Trat. de Argentina* (Buenos Aires, 1911), II, 541–
550. Da Rocha, *Leyes Nac. de Arg.* (Buenos Aires, 1918),
VI, 357–362. 76 *British and Foreign State Papers* 309–313.
U. S. For. Rel., 1887, pp. 47–53. Martens, *Nouv. Rec. Gén.
de Traités*, 2° Sér., XII, 584–592. Ratified by Argentina,

Law #1756, Nov. 9, 1885; ratified by Brazil, Dec. 21,
1885; ratifications exchanged at Rio de Janeiro, Mar. 4,
1886.

[11] *Trat. de Argentina* (Buenos Aires, 1911), II, 637–
642. Moore, *Int. Arbitrations* (Washington, 1898), V, 4688–
4689. 81 *British and Foreign State Papers* 254–255. *Arch.
Dipl.*, 2° Sér., XXXII, 182. Ratified by Argentina, Law
#2646, Oct. 23, 1889; approved by the Emperor of Brazil,
Nov. 2, 1889; ratifications exchanged at Rio de Janeiro,
Nov. 4, 1889.

[12] Extended for six months from Aug. 11, 1893, by
protocol signed at Rio de Janeiro, June 10, 1893. Ratified
by Argentina, Law #2959, Aug. 26, 1893.

the reports of the 1885 commission the parties could not agree on an amicable solution. The Brazilian empire was overturned and the republic proclaimed on November 15, 1889; and renewed negotiations for direct settlement resulted in the signing by Quintino Bocayuva, Brazilian minister of foreign relations, Baron de Alençar, Brazilian minister to Argentina, Estanislao S. Zeballos, Argentine minister of foreign relations, and Enrique B. Moreno, Argentine minister to Brazil, at Montevideo on January 25, 1890,[13] of a treaty dividing the disputed territory between the parties across the *divortia aquarum* of the Iguazú and the Uruguay, making use so far as possible of natural bounds, and preserving settlements of each nation as they existed. There were manifestations of approval and celebrations in Argentina,[14] where Congress ratified the treaty without discussion, but it was rejected on August 10, 1891, by the Brazilian House of Deputies by a vote of 142 to 5. Argentina thereupon insisted that the previously agreed arbitration be immediately proceeded with. In the treaty of 1889 it was stipulated that the frontier must be constituted of the rivers which Argentina or Brazil had designated, and the arbiter was invited to decide for one of the parties as he should judge just, in view of the arguments and documents which they might produce. The cases were to be presented within twelve months of receipt of the arbiter's acceptance, and the award to be made within twelve months from the presentation of the later case. President Benjamin Harrison accepted the office of arbiter on July 2, 1892.[15] The Argentine case was prepared by Dr. Estanislao S. Zeballos, minister at Washington, the Brazilian case by a special mission headed by the (second) Baron de Rio Branco, and they were submitted to the United States secretary of state on February 10, 1894,[16] but they were not exchanged. Argentina at one time contended, among other things, that the principle of *uti possidetis*, proper between nations whose territory was formerly under a common sovereignty,[17] had no place in a controversy between states whose territory had always belonged to different nations and whose boundary had been the subject of international treaties and agreements; but later contended that the principle favored her in the Misiones territory. On February 6, 1895, the United States secretary of state delivered to the repre-

[13] *Trat. de Argentina* (Buenos Aires, 1911), II, 652-654. Estanislao S. Zeballos, *Cuestiones de Límites* (Buenos Aires, 1892), pp. 1-235. *La Cuestión Misiones* (Buenos Aires, 1892). *Arch. Dipl.*, 2ᵉ Sér., XLIII, 211.

[14] *Tratado de Misiones, Resumen General de las Fiestas, 1889-90* (Buenos Aires, 1890).

[15] *U. S. For. Rel.*, 1892, pp. 1-4, 17-19.

[16] Estanislao S. Zeballos, *Arbitration on Misiones: Argentine Evidence* (New York, 1893), Vol. 1. *Idem., Argentine Republic upon the question with Brazil in regard to the Territory of Misiones* (Washington, 1894), with documents and maps under title of "Argentine evidence." Rio Branco, *Brazilian-Argentine Boundary Question* (New York, 1894), 6 vols. Alejandro Guesalaga, "Le Litige des Missions," *Rev. d'Hist. Dipl.*, 8ᵉ Année (1894), pp. 75-80. Moore, *Int. Arbitrations* (Washington, 1898), II, 1969-2026.

[17] *Cf.* Peru's argument in 1867, §6, this chap., *infra.*

sentatives of the parties in Washington the award of President Grover Cleveland dated February 5, 1895,[18] which decided that the boundary line was the rivers Pepirí (also called Pepirí-Guazú) and San Antonio, the rivers designated by Brazil, denominated the westerly system, supported by the report of the commissioners in 1759, by the report of the joint survey made in 1788 under the treaty of 1777, and by the map and report of the survey made in 1887 by the joint commission under the treaty of 1885. The award thus favorable to Brazil was loyally accepted by Argentina. On August 9, 1895,[19] there was signed at Rio de Janeiro a protocol for carrying out the award by the placing of boundary posts along the line, and on October 1, 1898,[20] a further protocol for placing marks at the mouth of each of the two rivers. Actual laying down of the boundary continued to prove difficult, and on October 6, 1898,[21] there was signed at Rio de Janeiro a treaty to complete the establishment of the line by amicable and direct agreement. The mixed commission, further instructed by a convention signed at Rio de Janeiro on August 2, 1900,[22] labored at setting up marks from November 3, 1900, to October 6, 1904, and the work so far was approved by an act signed at Rio de Janeiro on October 4, 1910,[23] accepting the line as marked from the mouth of the Quarahim on the left or Brazilian (east) bank of the Uruguay, continuing by the thalweg of the Uruguay and the Pepirí-Guazú by the highest land between its principal source and that of the San Antonio and thence by the thalweg of the San Antonio and the Iguazú to the confluence of the Igauzú with the Paraná, and assigning to Argentina twenty-nine and to Brazil twenty-four of the small islands or groups of islands in the Uruguay from the confluence of the Quarahim to the mouth of the Pepirí-Guazú, and to Argentina three and to Brazil two of the groups in the Igauzú below the confluence of the San Antonio. On the same day, October 4, 1910,[24] there was signed at Buenos Aires a convention complementary to the treaty of October 6, 1898, which specified that the line at the confluence of the Quarahim with the Uru-

[18] *U. S. Treaty Series*, No. 5. *U. S. For. Rel.*, 1895, Part I, pp. 1-3. 87 *British and Foreign State Papers* 697-702. *Trat. de Argentina* (Buenos Aires, 1912), X, 30-34.

[19] Trat. de Argentina (Buenos Aires, 1911), II, 655-656. 87 *British and Foreign State Papers* 1209-1210.

[20] *Trat. de Argentina* (Buenos Aires, 1911), II, 666-667.

[21] *Ibid.*, II, 668-672. Da Rocha, *Col. Com. Leyes Nac.* (Buenos Aires, 1918), XII, 191-193. 90 *British and Foreign State Papers* 85-87. Ratified by Argentina, Law #3804, Sept. 25, 1899; sanctioned by Brazil by Decree #587, Aug. 5, 1899; ratified by Brazil, Oct. 26, 1899; ratifications exchanged at Rio de Janeiro, May 26, 1900;

promulgated by Brazil, Decree #3667, May 31, 1900.

[22] *Trat. de Argentina* (Buenos Aires, 1911), II, 673-676.

[23] *Trat. de Argentina* (Buenos Aires, 1911), II, 716-747. *La Frontera Argentino-Brasileña, Estudios y Demarcación General* (Buenos Aires, 1910), 2 vols. Fernando Antonio Raja Gabaglia, *As Fronteiras do Brasil* (Rio de Janeiro, 1916), pp. 256-263. 103 *British and Foreign State Papers* 341-355. Martens, *Nouv. Rec. Gén de Traités*, 3° Sér., VII (1913), 783-798. *U. S. For. Rel.*, 1907, Part I, pp. 22-23.

[24] *Trat. de Argentina* (Buenos Aires, 1911), II, 713-715.

guay should pass between the right (west) bank of the Uruguay and the Brazilian island of Quarahim, thence by the median line of the Uruguay to
opposite the Argentine mouth of the Miriñay, and thence by the thalweg of
the Uruguay to the confluence of the Pepirí-Guazú. In commemoration of the
arbitral award the town of Clevelandia was established by Brazil, twenty-five
miles west of Palmas. J. P. Rodrigues Alves, Brazilian ambassador to Argentina, and Antonio Sagarve, acting Argentine minister of foreign relations
signed at Buenos Aires on December 27, 1927, another complementary convention regulating the frontier at Quarahim south of the Brazilian island, but
this convention still is pending approval by the Argentine Congress and has
not been ratified.

The nationality of 11,500 square miles of territory depended upon which
of two pairs of rivers 100 miles apart was the pair named in an express
boundary agreement, and this was settled by neutral arbitration. The demarcation has since been completed as agreed, and this border may be considered as permanently settled.

3A. ARGENTINA–CHILE. LOS ANDES

The northern 300 miles of the present boundary between Argentina and
Chile, from about 23° to 26°52′45″ S., was involved in the controversy between Argentina and Bolivia until their treaty of May 10, 1889,[1] and the
Argentine-Chilean agreement of April 17, 1896,[2] contemplated the coöperation of Bolivia in the settlement of that portion of the line. On September
17, 1898,[3] the experts of Argentina and Chile concluded definitely that they
could come to no common agreement and suspended consideration of this section. On November 2, 1898,[4] it was agreed that the problem should be
studied for not over ten days by an international conference in Buenos Aires
of ten delegates, five designated by each country, their conclusions, if reached,
not to be obligatory but to require a decision by each government; and if such
conference should reach no decision in three sessions, a demarcation commission of one Argentine delegate, one Chilean delegate, and the then United
States minister to Argentina should proceed within three days by majority
to trace the line in final form; the result in any event to be communicated to
Bolivia. The Conference of Ten met in Buenos Aires on March 1 and March 9,

---

[1] See §1, this chap., *supra*. [2] See §3B, this chap., *infra*.
[3] *Trat. de Argentina* (Buenos Aires, 1911), VII, 192.
90 *British and Foreign State Papers* 1028.

[4] *Trat. de Argentina* (Buenos Aires, 1911), VII, 212–
244. *Recop. de Trat. de Chile*, Ed. Ofic. (Santiago, 1908),
V, 20–30. 97 *British and Foreign State Papers* 550–553.

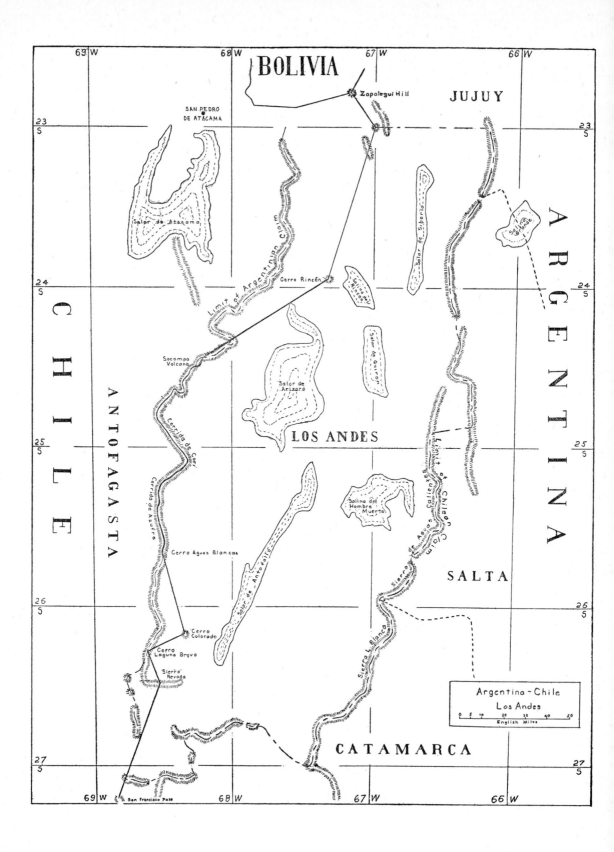

BOLIVIA

JUJUY

ARGENTINA

Zapalegui Hill

SAN PEDRO
DE ATACAMA

Salar de Atacama

Salar Grande

Limit of Argentinian Claim

Cerro Rincón

Salar del Rincón

Salar de Siberia

Salar de Quirón

Socompa Volcano

Salar de Arizaro

Corrida de Cori

LOS ANDES

ANTOFAGASTA

CHILE

Corrida de Azufre

Salina del Hombre Muerto

Limit of Chilean Claim

Sierra de Agua Saliente

Cerro Aguas Blancas

Salar de Antofalla

SALTA

Cerro Colorado

Cerro Laguna Brava

Sierra
Nevada

Sierra Blanca

Argentina-Chile
Los Andes

0 5 10   20   30   40   50
English Miles

CATAMARCA

San Francisco Pass

and the two separate proposals for adoption of a line were both rejected by a vote of five to five; whereupon the conference decided unanimously that each delegation should communicate this result to its government. José E. Uriburu for Argentina and Enrique MacIver for Chile were designated to act as the respective representatives on the demarcation commission under the alternative agreement. William I. Buchanan was the United States minister to Argentina, and after communicating with his government and getting President McKinley's permission,[5] he accepted office on the commission on February 23, 1899. The demarcation commission of three met in Buenos Aires on March 21, 22, 23 and 24, 1899,[6] and after ascertaining from both countries that the question submitted to the arbitration of the British government did not touch the line north of 26°52′45″, proceeded on March 24, 1899, to determine the line between 23° and 26°52′45″ as entrusted to them. The complete propositions of Argentina and Chile were both rejected by the vote of the opposing representative and Minister Buchanan, who then presented his own proposal for the line, in seven sections. The first, from the intersection of the 23° S. parallel and the 67° W. meridian to Cerro Rincón, and the fourth from Cerro Aguas Blancas to Cerro Colorado, were carried by Buchanan and the Chilean representative; the second and third, from Cerro Rincón through Socompa Volcano to Cerro Aguas Blancas and the fifth and sixth, from Cerro Colorado through Cerro Laguna Brava to Sierra Nevada, were carried by Buchanan and the Argentine representative; and the seventh, from Sierra Nevada to the point which should be fixed by the British arbiter as the beginning of the southern portion, which turned out three years and eight months later to be the mark in San Francisco Pass at 26°52′45″, was carried unanimously. By a convention signed at Buenos Aires on January 9, 1903,[7] it was agreed to ask the British government to commend to the commission named to mark the line determined by King Edward's award of November 20, 1902, or to another commission it might name, the marking also of the northern part of the line as established by the demarcation commission in its award of March 24, 1899; but on November 5, 1903,[8] it was determined, subject to the consent of the British government, to entrust the demarcation of the northern portion to a mixed commission of engi-

[5] *U. S. For. Rel.*, 1898, pp. 2–4, 179–181; *ibid.*, 1899, pp. 3, 7.
[6] *Trat. de Argentina* (Buenos Aires, 1911), VII, 245–256. *Recop. de Trat. de Chile* (Santiago, 1908), V, 96–136. 96 *British and Foreign State Papers* 379–383. *Rev. de dr. int. et de lég. comp.*, 2e Sér. (1902), IV, 636. *Chilo-Argentine Boundary, the Puna of Atacama; Memorandum* (Washington, 1899).

[7] *Trat. de Argentina* (Buenos Aires, 1911), VII, 291–292. 96 *British and Foreign State Papers* 416–417; 97 *ibid.* 554.
[8] *Trat. de Argentina* (Buenos Aires, 1911), VII, 319–320. *Recop. de Trat. de Chile* (Santiago, 1913), VI, 48–49. 97 *British and Foreign State Papers* 555.

neers designated by the respective governments, and to submit to the decision of His Britannic Majesty's government any points of disagreement which might arise and could not be settled by the respective chancelleries. By a convention signed at Buenos Aires, May 2, 1904,[9] it was agreed that the boundary north of the 23° parallel, as left between Argentina and Chile by the Argentina-Bolivia adjustment of 1893, should be a straight line from the point of intersection of that parallel with the 67° W. meridian to the highest peak of the Zapaleri hill, indicated as such in the plan drawn by the Argentina-Bolivia boundary commission. The demarcation of this line as well as of the portion between 23° and 26°52′45″ was entrusted, with instructions,[10] to the mixed commission of engineers under the agreement of November 5, 1903, and that commission was authorized to submit [11] to the respective governments proposals to substitute on the basis of an equitable compensation for the straight lines indicated in the award such natural boundaries as might offer a more permanent frontier. The demarcation of the whole northern section was substantially finished in 1905.[12]

The stipulation for a frontier along the cordillera by the most lofty peaks which divide the waters turned out to be equivocal when it was found that the highest ridge was not in all places the watershed and it was resolved by the compromise line drawn by an arbiter. Taken in conjunction with the prior adjustments of both countries with Bolivia, this boundary has given rise to no further difficulties and seems permanently settled.

3B. Argentina–Chile. Patagonia

Although the Chilean constitutions of 1823, 1828, and 1833 all declared that the territory of Chile extended from the Andes to the Pacific and south to Cape Horn, the Araucanians successfully discouraged settlement or exploration southward overland, and the government was too much occupied with matters nearer at hand to concern itself greatly with the bleak territory about the Strait of Magellan and beyond. In 1843 the Chilean schooner *Ancud* sailed south from Chiloé Island, and on September 21 established a settlement called Bulnes at Puerto del Hambre (Port Famine) on Brunswick Peninsula, moved in 1849 to Punta Arenas on the eastern shore of the peninsula.

[9] *Trat. de Argentina* (Buenos Aires, 1911), VII, 331–333. *Recop. de Trat. de Chile* (Santiago, 1913), VI, 118–135. *U. S. For. Rel.*, 1904, pp. 40–41. Approved by Argentina, Law #4330, Aug. 25, 1904.

[10] *Trat. de Argentina* (Buenos Aires, 1911), VII, 323–330. 97 *British and Foreign State Papers* 556–561.

[11] *Trat. de Argentina* (Buenos Aires, 1911), VII, 334–337. Approved by Argentina, Law #4331, Aug. 25, 1904.

[12] *Trat. de Argentina* (Buenos Aires, 1911), VII, 344–348. *Recop, de Trat. de Chile* (Santiago, 1913), VI, 177–193, 201–205. Luis Risopatrón S., *La Linea de Frontera en la Puna de Atacama* (Santiago, 1906).

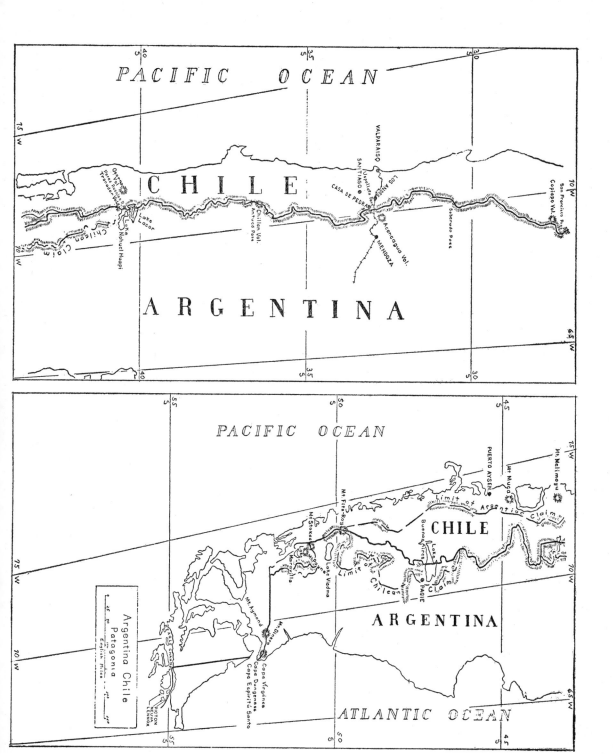

Argentina as soon as she heard of the settlements protested by note of December 15, 1847, that the peninsula belonged to her, but the matter was not followed up. A treaty of friendship, commerce, and navigation between the Argentine Confederation and Chile signed at Santiago on August 30, 1855,[1] provided that (Article 39) both parties recognized as the boundaries of their respective territories those which they had at the time of being separated from Spanish domination in 1810, and agreed to postpone the questions which had arisen or might arise on that subject to be later discussed peacefully and amicably, without recourse ever to violent measures, and in the event of not arriving at a complete agreement, to submit the decision to the arbitration of a friendly nation. Reference to the boundaries of 1810 in fact offered no solution of the problem, for throughout the dependency period the territory had not been inhabited by any Spaniards, and neither the viceroys of Buenos Aires nor the captains-general of Chile had concerned themselves about it.

Guano of commercial value was discovered in the southern region in 1870, and in 1872 coal deposits on the Atlantic coast. Chile attempted to treat the territory as her own, as far north as the Gallegos river, whereupon Argentina again protested. There were several clashes and incidents, and the dispute continued, becoming especially acute in 1873; from 1876 to 1879 various conferences were held and proposals exchanged [2] with little result until, with the war with Peru impending, Chile felt it wise to make some concessions. With the mediation of the United States, through Thomas O. Osborn, United States minister at Buenos Aires, and Thomas A. Osborn, United States minister at Santiago,[3] a treaty to settle amicably and honorably the boundary controversy was signed at Buenos Aires on July 23, 1881,[4] which provided that (Article 1) the boundary between Argentina and Chile was from north to

[1] *Trat. de Argentina* (Buenos Aires, 1911), VII, 28–53. 49 *British and Foreign State Papers* 1200–1213. Ratified by Argentina, Law #55, Oct. 1, 1855, Executive, Jan. 31, 1856; ratified by Chile, Apr. 5, 1856; ratifications exchanged at Santiago, Apr. 29, 1856; denounced by Chile Oct. 25, 1866 to take effect Apr. 29, 1868.

[2] *Trat. de Argentina* (Buenos Aires, 1911), VII, 95–117. *U. S. For. Rel.*, 1873, pp. 38–39, 104–117; *ibid.*, 1876, pp. 7–9; *ibid.*, 1878, pp. 9–10, 86–87; *ibid.*, 1879, pp. 13–15, 147–148. *Arch. Dipl.*, 1876–77, IV, 324–327, 373–374; *ibid.*, 1878–79, III, 302–303, 322–328. *Cuestión de Límites con Chile, Min. de Rel. Est.* (Buenos Aires, 1873–77), 3 vols. *Cuestión Chileno-Argentina, Notas Diplomaticas y otras Escritas en defensa de los Derechos de la República Argentina* (Buenos Aires, 1877). Gaspar Toro, *La Diplomacia Chileno-Arjentina en la Cuestión de Límites* (Santiago, 1878). Miguel Luís Amunátegui, *La Cuestión de Límites entre Chile i la República Argentina* (Santiago, 1879–80),

3 vols. Antonio Bermejo, *La Cuestion Chilena y el Arbitrage* (Buenos Aires, 1879). B. Vicuña Mackenna, *La Patagonia* (Santiago, 1880). Vicente G. Quesada, *La Cuestión de Límites con Chile* (Buenos Aires, 1881). Bernardo de Irigoyen, *Question des Limites entre la République Argentine et le Chili* (Buenos Aires, 1881).

[3] *U. S. For. Rel.*, 1881, pp. 6–18, 130–131, 134–135.

[4] *Trat. de Argentina* (Buenos Aires, 1911), VII, 118–127. *Recop. de Trat. de Chile* (Santiago, 1894), II, 120–125. 72 *British and Foreign State Papers* 1103–1105. Martens, *Nouv. Rec. Gen. de Traités*, 2e Sér., XII, 491–494. M. A. Pelliza, *La Cuestión del Estrecho de Magallanes, Cuadros Históricos* (Buenos Aires, 1881). Bernardo de Irigoyen, *Discurso del Min. de Rel. Ext.* (Buenos Aires, 1882). Ratified by Argentina, Law #1116-1/2, Oct. 11, 1881; ratifications exchanged at Santiago, Oct. 22, 1881; promulgated by Chile, Oct. 26, 1881.

south to the 52° parallel the cordillera of the Andes, the frontier line to run by the most lofty peaks of said chains which divide the waters and to pass between the slopes which incline to one side and the other; difficulties which might arise from the existence of certain valleys formed by the bifurcation of the cordillera in which the dividing line of the waters may not be clear to be settled amicably by two experts, one named by each party, and if these could not agree, by a third expert named by both governments; (Article 2) in the southern part of the continent and north of the Strait of Magellan the boundary should be a line from Point Dungeness overland to Mount Dinero, thence toward the west, following the greatest elevations of the chain of hills to the top of Mount Aymond, thence to the intersection of meridian 70° with the parallel 52° and thence to the west along such parallel to the *divortia aquarum* of the Andes, territories to the north of such line to belong to Argentina and to the south to Chile; (Article 3) in Tierra del Fuego the line should start from Cape Espíritu Santo at 52°40' S. and run southward along the meridian 68°34' W. to Beagle Channel, the part of Tierra del Fuego thus divided to the west to be Chilean, to the east Argentine; the island of Los Estados (Staten) and small islands very near it and the other islands in the Atlantic to the east of Tierra del Fuego and the east coasts of Patagonia to belong to Argentina, all the islands to the south of Beagle Channel to Cape Horn and those west of Tierra del Fuego to belong to Chile; (Article 5) the Strait of Magellan to remain neutralized [5] forever, free navigation of it to be assured for the flags of all nations [6] and no coast fortifications or military defenses to be erected which might threaten this arrangement; and (Article 6) any question which might unfortunately arise whether in this or any other matter to be submitted to the judgment of a friendly power, in any case the boundary described therein remaining immovable. The provision in Article 1 as to the line passing between the slopes (*vertientes*) was added by the Argentine government to the draft treaty as proposed by Chile, but instead of solving the difficulty only made more impossible the running of a line by the most lofty peaks which divide the waters,[7] whether or not anything different was meant from the *divortia aquarum* used later in the treaty.

[5] Oppenheim, *Int. Law* (4th ed., London, 1926–28), I, 413; II, 149. *Wheaton's Elements of International Law*, ed. and enl. by A. Berriedale Keith (6th Eng. ed., London, 1929), I, 384. Naval War College, *International Law Situations*, 1931, pp. 55–56.

[6] Moore, *Dig. Int. Law* (Washington, 1906), I, 664.

[7] Eduardo de la Barra, *El Problema de los Andes* (Buenos Aires, 1895), Henri S. Delachaux, "La Question des Limites Chilo-Argentines," *Annales de Géog.* (Paris, 1898), XXXIII, 239–262. Manuel A. Montes de Oca, *El Divortium Aquarum Continental ante el Tratado de 1893* (Buenos Aires, 1899). Henri-Alexis Moulin, *Le Litige Chilo-Argentin* (Paris, 1902). Emilio Lamarca, *Reports on Conflicting Translations* (Buenos Aires, 1902). L. Gallois, "Les Andes de Patagonie," *Annales de Géog.* (Paris, 1901), X, 232–259. Rafael Torres Campos, "Explicación histórico-geográfica," *Bol. de la Real Soc. Geog.*, XLIV (1902), 600–604.

Negotiations for the actual demarcation under this treaty of 1881 dragged along until a convention was signed in Santiago on August 20, 1888,[8] which provided for the appointment within two months of the experts referred to, with five assistants each, and a meeting at Concepción within forty days after their nomination to agree on the work and proceed with the demarcation. Numerous difficulties appeared and an additional and clarifying protocol was signed at Santiago on May 1, 1893,[9] which provided that (Article 1) under the principle of Article 1 of the Treaty of 1881, Argentina should have in perpetuity as her property and under her absolute dominion all the lands and all the waters, to wit, lakes, lagoons, rivers, parts of rivers, streams, springs, to the east of the line of the most lofty peaks of the cordillera of the Andes which divide the waters, and Chile the same to the west of that line; (Article 2) Argentina should keep her dominion and sovereignty over all the territory to the eastward of the principal chain of the Andes to the Atlantic coast, and Chile the same to the westward to the Pacific coast, with absolute sovereignty to each over the respective littoral, so that Chile might not claim any point on the Atlantic nor Argentina on the Pacific, except that in the southern peninsula near the 52° parallel if the cordillera appeared mingled among the channels of the Pacific, the experts should make a study of the land to fix a dividing line which should leave to Chile the shores of those channels; (Article 4) the demarcation of Tierra del Fuego should commence simultaneously with that of the cordillera, starting from the point called Cabo Espíritu Santo, on the central one of three hills visible, which is the highest, placing there the first mark and proceeding southward. On February 8, 1894,[10] Argentina and Chile signed a protocol for the construction and maintenance of a carriage road from railhead on either side to the boundary line in Uspallata Pass.

An agreement signed at Santiago on September 6, 1895,[11] provided that mixed subcommissions of assistant experts should leave for the frontier between October 15 and November 1, 1895. But so long as the equivocal original phrase, "the most lofty peaks of the Andes which divide the waters," was retained, no real solution of the boundary difficulty was possible, however much the parties might profess to desire it. With Argentina claiming to

[8] *Trat. de Argentina* (Buenos Aires, 1911), VII, 144–150. *Recop. de Trat. de Chile* (Santiago, 1894), II, 331–334. 82 *British and Foreign State Papers* 684–686. Ratified by Argentina, Law #2488, Aug. 17, 1889; ratifications exchanged at Santiago, Jan. 11, 1890; promulgated by Chile, Jan. 15, 1890.

[9] *Trat. de Argentina* (Buenos Aires, 1911), VII, 151–159. *Recop. de Trat. de Chile* (Santiago, 1894), II, 392.

Ratified by Argentina, Law #3042, Dec. 14, 1893; ratifications exchanged at Santiago, Dec. 21, 1893; promulgated by Chile, Dec. 21, 1893.

[10] *Trat. de Argentina* (Buenos Aires, 1911), VII, 160–164. 87 *British and Foreign State Papers* 77.

[11] *Trat. de Argentina* (Buenos Aires, 1911), VII, 182–183. *Recop. de Trat. de Chile* (Londres, 1898), III, 280–281. Approved by President Uriburu of Argentina, Oct. 21, 1895.

the line of highest peaks and Chile insisting the line should follow the watershed and neither country willing to yield its interpretation, the popular fervors of nationalism soon became aroused and at times the dispute came to the verge of war.[12]

Finally Norberto Quirno Costa, Argentine minister, and Adolfo Guerrero, Chilean minister of foreign relations, signed at Santiago on April 17, 1896,[13] an agreement, to facilitate loyal execution of the existing treaties fixing an immovable boundary between the two countries, which provided that the demarcation should be extended in the cordillera of the Andes to the 23° parallel and the line traced from that parallel to 26°52'45" S. with the government of Bolivia, which should be invited to join; and if any differences should occur between the experts in fixing the marks south of 26° 52'45" or in the neighborhood of parallel 52° which could not be amicably settled, they should be submitted to the judgment of the government of Her Britannic Majesty as arbiter; the provisions of the Treaty of 1881 and the Protocol of 1893 to be strictly applied, and the situation of the San Francisco Pass boundary mark[14] between the 26° and 27° parallels not to be considered final. Following this agreement, the experts still made efforts to come to direct accord, but thenceforward treated the problem somewhat differently as to the 275-mile portion of the line from 23° to 26°52'45" S., to be worked out in coöperation with Bolivia,[15] and the portion of 1,750 miles from 26°52'45" to and about 52°, for British arbitration if necessary. The virtual deadlock continued until in September 1898[16] the experts came to the definite conclusion that no further progress could be made as to the line where the highest peaks and the watershed did not coincide, and concrete statements of their respective positions were drawn up.[17]

On October 1, 1898, the representatives of the two countries agreed on the four stretches of the boundary from 27°2'50" S. to 40°6'1" S., from 40°9' 39" S. to 41°12'18" S., from 48°53'10" S. to 50°38'10" S., and from 52° S. to

[12] Doc. Dipl. Fr., 2e Sér., I, 680.

[13] Trat. de Argentina (Buenos Aires, 1911), VII, 184–187. Recop. de Trat. de Chile (Londres, 1898), III, 314–320. 88 British and Foreign State Papers 553–554. Rev. de dr. int. et de lég. comp., 2e Sér., IV (1902), 629–630. Rec. des Cours, VIII (1925), 306–310; XXXV (1931), 415–417. U. S. For. Rel., 1896, pp. 32–34; ibid., 1898, pp. 1–2. Moore, Int. Arbitrations (Washington, 1898), V, 4854–4855. Approved by President Uriburu of Argentina, Apr. 27, 1896.

[14] Alejandro Bertrand, Estudio Técnico de la Demarcación de Límites (Santiago, 1895).

[15] See §3A, this chap., supra.

[16] Trat. de Argentina (Buenos Aires, 1911), VII, 190–

211. Recop. de Trat. de Chile (Santiago, 1908), V, 11–19. 90 British and Foreign State Papers 1027–1030. Martens, Nouv. Rec. Gén. de Traités, 2e Ser., XXXII, 394–397. Approved by Decree, Oct. 11, 1898.

[17] Ernesto Quesada, La Política Chilena en el Plata (Buenos Aires, 1895). Alejandro Alvarez, "La Theorie de l'Arbitrage Permanent et le Conflit de Limites entre le Chili et la République Argentine," Rev. Gén. de dr. int. pub., V (1898), 422–444. Ernesto Quesada, La Política Argentina respecto de Chile (Buenos Aires, 1898). Ramón Serrano Montaner, Límites con la República Arjentina, ed. rev. (Santiago, 1898). Luis V. Varela, Historia de la Demarcación de sus Fronteras (Buenos Aires, 1899), 2 vols. Luis V. Varela, Ante el Arbitro (Buenos Aires, 1901).

54°56′ S., leaving open for arbitration only the four sections at the mark in San Francisco Pass from 26°52′45″ S. to 27°2′50″ S., the region of Lake Lacar from 40°6′1″ S. to 40°9′39″ S., the line from Pérez Rosales Pass at 41°12′18″ S. to Monte Fitz-Roy near Lake Viedma at 48°53′10″ S. and the region north-east of the estuary of La Última Esperanza from 50°38′10″ S. to 52° S. Queen Victoria, having been invited on June 15, had accepted on July 11, 1896, the office of arbiter if any case should arise for decision under the agreement, and on November 23, 1898, formal steps were taken by both countries to submit the dispute. The Argentine case was delivered to the Marquis of Salisbury, British minister of foreign affairs, on January 17, 1899,[18] and the Chilean reply a little later.[19] While awaiting the award,[20] the two countries cleared up minor points as to the form of establishing marks and the mutual cancellation of claims in the disputed territories. Queen Victoria named an English commission of one lawyer and three engineers [21] to examine the question, but before they reported she died, on January 22, 1901. Both countries agreed to accept King Edward VII as arbiter in her place, and by a convention signed at Santiago on May 28, 1902,[22] asked further that he should name a commission to fix on the ground the boundaries which he might ordain in his decision. Sentiment in the two countries grew very warm, and might have led to war but for diplomatic pressure exerted by Great Britain at both Buenos Aires and Santiago and a hastening of the award, handed down on November 20, 1902.[23] The decision, without giving any reasons, did not adopt the line proposed by either party, but established a compromise line between them, awarding 15,450 square miles to Argentina and 20,850 square miles to Chile. Some Chileans thought that in drawing the compromise line the arbiter had exceeded his power,[24] and further that the line showed deviations westward in favor of Argentine settlements, as in the valleys of Lacar, 16 de Octubre, Cholila, and others, which had been unoccupied when the dispute first arose. The British government named a commission of five artillery and engineer officers [25] who with Argen-

[18] *Argentine-Chilian Boundary in the Cordillera de los Andes* (London, 1900–02), 11 vols.

[19] *Chilean-Argentine Boundary Arbitration* (London, 1901–02), 6 vols. (Paris, 1902), 7 vols.

[20] *Trat. de Argentina* (Buenos Aires, 1911), VII, 257–266. *Recop. de Trat. de Chile* (Santiago, 1908), V, 251–253, 257–267, 271–275.

[21] Lord Edward Macnaghten, Major General John C. Ardagh, Colonel Sir Thomas Hungerford Holdich, and Major E. H. Hills.

[22] *Trat. de Argentina* (Buenos Aires, 1911), VII, 286–287. *Recop. de Trat. de Chile* (Santiago, 1913), VI, 39–47, 59–60. *U. S. For. Rel.*, 1902, pp. 18–23, 126–128. Ratified by Argentina, Law #4094, July 30, 1902.

[23] *Trat. de Argentina* (Buenos Aires, 1912), X, 35–49. *Recop. de Trat. de Chile* (Santiago, 1913), VI, 20–38. *U. S. For. Rel.*, 1899, pp. 1–5. 95 *British and Foreign State Papers* 162–164. *Rec. des Cours*, XXXII (1930), 766–767; *ibid.*, XXXIV (1930), 405.

[24] Luis Orrego Luco, *La Cuestión Argentina* (Santiago, 1902), 2 vols. Alejandro Alvarez, "Des Occupations de Territoires Contestés," *Rev. gén. de dr. int. pub.*, X (1903), 674–687.

[25] Colonel Sir Thomas Hungerford Holdich and Captains H. L. Crosthwait, Bertram Dickson, C. L. Robertson, and W. M. Thompson.

tine and Chilean aids and experts proceeded to the line in January 1903 and between then and the end of March set up eighty-eight marks in the four disputed sections. Minor difficulties which arose between the experts of the two countries who placed 608 marks on the agreed remainder of the line were cleared up by brief direct agreements[26] between the two countries.

On April 5, 1910,[27] the Trans-Andean railroad, begun in 1886, was opened under the Uspallata Pass, passing through the nearly two-mile-long Cumbre tunnel and providing when in operation rail connection between Buenos Aires and Santiago de Chile, with changes to and from narrow gauge at Mendoza and Los Andes. By a convention on frontier police signed at Buenos Aires on October 13, 1919,[28] it was agreed that police in hot pursuit of delinquents, except for political crimes, might cross the frontier, with immediate notice and surrender of the captives to the country in whose territory they were taken, pending extradition.

A treaty stipulation that the frontier should run along the most lofty peaks which divide the waters caused difficulty in four places along the 2,900-mile boundary (1,900 miles by air line from San Francisco Pass to Beagle Channel), where the highest ridge proved not to be the watershed; and a compromise line drawn by an arbiter divided the 36,300 square miles of territory involved. The hope for boundary peace along the frontier symbolized by the Christ of the Andes [29] has proved justified for thirty years, and except for a possible difficulty as to the three islands in the entrance to Beagle Channel at the extreme south end of the line,[30] this boundary may be thought to be permanently settled.

4. ARGENTINA–PARAGUAY. CHACO CENTRAL

Following the end of the war between Paraguay and the Argentine Confederation with the downfall of Rosas on February 3, 1852, his successor, General Justo José de Urquiza, negotiated with Dictator Carlos Antonio López a treaty of boundaries, commerce, and navigation, signed at Asunción,

[26] *Trat. de Argentina* (Buenos Aires, 1911), VII, 321–322. Luis Risopatrón S., *La Línea de Frontera* (Santiago, 1903-07-11), 3 vols. *La Frontera Argentino-Chilena, Documentos de la Demarcación* (Buenos Aires, 1908), 2 vols.

[27] *Trat. de Argentina* (Buenos Aires, 1925), I, 364–368. *Arch. Dipl.*, 3ᵉ Sér., CXIII, 480. *Nat. Geog. Mag.*, XXI, 397-417.

[28] *Trat. de Argentina* (Buenos Aires, 1925), I, 369–370.

[29] A large statue of bronze cast from old Spanish cannon, erected on the boundary line beside the road in Uspallata Pass at an altitude of 12,000 feet. It was paid for by popular subscription, after a campaign largely by women, in which Senora Angela de Costa, president of the Christian Mothers' Association in Argentina, was especially prominent; and it was unveiled on Mar. 13, 1904. See letter by Alice Stone Blackwell dated Jan. 7, 1929; *Cong. Rec.*, LXX, 1579, Jan. 11, 1929. Rotary Club members from Argentine, Chile, and Uruguay met at the monument on Jan. 17, 1937, and affixed to the base a bronze plaque bearing in Spanish the inscription: "Sooner shall these mountains crumble into dust than the peoples of Argentina and Chile break the peace which at the feet of Christ the Redeemer they have sworn to maintain." (See Frontispiece.)

[30] See chap. II, § 16, *infra.*

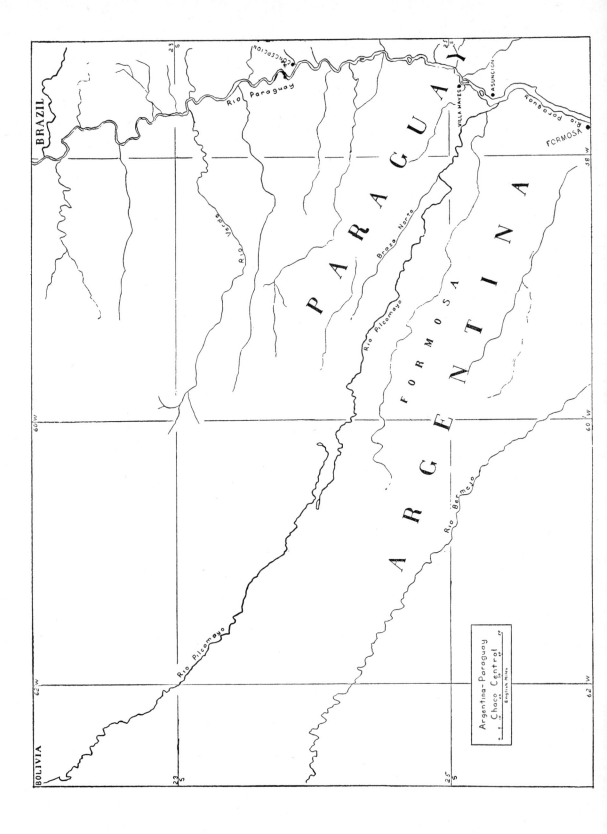

BRAZIL

BOLIVIA

PARAGUAY

ARGENTINA

FORMOSA

CONCEPCION

Rio Paraguay

Rio Verde

Brazo Norte

Rio Pilcomayo

VILLA HAYES

ASUNCION

Rio Pilcomayo

FORMOSA

Rio Pilcomayo

Rio Bermejo

Rio Porobojod

23 S

25 S

60 W

62 W

38 W

60 W

62 W

23 S

25 S

Argentina - Paraguay
Chaco Central

English Miles

July 15, 1852,[1] which provided that (Article 1) the Paraná should be the boundary between Argentina and Paraguay from the Brazilian possessions to two leagues above the lower mouth at the island of the Atajo; (Article 2) the island of Yaciretá should continue to belong to Paraguay, Apipé to Argentina, and the other islands whether dry or overflowed to the territory to which they were more adjacent; (Article 4) the Paraguay from bank to bank to its confluence with the Paraná belonged in perfect sovereignty to Paraguay; (Article 5) navigation of the Bermejo was to be perfectly common to the two states; (Article 6) the landward (west) shore from the mouth of the Bermejo to the Atajo was to be neutral territory for the width of one league, so that neither state could station there military cantonments or police guards, even for the purpose of watching the barbarians that inhabited that shore; (Article 7) Argentina conceded to Paraguay free navigation of the Paraná and its affluents; (Article 8) Paraguay conceded to Argentina free navigation of the Paraguay and its affluents; and (Article 12) Paraguay would, in the event of being requested by Argentina to do so pursuant to a previous understanding, provide and secure a port on the Pilcomayo as high up as it might be navigable, so that from it the shortest possible land route might be afforded to commerce through Paraguayan territory to the frontier of Bolivia.

The Argentine Congress on June 4, 1856,[2] approved the act of recognition of the independence and sovereignty of Paraguay by the provisional director of the Argentine Confederation on July 17, 1852, with reservation of that part of such act which referred to territorial boundaries, whose final adjustment was declared to be still pending. On July 29, 1856,[3] there was signed at Asunción a treaty of friendship, commerce, navigation, and boundaries which provided that (Article 17) the navigation of the Paraná, Paraguay, and Bermejo should be free to the merchant and war vessels of both countries; (Article 24) the adjustment of boundaries should be postponed; and (Article 25) the island of Apipé in the Paraná should belong to Argentina and the island of Yasiretá to Paraguay. Paraguay continued to claim and exercise jurisdiction over a portion of the Misiones territory, from the Iguazú down to Candelaria.

On the death of López on September 10, 1862, he was succeeded as dic-

[1] *Trat. de Argentina* (Buenos Aires, 1912), IX, 69–74. 42 *British and Foreign State Papers* 1256–1258. Ratified by Provisional Director of Argentina, General Justo José de Urquiza, July 17, 1852; ratified by President Carlos Antonio López, July 19, 1852; ratifications exchanged at Asunción, Sept. 14, 1852.

[2] *Trat. de Argentina* (Buenos Aires, 1912), IX, 87.
[3] *Trat. de Argentina* (Buenos Aires, 1912), IX, 89–103. 46 *British and Foreign State Papers* 1305–1310. Ratified by Argentina, Law #102, Sept. 30, 1856; ratified by Paraguay, Oct. 15, 1856; ratifications exchanged at Paraná, Nov. 6, 1856.

tator by his eldest son, Francisco Solano López, who was chosen president for ten years in October 1862. On April 13, 1865, López proclaimed the annexation of Corrientes province, fired on and captured two small Argentine government steamers, the *Gualeguay* and the *Veinte-Cinco de Mayo*, at Corrientes,[4] and declared war on Buenos Aires. The secret treaty of May 1, 1865,[5] between Argentina, Brazil, and Uruguay for the war against Paraguay provided that (Article 16) after the conclusion of permanent boundary treaties Argentina should be separated from Paraguay by the Paraná and the Paraguay up to their meeting with the frontiers of Brazil, which were at Bahia Negra on the right (west) bank of the Paraguay. This would have given to Argentina Misiones and the entire Chaco from the Bermejo up to Bahia Negra. After this treaty became known, its territorial provisions especially evoked protests from Peru[6] and some of the other South American nations.[7] After the death of Francisco Solano López on March 1, 1870, and the end of the Five Years' War, the provisional government of Paraguay made a preliminary agreement of peace with Argentina and Brazil, signed at Asunción, on June 20, 1870,[8] by which the provisional government accepted in substance the Treaty of May 1, 1865, but reserved full liberty to propose and maintain, in the final arrangements as to boundaries, whatever they might deem to be in conformity with the rights of the republic of Paraguay; and the Argentine plenipotentiary agreed to the reservation, declaring that his government had expressly stated in its notes as to the occupation of Villa Occidental that it would not avail itself of its rights as conqueror to solve the question of boundaries but would terminate the question by an amicable agreement in view of the titles of both parties. In the ensuing negotiations Brazil supported Paraguay in her objection to ceding Villa Occidental and the Gran Chaco to Argentina, and, thus encouraged, Paraguay persisted in her resistance.[9] After Brazil had made her own separate treaties with Paraguay, she agreed with Argentina at a conference in Rio de Janeiro on November 19, 1872,[10] that Argentina should negotiate her own treaties with Paraguay, including one as to frontiers, subject to the Treaty of May 1, 1865. A treaty signed at Rio de Janeiro in 1875 failed of approval by the Paraguayan government, but following conferences at Buenos Aires with representatives of Brazil and Paraguay,[11] a treaty of

[4] *U. S. Dipl. Corr.*, 1867, Part II, pp. 710–711, 726.

[5] See §1, n. 2, this chap., *supra*.

[6] Ricardo Aranda, *Col. de Trat. del Peru* (Lima, 1907), X, 467–475.

[7] Bolivia: Ricardo Aranda, *Col. de Trat. del Peru* (Lima, 1911), XIV, 94–97.

[8] 63 *British and Foreign State Papers* 322–325.

[9] *U. S. For. Rel.*, 1872, pp. 29–30, 35–40, 43; *ibid.*, 1875, I, 36–41.

[10] 68 *British and Foreign State Papers* 83–86. Hildebrando Accioly, *Actos Int. Vig. no Brasil* (Rio de Janeiro, 1927), pp. 296–297.

[11] *Trat. de Argentina* (Buenos Aires, 1912), IX, 115–172.

peace was signed by Bernado de Irigoyen, Argentine minister of foreign relations, and Facundo Machain, Paraguayan minister of foreign relations,
at Buenos Aires on February 3, 1876,[12] by which it was agreed that (Article
2) the final frontier between the two nations should be set forth in a special
treaty to be signed simultaneously; (Article 6) indemnities and claims were
to be fixed by a mixed commission; (Article 12) navigation of the Paraná,
Paraguay, and Uruguay (Article 13) not including their tributaries nor internal trade, was to be free to the trade of all nations; (Article 14) vessels
of war of the river states should enjoy free passage, but those of nations not
bordering on the rivers might go only as far as each river state within its
own boundaries should permit; and (Article 20) Argentina in accordance
with the Treaty of May 1, 1865, bound herself to respect forever the independence, sovereignty, and integrity of the Republic of Paraguay. The
boundary treaty of the same day, February 3, 1876,[13] provided that (Article 1) Paraguay should be divided from Argentina on the east and on the
south by the mid-channel of the main stream of the Paraná from its confluence
with the Paraguay to the boundary of Brazil, on its left (east) bank, the
island of Apipé to belong to Argentina and the island of Yasiretá to Paraguay, as declared in the Treaty of 1856; (Article 2) Paraguay should be divided from Argentina on the west by the mid-channel of the main stream of
the Paraguay from its confluence with the Paraná, the Chaco as far as the
main channel of the Pilcomayo, which empties into the Paraguay at 25°
20' S., according to the map of Mouchez,[14] and at 25°22' S. according to the
map of Brayer,[15] being definitely recognized as belonging to Argentina;
(Article 3) the island of Atajo or Cerrito should belong to Argentina and the
remaining permanent or temporary islands in either the Paraná or the Paraguay to Argentina or Paraguay according to their position with reference to
one or the other republic in conformity with the principles of international
law which guide such matters, the channels between the islands, including
Cerrito, to be common to the navigation of both states; (Article 6) of the
territory between the main arm of the Pilcomayo and Bahia Negra, Argentina definitely renounced all claim or right over the section between Bahia

[12] *Ibid.*, 173-184. *Col. de Trat. del Paraguay*, Pub.
Ofic. (Asunción, 1890), pp. 14-19. 68 *British and Foreign
State Papers* 86-91. Martens, *Nouv. Rec. Gén. de Traités*,
2ᵉ Sér., III, 487-492. Martens et Cussy, *Rec. Man. et
Prat. de Traités* 2ᵉ Sér., II, 522-527. Ratified by Argentina, July 7, 1876; ratified by Paraguay, Aug. 24, 1876;
ratifications exchanged at Buenos Aires, Sept. 13, 1876.

[13] *Trat. de Argentina* (Buenos Aires, 1912), IX, 196-
203. *Col. de Trat. del Paraguay* (Asunción, 1885), pp.
32-36. *U. S. For. Rel.*, 1876, pp. 9-10. Moore, *Int. Arbi-*

trations (Washington, 1898), V, 4783-4785. 68 *British
and Foreign State Papers* 97-100. Martens, *Nouv. Rec.
Gén. de Traités*, 2ᵉ Sér., IX, 748-751. *Arch. Dipl.*, 1876-77,
III, 176-179. Ratified by Argentina, Law #770, July 7,
1876; ratified by Paraguay, Aug. 24, 1876; ratifications
exchanged at Buenos Aires, Sept. 13, 1876.

[14] E. Mouchez, 1862. See *La Cuestión del Rio Putumayo*, Min. de Rel. Ext. (Asunción, 1927).

[15] Lucien de Brayer, 1863. See *La Cuestión del Rio
Putumayo*, Min. de Rel. Ext. (Asunción, 1927).

Negra and the river Verde, at 23°10' S. according to Mouchez' map; and the proprietorship or right over the territory of the second section, between the Verde and the main arm of the Pilcomayo, including Villa Occidental, was to be submitted to the arbitration of the President of the United States, or another arbiter if he should not accept; (Article 8) cases to be submitted within twelve months of the arbiter's acceptance; (Article 10) the arbiter's decision to be final and binding on both states; and (Article 12) either state receiving the territory should respect the property and possessions of the other and pay for public buildings taken over. By this treaty Paraguay gave up all claim to any of the Misiones territory [16] east of the Paraná, to the Middle Chaco south of the Pilcomayo and to the island of Atajo or Cerrito at the confluence of the Paraná and the Paraguay, and Argentina agreed to evacuate Villa Occidental and resigned her claim to the Chaco Boreal north of the Verde. President Ulysses S. Grant was asked by the president of Paraguay on January 13, and by the president of Argentina on January 25, 1877, if he would be the arbiter, and President Rutherford B. Hayes accepted the office on March 28, 1877.[17] The Argentine case was delivered by Minister Manuel R. Garcia on March 25,[18] and the Paraguayan case by Minister Benjamin Aceval on March 27, 1878,[19] to William M. Evarts, secretary of state, in Washington. On November 13, 1878, Secretary Evarts transmitted to the ministers of the two countries in Washington copies of the award of President Hayes dated November 12, 1878,[20] deciding that Paraguay was legally and justly entitled to the territory between the Pilcomayo and the Verde rivers and to the Villa Occidental situated therein, stating no western boundary and giving no reasons for the decision. Paraguay in appreciation of her victory changed to Villa Hayes [21] the name of Villa Occidental, which had been founded by decree of May 14, 1855,[22] with French colonists from Bordeaux as Nueva Bordeos.

Use of the Pilcomayo (Pilco-Mayu) river as the southern boundary of the disputed territory in the submission and in the award seemed clear enough on paper, but in practical application to the ground left doubts which

[16] Belisario Saravia, *Memoria sobre los Límites entre la República Argentina y el Paraguay* (Buenos Aires, 1867).

[17] Moore, *Int. Arbitrations* (Washington, 1898), II, 1923–1944.

[18] *U. S. For. Rel.*, 1878, pp. 17–18. *Cuestión de Límites entre la República Argentina y el Paraguay, Ojeada Retrospectiva* (Buenos Aires, 1880).

[19] *U. S. For. Rel.*, 1878, pp. 709–710. Benjamin Aceval, *Chaco Paraguayo, Memoria Presentada al Arbitro* (Asunción, 1896).

[20] *Trat. de Argentina* (Buenos Aires, 1912), X, 25–29. *U. S. For. Rel.*, 1878, pp. 710–712. *U. S. Treaty Series* no. 390. 69 *British and Foreign State Papers* 600–601. Martens, *Nouv. Rec. Gén. de Traités*, 2e Sér., XII, 472–474. *Rev. de Der. Int.* (Habana), XV (1929), 5–27. *Rev. de dr. int. et de lég. comp.*, 2e Sér., IV (1902), 560.

[21] Law of May 13, 1879. *Reg. Ofic. del Paraguay* (Asunción, 1887), II, 500–501.

[22] *Appendix and Documents Annexed to the Memoir filed by the Minister of Paraguay* (New York, 1878), pp. 174–178, 355–361.

caused serious further difficulty, for the river was one of the geographical unknowns of South America. Its headwaters, in Tarija and Chuquisaca, and the neighborhood of its mouth, on the Paraguay, had been known for many years, but its interior course across the flat marshy lands of the Chaco, spreading out into wide swamps and dividing into inconstant channels, remained a puzzle. The scattered groups of Indians were fierce and intractable and combined with the waters to make exploration difficult. Crevaux was treacherously killed by the Tobas while making his way down stream in 1882; Ibaretta was defeated in his attempts at exploration in 1898, as were numerous others after him. Thouar, a Frenchman, made his way from the upper Pilcomayo to Asunción, and was for a long time the only white man to get through. Pages, a captain in the Argentine navy, tried to ascend, building dams below his small steamer to secure a navigable depth of water, but finally had to abandon his vessel in the marshes. In 1905 Gunnar Lange with thirty men undertook a thorough survey of the river and attained 700 miles from its mouth.

Carlos Rodríguez Larreta, Argentine minister of foreign relations, and José Z. Caminos, Paraguayan minister at Buenos Aires, signed on September 11, 1905,[23] an agreement for a mixed commission of four experts, two appointed by each party, to make the necessary studies and report which was the principal arm or channel of the Pilcomayo, the two governments to examine the map and report in Buenos Aires and determine what should be considered the boundary according to the Hayes award. On February 1, 1907,[24] a modifying agreement changed the mixed commission to consist of two experts, one appointed by each party. Argentina appointed D. Krausse and Paraguay Elias Ayala, and these two explored the region of the river, surveyed its north and south branches, and united in a report [25] which Honorio Pueyrredón, Argentine minister of foreign relations, on April 12, 1921, submitted to the Paraguayan minister in Buenos Aires, with an exposition to which the Paraguayan minister of foreign relations replied in March 1925, and there the matter has since rested.

East of the confluence of the Paraguay, the Paraná up to the Iguazú forms the boundary between Argentina and Paraguay, and no dispute over the channel, median line, or thalweg has yet arisen. Navigation is common

[23] *Trat. de Argentina* (Buenos Aires, 1912), IX, 284–285. 98 *British and Foreign State Papers* 770–771. Martens, *Nouv. Rec. Gén. de Traités*, 3e Sér., VI, 611–612.

[24] *Trat. de Argentina* (Buenos Aires, 1912), IX, 286–287. Martens, *Nouv. Rec. Gén. de Traités*, 3e Sér., VI, 612.

[25] *La Cuestión del Rio Pilcomayo, Min. de Rel. Ext.* (Asunción, 1927). E. A. Fretes, *El Paraguay en el primer cincuentenario del fallo arbitral del presidente Hayes* (Asunción, 1932).

to the two countries and Brazil by treaties elsewhere discussed. A vast tract of 1,000,000 hectares (2,471,000 acres) of forest and hills on the west bank of the Paraná for 300 kilometers (186 miles) from near Guayra Falls to San Lorenzo, granted to Domingo Barthe, a French Basque boatman who made himself acceptable to the government and greatly prospered, has been kept unsettled, except for occasional watch villages, and is not allowed to have commerce with or use the steamers that serve the Argentine east bank.

An issue of doubtful paper boundaries of the province of Chiquitos in the north of the viceroyalty of the Plata against marginal settlement and control from the province of Paraguay in the same viceroyalty was adjudged by a neutral arbiter to call for a boundary along a river whose source and mouth were known; but when the middle course of that river proved to be swampy and wandering, with the main channel doubtful, further agreement was required. With the advent of the struggle with Bolivia, Paraguay allowed further discussion with Argentina to lapse, but when the Bolivian frontier is fixed, the question of which channel of the Pilcomayo forms the southern boundary of the Chaco Boreal with Argentina will come up again to be formally settled.

5. Argentina–Uruguay. La Plata

The Rio de la Plata, an arm of the sea muddy and fresh for miles out of sight of land, is 135 miles across at its outer capes and 25 miles wide at the confluence of the Paraná and the Uruguay, 200 miles inland, but despite its size is claimed by Argentina and Uruguay to belong to them as littoral nations and to be no part of the high seas.[1] Martín García is a nearly circular rocky island about two miles in circumference, at most 200 feet above sea level, at the head of the Plata and the mouth of the Paraná and a little below the mouth of the Uruguay, two miles from the Uruguayan shore, seven from the Argentine, at 34°11′25″ S. 58°15′38″ W. As a reward for valiant service in helping to oust the British from Buenos Aires in 1807, Charles IV bestowed the island of Martín García upon Antonio Tejo.

The preliminary convention of peace between the United Provinces of the Rio de la Plata and the Emperor of Brazil, signed at Rio de Janeiro on August 27, 1828,[2] provided for the independence of the province of Monte-

[1] Elihu Root, *North Atlantic Coast Fisheries Arbitration* (Cambridge, 1917), p. xcviii. Philip C. Jessup, *Law of Territorial Waters* (New York, 1927), p. 379. Uruguayan Laws of July 11, 1895, July 20, 1900, and Dec. 12, 1906; *Col. Leg. del Uruguay* (Montevideo), XVIII (1896), 194–197; *ibid.*, XXIII (1901), 360–361;

ibid., XXIX (1907), 819–821.
[2] *Col. das Leis do Brazil*, 1828 (Rio de Janeiro, 1878), pp. 121–132. *Col. Leg. del Uruguay* (Montevideo, 1930), I, 84–89. 15 *British and Foreign State Papers* 935–944. Martens, *Nouv. Rec. de Traités*, VI, 686–691. Ratifications exchanged at Montevideo, Oct. 4, 1828.

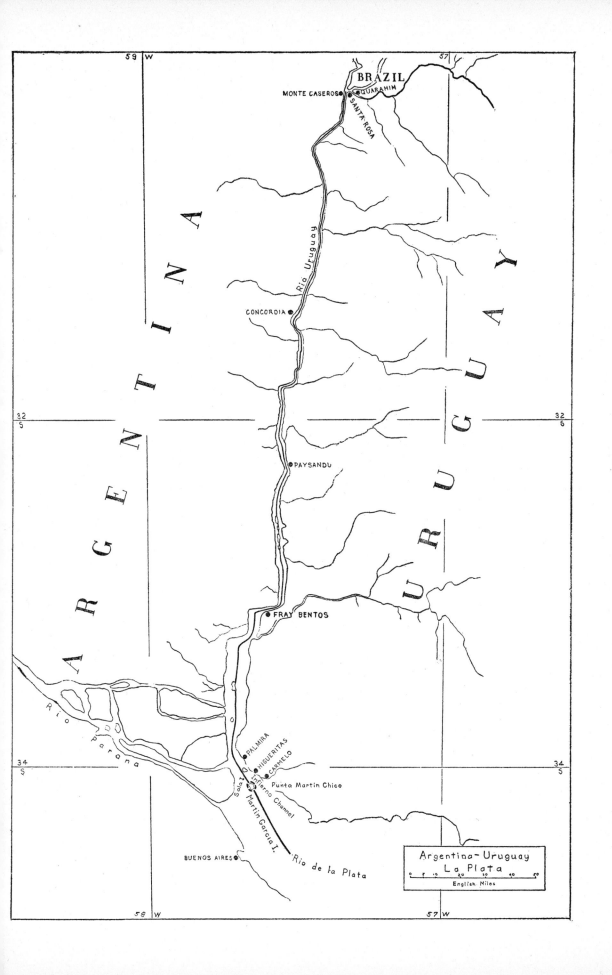

BRAZIL

MONTE CASEROS● ●QUARAHIM

SANTA ROSA

ARGENTINA

URUGUAY

Rio Uruguay

CONCORDIA ●

32
S

32
S

● PAYSANDU

● FRAY BENTOS

Rio
Parana

PALMIRA ●
●HIGUERITAS
● CARMELO

34
S

Salala

Infierno Channel
Punta Martin Chico

34
S

Martin Garcia I.

BUENOS AIRES ●

Rio de la Plata

Argentina-Uruguay
La Plata

0   5   10   20   30   40   50

English Miles

59 W

57 W

59 W

57 W

video or the Cisplatine province without reciting any boundaries for Uruguay, but assumed (Article 12) that troops on the right (south or west) bank of the Plata or the Uruguay would be outside the territory of the province of Montevideo. The convention between Brazil and Uruguay signed on December 25, 1828,[3] providing that the Quarahim should be the provisional boundary line between the two countries did not concern itself with the southern boundary of Uruguay. In November 1837 [4] France came into conflict with Dictator Juan Manuel de Rosas over a decree requiring resident Frenchmen to serve in the Buenos Aires militia, and various claims for injuries and failure of justice. Diplomatic representations made no practical headway, and Rear Admiral L. Le Blanc on March 28, 1838,[5] declared a blockade of the port of Buenos Aires and all the Argentine shore from May 10, 1838; and on October 11, 1838,[6] a French landing party from the *Bordelaise* took possession of Martín García Island. France in March 1839[7] on inquiry by England disclaimed any intention of appropriating the island permanently or of altering its possession as between Argentina and Montevideo. Peace efforts by the United States [8] through Captain John B. Nicolson, commanding the United States frigate *Fairfield,* failed, but Great Britain exerted her good offices,[9] and the difficulties were adjusted in a convention of October 29, 1840,[10] by which the government of Buenos Aires agreed to pay indemnities at a figure to be fixed by six arbitrators and to continue to recognize the absolute independence of Uruguay, and France agreed to raise the blockade of Argentine ports and to evacuate the island of Martín García within eight days after ratification of the convention by the government of Buenos Aires. Uruguayans under Lieutenant-Colonel Francisco Anzani sent by General Giuseppe Garibaldi seized and occupied Martín García Island on September 5, 1845. Great Britain blockaded Buenos Aires on September 24, 1845, and occupied the island, but by a convention signed at Buenos Aires November 24, 1849,[11] agreed to evacuate it. Uruguay occupied it again, but shortly after the fall of Rosas, Acting President Bernardo P. Berro of Uruguay on February 28, 1852, ordered the island returned to Argentina, and

[3] See §14, this chap., *infra.*

[4] 26 *British and Foreign State Papers* 920–1023, 1081–1083.

[5] *Ibid.*, 727–728, 1069–1070. Martens, *Nouv. Rec. de Traités*, XV, 502–504. *Amer. J. Int. Law*, III (1909), 298. Naval War College, *International Law Situations*, 1931, p. 95.

[6] 26 *British and Foreign State Papers* 992–993, 1024.

[7] 27 *ibid.*, 195–196.

[8] 31 *ibid.*, 790–801. William S. Robertson, *Hispanic-American Relations with the United States* (New York,

1923), pp. 143–145.

[9] 31 *British and Foreign State Papers* 1080.

[10] *Col. de Trat. celebrados por la República Argentina* (Buenos Aires, 1884), I, 212–223. de Clercq, *Rec. des Traités* (Paris, 1880), IV, 591–594. Ratifications exchanged at Paris, Oct. 15, 1841.

[11] *Col. de Trat. celebrados por la República Argentina* (Buenos Aires, 1884), I, 258–267. 37 *British and Foreign State Papers* 7–11. Ratifications exchanged at Buenos Aires, May 15, 1850.

possession was turned over on March 17, 1852. On October 3, 1852, the new government of the Argentine Confederation, against the will of the Buenos Aires government,[12] which desired to keep control of the rivers and customs dues in its own hands, issued a decree[13] looking toward freer river navigation; and on July 10, 1853, the Confederation signed at San José de Flores with the United States,[14] Great Britain,[15] and France[16] treaties permitting the free navigation by all nations of the Paraná and the Uruguay wherever they belonged to the Confederation.

After the occupations by France and Great Britain, the states of the Plata took alarm at the possibility of the permanent seizure of Martín García island by a European power. Accordingly in the ensuing treaties between the allies,[17] aside from the disputed question of fortification,[18] there was included the specific agreement (Article 18) that each party would oppose by all means that the sovereignty of Martín García should cease to belong to one of the states of the Plata, interested in the free navigation of that river; and in the three Argentine treaties of 1853 for free river navigation the parties agreed (Article 5) to use their influence to the end that the island should not be retained or held by any state of the Plata or its confluents which had not adhered to the principle of their free navigation.

The constitution adopted by the state of Buenos Aires, April 11, 1854,[19] recited that its territory was bounded on the northeast and east by the Paraná, the Plata, and the Atlantic, including the islands of Martín García and others adjacent to its coasts, and in the interprovincial struggle in 1859 the Argentine Confederation asked Brazil to aid in dislodging the forces of Buenos Aires from the island. Brazil and the Argentine Confederation made with Uruguay at Rio de Janeiro on January 2, 1859,[20] a treaty of alliance agreeing that Uruguay should not have the power of incorporating or confederating with either of the others or of diminishing on any pretext whatever the territory which then belonged to it; the other two declared

[12] 49 *British and Foreign State Papers* 1261-1273.

[13] 42 *ibid.*, 1313-1315. Moore, *Digest Int. Law* (Washington, 1906), I, 640. *Wheaton's Elements of International Law*, ed. by A. Berriedale Keith (6th Eng. ed., London, 1929), I, 396.

[14] *Col. de Trat. celebrados por la República Argentina* (Buenos Aires, 1884), I, 358-365. *United States Treaty Series*, No. 3. Malloy, *Treaties of the United States* (Washington, 1910), I, 18-20. 42 *British and Foreign State Papers* 718-720. *Rev. de Der. Int.* (Havana), V (1924), 422-425. Ratifications exchanged at Paraná, Dec. 20, 1854.

[15] *Col. de Trat. celebrados por la República Argentina* (Buenos Aires, 1884), I, 366-373. 42 *British and Foreign State Papers* 3-6. Ratifications exchanged at Paraná, Mar. 11, 1854.

[16] *Col. de Trat. celebrados por la República Argentina* (Buenos Aires, 1884), I, 374-382. 44 *British and Foreign State Papers* 1071-1073. Martens, *Nouv. Rec. Gén. de Traités*, 2ᵉ Sér., X, 294-295. Ratifications exchanged at Paraná, Sept. 21, 1854.

[17] Brazil-Uruguay, treaty of Oct. 12, 1851. See §14, this chap., *infra*. Argentina-Brazil, treaty of March 7, 1856. See §2, note 3, this chap., *supra*.

[18] Protocol of Feb. 25, 1864. *Trat. de Argentina* (Buenos Aires, 1901), I, 137-138. *U. S. For. Rel.*, 1874, 73-80; *ibid.*, 1875, I, 4, 24, 36.

[19] 46 *British and Foreign State Papers* 843-859.

[20] *Col. de Trat. del Uruguay*, Pub. Ofic. (Montevideo, 1923), I, 473-485. 49 *British and Foreign State Papers* 1234-1238.

themselves perpetually obliged to defend the independence and integrity of Uruguay, that republic was declared and guaranteed as a state absolutely and perpetually neutral between them, and none was to harbor revolutions or conspiracies against either of the others or their governments. This treaty was not ratified by any of the party nations.

Argentina insisted in 1874–75 on her right to fortify and arm Martín García Island,[21] against Brazil's protest that such action threatened free navigation of the Paraná and the Uruguay and was therefore contrary to existing treaties, especially those of July 10, 1853. In 1877 vaguely and in 1888 more definitely Uruguay considered the commercial desirability of improving the Infierno Channel, rediscovered in 1884, northeast of the island between it and Punta Martín Chico on the Uruguayan shore, and surveys under Engineer Duclout were completed in 1892, but no actual dredging or marking was undertaken. The vast amount of sediment brought down by the Paraná and the Uruguay is slowly but steadily raising the bottom of the entire southerly portion of the Plata, and the channels on the north side are the easiest to maintain of a depth to admit ocean-going vessels.

Argentina and Uruguay signed at Montevideo on August 14, 1888,[22] a convention declaring the profession of pilot in the Plata free to those licensed by either nation, and permitting any such pilots to cruise to any distance up the river or beyond the Capes and to offer their services to ships inbound to Uruguayan or Argentine ports, ships in the river or outside the Capes being permitted to take a pilot of either nationality, but those leaving a port to employ a pilot of the nationality of that port. In 1895 Argentina became interested in better navigation to the upper rivers and made surveys of the Plata, but it was not until 1899 [23] that a law in support of the construction and development of a commercial port at Rosario de Santa Fé called for the maintenance by the national government of a minimum depth of 5.80 meters (19 feet) of water at ordinary low tide in the Martín García passage. In 1901 Argentina set up along this channel forty-four lighted buoys, and has since attended to the dredging and marking required to keep it open for navigation, as well as the channels from Buenos Aires out to it, and towards Montevideo and the open sea. In November 1907 [24] the deten-

---

[21] *U. S. For. Rel.*, 1874, pp. 73–81, 84; *ibid.*, 1875, I, 4, 24, 107, 110.

[22] *Col. de Trat. del Uruguay* (Montevideo, 1925), III, 607–609. Ratifications exchanged at Montevideo, Nov. 13, 1891.

[23] Law #3885, of Dec. 20, 1899. Da Rocha, *Leyes Nac.* (Buenos Aires, 1918), XII, vol. 1, pp. 276–279.

[24] Setembrino E. Pereda, *Una Cuestón Histórica, La Isla de Martín García Uruguaya y no Argentina* (Montevideo, 1907). *Amer. J. Int. Law*, I (1907), 984–988. José Leon Suarez, *La Isla de Martín García, Legitimidad del dominio argentino* (Buenos Aires, 1907). Agustin de Vedia, *Martín García y la Jurisdiccion del Plata* (Buenos Aires, 1908).

tion by the Argentine authorities at the island of a small Uruguayan steam
fishing boat gave rise to a diplomatic incident between the countries which
threatened for a time to lead to serious conflict. Dr. Estanislao S. Zeballos
denounced the 1899 treaty [25] of obligatory and unconditional arbitration
with Uruguay as an error on the part of Argentina; and others asserted that
the question of the river boundary was so vital to Argentina that it could
not be submitted to arbitration. A protocol signed by Dr. Gonzalo Ramírez,
Uruguayan minister to Argentina, and Dr. Roque Sáenz Peña, Argentine
minister to Italy, at Montevideo on January 5, 1910,[26] provided that the
navigation and use of the waters of the Plata should continue without alteration as up to the present time, and that any difference which might arise with
respect to them should be overcome and resolved with the spirit of cordiality
and good harmony which had always existed between the two countries.

An unratified convention between Argentina and Uruguay signed at
Montevideo on July 29, 1912,[27] provided that vessels engaged in coastwise
trade along the Plata and its affluents should receive the same facilities and
privileges which the national laws of each nation granted to vessels under its
own flag. A convention signed at Montevideo on April 11, 1918,[28] arranged
for the institutes of military geography of the two countries to carry out
jointly triangulation of the frontier river Uruguay from the mouth of the
Quarahim to the mouth of the Uruguay in the estuary of the Plata, as a
basis for fitting together sheets of the 1:1,000,000 map of this zone.

Whether the line of division in the wide shallow estuary that lies between these countries should run close to the shore of the smaller inside the
channel maintained by the other, down the thread of the stream or thalweg if determinable, or down the center of the water surface is still unsettled,[29] but the two countries are essentially friendly and while Argentina is
willing to keep the channel navigable and Uruguayan fishermen are not in-
terfered with there seems little likelihood of the dispute becoming acute.
Although probably not arbitrable, it may be expected to be adjusted in the
not very remote future by special agreement.

[25] See chap. III, §8, infra.

[26] Trat. de Argentina (Buenos Aires, 1912), IX, 624–625. Col. de Trat. del Uruguay (Montevideo, 1928), V, 459–460. 103 British and Foreign State Papers 357. Martens, Nouv. Rec. Gén. de Traités, 3e Sér., VI, 876–877. Amer. J. Int. Law, IV (1910), 430–431, Supp., 138–139.

[27] Col. de Trat. del Uruguay (Montevideo, 1928), V, 741–743. Amer. J. Int. Law, VII (1913), Supp., 166–167.

[28] Trat. y Conv. Vig. en la Nación Argentina (Buenos Aires, 1925), I, 810–812. Comp. de Leyes y Decr. del Uru-

guay (Montevideo, 1930), XLIX, 148–150. League of Nations Treaty Series, No. 385, XIV, 368–373. 114 British and Foreign State Papers 567–568. Approved by Argentina, Law #11175, Sept. 30, 1921; ratified by Argentine Executive, Nov. 25, 1921; ratified by Uruguayan Executive, June 13, 1919; ratifications exchanged at Buenos Aires, Feb. 3, 1922; promulgated by Uruguay, Feb. 11, 1922.

[29] Lester H. Woolsey, "Boundary Disputes in Latin America," Amer. J. Int. Law, XXV (1931), 332.

6. Bolivia–Brazil. Acre–Abuná

The Treaty of San Ildefonso of October 1, 1777,[1] ran the line between Portuguese and Spanish territory up the Paraguay to the Lake of Xarayes, across that lake to the mouth of the Jaurú, then in a straight line to the south bank of the Guaporé or Itenes, opposite the mouth of the Sararé, or other river near if found more easy and certain, down the Guaporé to its junction with the Mamoré, down the Mamoré and the Madeira to a point equidistant from the Marañón or Amazon and the mouth of the Mamoré, and thence by an east-west line to the east bank of the Javary. In 1837[2] the Brazilian president of the province of Matto Grosso complained that the Bolivian authorities in the district of Chiquitos had assigned portions of land in Matto Grosso as if they lay within Bolivia, and Brazil asked the Bolivian minister of foreign relations to send out the necessary orders for preserving the boundary according to the Treaty of October 1, 1777, until a new treaty should be concluded. Long pending negotiations for a boundary treaty were broken off in 1863[3] when Brazil, starting from Bahia Negra, wished to draw the line west of lakes Mandioré, Gaiba, and Overaba, while Bolivia, resting on the Treaty of 1777, wanted the line to be the Paraguay from below Bahia Negra to the mouth of the Jaurú, dividing the lakes equally or, as they were west of the principal channel of the Paraguay, making them entirely Bolivian; but the next government of Bolivia, under General José Mariano Melgarejo, came to an agreement with Brazil. By a treaty signed at La Paz on March 27, 1867,[4] recognizing as a basis for the boundary the *uti possidetis*, the line was run from the Paraguay in 20° 10′ S. through the center of Bahia Negra to its head; thence in a straight line to the Lake of Cáceres and across its center; thence to Lake Mandioré and through its middle, as also through the middles of lakes Gahiba and Uberaba in as many straight lines as necessary, so that the highlands of Pedras de Amolar and Insua should be left on the Brazilian side; from the north end of Lake Uberaba in a straight line to the south end of Corrixa-Grande, preserving the towns on either side as they were; from the end of Corrixa-Grande in a straight line to the Morro da Boa-Vista and to Quatro Irmãos; thence also in a straight line to the sources of the Verde; down the Verde to

[1] Articles 9, 10 and 11. See §2, this chap., *supra*.
[2] 27 *British and Foreign State Papers* 1416.
[3] 55 *ibid.*, 862. *Mariano Reyes Cardona, Cuestión de Límites entre Bolivia i el Brasil* (Sucre, 1868).
[4] *Rel. do Min. das Rel. Ext.* (Maio, 1868), p. 11; Annexo pp. 63–72. 59 *British and Foreign State Papers* 1161–

1169. *Arch. Dipl.*, 1869, III, 1074–1081. Martens, *Nouv. Rec. Gén. de Traités*, XX, 613–621. Ratified by Bolivia, Law of September 21, 1868; ratified by Brazil, June 16, 1867; ratifications exchanged at La Paz, Sept. 22, 1868; promulgated by Brazil, Decree #4280, Nov. 18, 1868.

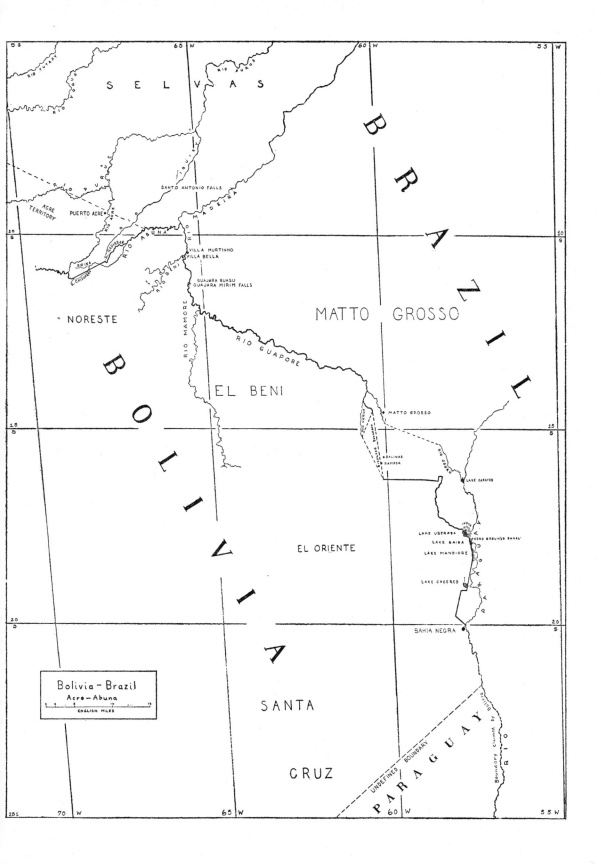

its confluence with the Guaporé; through the middle of the Guaporé and of the Mamoré as far as Beni, where the Madeira begins; from the Madeira west by a line from its left (west) bank along the parallel at 10°20′ S. to the Javary; or if the sources of the Javary are north of 10°20′ S., from the said latitude on the Madeira in a straight line to the principal source of the Javary. Each party within six months was to name a commissioner to mark out the line where necessary; more natural or convenient boundaries were to be followed, with an exchange of territory, where advantageous or to give space to any existing hamlet or public establishment; communication over the frontier to be free; waters of navigable rivers through Brazilian territory to the ocean to be free to Bolivian commerce, and of Bolivian navigable rivers to be free to Brazilian commerce; navigation of the Madeira above the waterfall of Santo Antonio to be permitted only to the parties, even should Brazil open the river up to that point to third nations; Brazil to grant at once to Bolivia under the same regulations as for Brazilians the use of any road which it might open from the first waterfall on the right bank of the Mamoré to the fall of Santo Antonio on the Madeira; reciprocal free passage and entry of vessels of war to be permitted in all rivers qualified for the entry of merchant vessels, except that as to the affluents of the Amazon a limit in number should be fixed. By explanatory notes exchanged on September 19, 1867, it was declared to be understood that although the boundary line passed through the middle of lakes Negra, Cáceres, Gahiba, Mandioré, and Uberaba the navigation of them and of Lake Gahiba-Mirim was common to the parties, subject to police regulations. By this treaty Bolivia acknowledged or cleared Brazil's title to some 540,000 square miles of territory on the Paraguay and Madeira rivers, and drew boundary lines on paper disregarding the natural bounds of the hydrographic basin through an unsettled and largely unknown region among the remote southwestern tributaries of the Amazon. Peru, whose boundaries with neither Bolivia nor Brazil were settled, thought her rights infringed in this treaty, and on December 20, 1867,[5] protested to the Bolivian minister of foreign relations that the principle of *uti possidetis*, while applicable between the Spanish-American states with a common origin,[6] had no proper place between countries derived from separate sovereignties, especially when there was an existing written agreement on the matter; that the Madeira commenced not

---

[5] *Anuario Admin. de 1868*, Ed. Ofic. (La Paz), Apen. pp. 385-404. Ricardo Aranda, *Col. de Trat. del Peru*, II, 381-385; *ibid.*, XIV, 918-922.

[6] *Cf.* Argentina's argument in 1894. §2, this chap., *supra*.

at Beni but at the confluence of the Guaporé with the Mamoré; that the abandonment of the line of the San Ildefonso Treaty would result in the absorption by Brazil of 90,000 square miles of territory in which were such important rivers as the Purús, the Yurua, and the Yutay; that according to the treaty of October 23, 1851,[7] with Brazil, the line between Brazil and Peru should be the course of the Javary south of Tabatinga to 9°30′ S. or to the source of that river if south of that parallel, so that according to this treaty between Bolivia and Brazil if the principal source of the Javary should turn out to be south of 10°20′ S. Brazil would invade Peruvian territory and if such source should be north of 10°20′ S. none of the three countries would own the parcel between the parallel 10°20′ S. on the Madeira and the parallel 9°30′ S. Bolivia, rejecting the protest on February 6, 1868, declared that the Itenes or Guaporé joined the Mamoré at 11°22′ S. 65°34′46″ W. and the Madeira began at the junction of the Mamoré and the Beni at 10°20′ S. 66°19′46″ W.; that there could be no unowned parcel, and that the treaty with Brazil did not infringe upon territorial rights of Peru. Following this treaty, Brazilian rubber gatherers from Manaos penetrated farther and farther into the unoccupied territory in search of the finest wild gum of the region and even worked as far as 12° S., clearly within Bolivian territory. Pedro II on August 27, 1868,[8] granted to George Earl Church, formerly a colonel in the United States Engineers, an exclusive privilege for fifty years, subject to purchase if desired by the government after thirty years, to organize a company and construct and operate a railway from the most advantageous point near to and below the falls of Santo Antonio along the right (southeast) bank of the Madeira to the most advantageous point near to and above the falls of Guajará-Mirim, with the grant of alternate lots of land along the line and exemption of construction material from import duties for the whole term and of export duties for twenty-five years. Colonel Church got the Bolivian government to lend its credit to a loan of from £1,500,000 to £2,000,000 for the enterprise, acquired some good English names, sold a considerable quantity of bonds in England, and let the construction contract to the Public Works Construction Company, Ltd., of London. The required railroad turned out to be 197 in-

[7] See §13, this chap., *infra*.

[8] Brazilian contract modified Dec. 7, 1869. Decree #4509 of Apr. 20, 1870. Approved by Law of Sept. 6, 1870. Time for completion extended to Apr. 20, 1884; Decree #6357, of Oct. 18, 1876. *Col. das Leis do Brasil*, XXXIII (1870), Parte II, 230–234; *ibid.*, XXXIX (1876), Parte II, 1056. *Anuario de Leyes de Bol.*, 1871, p. 74.

Actos Admin. del Gob. Prov. de Bol., 1870–71 (La Paz), pp. 204–205. 63 *British and Foreign State Papers* 254–259. National Bolivian Navigation Co. chartered by U. S. Congress, Act of June 29, 1870, c. 168; 16 *U. S. Stat. L.* 168–169. Madeira and Mamoré Co., Ltd., incorporated in England, Mar. 1, 1871.

stead of 150 miles long, money became scarce, disputes broke out between the companies and the two countries,[9] and the English company failed to perform its contract. The construction was then given to Philip and Thomas Collins, railroad contractors of Philadelphia, Pennsylvania, who sent out a large party of Americans to the scene in 1878. They struggled gamely with the difficulties of food, climate, illness, hostile savages, and money shortage, but the work finally collapsed on February 17, 1879, and the American colony at Santo Antonio left on August 19 and reached New York, September 29, 1879.[10]

In 1872 [11] some of the Argentine legalists, in connection with the protocol and discussion concerning the boundary with Bolivia, advanced a claim to the entire Chiquitos and Mojos territories, on the theory that the possession of the original province and later viceroyalty of the Plata ran north, west of the Tordesillas line, to meet on the upper Amazon the 1568 grant of Diego Hernández de Zerpa; but neither Bolivia, Brazil, nor Peru made any pretense of treating this claim seriously, and it was not officially urged.

The two commissioners contemplated by the Treaty of 1867 were finally appointed and mapped part of the line, but, finding themselves unable to agree on other portions, suspended operations and reported to their respective governments, which failed to resolve the matter, and the commission did no further work on the demarcation. A new dispute arose as to the source of the Javary, and it was on March 14, 1874,[12] fixed at 6°59'29.5" S. 74°6'26.67" W. by a mixed commission (Guillermo Black and Barón de Teffé); corrected on November 17, 1877,[13] to 7°1'17.5" S. 74°8'27.07" W. by another mixed commission (Guillermo Carlos Lassanse and Frederico Ferreira de Oliveira); and rectified in 1898 by the Brazilian Augusto da Cunha Gomes [14] to 7°11'48" S. 73°47'44" W. In 1890 [15] Bolivia created in the northern region two national delegations of the Madre de Dios and of the Purús; combined into one, the Noroeste, in 1893; [16] and in 1898 she undertook to enforce her revenue laws by establishing a customs house at Puerto Acre (Porto Alonso) near the Brazilian frontier. In July 1899 the

[9] Wilson v. Church, Law Rep. (1878) 9 Ch. Div. 552; 13 Ch. Div. 1. 39 Law Times Rep., N. S. (1878) 413; 41 ibid. (1879) 50, 296. 48 L. J. Rep., Chan. (1879) 690. 5 App. Cases (1880) 176.

[10] George E. Church, The Route to Bolivia via the River Amazon; a Report to the Governments of Bolivia and Brazil (London, 1877). Neville B. Craig, Recollections of an Ill-fated Expedition (Philadelphia and London, 1907).

[11] See §1, this chap., supra.

[12] Col. de Doc. que apoyan el Alegato de Bolivia en el Juicio Arbitral con Peru (Buenos Aires, 1906), II, 559–563.

[13] Ibid., 557–559.

[14] Augusto da Cunha Gomes, Commissão de Limites entre o Brasil e a Bolivia, Re-exploração do Rio Javary (Rio de Janeiro, 1899). José Manoel Cardoso de Oliveira, Actos Dipl. do Brasil (Rio de Janeiro, 1912), II, 255.

[15] Law of Oct, 28, 1890. Anuario de Leyes, 1890, Ed. Ofic. (La Paz, 1891), pp. 255-257.

[16] Decree of May 16, 1893. Anuario de Leyes, 1893, pp. 119-123. Order of Mar. 31, 1896. Anuario de Leyes, 1896, pp. 60-61.

Brazilian rubber gatherers in the region refused to recognize the Bolivian authorities, armed their employees, numbering from 15,000 to 30,000, seized Puerto Acre, and on July 14, 1899,[17] under a Spanish adventurer named Luís Gálvez Rodríguez de Arias proclaimed the independent state of Acre. Bolivia sent two military expeditions to put down the uprising, and, after sanguinary clashes between the soldiers and the Acreans, Bolivian authority was reëstablished in April 1901, and "President" Gálvez solemnly resigned his title for an indemnity of 420 contos of reis ($25,300).

In protocols of February 19, 1895,[18] May 10, 1895,[19] October 30, 1899,[20] and August 1, 1900,[21] and acts in 1896[22] for demarcation of the line between the Madeira and the source of the Javary, Brazil appeared to agree that the Acre was Bolivian territory, and she refused to recognize the Republic of Acre or to take part in the military pacification of the territory. Bolivia tried in vain to get Brazil to assist her officials, uncomfortable in the low lands,[23] in pacifying the Acre as a piece of property claimed by both and held by Bolivia provisionally under the protocols; and without success offered administration and a share in the revenues to a citizen of Rio de Janeiro if he would first reëstablish order.

On May 17, 1901,[24] Bolivia approved a proposition of the Bolivia Trading Company[25] to introduce within six months a limited number of acclimated laborers with families as colonists into the Noroeste territory for a concession of five hectares (12.35 acres) of land in the department of Beni for each laborer. In September 1901 a mixed commission (Ballivián-Cruls) fixed the source of the Jaquirana at 7°6'55" S., 73°47'30" W. On July 11, 1901,[26] there was signed in London by Felix Avelino Aramayo, Bolivian minister to England, and Frederick Willingford Whitridge of New York, representing the Bolivian syndicate, after a declaration of English and United States precedents for "chartered companies," a concession of exclusive option for five years to purchase outright for ten centavos per hectare (2.47 acres) all or part of the lands included in the Acre territory, bounded north by Brazil, west by Peru, south by the Abuná and a line drawn from the sources of that river to

[17] Ricardo Aranda, *Col. de Trat. del Peru*, XIV, 907–918.

[18] *Col. de Doc. que apoyan el Alegato de Bolivia en el Juicio Arbitral con Peru* (Buenos Aires, 1906), II, 563–564.

[19] *Annexo ao Rel. do Min. das Rel. Ext.* (Rio de Janeiro, 1900), Parte 2ª, pp. 75–76.

[20] *Ibid.*, Parte 2ª, p. 76. *Anuario de Leyes, 1899*, pp. 288–289.

[21] Lopes Gonçalves, *A Fronteira Brasileo-Boliviana pelo Amasonas* (Lisboa, 1901), pp. 117–119.

[22] *Col. de Doc. que apoyan el Alegato de Bolivia en el Juicio Arbitral con Peru* (Buenos Aires, 1906), II, 566–575.

[23] *U. S. For. Rel.*, 1902, pp. 105–106.

[24] *Anuario de Leyes, 1901*, pp. 161–163.

[25] Incorporated in Jersey City, New Jersey; represented by Baron Arnous de Riviére, William J. Jennings, George MacTaggart, and Henry Clay Beauchamp.

[26] *Rev. gén. de dr. int. pub.*, XI (1904), 158–160. Moore, *Dig., Int. Law* (Washington, 1906), I, 646–647.

the confluence of the Inambari and the Madre de Dios; with the right to navigate freely and undisturbed on all the rivers and navigable waters of the territory and the exclusive right to charge and collect for navigation concessions; with all mining rights in the territory, all Bolivian mining laws being suspended there for the term of the contract; freedom from all tax except 10 per cent of the net annual profits; the right to construct, maintain, and operate wharves, railroads, telegraphs, electric power plants, and any other construction the syndicate might think useful, and to maintain a police force; the absolute exclusive and independent right, power, and authority for thirty years to collect all revenues, taxes, charges, and contributions of every kind, and to use all the public or state lands, edifices, property, and rights of all sorts, except those which belonged to Bolivia as a sovereign power, to pay over 60 per cent of the revenue so collected to the government and retain 40 per cent for the syndicate; all so that the condition of the syndicate by the concession should be that of a local government subordinate to the government of the state; the concession not to be transferable to any state or foreign government and to be transferable to any other company or syndicate only with the previous approval of the Bolivian Congress. Peru protested against this broad concession as amounting practically to a partial alienation of sovereignty to a foreign corporation without international responsibility; and an invitation in April 1902 by Bolivia to Brazil to participate in the subscription to the Bolivian syndicate was declined by Brazil, with a warning to investors in Berlin, where Baron Rio Branco was then Brazilian minister, against risking their capital in the enterprise, since the Acre boundaries were in dispute not only with Bolivia but with Peru. The concession was ratified by the Bolivian Congress in special session on December 21, 1901,[27] and President José Manuel Pando declared in his message of August 1902 Bolivia's intention of carrying out the contract. Brazil thereupon undertook "reprisals" by recalling her consul in Porto Alonso and on August 8, 1902,[28] closing all the Amazon rivers to commerce in transit to or from Bolivia. France, Germany, Great Britain, Switzerland, and the United States protested to Brazil against the closing of the Amazon as an injury to their commerce with Bolivia, and on February 20, 1903,[29] Brazil restored commercial transit with Bolivia except for munitions of war and goods cleared for foreign countries at Bolivian river ports. In January 1903 [30] the Brazilian colonists in the territory took up arms again

[27] *Anuario de Leyes,* 1901, pp. 452–464.
[28] 95 *British and Foreign State Papers* 774.
[29] *Rel. do Min. das Rel. Ext.,* 1902–1903, pp. 22–26; *ibid.,* Annexo I, pp. 84–135. 96 *British and Foreign State*

Papers 388.
[30] *Rel. do Min. das Rel. Ext.,* 1902–1903, pp. 4–13; *ibid., Annexo* I, pp. 48–62.

under Plácido de Castro, and war between Bolivia and Brazil seemed imminent. After one unsuccessful expedition had been sent, President Pando, who had previously personally explored the Acre territory, turned over his office to Vice-President Aníbal Capriles and in person led the campaign from January 26 to August 3, 1903. Bolivia accepted Brazil's offer to undertake the pacification of the territory and to assume its provisional occupation and administration; and by a preliminary agreement for a *modus vivendi* during negotiations for four months, later extended for three more, signed at La Paz on March 21, 1903,[31] Brazilian troops occupied the contested territory east of the Purús between the Cunha Gomes line and 10°20' S., and interposed between the Acreans and the Bolivian forces south of that parallel on the Orton, with advanced posts as far as the Abuná. The Bolivian syndicate relinquished its concession for an indemnity of £110,000 paid by Brazil,[32] and Brazil proposed to Bolivia first to buy and then to exchange the Acre territory, and under the name of an exchange a settlement was finally reached.[33] By a treaty signed by Baron Rio Branco, Brazilian minister of foreign relations, Joaquim Francisco de Assis Brazil, Brazilian minister to the United States, Fernando E. Guachalla, Bolivian special minister to Brazil, and Claudio Pinilla, Bolivian minister of foreign relations, at Petropolis on November 17, 1903,[34] it was agreed that the boundary line between Bolivia and Brazil should run (Sec. 1) from 20°8'35" S. opposite the outlet of the Bahia Negra into the Paraguay up the Paraguay to a point on its right (west) bank nine kilometers (5.6 miles) in a straight line from the Fort of Coimbra, that is, at approximately 19°58'5" S. 57°47'40" W., according to the map of the frontier made by the mixed boundary commission of 1875; thence on the right (west) bank of the Paraguay by a straight line four kilometers (2.5 miles) in the direction of 27°1'22" northeast from the mark at the head of Bahia Negra to a point more or less at 19°45'36.6" S. 58°4'12.7" W., thence by the line fixed by the mixed commission of 1875 up to 19°2' S.; thence eastward along that parallel to the Concepción stream, down the Concepción to its mouth on the southern bank of the outlet of Lake Cáceres, also called the Tamengos; up this outlet to the meridian which traverses the end of the Tamarinderia and northward by that meridian to 18°54' S.;

[31] *Ibid.*, 48–75. *U. S. For. Rel.*, 1903, pp. 34–36.

[32] *Rel. do Min. das Rel. Ext.*, 1902–1903; pp. 16–21, 26–28; *ibid.*, Annexo I, pp. 40–47.

[33] Thaumaturgo de Azevedo, *O Acre, Limites com a Bolivia* (Rio de Janeiro, 1901). *Bolivia-Brasil; Soc. Geog. de La Paz* (La Paz, 1903). *Brazil and Bolivia Boundary Settlement* (New York, 1904).

[34] *Trat. Vig.* (Bolivia, 1925), I, 150–163. *Rel. do Min.*

das Rel. Ext., 1902–1903; pp. 48–50. 96 *British and Foreign State Papers* 383–387. *U. S. For. Rel.*, 1904, pp. 98, 104–108. Moore, *Dig. Int. Law* (Washington, 1906), I, 646–648; *ibid.*, VI, 440–442. Martens, *Nouv. Rec. Gén. de Traités*, 3e Sér., III, 62–70. Ratified by Bolivia January 6, 1904; sanctioned by Brazil, Decree #1179, Feb. 18, 1904; ratifications exchanged at Rio de Janeiro, Mar. 10, 1904; promulgated by Brazil, Decree #5161, Mar. 10, 1904.

thence westward along that parallel to the existing frontier; (Sec. 2) along the existing frontier to 18°14′ S., thence eastward along that parallel to the outlet of Lake Mandioré; up that outlet and across the lake in a straight line to the point on the old frontier equidistant from the two existing marks; thence by the old line to the mark on the northern shore; (Sec. 3) from the northern mark on Lake Mandioré in a straight line in the same direction as at present to 17°49′ S.; thence along that parallel to the meridian at the southeast end of Lake Gahiba; along that meridian to the lake and across the lake in a straight line to the point on the old frontier equidistant from the two existing marks; thence by the old line to the entrance of the Pedro Segundo Canal, also recently called the Pando; (Sec. 4) along the boundary fixed by Article 2 of the Treaty of March 27, 1867, from the southern entrance of this canal or the Pando to the confluence of the Beni and Mamoré; (Sec. 5) from that confluence down the Madeira to the mouth of the Abuná, its affluent on the left (west) bank, and up the Abuná to 10°20′ S.; thence along that parallel westward to the Rapirrán, and up that river to its principal source; (Sec. 6) from the principal source of the Rapirrán along the parallel of that source westward to the Iquiry; up the Iquiry to its source; thence to the Bahia stream by the most pronounced features of the country or by a straight line as should appear most expedient to the demarcation commissioners; (Sec. 7) from the source of the Bahia stream down that stream to its mouth on the right (south) bank of the Acre or Aquiry, and up the Acre to its source, if such source is not west of 69° W., and thence along the meridian of that source to 11° S., and thence west along that parallel to the Peruvian frontier; or, if the Acre, as appears certain, crosses 69° W. and runs in turn north and south of said 11° S. parallel, more or less following it, the line shall be the channel of that river to its source, and along the meridian of such source to 11° S., and thence westward along that parallel to the Peruvian frontier; but if west of said 69° W. the Acre runs continuously to the south of 11° S., the frontier shall run from that river along 69° W. to the point of intersection with 11° S. and thence along that parallel to the Peruvian frontier. (Article 2) Private rights in the territories thus transferred were to be respected, and claims were to be examined and adjudged by an arbitral tribunal of one representative of each country and as president a foreign minister accredited to Brazil, to be chosen by the parties; (Article 3) on account of the inequality of the areas exchanged, Brazil was to pay in London to Bolivia an indemnity of £2,000,000 in two equal instalments, one three months after the exchange of ratifications (paid on June 10, 1904), and the other on March 31, 1905; (Article 4) a mixed commission appointed by the two governments within a year from the exchange of ratifications should within six months of its nomination commence the demarcation of the frontier, any disagreement which could not be settled by the two governments to be submitted to the arbitral decision of a member of the Royal Geographical Society of London chosen by the president and council of that society; (Article 5) the parties were to conclude within eight months a treaty of commerce and navigation based on the principle of the most complete liberty of land transit and river navigation perpetually for both countries, subject to local regulations, and (Article 6) each might have agents attached to the customhouses of the other on the frontier. Brazil further undertook (Article 7) to construct and to endeavor to finish within four years a railway from the Port of Santo Antonio on the Madeira to Guajará-Mirim on the Mamoré, with a branch through Villa Murtinho or some place nearby in the state of Matto Grosso to Villa Bella in Bolivia at the confluence of the Beni and Mamoré, to be used by both countries with equal rights and privileges; and (Article 8) to treat directly with Peru as to the frontiers in the territory between the source of the Javary and 11° S., and endeavor to arrive at an amicable settlement of the dispute, no responsibility to rest with Bolivia in any case; (Article 9) differences as to the interpretation and execution of the treaty to be referred to arbitration.

By this treaty of Petropolis, Bolivia relinquished [35] to Brazil all rights over the rubber-producing Acre territory not only in places where possession had been contested but also an area south of 10° 20' S. to the Aquiry in which Bolivian rights had never been disputed, in exchange for £2,000,000, a parcel of 890 square miles in the angle south of the confluence of the Abuná and the Madeira, and communication for the Beni and Mamoré valleys by rail around the 200 miles of falls on the Madeira to connect with the lower Amazon and the ocean commerce of the world. Part of the area thus acquired by Brazil included some of the territory which Bolivia had by treaties in 1902 agreed with Peru to submit to the arbitration of Argentina,[36] and Peru was thus obliged to take up with Brazil settlement of a portion of the line.[37]

The Arbitral Claims Tribunal [38] contemplated by the treaty was installed

[35] H. A. Moulin, "L'Affaire du Territoire d'Acre," *Rev. gén. de dr. int. pub.*, XI (1904), 150–191. Fernando Antonio Raja Gabaglia, *As Fronteiras do Brasil* (Rio de Janeiro, 1916), pp. 269–278.

[36] See §9, this chap., *infra.*
[37] See §13, this chap., *infra.*
[38] Carlos V. Romero, delegate of Bolivia; Carlos A. de Carvalho, delegate of Brazil.

at Rio de Janeiro on May 20, 1905,[39] with Monsignor Julio Tonti, the papal nuncio at Rio de Janeiro, as the third member and president. Doubt very quickly arose over the powers of the president in case of a tie between the other two members, and work was suspended on May 20, 1906. By a protocol signed at Rio de Janeiro, February 6, 1907,[40] it was provided that the work of the tribunal should proceed again for one year with Monsignor Alexandre Bavona, Tonti's successor as papal nuncio at Rio de Janeiro, as the third member and president. Without mention of the previous difficulty, the tribunal [41] functioned from November 3, 1908, to November 3, 1909,[42] dealt with 100 cases (26 against Bolivia, 54 against Brazil, and 20 against both), and determined indemnities to be paid by each state to the other. A protocol of instructions of February 6, 1907, for the mixed demarcation commission called for a meeting of the representatives of both countries at Corumbá in Matto Grosso within six months, thence to proceed to the demarcation of the frontier from Bahia Negra to the entrance of the Pedro Segundo Canal or the Pando; any differences between the Bolivian and Brazilian commissions to be submitted to the decision of the respective governments, who would proceed in conformity with the provision for arbitral decision by a member of the Royal Geographical Society.

On November 14, 1906,[43] Brazil on public bids made a contract with civil engineer Joaquin Catramby for the construction of the Madeira-Mamoré railroad, and on January 30, 1908,[44] authorized the transfer of his contract to the Madeira-Mamoré Railway Company,[45] which went on constructing the road and on February 25, 1909,[46] leased it from the government for sixty years from January 1, 1912. Competition from the cultivated plantations of the Far East has made wild rubber gathering unprofitable, and white men are gradually retiring from the region. The railroad now runs two trains a month each way, staying at Abuná over Thursday nights.

A treaty of commerce and navigation signed at Rio de Janeiro, August 12, 1910,[47] after the receipt of certain suggestions from the Pope, to carry

[39] Carlos V. Romero, *Informe dirigido a su Gobierno* (Buenos Aires, 1906). José Armando Mendez, *Defensa de los Derechos de Bolivia* (Buenos Aires, 1906). *Rec. de Cours*, VI (1925), 230-231. Clunet, *J. du dr. int. privé*, XXXVII (1910), 747-748.

[40] *Trat. Vig. de Bolivia* (Santiago, 1908), pp. 85-92. Sanctioned by Brazil, Decree #1721, Sept. 16, 1907.

[41] Claudio Pinilla, delegate of Bolivia; Ubaldino do Amaral, delegate of Brazil.

[42] Helio Lobo, *O Tribunal Arbitral Brasileiro-Boliviano* (Rio de Janeiro, 1910).

[43] Authorized by Decree #6103, Aug. 7, 1906. *Col.*

das Leis do Brazil, 1906, II, 732-739. Decree #6755, Nov. 28, 1907.

[45] Incorporated in Portland, Maine, Aug. 6, 1907; filed last return, 1931; excused, Mar. 17, 1932.

[46] Decree #7344. *Col. das Leis do Brazil*, 1909, II, 150-160. Decree #7433, June 3, 1909. *Ibid.*, pp. 522-533.

[47] *Trat. Vig.* (Bolivia, 1925), I, 180-200. Martens, *Nouv. Rec. Gén. de Traités*, 3e Sér., VII, 632-638. *Amer. J. Int. Law*, XXVII (1933), 287. Ratifications exchanged at La Paz, July 29, 1911.

out the principle of free transit recognized in the Treaty of Petropolis provided that the merchant vessels of all nations might navigate freely not only on the Paraguay between the frontier of Bolivia and Brazil south of Coimbra and the Brazilian port of Corumbá as theretofore but also in the Tamengo Canal and Lake Cáceres between Corumbá and the Bolivian Puerto Guachalla on that lake, and that the war vessels of each country might go freely between river ports specifically designated. By an accord signed at Petropolis on February 10, 1911,[48] it was agreed that the instructions of February 6, 1907, should apply to the new work of demarcation. The railroad from Santo Antonio to Guajará-Mirim was duly completed, but the branch through Villa Murtinho or a nearby place to Villa Bella was not built. By a protocol signed at Rio de Janeiro on December 28, 1912,[49] canceling one of November 14, 1910,[50] it was agreed that such branch should start from Guarjará-Guasú or some more suitable point near Guajará-Mirim, the terminal of the main line, cross the river on a bridge to be built by Brazil, and end on the Bolivian frontier, where it should connect with a railroad which Bolivia undertook to construct to Riberalta.

Two protocols signed at La Paz, September 3, 1925,[51] agreed that the boundary from the crest of the hill of Cuatro Hermanos should run in the direction of the principal source of the Verde, diverging only so far as necessary to preserve to Brazil its historic possession of the hamlets of Ramada, Cacimba, and Salinas, with a mixed commission to mark such line as soon as possible; and distributed thirteen small islands in the Madeira to the country owning the nearer shore, seven to Brazil and six to Bolivia. On the same day, September 3, 1925,[52] there were signed in Rio de Janeiro a protocol agreeing to transfer the sum up to £2,000,000 which Brazil would have to spend on railroad construction under the treaty of November 17, 1903, to connect northeastern Bolivia with the Brazilian region of the Madeira, to building a connection between the Brazilian railroad system on the Paraguay at Porto Esperanza and the Bolivian system from Santa Cruz de la Sierra as recently planned to be extended to Puerto Ichilo; and another protocol[53] agreeing that the boundary line should run from the principal source of the Rapirrán to the mouth of the Chipamanu in such manner as to divide, when-

[48] *Trat. Vig.* (Bolivia, 1925), I, 204–208.

[49] *Ibid.*, 208–211. *Arch. Dipl.*, CXXX (1914), 381–383. Martens, *Nouv. Rec. Gén. de Traités*, 3e Sér., IX, 511–512. Approved by the Bolivian Cabinet, Feb. 18, 1913; sanctioned by Brazil, Decree #3418A, Dec. 12, 1917.

[50] *Trat. Vig.* (Bolivia, 1925), I, 201–203. Approved by

the Bolivian Cabinet, Aug. 1, 1911; not approved by Brazil.

[51] *Trat. Vig.* (Bolivia, 1925), III, Apen. 16–23. Approved by the Bolivian Cabinet, Sept. 3, 1925.

[52] *Trat. Vig.* (Bolivia, 1925), III, Apen. 23–27. Approved by the Bolivian Cabinet, Sept. 3, 1925.

[53] *Trat. Vig.* (Bolivia, 1925), III, Apen. 28–31. Approved by the Bolivian Cabinet, Sept. 3, 1925.

ever possible, the waters which flow to the Acre from those which flow to the Abuná, and from its mouth by the Chipamanu up to the mouth of the Ina, thence to the eastern source of the Bahia stream, in a straight line so far as possible, but so as to leave entirely to Brazil the whole course of the Ina and to Bolivia the whole course of the Chipamanu from such confluence; and from the eastern source of the Bahia stream by such stream to the Acre basin.

These protocols were substantially carried into a treaty signed at Rio de Janeiro on December 25, 1928,[54] providing that (Article 1) the frontier between the principal source of the Rapirrán and the Bahia stream should run from such principal source in a straight line to the mouth of the Chipamanu; thence up the Chipamanu to its principal source; thence in a straight line to the source of the eastern arm of the Bahia stream; thence down that eastern arm and the Bahia stream to its mouth in the Acre; (Article 2) in the Madeira zone, that is, from the confluence of the Beni and the Mamoré to the mouth of the Abuná, the frontier should run by the line equidistant from the banks, the islands and islets nearer the Brazilian side to belong to Brazil, those nearer the Bolivian side to Bolivia, according to the maps drawn up in 1914 by the Brazil-Bolivia mixed commission, seven (named) to Brazil, and six (named) to Bolivia; (Article 3) from the last point of the demarcation of 1877 where a mark was set up, the frontier should run eastward by the parallel of such mark until it should meet a straight line drawn between the crest of the hill of Cuatro Hermanos and the principal source of the Verde; thence by such straight line northward to such source of the Verde, to be marked; a mixed demarcation commission to be named by the two governments as soon as possible after the exchange of ratifications, to inspect the whole frontier line, repair old marks destroyed, erect again fallen ones, and select points where, for greater clarity of the dividing line and the respective possessions of the two countries, new marks ought to be placed; in short, to carry out all necessary demarcation operations on such frontier line; (Article 4) instructions for the mixed demarcation commission to be determined by exchange of notes; (Article 5) the railroad construction under the terms of the treaty of November 17, 1903, not to be completed, but in place thereof Brazil by a payment of £1,000,000 within six months after the exchange of ratifications to assist in carrying out a plan of railroad construction which, linking Cochabamba to Santa Cruz de la Sierra, should extend thence on one side to a port

[54] *Col. de Actos Int.* (Rio de Janeiro, 1929), No. 12. 128 *British and Foreign State Papers* 677–680. João Ribeiro, *As Nossas Fronteiras* (Rio de Janeiro, 1930), pp. 63–76. Sanctioned by Brazil, Decree #5649, Jan. 8, 1929; ratified by Brazil, Feb. 19, 1929; ratified by Bolivia, June 7, 1929; ratifications exchanged at Rio de Janeiro, June 27, 1929; promulgated by Brazil, Decree #18838, July 9, 1929.

in the Amazon basin and on the other to a port on the Paraguay at a place which permits contact with the Brazilian railroad system. The latter section might be provisionally built as a modern highway and afterwards changed to a railroad, Brazil to have the right to hasten such change if she wished, in a manner to be agreed on by the two governments. On the date of signing this treaty there were exchanged notes in which Bolivia recorded and Brazil acknowledged notice of Bolivia's claim to the whole western bank of the Paraguay from Bahia Negra southwards, then occupied by Paraguay, and confirming as to Bolivia Brazil's sovereignty over the east bank of the Paraguay between the outlet of Bahia Negra and the mouth of the Apa.

Minor difficulties over shallow lakes or broad places in a sluggish river were early adjusted by treaty in the larger nation's favor; and the major contest over ownership of a then profitable rubber region, explored and rudimentarily settled by voyaging pioneers, later involving an elusive river source, was finally disposed of by purchase. Bolivia's preoccupation with the struggle with Paraguay has prevented any work being done in connection with the latest demarcation, but the whole boundary seems to be now fairly closely settled, on paper, and it may be expected that actual marking on the ground will proceed without mishap when the Chaco Boreal or Paraguayan frontier has been definitely determined.

7. BOLIVIA–CHILE. ANTOFAGASTA

Early boundary negotiations with Bolivia which had lapsed were reopened in 1858 by President Manuel Montt of Chile, with a view "not to any increase of territory but to preserve what we possess and what we have always possessed,"[1] but dragged along[2] until the realization of the common danger to the Pacific nations from Spain inspired both sides with a greater tractability. A treaty signed by Álvaro Covarrubias, Chilean secretary of foreign relations, and Juan Ramón Muñoz Cabrera, Bolivian minister, at Santiago on August 10, 1866,[3] provided that the boundary line in the desert of Atacama should thereafter be the 24° S. parallel from the shore of the Pacific to the eastern boundary of Chile, so that Chile on the south and Bo-

[1] 50 *British and Foreign State Papers* 1029. Miguel Luis Amunátegui, *La Cuestion de limites entre Chile i Bolivia* (Santiago, 1836). Manuel M. Salinas, *Impugnación a la Cuestión de Limites entre Chile i Bolivia* (Sucre, 1863).

[2] 55 *British and Foreign State Papers* 860–861.

[3] José R. Gutiérrez, *Col. de Trat. de Bol.* (Santiago, 1869), pp. 20–23. *Recop. de Trat. de Chile* (Santiago, 1894), II, 22–28. *U. S. Dipl. Corr.*, 1864, IV, 173–179. 56 *British and Foreign State Papers* 717–719. *Arch Dipl.*, 1866, IV, 183–185. Martens, *Nouv. Rec. Gén de Traités*, XX, 609–612. Ratified by Bolivia, Nov. 10, 1866; ratifications exchanged at Santiago, Dec. 9, 1866; promulgated by Bolivia, Jan. 4, 1867; promulgated by Chile, Dec. 13, 1866.

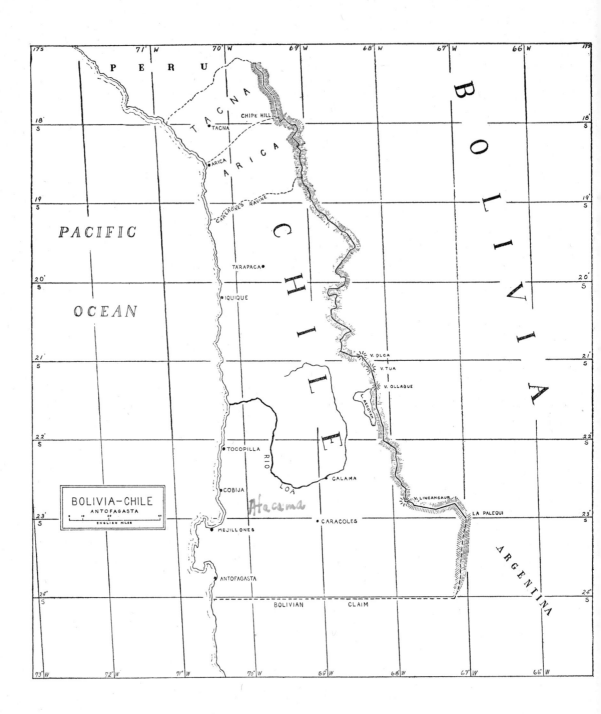

livia on the north should have possession of and dominion over the territories
which extend to such parallel, being able to exercise in them all the acts of
jurisdiction and sovereignty which belong to the owner of the soil; exact fix-
ation of the demarcation line should be made by a commission of competent
experts, half of whose members should be named by each party, the line
when fixed to be marked on the ground by visible and permanent signs at joint
expense; (Article 2) notwithstanding the foregoing territorial division, the
parties should divide equally the proceeds of exploitation of the guano deposits found in Mejillones and other deposits of the same fertilizer which may
be found in the territory between 23° S. and 25° S. and also the export
duties collected on minerals extracted from the same stretch of territory;
(Article 3) Bolivia should open the bay and port of Mejillones and establish a custom house there, in which one or more Chilean treasury employees
might officiate, and so for Bolivia in any collection office established by Chile
in the territory between 24° S. and 25° S.; (Article 4) all produce of the territory between 24° S. and 25° S. exported through the port of Mejillones
should be free of all export tax, and natural produce of Chile imported
through the port of Mejillones should be free of import tax; (Article 5) a
system for exploitation or sale of the guano and for the export duties on
minerals should be fixed by agreement between the parties; (Article 6) the
republics agreed not to transfer their rights to the possession or dominion of
the territory divided between them by the present treaty to any other state,
corporation, or private individual; in case either desired to sell, the purchaser
could only be the other party; and (Article 7) for the damages which the
matter of this boundary had, as was known, caused the individuals who
jointly were the first seriously to exploit the guano deposits of Mejillones,
whose operations were suspended by the Chilean authorities on February 17,
1863, the parties would give them in equity 80,000 pesos. As most of the
desert of Atacama had been in the possession of Bolivians, this arrangement
disregarded the principle of the _uti possidetis_ of 1810, Bolivia abandoning her
previous claim to territory on the Pacific down to the Salado river at 26°20′
S. and giving Chileans an interest as far north as 23° S., in a manner which
later supported substantial claims of their country in this rich revenue-pro-
ducing region. The two commissioners[4] under this treaty fixed the lines of the
23° and 24° parallels and signed a declaratory act at Antofagasta on February 10, 1870.[5]

[4] Juan Mariano Mujía for Bolivia, Amado Pissis for Chile.

[5] Luis Risopatron S., _La Linea de Frontera con la República de Bolivia_ (Santiago, 1911), pp. 16–19.

The business of digging and exporting nitrate from the region around Salinas in the littoral had been gradually growing, and on April 13, 1872, President Morales granted to the Compañía de Salitres y Ferrocarril de Antofagasta, a Chilean company domiciled at Valparaiso, following concessions of September 2, 1868, and September 13, 1870, a large parcel of land from which nitrate might be extracted, under regulations established by him on January 8, 1872,[6] which declared all deposits of inorganic nonmetalliferous substances property of the state but permitted their extraction under license awarded to the bidder most advantageous to the Treasury. By a convention signed at La Paz December 5, 1872,[7] to fulfill the treaty of August 10, 1866, it was agreed that the eastern boundary of Chile mentioned in Article 1 was the highest summit of the Andes, and therefore the boundary between Chile and Bolivia was 24° S. from the Pacific Ocean to the summit of the Andes; (Article 2) in order to determine by visible marks the situation of the mines and ore-producing places to be worked in common, in the area bounded north by 23° S., south by 25° S., east by the summit of the Andes and west by the Pacific, each party would appoint a commissioner, who as experts should proceed to fix and determine such places, if in disagreement they to appoint a third as umpire and if in disagreement on the appointment, the emperor of Brazil to designate such umpire; further details of the fiscal operations were agreed upon, and both governments were to go on negotiating in a pacific and friendly way for the revision and abrogation of the treaty of August 10, 1866, and the substitution of another better calculated to promote mutual interests, on the unchangeable basis of the 24° parallel and the highest summits of the Andes. By a law of November 11, 1872, Congress directed the Bolivian government to negotiate for an alliance with Peru, and there was for a time a chance that Argentina might join them.[8] President Frias amended the regulations on December 31, 1872,[9] limiting more strictly the area which might be assigned to one person, and imposing an annual tax of thirty or forty bolivianos (according to surface conditions) for the patent for each unit area worked.

On February 6, 1873,[10] there was signed at Lima a treaty of defensive alliance by which Bolivia and Peru united mutually to guarantee their inde-

[6] *Anuario de Leyes de 1872*, pp. 5-8.

[7] *Ibid.*, 1873, p. 76. Ricardo Aranda, *Col. de Trat. del Peru*, XIV, 261-264. *U. S. For. Rel.*, 1872, pp. 64-65; ibid., 1874, pp. 194-198. 65 *British and Foreign State Papers* 275-277. *Arch. Dipl.*, 1875, II, 357-359. Martens, *Nouv. Rec. Gén. de Traités*, 2e Sér., III, 486-487. Lucos Palacios, *Chile y Bolivia, El Protocolo Diplomático de 5 de diciembre de 1872* (La Paz, 1873). Approved by Chile,

Jan. 8, 1873.

[8] Pedro Yrigoyen, *La Alianza Peru-Boliviano-Argentina* (Lima, 1921). Pedro Yrigoyen, *La Adhesión de la República Argentina al tratado de alianza defensiva* (Lima).

[9] *Anuario de Leyes de 1872*, pp. 244-248.

[10] *Anuario de Leyes de 1879*, pp. 83-86. 70 *British and Foreign State Papers* 214-216. Ratifications exchanged at La Paz, June 16, 1873.

pendence, sovereignty, and the integrity of their respective territories, binding them to defend themselves from all foreign aggression, especially in cases of offense consisting of acts tending to deprive either nation of a portion of its territory or to submit it to a protectorate, sale or cession of territory, or to establish over it any right which might injure or offend the full exercise of its sovereignty and independence; the *casus foederis* once declared, the two nations were to act together in breaking off relations, closing their ports, operating sea or land forces and making peace; they were to make no boundary treaties or other territorial arrangements without the other nation first knowing of them; and to keep the treaty secret [11] until they should both deem its publication necessary. On November 27, 1873,[12] President Ballivián approved an adjustment offered by Belisario Peró, representing the directors of the Antofagasta company, of reducing the area of their concession, continuing it for fifteen years from January 1, 1874, and because of the disadvantageous conditions of transportation in competition with the industry in Tarapacá, Peru, permitting the company to bring the nitrate down free on their own railroad, on condition of exporting it all through Antofagasta, and paying annually forty bolivianos for the patent for each unit area.

A treaty signed at Sucre, August 6, 1874,[13] and a supplementary protocol as to arbitration signed at La Paz, July 21, 1875, declared that the 24° parallel from the sea to the cordillera of the Andes at the *divortia aquarum* was the boundary, provided for the location of the Caracoles or other mining regions by commissioners as before, promised the freedom of minerals in the common zone from any increased taxes for twenty-five years and derogated all parts of the treaty of August 10, 1866. When the Peró agreement of November 27, 1873, eventually came before the National Constituent Assembly for approval the legislators thought they saw a good opportunity to increase the public revenue and accordingly granted their consent by a law of February 14, 1878,[14] on condition of payment by the company of a tax of ten cents on each quintal (100 pounds) of nitrate exported. This measure set off a train of far-reaching consequences, in the end most disastrous for Bolivia. The Antofagasta company protested the new tax, refused to pay, and appealed to the Chilean government for aid. As a result of diplomatic

[11] *Rev. de Der., Hist. y Letras*, LXXI (1922), 491–499.

[12] *Anuario de Leyes de 1873*, pp. 185–187.

[13] *Anuario de Leyes de 1874*, pp. 213–218. *Recop. de Trat. de Chile* (Santiago, 1894), II, 101–107. 71 *British and Foreign State Papers* 897–906. Ricardo Aranda, *Col. de Trat. del Peru*, XIV, 82–93. *Tratado de Limites entre Bolivia y Chile*, 1874–75 (La Paz, 1875). *Rev. de dr. int. et de lég. comp.*, 2e Sér., IV (1902), 379–380. Ratified by Bolivia, Nov. 12, 1874, with modifications; ratifications exchanged at La Paz, July 28 and Sept. 22, 1875; promulgated by Chile, Oct. 25, 1875.

[14] *Anuario de Leyes de 1878*, p. 43. Approved by President Daza, Feb. 23, 1878.

representations by Chile on November 8, 1878, enforcement of the tax was suspended, but on December 17, 1878,[15] President Daza through the secretary of the treasury ordered the prefect of the department of Cobija to proceed to collect the tax. Chile was continuing negotiations at La Paz, when President Daza on February 1, 1879,[16] ordered the rescission of the Peró agreement of November 27, 1873, and the suspension of the law of February 14, 1878. An expeditionary force from Chile on the ironclad *Blanco Encalada* on February 14, 1879, took possession of the ports of Antofagasta, Mejillones, and Caracoles, and on February 26, 1879,[17] President Daza declared that because of the occupation a state of war existed with Chile, and Chileans were expelled from Bolivia and their goods confiscated.[18] The Chileans took possession of the port of Cobija, and captured Calama by assault. Chile asked Peru to proclaim her neutrality, and no such declaration being forthcoming Chile declared war on Peru and Bolivia on April 5, 1879,[19] whereupon President Mariano I. Prado of Peru proclaimed on April 6, 1879,[20] the existence of the *casus foederis* and the consequent coming into effect of the treaty of February 6, 1873. Attempts of the United States [21] and other nations to restore peace were unsuccessful. A force of Peruvian soldiers was routed by the Chileans at San Francisco Hill, near Pisagua, and soon afterwards the Chileans defeated a combined Peruvian-Bolivian army at Tarapacá. President Daza fled on December 27, 1879, and, although Peru prolonged the war until 1881, Bolivia was able to take little further part.

At the end of the war Chile considered all previous territorial arrangements abrogated; her military possession of the Bolivian department of Atacama became permanent, and Bolivia remained without any port of her own on the Pacific. An agreement for a truce signed at Valparaiso on April 4, 1884,[22] with complementary protocols of April 18 and May 30, 1885,[23] provided that the state of war was terminated and could not be renewed without one year's notice; while the truce remained in force, Chile was to govern po-

---

[15] *Anuario de Leyes de 1878*, p. 303.
[16] *Anuario de Leyes de 1879*, pp. 21–23. *Amer. J. Int. Law*, III (1909), 304.
[17] *Anuario de Leyes de 1879*, p. 48. 71 *British and Foreign State Papers* 926–933.
[18] Alphonse Rivier, *Principes du Droit des Gens* (Paris, 1896), II, 231. Moore, *Dig. Int. Law* (Washington, 1906), VII, 192.
[19] Laws of Apr. 3 and Apr. 4, 1879; *Bol. de las Leyes de Chile* (Santiago, 1879), pp. 107–109. 70 *British and Foreign State Papers* 184–185, 341–360. *U. S. For. Rel.*, 1879, pp. 148–180; *ibid.*, 1880, pp. 75–82; *ibid.*, 1881, pp. 76–95. *Arch. Dipl.*, 1878–79, III, 241–255, 257–258, 297–302, 306–322. Santiago Vaca Guzmán, *La Usurpación en el Pacífico* (Buenos Aires, 1879). *Cuestión Chileno-Boliviana*,

Min. de Rel. Ext. (Santiago, 1879).
[20] Ricardo Aranda, *Col. de Trat. del Peru* (Lima, 1892), IV, 208–209. 70 *British and Foreign State Papers* 692.
[21] *The War in South America and Attempts to Bring About a Peace* (Washington, 1882).
[22] *Anuario de Leyes de 1885*, pp. 14–18. *Recop. de Trat. de Chile* (Santiago, 1894), II, 167–175. Ricardo Aranda, *Col. de Trat. del Peru*, IV, 680–689. 75 *British and Foreign State Papers* 367–370. Martens, *Nouv. Rec. Gén. de Traités*, 2e Sér., X, 610–614. Ratified by Chile, Nov. 29, 1884; ratifications exchanged at Santiago, Nov. 29, 1884; promulgated by Bolivia, Jan. 16, 1885; promulgated by Chile, Dec. 2, 1884.
[23] *Recop. de Trat. de Chile* (Santiago, 1894), II, 255–263.

litically and administratively according to Chilean law the territory from the
23° parallel (north 100 miles) to the mouth of the Loa on the Pacific, having
for eastern boundary a straight line from Zapalegui at the intersection of the
boundary with Argentina to the volcano Licancaur; thence by a straight
line to the peak of the extinct volcano Cabana; thence by another straight
line to the most southerly bay head in Lake Ascotán; thence by another
straight line which crossing such lake ended at the volcano Ollagüe, thence
by another straight line to the volcano Túa, and thence by the dividing line
between the department of Tarapacá and Bolivia; in case difficulties should
arise, both parties should appoint a commission of engineers to fix the boundary thus described; claims for damages were to be arbitrated by a commission of three, one member appointed by each party and the third by the
neutral representatives accredited to Chile; (Article 6) collections at the Arica
custom house to be divided, 25 per cent to the customs service for Chile's
part in the clearance, 75 per cent to Bolivia, of which Chile would retain 40
per cent for payments of indemnities which might be due from Bolivia and
for the Chilean loan of 1867 to Bolivia, 35 per cent to be paid over to Bolivia.
By this agreement Bolivia lost control of the nitrate territory and her only
Pacific seaports.[24]

A treaty of peace and friendship signed by Luis Barros Borgoño, Chilean
minister of foreign relations, and Heriberto Gutiérrez, Bolivian minister, at
Santiago on May 18, 1895,[25] provided that Chile should continue to enjoy
in absolute and perpetual dominion the possession of the territory which she
had until then been governing under the provisions of the truce of April 4,
1884, wherefore Chile's sovereignty was recognized over the territory south
of the Loa from its mouth on the Pacific to the 23° parallel and bounded on
the east by the series of straight lines fixed in Article 2 of the truce agreement; (Article 2) Chile assumed and agreed to pay the obligations recognized by Bolivia in favor of the mining companies of Huanchaca, Corocoro,
and Oruro and the balance of the Bolivian loan raised in Chile in 1867, less
the sums already paid on this account under Article 6 of the truce agreement; and also the following encumbrances on the Bolivian coast: the bonds
issued for the construction of the railroad from Mejillones to Caracoles (under contract of July 10, 1872), the obligation in favor of Pedro López Gama,

[24] The Antofagasta-La Paz railroad was completed in
1892. As to inheritance rights in Antofagasta after the
transfer to Chile, see Clunet, *J. de dr. int. privé*, XXXV
(1908), 229–231.

[25] *Recop. de Trat. de Chile* (Londres, 1898), III, 282–
286. 88 *British and Foreign State Papers* 755–757. *U. S.*

For. Rel., 1896, pp. 27–29. Martens, *Nouv. Rec. Gén. de
Traités*, 2e Sér., XXXIV, 345–347. Ratified by Bolivia,
Dec. 10, 1895; ratified by Chile, Dec. 31, 1895; ratifications exchanged at Santiago, Apr. 30, 1896; promulgated
by Bolivia, July 26, 1896; promulgated by Chile, May 1,
1896.

then represented by Alsop and Company of Valparaiso, the obligation in favor of Henry G. Meiggs, represented by Edward Squire, arising from the contract of May 20, 1876, with Bolivia for lease of the government nitrate deposits at Toco, and the obligation in favor of the family of Juan Garday; (Article 3) except these enumerated, Chile recognized no obligations or responsibilities of any sort against the described territory, whatever their nature or origin; Chile was released from the obligations under Article 6 of the truce agreement, the receipts of the custom house at Arica to be absolutely free and Bolivia to have power to establish her custom houses in such place and manner as seemed to her convenient; (Article 4) a commission of engineers was to be named to adjust any difficulties of demarcation which might arise on the spot as to the frontier described in Article 1 or on the traditional frontier between the department of Tarapacá, now Chilean, and Bolivia; any disagreement which could not be settled by the direct action of the governments was to be submitted to the decision of a friendly power. The special treaty as to exchange of territory of May 18, 1895,[26] provided that if in consequence of the plebiscite which had to be held according to the Treaty of Ancón or by direct arrangements Chile should acquire permanent dominion and sovereignty over the territories of Tacna and Arica, she would transfer them to Bolivia in the same form and with the same extent with which she acquired them, and Bolivia would pay as indemnity for such transfer 5,000,000 pesos, the 40 per cent net proceeds of the custom house at Arica being specially pledged for such payment; (Article 2) if such cession were made, it was understood that Chile would advance her frontier north of Camarones to the Vitor ravine, from the sea up to the boundary then separating that region from Bolivia; (Article 3) for the foregoing purpose, Chile promised to use all her efforts separately or with Bolivia to obtain complete property over the territories of Tacna and Arica; (Article 4) if Chile could not obtain in the plebiscite or by direct arrangements complete sovereignty over the zone including the cities of Tacna and Arica, she undertook to cede to Bolivia the Vitor cove as far as the Camarones or other similar ravine and to pay 5,000,000 pesos; (Article 5) a special agreement should determine the exact boundaries of the ceded territory; (Article 6) if in the ceded zone thereafter there should be discovered nitrate deposits, they could absolutely not be exploited or assigned until after the exhaustion of all the nitrate deposits existing in the territory of Chile, unless by special agreement of both governments another provision should be made; and (Article 7) the treaty was to be kept in reserve and not published without the agreement

[26] *Recop. de Trat. de Chile* (Londres, 1898), III, 295–297. 88 *British and Foreign State Papers* 1328–1329.   Ratifications exchanged at Santiago, Apr. 30, 1896.

of both parties. The treaty was, however, published by strangers without authority, whereupon the Chilean Ministry of Foreign Relations published it. A supplementary protocol signed at Sucre on December 9, 1895,[27] declared that the treaties of peace and of transference of territory were to be taken together as indivisible, the cession of Bolivia's coast to Chile was to be of no effect unless Chile delivered to Bolivia within two years the seaport on the Pacific spoken of in the latter treaty, Chile should use every legal recourse under the Treaty of Ancón or by direct negotiation to acquire the port and territories of Arica and Tacna, and, if she could not, her obligation was not fulfilled by delivering Vitor or other similar cove unless she also delivered a port and zone which should amply satisfy the present and future necessities of the commerce and industries of Bolivia; and Bolivia recognized no obligations or responsibilities of any sort arising from the territories which she should cede to Chile. An aclaratory protocol of April 30, 1896,[28] declared further that the agreed delivery of Vitor or other similar cove required a port sufficient to satisfy the necessities of commerce; and that both countries would endeavor to get their respective congresses to agree to the foregoing treaties and protocols, as well as one of May 28, 1895, relating to the liquidation of money obligations. The protocols, however, failed of approval, and as by notes exchanged on April 29–30, 1896, the Bolivian minister in Santiago and the Chilean minister of foreign affairs agreed that failure to approve them by either congress would show a disagreement as to the fundamental bases of the treaties of May 18, 1895, which would render them totally inefficacious, those treaties, although ratifications had been exchanged, were considered never to have come into effect and were not executed.[29] Peru upon learning of these treaties made strong protest at their terms so far as they concerned the territories of Tacna and Arica.

A treaty signed by Alberto Gutiérrez, Bolivian minister, and Emilio Bello Codecido, Chilean minister of foreign relations, at Santiago on October 20, 1904,[30] in execution of Article 8 of the truce agreement, provided that (Article 1) peace should be reëstablished and the truce regime ended; (Article 2) the absolute and perpetual dominion of Chile over the territories occupied by

[27] Recop. de Trat. de Chile (Londres, 1898), III, 298–299. 88 British and Foreign State Papers 1329–1330.

[28] Anuario de Leyes de Bol., 1897, p. 378. Recop. de Trat. de Chile (Londres, 1898), III, 299–302. 88 British and Foreign State Papers 1330–1333.

[29] Documentos oficiales relativos a los Límites entre Chile, Bolivia i la República Argentina (Santiago, 1898). Julio César Valdés, Bolivia y Chile (Santiago, 1900). Alcibíades Guzmán, Fronteras de Bolivia (La Paz, 1902).

[30] Tratados Vigentes (Bolivia, 1925), I, 272–284. Recop. de Trat. de Chile (Santiago, 1913), VI, 147–165. 98

British and Foreign State Papers 763–769. Martens, Nouv. Rec. Gén. de Traités, 3ᵉ Sér., II, 174–179. Manifesto á la Nación; Ampliación sobre el Tratado Gutiérrez-Bello Codecido (Sucre, 1905). Ratified by Bolivia, Feb. 4, 1905; ratifications exchanged at La Paz, Mar. 10, 1905; promulgated by Bolivia, Mar. 10, 1905; promulgated by Chile, Mar. 21, 1905. Protocols of Oct. 20, 1904, and Sept. 10, 1905, and notes of Nov. 16/17, 1904, concerned commercial provisions; and notes exchanged on Oct. 21, 1904, agreed that Chile should settle directly with the creditors under Article 5, relieving Bolivia of all further responsibility.

her under Article 2 of the truce agreement was recognized; and the boundary from south to north between Bolivia and Chile should run through ninety-six points specified, from (1) the highest peak of Zapalegui hill by (2) the highest peak of the detached ridge southward of Guayaques hill at about 22°54′ S., (5) the volcano Licancábur, (15) the northern peak of the extinct volcano on the Silaguala hills, (17) Inacaliu or Cajón hill, (19) the ridge of the Ascotán or Jardín hill, (21) the peak of the volcano Ollagüe, (25) the volcano Olca, and (95) the Santuario, north of the Maure, northwest of the confluence of that river with another which comes from the north two kilometers northwest of the Maure posthouse, and thence (96) northwest by the ridge which leads to the boundary mark on Chipe or Talacollo hill, the last point of the frontier, each party to recognize (without any obligations of indemnity) private rights acquired in the territory affected (as at Chilcaya, Ascotán, and south of the Loa); (Article 3) the parties agreed to unite the port of Arica with the plateau above La Paz by a railroad whose construction was to be contracted for at Chile's expense within one year, ownership of the Bolivian portion to be transferred to Bolivia at the end of fifteen years from its completion; Chile to pay under special agreements, to be made, not over £100,000 annually or £1,700,000 in all (including the cost of the Bolivian section of the Arica railroad) on account of the obligations incurred by Bolivia for guaranteeing 5 per cent of the capital that might be invested in the construction within thirty years of the railroads from Uyuni to Potosí, Oruro to La Paz, Oruro by Cochabamba to Santa Cruz, La Paz to the region of Beni and Potosí by Sucre and Lagunillas to Santa Cruz; (Article 4) Chile to pay Bolivia £300,000 in two equal installments, one six months after the exchange of ratifications and the other one year after the first payment; (Article 5) Chile to assign 4,500,000 gold pesos to the final settlement of the Bolivian obligations (as specified in Article 2 of the peace treaty of May 18, 1895); (Article 6) Chile recognized in favor of Bolivia in perpetuity the fullest and free right of commercial transit through Chilean territory and ports on the Pacific, to be regulated by special agreements; (Article 7) Bolivia to have the right to establish custom-house agencies at such ports as she might select, indicating now Antofagasta and Arica; (Article 12) all questions which might arise to be submitted to the arbitration of the Emperor of Germany; and various commercial provisions. By an aclaratory protocol of November 15, 1904,[31] Bolivia recognized the absolute and perpetual dominion of Chile over

---

[31] *Tratados Vigentes* (Bolivia, 1925), I, 290–292. *Recop. de Trat. de Chile* (Santiago, 1913), VI, 173–176.

Ratifications exchanged at Santiago, Apr. 16, 1907; promulgated by Chile, May 6, 1907.

the territory between 23° S. and 24° S. from the sea to the existing boundary with Argentina. Peru protested to both countries against the terms of this treaty, and declared that its provisions could in no way diminish her rights to Tacna and Arica. A convention signed at La Paz on June 27, 1905,[32] provided for the construction of the railroad from Arica to Viacha junction under Article 3 of the treaty of October 20, 1904. A protocol signed at La Paz on July 24, 1905,[33] arranged for a mixed commission of engineers to mark the line, with submission of difficulties that could not be solved by the governments to the decision of the emperor of Germany. William II declined to act as arbiter under Article 12 of the Treaty of October 20, 1904, and by protocol signed at Santiago on April 16, 1907,[34] the two countries agreed that the Permanent Court of Arbitration at the Hague should hear all questions which might arise upon the meaning or execution of that treaty. By a convention signed at Santiago on May 1, 1907,[35] minor changes were agreed to at two points on the line. A protocol signed at Santiago on May 26, 1908,[36] after making various provisions as to freight charges on the Arica-Viacha railroad provided that (Article 5) in place of the guarantee established in Article 3 of the treaty of October 20, 1904, Chile should pay annually (1) £22,500 on each September 30 after the completion and opening to traffic of the line (125 miles) from Oruro to Viacha, (2) another £22,500 on each April 1 after the opening to traffic of 250 kilometers (155 miles) of the railroads in connection with the railroad from Oruro to La Paz, and (3) finally £10,000 after the termination of the branch to connect the Oruro-Viacha line with the Arica-La Paz railroad near the Desaguadero; (Article 6) all to be paid until the total without interest should amount to the £1,-700,000 contemplated by Article 3 of the Treaty of October 20, 1904, less the value of the Bolivian section of the railroad from Arica to Bolivia. A convention for commercial traffic signed at Santiago on August 6, 1912,[37] provided for the conduct of freight and travelers' baggage destined for Bolivia or from Bolivia to foreign countries more freely through the custom houses, Bolivia having removed her agency from Antofagasta to Uyuni. The railroad from Arica to Viacha junction was completed and opened to traffic May 13,

[32] *Tratados Vigentes* (Bolivia, 1925), I, 299–303. Martens, *Nouv. Rec. Gén. de Traités*, 3e Sér., VI, 603–606.

[33] *Ibid.*, 606–608.

[34] *Tratados Vigentes* (Bolivia, 1925), I, 314–316. Martens, *Nouv. Rec. Gén. de Traités*, 3e Sér., II, 184. Ratified by Bolivia, Dec. 29, 1910.

[35] Luis Risopatron S., *La Linea de Frontera con la República de Bolivia* (Santiago, 1911), pp. 384–385.

[36] *Tratados Vigentes* (Bolivia, 1925), I, 317–323. Re-

cop. de Trat. de Chile (Santiago, 1913), VI, 734–739. Martens, *Nouv. Rec. Gén. de Traités*, 3e Sér., VI, 609–610. Ratified by Bolivia, Jan. 25, 1911; ratifications exchanged at La Paz, Sept. 20, 1911; promulgated by Chile, Law #2569, Nov. 16, 1911.

[37] *Tratados Vigentes* (Bolivia, 1925), I, 335–346. 106 *British and Foreign State Papers* 899–903. Martens, *Nouv. Rec. Gén. de Traités*, 3e Sér., XV, 499–503. Ratifications exchanged at Santiago, Mar. 23, 1914.

1913,[38] and the Bolivian section was to be turned over to Bolivia on May 13, 1928, according to Article 3 of the treaty of October 20, 1904.

It was recognized by Bolivia, Chile, and Peru that Bolivia had no real chance of recovering any of the Antofagasta or Tarapacá regions while Chile held Tacna and Arica, since to give Bolivia a strip or passage of her own to the sea in either of those regions would cut Chile off from continuity on land with some of her own territory. The Bolivian government in 1918 announced that neither Chile nor Peru had a conclusive right to the provinces of Tacna and Arica and that Bolivia should be granted an outlet to the Pacific through a port in those provinces, preferably Arica, basing the claim partly upon geographical proximity and economic considerations and partly upon the allegation that before independence Tacna and Arica had always been considered as belonging to the audiencia of Charcas.[39] A particularly aggressive reassertion of her claim by Bolivia brought a sharp denial from Peru, anti-Peruvian disorders in La Paz, March 14, 1920,[40] and threatened mobilization of the Peruvian army. A belief that the government was quietly negotiating with Chile for an understanding about an outlet to the Pacific seems to have had something to do with precipitating the bloodless revolution in La Paz on July 12–13, 1920,[41] when President José N. Gutiérrez Guerra was deposed and a provisional junta was set up under Bautista Saavedra.

Bolivia by petition,[42] presented November 1, 1920,[43] to the first Assembly of the League of Nations, invoked Article 19 of the Treaty of Versailles to obtain from the League a revision of the peace treaty of October 20, 1904, on the grounds of (1) compulsion under which the treaty was imposed; (2) nonperformance by fault of Chile of some fundamental points of the treaty; (3) the permanent threat of war arising from the existing situation, and (4) Bolivia's complete deprivation by the treaty of all access to the sea. The United States in May 1920 [44] requested Brazil to suggest to the League Council that it not take cognizance at that time of the dispute to be referred to the League by Bolivia. Bolivia asked on December 15, 1920, that her request go

---

[38] *Tratados Vigentes* (Bolivia, 1925), I, 347–349.

[39] Arturo Arenas B., *Bolivia en al Pacífico* (La Paz, 1920). Prescott, *El Problema Continental* (La Paz, 1921). Luis Barros Borgono, *La Cuestión del Pacifico y las Nuevas Orientaciones de Bolivia* (Santiago, 1922); in English (Baltimore, 1924). E. Diez de Medina, *La Cuestion del Pacifico y la Politica Int. de Bolivia* (La Paz, 1923). Vicente Mendoza Lopez, *El Litoral de Bolivia ante el Derecho Int.* (La Paz, 1924). Conrado Rios Gallardo, *Después de la Paz* (Santiago, 1926). Luis Espinoza y Saravia, *Después de la Guerra* (La Paz, 1928; 2ᵃ ed., La Paz, 1929).

[40] *U. S. For. Rel.*, 1920, I, 324–340.

[41] *Ibid.*, I, 372–386.

[42] *Cf.* Peru's request, 1920. §19, this chap., *infra.*

[43] *Monthly Summary of the League of Nations*, 1921, I, 69, 123–124. *Second Assembly, Verbatim Records*, Sept. 15, p. 2; Sept. 28, pp. 2–5. *Journal of the Second Assembly*, pp. 122–123, 134, 218. *League of Nations Documents*, 1921, VII, A73. José Carrasco, *Bolivia ante la Liga de las Naciones* (Lima, 1920); in English (London, 1920); in French (Nancy, 1921). Raymond Poincaré, *La Cuestión del Pacífico y la Liga de las Naciones* (Paris, 1921).

[44] *U. S. For. Rel.*, 1920, I, 341.

on the agenda of the second (1921) session of the Assembly. The Chilean delegation in letters of December 17, 19, and 28, 1920, objected to the competence of the League to admit the petition on the grounds that a treaty could not be revised except with the consent of the parties to it, that the treaty of 1904 could not be revised under Article 19 of the Covenant because it had been already executed, and that by reason of the reservation in Article 21 of the Covenant the Assembly could not concern itself with matters exclusively American; and moved the "previous question" to Bolivia's proposal to include this item in the agenda of the second Assembly. The officers of the Assembly referred the question of the powers of the Assembly under Article 19 of the Covenant to a committee of three jurists, Vittorio Scialoja of Italy, Francisco José Urrutia of Colombia, and Manuel de Peralta of Costa Rica. Sr. Urrutia declined the honor because he was still technically Colombia's minister to Bolivia, and M. A. A. H. Struycken of the Netherlands was named in his stead. The committee reported unanimously on September 22, 1921, that Bolivia's petition as presented was inadmissible, since the Assembly of the League could not by itself modify any treaty, which only the parties might do; and Article 19 gave the Assembly the power only to invite members of the League to examine afresh certain treaties which might have become inapplicable by radical material or moral transformations or certain international situations whose continuance might endanger the peace of the world. The Chilean delegate, Agustín Edwards, told the Assembly that Chile's earnest wish was that Bolivia might be happy and prosperous, and that she would welcome direct negotiations for facilitating Bolivia's development. The Bolivian delegation under Carlos Victor Aramayo declared that it accepted the conclusions of the committee of jurists and did not insist that the request of November 1, 1920, be placed on the agenda, but reserved Bolivia's right to submit afresh her demand to the League. Edwards replied that Bolivia could reserve no right not to carry out the treaty or bring it up again before the League, to which Avelino Aramayo responded that Bolivia had the right to renew her request and could not renounce it in any form. While the withdrawal of the request for the record was based on the report of the committee of jurists, the reservation in Article 21 of the Covenant as to the validity of international engagements, such as regional understandings like the Monroe Doctrine, for securing the maintenance of peace, and the suggested adverse attitude of the United States, are supposed to have influenced the decision.

Title to territory acquired by war, comprising the entire sea coast of the vanquished, was confirmed on a permanent basis by peace treaties, but on the disappearance of the nitrate market the accession lost most of its practical value. With pressure gradually increasing on the South American nations to become better friends with their neighbors, it is not impossible that after the settlement of the Chaco Boreal boundary, presumably not entirely to Bolivia's satisfaction, Chile might offer her some compensation in a corridor near Arica, Peru probably being quite willing to give her consent, a necessary prerequisite of any cession according to the complementary protocol of June 3, 1929,[45] between Chile and Peru.

8. BOLIVIA–PARAGUAY. CHACO BOREAL

After the award by President Hayes on November 12, 1878,[1] decided that as against Argentina Paraguay was entitled to the territory between the Pilcomayo and the Verde, Bolivia sought a settlement with Paraguay of an old claim by Bolivian publicists to the whole Chaco Boreal, including the awarded area, upon the ground that the audiencia of Charcas had always exercised jurisdiction down to the right (west) bank of the Paraguay; and Bolivia undertook to find support for the claim in the old Spanish archives. Bolivia sent Antonio Quijarro to Asunción, where he signed with José Segundo Decoud, Paraguayan minister of foreign relations, on October 15, 1879,[2] a treaty providing that the boundary should be a line along the parallel (22°05′ S.) from the mouth of the Apa to the Pilcomayo, and by the middle of the principal channel of the Pilcomayo or its most important branch, with a special convention to be agreed upon for a demarcation commission. By this arrangement Paraguay yielded to Bolivia the territory on the west side of the Paraguay from Bahia Negra 125 miles south to opposite the mouth of the Apa, and Bolivia gave up her claim to all of the Chaco Boreal south of 22° 6′45″. This treaty was not ratified by either country, and Bolivia later claimed that the whole arrangement was canceled.

Authorized by Bolivia,[3] Miguel Suárez Arana on July 16, 1885, founded Puerto Pacheco at Bahia Negra on the west bank of the Paraguay, sixty miles north of Fuerte Olimpo. A treaty signed by Isaac Tamayo, Bolivian special minister, and Benjamin Aceval, Paraguayan minister of foreign rela-

---

[45] See §19, this chap., *infra.*

[1] See §4, this chap., *supra.*

[2] Approved by Bolivian National Convention on Aug. 3, 1881, on the condition of obtaining on the east bank of the Pilcomayo and south of the swamps territory sufficient to found one or more ports; approved unconditionally by Bolivian Congress, Nov. 12, 1886; ratified by Gregorio Pacheco, President of Bolivia, Nov. 23, 1886. Telmo Ichaso, *Antecedents del Tratado de Límites celebrado con la República del Paraguay* (Sucre, 1894), pp. 1–3.

[3] Decree of Nov. 18, 1884; Resolution of Dec. 1, 1884. *Anuario de Leyes de 1884*, pp. 251–255.

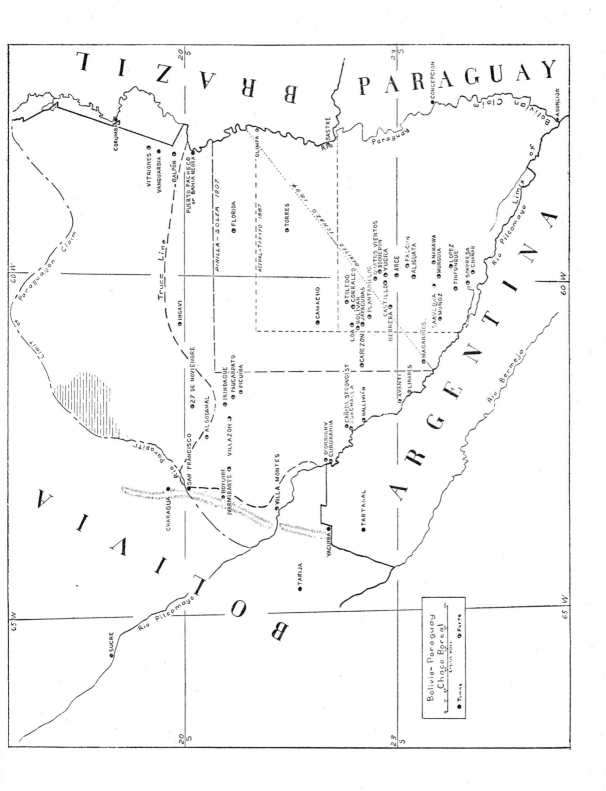

Bolivia-Paraguay
Chaco Boreal

● Towns   ● Forts

tions, at Asunción on February 16, 1887,[4] considered the disputed area in three sections, (1) Paraguay to have the region between the principal branch of the Pilcomayo, which empties opposite Lambaré at 25°21′ S. according to the map of Mouchez,[5] and a line parallel to the equator which runs from the (west) bank of the Paraguay opposite the middle of the mouth of the Apa to the meridian 60°39′46″ W.; (2) the region between the parallel of the Apa and the parallel one league north of Fuerte Olimpo west to the same meridian 60°39′46″ W. to be submitted to the arbitral decision of King Leopold II of Belgium or another arbiter to be chosen by the parties; and (3) Bolivia to have the region between the parallel one league north of Fuerte Olimpo and Bahia Negra; but this treaty was never ratified. In December 1887 [6] Puerto Pacheco was seized and five Bolivians captured by the Paraguayan Sergeant-Major Ángel Giménez and a small guard from Fort Olimpo; diplomatic relations were broken off, and a sharp correspondence ensued. Paraguay on January 13, 1888, made a decree purporting to extend her jurisdiction on the west bank of the Paraguay to Bahia Negra and ordering the occupation of Fuerte Olimpo by a military garrison. Under the good offices of Uruguay, diplomatic relations were resumed on July 31, 1889, and Gregorio Benítez, Paraguayan minister of foreign relations, and Telmo Ichaso, Bolivian minister, in a preliminary convention signed at Asunción on August 3, 1894, agreed in declaring the complete lapse of the Decoud-Quijarro treaty of October 15, 1879, and the Aceval-Tamayo treaty of February 16, 1887. The same two ministers signed at Asunción on November 23, 1894,[7] a treaty which provided that the boundary line should run across the Chaco from a point three leagues north of Fuerte Olimpo on the right bank of the Paraguay southwest in a straight line to the principal branch of the Pilcomayo at its intersection with the meridian 61°28′ W., a mixed commission to fix the boundary thus agreed upon. This treaty also was never ratified, and feeling on both sides grew more bitter until war was averted only by a revolution in Paraguay on May 1, 1898, which deposed the bellicose President Juan Bautista Eguzquiza. Negotiations under Argentine auspices were reopened [8] and Claudio Pinilla,

[4] Telmo Ichaso, *Antecedentes del Tratado de Límites celebrado con la República del Paraguay* (Sucre, 1894), pp. 4–9. "Para la Historia Diplomática," *Rev. de Der. y Cien. Soc.* (Asunción, 1930), III, Num. 11, pp. 97–123. Approved by the Bolivian Congress, Nov. 23, 1888.

[5] Probably E. Mouchez, 1862. See §4, this chap., *supra.*

[6] *Notas Cambiadas* (Asunción, 1888). *U. S. For. Rel.*, 1888, Part II, pp. 1357–1358. *Arch. Dipl.*, 2ᵉ Sér., XXX, 135–151, 359–360; *ibid.*, XXXII, 182–183; *ibid.*, XXXIV, 111; *ibid.*, LIV, 247.

[7] Telmo Ichaso, *Antecedents del Tratado de Límites* (Sucre, 1894), pp. 319–320. Manuel Bernárdez, *El Tratado de la Asunción* (Montevideo, 1894). Gregorio Benites, *Exposición de los Derechos del Paraguay* (Asunción, 1895). Postponed indefinitely by Paraguayan Congress, May 19, 1896.

[8] *U. S. For. Rel.*, 1906, Part II, p. 1429; *ibid.*, 1907, Part I, pp. 85–89. Cecilio Baez, *The Paraguayan Chaco* (New York, 1904). Fulgencio R. Moreno, *El Problema de las Fronteras* (Buenos Aires, 1927). Miguel Mercado Moreira, *El Chaco Boliviano* (Cochabamba, 1928). *Actos*

Bolivian minister of foreign relations, and Adolfo L. Soler, Paraguayan ex-minister of foreign relations, signed at Buenos Aires on January 12, 1907,[9] a protocol which described the area to be submitted in arbitration to the president of Argentina as included between the 20°30′ S. parallel and the north line which Paraguay supported in her claims, and in the interior between 61°30′ and 62° W.; and (Article 7) both countries agreed not to advance their existing possessions. It was later declared by Bolivia that this was intended to apply to the possessions in the whole Chaco; by Paraguay, only to possessions in the two arbitral zones. This protocol, although approved, was not ratified, and the Bolivian negotiator, Emeterio Cano, died in Asunción in November 1907 before any treaty of arbitration was agreed on.

Ricardo Mujía, Bolivian minister, and Eusebio Ayala, Paraguayan minister of foreign relations, signed at Asunción on April 5, 1913,[10] a protocol, which Paraguay later claimed superseded all previous ones, in which the parties promised to negotiate a final boundary treaty within two years by direct arrangement if possible, and if not to submit the boundary question to a legal arbitration; and meanwhile to maintain the *status quo* stipulated in the agreement of January 12, 1907, which was terminated, both parties declaring that they had not modified their respective positions since that date. Bolivia afterwards asserted that the word "positions" in this protocol was substituted by Paraguay for the word "possessions" in the corresponding clause of the 1907 protocol, without agreement between the negotiators, and that Dr. Mujía inadvertently failed to notice the change.[11]

By a protocol signed at Asunción on July 19, 1915,[12] the time for making the final treaty was extended to July 28, 1916, and the continuation of the *status quo* was to be the subject of special stipulation in the arbitration treaty to be signed if the parties could not come to direct agreement. The time was by a protocol signed at Asunción on November 21, 1916,[13] further extended to June 15, 1917, agreed by both countries to be the end for boundary negotiations between them, all the conditions of the protocol of April 5,

---

y Documentos de las Conferencias . . . en Buenos Aires, Min. de Rel. Ext. (La Paz, 1929). Elias Ayala, *Paraguay y Bolivia en el Chaco Boreal* (Asunción, 1929). José Aguirre Achá, *The Arbitration Zone in the Bolivian-Paraguayan Dispute through the Diplomatic Negotiations* (La Paz, 1929).

[9] *U. S. For. Rel.,* 1907, Part I, pp. 87–88. *Protocolos y Notas Cambiadas, Min. de Rel. Ext.* (Asunción, 1927), pp. 3–4. Manuel Domínguez, *Informe del Plenipotenciario Paraguayo* (Asunción, 1929). Approved by the Bolivian government, Mar. 6, 1907; approved by the Paraguayan government, Mar. 11, 1907.

[10] *Trat. Vig.* (Bolivia, 1925), I, 578–580. 107 *British and Foreign State Papers* 604. *U. S. For. Rel.,* 1914, pp. 27–29. Martens, *Nouv. Rec. Gén. de Traités,* 3ᵉ Sér., X, 253. Approved by the Bolivian Cabinet, July 28, 1913; ratifications exchanged, July 28, 1913.

[11] In Spanish, *posiciones* for *posesiones,* a difference of only two letters; and in Spanish-American pronunciation almost *idem sonans.*

[12] *Trat. Vig.* (Bolivia, 1925), I, 581–583. Approved by the Bolivian Cabinet, Aug. 17, 1915.

[13] *Trat. Vig.* (Bolivia, 1925), I, 584–586. Approved by the Bolivian Cabinet, Jan. 15, 1917.

1913, to be in continuous effect until that date. By act signed by Ricardo Mujía, Bolivian minister, and Fulgencio R. Moreno, special Paraguayan minister, at Asunción at five P.M. on June 15, 1917,[14] the two countries agreed to extend the protocol of November 21, 1916, in all its terms to give time to conclude the negotiations then under way, and that after a reasonable time either party might with not less than thirty days' notice fix a definite date for the conclusion of the negotiations, in which thirty days the countries should come to direct agreement if possible and if not arrange for arbitration according to the current protocol of April 5, 1913. In July 1917 Mujía was called back to La Paz to become minister of foreign relations in the cabinet of President José N. Gutiérrez Guerra, but Moreno was sent as Paraguayan minister to Bolivia and on June 7, 1918, the negotiations between them were renewed at La Paz. On June 17, 1918,[15] they signed an act extending the time for negotiation to the day of defining any of the propositions for direct agreement, until which date there should be in continuous force the stipulations of the protocol of November 21, 1916, and the act of June 15, 1917.

Conversations held at Montevideo on May 3, 1923,[16] contemplated the setting up of a permanent arbitration commission, but nothing was accomplished. A project for a pipe line from Bolivia across the Chaco to the Paraguay was said to have been abandoned by the oil company as impracticable in 1922; and in 1925 a survey was made for a pipe line from the Tarija region across the Pilcomayo into northern Argentina. Both countries gradually advanced their lines of occupation until they averaged fifteen miles apart, more or less along the 60° W. meridian, with fourteen fortified blockhouses and stockades on the front line on each side. Paraguay granted lands and encouraged settlements along the west bank of the Paraguay, recognized Argentine owners of grazing areas on the drier tracts north of the Pilcomayo, and authorized the Mennonite immigration farther northward and inland in 1927 and thereafter. Negotiations were revived at Buenos Aires, and Argentina attempted mediation without success, for Bolivia held out for the line discussed in 1913 and Paraguay for the 1907 line as the basis for negotiations. On February 26, 1927, Bolivian soldiers at Fortin Sorpresa undertook to arrest the Paraguayan Lieutenant Adolfo Rojas Silva, who with three Paraguayan soldiers and a Guaraní guide had entered the enclosure, whereupon he and one of the soldiers started to run but were pursued by one or more

14 *Trat. Vig.* (Bolivia, 1925), I, 586–588. *Cuestión de Límites con Bolivia. Negociaciones Diplomáticas, 1915–1917*, Ministerio de Relaciones Exteriores (Asunción, 1917; Tomos 3, 2ª ed., Asunción, 1928). Miguel Mercado

Moreira, *El Chaco Boreal* (La Paz, 1929).
15 *Trat. Vig.* (Bolivia, 1925), I, 592–595.
16 Cornelio Rios, *Cuestión de Límites entre el Paraguay y Bolivia* (Buenos Aires, 1925).

Bolivians, and in the ensuing exchange of shots Lieutenant Rojas was killed.

By a protocol signed by Alberto Gutiérrez, Bolivian minister of foreign relations, and Lisandro Díaz León, national deputy of Paraguay, at Buenos Aires on April 22, 1927,[17] both countries accepted the good offices of Argentina and undertook to send representatives to Buenos Aires within ninety days. Conferences were held in Buenos Aires from September 29 to December 27, 1927, and included, among other proposals, the establishment of a neutral zone in the Chaco from which troops of both nations would withdraw. After further conferences from May to July 13, 1928,[18] it was announced in Buenos Aires that the representatives were unable to agree, and Argentina suggested that the two countries should submit the question to arbitration and meanwhile withdraw their forces from the frontier. On July 12, 1928, Bolivia issued a statement on the settlement of a tax dispute with the Standard Oil Company of Bolivia, a subsidiary of the Standard Oil Company of New Jersey[19] and holder of a concession in southeastern Bolivia, by which the company advanced to Bolivia on acccount of future taxes the sum of 1,000,-000 bolivars ($362,978) and was to be credited for taxes up to and including 1936; but a succeeding administration attempted to repudiate the arrangement and demanded 1,500,000 bolivars more, upon which suit was brought and so far as announced the matter was still unsettled at the time of the final confiscation decree of March 1937, hereafter described.

It was announced in La Paz on August 9, 1928, that no agreement was in sight but that the delegates of both countries were confident that the dispute would be settled peacefully unless there was armed aggression by one of the parties. On December 5, 1928,[20] Paraguayan troops from Galpón seized and destroyed the Bolivian advance post of Fortin Vanguardia at 19°35′ S. 58°11′ W. in territory claimed by both countries; and on December 6, 1928, Bolivia captured the Paraguayan Fortin Boquerón, 225 miles northwest from Asunción. Bolivia on December 9 recalled her minister from Asunción and gave the Paraguayan minister in La Paz his passports. The Council of the League of Nations was meeting in its fifty-third session, at Lugano, and on the strength of press reports of the trouble requested its acting president, Aristide Briand of France, on December 11[21] to telegraph both

[17] Protocolos y Notas Cambiadas, Min. de Rel. Ext. (Asunción, 1927), pp. 35-36. Ratified by Bolivia, June 30, 1927.

[18] 133 British and Foreign State Papers 166-168.

[19] Carlos R. Santos, Conflicto Paraguayo-Boliviano (2ª ed., Asunción, 1932).

[20] Documentos relativos a la Agresión del Paraguay contra el Fortín Boliviano Vanguardia, Min. de Rel. Ext. (La Paz, 1929). Julio Oroza Daza, Los ataques a los Fortines Vanguardia y Boquerón (Buenos Aires, 1929). Bull. of Int. News (London, 1928), V, 282-284.

[21] League of Nations Documents, 1928, VII, 1: C 619, M 195; ibid., 1929, VII, 1: C 16, M 13.

governments reminding them of their solemn pledge to seek by pacific means the solution of disputes arising between them. Both replied with detailed statements of their positions, and President Briand on December 21 reported to the members of the Council that he had seen the Argentine and United States chargés d'affaires in Paris, and as Bolivia and Paraguay had accepted the good offices of the Pan-American Arbitration Conference no extraordinary session of the Council would be necessary.

The American International Conference on Conciliation and Arbitration was meeting at Washington from December 10, 1928, to January 5, 1929; and on December 10, 1928,[22] the conference, including representatives of Bolivia and Paraguay, unanimously resolved to express telegraphically to the governments of the sister republics of Bolivia and Paraguay the lively hope that their differences might be adjusted peacefully and in a spirit of justice, concord, and fraternity; to remind them cordially and respectfully in accordance with the tradition of this continent and the general practices of modern international law that nations in circumstances such as theirs had at their disposal adequate and efficacious organizations and means for finding solutions which should harmonize the preservation of peace with the rights of states; and to appoint a committee to report to the conference upon the conciliatory action which might opportunely be lent in coöperation with the forces seeking an amicable solution of the problem. The committee reported that the full conference ought to decide on the line of conduct to be followed, but suggested, and the conference thereupon on December 14 [23] voted, that it tender its good offices to the two countries to bring about conciliatory measures. Frank B. Kellogg, United States secretary of state, president of the conference, extended the offer to Eduardo Díez de Medina, Bolivian minister, and Juan Vicente Ramírez, Paraguayan chargé d'affaires, and they accepted. On January 3, 1929,[24] they signed at Washington a protocol agreeing to create a commission of investigation and conciliation composed of two delegates each of Bolivia and Paraguay and one delegate each designated by the governments of the United States, Mexico, Colombia, Uruguay, and Cuba, to investigate what had happened, hearing both sides, and within six months to propose methods for adjusting amicably the incident under condi-

[22] Sixth Resolution. *Rev. de Der. Int.* (Havana), XV (1929), 130-131.

[23] Seventh Resolution. *Rev. de Der. Int.* (Havana), XV (1929), 131-132.

[24] J. Isidro Ramírez, *Alrededor de la Cuestión Paraguayo-Boliviana* (Lima, 1930). *Amer. J. Int. Law,* XXIII (1929), 110-112; *ibid.,* XXIV (1930), 122-126. 133 *British and Foreign State Papers* 169-171. *Int. Conciliation,*

1929; No. 249, pp. 195-217. *Rev. de Der. Int.,* (Havana), XV (1929), 135-137. *Rev. gen. de dr. int. pub.,* XXXVI (1929), 528-553, 587-588. *L'Europe Nouvelle,* 1929, 12e Année, pp. 389-397. Fernando Gonzales Roa, *Comisión de Investigación y Conciliación, Informe del Delegado Mexicano* (Mexico, 1930). "Documentos y Crónicas," *Rev. de Der. y Cien. Soc.* (Ascunción, 1929) Año II, Nums. 7-8, pp. 148-156.

tions satisfactory to both parties, or, if that should not be possible, to report the result of its investigation and its efforts to adjust the incident; to be empowered, if conciliation could not be arranged, to establish the responsibilities which appeared as the result of its investigation according to international law; both governments promised to suspend hostilies and to cease all concentration of troops at the points of contact of the military defenses of the two countries until the pronouncement of the commission; and it was declared to be understood that the protocol did not include or affect the question between the two countries of territory according to Bolivia or of boundaries according to Paraguay, or the existing agreements in force between them. A place on the commission is supposed to have been offered to Argentina and declined by President Hipólito Irigoyen, Argentina preferring to work alone, and Uruguay was then named. The conference on January 4, 1929,[25] congratulated the two countries on signing the protocol and thanked its committee for the efficient and noble manner in which it had discharged its task. The commission[26] met on March 13, 1929, in Washington and prepared to commence the investigation,[27] but first arranged by resolutions of May 13 and May 24, 1929,[28] for the repatriation of all the other's nationals held by each country since December 1928, which was accomplished by delivery of the Paraguayans on June 30 at Formosa and of the Bolivians on July 8 at Puerto Suarez, with the assistance and coöperation of Argentina and Brazil. On May 31 the neutral members proposed to the Bolivian and Paraguayan commissioners to prepare in a spirit of amity plans for conciliation, and the offer was accepted, excluding direct settlement of the fundamental question. On September 12 the commission unanimously adopted a resolution on conciliation, reciting the agreement of both parties to (1) mutual forgiveness of the offenses and injuries caused by each to the other; (2) reëstablishment of the state of things in the Chaco on the same footing as prior to December 5, 1928, by restoration by Paraguay of the buildings of Fortín Vanguardia and abandonment by Bolivian troops of Fortín Boquerón without the presence of Paraguayan authorities, without prejudgment of the pending territorial or boundary dispute; and (3) renewal of diplomatic relations. The commission resolved that, as conciliation had been effected, it was

[25] Ninth Resolution. *Rev. de Der. Int.* (Havana), XV (1929), 132–133.

[26] David Alvéstegui and Enrique Finot of Bolivia, Enrique Bordenave and Francisco C. Chaves of Paraguay, Raimundo Rivas of Colombia, Manuel Márquez Sterling of Cuba, Fernando González Roa of Mexico, Guillermo Ruprecht of Uruguay, and Frank R. McCoy of the United States, chosen chairman at the first meeting.

[27] *Foreign Affairs*, VII (1929), 650–655. *Bull. Pan-Amer. Union*, LXIII (1929), 753–760, 1077–1097. *Rev. de Der. Int.* (Havana), XVI (1929), 176–185.

[28] *U. S. Tr. Inf. Bull.*, May, 1929, No. 3, pp. 15–18; July, 1929, No. 5, pp. 33–34.

unnecessary to proceed with the investigation or to render a report, and acknowledged that it had not established responsibilities. The neutral commissioners proposed arbitration which both countries accepted in principle, subject to observations as to its application, promising to transmit the proposed convention of arbitration to their foreign offices; and the commission held its final meeting on September 13, 1929.[29]

Conferences held in Buenos Aires in 1929 with Daniel Sánchez Bustamante, former Bolivian minister of foreign relations, as head of the Bolivian delegation, resulted in nothing. On January 16, 1930, there was a clash between Bolivian and Paraguayan patrols at Isla Poi, and one Paraguayan soldier was killed. M. Auguste Zaleski of Poland, acting president of the League Council, telegraphed both countries on January 23 [30] urging pacific procedure; both answered with assurances of their pacific intentions, and the League again extended and received congratulations on its great service to peace. A protocol setting May 1, 1930, for the renewal of diplomatic relations was signed by Alberto Díez de Medina, minister of Bolivia, and Higinio Arbo, minister of Paraguay, at Montevideo on April 4, 1930,[31] and new ministers were officially received in both countries on May 21, 1930.

In June, 1931,[32] Pablo M. Insfrán, Paraguayan chargé d'affaires in Washington, gave out a statement charging Bolivia with militaristic intentions. The Paraguayan government declined to disavow the statement, and although on June 25 the representatives of Colombia, Cuba, Mexico, Uruguay, and the United States in identic notes to Bolivia and Paraguay offered their services to compose the situation, Luis Fernando Guachalla, Bolivian minister to Paraguay, left Asunción on July 5 and Rogelio Ibarra, Paraguayan minister to Bolivia, was withdrawn from La Paz. Argentina offered to mediate, and Paraguay accepted on July 12. To a further Argentina offer to use her good offices to settle the basic dispute, Bolivia replied that she preferred direct negotiations to that end. On August 6 [33] the five neutrals jointly suggested to Bolivia and Paraguay the negotiation of a nonaggression pact in the Chaco. The Argentine efforts were making progress until on September 6, 1931,[34] a Paraguayan patrol of twelve horsemen attacked Agua Rica, an outpost of the Bolivian Fortín Nataniel Murguía, and a few soldiers were killed and wounded on each side. On September 25 there was another clash

[29] *Bull. Pan American Union*, LXIII (1929), 1077–1097.

[30] *League of Nations Documents*, 1930, VII, 1: C 122, M 40.

[31] *U. S. Tr. Inf. Bull.*, May 1930, No. 8, pp. 4–5.

[32] *Bol. del Min. de Rel. Ext.* (La Paz, 1931), V,

No. 10, 66–69. *Aff. Étrangères* (Paris), 1931, 1e Année, pp. 301–302.

[33] *U. S. Tr. Inf. Bull.*, August, 1931, No. 23, pp. 7–8.

[34] *League of Nations Off. Journal*, 1932, 13th Year, p. 151.

near Fortin Samaklay, with seventeen dead and nine wounded. Other fights followed, and feeling rapidly rose in both countries. To the proposal by the five neutrals that negotiations concerning the proposed nonaggression pact begin in Washington on October 1, both countries suggested postponement. On October 16 [35] the five neutrals asked the other American nations to join them in an appeal to the two countries to sign a nonaggression pact, and on October 19 all the nineteen neutral American nations joined in the appeal.

There was a student movement in Asunción in favor of war with Bolivia, and President José Patricio Guggiari was forced to resign on October 26, 1931, because he tried to suppress it, but he returned to office on January 26, 1932. Negotiations for the nonaggression pact were begun in Washington on November 11, 1931,[36] and continued until the end of May 1932, when a proposed pact was submitted to the two governments. On June 15, 1932, a small Bolivian road-surveying detachment preparing to camp on the west bank of Lake Chuquisaca was objected to by a Paraguayan corporal who with his squad of five soldiers was stationed on the other shore in Fortin Pitiantuta (Mariscal Carlos Antonio López) at 60° 20′ W., whereupon the Bolivians drove out the Paraguayans and occupied the Fortin, and the war was on.[37] When Paraguay heard of the event, a considerable detachment was sent, and recaptured the place on July 15, 1932. Bolivian national honor thus became involved, and on July 31 Bolivian troops captured Fortin Boquerón from a Paraguayan garrison of a lieutenant and eighty men, and a little later Fortins Corrales and Toledo. On August 2 Paraguay protested to the League of Nations that Bolivia had violated Articles 10 and 11 of the Covenant, and in reply to a League telegram agreed to arbitrate the dispute, but Bolivia, while "not declining," insisted that Paraguay had committed the first act of aggression on June 29.[38] On August 3, 1932, all the other members of the Pan American Union sent an identic note to Bolivia and Paraguay in which they laid down the principle that they would not recognize territorial gains in the Chaco made by force of arms. Representatives of the two countries and the five neutrals,[39] joined by representatives of Argentina, Brazil, Chile, and Peru, met in Washington on August 10 to continue efforts to adjust the dispute and the nine neutrals insisted upon an armistice. The

[35] U. S. Tr. Inf. Bull., October, 1931, No. 25, pp. 6-7.

[36] Bull. Pan Amer. Union, LXV (1931), 1213-1216.

[37] John W. White, "Warfare in the Chaco Jungle," Current History, XXXVIII (1933), 41-46. Elmer Davis, "Paradigm in Paraguay," New Republic, Feb. 22, 1933.

[38] League of Nations Off. Journal, 1932, 13th Year, pp. 1573-1586, 1720-1721, 1760-1761, 1923-1925, 1944-1946, 1951-1955, 1967-1969, 1986-1987, 1993-2000.

[39] Eduardo Díez de Medina and Enrique Finot for Bolivia; Juan José Soler and César A. Vasconcelos for Paraguay; Fabio Lozano of Colombia; José T. Baron of Cuba; Herrera de Huerta of Mexico; J. Varela of Uruguay; Francis White, United States assistant secretary of state, chairman.

four adjoining countries had signed an agreement to preserve strict neutrality in case of war, and Argentina withdrew from Paraguay her military mission under Colonel Schweitzer which had in 1930 replaced a French mission. Fortin Pitiantuta was recaptured by the Paraguayans on August 12, and the desired truce ended before it had begun. On August 29, 1932, the neutrals in Washington proposed a sixty-day truce beginning September 1, which Paraguay rejected, as she did also a proposal by Bolivia for a thirty-day truce, on the ground that both were based on maintenance of the *status quo,* which meant that Bolivia would retain possession of Fortins Boquerón, Corrales, and Toledo. On September 7 the Bolivians took Fortin Falcón (Rojas Silva). On September 9 some 10,000 Paraguayan troops attacked Fortin Boquerón, much strengthened and defended by 1,000 Bolivians, and after a real siege, almost daily costly assaults, and shortage of water on both sides, they captured it on September 29 with half the garrison. The neutrals on September 14 proposed immediate cessation of hostilities and a demilitarized zone twenty kilometers (12.4 miles) wide between the combatants. Argentina on September 26 sent a note to the commission of neutrals meeting in Washington, taking the position that the neutrals had no right to use force or compulsion against either Bolivia or Paraguay and that their efforts should be limited to the use of good offices and moral influence. Bolivia evacuated Fortins Toledo and Corrales; the Paraguayans announced on October 2 that they had taken Fortins Yucra, Ramírez, 14 de diciembre, and Lara; and on October 23 they captured Fort Arce, field headquarters of the Bolivian army in the Chaco. The five neutrals on October 14, 1932, published telegraphic correspondence with the League of Nations tending to dispel rumors that the League was attempting to interfere in the negotiations; and on October 27 conferences were resumed on a plan to which Paraguay had assented on October 14 and Bolivia on October 26 for separation of the armies in the Chaco, demobilization of the reserves on both sides, reduction of the regular armies to a fixed maximum, the sending of a neutral commission to the Chaco to see that the conditions were complied with, and direct negotiations for settlement by arbitration. On November 6 the Paraguayans captured Fortin Platanillos, forty-three miles west of Boquerón and forty-four miles northwest of Arce; on November 7 Fortin Bolívar, twenty-five miles farther north; and on November 9 they occupied Fortin Loa, sixty-nine miles north of Platanillos, and Fortin Jayacuba. In all the Paraguayans captured thirty positions in October and November and pushed the Bolivian line back fifty-six miles north and fifty miles west. The Paraguayan attack in the south on Fort Nanawa (Presi-

dente Ayala) and Fortins Samaklay (Agua Rica), Saavedra, and Murguía
was finally halted. General Hans Kundt, a German officer who had formerly trained the Bolivian army and left the country on the overthrow of
President Siles in May 1930, sailed from New York on November 17 and
reached La Paz, December 6, 1932. On November 25 the League of Nations
by cable urged both countries and the neutrals in Washington that the proposed military commission to effect a truce be set up at once by the neutrals
in accordance with their proposals of September 14. Paraguay on November
28 notified the League that it was willing to stop the fighting if effective guarantees were established, and Bolivia on December 1 replied to the League
cable that she was willing to suspend hostilities at once but was the country
aggrieved and on the defensive and could not acept the condition of abandonment of the disputed territory, as imposed by Paraguay in negotiations with
the neutrals. On December 10 the Paraguayan offensive was repulsed at
Kilometer Siete (Campo Jordán) on the Alihuatá road, northeast of Fortin
Saavedra. On that day General Kundt left La Paz for the front, and on December 13 the Bolivians took the offensive, after having been on the defensive since September 29, and recaptured Fortin Platanillos, Fortin Loa on
December 15, Fortin Jayacuba on December 20, and Fortin Bolívar on December 21. On December 31, 1932, the Bolivians took Fortin Duarte, one
of the outposts of Nanawa, and on January 3, 1933, Paraguay admitted the
abandonment of Fortin Corrales. Paraguay on December 17 refused as un-
just and openly favorable to Bolivia a new neutral proposal advanced on December 15 for suspension of hostilities within forty-eight hours, withdrawal of
Paraguayan forces to the Paraguay river and of Bolivian forces to a line from
Fort Ballivián to Fortin Vitriones, demobilization of the armies, policing of the
evacuated zone by a small force from each country with a central zone between
them, and arbitration by geographical experts or the World Court; and under
instructions of December 19 from his government Dr. Juan José Soler, the
Paraguayan delegate to the neutrals in Washington, withdrew from the negotiations and sailed from New York on December 31. The League of Nations on December 17, 1932, broadcast an appeal in Spanish, French, and
English for cessation of hostilities. On December 20 Bolivia replied to the
neutrals that in view of Paraguay's absolute rejection of the proposal, the Bolivian government did not believe it useful to touch on any of the points. The
neutrals announced on December 20 in reply to Paraguay that the proposal
was not intended to examine titles or decide rights; and on December 23
added that, though Paraguay now objected to the Ballivián-Vitriones line, in

August 1932 she considered adequate the positions of June 1, 1932, which were much nearer the Paraguay river. The neutrals on December 31 in an identic note asked the ABCP countries (Argentina, Brazil, Chile, and Peru) what steps they were prepared to take to bring about peace. United States bankers were said in 1932 to have lent Bolivia $20,000,000 for the purchase of arms, mostly in Great Britain; but on January 10, 1933,[40] President Herbert Hoover in a message to the United States Congress urged ratification of the Geneva convention of June 17, 1925, or if that was impossible, as seemed to be the case, legislation conferring upon the president authority in his discretion to limit or forbid shipment of arms from the United States for military purposes in cases where coöperation could be secured with the principal arms-manufacturing nations. On January 8, 1933, the Bolivians captured Fortin Pitiantuta and a new Fortin López, one of the outposts of Nanawa. On January 25 the Standard Oil Company of New Jersey announced that Bolivia had commandeered motor and animal transport equipment belonging to its Bolivian subsidiary, for which the company had claimed reimbursement, but denied that it was aiding Bolivia financially or materially in the war, or that it was interested in or contemplated a pipe line from its holdings in Tarija to the Paraguay river. Simon Patino, owner of the richest tin mines in Bolivia, of course loyally supported his country.

The ministers of foreign relations of Argentina and Chile met at Mendoza on February 1 and on February 2, 1933,[41] signed a confidential plan which they communicated to Brazil and Peru, and the four states submitted it to Bolivia and Paraguay on February 24, 1933. The Act of Mendoza called for the immediate cessation of hostilities, withdrawal of troops from the contact zone, demobilization, an economic conference as to transit facilities for landlocked countries or frontier regions, and settlement of the substantive question by arbitration. Paraguay accepted on February 27, with amendments, and Bolivia on March 1 answered with different proposals. This attempt at mediation by the ABCP group thereupon came to an end.

On March 6, 1933,[42] the Paraguayan Congress passed a law authorizing the president to declare the republic in a state of war with Bolivia. On March 6 [43] the representatives of the Irish Free State, Guatemala, and Spain, as a committee of three set up by the Council on September 23, 1932, asked the

[40] *Congressional Record*, vol. LXXVI, Part 2, 1448, 1546.

[41] *Libro Blanco*, II Parte, Min. de Rel. Ext. (Asunción, 1933).

[42] Law #1302. *Diario Ofic.* (Asunción), March, 1933, Num. 2151, p. 2. Approved by President Eusebio Ayala, Mar. 17, 1933.

[43] *League of Nations Off. Journal*, 1933, 14th Year, pp. 253–263, 373–381, 623–626, 632–634, 752–789, 849, 1072–1079, 1082–1099, 1552–1554, 1556–1593. *Cf.* §21B, note 10, *infra*.

League of Nations to place the dispute on the agenda of a meeting of the Council under Article 11 of the Covenant. The ABCP group made peace proposals which were announced on March 8 to have been accepted by Bolivia only on conditions, including a revision of the Hayes arbitral award, which were unacceptable to Paraguay; and a plan for the exchange of prisoners under Uruguay's auspices also failed. On March 12 General Kundt with 40,-000 troops started a general offensive which resulted in the capture of Fortin Alihuatá, a Paraguayan base, and on March 17 of Campo Jordán (Kilometer Siete), but failed to take Fortin Toledo. On May 4, 1933, the ABCP group announced that it had abandoned its peace efforts, but Bolivia immediately asked for the continuance of their good offices and those of the neutrals in Washington, and suggested that Paraguay define her territorial claims so as to bring about a final solution of the Chaco problem, not merely a truce that might end in a resumption of hostilities. A meeting was called for May 8 in Washington, with representatives of the ABCP group invited; but Argentina and Peru were not represented because they had notified Bolivia that their good offices had ceased. On May 10, 1933,[44] President Ayala declared the republic in a state of war with Bolivia, and a state of siege for the whole territory for the duration, of which notice was to be given the League of Nations and individual governments. Declarations of neutrality were issued by Argentina, Chile, and Uruguay on May 13, by Peru on May 14, and by Brazil on May 25. On May 27 Argentina closed Puerto Irigoyen, Ingeniero Juárez, and the whole frontier with Bolivia along the Pilcomayo to shipments of munitions, foodstuffs, and all kinds of supplies; but on May 30 Chile officially notified Bolivia that the port of Arica would remain open to her under existing treaty obligations.[45]

On May 11, 1933, the League of Nations by cable asked both countries if they would accept an arbitral decision, and the meeting of neutrals in Washington on May 12 promised the League its coöperation. On May 15 Paraguay agreed to arbitration, and on May 16 Bolivia, with the qualification that she desired to avoid temporary palliatives which might soon lead to fresh conflict. The Council of the League met in special session on May 15 and on May 20 adopted a report which asserted the authority of the League over its South American members and stated that the frontier between the disputants must be settled by this authority; involving (1) cessation of hostilities, (2) withdrawal of Paraguay's declaration of a state of war, and (3)

[44] Decree #47451. *Diario Oficial*, May, 1933, Num. 2166, pp. 8-9. *Affaires Étrangères*, 1933, 3e Année, pp. 306-310.
[45] See §7, this chap., *supra*.

arbitration of the questions at issue, with an international commission to proceed to the spot, supervise the cessation of hostilities, prepare for arbitration, and report upon the facts in dispute. Paraguay immediately accepted the report without reservations; and Bolivia on May 27 replied agreeing to accept the proposals provided peace were not imposed but negotiated freely; repeating her desire for a complete settlement rather than a dilatory adjustment which would prove unworkable; and stating her opinion that the efforts of the proposed commission would be sterile and that it would be desirable for the efforts of the neutrals to be continued. Paraguay on June 6 suggested to the League the immediate cessation of hostilities, the withdrawal of both armies and the dispatch of a League commission to fix responsibility, with a recommendation of access to the sea for both countries. Argentina on June 8, 1933, refused Bolivia's request that she reopen Puerto Irigoyen. Bolivia on June 10 deplored Paraguay's persistence in her territorial pretensions to the Chaco and on June 13 urged the League to endeavor to discover some means of direct negotiations with Paraguay with a view to concluding an arbitration agreement, as a condition on which all further action must depend. On June 15 Paraguay definitely accepted the League's proposals, asking for effective assurances to prevent further clashes, and Bolivia asked the League to induce Paraguay to reduce her claim so that negotiations would be possible. Although there were reports from Buenos Aires and Rio de Janeiro on June 20 and 21 that Bolivia was trying to persuade Chile to initiate new negotiations and that Paraguay had invited Brazil to act as mediator, no further efforts by the ABCP group appeared. On June 22 the League committee found Bolivia's acceptance of the League's proposal to send a commission to the Chaco unacceptable as altering the original proposal, as accepted by Paraguay, but on June 23 it was reported from Geneva that the committee had agreed with the Bolivian point that cessation of hostilities and preliminary agreement on the arbitral zone must come simultaneously. The neutrals in Washington voted on June 27 to suspend their activities and affirmed their support of the League's efforts. On June 28 Paraguay instructed her delegate at Geneva to insist that the termination of hostilities must precede any discussion of arbitration.

On July 6, 1933, General Kundt with 25,000 men started an offensive directed at Fort Nanawa. On July 19 the League commission was appointed, with representatives of Spain, France, Great Britain, Italy, and Mexico, after the United States had declined. On July 26 it was announced that Paraguay with the accord of Bolivia had proposed to the League Council that the ABCP

group be given a mandate to intervene in the Chaco question by the appointment of an investigating commission of five persons, in an endeavor to suggest
a formula calculated to establish and guarantee a lasting and just peace. On
August 25 it was announced at La Paz that Bolivia had accepted the proposal of the ABCP countries for a simultaneous agreement on an armistice and
arbitration in the Chaco war, pending Paraguay's acceptance of the formula.
On August 26 Afranio de Mello Franco, Brazilian minister of foreign relations, notified the League that the ABCP group hoped to be able to accept
the League mandate, and were still negotiating; but on August 27 Carlos
Saavedra Lamas, Argentine minister of foreign relations, expressed pessimism
as to the outcome and added that this effort to establish peace in the Chaco
was positively the last in which Argentina would participate. On September
30 the ABCP nations formally notified the League that they could not serve
as mediators in the Chaco dispute, and after the utmost effort in complete
unity of purpose sincerely lamented their inability to propose an acceptable
formula of peace. Later Dr. Saavedra Lamas stated that the Argentine and
Chilean foreign offices thought they were signing a formula under which the
arbiter would determine the zone to be arbitrated, while the formula sent by
Brazil to Asunción and La Paz proposed integral arbitration, to which Bolivia
was apparently irrevocably opposed. A new peace plan reported on September 27, 1933, as having been sent by Brazil to Bolivia and Paraguay, propos-
ing an arbitral zone of the area bounded by the Pilcomayo on the south, the
Paraguay on the east, 20° S. on the north, and 62° W. on the west, was
flatly rejected by Paraguay. Paraguay, who had been pointing out that she
was so far from militaristic that her highest commander and head of her
forces in the field was a colonel, on September 29 promoted Colonel José
Felix Estigarribia to brigadier general. The League proceeded with its un-
accepted plans for sending a commission to the Chaco, and at the conclusion
of the seventh Pan-American Conference [46] at Montevideo on December 26,
1933, Delegate Alfonso López of Colombia declared that they were turning
over to the League of Nations what the conference was incapable of settling.
The League commission [47] met in Montevideo on November 3, 1933, conferred
there with Casto Rojas, delegate of Bolivia, and Gerónimo Zubizarreta, delegate of Paraguay, and on January 1, 1934, transferred its activities to Buenos
Aires. President Gabriel Terra of Uruguay, United States Secretary of State

[46] *U. S. Tr. Inf. Bull.*, January, 1934, No. 52, p. 3.
Rev. de Der. Int. (Havana), XXV (1934), 74, 177.
[47] Julio Alvarez del Vayo of Spain, chairman; Major-
General Henri Freydenberg of France; General Alexander
B. Robertson of England; Count Luigi Aldrovandi of Italy;
and Major G. Raúl Rivera Flandes of Mexico.

Cordell Hull, and other delegates at Montevideo did, however, induce Bolivia and Paraguay to agree to a truce from midnight on December 19 to midnight on January 6, 1934. A heavy Paraguayan drive had captured Fortins Alihuatá on December 10, Samaklay on December 12, Murguía and Saavedra on December 13, and a few days later Fort Muñoz and Fortins Sorpresa and Corrales. The extent of the Bolivian disaster resulted in the removal of General Kundt and the appointment as commander in chief with the rank of general of Colonel Enrique Peñaranda del Castillo. It was reported that the Indians of a remote Bolivian settlement in uncivilized hatred of war rose against two conscription officers and killed them, whereupon a punitive company was sent, which with machine guns and bayonets wiped out the entire population of the village, including women and children. The League commission as its final effort on February 24, 1934,[48] recommended to both countries a draft of a treaty of peace to which objections were stated by Paraguay on March 3 and by Bolivia on March 6. The preamble of the proposed treaty baldly called the existing situation between Bolivia and Paraguay a state of war, the first time it had been officially recognized as such by any League organ; and its adoption by the Council would seem to have meant a declaration *ipso facto* that one or both of the parties had violated Article 12, 13, or 15 of the Covenant, in which case, according to Article 16, the members of the League must immediately sever all relations with the offending country. The proposed treaty, made public on March 4, provided that the Bolivian troops should retire from 125 to 175 miles to the Villa Montes-Robero line, the Paraguayans 250 miles to the Paraguay River; each army should be reduced to 5,000 men within three months; the lower Pilcomayo region to 61°30′ W. and 20° N. would be patrolled by Paraguayan police, the upper Pilcomayo to 62° E. and 19°30′ S. by Bolivian police; a neutral zone of about 40 miles would be policed as provided by the League Council; war prisoners would be repatriated, with arbitration of any difficulties by the International Red Cross, and the Permanent Court of International Justice should render final judgment as to the frontier between the two countries.

Two Paraguayan columns advancing westward on parallel lines captured Fortins Cabezón on February 12, 1934, Magariños and Linares on March 3 and La Señora on March 5, thus pushing the Bolivians west of the 62° W. meridian which had much earlier been proposed as the western limit of the neutral zone. The League commission sailed from Montevideo on March 14,

[48] *League of Nations Off. Journal*, 1934, 15th Year, pp. 242–271, 748–867, 1530–1611.

leaving the situation practically unchanged. On March 28 Paraguay announced a victory at Cañada Tarija, northwest of Camacho and 186 miles
east of Villa Montes, the road head and Bolivian supply point for all the
Chaco. On May 12 [49] the League commission issued an outspoken report on
the war, declaring arms and materials were supplied to the belligerents by
American and European countries and urging a complete embargo on arms
shipments to both nations. President Franklin D. Roosevelt on May 18, 1934,
sent a message to the United States Congress urging legislation for the supervision and control of the arms traffic; a joint resolution giving the president,
under certain conditions, power to prohibit the sale of arms or munitions in
the United States was enacted on May 28, 1934,[50] and, on the same day,
President Roosevelt issued a proclamation forbidding the sale of arms and
munitions (including war airplanes) to Bolivia and Paraguay. Secretary Hull
on June 13 pointed out to Enrique Finot, Bolivian minister at Washington, in
answer to a protest made by him on June 1, that the embargo dealt with the
sale of arms to the belligerents in the United States, and so did not violate
the commercial treaty with Bolivia of May 13, 1858, which dealt with importation and exportation; and further ruled on June 16 and July 27 [51] that the
embargo did not cover sales completed and paid for in whole or in part before May 28, against which Paraguay protested. On May 24 the Standard
Oil Company of New Jersey issued a fresh denial that it was interested in a
pipe line across the Chaco to the Paraguay, but on May 30, 1934,[52] and again
on January 17, 1935, Senator Huey P. Long of Louisiana charged on the floor
of the United States Senate that the company was aiding Bolivia against Paraguay. In July 1934 the Paraguayan Foreign Office announced that it would
present to the League of Nations a memorial charging that the Standard Oil
Company was backing Bolivia in the war, alleging that the company's concessions from Bolivia in the fields around Villa Montes and Cumiri had increased from 386,000 to 2,703,000 square miles since the war began; and
Walter C. Teagle, president of the company, wrote the League denying the
charges. On July 30 the governing board of the Pan American Union, of
which Secretary Hull was chairman, adopted a resolution calling on all neutral American governments to indicate their attitude on unified action to
bring the Chaco conflict to a close through arbitration.

[49] *League of Nations Documents*, 1934, VII, 1: C 154, M 64; *ibid.*, VII, 2: C 186, M 75; *ibid.*, VII, 5: C 255, M 104; *ibid.*, VII, 6: C 314, M 140; *ibid.*, VII, 7: A 19; *ibid.*, VII, 9: A 22; *ibid.*, VII, 13: A (Extr.) 5.
[50] Pub. Res. #28. 48 *U. S. Stat. L.* p. 811, 1744. *Cong. Rec.*, LXXVIII, Part 8, 9072, 9095; *ibid.*, Part 9, 9373–9375, 9432–9433. *U. S. Tr. Inf. Bull.*, May,

1934, No. 56, 6–10. Russell M. Cooper, *American Consultation in World Affairs* (New York, 1934), pp. 109–191.
[51] U. S. Dept. of State, *Press Releases*, XI (1934), No. 252, 71–74; *ibid.*, No. 259, 196–198.
[52] *Cong. Rec.*, LXXVII, 9942–9945; *ibid.*, LXXIX, 1044–1055.

Chile's interpretation of her treaty with Bolivia as not permitting her to stop the transit of munitions through Arica, the presence of retired Chilean army officers in Bolivia as instructors and the movement of Chilean laborers to work in Bolivian tin mines until prohibited by a new Chilean law, caused Paraguay to feel that Chile was favoring Bolivia, and a campaign in July 1934 in the newspapers of Asunción charging that Miguel Cruchaga Tocornal, Chile's foreign minister, had important economic interests in Bolivia, and making personal attacks on President Arturo Alessandri, led to Chile's withdrawal on August 12 of Enrique Gallardo Nieto, her minister at Asunción. Paraguay transferred Isidro Ramírez, her minister at Santiago, to Lima, and there were no diplomatic relations between Chile and Paraguay until with the mediation of friendly nations the difficulty was smoothed over on September 18 and ministers were again appointed. On August 9 Dr. Felix Palavicini of Mexico declared that Chile, helped by the United States, was backing Bolivia, and that Argentina,[53] helped by Great Britain, was backing Paraguay.

In their sixth drive the Paraguayans captured Fortins Picuiba on August 15, 1934, Loma Vistosa, which they renamed Senador Long, on August 16, and 27 de noviembre on August 19, the last two being on the main road from Amboro on the Parapiti to Ingavi and northeastward to Robore, Fortins Algodonal, Muro on August 25, Ibamirante on August 26, and Capitán Pascoe and Santa Elena on September 8, finally reaching a point within fifty-eight miles of the Bolivian general headquarters at Villa Montes. On August 25 the Roman Catholic archbishops of the ABCP nations united in an appeal to the presidents of Bolivia and Paraguay to end the war during the Eucharistic Congress to be held in Buenos Aires October 10–14, 1934; and both presidents replied that they would make every effort to seek an honorable peace. The replies were forwarded to Rome, where it was said that members of the Pope's entourage were elated at their tone. On August 29 Bolivia and Paraguay filed with the League of Nations statements of their claims in the Chaco as required by Article 15 of the Covenant, under which the Assembly was to examine the conflict. On August 31, 1934, Paraguay accepted the proposal of Argentina, Brazil, and the United States for the cessation of hostilities while peace terms were discussed at Buenos Aires, but Bolivia would not agree, except on condition of being assured an outlet through the Paraguay river, which Paraguay was unwilling to consider. On September 5 Paraguay announced the capture of Fortins Vanguardia and Castillo on the upper Paraguay north of Bahia Negra. On September 14 Argentina closed

[53] Benjamin Villafañe, *Pasado y Presente* (Buenos Aires, 1933).

the Standard Oil Company's wireless station at Tartagal in Salta Province near the Bolivian frontier on a postal inspector's report of suspicious activities that threatened Argentine neutrality and the sending of messages through the Southern Radio Corporation's station at Yacuiba, Bolivia, to New York and Buenos Aires without paying Argentine telegraph tolls. José Maria Cantilo, Argentina's delegate to the League of Nations, told the Assembly on September 16 that Bolivia and Paraguay had accepted Saavedra Lamas' seven-point project in principle, whereupon Bolivia announced that the negotiations were still exploratory and confidential, and Paraguay declared that she had accepted the arbitration concept without reservations or restrictions of any kind. On September 17 Saavedra Lamas suspended Argentina's peace efforts, against the desires of Brazil and the United States, to permit the centralization of negotiations in the League of Nations at the new session of the Assembly. The Juridical Committee of the League agreed on September 18, 1934, to concentrate on conciliation and decided on September 22 that Article 15 of the Covenant gave the Assembly the right to proceed with an inquiry. Bolivia asked the League to place the question of the arms embargo on the agenda of the next session of the Council. On September 19 France and Great Britain in the Council denounced the war and declared that the League must act to stop it; and the Council referred the dispute and the question of the arms embargo to the Assembly, with a consultative committee of twenty-two under the presidency of Dr. Stephan Osusky of Czechoslovakia to report to a special session of the Assembly on November 20, 1934. On September 28 the League's committee entrusted the efforts for settlement to a subcommittee of five.[54] On October 1 Bolivia announced that she would not accept any proposal for the cessation of hostilities unless it was accompanied by a definite solution of the territorial dispute. The Paraguayans captured Fort Ingavi, seventy-five miles northeast of Picuiba, on October 6, but the Bolivians took Fortins Villazón and Irindague on November 11 and 27 de noviembre on November 12, and temporarily pushed the Paraguayans back from Algodonal, Carandaiti, and the oil region.

Spain proposed to the Chaco committee of the League that Brazil and the United States be invited to participate in the League's efforts for conciliation, which the committee modified to a resolution on November 12, 1934, authorizing the chairman to seek the two nations' coöperation at the most appropriate time. The resolution was forwarded to Rio de Janeiro and Washington on November 13, and the United States through Prentiss Gilbert,

[54] Representatives of Argentina, Chile, Mexico, Peru, and Venezuela, with Dr. Francisco Castillo Nájera of Mexico as chairman.

consul at Geneva, answered on November 15, 1934,[55] that it did not deem that particular moment opportune for collaboration with the committee, but if in the future a time should arrive when its coöperation with the League endeavors would appear to prove useful, it would so inform the League and at the same time indicate the form in which the coöperation might be offered. Paraguay on November 17 captured Fort Ballivián, which she had been heavily attacking since May 14 with costly struggles at Cañadas Tarija, El Carmen, Chile, and Strongest (the last named for Bolivia's best soccer team, which volunteered in a body). Ten thousand Bolivians were made prisoners, and others fled across the Pilcomayo into Argentina and were interned. Paraguay captured on November 22 Fortins Guachalla and Beatriz, on November 23 Fortin Celina, and on December 2 Fortin La Puerta, but was unable to take Fort D'Orbigny, most northwestern of the Ballivián group, opposite the corner of the Argentine boundary where it turns west from the Pilcomayo.

On November 24, 1934, the Assembly of the League in special session adopted unanimously the report of its committee, as modified since its first publication on November 18, "recommending a peaceful solution of the conflict" and providing for a neutral commission of six members (to be designated by Argentina, Brazil, Chile, Peru, Uruguay, and the United States) to supervise demobilization by both belligerents, a peace conference to be held in Buenos Aires, and an advisory committee of twenty-three members [56] to meet in Geneva not later than December 20 with power to ask the World Court's advisory opinion on anything it desired. The Bolivian president, Daniel Salamanca, a Republican, went to general headquarters at Villa Montes after the fall of Ballivián with the reported intention of removing General Peñaranda as commander in chief and appointing General José L. Lanza, a former minister of war who resigned as chief of staff on January 6, 1933, to give General Kundt a free hand. President Salamanca on November 28, 1934, was forced to resign, perhaps after having been made prisoner by the troops upon the instigation of their officers, indignant at his demand that they win more of the battles, and Vice-President José Luis Tejada Sórzano, a Liberal, assumed the presidency in La Paz in a coup apparently designed to prevent the inauguration on March 5, 1935, of the newly elected Republican president, Franz Tamayo. Paraguay on December 1 proclaimed an offer of peace to Bolivia if the new government would stop hostilities.

[55] U. S. Dept. of State, *Press Releases*, XI (1934), No. 268, pp. 299–300.

[56] Representatives of Argentina, Australia, Chile, China, Colombia, Cuba, Czechoslovakia, Denmark, Ecuador, France, Great Britain, Irish Free State, Italy, Mexico, Peru, Poland, Portugal, Russia, Spain, Sweden, Turkey, Uruguay, and Venezuela.

On December 7, 1934,[57] the United States through its consul at Geneva replied to the League of Nations that not being a member of the League it could not collaborate with the advisory committee but was willing to maintain informal contact with its members for purposes of information if agreeable to the committee; that it would coöperate with the neutral supervisory commission by appointing a member to participate in the labors on American soil without power to vote or to commit the United States except under specific instructions from the government of the United States; and that when invited by Argentina it would be happy to accept and participate in the conference of American states at Buenos Aires within one month from the cessation of hostilities; all contingent upon acceptance of the recommendations of the Assembly by Bolivia and Paraguay and the consequent cessation of hostilities. On December 10 Bolivia accepted the League's peace plan without reservations, but on December 18 Paraguay rejected the plan as not providing guarantees against a renewal of hostilities during the proposed negotiations, or for any investigation of responsibility for the original aggression, and because Paraguay could not permit litigation over territory already given her by the Hayes arbitral award; and again the League efforts came to nothing. In new drives the Paraguayans captured Fortins Samaihuata and Florida on December 7, 1934, Picuiba, Loma Vistosa, and Irindague on December 8, Villazón and 27 de noviembre on December 12, Ispdoirenda on December 24, and beginning December 28 made heavy attacks on the whole sixty-mile front from Carandaiti in the north through Capirenda to Villa Montes, the Bolivian base on the Pilcomayo, which resulted in the abandonment by the Bolivians of Carandaiti on January 22, 1935, and Boyuibe on January 29; but all attempts to capture Villa Montes failed and the Paraguayans withdrew on February 25 toward the Parapiti. On January 16 the advisory committee of the Assembly of the League unanimously voted to recommend to all League members a lifting of the arms embargo from Bolivia because of Paraguay's reply constituting nonacceptance of the League's peace plan, and to strengthen the embargo against Paraguay; and a report of the recommendation was transmitted to Brazil and the United States. Asunción newspapers charged E. H. R. Vigier of France, secretary of the League commission that went to South America in 1933, and Julian Nogueria of Uruguay with having unduly influenced the committee's action. The three months within which under Article 12 of the Covenant Paraguay had the opportunity to accept the League's proposals ended on February 24, and on February 23 Paraguay an-

[57] U. S. Dept. of State, *Press Releases*, XI (1934), No. 271, pp. 333-335.

nounced that she would quit the League. Under the Covenant, her resignation would not be effective for two years, but meanwhile she would ignore the League.

The Bolivian Congress in a special session on March 7, 1935, amended the constitution to make the term of the president begin on August 16 instead of March 5, and authorized the administration of President Tejada to promulgate all necessary decrees for governing the country and carrying on the war until the next regular meeting of Congress on August 6. On March 12 Ecuador, supported by Venezuela, came out at Geneva strongly for full application of sanctions by the League, but Uruguay on March 13 announced that she would refuse to apply the arms embargo against Paraguay so long as neighboring countries did not apply it against Bolivia; and Argentina and Chile, also opposing sanctions, were working outside the League in secret negotiations involving security guarantees by them to the disputants. The committee of the Assembly of the League on March 15 unanimously adopted a resolution convoking a special Assembly for May 20 to consider the question of further application of the Covenant, and giving Argentina and Chile on their written request and responsibility, supported and shared by Peru and Brazil, until May 20 to render sanctions and the proposed Assembly unnecessary by ending the war. On March 23 Brazil announced that it had not approved Argentina's move and would remain aloof from it, and that the participation of the United States was an essential condition of her own collaboration in the negotiations, whereupon Argentina and Chile formally invited the United States to coöperate in their efforts.

On April 16, 1935, the Paraguayans captured Charagua, west of the Parapiti in Santa Cruz Province, 110 miles north of Villa Montes, but after a week's hard fighting along a 120-mile front, the Bolivians retook Charagua on April 23, pressed the Paraguayans back in the Boyuibe sector in the center, and in the next few days recaptured Santa Fé and eight other forts in the Parapiti region. Brazil, perhaps because of the omission of her name — by mistake, it was said — from the list of countries to be included in a proposed Chaco economic conference, declined on April 11 an invitation from Argentina and Chile to join them, Peru, and the United States in new negotiations, though avowing her willingness always to coöperate in the maintenance of peace in South America. After further urging by all four countries, however, seconded by Great Britain and Italy, Brazil reconsidered and early in May accepted the invitation; and on May 10 the five countries unanimously asked Uruguay to join them. The six nations proposed to Bolivia and Paraguay that their ministers of foreign relations meet in Buenos Aires in a direct effort to arrange a peace, and Paraguay accepted at once, Bolivia on May 16. The United States on May 17 designated Hugh S. Gibson, former ambassador to Brazil, as her representative, and he reached Buenos Aires on June 9.[58] A special Assembly of the League of Nations to consider the Chaco situation met in Geneva on May 20, and Maxim Litvinoff of Russia, presiding, urged settlement through mediation, to keep the Covenant intact; but the Assembly on May 21, influenced by a mixture of pacifism, political opportunism, and timidity, decided to postpone final decision on application of the Covenant until it was seen what success the six powers should have. The Bolivian delegation, headed by Minister of Foreign Relations Tomás Manuel Elio, and former-President Bautista Saavedra, reached Buenos Aires May 25, 1935, and at once announced that they would ask the conference to consider directly the fundamental underlying question of the frontier. Paraguayan officials, under Luis A. Riart, minister of foreign relations, announced as in 1928 that they would not debate any terms of peace until hostilities were ended under some guarantee against their renewal. It was reported from Buenos Aires on May 29 that Bolivia had agreed to a thirty-day truce, but Paraguay refused. On June 9 the six mediators announced in Buenos Aires that arrangements for peace had been reached; Paraguay accepted at once, Bolivia on June 11, and the agreement was signed at the Casa Rosada in Buenos Aires on June 12, 1935. The protocol provided that (Article 1) the president of Argentina should be requested by the mediating group to convene immediately the peace conference, to settle the practical questions which might arise in the execution of measures for the cessation of hostilities, to promote the settling of differences between the parties by direct agreement or if direct negotiations should fail, at a time to be determined by the peace conference, by juridical arbitration by the Permanent Court of International Justice, and to form an international commission to render an opinion on the responsibilities of any order and kind arising from the war, any conclusions of this opinion not accepted by either party to be settled definitely by the Permanent Court; (Article 2) there should be a definite cessation of hostilities based on the then positions of the belligerent armies to be fixed (a) during a twelve-day truce in which a neutral military commission composed of representatives of the mediating nations should fix intermediate lines between the positions, to begin at midnight on the day the commission was ready to begin its mission,

---

[58] Alexander W. Weddell, minister to Argentina, represented the United States in the negotiations until Gibson's arrival, and by preventing an adjournment for "study" was credited with saving the negotiations from collapse on June 9.

and (*b*) extended by the peace conference until the final execution of the measures of security next provided for; (Article 3) there should be adopted (Sec. 1) the demobilization of the armies within ninety days, (Sec. 2) to a maximum of 5,000 effectives, (Sec. 3) the obligation not to make new purchases of war material except for replacement, and (Sec. 4) the pledge of "non-aggression"; (Article 4) the declaration of August 3, 1932, regarding territorial aggression was recognized by the belligerents; and (Article 5) firing was suspended from noon June 14, 1935. By an additional protocol signed at the same time, the parties requested the mediation commission to send the neutral military commission to the scene of operations immediately, to arrange for the suspension of firing and start the work of drawing the lines separating the armies; and if the principal protocol should not be ratified, the suspension of firing under Article 5 should cease *ipso facto*. The mediating group disbanded, on June 21 the Bolivian Congress approved the protocol by a vote of 69 to 3, and on the same day the neutral military commission of twelve, composed of military attachés and other officers of the six neutral nations, began to assemble at Villa Montes, the Bolivian field headquarters, and at Ivamirante, the Paraguayan headquarters on the Parapiti front, connected by telephone on June 15. On July 3 demobilization of both armies in the Chaco began under the supervision of the neutral military commission, which a week later provided for the reëstablishment of the main road between Villa Montes and Boyuibe, connecting with Santa Cruz, and the return of settlers to regions from Villa Montes along the Santa Fé river, then included in the new neutral zone. On July 8 a further demobilization agreement was signed. On July 15 Generals Peñaranda and Estigarribia had their first direct conference, under the auspices of the commission, and discussed the policing of the neutral zone; and they met again on July 19 at Puesto Marino and exchanged champagne toasts. The Peace Conference met in Buenos Aires on July 15, made up of the foreign ministers of Argentina (as president), Bolivia, Chile, Paraguay, Peru, and Uruguay and the United States minister to Brazil, Hugh S. Gibson.

On July 28 it was announced that Paraguay had released 10,000 Bolivian prisoners of war among those last captured in the Izozog swamps along the upper Parapiti River, never sent to Asunción but permitted to return to their homes. During July Bolivia demobilized 11,000 soldiers.

On August 11 it was reported that Ambassador Gibson, as chairman of the Peace Conference committee on exchange and repatriation of war prisoners, contrary to the report of Sr. Ruiz Moreno, the Argentine member whom he had appointed a subcommittee to trace usages and precedents, had proposed that all prisoners on both sides be freed at once by the neutral military commission; to which Bolivia, holding 2,500 Paraguayans, agreed but Paraguay, claiming to hold 25,000 Bolivian prisoners in Paraguay, was willing only to exchange grade for grade and man for man, until final peace should be signed. On August 16 the commission reported that Bolivia had demobilized nearly 19,000 soldiers and Paraguay more than 30,000. On August 22 there was sent out from Buenos Aires a rumor that Paraguay was ready to assist a rebellion and secession of the Bolivian provinces of Beni and Santa Cruz to set up a new independent republic of Santa Cruz, with Santa Cruz City as capital and a total population of about 400,000. The negotiations as to repatriation of prisoners got nowhere, and after demonstrations of protest in La Paz, Paraguay on September 15 ordered mobilization of five classes of reserves, to include all youths between eighteen and twenty-two. The ninety-day demobilization period expired on October 3, and on September 29 the commission announced that Bolivia had demobilized 49,490 soldiers and Paraguay 43,500, leaving only 5,000 men on each side in the Chaco.

On October 12 Spruille Braden of New York, who had been sent to Buenos Aires in July as a delegate to the Pan-American Commercial Conference, was appointed by United States Secretary of State Cordell Hull as an additional delegate of the United States to the Chaco Peace Conference, to assist Ambassador Gibson especially on economic questions, and he sailed from New York on October 25. An additional protocol signed at Buenos Aires and published on October 21 provided for an international investigation commission, of one member from a neutral government to be named each by Bolivia and Paraguay and the third member and president to be a "magistrate of the Supreme Court or some other high judicial official of the United States." On October 25 the Peace Conference announced in Buenos Aires that Bolivia and Paraguay had both immediately rejected the conference's draft of a treaty of peace, dividing the Chaco by a frontier line from Bahia Negra to Fort d'Orbigny, with a neutral zone 30 kilometers wide on each side, Paraguay to grant Bolivia a free port zone at Puerto Casado and the use of the railroad running thence westward. On November 1 the Peace Conference formally declared that the war had terminated; but had been unable to make any progress toward a definite solution of the conflict.

On November 12, 1935, it was reported that forty-nine Bolivian officers had escaped from a prison camp at Paraguari, twenty-five miles southeast of Asunción and twenty-five miles from the Paraguay river. On November 14 [59] President Roosevelt revoked, effective November 29, the United States em-

[59] U. S. Tr. Inf. Bull., Nov., 1935, No. 74, pp. 5–7.

bargo on the sale of arms and munitions to Bolivia and Paraguay, predicated on their agreement not to import war material pending the conclusion of a formal treaty of peace. On January 21, 1936, it was announced by the Peace Conference that the two countries with the six neutrals had signed a new pact providing for the release of all war prisoners and the renewal of diplomatic relations, Bolivia to pay Paraguay 2,800,000 Argentine pesos and Paraguay to pay Bolivia 400,000 Argentine pesos, for the maintenance of war prisoners. Bolivia deposited with the Peace Conference a check for £132,231 on March 4, payable to Paraguay as soon as the military commission certified that all Bolivian prisoners had been repatriated. An extraordinary joint session of the Bolivian Congress met in La Paz on February 2 and on February 8 ratified the protocol of January 21; and the Paraguayan Congress ratified it on February 9–15.

A revolt in Paraguay on February 17, 1936, expressed the army's repudiation of the peace arrangements; and though the new regime promised to honor all agreements actually made, the government on February 23 canceled the credentials of all Paraguayan delegates and attachés at the Peace Conference, but promised to reorganize the delegation when diplomatic relations had been reëstablished between the new government and the six neutral mediator nations. The neutrals on February 28 agreed to act jointly and to refuse diplomatic recognition of the new government until it formally agreed to abide by the peace protocols already signed.

A revolt in Bolivia resulted in President Tejada's resignation on May 17, 1936, and appeared to be in part the result of an effort by a group of army officers to bring about more satisfactory peace terms.

The Peace Conference arranged for the transport of about 16,500 Bolivian prisoners in batches of 1,500 by boat from Asunción to the Argentine town of Formosa, thence 500 miles by rail to Yacuiba, and by motor truck to Bolivian headquarters at Villa Montes, whence they were to be removed by Bolivia so that not more than 1,500 would be concentrated in Villa Montes at one time. The Paraguayan prisoners were to be returned in similar fashion, starting from Villazón in southern Bolivia. A total of 63 officers and 1,886 men were returned to Paraguay, the last contingent of 651 men reaching Asunción on June 13, 1936. Approximately 16,000 Bolivians were sent back by Paraguay, the last group of 1,000 men leaving Asunción on July 3, 1936. On August 21, 1936, the peace conference got the two delegations to sign an agreement for the renewal of diplomatic relations between the countries. Bolivia charged that Paraguay had officially announced the capture of

25,000 prisoners, but army officers representing the six neutral mediators found that Paraguay had never had that many and had returned all prisoners still in captivity, and the peace conference paid the indemnity check over to Paraguay. Announcement of the establishment of a neutral zone that would necessitate the withdrawal of Paraguayan troops east of the Villa Montes-Santa Cruz road brought a flat refusal from Paraguay, and the recall by Bolivia on October 4, 1936, of Tomás Manuel Elio, chief of the Bolivian delegation to the Peace Conference, until Paraguay should agree. On March 29, 1936, Paraguay announced that she would not permit the impasse in the Chaco conference of six neutrals [60] to be discussed at the proposed inter-American peace conference in Buenos Aires, and the subject was kept off the public program; but at the final session on December 23, 1936, in response to a resolution offered by Harmodio Arias of Panama, urging the two countries to make a gesture of reconciliation, Foreign Minister Enrique Finot of Bolivia and Foreign Minister Juan Stefanici of Paraguay in formal addresses pledged their countries to settle the dispute by pacific means. The revolt in La Paz on July 13, 1937, which ousted Provisional President David Toro and put in his place Lieutenant Colonel German Busch was said to have been caused by discontent with the government's management of internal affairs, solely, and to have no probable effect on the stagnated peace negotiations. The Bolivian delegate, David Alvestegui, telegraphed his resignation at once, but was asked by President Busch to remain at his post, with complete approval of his activities, and he decided to stay.

On January 27, 1936, a federal grand jury in New York indicted the Curtiss-Wright Export Corporation, the Curtiss Aeroplane Motor Company, the Barr Shipping Company, John S. Allard, Robert R. Barr, Samuel J. Abelow, and Clarence W. Webster for conspiracy to "defraud the United States of and concerning its governmental function and of the right to administer the Bureau of Customs of the Treasury Department" in violation of the neutrality joint resolution of Congress of May 28, 1934, and the president's proclamation of the same day,[61] in connection with an alleged shipment between May 29 and September 28, 1934, of fifteen machine guns for Bolivia, packed in thirteen cases containing three Curtiss Hawk planes and two Curtiss Falcons sent via Lima, Peru to La Paz. On May 4, 1936, a federal grand jury indicted the American Armament Corporation, Miranda Brothers, Inc.,

[60] Argentina, Brazil, Chile, Peru, the United States, Uruguay.

[61] The joint resolution of Congress and the presidential proclamation are valid and lawful. U. S. v. Curtiss-Wright Export Corp. (1936), 299 U. S. 304, 57 S. Ct. 216, 81 L. Ed. 166; reversing (1936) 14 F. Supp. 230. See Columbia Law Review, XXXVI (1936), 1162; Harvard Law Review, L (1937), 691.

Alfred J. Miranda, Jr., and Ignacio J. Miranda for conspiracy to "defraud
the United States of its governmental function and right to administer the
Bureau of Foreign and Domestic Commerce" in connection with an alleged
shipment between December 14 and 28, 1934, of 1,515 cases of aerial bombs,
detonators, and capsules from Philadelphia to Bolivia, via Arica in Chile.

By decree of March 16, 1937, the government undertook to cancel the
Standard Oil Company's concession and to confiscate all its holdings in Bolivia, on the ground of fraud in exporting petroleum without paying the 11 per
cent royalty due to the amount of 3,000,000 pesos. The original concession
gave the company exploration rights in virtual partnership with the government to 2,500,000 acres, mostly in the foothills between Santa Oruz and
Villa Montes. The final controversy dates from November 1935, when the
company was accused of smuggling oil out of the country by a secret pipe
line across the Argentine frontier; a charge which an Argentine commission
reported had no basis in fact.

The only international war South America had for fifty years actually
broke out over frontier armed clashes, but was rooted in the historical issue
between documentary [62] inconclusive and sometimes inconsistent boundaries
of the old territory of the audiencia of Charcas, and alleged settlement, occupation, and control from the original province of Paraguay. The resulting
sacrificial strife fostered on both sides by selfish politicians and noisy pa-
triots backed by academic legalists involved an area of about 115,000 square
miles, in parts good for grazing lands but largely periodically inundated jungle, with indications of oil and minerals in the higher western part. Despite
her experience in the decimating López war, Paraguay again stripped herself
by sending school boys into the fatal swamps, and Bolivia shipped intermin-
able train loads of meek and stolid upland Indians and her none too numerous white sons to their death in the jungle. After three years of war in which
never more than 100,000 men were engaged at one time, it was estimated that
there had been total casualties of 250,000, of which Bolivia with a population of 2,911,000 (14.6 per cent white, 30.9 per cent mixed, 54.5 per cent in-
digenous) had 55,000 killed and 83,000 ill or wounded; and Paraguay with
a population of 836,000 (85 per cent full or part Guarani) had 45,000 killed
and 67,000 ill or wounded. Through all the professions of a will to peace, the
tangle of attempted mediation by the League of Nations, the five neutrals,

[62] Leopoldo Ramos Giménez, *Chaco a través de los Siglos en los Mapas de la Colección Rio Branco* (Rio de Janeiro, 1933). Carlos E. Grez Pérez, *La Prueba de los Mapas en el Conflicto del Chaco* (Santiago, 1933). Pizarro Loureiro, *O Chaco Boreal* (Rio de Janeiro, 1933). René Ballivián C., *El Problema del Chaco, Un Resumen* (Santiago, 1933).

the ABCP powers, the Roman Catholic archbishops, and single-handed efforts, the belligerents' respective demands were substantially unchanged from the first. Bolivia maintained that the dispute involved a territorial question and insisted that a definition of the area of any (limited) arbitration should precede the suspension of hostilities; Paraguay held that the dispute involved a boundary question, not including any of the territory in the Hayes award, and demanded a suspension of hostilities with guarantees before an (unlimited) arbitration agreement. From the outset national feeling was too intense to make it likely that any solution would be accepted from an outside source; the end had to come naturally, as in most wars, from a stalemate or from the utter exhaustion of one combatant and satiety of the other with the fulfillment of most of its desires. The Bolivians may want to govern, but they would not themselves happily settle or live in, the wet lowlands; and the river-dwelling Paraguayans would be just as unhappy permanently on the high tableland or even the slopes of the mountains or foothills. What boundary between the two countries will be finally agreed upon in the direct peace negotiations or by decision of the Permanent Court it is not possible to foresee in detail, but it seems safe to predict that the southern part of the line will run not far from the eastern foot of the mountains; and that notwithstanding the sentiment expressed in Article 4 of the peace protocol, all concerned, including the members of the Pan American Union, will eventually, when it comes right down to taking actually conquered ground away from the victor, more or less gracefully recede from the principle stated in the note of August 3, 1932, that they would not recognize territorial gains in the Chaco made by force of arms. The quibble that the new territorial adjustment will in some measure at least have been agreed upon by treaty between the two countries may very likely prove a useful face-saver; and the explosive question of original responsibilities will probably be eluded by the peace conference and the Permanent Court as by all prior assemblies.

9. BOLIVIA–PERU. ACRE–MADRE DE DIOS

The dispute dates from the creation of Bolivia as an independent state. President Antonio José de Sucre procured to be signed at Chuquisaca on November 15, 1826,[1] a boundary treaty with Peru which provided that the dividing line of the two republics, starting from the Pacific, should be (Article 1) the cliff of Los Diablos or Cape Sama or Laquiaca, at 18° S., between the

---

[1] Ricardo Aranda, *Col. de Trat. del Peru*, II, 165-170.

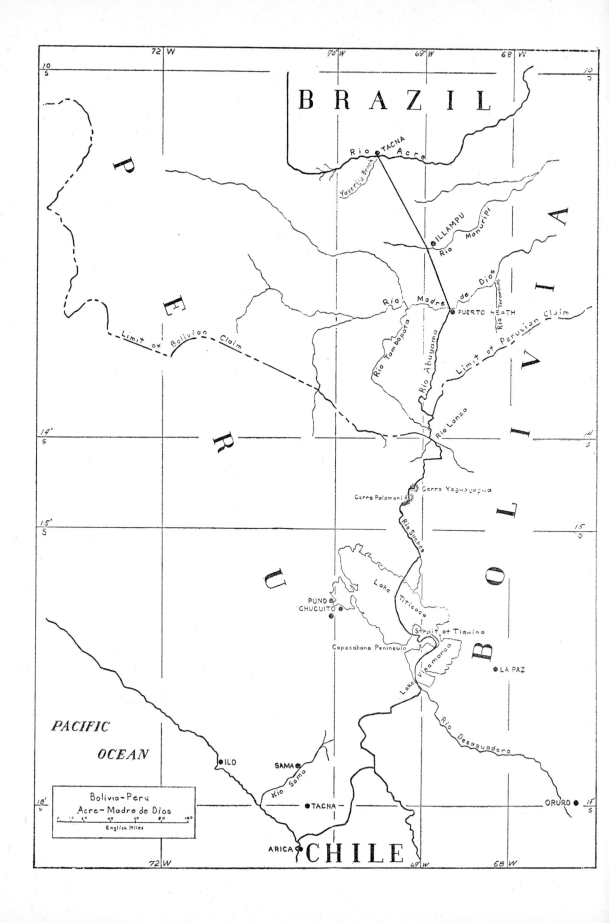

ports of Ilo and Arica, as far as the town of Sama, thence by the deep ravine in the Sama valley to the cordillera of Tacora, leaving to Bolivia the port of Arica and the others between 18° S. and 21° S., and all the territory belonging to the province of Tacna and the other towns situated south of that line; (Article 2) thence to the river Desaguadero the dividing line should be the old boundaries between the provinces of Parajes of Bolivia and Chucuito of Peru; (Article 3) thence the Desaguadero to its origin in Lake Chucuito, thence by the coast line of the west part of that lake, called Vinamarca, to the strait of Tiquina, which is where that lake is divided from Lake Titicaca; thence by the east coast of Lake Titicaca to the beginning of the province of Omasuyos, so that there remained to Peru the town of Copacabana and its territory, Lake Titicaca and all its islands, and to Bolivia Lake Vinamarca and all its islands, navigation and fishing in the lakes remaining common to both republics; (Article 4) from the beginning of the province of Omasuyos the boundaries should be those which divided that province and that of Larecaja, also belonging to Bolivia, from the provinces of Huancané, Azángaro, and Carabaya of Peru, as far as the Missions of the Gran Patiti and the river of that name, leaving consequently to Peru the province of Apolobamba or Caupolicán and its territory; (Article 5) public property to belong to the state in which the place of its location should fall; (Article 6) private property to be respected by each state; and (Article 10) Bolivia in indemnization of the value of the ports and coast territories received from Peru from 18° S. to 21° S. on the Pacific undertook to satisfy the sum of 5,000,000 pesos to Peru's foreign creditors in the instalments and on the terms which Peru had agreed. The Council of Government of Peru, however, thought the provisions of this treaty exclusively favorable to Bolivia, because the promise to pay a portion of Peru's foreign debt was no adequate compensation, under the precarious circumstances of Bolivia's own debt, for the ports and territories; and the undesirable territories of Apolobamba and Copacabana were no suitable indemnity. Peru accordingly notified the Bolivian minister on December 18, 1826, that the treaty could not be ratified. A preliminary treaty of peace was signed between Peru and Bolivia at Piquisa on July 6, 1828,[2] in which it was agreed that all Colombian soldiers should leave the Bolivian army, the Peruvian army should occupy the department of Potosí until the day of meeting of a Bolivian Constituent Congress and then commence its march through the department of Cochabamba for La Paz and Oruro; and neither country was to enter into friendly relations with Brazil

[2] 15 *British and Foreign State Papers* 1221-1227.

until that empire had made peace with Argentina. No final agreement had been reached when General Sucre resigned on August 2, 1828, and unfortunately for Bolivia his successor, General Andrés Santa Cruz, elected August 12, 1828, disapproved the 1826 arrangement and failed to press it on Peru before or after his wars.[3] Another preliminary treaty of peace was signed at Tiquina, August 25, 1831.[4] The final treaty of peace signed with Chile's mediation at Arequipa on November 8, 1831,[5] provided that (Article 10) neither republic might intervene directly or indirectly under any pretext in the internal affairs of the other; (Article 16) a commission should be named by both governments for the purpose of drawing up a topographical map of their frontiers, and another for the statistics of the villages located on them, in order that without detriment to the two states such cessions might be reciprocally made as should be necessary for an exact and natural demarcation of their boundaries, which ought to be rivers, lakes, or mountains, it being understood that neither country would refuse to make such cessions as might be desirable to accomplish this end, on condition of giving mutually suitable indemnities or compensations satisfactory to both parties; (Article 17) until this was carried out, the existing boundaries were to be recognized and respected; (Article 18) claims to be settled by two commissioners, any upon which they could not agree to be submitted to the decision of an arbiter, for which office both governments named the United States; and (Article 21) the parties would ask Chile, the United States, or any free European nation, in that order, to guarantee the fulfillment of all the articles of the treaty.

A treaty of aid signed at La Paz on June 15, 1835,[6] placed Peru, until completely pacified, under General Andrés Santa Cruz, dictator of Bolivia, and he invaded Peru and after defeating General Gamarra at Yanacocha on August 13, 1835, styled himself Protector of the States of South and North Peru. On February 7, 1836, he defeated Felipe Santiago Salaverry at Socabaya, near Arequipa, and at Sicuaní on March 17, 1836,[7] he caused the Assembly of South Peru, of twenty-three deputies for the departments of Arequipa, Ayacucho, Cuaco, and Puno, to declare the independence of the South Peruvian state and to seek confederation with the states of North Peru and Bolivia. At Huaura on August 6, 1836,[8] an assembly of the North

[3] Ricardo Aranda, *Col. de Trat. del Peru*, XIII, 277–354.
[4] *Ibid.*, II, 176–179. 19 *British and Foreign State Papers* 1380–1383.
[5] Ricardo Aranda, *Col. de Trat. del Peru*, II, 180–186, 198–204. 19 *British and Foreign State Papers* 1383–1390, 1396–1397. Martens, *Nouv. Rec. de Traités*, X, 420–431. Ratified by Bolivia, Aug. 31, 1832; ratified by Peru, Mar. 20, 1833.

[6] Ricardo Aranda, *Col. de Trat. del Peru*, II, 206–208.
[7] *Const. Pol. del Peru* (Lima, 1922), pp. 191–194. Ricardo Aranda, *Col. de Trat. del Peru*, II, 217–220. 24 *British and Foreign State Papers* 770–775.
[8] *Const. Pol. del Peru* (Lima, 1922), pp. 194–199. Ricardo Aranda, *Col. de Trat. del Peru*, II, 221–225. 24 *British and Foreign State Papers* 776–779.

of twenty deputies for the departments of Amazonas, Junín, Libertad, and Lima declared the independence of the North Peruvian state, under Santa Cruz as supreme protector. On October 28, 1836,[9] in Lima Santa Cruz proclaimed the establishment of the Peru-Bolivian Confederation, composed of the North Peruvian state, the South Peruvian state and the republic of Bolivia. Representatives of North Peru, South Peru, and Bolivia met at Tacna, and on May 1, 1837,[10] agreed upon a treaty to be the pact and fundamental law of the Peru-Bolivian Confederation, under which each republic was to have at least one principal port for the maintenance of trade with foreign nations. Santa Cruz was defeated by General Agustín Gamarra and Chileans under General Manuel Bulnes at Yungay on January 20, 1839; and on February 20, 1839,[11] at Arequipa he resigned as protector of the Peru-Bolivian Confederation and as president of Bolivia. The Confederation was dissolved, and Santa Cruz, after stirring up trouble for a number of years, was in 1845 exiled to Europe.[12]

By the preliminary convention of peace signed at Cuzco on August 14, 1839,[13] the governments promised that (Article 4) they would arrange a joint demarcation of boundaries, fixing as a base the river Desaguadero, which was the natural bound and the only one which should serve as a point of departure for the operation, and (Article 5) the republics would make reciprocal just and equitable indemnities for such part of the territory as might in the arrangement of boundaries remain subject to a new sovereignty. Gamarra, after becoming president of Peru, undertook to invade Bolivia, but he was killed and the Peruvians were defeated at Ingavi on November 18, 1841, by the Bolivians under General José Ballivián. With the mediation of Chile, a preliminary treaty of peace was signed at Puno on June 7, 1842,[14] the Bolivian army withdrew from Peruvian territory and the *status quo* was restored. The treaty of friendship and commerce signed at Arequipa on November 3, 1847,[15] repeated the provisions of Article 16 of the treaty of November 8, 1831; and the Peruvian ratification explained (Article 1) that the demarcation of boundaries so agreed on should have for its sole object the restitution of the lands which were in confusion on the then frontiers, not

[9] *Const. Pol. del Peru* (Lima, 1922), pp. 199–200. Ricardo Aranda, *Col. de Trat. del Peru*, II, 226–228. 24 *British and Foreign State Papers* 779–780.

[10] Ricardo Aranda, *Col. de Trat. del Peru*, II, 228–239. 27 *British and Foreign State Papers* 1360–1369.

[11] Ricardo Aranda, *Col. de Trat. del Peru*, II, 249. 27 *British and Foreign State Papers* 1369–1380.

[12] 34 *ibid.*, 1113–1115; 35 *ibid.*, 698.

[13] Ricardo Aranda, *Col. de Trat. del Peru*, XIII, 504–592.

[14] *Ibid.*, II, 283–285. 32 *British and Foreign State Papers* 1400–1401. Ratified by President Manuel Menendez, June 15, 1842.

[15] Article 3. Ricardo Aranda, *Col. de Trat. del Peru*, II, 286–294. 36 *British and Foreign State Papers* 1137–1143. Ratified with modifications by Ramón Castilla, president of Peru, Nov. 9, 1847; not ratified by Bolivia as modified.

that of ceding territory by way of transfer or compensation of any kind, but solely for establishing its ancient landmarks with a view of avoiding doubts and confusion. The new treaty signed at Sucre on October 10, 1848,[16] provided that there should be named by both governments a commission to draw up a topographic map of their frontiers, with the purpose of restoring to each state the lands in confusion on the then frontiers, reëstablishing for that purpose the ancient boundary marks, to avoid doubts and confusion in the future, both states undertaking to preserve the territory which had always belonged to them and not to seek or request any territory of the other, by way of cession, compensation, or other motive of any sort. In the treaty of peace and friendship signed at Lima on November 5, 1863,[17] the parties with the purpose of removing every ground for ill feeling between them agreed to arrange definitely the boundaries between their respective territories, naming within an agreed time after the exchange of ratifications a mixed commission to draw up a topographic map of the frontiers and execute the demarcation with regard to the data and instructions which should be given in due course by both parties and whose labors should be taken into account for a boundary treaty to be executed promptly thereafter; and meanwhile the existing boundaries should be recognized and respected. The treaty of commerce and customs signed at Lima on September 5, 1864,[18] provided that Bolivia should construct in the southern part of Lake Titicaca included in her territory in the most suitable bays firm wharves at which the Peruvian steamers might readily tie up and unload.

The boundary treaty of March 27, 1867,[19] between Bolivia and Brazil caused Peru to protest on December 20, 1867,[20] to Bolivia against the infringement of Peru's rights on the frontier between the Madeira and the Javary, but the treaty was not amended or suspended. The treaty of defensive alliance of February 6, 1873,[21] between Bolivia and Peru provided (Article 8) that neither party would grant to or accept from any nation or government any protectorate or overlordship which should threaten its independence or sovereignty, nor cede or alienate in favor of any nation or gov-

---

[16] Article 3. Ricardo Aranda, *Col. de Trat. del Peru,* II, 294–302. Ratified by Peru, Dec. 11, 1848; ratifications exchanged at Oruro, Nov. 7, 1849; promulgated by Peru, Dec. 24, 1849.

[17] Articles 22 and 23. *Trat. Vig.* (Bolivia, 1925), II, 1–18. Ricardo Aranda, *Col. de Trat. del Peru,* II, 303–312. Ratified by Bolivia, Oct. 7, 1864; ratified by Peru, Jan. 20, 1865; ratifications exchanged at Lima, Jan. 21, 1865; promulgated by Bolivia, Apr. 12, 1865.

[18] Article 12. Ricardo Aranda, *Col. de Trat. del Peru,*

II, 317–323, 389–398. Ratified by Bolivia, Oct. 22, 1864; ratified by Peru, Jan. 20, 1865; ratifications exchanged at Lima, Jan. 21, 1865; promulgated by Bolivia, Apr. 12, 1865.

[19] See §6, this chap., *supra.*

[20] Ricardo Aranda, *Col. de Trat. del Peru,* II, 381–385. Mariano Felipe Paz Soldán, *Verdaderos Límites entre el Perú y Bolivia* (Lima, 1878). Bautista Saavedra, *El Litigio Perú-Boliviano* (La Paz, 1903).

[21] See §7, this chap., *supra.*

ernment any part of its territories except for better demarcation of its boundaries, nor conclude any boundary treaty or other territorial arrangement without the previous knowledge of the other party. A supposed invasion by a Bolivian official of the Peruvian district of Yunguyo in the department of Puno gave rise to a diplomatic correspondence in 1875.[22] The unratified protocol signed at Lima June 11, 1880,[23] setting forth the preliminary bases for the proposed federal union of Bolivia and Peru, in which the existing departments of both countries were to be made autonomous states, provided further (Article 2) that the departments of Tacna and Oruro should form the state of Tacna de Oruro and the departments of Potosí and Tarapacá the state of Potosí de Tarapacá; and the regions of the Chaco and Beni in Bolivia and La Montaña in Peru, as well as other territories in analogous conditions, should form federal districts subject to special regulations and to the direct government of the union.

The preliminary boundary treaty signed by Manuel Maria del Valle, Peruvian minister, and Juan C. Carrillo, president of Bolivia, at La Paz on April 20, 1886,[24] provided that (Article 1) the parties should each name a national commission duly authorized for the purpose of studying the frontiers of the two republics and fixing them according to justice and the common interest of the parties; (Article 2) the national commissions should maintain without alteration the clearly established frontiers, according to which both nations were then in tranquil possession of the separate territories on either side of the frontiers; (Article 3) the Bolivian and Peruvian settlements established in the frontier territories should always remain part of the nation to which they then belonged; (Article 4) on doubtful, vague, or disputed points, the commissions, working together, should determine the dividing line according to the rights of dominion, possession, and use which might be pertinent, or in the absence of such rights, they should arrange the line according to equity and the reciprocal interest of the parties; (Article 5) in such cases the commissions should establish preferably, subject to compensations if necessary, natural boundaries such as rivers, high peaks of the cordillera and mountains, ravines and narrow passes; on the plains the territories should be separated by straight lines, with natural points of departure and intersection wherever possible; (Article 9) if deliberation between the parties should not suffice to resolve disagreements between the commissions and consequently the

---

[22] Ricardo Aranda, *Col. de Trat. del Peru*, XIV, 215–229.

[23] *Ibid.*, II, 448–452.

[24] *Ibid.*, 462–471. Martens, *Nouv. Rec. Gén. de Traités*, 2e Sér., XV, 770–774. Abel Iturralde, *Col. de Artículos* (La Paz, 1897). Ratified by Bolivia with a reservation, Oct. 26, 1886; ratified by Peru with a reservation, Sept. 13, 1886; ratifications not exchanged.

demarcation should be suspended at one or more disputed points, determination of the dividing line at such points should be submitted to the judgment of an arbitral tribunal, meanwhile leaving in effect the boundaries where agreed upon; (Article 10) until a definite treaty was made and approved, the existing boundaries should be maintained and respected; and (Article 11) in the regions of the upper Amazon there should be recognized in favor of Bolivia and Peru the right of full and free navigation on the rivers which transverse the territory of both nations and on those which separate them on their two banks, whether such rivers are affluents or principal ones into which the others empty. A complementary protocol signed at La Paz, April 24, 1886, provided that each national commission should be composed of two authorized commissioners, a competent engineer and suitable employees, only the national commissioners to deliberate; to sit at La Paz and Puno; to be named within six months of the exchange of ratifications, and in case of disagreement the deciding arbiter to be the government of the Spanish nation.

Peru protested strongly against the territorial provisions of the protocols of 1895 [25] between Bolivia and Brazil and of the treaties of May 18, 1895,[26] between Bolivia and Chile, which finally were not carried out. Further disagreements arose in 1897 [27] over a customs house established by Bolivia at Puerto Heath (Puerto Pardo) on the Madre de Dios, and in 1899 [28] over certain rubber concessions granted by Bolivia in territory occupied by the Chuncha and Mojos Indians and claimed by Peru; but the polemics in the press gradually cooled and arbitration was suggested.

Eliodoro Villazón, Bolivian minister of foreign relations, and Felipe de Osma, Peruvian minister, signed at La Paz on September 23, 1902,[29] a treaty which provided that (Article 1) demarcation of the frontier should proceed from its intersection with the boundary of the territories occupied by Chile under Article 3 of the treaty of peace of (Ancón) October 20, 1883,[30] on the west to (the snow peaks of Palomani, changed on the exchange of ratifications to) the place at which the line of the existing frontier joined the river Suches, on the east, taking care that in this region the terminal point of the dividing line should be fixed in conformity with the studies and reports of the demarcation commission, the adjustment of the question as to the rest of

---

[25] See §6, this chap., *supra.*

[26] See §7, this chap., *supra.*

[27] Nicolás Armentia, *Límites de Bolivia con el Perú por la parte de Caupolicán* (La Paz, 1897). *Rev. de dr. int. et de lég. Comp.*, XXIX (1897), 665-668.

[28] Ricardo Aranda, *Col. de Trat. del Peru*, XIV, 774-781, 876-907.

[29] *Trat. Vig.* (Bolivia, 1925), II, 94-100. *Actos Int. del Peru* (Lima, 1916), Num. 63. *U. S. For. Rel.*, 1904, pp. 684-685. *Arch. Dipl.*, 3e Sér., XCVIII, 21-26. Martens, *Nouv. Rec. Gén. de Traités*, 3e Sér., II, 836-838. Ratified by Bolivia, Jan. 14, 1904; ratified by Peru, Jan. 20, 1904; ratifications exchanged at La Paz, Mar. 9, 1904.

[30] See §19, this chap., *infra.*

the frontier to be reserved for another special convention; (Article 2) the parties also to proceed in accordance with the stipulations of this treaty with the demarcation of the line which separated the Peruvian provinces of Tacna and Arica from the Bolivian province of Carangas as soon as the former two should return to the full sovereignty of Peru; (Article 3) the frontier indicated in Article 1 to be studied by a mixed demarcation commission, of one national commissioner for each party, a geographical engineer, an assistant engineer, a secretary, and necessary personnel, to be set up at once after the exchange of ratifications, and (Article 7) if the parties could not resolve directly the points of disagreement between the respective commissions, they should be submitted to arbitration. The same ministers signed at La Paz on December 30, 1902,[31] a treaty for arbitration "juris" of the boundary question (Article 1) by the government of the Argentine Republic, to obtain a final inappealable decision according to which the whole territory which in 1810 belonged to the jurisdiction or district of the old audiencia of Charcas,[32] within the limits of the viceroyalty of Buenos Aires, by acts of the former sovereign, should belong to Bolivia, and all the territory which on the same date and by acts from the same source belonged to the viceroyalty of Lima should belong to Peru; (Article 2) the treaty of September 23, 1902, having settled the demarcation and setting up of posts on the frontier which runs between the Peruvian provinces of Arica and Tacna and the Bolivian province of Carangas on the west to (as changed) the place at which the line of the existing frontier joins the river Suches, that section is excepted from this treaty; (Article 3) the arbiter for its decision should take into account the laws of the Indies, cédulas, royal orders, the Intendente Ordinances, diplomatic acts relating to the demarcation of frontiers, maps, official descriptions, and in general all documents which, having an official character, might have been used to give the true significance and effect to such royal provisions; (Article 4) if the royal acts and provisions should not define the dominion of any part of the territory in a clear manner, the arbiter should resolve the question equitably, approximating so far as possible their meaning and the spirit which inspired them; (Article 5) possession of territory by one of the parties could not be asserted or prevail against rights or royal provisions which established the contrary; (Article 7) one year after the arbi-

[31] *Trat. Vig.* (Bolivia, 1925), II, 100–107. *Actos Int. del Peru* (Lima, 1916), Num. 86, pp. 7–10. 100 *British and Foreign State Papers* 803–804. *U. S. For. Rel.*, 1904, pp. 685–686. *Arch. Dipl.*, 3e Sér., XCVIII, 26–32. Martens, *Nouv. Rec. Gén. de Traités*, 3e Sér., III (1910), 50–52. Ratified by Bolivia, Jan. 14, 1904; ratified by Peru, Jan. 28, 1904; ratifications exchanged at La Paz, Mar. 9, 1904.
[32] *Limites de la Audiencia de Charcas, Notas Cambiadas* (La Paz, 1904).

ter's acceptance, the states should submit their expositions and documents; (Article 9) as soon as the decision should be given, the legal territorial boundary between the two republics should be considered definitely and compulsorily established; and (Article 10) any points not regulated by this treaty should be governed by the general arbitration treaty of November 21, 1901.[33] Bolivia signed with Brazil on November 17, 1903,[34] the treaty of Petropolis, by which the boundary settled between those countries included the line from the source of the Acre or Aquiry along the meridian of that source to 11° S. and thence west by the river or along the 11° S. parallel to the Peruvian frontier, thus transferring to Brazil [35] some of the northern part of the territory which it had been agreed by these treaties of 1902 should be submitted to the arbitration of Argentina, and forcing Peru to enter into new negotiations with Brazil as to that portion of the line.[36] On July 6, 1904, the ministers of Bolivia and Peru at Buenos Aires asked José A. Terry, Argentine minister of foreign relations, if his government were willing to accept the office of arbiter; and on July 13 [37] the Argentine president, Julio A. Roca, accepted, expressing his appreciation of the proof of confidence reposed in his government by the two friendly nations. On July 11, 1905, Bolivia requested and Peru agreed to an extension of ten months in the time within which the cases were to be submitted to the arbiter, and President Manuel Quintana of Argentina on July 14, 1905,[38] ordered that the time should expire May 15, 1906. He died in office on March 12, 1906, and was succeeded by Vice-President José Figueroa Alcorta. The printed cases [39] were presented to the Argentine government on May 15, 1906, by Eliodoro Villazón, Bolivian minister, and Victor M. Maúrtua, Peruvian minister, followed by an answer by Peru, August 15, 1907,[40] and a reply by Bolivia, September 15, 1907.[41]

In June 1906 [42] ex-President José Manuel Pando, Bolivian governor of the Beni and Noroeste region, was reported to have occupied some of the Madre de Dios territory near Puerto Heath claimed by Peru; whereupon Peru protested to Bolivia on the ground that the area formed part of the

[33] See chap. III, §15, infra.
[34] See §6, this chap., supra.
[35] Rev. Gén. de dr. int. pub., XIII (1906), 309-324. Euclydes da Cunha, Peru vs. Bolivia (Rio de Janeiro, 1907). Euclydes da Cunha, La Cuestión de Límites entre Bolivia y el Peru (Buenos Aires, 1908). El Istmo de Fiscarrald, Junta de Vias Fluviales (Lima, 1904). Nuevas Exploraciones en la Hoya del Madre de Dios, Junta de Vias Fluviales (Lima, 1904).
[36] See §13, this chap., infra.
[37] Arch. Dipl., 3e Sér., XCVIII, 33.
[38] Actos Int. del Peru (Lima, 1916), Num. 86, pp.

10-13.
[39] Alegato de Bolivia, Col. de Documentos (2 vols.). Bautista Saavedra, Defensa de los Derechos de Bolivia (Buenos Aires, 1906), 2 vols. Exposición de la República del Peru . . . en el Juicio de Limits con la Republica de Bolivia (Barcelona, 1906), 2 vols. Victor M. Maurtua, Juicio de Límites entre el Perú y Bolivia. Prueba Peruna (Barcelona and Madrid, 1906), 12 vols. and maps.
[40] Contestación (Buenos Aires, 1907).
[41] Nueva Prueba; Tacha de Pruebas (Buenos Aires, 1907).
[42] U. S. For. Rel., 1906, Part I, p. 106.

territory then actually under consideration by the arbiter. Bolivia, after complaining to the arbiter in May 1907, agreed to withdraw if Peru would also withdraw from such portion of the disputed territory as was then occupied by her; and the incident was closed by explanations in August 1907.

President Figueroa Alcorta appointed an advisory commission [43] of three to fix the proceedings to be followed, receive the expositions of the case, statements of claims, and proofs, and to assist the arbiter; and at Buenos Aires on July 9, 1909,[44] made his award, dividing the 55,000 square miles of contested territory 22,000 to Bolivia and 33,000 to Peru. Reciting that the parties empowered the arbiter to fix the dividing line between the audiencia of Charcas and the viceroyalty of Lima in 1810 so far as the respective territorial rights were concerned; that it was the territorial border between the two republics which the arbiter was to determine; that having most carefully examined the titles adduced by the two parties the arbiter did not find sufficient ground for considering as the dividing line between the audiencia of Charcas and the viceroyalty of Lima in 1810 either of the demarcations claimed in the respective cases of the contending states; and that in reality the disputed zone was in 1810 and until a recent time entirely unexplored, for which reasons there should be applied the provisions (Article 4) which authorized the arbiter to decide the question equitably, the award drew the frontier line from the intersection of the existing frontier with the Suches, across Lake Suches to the hill of Palomani Grande; thence to the lakes of Yaguayagua and through the river Yaguayagua to the San Juan del Oro or Tambopata; thence down that river to the mouth of the Lanza or Mosoc Huaico; from the confluence of the Tambopata with the Lanza to the western headwaters of the Abuyama or Heath; thence down the Heath to its emptying into the Amarumayo or Madre de Dios; down the bed of the Madre de Dios to the mouth of the Toromonas, an affluent on the right (south) side; from the confluence of the Toromonas with the Madre de Dios by a straight line to the intersection of the Tahuamanu with the 69° W. meridian and north on this meridian to the border of the territorial sovereignty of a nation not a party to the arbitraion treaty of December 30, 1902; the territories east and south of this line of demarcation to belong to Bolivia, those to the west and north to Peru. An advance summary of the decision appeared in the public press in Lima and was known in La Paz, and the Bolivian minister on in-

[43] Drs. Antonio Bermejo, Manuel Augusto Montes de Oca, and Carlos Rodríguez Larreta, with Horacio Beccar Varela as secretary.

[44] *Libro Azul, Min. de Rel. Ext.* (Buenos Aires, 1909).

Trat. de Argentina (Buenos Aires, 1912), X, 50–84. *Actos Int. del Peru* (Lima, 1916), Num. 86, pp. 13–20. 105 *British and Foreign State Papers* 572–578. Martens, *Nouv. Rec. Gén. de Traités*, 3e Sér., III 53–59.

structions from his government declined to attend at the Argentine ministry of foreign relations at the appointed time to receive his copy of the award, causing a complaint of discourtesy from the Argentine government and a severance of diplomatic relations by Argentina from July 21, 1909, to January 9, 1911.[45] There were popular demonstrations in La Paz against the Argentine and Peruvian legations, and Bolivia protested [46] that the award was not according to the terms of the treaty of arbitration, in that under the submission the arbiter had no jurisdiction to draw a new line, different from that of either of the parties, dividing the disputed area. Daniel Sánchez Bustamante, Bolivian minister of foreign relations, and Solón Polo, Peruvian minister, however, signed at La Paz two protocols, one dated September 15, 1909,[47] agreeing to accept the award, and the other dated September 17, 1909,[48] effecting exchanges and cessions of territories which by mutual consent the countries considered necessary so that the frontiers should be settled in a manner to secure their safety and prevent all future misunderstanding, and agreeing to appoint within six months joint boundary commissions to mark the actual line. By this agreement the boundary line was to run from the junction of the existing frontier with the Suches, across Lake Suches, and across the hills of Palomani Tranca, Palomani Kunca, the summit of Palomani, and the cordillera of Yaguayagua; thence along the cordilleras of Huajra, Lurini, and Ichocorpa, following the watershed between the Lanza and the Tambopata as far as 14° S.; thence along that parallel to the Mosoj-Huaico or Lanza; thence along the Lanza to its confluence with the Tambopata; from such confluence to the western source of the Heath; thence down the Heath to the Amarumayo or Madre de Dios; from the confluence of the Heath and the Madre de Dios by a geodesic line from the mouth of the Heath to the west of Illampu barracks on the Manuripi, leaving that place on the Bolivian side; thence to the confluence of the Yaverija stream

[45] U. S. For. Rel., 1909, pp. 10–12. Martens, Nouv. Rec. Gén. de Traités, 3e Sér., VI, 509–510. 104 British and Foreign State Papers 664.

[46] Oscar F. Arrus, El Laudo Argentino (Lima, 1909). Adolfo Ballivián, El Laudo Argentino (La Paz, 1909). Eduardo Díez de Medina, El Laudo Argentino (La Paz, 1909). Javier Prado y Ugarteche, El Fallo Arbitral (Lima, 1909). M. G. Sánchez Sorondo, El Litigio Peru-Boliviano (Buenos Aires, 1909). Estanislao S. Zeballos, The Bolivian Question, an Interview (Buenos Aires, July 31, 1909). Documentos que Justifican la Actitud de Bolivia (New York, 1909). U. S. For. Rel., 1909, pp. 12–13, 502–507. Amer. J. Int. Law, III (1909), 949–953, 1029–1036. Rev. gén. de dr. int. pub., XVI (1909), 368–372; ibid., XVII (1910), 105–136, 225–256. Rec. des Cours, XXXV (1931), 390–391, 417–420.

[47] Actos. Int. del Peru (Lima, 1916), Num. 86, pp. 21–22. 105 British and Foreign State Papers 578–580. Martens, Nouv. Rec. Gén. de Traités, 3e Sér., III, 59–61.

[48] Trat. Vig. (Bolivia, 1925), II, 116–121. Actos Int. del Peru (Lima, 1916), Num. 86, pp. 3–6. El Arbitraje, Docs. Dipl., Min. de Rel. Ext. (La Paz, 1909). 105 British and Foreign State Papers 580–581. Alexandre van der Burch, L'Arbitrage du Gouvernement Argentine (Bruxelles, 1909). Martens, Nouv. Rec. Gén. de Traités, 3e Sér., III, 61–62. Juan Angulo Pnente Arnao, Historia de los Límites del Peru (Lima, 1927), pp. 145–167. Ratified by Bolivia, Oct. 28, 1909; ratified by Peru, Res. #1138, Oct. 26, 1909; ratifications exchanged at La Paz, Nov. 9, 1909.

with the Acre; all the territories to the east of these lines becoming definitely and perpetually the property of Bolivia, those lying west of the same lines definitely and perpetually the property of Peru. This agreement fixed 125 miles of the boundary farther to the southwest than the line of the award, from the confluence of the Heath and the Madre de Dios to the northern end of the frontier at the confluence of the Yaverija and the Acre (Aquiry) and the south boundary of the territory ceded by Bolivia to Brazil by the Petropolis treaty of November 17, 1903.[49]

In 1910 there were conflicts between armed bodies of Bolivians and Peruvians in the Manuripi region; and Severo Fernandez Alonso, Bolivian minister, and Germán Leguía y Martínez, Peruvian minister of foreign relations, signed at Lima on March 30, 1911,[50] a protocol reciting the regret of both governments for the events on the Manuripi, without direct support on either side, and agreeing that each government should appoint a commission to investigate, receive claims and proofs, and report within six months, whereupon the governments would try to reach a friendly settlement and if they could not, would submit the matter to the unappealable arbitral decision of the Hague International Court; meanwhile, to avoid collisions or conflicts between the military forces of the two states, the Peruvian garrison should continue to occupy the point at the junction of the Mavila ravine with the Manuripi and two kilometers more eastward, and the Bolivian garrison should continue to occupy the Illampu building and two kilometers more westward, the whole intermediate zone being neutralized; the demarcation under the protocol of September 17, 1909, to proceed as rapidly as possible, with a friendly agreement if possible as to the line from the mouth of the Heath to the west of Illampu barracks on the Manuripi and thence to the confluence of the Yaverija with the Acre and as to any other points of difference. The same ministers signed at Lima on April 15, 1911,[51] a protocol of instructions for the demarcation mixed commission, of one chief, one assistant chief, engineers, and civil or military aids from each government, to deal with the frontier in four sections, set up marks, refer any difficulty which they could not settle through the president to the directors of the Royal Geographical Society of London, whose decision should be final, keep a daily record of their

[49] See §6, this chap., *supra*.

[50] *Trat. Vig.* (Bolivia, 1925), II, 121-125. *Actos Int. del Peru* (Lima, 1916), Num. 105 4-6. 105 *British and Foreign State Papers* 581-583. Martens, *Nouv. Rec. Gén. de Traités*, 3e Sér., VII, 897-899. Approved by Bolivian Cabinet, Aug. 1, 1911.

[51] *Trat. Vig.* (Bolivia, 1925), II, 126-132. *Actos Int. del Peru* (Lima, 1916), Num. 105, pp. 6-9. 105 *British and Foreign State Papers* 583-587. Martens, *Nouv. Rec. Gén. de Traités*, 3e Sér., VII, 899-902. Approved by Bolivian Cabinet, Aug. 1, 1911.

proceedings and make a map. The Peruvian government appointed British army officers [52] nominated by the Royal Geographical Society of London to four of the six places on its commission, and they left England on January 4, 1911, arrived in Lima, February 1, and Arequipa, April 14, and worked on the actual survey and placing of boundary marks from June 8 to October 25, 1911, April 14 to November 3, 1912, and May 16 to September 1913. The Bolivian commission included two French officers; [53] and joint records of operations ran from June 2, 1911, to December 15, 1913. [54]

A protocol signed at La Paz on May 6, 1912, [55] modified that of March 30, 1911, by entrusting to the demarcation mixed commission the marking of the frontier between the mouth of the Heath and the mouth of the Yaverija according to the treaty of September 17, 1909, and the protocol of April 15, 1911, and agreed that the demarcation of the frontier between the Manuripi and the Acre should begin during 1912; and by a protocol signed at La Paz on December 19, 1916, [56] it was agreed that iron boundary posts might be substituted for wooden ones and that the mixed commission should begin its work in May 1917. Tree trunks set up in a small circle of piling filled with earth were hidden by the brush and partly washed away the next year, and exposed wood lasts not over four years in the wet climate. Eduardo Díez de Medina, Bolivian minister of foreign relations, and Manuel Elias Bonnemaison, Peruvian minister, signed at La Paz on June 2, 1925, [57] a protocol for the demarcation by a mixed commission to consist of a national commissioner, a first geographic engineer, and an assistant engineer for each country, of the frontier in three sections, from the point where it was begun by the former demarcation mixed commission, at the confluence of the Pachasili stream with the Suches, at about 15°15′32″ S. 69°8′ W. across the land and Lake Titicaca to the boundary of the territories(province of Tacna) occupied by Chile under the Peace Treaty of 1883.

In October 1935 it was reported that the governments of Bolivia and

[52] Lieutenant Colonel Arthur James Woodroffe, Chief of the Commission (until 1912); Major Harry Stanley Toppin (chief after 1912); Captain M. R. C. Nanson; and Lieutenant Clive G. Moores. The Peruvian members were Naval Captain José Maria Olivera and Naval Lieutenant Ernesto Salaverry.

[53] Lieutenant Colonels Charles Mailles and Camille Vincent. The Bolivian members were Dr. Lino Romero, Chief; Lieutenant Colonel P. H. Fawcett; Lieutenant Colonel Oscar Mariaca Pando; and Captain Casto Segundo Gonzalez.

[54] *Bol. del Min. de Rel. Ext.* (Lima, 1912), Num. 45, pp. 47-63. "Peru-Bolivia Boundary Commission, 1911-1913," *Royal Geog. Soc. of London* (Cambridge, 1918).

[55] *Trat. Vig.* (Bolivia, 1925), II, 134-136. *Actos Int. del Peru* (Lima, 1916), Num. 105, pp. 3-4. *U. S. For. Rel.*, 1912, p. 1279. Martens, *Nouv. Rec. Gén. de Traités*, 3e Sér., IX, 606. Approved by Bolivian Cabinet, Aug. 19, 1912.

[56] *Trat. Vig.* (Bolivia, 1925), II, 159-161. *Mem. del Min. de Rel. Ext.*, 1917, pp. 53-56. *Anuario de la Leg. Peruana*, Ed. Ofic. (Lima, 1918), XII, 243. Martens, *Nouv. Rec. Gén. de Traités*, 3e Sér., XXIII, 528. Approved by Bolivian Cabinet, Dec. 30, 1916.

[57] *Trat. Vig.* (Bolivia, 1925), II, 164-170. *Mem. del Min. de Rel. Ext.* (Lima, 1925), p. 23. Martens, *Nouv. Rec. Gén. de Traités*, 3e Sér., XXIII, 534-537. Approved by Bolivian Cabinet, June 8, 1925.

Peru were interested in joint plans to develop the Lake Titicaca region by bringing United States fisheries experts to introduce new edible species into the lake and its ten tributary rivers and to report on a large hatchery project. On January 30, 1936, it was announced from Lima that there had been signed a preliminary convention for a mixed scientific commission to study the fisheries question.

Lack of exploration, occupation, or proved actual control on the ordained border between the audiencia of Charcas in the viceroyalty of Buenos Aires and the viceroyalty of Peru resulted in a compromise arbitral award so unsatisfactory that the line was subsequently adjusted by voluntary agreements. This boundary appears now to be practically marked and substantially settled, and the territory probably will not for a long time become of sufficient importance for either country to seek a violent readjustment.

10. BRAZIL–COLOMBIA. APAPORIS

Brazilian travellers and rubber hunters very early explored the valleys north of the Amazon, especially those of the Rio Negro and its tributaries, and established numerous trading posts and small settlements before the New Granadans thought of pushing down from the eastern cordillera to the river lowlands. The Treaty of San Ildefonso of October 1, 1777,[1] provided that the boundary line between Spanish and Portuguese possessions in this region should run down the Javary to the Marañon or Amazon, down the Amazon to the westernmost mouth of the Yapurá, up the Yapurá far enough to include the Portuguese establishments on its banks and those of the Negro and on the channel between them and thence by the mountains which form the divide between the Orinoco and the Amazon. The largely unknown and wholly undetermined situation of the boundary line was long a source of anxiety to successive governments of Colombia,[2] and supposed encroachments by Brazil occasioned numerous protests; but despite various periods of negotiation since 1826 and a proposal by Colombia of arbitration in 1882[3] no agreement was reached. The Spanish award of March 16, 1891,[4] in the Colombia-Venezuela arbitration moved the end of the boundary between those countries eastward from the disputed source of the Memachi to the island of San

[1] Articles 11 and 12. See §2, this chap., *supra*.

[2] Pedro Moncayo, *Colombia i el Brasil, Cuestión de Límites* (Valparaiso, 1862), pp. 5–39. José Maria Quijarro Otero, *Memoria Hist. sobre Límites entre Colombia y Brasil* (Bogotá, 1869). *U. S. For. Rel.*, 1880, p. 310. 50

British and Foreign State Papers 1044.

[3] José Manoel Cardoso de Oliveira, *Actos Dipl. do Brasil* (Rio de Janeiro, 1912), II, 111–112. *Anales Dipl. y Consul-de Col.* (Bogotá, 1901), II, 625–680.

[4] See §22A, this chap., *infra*.

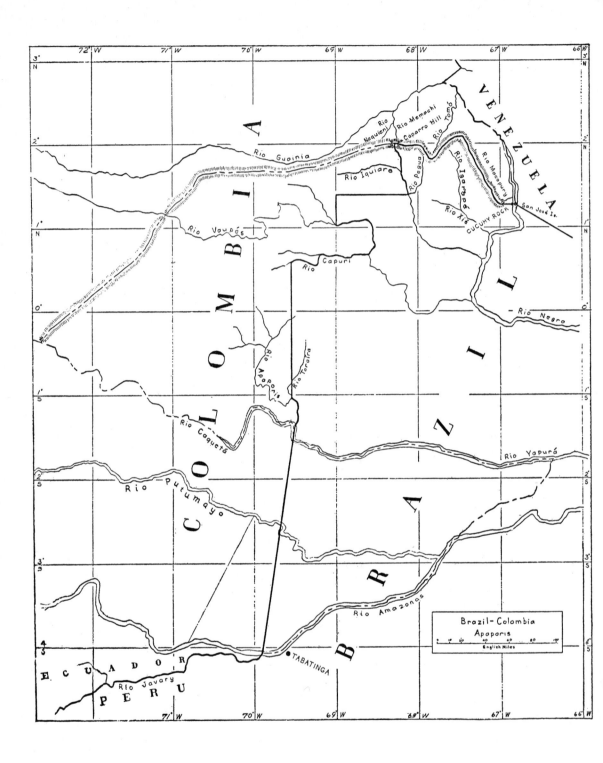

Brazil-Colombia
Apaporis
English Miles

José in the Negro, near Cucuhy rock, so that Colombia instead of Venezuela [5] thereafter bounded with Brazil between those points.

Enéas Martins, Brazilian special minister, directed by Baron do Rio Branco, Brazilian minister of foreign relations, and Alfredo Vazquez Cobo, Colombian minister of foreign relations, signed at Bogotá on April 24, 1907,[6] a treaty of boundaries and navigation providing that (Article 1) the frontier between Cucuhy rock on the Negro and the confluence of the Apaporis on the left (north) bank of the Yapurá or Caquetá should be (Sec. 1) from the island of San José opposite Cucuhy rock westward from the right (west) bank of the Negro at 1°13′51.76″ N. 66°55′ W.; thence by a straight line to the head of the rivulet Macacuny (or Macapury), an affluent wholly in Colombian territory on the right (west) bank of the Negro or Guainia; (Sec. 2) thence by the *divortium aquarum* to pass between the head of the Igarapé Japery, an affluent of the Xié, and the head of the Tomó, an affluent of the Guainia at 2°1′26.65″ N. 67°43′ W.; (Sec. 3) thence westward by the crest of the winding ridge which separates the waters which go to the north from those which go to the south to Caparro hill; thence always by the crest dividing the waters which go to the Guainia from those which flow to the Cuiary (or Iquiare), to the principal source of the Memachi, an affluent of the Naquieni, which in turn is an affluent of the Guainia, at 2°1′27.03″ N. 68°20′ W.; (Sec. 4) thence along the crest of the ridge to the principal head of the affluent of the Cuiary which is nearest the head of the Memachi, and down such affluent to its confluence with the Cuiary; (Sec. 5) thence by the thalweg of the Cuiary to the place where the Pegua, an affluent on the left (east) bank, enters, and from the confluence of the Pegua and the Cuiary westward by the parallel of such confluence to the meridian which passes through the confluence of the Kerary (or Cairary) and the Vaupés; (Sec. 6) thence down that meridian to such confluence; thence by the thalweg of the Vaupés to the mouth of the Capury, an affluent on the right (south) bank of the Vaupés near the Jauarité cascade; (Sec. 7) from the mouth of the Capury west by the thalweg of the Capury to its source near 69°30′ W. and down by the meridian of such source to the Taraíra; thence by the thalweg of the Taraíra to its confluence with the Apaporis and by the thalweg of the

[5] See §15, this chap., *infra.*

[6] *Trat. Pub. de Colombia,* Ed. Ofic. (Bogotá, 1913), II, Apen., pp. 8-13. 100 *British and Foreign State Papers* 810-812. *U. S. For. Rel.,* 1907, Part I, pp. 108-113, 292; *ibid.,* 1908, p. 51. Martens, *Nouv. Rec. Gén. de Traités,* 3ᵉ Sér., I, 786-788. *Tratado de Limites e Navagação e Modus Vivendi,* Min. das Rel. Ext. (Rio de Janeiro, 1908). *Tratado sobre Limites y Libre Navegación y Convenio sobre*

"Modus Vivendi," *Documentos,* Min. de Rel. Ext., Ed. Ofic. (Bogotá, 1908). Fernando Antonio Raja Gabaglia, *As Fronteiras do Brasil* (Rio de Janeiro, 1916), pp. 285-287. Sanctioned by Brazil, Decree #1866, Jan. 9, 1908; ratified by Colombia, Law #24, May 17, 1907; ratifications exchanged at Rio de Janeiro, Apr. 20, 1908; promulgated by Brazil, Decree #6932, Apr. 23, 1908.

Apaporis to its mouth in the Yapurá or Caquetá, where the part of the frontier established by this treaty ended, thus defining the line from Cucuhy rock to the mouth of the Apaporis, the rest of the disputed frontier remaining subject to later arrangement in case Colombia should be favored in its other controversies with Peru and Ecuador; (Article 2) a mixed commission to be named within one year after the exchange of ratifications should proceed to the demarcation of the frontier established in this treaty, and protocols should settle the formation and instructions of such commission, it being agreed that where necessary, in the absence of natural features of the ground to close and complete the frontier, the boundary should follow parallels and meridians in preference to any oblique lines; (Article 3) any differences between the respective commissioners to be submitted to their governments and if they could not come to a direct agreement, to the decision of an arbiter; and (Article 4) the parties should conclude within twelve months a treaty of commerce and navigation based on the principle of the fullest liberty of land transit and river navigation by both nations, in the whole course of the rivers which rise or flow within the region of the line of frontier thus established, subject to fiscal and police regulations no more burdensome for the nationals of the other country than for those of the country making them, Colombian vessels to have free communication with the ocean by the Amazon. By this treaty Colombia relinquished to Brazil territory which Colombia had previously claimed in the valley of the Içana and on the Sierra Arara east of the Apaporis between the Vaupés and the Caquetá.

Also on April 24, 1907,[7] the same ministers signed at Bogotá a convention of *modus vivendi* in the Putumayo, in which it was agreed that Colombian and Brazilian merchant vessels might communicate freely with the ports which either country had established or might establish on the Içá or Putumayo, exempt from all dues except for lighthouses and the like aids to navigation, subject to fiscal and police regulations; Colombian vessels destined for navigation of the Putumayo might communicate freely with the ocean by the Amazon; and war vessels for waters under the jurisdiction of either country might pass freely through the waters of the other, subject to previous notice of their number.

Luis Tanco Argáez, Colombian minister, the Baron of Rio Branco, Brazilian minister of foreign relations, and Enéas Martins, Brazilian special min-

---

[7] *Trat. Pub. de Colombia*, Ed. Ofic. (Bogotá, 1913), II, Apen., pp. 20-21. 100 *British and Foreign State Papers* 809-810. *U. S. For. Rel.*, 1907, Part I, pp. 110-111. Martens, *Nouv. Rec. Gén. de Traités*, 3° Sér., I, 789-790. Approved by Colombian Executive, April 3, 1908. See note 6, preceding.

ister to Colombia, signed at Rio de Janeiro on August 21, 1908,[8] a treaty of commerce and river navigation providing that the navigation of the rivers recognized as common to Brazil and Colombia by the boundary treaty of April 24, 1907, should be completely free for the merchant vessels of both nations, and the Yapurá or Caquetá for war vessels in a number to be limited by common accord; and for the war vessels of Colombia, the Amazon, and other rivers which Brazil had opened or might thereafter open to the commerce of all nations, other than by special agreement between the two countries.

On June 8, 1914,[9] Francisco Jose Urrutia, Colombian minister of foreign relations, called the attention of the Brazilian chargé d'affaires at Bogotá, to Article 1 (meaning Article 2) of the treaty of April 24, 1907, calling for a mixed commission to mark the frontier and requested him to ask his government for instructions to sign the special protocols necessary to constitute and instruct the demarcation commission. Nothing definite was accomplished and the negotiations for the demarcation dragged on without practical result.

On learning of the Colombia-Peru treaty of March 24, 1922,[10] Brazil made friendly but formal observations to Peru, that the parties to that treaty were attempting to deal in part with territory which Brazil claimed as against Peru and had never settled with Colombia, especially the area to the east of the Apaporis-Tabatinga line described in the Brazil-Peru treaty of October 23, 1851.[11] This protest seemed to block Peru's further favorable consideration of the 1922 treaty, and Colombia presently asked the United States to see what could be done toward satisfying Brazil. Secretary of State Charles E. Hughes conducted complicated negotiations which finally resulted in the signing in Washington on March 4, 1925,[12] of an act in which Brazil agreed to withdraw her observations as to the 1922 Colombia-Peru treaty, and as soon as that treaty should be ratified by both governments, Colombia agreed to conclude with Brazil a treaty recognizing as their frontier the village of Tabatinga and thence northward a straight line to meet the River Yapurá at its junction with the Apaporis, Brazil in the same treaty to establish in perpetuity in favor of Colombia freedom of navigation on the Amazon and other rivers common to both countries.

Ratifications of the Colombia-Peru treaty of March 24, 1922, were

[8] *Trat. Pub. de Colombia* (Bogotá, 1913), II Apen., 13-19. *Coll. das Leis do Brasil de 1910* (Rio de Janeiro, 1915), II (Parte 1), 658-666. Martens, *Nouv. Rec. Gén. de Traités*, 3° Sér., IV, 312-318. Sanctioned by Brazil, Decree #2247, Apr. 27, 1910; ratified by Colombia, Law #1, Mar. 5, 1909; ratifications exchanged at Bogotá, Aug.

6, 1910; promulgated by Brazil, Decree #8252, Sept. 26, 1910.

[9] *Trat. de Colombia* (Bogotá, 1914), 155-156.
[10] See §21B, this chap., *infra.*
[11] See §13, this chap., *infra.*
[12] See §21B, this chap., *infra.*

exchanged at Bogotá on March 19, 1928; and pursuant to the Hughes agreement, Laureano Garcia Ortiz, Colombian minister, and Octavio Mangabeira, Brazilian minister of foreign affairs, signed at Rio de Janeiro on November 15, 1928,[13] a treaty to complete the determination of the common frontier southward from the mouth of the Apaporis and to establish regulations for river navigation to be reciprocally guaranteed forever free; providing (Article 1) that the frontier from the mouth of the Apaporis on the Yapurá or Caquetá, at the end of the line stipulated in the treaty of April 24, 1907, should be a straight line from such mouth to the left (west) bank of the Amazon (opposite) the Brazilian town of Tabatinga; (Article 2) a mixed commission should proceed within two years after the exchange of ratifications to mark by durable posts the frontier designated in the former treaty and in this one; to erect in places where the frontier may not be formed by sufficient natural features, such as streams of water or ridges, stone or cement posts, columns, or other durable signs so that the frontier line might be exactly recognized at any time; (Article 4) to facilitate the work, the mixed commission was authorized to make necessary modifications and compensations in the frontier line, so far as indispensable for clarity and permanence of the line or for reasons of manifest and reciprocal convenience, recognized by both parties; (Article 5) both parties recognized reciprocally forever the right of free navigation in the Amazon, Yapurá or Caquetá, Içá or Putumayo, and all the affluents or confluents of those rivers, subject to fiscal and police regulations equal for the nationals of both parties; (Article 6) war vessels to be included, subject to previous notice of their number and nature.

By notes exchanged at Bogotá on March 7 and 12, 1930,[14] it was agreed that each government should name a commission of one chief and as many assistants as necessary to meet in Belém do Pará within ninety days and form a demarcation mixed commission to proceed to the frontier and set up posts, submitting any differences to the two governments, and drawing up a map and a report, considering the use of aerophotography to save time, labor, and expense, especially in the zones of the (a) straight line between Tabatinga and the mouth of the Apaporis, (b) Taraíra for most of its length, (c) Capurí or Paporí, (d) Kerari and (e) Cuyari or Iquiare with its affluent from Caparro hill. Colombia appointed her commission, of which part went in September

[13] Coll. de Actos Int., Min. das Rel. Ext. (Rio de Janeiro, 1930), No. 22. Coll. das Leis do Brasil de 1930, I, 31–38. Martens, Nouv. Rec. Gén. de Traités, 3e Sér., XXV, 674–677. Sanctioned by Brazil, Decree #5655, Jan. 9, 1929; ratified by Brazil, Nov. 12, 1929; ratified by Colombian Executive, Jan. 7, 1930; ratifications exchanged at Bogotá, Jan. 9, 1930; promulgated by Brazil, Decree #19104, Feb. 11, 1930.

[14] Coll. de Actos Int., Min. das Rel. Ext. (Rio de Janeiro, 1930), No. 27.

1930 to Rio de Janeiro to settle the technical phases of the work, and the rest set out in February 1931 for Manaos, and it is understood that the actual demarcation is proceeding annually.

The viceroyalty of Nueva Granada theoretically extended southward presumably to the San Ildefonso line, but before the Spaniards had taken possession or even explored that region, Brazilian traders pushed in and established scattered settlements, and the subsequent treaty adjustment had to recognize accomplished occupation. This boundary now appears to be settled in detail and finally.

11. BRAZIL–ECUADOR. IÇA

Spain and Portugal by the Treaty of San Ildefonso of October 1, 1777,[1] provided that the boundary between their possessions should run from a point on the Javary due west of the point on the Madeira equidistant from the Marañon or Amazon and the mouth of the Mamoré down the Javary to the Marañon or Amazon, down the Amazon to the westernmost mouth of the Yapurá, far enough to include the Portuguese establishments on its banks and those of the Negro and on the channel between them and thence by the mountains which form the divide between the Orinoco and the Amazon. Colombia and Peru were in dispute over their boundaries in this region,[2] and with her creation in 1830 as an independent state Ecuador inherited from Colombia the western portion of the boundary difficulty with Peru, and had for her own part to maintain her supposed rights against her larger neighbors on either side who, she felt, were both always ready to confine her so far as possible to the mountain region and the Pacific slope. Before, however, Ecuador's frontiers were settled with either Colombia[3] or Peru,[4] Brazil succeeded, after negotiations reopening those begun at Quito in 1853, in obtaining from Ecuador release of her claim to an area which protruded into Brazilian territory between the Caquetá and the Amazon, for most of which Brazil in 1928 obtained further title from Colombia.[5]

The Baron of Rio Branco, Brazilian minister of foreign affairs, and Carlos R. Tobar, Ecuadorian minister, signed at Rio de Janeiro on May 6, 1904,[6] a treaty which provided that (Article 1) if the frontier dispute between Peru

[1] Articles 11 and 12. See §2, this chap., *supra*.
[2] See §21A, this chap., *infra*.
[3] See §20, this chap., *infra*.
[4] See §23, this chap., *infra*.
[5] See §10, this chap., *supra*.
[6] *Coll. das Leis de 1905*, I (Parte 2), 211–214. 97

British and Foreign State Papers 688–689. Martens, *Nouv. Rec. Gén. de Traités*, 2e Sér., XXXIV, 519–520. *Arch. Dipl.*, 4e Sér., CXXX, 380. Sanctioned by Brazil, Decree #1310, Dec. 28, 1904; ratified by Ecuador, Oct. 12, 1904; ratifications exchanged at Rio de Janeiro, May 16, 1905; promulgated by Brazil, Decree #5531, May 18, 1905.

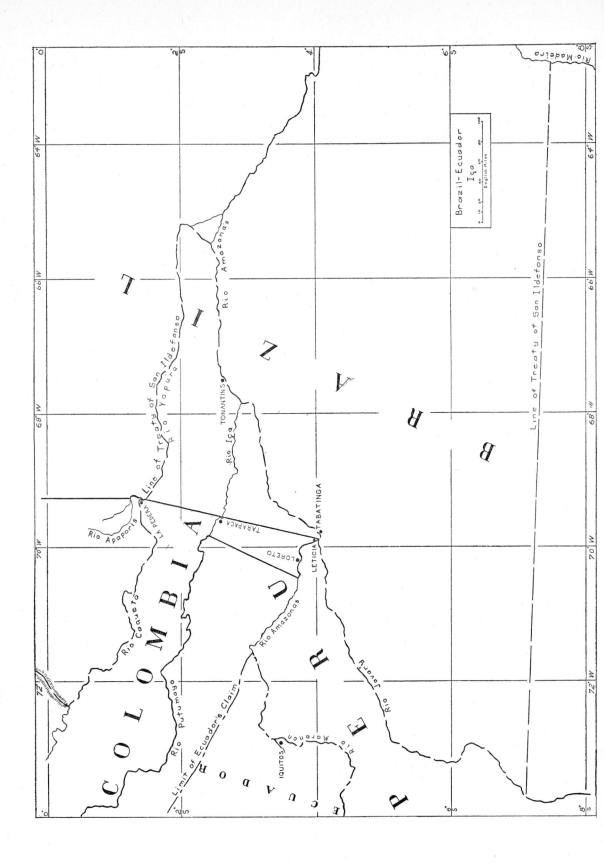

Brazil-Ecuador
Iça

English Miles

and Ecuador should terminate according to her expectations in favor of
Ecuador, the frontier between Brazil and Ecuador should be that established
by Article 7 of the convention of October 23, 1851, between Brazil and Peru
as modified by the agreement of February 11, 1874, for the exchange of territories along the Iça or Putumayo; that is, the frontier should be, wholly or
partly, according to the outcome of the Ecuador-Peru dispute, the geodesic
line from the mouth of the Santo Antonio stream on the left (north) bank
of the Amazon between Tabatinga and Leticia, and terminating at the confluence of the Apaporis with the Yapurá or Caquetá, except the section of the
Iça or Putumayo intersected by such line and there the bed of that river
between the points of intersection should form the dividing line; and (Article 2) the parties declared that in this treaty they had no intention of
prejudicing any right which might be afterwards established by the other
neighboring countries; that is to say, they had no intention of modifying the
boundary questions pending between Brazil and Colombia and between Ecuador, Colombia, and Peru, nor had Brazil any such intention when negotiating
with Peru [7] the convention of October 23, 1851. This resulted in clearing
the way for Brazil's arrangements with Colombia and Peru, and by the
1922 agreement between these two [8] Ecuador no longer has any frontier
bounding with Brazil.

The absence of definite records as to the boundary between the Viceroyalties of New Granada and of Peru or proof of control of the border region
made it especially difficult for the smallest nation to maintain her claims
against her three larger neighbors, and she finally relinquished the remotest
part of the area to the most definitely insistent and probably least dangerous
claimant.

12. BRAZIL–PARAGUAY. APA

The Spanish-Portuguese boundary northeast of Asunción had been fixed
in the Treaty of San Ildefonso of October 1, 1777,[1] to run from the mouth of
the Curituba up the Paraná to the Igurey,[2] up the Igurey to its chief source,
then by a straight line to the head of the nearest river that empties into the
Paraguay, down that river to the Paraguay and up the Paraguay to the Lake
of Xarayes. After independence the boundary remained unsettled, although
in turn both countries tried to obtain a settlement. Brazil sought persist-
ently to gain access to her interior region of southern Matto Grosso by the

[7] See §13, this chap., *infra.*
[8] See §21B, this chap., *infra.*

[1] Articles 8 and 9. See §2, this chap., *supra.*
[2] Felix de Azara, *Correspondencia Oficial e Inédita,*
1784-1795 (1ª ed., Buenos Aires, 1836).

Paraná and the Paraguay, claiming natural and necessary rights in them as international rivers, but Dictator Carlos Antonio López, in control of the lower rivers from 1841 to 1862, for a time refused to allow any Brazilian vessels to ascend and would open no ports on the Paraguay north of Asunción. With the overthrow of Rosas in Argentina in 1852 the Paraná was declared free for navigation to vessels of all nations by Argentine law and by treaties to which Argentina, Brazil, and Uruguay were parties, though Paraguay was not. A convention signed at Rio de Janeiro on April 6, 1856,[3] provided that as soon as circumstances should permit and within six years representatives of the parties should examine and agree to the boundary line and that until a final agreement should be concluded the existing *uti possidetis* was to be respected. By a treaty signed at Rio de Janeiro on April 6, 1856,[4] each party granted to the merchant vessels of the other free navigation of the Paraná and Paraguay in the parts bordered by each, so that navigation of the rivers in the parts bounded by both nations remained common to both. Paraguay granted to Brazil the right for two warships of not over 600 tons and carrying not more than eight guns each to ascend and descend freely without previous notice and consent the Paraguay and Paraná in those parts belonging to Paraguay and to enter all ports open to foreign flags; and reciprocally Brazil granted to Paraguay under the same conditions the right for two warships to enter the ports of Brazil open to foreign flags in the Paraguay and Paraná. These provisions for free transit upon the two rivers were to be permanent, though the other stipulations of the treaty, relating chiefly to commerce and contraband, were to be in force only for six years. The number of warships allowed in the Paraguay was raised to three, and the limits of two in the Paraná and of tonnage and armament for all were revoked by an additional convention signed at Asunción, February 12, 1858.[5]

Francisco Solano López, who became dictator on his father's death September 10, 1862, sought to settle Paraguay's boundary east of the Paraguay by treaty with Brazil, but Pedro II held off, and the expanding empire asserted a claim to territory south of the Branco (opposite Fuerte Olimpo), but recognized that west of the Paraguay the northern boundary of Paraguay began opposite the Negro.

[3] José Manoel Cardoso de Oliveira, *Actos Dipl. do Brasil* (Rio de Janeiro, 1912), I, 210. 46 *British and Foreign State Papers* 1304-1305. Martens et Cussy, *Rec. Man. et Prat. de Traités*, VII, 522. Sanctioned by Brazil, Decree #1783, July 14, 1856.

[4] Antonio Pereira Pinto, *Apontamentos para o Direito Int.* (Rio de Janeiro, 1866), III, 434-490. Martens et Cussy, *Rec. Man. et Prat. de Traités*, VII, 516-521. 46

British and Foreign State Papers 1299-1304. Ratifications exchanged at Asunción, June 13, 1856. A similar treaty signed at Asunción on Apr. 27, 1855, failed of ratification. 49 *British and Foreign State Papers* 1195-1200.

[5] Antonio Pereira Pinto, *Apontamentos para o Direito Int.* (Rio de Janeiro, 1869), IV, 95-148. 49 *British and Foreign State Papers* 1274-1288. Ratifications exchanged at Rio de Janeiro, Apr. 30, 1858.

In connection with the troubles in Uruguay, on November 11, 1864, Dictator Francisco Solano López of Paraguay caused his gunboat *Tacuari* to halt a little way up the river and to force to return to a mooring off Asunción the Brazilian commercial steamer *Marquez de Olinda,* making its regular trip up the Paraguay to Corumba in Matto Grosso. Brazil broke off diplomatic relations on November 12, 1864,[6] López sent up the Paraguay an expedition which easily captured the defenseless principal southern river settlements in Matto Grosso, and the Five Years' War began in February 1865.[7] Brazil sent a naval force up the Paraná on April 24 [8] to blockade the ports and coast of Paraguay, and closed to all foreign vessels all the ports of Matto Grosso province.

The treaty of alliance of May 1, 1865,[9] between Argentina, Brazil, and Uruguay provided that after the conclusion of permanent boundary treaties Brazil should be separated from Paraguay on the side of the Paraná by the first river below the Cataract of the Sete Quedas, which according to the last map of Manchez [10] was the Igurey, and thence by the course of the Igurey from its mouth up to its source; on the side of the left (east) bank of the Paraguay, by the Apa from its mouth to its source; in the interior, by the crest of the Maracayú mountains, the streams on the east to belong to Brazil and those on the west to Paraguay, and by lines drawn as straight as possible from those mountains to the sources of the Apa and of the Igurey. This gave Brazil clear title to all southern Matto Grosso from the Paraná to the Paraguay north of the Igurey and the Apa instead of the Branco as claimed by Paraguay. This treaty was to have been kept secret until the principal object of the alliance had been attained, but it was published in England before the war was a year old. Dr. C. de Castro, foreign minister of Uruguay, referred to the treaty in a note of June 21, 1865, to W. G. Lettsom, British minister at Montevideo, announcing the departure of General Flores to put himself at the head of the national army as stipulated, whereupon Great Britain apparently became solicitous to know what had been arranged concerning Paraguay. Castro delivered a copy of the treaty to Lettsom, who transmitted a translation on June 27, 1865, to Earl Russell in London; and when on March 2, 1866, the House of Commons in an address to the Queen asked that further correspondence "relative to the War

---

[6] *Arch. Dipl.,* 1865, II, 219–223, 224–225, 237–239.

[7] *U. S. Dipl. Corr.,* 1866–67, II, 278–281, 283–284. 55 *British and Foreign State Papers* 294; 66 *ibid.,* 1179–1352. *Arch. Dipl.,* 1865, II, 237–239. *Rev. Der. Int.* (Havana), VII (1925), 18–19.

[8] 55 *British and Foreign State Papers* 296.

[9] Article 16. See §4, this chap., *supra.*

[10] Probably E. Mouchez, 1862. See §4, note 14, this chap., *supra.*

in the River Plate" be laid before it, the translation of treaty and protocol
was included in the return of the address presented by Mr. A. H. Layard
of Southwark on March 20, 1866,[11] and with the rest of the papers was ordered to lie on the table and be printed. The terms of the treaty became
known in South America, and Peru protested in a note to the three signatories on July 9, 1866,[12] against the allied claim of right to overthrow and
destroy the government of another nation. Efforts by the United States and
other powers at mediation during 1867 and 1868 [13] met with no success
against the allies' determination that López must go. The protests of Peru
and others against the 1865 treaty did not prevent its being substantially
carried out, after the death of López on March 1, 1870, and the end of the
war. In the preliminary protocol of peace signed at Asunción on June 20,
1870,[14] with Argentina and Brazil, the provisional government of Paraguay
by a triumvirate installed August 15, 1869,[15] accepted in substance the treaty
of May 1, 1865, but reserved full liberty to propose and maintain, in the final
arrangements as to boundaries, whatever they might deem to be in conformity with the rights of the republic of Paraguay. The Brazilian plenipotentiary agreed to the reservation and declared it not to be the intention of
the allied governments to gain territory by the right of conquest, but only
to exact what was their perfect right, respecting also the territorial integrity
of Paraguay. A treaty of peace was signed at Asunción on January 9, 1872,[16]
by which it was agreed that boundary lines between the two nations should
be adjusted and defined in a special treaty; navigation of the Paraguay,
Paraná, and Uruguay, not including their affluents or internal trade, was to
be free to the commerce of all nations, and vessels of war of the river states
should enjoy free passage, but those of nations not bordering on the rivers
might go only as far as each river state within its own boundaries should
permit; indemnities and claims were to be fixed by a mixed commission; and
Brazil in accordance with the Treaty of May 1, 1865, bound itself to respect
perpetually the independence, sovereignty, and integrity of the republic of
Paraguay and to guarantee them for five years.

João Mauricio Wanderley, Baron of Cotegipe, Brazilian minister, and

[11] *Journal of the House of Commons*, CXXI, 128, 181.
Command Papers, 1866, LXXVI, No. 199.

[12] *U. S. Dipl. Corr.*, 1866–67, Part II, pp. 599–601.

[13] *Ibid.*, 1867, Part II, pp. 705–733; *ibid.*, 1868, Part
II, pp. 228–248. *Arch. Dipl.*, 1868, IV, 1682–1692, 1697–
1702; *ibid.*, 1869, I, 287–291; *ibid.*, 1870, 322–325.

[14] 63 *British and Foreign State Papers* 322–325.

[15] Rafael C. Vallejos, *Recop. de Leyes del Paraguay*
(Asunción, 1892), pp. 558–559.

[16] *Col. de Trat. del Paraguay*, Pub. Ofic. (Asunción,
1890), pp. 3–7. 62 *British and Foreign State Papers* 277–
281. Martens, *Nouv. Rec. Gén. de Traités*, 2ᵉ Sér., IV,
568–572. Ratified by Brazil, Mar. 26, 1872; ratified by
Paraguay, Feb. 12, 1872; ratifications exchanged at Rio de
Janeiro, Mar. 26, 1872.

Carlos Loizaga, Paraguayan senator, signed at Asunción on January 9, 1872,[17] a boundary treaty providing that (Article 1) the dividing line should be the bed or channel of the Paraná from the beginning of the Brazilian possessions at the mouth of the Iguazú to the Great Cataract of the Sete Quédas on the Paraná; thence by the ridge of the Sierra of Maracayú to its end; thence by a straight line, or a line as nearly straight as possible, by the most elevated ground to the Sierra of Amambay; thence by the highest ridge of this sierra to the principal source of the Apa and down by the channel of the Apa to its mouth on the east bank of the Paraguay; all the slopes which incline north and east to belong to Brazil, those which incline south and west to Paraguay; the island of Fecho dos Morros to belong to Brazil; and (Article 2) demarcation commissioners to be named within three months by common agreement of both parties; (Article 3) if one should fail, the demarcation to be made by the other and become valid after inspection and approval by a commissioner to be named by the governments of Argentina and Uruguay. This confirmed to Brazil the territory north of the Apa for one hundred miles substantially as promised her in the treaty of 1865 and ended further claim by Paraguay to run the northern line by the river Branco in accordance with her previous interpretation of the Treaty of San Ildefonso.

The Brazilian commissioner [18] left for Asunción on July 16, 1872, and the work of demarcation was finished November 14, 1874. By a protocol signed at Asunción, January 7, 1874,[19] it was agreed that the stream called Estrella was in fact the principal source of the Apa, and that the frontier line should pass through it.

The frontier being definitely established in the portion from the mouth of the Iguazú in the Paraná to the mouth of the Apa in the Paraguay, Octavio Mangabeira, Brazilian minister of foreign relations, and Rogelio Ibarra, Paraguayan minister, signed at Rio de Janeiro on May 21, 1927,[20] a complementary boundary treaty which provided that (Article 1) from the confluence of the Apa in the Paraguay to the entrance or outlet of Bahia Negra the frontier should be formed by the bed of the Paraguay, the left (east) bank

[17] *Annexo ao Rel. do Min. das Rel. Ext.* (Rio de Janeiro, 1900), Parte II, pp. 201-202. *Col. de Trat. celebr. por Paraguay* (Asunción, 1885), pp. 11-13. 62 *British and Foreign State Papers* 282-284. *U. S. For. Rel.*, 1872, pp. 29-30, 35-40, 43, 91-109; *ibid.*, 1873, Part I, pp. 47-50. Martens, *Nouv. Rec. Gén. de Traités*, 2ᵉ Sér., IV, 573-574. Ratified by Brazil, Mar. 26, 1872; ratified by Paraguay, Jan. 26, 1872; ratifications exchanged at Rio de Janeiro, Mar. 26, 1872; promulgated by Brazil, Decree #4911, Mar. 27, 1872.

[18] Colonel of Engineers Rufino Enéas Gustavo Galvao, afterwards Baron of Maracajú. *Relatorio do Min. das Rel. Est.*, December, 1872; *ibid.*, May 14, 1875.

[19] *Arch. Dipl.*, CXXX, 380. Fernando Antonio Raja Gabaglia, *As Fronteiras do Brasil* (Rio de Janeiro, 1916), pp. 263-269.

[20] *Coll. de Actos Int.* (Rio de Janeiro, 1930), No. 20. 127 *British and Foreign State Papers*, Part II, pp. 145-147. Sanctioned by Brazil, Decree #5431, Jan. 10, 1928; ratified by Brazil, Oct. 29, 1929; ratified by Paraguay, Oct. 31, 1929; ratifications exchanged at Rio de Janeiro, Nov. 25, 1929; promulgated by Brazil, Decree #19018, Dec. 3, 1929.

to belong to Brazil and the right (west) bank to Paraguay; (Article 2) except for Fecho dos Morros, which is Brazilian, the other islands situated on the east or west side of the frontier line, determined by the middle of the principal channel of the river, of greatest depth and most easy and free for navigation, as accepted at the time of demarcation and according to the studies made, should belong respectively to Brazil or to Paraguay, islands formed in the future to be adjudicated according to the same criterion; and (Article 3) a mixed commission, named by the two governments as soon as possible after exchange of ratifications, should draw up a map of the river Paraguay, with its islands and channels, from the Apa to the entrance of Bahia Negra, make necessary soundings and measurements and place marks on the principal islands and points they deemed most suitable. A protocol of instructions for the demarcation mixed commission was signed at Rio de Janeiro, May 9, 1930,[21] and by notes exchanged at Asunción November 30–December 9, 1931, it was agreed that the commission should meet at Asunción on May 15, 1932.

The Chaco Boreal war with Bolivia has prevented any work from yet being done on this demarcation along the Paraguay from the Apa to Bahia Negra, but it is improbable that Paraguay will permit Bolivia to retain any rights on this part of the river, and the agreement as made with Brazil will presumably eventually be carried out. The arrangement amounted to regularizing by treaty the occupation by early settlers as sanctioned by a successful war, discarding the loser's identification of a river imperfectly described in the San Ildefonso Treaty.

13. BRAZIL–PERU. ACRE–PURÚS

The Treaty of San Ildefonso of October 1, 1777,[1] separated the Spanish and Portuguese possessions by a line from the Madeira at a point midway between the Amazon and the mouth of the Mamore due west to the east bank of the Javary, down the Javary to the Marañon or Amazon, and down the Amazon to the westernmost mouth of the Yapurá. Peru early asserted claims to lands east of the Javary and resisted application of the San Ildefonso line to determine her rights on this frontier. The geographical natural boundary would cut down Peru's possessions still further, for from Lake Titicaca the divide runs northwest above the headwaters of the Purús, west-

[21] *Coll. de Actos Int.* (Rio de Janeiro, 1932), No. 44. João Ribeiro, *As Nossas Fronteiras* (Rio de Janeiro, 1930), pp. 49-58.

[1] Article 11. See §2, this chap., *supra*.

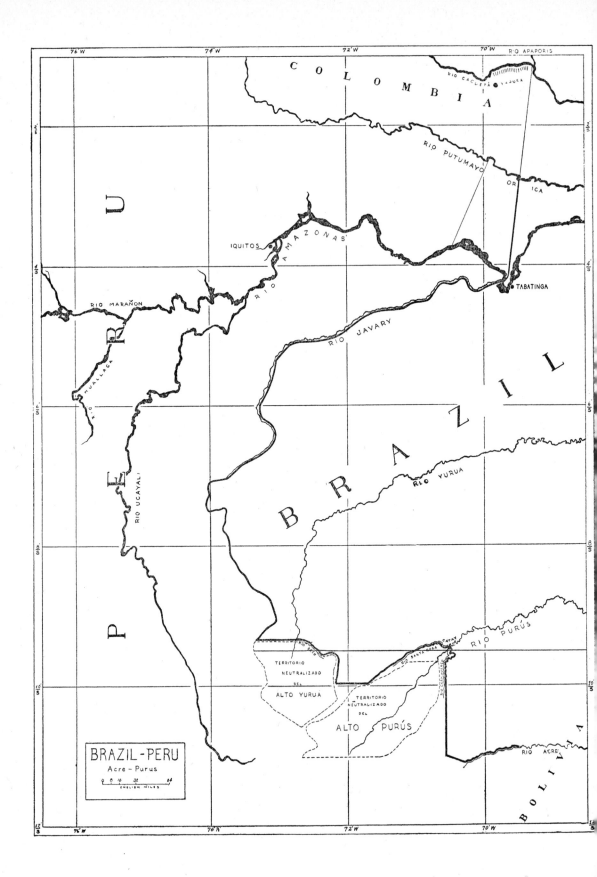

ward around the head of the Ucayali valleys, and thence northward to the
Ecuador border west of the Ucayali, and 100 miles west of the beginning of
the Javary. A treaty of friendship, commerce, and navigation signed at Lima
July 8, 1841,[2] affirmed (Article 14) the necessity of demarcation of the exact
boundary which should divide Brazil from Peru, and agreed that the parties
would carry into effect as soon as possible conciliatory, pacific, and amicable
measures, in conformity with the *uti possidetis* of 1821, by common agreement, with an exchange of lands or other indemnities where necessary, to fix
the dividing line in the most exact and natural manner and most in accord
with the interests of both nations. The Bolivia-Peru war intervened, and
Brazil never ratified this treaty, but when peace was restored and settlements
had been negotiated with Colombia and Ecuador, Dictator Ramón Castilla
caused negotiations to be reopened with Brazil.

Bartolomé Herrera, acting Peruvian minister of foreign relations, and
Duarte da Ponte Ribeiro, Brazilian minister to the republics of the Pacific,
signed at Lima on October 23, 1851,[3] a convention of commerce and river
navigation (with four separate articles of the same date as to steam navigation concessions) providing (Article 7) that, to prevent doubts respecting the
frontier, the parties accepted the principle of *uti possidetis* as that according
to which the boundaries should be adjusted, and consequently they recognized respectively as frontier the town of Tabatinga and thence a straight
line to the north to the Yapurá opposite its confluence with the Apaporis,
and from Tabatinga south the Javary from its confluence with the Amazon;
a mixed commission named by both governments to lay down the frontier
according to the principle of *uti possidetis* and to propose nevertheless such
exchanges of territory as they should think suitable to fix the most natural
and convenient boundaries for both nations. A river convention signed at
Lima, October 22, 1858,[4] provided (Article 17) that within twelve months
from the exchange of ratifications both countries would name the mixed commission which according to Article 7 of the treaty of October 23, 1851,
should lay down and mark the frontier. The first commission, named in

[2] Ricardo Aranda, *Col. de Trat. del Peru*, II, 507–
514.

[3] José Manoel Cardoso de Oliveira, *Actos. Dipl. do
Brasil* (Rio de Janeiro, 1912), I, 166-167. *Annexo ao
Relatorio do Min. das Rel. Ext.* (Rio de Janeiro, 1900),
Parte II, p. 208. *Actos Int. del Peru* (Lima, 1915), Num.
2. Ricardo Aranda, *Col. de Trat. del Peru*, II, 514-520.
42 *British and Foreign State Papers* 1308-1312. Martens et
Cussy, *Rec. Man. et Prat. de Traités*, VI, 640-642. Ratified
by Brazil, Mar. 18, 1852; ratified by Peru, Dec. 1, 1851;

ratifications exchanged at Rio de Janeiro, Oct. 18, 1852.
Articles 1-6 denounced by Peru, Apr. 24, 1885. Ricardo
Aranda, *Col. de Trat. del Peru*, II, 634-636.

[4] José Manoel Cardoso de Oliveira, *Actos Dipl. do Brasil*
(Rio de Janeiro, 1912), I, 254-258. *Actos Int. del Peru*
(Lima, 1915), Num. 4. Ricardo Aranda, *Col. de Trat. del
Peru*, II, 520-526. Ratified by Brazil, Apr. 5, 1859; rati-
fied by Peru, Apr. 1, 1859; ratifications exchanged at Paris,
May 27, 1859; promulgated by Brazil, Decree #2442,
July 16, 1859.

1861,[5] broke up [6] over the tracing of the line, and a second one met in joint conference on September 13, 1865,[7] and began the demarcation on July 28, 1866. Some members of the field party were massacred by the Indian savages on the Javary in 1866. A masaranduba wooden post for the northernmost mark on the right (south) bank of the Yapurá opposite the mouth of the Apaporis was set up at 1°31′29.5″ S. 69°24′55.5″ W. on August 25, 1872.[8]

By a convention signed at Lima, February 11, 1874,[9] reciting that the frontier line as traced from the slopes of Igarapé at Santo Antonio de Tabatinga to the Yapurá crossed a bend of the Içá or Putumayo twice in a short distance between two specified marks,[10] it was agreed that between those marks the frontier should follow the bed of the river between the Peruvian and Brazilian islands, leaving the right (west) bank to Peru and the left (east) bank to Brazil. The work was terminated on March 14, 1874,[11] by the setting up of a final mark on the right (southeast) bank of the Javary. Colombia protested by a note of March 15, 1875,[12] against the demarcation of the line from Tabatinga north to the Yapurá, and especially the position of the mark on the bank of the Putumayo placed July 26, 1873, at 2°52′12″ S. 62°41′10″ W., but both Brazil and Peru maintained its correctness. A diplomatic agreement signed at Lima, September 29, 1876,[13] provided for free navigation by the merchant and war vessels of both nations on the Içá or Putumayo, where it was the property of either or held in common by both nations, subject to fiscal and police regulations as for nationals, and free access by Peruvian vessels to and from the Amazon and the ocean; war vessels to be subject to limitation in number. A treaty of commerce and navigation signed at Rio de Janeiro, October 10, 1891,[14] agreed that (Article 1) navigation of the rivers common to Brazil and Peru and of the Javary and its affluents should be free for the vessels of both nations, sub-

[5] Naval Captain José da Costa Azevedo, afterwards Baron of Ladario, for Brazil; Admiral Ignacio Mariategui for Peru.

[6] José da Costa Azevedo, *Breve resposta as Arguições* (Rio de Janeiro, 1863).

[7] Costa Azevedo for Brazil; naval captain Francisco Carrasco for Peru.

[8] Ricardo Aranda, *Col. de Trat. del Peru*, II, 554–570.

[9] *Col. das Leis do Brazil de 1875* XXXVIII, Parte 2, 794–796. *Actos Int. del Peru* (Lima, 1915), Num. 15. 65 *British and Foreign State Papers* 630–631. Sanctioned by Brazil, Law #2583, June 12, 1875; ratified by Brazil, Aug. 11, 1875; ratified by Peru, Apr. 13, 1875; ratifications exchanged at Lima, Sept. 23, 1875; promulgated by Brazil, Decree #6034, Nov. 20, 1875.

[10] From 2°46′11.5″ S. 69°39′10.85″ W. on the left (north) bank downstream southward to 2°53′12.8″ S.

69°40′28.55″ W. on the right (south) bank. Ricardo Aranda, *Col. de Trat. del Peru*, II, 570–577.

[11] *Ibid.*, 580–611.

[12] *Ibid.*, 611–614.

[13] *Annexo ao Relatorio do Min. das Rel. Ext.* (Rio de Janeiro, 1900), Parte II, pp. 212–216. *Actos Int. del Peru* (Lima, 1915), Num. 21. Ricardo Aranda, *Col. de Trat. del Peru*, II, 619–625, 631–634.

[14] *Annexo ao Relatorio do Min. das Rel. Ext.* (Rio de Janeiro, 1900), II, 217–221. *Coll. das Leis do Brazil de 1896*, II, 350–360. Martens, *Nouv. Rec. Gén de Traités*, 2e Sér., XXII, 217–223. Sanctioned by Brazil, Decree #203, Aug. 20, 1894; ratified by Peru, Oct. 30, 1894; ratifications exchanged at Lima, Mar. 18, 1896; promulgated by Brazil, Decree #2269, Apr. 30, 1896. Denounced by Brazil, May 18, 1904; ceased to be in effect May 18, 1905; Brazilian Decree #5531A, May 18, 1905.

ject to regulations established or to be established by the two countries; (Article 21) the official value of goods for customs duties should be based upon the price at Manaos, the most important market nearest to the Javary; (Article 29) importations for Iquitos or any other port of the Peruvian Marañon or Amazon might be entered at Tabatinga; and (Article 39) the river convention of October 22, 1858, was abrogated. In 1896 it appeared that the position of the 1874 mark on the Javary was erroneous, and May 28, 1897,[15] in a protocol signed at Rio de Janeiro it was agreed to correct it and to replace destroyed marks.

After Bolivia's interest in the Acre region had been transferred to Brazil by the treaty of Petropolis of November 17, 1903,[16] while arbitration by Argentina of the Bolivian-Peruvian dispute was pending,[17] the relations of Brazil with Peru became strained, and there were conflicts between Brazilians and Peruvians in the region of the upper Yuruá and Purús which threatened to become serious. On May 16, 1904,[18] Brazil prohibited the transit of arms and munitions to Peru by way of the Amazon, and Peru protested against the general prohibition and that the particular shipment stopped was intended for commercial and not military purposes. The Baron of Rio Branco, Brazilian minister of foreign relations, and Hernán Velarde, Peruvian minister, signed at Rio de Janeiro on July 12, 1904,[19] a protocol of provisional agreement which provided that (Article 1) the diplomatic negotiations for a direct agreement on fixing the boundary from the source of the Javary to 11° S. should commence on August 1 and close on December 31, 1904;[20] (Article 2) it was the sincere purpose of both governments to resort to the good offices or the mediation of some friendly government or the decision of an arbiter if within the specified time they did not reach a direct satisfactory agreement; (Article 3) during the discussion there should remain neutral the disputed territories of (a) the basin of the upper Yuruá from its headwaters and higher affluents down to the mouth and left (west) bank of the Breu and thence westward along the parallel of the confluents of the Breu to the western edge of the basin of the Yuruá and (b) the basin of the upper Purús from the 11° S. parallel to Catay; (Article 4) the policing of the two neutral territories should be done by a mixed commis-

[15] José Manoel Cardoso de Oliveira, *Actos Dipl. do Brasil* (Rio de Janeiro, 1912), II, 246, 256.

[16] See §6, this chap., *supra.*

[17] See §9, this chap., *supra.*

[18] Moore, *Dig. Int. Law* (Washington, 1906), I, 647–648.

[19] José Manoel Cardoso de Oliveira, *Actos Dipl. do Brasil* (Rio de Janeiro, 1912), II, 324–325. 97 *British and Foreign State Papers* 689–691. *U. S. For. Rel.,* 1904, pp. 109–110. Arturo Pérez Figuerola, *Nuestra Cuestión de Límites con el Brasil* (Lima, 1905). John Bassett Moore, *Brazil and Peru Boundary Question* (New York, 1904).

[20] Time extended by agreements to May 31, 1905, to Sept. 30, 1907, to May 31, 1908, and finally to Sept. 30, 1909.

sion of a major or captain, a captain or lieutenant, and an escort of fifty men of each country; (Article 9) each government should also nominate a special commissioner for the upper Purús and one for the upper Yurúa, to form two other mixed commissions which should make a rapid reconnaissance of the two rivers in the neutral territories; and (Article 12) both governments declared that the agreement did not in any wise affect the territorial rights which each reserved. An arbitral tribunal of three to examine and resolve within one year all claims of Brazilian and Peruvian citizens for damages or violence suffered in the region since 1902 was provided for in a convention also signed at Rio de Janeiro on July 12, 1904.[21] Reports [22] of the survey mixed commissions, which left Manaos on March 24 and April 11, 1905, showed greater penetration of both the Yuruá and Purús into the mountain region (La Montaña) of Peru than had been theretofore known or expected. An agreement signed at Lima on April 15, 1908,[23] provided for free navigation of the Yapurá or Caquetá by vessels of both nations, subject to fiscal and police regulations.

The long controversy was settled, after the receipt of certain suggestions from the Pope, when Hernán Velarde, Peruvian minister, and the Baron of Rio Branco, Brazilian minister of foreign relations, signed at Rio de Janeiro on September 8, 1909,[24] a treaty of boundaries, commerce, and navigation which provided that (Article 1) the frontier already being marked, in execution of Article 7 of the treaty of October 23, 1851, from the source of the Javary to the Caquetá or Yapurá, the boundary should be established from such source of the Javary southward (Sec. 1) by the dividing line [25] of the waters which flow to the Ucayali from those which flow to the Yuruá as far as 9°24′36″ S., which is the parallel of the mouth of the Breu, an affluent on the right (east) bank of the Yuruá; (Sec. 2) thence eastward by that parallel to the confluence of the Breu and up by the bed of that river to its principal headwaters; (Sec. 3) thence southward by the line which divides

[21] 97 British and Foreign State Papers 692–693. U. S. For. Rel., 1904, p. 111. Anibal Maúrtua, Arbitraje Int. entre el Perú y el Brasil (Buenos Aires, 1907). Clunet, J. du dr. int. privé, XXXVII (1910), 1395.

[22] Informes de las Comisiones Mixtas; Lima, 1906.

[23] Coll. das Leis do Brazil de 1912 (Rio de Janeiro, 1915), I (Parte 2), 304–307. Actos Int. del Peru (Lima, 1916), Num. 83. 102 British and Foreign State Papers 912. Sanctioned by Brazil, Decree #2098, Sept. 4, 1909; ratified by Peru, Nov. 28, 1911; ratifications exchanged at Rio de Janeiro, Jan. 13, 1912; promulgated by Brazil, Decree #9391, Feb. 28, 1912.

[24] Coll. das Leis do Brazil, 1910 (Rio de Janeiro, 1913), I (Parte 2), 671–677. Actos Int. del Peru (Lima, 1916), Num. 88. 102 British and Foreign State Papers 199–202. Martens, Nouv. Rec. Gén. de Traités, 3° Sér., VI, 849–852.

O Tratado de 8 de set. de 1909 (Rio de Janeiro, 1910). Límites entre el Perú y el Brasil, Antecedentes del Tratado de 8 de set. de 1909 (Lima, 1909). Dunshee de Abranches, Limites com o Perú (Rio de Janeiro, 1910). Fernando Antonio Raja Gabaglia, As Fronteiras do Brasil (Rio de Janeiro, 1916), pp. 278–284. João Ribeiro, As Nossas Fronteiras (Rio de Janeiro, 1930), pp. 81–85. Juan Angulo Puente Arnao, Historia de los Límites del Perú (Lima, 1927), pp. 126–145. Amer. J. Int. Law, XXVII (1933), 287. Sanctioned by Brazil, Decree #2249, Apr. 29, 1910; ratified by Brazil, Apr. 29, 1910; ratified by Peru, Res. #1225, Jan. 15, 1910; ratifications exchanged at Rio de Janeiro, Apr. 30, 1910; promulgated by Brazil, Decree #7975, May 2, 1910.

[25] This includes the westernmost point of Brazil, at 7°12′85″ S. 73°59′32″ W.

the waters which flow westward to the upper Yuruá from those which flow
northward to the same river, and passing between the headwaters of the Tarahuacá and the Envira on the Brazilian side and of the Piqueyaco and the
Toroyuc on the Peruvian side, by the *divortium aquarum* between the Envira and the affluent on the left (northwest) bank of the Purús called Curanja
or Curumabá, whose basin should belong to Peru, to the source of the Santa
Rosa or Curinahá, also an affluent on the left (northwest) bank of the Purús; if
the headwaters of the Tarahuacá and the Envira should be south of the 10°
parallel the line should intersect those rivers following that parallel of 10°
and continue by the *divortium aquarum* between the Envira and the Curanja or Curumabá to the source of the Santa Rosa; (Sec. 4) thence down
by the bed of the Santa Rosa to its confluence on the left (northwest) bank
of the Purús; (Sec. 5) opposite the mouth of the Santa Rosa to the middle
of the deepest channel of the Purús, and thence southward up the thalweg of
the Purús to the confluence of the Chambuyaco, its affluent on the right
(southeast) bank between Catbi and the Santa Rosa; (Sec. 6) from the
mouth of the Chambuyaco up by the bed of that stream to its source;
(Sec. 7) from the source of the Chambuyaco southward on the meridian of
that source to the left (north) bank of the Acre or Aquiry or, if the source
of that river should be further east, to the 11° parallel; (Sec. 8) if such
meridian of the source of the Chambuyaco crosses the Acre, the frontier
should continue from the point of intersection by the bed of the Acre down
to the point where the Peru-Bolivia frontier begins on the right (south) bank
of the Acre; (Sec. 9) if the meridian of the source of the Chambuyaco does
not cross the Acre, that is to say, if the source of the Acre is east of that meridian, the frontier should continue from the intersection of that meridian with
the 11° parallel by the most pronounced natural features of the land or by a
straight line, as might seem more suitable to the demarcation commissioners
of both countries, to the source of the Acre and thence down the bed of the
Acre to the point where the Peru-Bolivia frontier begins on the right (south)
bank of the Acre; (Article 2) a mixed commission named by the two governments within one year from the exchange of ratifications should proceed within
six months to the demarcation of the frontier lines thus described; (Article 3)
disagreements between the commissioners which cannot be amicably settled by
the two governments should be submitted to the arbitral decision of three
members of the Academy of Sciences of the Institute of France or of the Royal
Geographical Society of London, chosen by the president of such institutions;
(Article 4) if the demarcation commissioners of either country failed to meet,
except by reason of *force majeure,* at the time and place designated the com-

missioners of the other party should proceed alone to the demarcation and the result of their operations should be obligatory on both countries; (Article 5) the parties would conclude within twelve months a treaty of commerce and navigation based on the principle of the fullest liberty forever of land transit and river navigation for both nations on all the course of the rivers which rise or flow within the bounds of the region crossed by the frontier line as described in Article 1, subject to uniform fiscal and police regulations; and Peruvian river vessels should communicate freely with the ocean by the Amazon; (Article 6) each country might maintain customs agents in specified frontier posts of the other; (Article 7) disagreements in the interpretation or execution of the treaty to be submitted to arbitration. By this treaty, of the 170,600 square miles in controversy, 155,600 square miles became Brazilian and 15,000 square miles remained with Peru. A protocol signed at Rio de Janeiro on April 19, 1913,[26] (in substitution for one of April 29, 1912) agreed on the organization of and instructions for the demarcation mixed commission.

As early as 1874[27] there was talk of a railroad across the Andes to connect the coast with the Brazilian frontier; but although a railroad is in operation from Lima over the cordillera 129 miles to Oroya, connecting there with the Cerro de Pasco line, there is yet only an automobile road from Oroya ninety-two miles down the eastern slope via Tarma to the Perené colony, and it is 350 miles thence by canoe down the Perené, the Tambo, and the Ucayali to the head of navigation near Pucalpa on the lower Ucayali; which is still fifty miles by land from the Brazilian frontier in the westernmost Acre territory and 750 miles by water to Tabatinga and the frontier on the Amazon. There is airplane service to Iquitos on the Amazon.

Complete early ignorance of the course and source of one river and the uppermost extent of the basins of two others, as relied on in early conventions, in a region of scant population and economic desertion gave rise to a dispute finally terminated by treaty. This boundary has been agreed upon and marked for its whole length, and may accordingly be supposed to be now permanently settled.

14. BRAZIL–URUGUAY. YAGUARÓN

As soon as the Treaty of Madrid was ratified, in February 1750, Portuguese troops swept westward across the fine pastures of western Rio Grande do Sul, removing from the Ibicuhy region the Jesuits and driving off or mas-

[26] *Actos Int. del Peru* (Lima, 1916), Num. 109. *Arch. Dipl.*, CXXX, 380, 381. Approved by Peru, June 24, 1913.   [27] *U. S. For. Rel.*, 1874, 91–92.

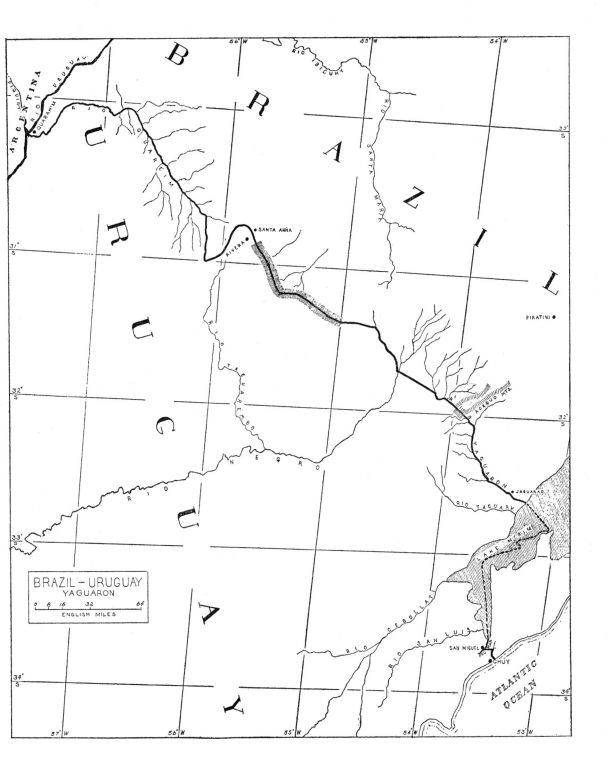

BRAZIL – URUGUAY
YAGUARON
0 8 16   32   64
ENGLISH MILES

sacring the unprepared Indians, who resisted as desperately as they could. When the treaty was annulled, in 1761, the Portuguese were confirmed in their retention of Colonia, which on the advice of the Marquis de Pombal they had never given up, and they withdrew from their formal claim to the Ibicuhy territory. The military operations they had so promptly undertaken, however, had nearly eradicated Spanish influence east of the upper Uruguay and it was never successfully reëstablished.

By the Treaty of San Ildefonso of October 1, 1777,[1] the southern end of the line between the Spanish and Portuguese possessions ran from the Atlantic[2] at Chuy creek and San Miguel Fort near the south end of Lake Mirim, which remained all Portuguese, around the west shore of that lake and across to the sources of the Negro, then northward, leaving all the rivers emptying into the Plata and the Uruguay and the Piratini and the Ibimini to the west Spanish, and Lagõa dos Patos, the Grande de San Pedro, the Yacuy, Tahim creek, Lake Manguera, San Gonzalo Fort, the Ararica, and the Coyacuy to the east Portuguese, to the Uruguay where the Piquiry or Pepiri-guazú enters it on the west (north) bank. In 1801 Portugal seized the Ibicuhy (Seven Missions) region from the Spaniards and conquered and retained it permanently; though the guerrilla chief José Gervasio Artigas from Argentina invaded the district in 1815 he was defeated and driven out in 1816. The northern boundary of the Cisplatine province as annexed to Brazil[3] was to be the Quarahim up to the ridge of Santa Anna, at the junction of the Santa Maria, and the Tacuarembo, the Yaguarón, Lake Mirim, San Miguel, and Chuy to the ocean.

General Sebastião Barreto for Brazil and General Fructuoso Rivera for Uruguay signed at Irebeasubá on December 25, 1828,[4] a convention which provided that the Quarahim should be the provisional boundary line until the two interested governments should settle the pending questions. This tentatively carried the limit of Uruguay's claim on the west some 300 miles south.

Among other treaties between Brazil and Uruguay of the same date there was signed at Rio de Janeiro, October 12, 1851,[5] a boundary treaty in which

[1] Articles 3 and 4. See §2, this chap., *supra.*
[2] Melitón González, *El Límite Oriental del Territorio de Misiones* (Montevideo, 1883), I, 185-322.
[3] Convention of July 31, 1921, between president and fifteen deputies at Montevideo and Baron de Laguna, representing John VI. Antonio Pereira Pinto, *Apontamentos para o Direito Int.* (Rio de Janeiro, 1864), I, 273-286. 8 *British and Foreign State Papers* 1017-1020, 1027-1030; 10 *ibid.,* 1012-1013.
[4] *O Tratado de 30 de outubro de 1909 entre os E. U. do Brasil e a Republica Oriental do Uruguay* (Rio de Janeiro, 1910), p. 12.
[5] *Annexo ao Relatorio do Min. das Rel. Ext.* (Rio de Janeiro, 1900), Parte II, pp. 270-274. *Col. de Trat. del Uruguay* (Montevideo, 1923), I, 215-220, 233-239. 40 *British and Foreign State Papers* 1151-1154. Martens et Cussy, *Rec. Man. et Prat. de Traités,* VI, 609-610. Pedro S. Lamas, *Nuestros Derechos Territoriales* (Buenos Aires, 1912). Ratified by Brazil, Oct. 13, 1851; ratified by Uruguay, Nov. 4, 1851; ratifications exchanged at Montevideo, Nov. 11, 1851.

the parties agreed (Article 1) to consider as abrogated and of no effect the several treaties and acts on which were founded the territorial rights on which they had up to that time relied in the demarcation of their boundaries, especially those rights which Brazil derived from the convention concluded at Montevideo, January 30, 1819,[6] and those which Uruguay derived from the reservation [7] at the end of Clause 2 of the treaty of incorporation of July 31, 1821; [8] (Article 2) to recognize as the basis for regulation of their boundaries the *uti possidetis* as set forth in such Clause 2; to wit, on the east the ocean, on the south the Plata, on the west the Uruguay, on the north the Quarahim as far as the Santa Anna ridge which divides the Santa Maria from the Tacuarembo Grande, and along the points of the Yaguarón, across Lake Mirim and by San Miguel to the Chuy, which empties into the ocean; (Article 3) in view of the insufficiency of the general terms of this description to determine fully the dividing line, to rectify such line to run (Sec. 1) from the mouth of the Chuy at the ocean up the Chuy for half a league, thence by a straight line passing south of Fort San Miguel and crossing the San Miguel river to the sources of the Palmar; thence by that river to the stream which the map of the Viscount of São Leopoldo calls the San Luis and the map of Colonel José Maria Reyes the India Muerta; thence to Lake Mirim and by the western shore of that lake to the mouth of the Yaguarón; (Sec. 2) thence by the right (south) bank of that river, following southward the branch which has its source in the valley of Acegua and the mountains of the same name; thence by a straight line crossing the Negro opposite the mouth of the San Luis and the San Luis to the Santa Anna ridge and the Haedo ridge at the source of the branch of the Quarahim called the Invernada on the map of the Viscount of São Leopoldo and without a name on the map of Colonel Reyes; and thence by such branch to the Uruguay, Brazil remaining owner of the island or islands in the mouth of the Quarahim in the Uruguay; (Article 4) Brazil, in exclusive possession of the navigation of Lake Mirim and the Yaguarón, to remain so according to the adopted basis of the *uti possidetis,* and Uruguay to cede to Brazil in complete sovereignty for ports on that lake half a league of land on one of the banks of the Sebolati which should be designated by the Brazilian commissioner, and another half league on one of the banks of the Tacuary selected in the same way, Brazil to be

[6] Antonio Pereira Pinto, *Apontamentos para o Direito Int.* (Rio de Janeiro, 1864), I, 251–267.

[7] Convention for the Incorporation of the Eastern Province of the Plata with the United Kingdom of Portugal, Brazil, and Algarve, signed at Montevideo: (translation) "without prejudice to the declaration which the Sovereign National Congress (of Brazil), our (Uruguay's) deputies being heard, shall make concerning the claims of this State (Uruguay) to the plains that are comprehended in the last demarcation made during the government of Spain." 8 *British and Foreign State Papers* 1027–1030.

[8] See n. 3, *supra.*

free to erect on such lands the works and fortifications which she thinks desirable; and (Article 5) to appoint one commissioner each, by common agreement, to proceed as soon as possible to the demarcation of the boundary line at the points where it may be necessary. In the treaty of commerce and navigation of October 12, 1851,[9] the parties agreed (Article 14) in principle upon declaring common the navigation of the Uruguay and the affluents of that river which belonged to them; (Article 15) to invite the other states bordering on the Plata and its affluents to join in a similar agreement to make navigation of the Paraná and the Paraguay free for all of them; (Article 18) to oppose by all means that the island of Martín García should cease to belong to one of the states of the Plata interested in its free navigation; and (Article 19) to destroy the reef of Salto Grande that impeded the free navigation of the Uruguay. A supplementary boundary treaty signed at Montevideo May 15, 1852,[10] provided that (Article 1) the boundary treaty of October 12, 1851, Article 3, Sec. 1, should be changed to run from the mouth of the Chuy at the ocean up the Chuy, thence by the point of San Miguel to Lake Mirim and along the western shore of Lake Mirim to the mouth of the Yaguarón, according to the *uti possidetis;* and (Article 2) the emperor gave up his right to the concession in Article 4 of two half-leagues of land.

By a protocol signed at Montevideo, April 22, 1853,[11] it was agreed that the dividing line agreed upon by the treaty of May 15, 1852, should be understood to run from the mouth of the Chuy at the ocean up the Chuy to its main defile, thence by a straight line to the main defile of the San Miguel stream; down that stream by its right (east) bank to the point of San Miguel on the south shore of Lake Mirim, and thence by the west shore of that lake to the mouth of the Yaguarón. In the treaty of commerce and navigation signed at Rio de Janeiro, September 4, 1857,[12] it was agreed (Article 17) that, in connection with the execution of the Treaty of October 12, 1851, Article 19, concerning the reef of the Great Cataract of the Uruguay, if the means indicated for destroying or avoiding that cataract should be considered impossible or very expensive in execution, they might be changed to a road

[9] Antonio Pereira Pinto, *Apontamentos para o Direito Int.* (Rio de Janeiro, 1866), III, 315-325. *Col. de Trat. del Uruguay* (Montevideo, 1923), I, 195-205. 40 *British and Foreign State Papers* 1145-1150. Martens et Cussy, *Rec. Man. et Prat. de Traités,* VI, 611-615. Ratifications exchanged at Montevideo, Nov. 11, 1851.

[10] *Annexo ao Relatorio do Min. das Rel. Ext.* (Rio de Janeiro, 1900), Parte II, pp. 274-275. *Col. de Trat. del Uruguay* (Montevideo, 1923), I, 241-246. 42 *British and Foreign State Papers* 1265-1267. Martens et Cussy, *Rec. Man. et Prat. de Traités,* VII, 57-59. Guaranteed by

Argentine Confederation, May 19, 1852; ratified by Brazil, June 10, 1852; ratified by Uruguay, July 5, 1852; ratifications exchanged at Rio de Janeiro, July 13, 1852.

[11] *Annexo ao Relatorio do Min. das Rel. Ext.* (Rio de Janeiro, 1900), Parte II, p. 276. Approved by Brazil, May 5, 1853; approved by Uruguay, Apr. 29, 1853.

[12] *Col. de Trat. del Uruguay* (Montevideo, 1923), I, 399-412. 49 *British and Foreign State Papers* 1215-1221. Ratifications exchanged at Rio de Janeiro, Sept. 23, 1858; denounced by Brazil to take effect, Jan. 1, 1861.

to unite in the best possible manner the navigable parts of the river separated by the reef, to be constructed by the company or individual offering
the best terms after public competition.

A treaty signed at Rio de Janeiro on September 4, 1857,[13] providing for
the cession by Uruguay to Brazil of an area around the outskirts of the Brazilian town of Santa Anna do Livramento sufficient to avoid division of private properties and conflicts and complications, and by Brazil to Uruguay
of an equal area of similar value and conditions at another point on the frontier, failed of ratification. The demarcation proceeded from November 1852
to March 1859. Brazil joined the Argentine Confederation in making with
Uruguay at Rio de Janeiro on January 2, 1859,[14] a treaty of alliance, but
it was not ratified by any of the party nations. By the Treaty of October
12, 1851, with the subsequent minor modifications of portions of the line, her
diplomats secured for Brazil a part of the desirable Misiones territory which
she had occupied after the Treaty of 1777 had acknowledged it to belong to
Spain, and gave Brazil exclusive rights of navigation on Lake Mirim and the
Yaguarón.

Rebels and political refugees have always made trouble across the artifi-
cial land border. On November 2, 1903,[15] the Brazilian Colonel Ataliva J.
Gomez, mayor of Santa Anna do Livramento in the state of Rio Grande do
Sul, attacked with detachments of regular army infantry and cavalry the
Uruguayan town of Rivera, in the province of the same name, separated from
Santa Anna only by a public highway, to effect the release of his brother,
Gentil Gomez, who had been imprisoned by the police judge of Rivera, but
was repulsed with a few casualties by a company of Uruguayan gendarmes;
and Brazil promptly removed him from command and appeased Uruguay.

Rufino T. Domínguez, Uruguayan minister, and the Baron of Rio Branco,
Brazilian minister of foreign relations, signed at Rio de Janeiro on October
30, 1909,[16] a treaty by which (Article 1) Brazil ceded to Uruguay (Sec. 1)
from the mouth of the San Miguel stream to the mouth of the Yaguarón,

[13] Col. de Trat. del Uruguay (Montevideo, 1922), I,
413–416.

[14] See §5, this chap., supra.

[15] Estanislao S. Zeballos, Bull. Arg. de Dr. Int. Privé
(Buenos Aires, 1903), 1e Année, 194–196.

[16] Coll. das Leis do Brasil de 1910, I (Parte 2), 692–
699. Col. de Trat. del Uruguay (Montevideo, 1928), V,
451–458. Comp. de Leyes del Uruguay (Montevideo,
1930), XXIX, 361–365. 102 British and Foreign State
Papers 204–207. Martens, Nouv. Rec. Gén. de Traités,
3e Sér., VI, 858–865. O Tratado de 30 de outubro de
1909 (Rio de Janeiro, 1910). Pinto da Rocha, O Tratado

de Condominio (Porto Alegre, 1910). Fernando Antonio
Raja Gabaglia, As Fronteiras do Brasil (Rio de Janeiro,
1916), pp. 252–256. João Bibeiro, As nossas Fronteiras
(Rio de Janeiro, 1930), pp. 27–32. Rec. des Cours, VIII
(1925), 300–306; ibid., XXXII (1930), 774. Sanctioned
by Brazil, Decree #2246, Apr. 26, 1910; ratified by Brazil,
Apr. 27, 1910; ratified by Uruguayan Legislature, Law
#3577, Nov. 13, 1909; ratified by Uruguayan Executive,
Apr. 27, 1910; ratifications exchanged at Rio de Janeiro,
May 7, 1910; promulgated by Brazil, Decree #7992, May
11, 1910.

that part of Lake Mirim included between its western shore and the new frontier which should cross longitudinally the waters of the lake according to the terms of Article 3 below, and (Sec. 2) in the Yaguarón the part of the bed included between the right or south bank and the dividing line determined in Article 4 below; and the parties agreed that (Article 2) the cession of the rights of sovereignty by Brazil based originally on the possession which she acquired and maintained since 1801 of the waters and navigation of Lake Mirim and the Yaguarón, and afterwards established and solemnly confirmed in the pacts of 1851, 1852, and 1853, should be made under the conditions, which Uruguay accepted, that (Sec. 1) subject to later agreement only Brazilian and Uruguayan vessels might navigate and trade in the waters of the Yaguarón and of Lake Mirim; (Sec. 2) Uruguay should maintain and respect, according to the principles of civil law, real property rights acquired by Brazilians or foreigners in the islands and islets which as the result of the new determination of the frontier should cease to belong to Brazil, and (Sec. 3) neither of the parties should establish forts or batteries on the shores of the lake, the banks of the Yaguarón, or on any of the islands which belong to them in those waters; (Article 3) from the mouth of the San Miguel stream, at the fourth Great Mark, placed there by the demarcation commission of 1853, the new frontier should cross longitudinally Lake Mirim to the crest of Rabotieso point on the Uruguayan shore, by a broken line composed of as many straight lines as necessary to preserve the median distance between the principal points on the two shores or, if the depth should be scanty, of as many straight lines as necessary to follow the principal channel of the lake; from the crest of Rabotieso point to the northwest as far as necessary to pass between the Tacuary islands, leaving on the Brazilian side the easternmost island and the two islets adjoining it; thence in the neighborhood of point Parobé, also on the Uruguayan shore, to the deepest channel and by such channel to opposite point Muniz, on the Uruguayan shore, and point of Los Latinos or Fanfa on the Brazilian shore; from that intermediate point, passing between point Muniz and the Brazilian island of Juncal to the mouth of the Yaguarón, where on the left or Brazilian shore is the fifth Great Mark of 1853 and on the right or Uruguayan shore the sixth intermediate mark; (Article 4) from the mouth of the Yaguarón the frontier should go up by the thalweg of that river to the confluence of the Lagoões stream on the left (north) bank; thence up the middle line between the banks of the Yaguarón and the middle line of the Yaguarón Chico or the Guaviyú, at the confluence of which is the sixth Great Mark of 1853, and finally up the bed of the Mina stream, indicated by the seventh and eighth intermediate marks; (Article 5) a mixed commission to be named by the two governments within one year from the exchange of ratifications should draw up a plan of that part of Lake Mirim south of the point of Juncal and also of the Yaguarón from its mouth to the Lagoões stream, making the necessary soundings and indispensable topographic and geodesic operations for the determination of the new frontier and marking it by buoys in the lake in the most suitable way; (Article 6) navigation in Lake Mirim and the Yaguarón should be free for merchant vessels of both nations, and for Uruguayan vessels there should be free transit also between the ocean and Lake Mirim by the Brazilian waters of the San Gonzalo, Lake of Los Patos, and the bar of the Grande de San Pedro, all subject to fiscal and police regulations, and not to communicate with the land of the other country except in case of *force majeure* or special license, other than at places where there were customs houses or fiscal and police offices; and (Article 9) Uruguayan war vessels might pass freely in Brazilian waters between the ocean and Lake Mirim and navigate like those of Brazil the Yaguarón and the lake or be stationed in their waters; but except in extraordinary circumstances, with advance notice to the other country, the parties undertook not to maintain in Lake Mirim and its affluents more than three small vessels of war or vessels armed for war, whose size, armament, and equipment should be the subject of special arrangement. By an almost unprecedented act of diplomatic generosity, Brazil thus spontaneously shared with Uruguay the navigation of Lake Mirim and the Yaguarón, which she had held exclusively since 1851.

Instructions for the demarcation mixed commission were agreed upon at Rio de Janeiro, January 17, 1913.[17] The line was further slightly modified by a convention signed at Rio de Janeiro, May 7, 1913,[18] providing that (Article 1) the frontier should run from the main defile of the San Miguel stream to its mouth in Lake Mirim by the middle line between the banks of such stream, in the same manner as that established for the division of the Yaguarón from the Lagoões stream to the confluence of the Mina stream, the two countries meanwhile to exercise jurisdiction in common in the waters of the San Miguel stream in this section; (Article 2) neither country to establish in time of peace fortifications upon the banks of the San Miguel stream; and (Article 3) marks to be erected in the main defile of the San Miguel. A convention

[17] *Col. de Trat. del Uruguay* (Montevideo, 1928), V, 761–766.

[18] *Ibid.*, pp. 767–769. 107 *British and Foreign State Papers* 610–611. Martens, *Nouv. Rec. Gén. de Traités*, 3ᵉ Sér., XX (1929), 511–512. Sanctioned by Brazil, Decree #2812, Oct. 23, 1913; ratified by Brazil, Mar. 25, 1914; ratified by Uruguay, May 12, 1914; ratifications exchanged at Rio de Janeiro, Aug. 12, 1914; promulgated by Brazil, Decree #11087, Aug. 19, 1914.

for better demarcation of the frontier was signed at Rio de Janeiro, December 27, 1916.[19] Instructions for the mixed commission created pursuant to this convention were agreed upon at Rio de Janeiro, September 2, 1919,[20] and the commission met at Rio Branco on January 10, 1920, and set about the demarcation.[21]

In connection with the adjustment of the debt owed by Uruguay to Brazil a treaty was signed at Rio de Janeiro, July 22, 1918,[22] which included (Articles 9–14) provisions for the construction by Uruguay and use free, except to trains, of an international foot, highway, and railroad bridge over the Yaguarón a little west of Lake Mirim from the Brazilian town of Yaguarón to or near the Uruguayan town of Rio Branco; and an accord by notes exchanged at Montevideo, November 17, 1926,[23] abolished the mixed commission and provided for the construction of the bridge by E. Kemnitz & Cia. under the supervision of the Uruguayan ministry of public works.

A claim based on occupation, disregarding the San Ildefonso line, was early pressed by the larger nation into a treaty, and later modified by voluntary grant of a condominium over locally important bodies of water at the ocean end of the line. This boundary as adjusted in detail by the successive treaties appears to be stable and may be considered definitely settled.

15. BRAZIL–VENEZUELA. AMAZONAS

The Treaty of San Ildefonso of October 1, 1777,[1] ran the northern part of the boundary between the Spanish and Portuguese possessions up the Yapura far enough to include the Portuguese establishments on its banks and those of the Negro and on the channel between them, and thence by the mountains which form the divide between the Orinoco and the Amazon, directing the line wherever possible to the north. Negotiations for demarcation of the line between Brazil and Venezuela began in 1843, and a treaty of friendship and boundaries was signed at Caracas, November 25, 1852,[2] in which (Article 2) the parties agreed upon and recognized as a basis for the determination of

[19] *Coll. das Leis do Brazil de 1919*, III, 2–6. Hildebrando Accioly, *Actos Int. Vig. no Brasil* (Rio de Janeiro, 1927), p. 259. *Bol. del Min. de Rel. Ext.* (Montevideo), V (1917), 130–134. Sanctioned by Brazil, Decree #3442, Dec. 27, 1917; ratified by Brazil, June 25, 1919; ratified by Uruguay, Law #6105, July 11, 1918; ratifications exchanged at Rio de Janeiro, June 26, 1919; promulgated by Brazil, Decree #13673, July 2, 1919.

[20] Hildebrando Accioly, *Actos Int. Vig. no Brasil* (Rio de Janeiro, 1927), p. 340. *Bol. del Min. de Rel. Ext.* (Montevideo), VII (1919), 958–963.

[21] Appropriation: Legislative Decree #3773, Executive Decree #13776, Sept. 27, 1919.

[22] *Coll. das Leis do Brasil de 1919*, II, 598–609. *Comp. de Leyes y Decr. del Uruguay* (Montevideo, 1930), XLIII, 193–199. *Bol. del Min. de Rel. Ext.* (Montevideo), VI, (1918), 1079–1102, 1239–1240. Sanctioned by Brazil, Decree #3620, Dec. 23, 1918; ratified by Uruguay, Dec. 12, 1918; ratifications exchanged at Rio de Janeiro, June 21, 1919; promulgated by Brazil, Decree #13658, June 25, 1919.

[23] *Relatorio do Min. das Rel. Ext. de 1926* (Rio de Janeiro, 1927), pp. 46–47, Annexo A, pp. 103–106.

[1] Article 12. See §2, this chap., *supra*.
[2] 49 *British and Foreign State Papers* 1213–1215.

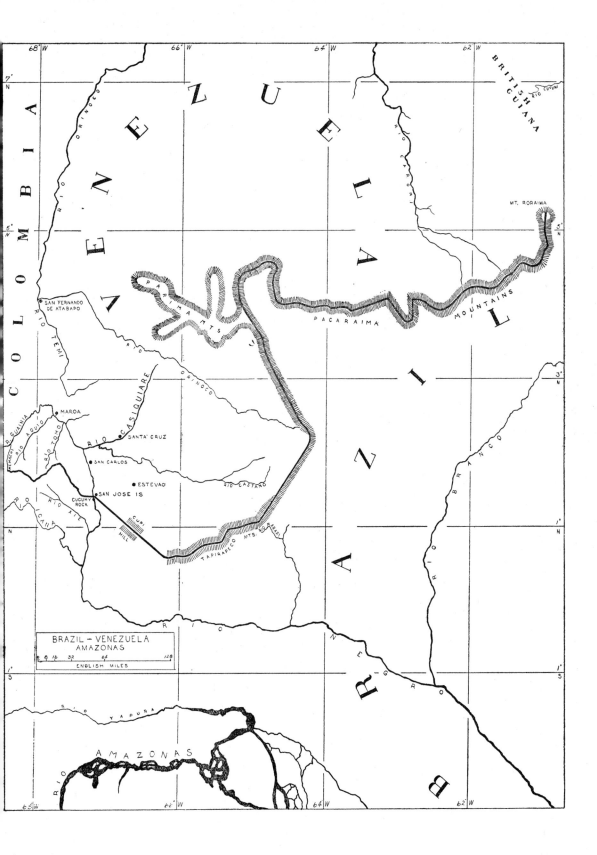

BRAZIL – VENEZUELA
AMAZONAS

0 8 16 32 64 128

ENGLISH MILES

the frontier between their respective territories the *uti possidetis,* and in conformity with that principle they declared and defined the boundaries to be (Sec. 1) from the sources of the Memachi by the highest ground past the sources of the Aquio and the Tomó, as well as those of the Guaicia and the Iquiare or Içana, so that all the streams which flow into the Aquio and the Tomó remained to Venezuela, while those which flow into the Guaicia, the Xié, and the Içana belonged to Brazil; thence across the Negro opposite the island of San José adjoining Cucuhy rock; (Sec. 2) from the island of San José in a straight line to cut the Maturaca channel at mid-water or such other point as the boundary commissioners might agree upon and which might conveniently divide that stream; thence by the group of high lands of Cupi, Imeri, Guay, and Urucusiro across the overland carry from the Castaño to the Marari; thence by Tapirapeco ridge to the crests of the Parima ridge, so that the waters which flow into the Padaviri, Marari, and Cababuri remained to Brazil, and those which flow into the Turuaca or Idapa or Xiaba belonged to Venezuela; (Sec. 3) thence along the crest of the Parima ridge as far as the angle made by that ridge with the Pacaraima ridge, so that all the streams which run into the Branco remained to Brazil and those which flow into the Orinoco belonged to Venezuela; thence along the highest summits of the Pacaraima ridge, so that the waters which flow into the Branco belonged as stated to Brazil and those which flow into the Essequibo, Cuyuní, and Caroní belonged to Venezuela, as far as the territories of the two states extend eastward; (Article 3) after ratification of this treaty each party should appoint a commissioner, and they in concert as soon as possible should proceed to demarcation of the line at such points as might be necessary; (Article 4) any doubts which occur to be amicably settled by both governments; (Article 5) any exchange of territory deemed advisable for fixing more natural or suitable boundaries for either nation to be arranged by new negotiations; and (Article 6) Brazil declared that in treating with Venezuela in regard to the territory situated west of the Negro drained by the Tomó and the Aquio, which though asserted by Venezuela to belong to her was nevertheless claimed by New Granada, it was not Brazil's intention to prejudice whatever rights New Granada might succeed in establishing over such territory. This treaty failed of ratification by Venezuela, but a new boundary and navigation treaty signed at Caracas, May 5, 1859,[3] omitting the declaration as to the *uti possidetis*

[3] *Coll. das Leis do Brasil de 1861,* XXII, Parte I, 44–50. José Manoel Cardoso de Oliveira, *Actos Dipl. do Brasil* (Rio de Janeiro, 1912), I, 265–266. *Annexo ao Relatorio do Min. das Rel. Ext.* (Rio de Janeiro, 1900),

Parte II, pp. 302, 306. *Recop. de Leyes,* Ed. Ofic. (Caracas, 1874), III, 721–724. *Col. de Trat. Pub. de Ven.,* Ed. Ofic. (Caracas, 1910), pp. 144–148, 343–345. 50 *British and Foreign State Papers* 1164–1169. Martens, *Nouv. Rec. Gén.*

basis, established (Article 2) the boundary in the same terms (Secs. 1, 2, and 3) as in the Treaty of November 25, 1852; agreed in the same way (Article 3) on a mixed commission for demarcation of the boundary, (Article 4) the amicable settlement of doubts, and (Article 5) possible exchange of territory, and made the same declaration as to rights claimed by New Granada west of the Negro; and provided further (Article 8) for free navigation by Brazilian vessels in the Negro, Guainia, Casiquiare, and Orinoco and by Venezuelan vessels in the Negro, Guainia, and Amazon, and to and from the ocean, subject to fiscal and police regulations, (Article 21) free from taxes except for lighthouses, buoys, and other aids to navigation. The boundary thus agreed upon from the principal source of the Memachi to opposite the island of San José was marked by the mixed commission which worked from January 7 to August 9, 1880,[4] and the Cupi high lands were surveyed by the Brazilian commission alone from 1882 to May 10, 1883. The first mixed commission before separating in 1880 erected in the center of the plaza of Maroa, on the left (northeast) bank of the Guainia, capital of the Centro department of Amazonas territory, Venezuela, a monument to commemorate the unalterable harmony which prevailed in the commission during its labors. Neither commission reached the Parima or Pacaraima high lands, but the positions of the mountain crests were guessed at. The Spanish award of March 16, 1891,[5] in the arbitration between Colombia and Venezuela fixed the southern end of the line between them at such point that Brazil's neighbor from the source of the Memachi to Cucuhy rock was no longer Venezuela but Colombia, and with her Brazil settled this portion of the frontier by the treaty of April 24, 1907.[6]

Alejandro Ibarra, Venezuelan minister of foreign relations, and Manoel de Oliveira Lima, Brazilian minister, signed at Caracas on December 9, 1905,[7] two protocols, of which the first approved and recognized the demarcation made in common in 1880 by the mixed commission of the frontier from Cucuhy rock to Cupi hill, and the second agreed (Article 1) that a mixed commission should verify the work of the Brazilian commission in 1882 to 1884

de Traités, XVII (Partie 2), 161-167. Arch. Dipl., 1861, IV, 161-167. Documentos Relativos a la Cuestión de Límites (Caracas, 1859). Dictamen del Consejo de Gobierno, 1844 (Caracas, 1860). Informe de la H. Comisión de Rel. Ext. del Senado (Caracas, 1860). Memoria . . . al Proximo Congreso (Caracas, 1860). Ratified by Brazil, Sept. 6, 1859; ratified by Venezuela, July 9, 1860; ratifications exchanged at Caracas, July 31, 1860; promulgated by Brazil, Decree #2726, Jan. 12, 1861.

4 Trat. Pub. de Venezuela, Ed. Conmem. (Caracas, 1927), III, 341-355.

5 See §22A, this chap., infra.

6 See §10, this chap., supra.

7 Coll. das Leis do Brazil de 1914, III, 282-284. Trat. Pub. de Venezuela (Caracas, 1925), II, 53-54. 106 British and Foreign State Papers 907-908. Martens, Nouv. Rec. Gén. de Traités, 3e Sér., IX, 763-764. Sanctioned by Brazil, Decree #1768, Nov. 6, 1907; ratified by Brazil, July 23, 1913; ratified by Venezuelan Legislature, July 22, 1907; ratified by Venezuelan Executive, July 25, 1914; ratifications exchanged at Caracas, July 28, 1914; promulgated by Brazil, Decree #11042, Aug. 5, 1914.

on the frontier from Cupi hill to the point on Mount Roraima where the three frontiers of Brazil, Venezuela, and British Guiana meet, preferential attention always being given to the division of the waters which run towards the basins of the Amazon, Orinoco, and Essequibo, respectively, and make the demarcation in accordance with the treaty of May 5, 1859, Article 2, Secs. 2 and 3; (Article 2) the two commissions to be appointed within three months and begin work within six months after ratification of the protocol by both governments. Before the exchange of ratifications and coming into effect of these protocols it was established that neither country had an exact knowledge of the true direction of the Cucuhy part of the frontier as marked in 1880, and it was agreed by a protocol signed at Caracas, February 29, 1912,[8] that each government should appoint a commissioner and sub-commissioner with the necessary assistants, and the mixed commission so constituted should erect durable posts on the left (east) bank of the Negro at the point (opposite the island of San José, at 1°13'51.76" N. 66°47'11.51" W. on the west bank) crossed by the line as indicated by the records of the Commission of 1880 and along the geodesic line from that point 52.54 miles to the Huá rapid in the Maturacá, at 0°45'3.37" N. 66°11'43.50" W.; the commissioners to meet at Manaos not later than April 15, 1912, and go up the Negro together. This mixed commission began work in 1914 and finished on January 23, 1915.[9]

Octavio Mangabeira, Brazilian minister of foreign relations, and José Abel Montilla, Venezuelan minister, signed at Rio de Janeiro on July 24, 1928,[10] a protocol reciting that the periods specified in the second protocol of December 9, 1905 (Article 2) had expired without the commissions having been constituted or the periods having been extended, and that the demarcations made in 1879–1880 and in 1914–1915 by mixed commissions should be completed, from the island of San José to the point on Mount Roraima where the frontiers of Brazil, Venezuela, and British Guiana meet, and agreeing to replace the second protocol of December 9, 1905, by provisions that (Article 1) each government should nominate a commission with the necessary staff to form a mixed commission to carry out the demarcation under instructions to be laid down in an exchange of notes; (Article 2) within three months the two commissions should meet at San Carlos on the Negro and

[8] *Limites do Brasil, Min. das Rel. Ext.*, 1913 (Rio de Janeiro, 1918), pp. 413–416. *Trat. Pub. de Venezuela* (Caracas, 1925), II, 474–476. 105 *British and Foreign State Papers* 938–940. *Arch. Dipl.*, 4e Sér., CXXX, 379, 380–381. Fernando Antonio Raja Gabaglia, *As Fronteiras do Brasil* (Rio de Janeiro, 1916), pp. 287–289.

[9] *Libro Amarillo de Venezuela* (Caracas, 1913), pp. xxi–xxii, 172–195.

[10] *Coll. das Leis do Brasil de 1929*, IV, 10–14. *Bol.*

del Min. de Rel. Ext. de Venezuela (Caracas, 1929), V, 311–317. *Libro Amarillo de Venezuela* (Caracas, 1929), pp. 56–59. 130 *British and Foreign State Papers* 447–449. João Ribeiro, *As Nossas Fronteiras* (Rio de Janeiro, 1930), pp. 111–115. Approved by Brazil, Decree #5664, Jan. 12, 1929; ratified by Venezuelan Legislature, May 31, 1929; ratified by Venezuelan Executive, June 24, 1929; ratifications exchanged at Rio de Janeiro, Aug. 31, 1929; promulgated by Brazil, Decree #18905, Sept. 17, 1929.

proceed together to the frontier; if either should fail, except for *force majeure,* the other should proceed by itself with the work, the result of its operations to be binding on both countries; (Article 3) the frontier described in the treaty of May 5, 1859 (Secs. 2 and 3) should be examined in detail by the mixed commission, the coördinates of positions established by the previous commissions to be verified and if necessary corrected; (Article 4) as many marks as appear necessary to be erected along the entire frontier; (Article 5) the two marks set up by the mixed commission of 1914–1915 near Cucuhy rock and the other two near the Huá gap should be considered permanent, though their latitude and longitude might be determined anew; and (Article 6) the boundary between the Huá gap and the Negro should run from such gap in a straight line in the direction indicated by the commission of 1914–1915 to a point at a distance from such gap equal to the distance between the island of San José and the most easterly of the marks erected by that commission on the Cucuhy side; thence in another straight line to such most easterly mark and thence also in a straight line in the direction of the mark opposite the island of San José to the right (west) bank of the Negro until it intersects the frontier between Venezuela and Colombia. An exchange of notes at Caracas, November 7, 1929,[11] established instructions for the mixed commission to meet at San Carlos on the Negro between December 10 and 20, 1929; at once to fix the position of Cupi hill; doubtful points or disagreements to be submitted to the two Governments, which should make every effort to settle them rapidly and amicably. The Brazilian commission left Rio de Janeiro, October 10, 1929, and reached Manaos, October 27, Cucuhy, November 30, and San Carlos, December 1, but the Venezuelan commission failed to arrive, and the Brazilians returned in January 1930 [12] after examining some of the marks placed by the previous commissions.

In September 1931 [13] reported discovery on July 14, 1931, from George G. Heye peak in the Parima range by Herbert Spencer Dickey, an explorer who left New York on April 1, of the source of the Orinoco some sixty miles northwest of where it was placed on current maps, with the supposed result of transferring a considerable parcel of territory from Venezuela to Brazil, was declared by Venezuela to have no juridical effect upon the frontier with Brazil until verified by the demarcation mixed commission.

Uncontested possession by each country of the mouths and most of the

[11] *Rel. do Min. das Rel. Ext.*, 1929 (Rio de Janeiro, 1930), Annexo A, pp. 15–19. *Bol. del Min. de Rel. Ext. de Venezuela,* V (1929), 317–323. *Libro Amarillo de Venezuela* (Caracas, 1930), pp. 77–88. *League of Nations Treaty Series,* no. 2288, CXIX, 428–439.

[12] *Rel. do Min. das Rel. Ext.*, 1929, Annexo A, pp. 20–26.

[13] *New York Times,* Sept. 15, 1931, p. 7, col. 1. *Libro Amarillo de Venezuela* (Caracas, 1932), I, 235–236. A. Hamilton Rice, *El Rio Negro (Amazonas)* (Cambridge, 1934).

basins of clear and separate river systems made it easy to agree on the watershed as the proper frontier line; the serious subsequent obstacles to demarcation arose from exploration difficulties rather than disputed rights and were resolved with notable amity. This boundary appears to be agreed upon in detail, and though the demarcation of the eastern portion has not been completed, its description is settled, and it seems unlikely that serious differences should arise over the remainder of the work, in unpopulated and not highly valuable territory.

16. BRAZIL–FRANCE. AMAPÁ

In 1635 Cayenne was founded by French traders; in 1643 the Cap Nord Company was formed at Rouen, and a large number of settlers under the Sieur de Brétigny went out to Cayenne, but after a series of hardships and struggles they were finally massacred by the Indians. Groenewegen, capable governor of Essequibo from 1645 to 1664, made friends with the Caribs and was able to explore the interior. Francis, Lord Willoughby of Parham, governor of Barbados, sent over from Barbados in 1650 an expedition of forty persons which founded Paramaribo under Anthony Rowse, who was governor there from 1651 to 1654. In 1652 Louis XIV granted to a new Cap Nord Company letters patent for the exclusive right of trading and settling in Guiana; and 800 persons under De Royville, a Norman, sailed from Havre to Cayenne, but this expedition also soon failed. In 1663 the Equinoctial Company sent 200 colonists out from La Rochelle to Cayenne, and under De la Barre they established the permanent settlement there. French Guiana passed under the control of the French Crown in 1674; Cayenne was captured by the Dutch Admiral Binckes in March 1676 and retaken by the French in October 1676.

By the Treaty of Utrecht[1] in 1713 Louis XIV, for France, wishing to be at peace with John V of Portugal, recognized that both banks of the Amazon, as well the south as the north, belong in full ownership, dominion, and sovereignty to the king of Portugal, and promised for himself, his successors and heirs never to form any pretension to the navigation or use of that river under any pretext whatever. At that time the imperfect state of exploring knowledge and the absence of fixed settlements of white men in the interior and upper Amazon basin made it plausible to consider the Amazon as entirely included within the limits of Brazil. This treaty provision was then

---

[1] See n. 9, this chap.. *infra.*

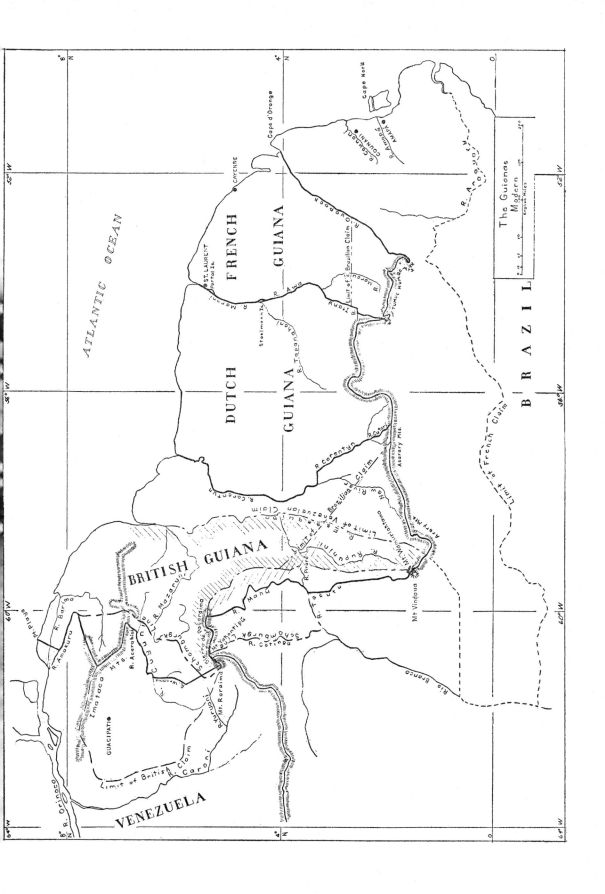

The Guianas
Modern

English Miles

in accord with the rule of international law giving the right of navigating an internal river wholly to the riparian state.[2]

Some 12,000 volunteer colonists, chiefly from Alsace and Lorraine, recruited by Choiseul, went to the valley of the Kourou in French Guiana in 1763, but found neither food nor water, and perished miserably, so that two years later but 918 were found alive and returned to France; in 1797 there landed on the Sinnamary 600 loyalists exiled from France, of whom two-thirds died. About 1777 the French founded a mission at Counani. French Guiana was attacked by the British and a Portuguese expedition from Pará in December 1808. After a vigorous defense by the French governor, Victor Hughes, Cayenne surrendered on January 14, 1809, and its possession was handed over to the Portuguese. By the treaties at the end of the Napoleonic Wars, French Guiana was awarded to the French [3] and turned over to them by the Portuguese in accordance with the Treaty of August 28, 1817.[4] In 1824 a settlement was established at Nouvelle Angoulême in French Guiana, and in 1853 a colony of free negroes was brought over from Africa. In 1854 French Guiana was made one of the places of confinement for convicts sentenced to eight years or more at hard labor,[5] and though for some years after 1867 most such convicts were sent to New Caledonia, in 1885 French Guiana was designated as a place for recidivists,[6] and since then free colonization has practically ceased.[7] In August 1936 the French government announced that it proposed to discontinue the use of French Guiana as a prison colony and that no more convicts would be sent there, anticipating formal action by the French Parliament on legislation still pending in October 1937. Seven or eight thousand prisoners in the colony were gradually to be sent to other prisons. *La Martiniere,* one of two prison ships which used to take out about 800 prisoners each twice a year from Marseilles, and which since 1921 had carried out more than 10,000 convicts, was sold by the government in March 1937 to a commercial shipping firm.

[2] Robert Phillimore, *Comm. upon International Law* (3rd ed., London, 1879), I (Secs. 155-160), 223-226. Charles Calvo, *Le Droit Int.* (5e éd., Paris, 1896), I, Sec. 302, 433-435. John B. Moore, *Dig. Int. Law* (Washington, 1906), Secs. 129-131, pp. 621-627. John Westlake, *International Law* (Cambridge, 1910), I, 145-148. L. Oppenheim, *International Law* (3rd ed., London, 1920), I, Secs. 176-177, 314-316. Paul Fauchille, *Traité de Droit Int. Pub.* (Paris, 1925), I (2e Partie, Secs. 520-525³), 422-468. Daniel Antokoletz, *Tratado de Der. Int. Pub.* (2ª ed., Buenos Aires, 1928), II (Sec. 350), 292-298. *Wheaton's Elements of International Law,* ed. by A. Berriedale Keith (6th Eng. Ed., London, 1929), I, 385.

[3] Treaty of Paris, May 30, 1814. 1 *British and Foreign State Papers,* I, 151-170.

[4] De Clercq, *Rec. des Traités de la France* (Paris, 1880), III, 102-103. Antonio Pereira Pinto, *Apontamentos para o Direito Int.* (Rio de Janeiro, 1864), I, 229-231. 4 *British and Foreign State Papers* 818-819. Martens, *Nouv. Rec. de Traités,* IV, 490-491. Ratifications exchanged, May 9, 1818.

[5] Law #1527, May 30, 1854; *Bull. des Lois,* 11e Sér., III, 1439.

[6] Law #15503, May 27, 1885; *Bull. des Lois,* 12e Sér., XXX, 1120.

[7] Separate parts are reserved for long term criminals and for recidivists. Decree #17904, Mar. 24, 1887; *Bull. des Lois,* 12e Sér., XXXIV, 829. Cayenne, Justice of the Peace, XCV 130 (Feb. 28, 1931).

There was signed at Lisbon, March 4, 1700,[8] a provisional treaty between France and Portugal by which it was agreed (Article 1) that the King of Portugal (Pedro II) should evacuate and demolish the forts of Araguari and Comau or Maçapa and the other forts on the bank of the Amazon toward Cape Nord and the shore of the ocean as far as the Oyapoc or Vicente Pinzón; (Article 2) neither French nor Portuguese might occupy or build new forts within the disputed territory, possession of which was left in suspense between the two crowns; (Article 4) the French might enter such lands as far as the bank of the Amazon which runs from the site of such forts Araguari and Comau or Maçapa to Cape Nord and the sea coast; and the Portuguese might enter the same lands to the bank of the Oyapoc or Vicente Pinzón which runs to the mouth of that river and sea coast; the French entering only by Cayenne and the Portuguese only by the Amazon; (Article 5) the French should be fully restored to Cayenne, and the Portuguese, so far as France was concerned, to Belém do Pará; (Article 7) any doubts on the meaning of the articles of this treaty or otherwise to be submitted to the two kings for amicable adjustment; and (Article 9) up to the end of 1701 both parties should search for and collect all information and documents which in conference should be recognized as necessary for better and more exact knowledge, and then should make a formal and final determination of the matter.

In the Treaty of Utrecht of April 11, 1713,[9] between Louis XIV of France and John V of Portugal (Article 10) it was recognized that both banks of the Amazon belonged to the Crown of Portugal and (Article 8) the Crown of France renounced all pretensions to any property in the lands of Cape Nord situated between the Amazon and the Japoc [10] or Vicente Pinzón. There is a river Oyapock empting into the Atlantic in the bay of Oyapoc at 4° 10′ N. immediately west of Cape d'Orange, and another river Araguary which empties into the Atlantic 220 miles farther to the southeast, just south of Cape Nord.

The Treaty of San Ildefonso of October 1, 1777,[11] described the northern and eastern end of the boundary between the Spanish and Portuguese possessions only as running by the mountains which form the divide between the Orinoco and the Amazon, directing the line wherever possible to the north.

[8] Carlos Calvo, *Col. Compl. de los Trat.* (Paris, 1862), II, 43–49.

[9] De Clercq, *Rec. des Traités de la France* (Paris, 1880), I, 14–15. Henri Vast, *Les Grands Traités* (Paris, 1899), III, 112–119. 4 *British and Foreign State Papers* 818. Joaquim Caetano da Silva, "Memoria sobre os Limites," *Rev. Trim. de Hist. e Geog.* (Rio de Janeiro, 1850), pp. 421–512. P. Vidal de la Blache, *La Riviere Vincent Pinzon* (Paris, 1902). *Rev. de dr. int. et de lég. comp.*, 2ᵉ Sér., III (1901), 81. Ratified by France, Apr. 18, 1713; ratified by Portugal, May 9, 1713.

[10] In Portuguese: *o Japoc.*

[11] Article 12. See §2, this chap., *supra.*

It will be observed that no termination is mentioned for this line either on the ocean or at any inland point, probably from a willingness on the part of both countries to keep alive any claims as far to the eastward and northward as they could; for although Spain [12] theoretically claimed and would still have liked to make effective her possession of all the country west of the old Tordesillas line ending on the ocean near the mouths of the Amazon, both she and Portugal were obliged to face the established reality of forbidden settlements northwest of that point by England, France, and Holland long before 1777. The unexecuted treaty of peace and friendship signed at Paris, August 10, 1797,[13] provided (Article 7) that the boundary between French and Portuguese Guiana should be the river called by the Portuguese Calsoene and by the French Vincent Pinzón, emptying into the ocean above Cape Nord, about 2°30′ N.; up such river to its source, and thence a straight line from such source west to the Branco; (Article 8) the mouths as well as the entire course of such river Calsoene or Vincent Pinzón to belong in full property and sovereignty to the French republic, with the right to Portuguese subjects settled near to and south of such river to use freely without tax its mouth, its course and its waters. The treaty of peace signed under the mediation of Spain at Badajoz, June 6, 1801,[14] provided that (Article 4) the boundary between the two Guianas should thereafter be the Arawari which empties into the ocean below Cape Nord, near Neuve and Penitence islands, at about 1° 20′ N.; thence by the Arawari from its mouth furthest from Cape Nord to its source, and thence by a straight line drawn from that source westward to the Branco, (Article 5) so that the north bank of the Arawari from its last mouth to its source and the lands to the north of the boundary line thus fixed should belong in full sovereignty to the French people; the south bank of that river from the same mouth and all the lands to the south of such boundary line should belong to Portugal; navigation of the river for its full length to be common to the two nations. This treaty was superseded by the unexecuted treaty of peace signed also under the mediation of Spain at Madrid, September 29, 1801,[15] which provided that (Article 4) the boundary between French and Portuguese Guiana should thereafter be the Carapanatuba which empties into the Amazon at about 0°20′ N., above Fort Maçapa; thence up

---

[12] See §24, this chap., *infra.*

[13] De Clercq, *Rec. des Traités de la France* (Paris, 1880), I, 329–334, 344–345. French Directional Decrees: confirmed, Aug. 11, 1797; nullified, Oct. 26, 1797.

[14] De Clercq, *Rec. des Traités de la France*, I, 435–437. Annulled by Prince Regent John from Rio de Janeiro,

May 1, 1808, and by treaty of Paris, May 3, 1814, Additional and Secret Article 3.

[15] De Clercq, *Rec. des Traités de la France*, I, 455–463. Expressly annulled by treaty of Paris, May 30, 1814, Additional and Secret Article 3.

that river to its source, thence bearing towards the great chain of mountains which makes the watershed; thence by the bending of such chain to its nearest point to the Branco at about 2°20′ N.

The Treaty of Amiens, March 25/27, 1802,[16] reproducing the Treaty of Badajoz, Articles 4 and 5, provided that (Article 7) the boundary of French and Portuguese Guiana should be the Arawari, which empties into the ocean below Cape Nord near Neuve and Penitence islands, at about 1°20′ N.; thence by the Arawari from its mouth furthest from Cape Nord to its source, and thence by a straight line drawn from that source westward to the Branco, so that the north bank of the Arawari from its east mouth to its source and the lands to the north of the boundary line thus fixed should belong in full sovereignty to France; the south bank of that river from the same mouth and all the lands to the south of such boundary line should belong to Portugal; navigation of the Arawari for its full length to be common to the two nations. By the final treaty of the Congress of Vienna, June 9, 1815 [17] (Article 107), the prince regent of Portugal and Brazil undertook to restore to France French Guiana up to the Oyapock, whose mouth was between 4° and 5° N., the boundary which Portugal had always considered as that fixed by the Treaty of Utrecht; declarations which by their argumentative nature appear to reveal doubts existing even then as to the identity of the Oyapock. By a convention between France and Portugal signed at Paris, August 28, 1817,[18] to carry out Article 107 of the treaty of the Congress of Vienna, (Article 1) Portugal promised to restore to France within three months French Guiana as far as the Oyapock, whose mouth was between 4° and 5° N. up to 322° east of the Island of Ferro (55°40′ W.); (Article 2) both parties to name at once commissioners to fix the boundary exactly, and to finish their work within one year or the parties to proceed amicably to some other arrangement under the mediation of Great Britain. This commission was never constituted.

In 1836 [19] France established provisionally a military post at Mapa on the right (southeast) bank of the Oyapock and Brazil on April 29, 1840, founded the colony of Dom Pedro II north of the Arawari; but by a neutralization convention of 1841 both countries agreed to abstain from all undertakings in the disputed territory. Fruitless conferences were held in Paris

[16] Martens, *Rec. des Prin. Traités* (Gottingue, 1831), VII, 402 at 407. Portugal was not a party and never adhered to this treaty.

[17] De Clercq, *Rec. des Traités de la France*, II, 567 at 610. 4 *British and Foreign State Papers* 818.

[18] De Clercq, *Rec. des Traités de la France*, III, 102–103. Antonio Pereira Pinto, *Apontamentos para o Direito Int.* (Rio de Janeiro, 1864), I, 229–231. 4 *British and Foreign State Papers* 818–819. Martens, *Nouv. Rec. de Traités*, IV, 490–491. Ratifications exchanged, May 9, 1818.

[19] 27 *British and Foreign State Papers* 1416; 28 *ibid.*, 1318; 29 *ibid.*, 717.

from August 30, 1855, to July 1, 1856.[20] In 1886 the inhabitants of Counani attempted to set up an independent republic, with Jules Gros, a Parisian geographer, as president, but because of internal dissensions the state lasted less than a year. Diplomatic negotiations continued with little result until 1895,[21] when the two nations agreed on a mixed commission to explore the territory. Early in 1895[22] one Trajane, a long-time French resident of Mapa, was imprisoned, and French washers of gold were said to have been robbed by Veiga Cabral, chief of the Brazilian adventurers in the region. The governor of French Guiana sent the French ship *Bengali* on May 11, 1895, from Cayenne to Counani to obtain Trajane's release and investigate the situation. Captain Lunier, with a company of marines, landed and marched fifteen miles inland to Mapa, where he and four marines fell in a sharp combat with the adventurers, many of whom were killed and the village destroyed.

The long negotiations were finally ended when Stephen Pichon, French minister, and Dionisio Evangelista de Castro Cerqueira, Brazilian minister of foreign relations, signed at Rio de Janeiro on April 10, 1897,[23] a convention for arbitration by the government of the Swiss Confederation, agreeing that (Article 1) France claimed that according to the true sense of Article 8 of the Treaty of Utrecht, the Japoc or Vicente Pinzón was the Arawari which empties into the ocean south of Cape Nord and whose thalweg should form the frontier; and Brazil claimed that according to the true sense of Article 8 of the Treaty of Utrecht, the Japoc or Vicente Pinzón was the Oyapock which empties into the ocean west of Cape d'Orange and whose thalweg should form the frontier; the arbiter to adopt in its sentence one or the other of those rivers or some river between them; (Article 2) France claimed that the interior boundary should be the line from the principal source of the principal arm of the Arawari westward parallel to the Amazon to the left (east) bank of the Branco and along (up) that river to the intersection with the parallel which passes through the extreme point of the Acaray mountains; and Brazil claimed that the interior boundary, of which a part was provi-

[20] Joaquim Caetano da Silva, *L'Oyapoc et l'Amazone: Question Brésilienne et Française* (Paris, 1861), 2 vols.; (2e éd., Rio de Janeiro, 1883; 3e éd., Paris, 1899). J. M. N. d'Azambuja, *Limites do Brazil com as Guyanas Franceza e Ingleza* (Rio de Janeiro, 1892), II, 15-134.

[21] 54 *British and Foreign State Papers* 983. *Arch. Dipl.*, 2e Sér., XXV, 316. José Alexandre Teixeira de Mello, *Subsidios . . . para o estudo da Questão de Limites* (Rio de Janeiro, 1895).

[22] E. Rouard de Card, "Le Différend Franco-Brésilien," *Rev. Gen. de dr. int. pub.*, IV (1897), 277-296. *Arch. Dipl.*, 2e Sér., LIV, 235-236. *U. S. For. Rel.*, 1895, Part

I, p. 70.

[23] *Coll. das Leis do Brazil de 1898*, I, Parte 2, 668-671. *Bull. des Lois de la Rep. Française* (Paris, 1899), LVII, No. 2015, pp. 2450-2451. 90 *British and Foreign State Papers* 952-953. *Arch. Dipl.*, 2e Sér., LXII, 363-365. Martens, *Nouv. Rec. Gén. de Traités*, 2e Sér., XXV, 335-336. *U. S. For. Rel.*, 1897, pp. 43-44. Clunet, *J. du dr. int.*, XLV (1918), 971. Sanctioned by Brazil, Decree #474, Dec. 8, 1897; ratified by France, Apr. 7, 1898; ratifications exchanged at Rio de Janeiro, Aug. 6, 1898; promulgated by Brazil, Decree #2967, Aug. 8, 1898; promulgated by France, Aug. 31, 1898.

sionally recognized by the convention of August 28, 1817, should be the parallel 2°24′ N. which starting from the Oyapock ends on the frontier of Dutch Guiana; the arbiter to adopt in its sentence one or the other of these lines or as an intermediate solution, from the principal source of the river adopted as being the Japoc or Vicente Pinzón to the Dutch frontier, the watershed of the Amazon basin, which in that region is constituted almost wholly by the crest of the Tumuc Humac mountains; (Article 3) printed cases to be submitted and exchanged in eight months (Article 4) with answers by each party if deemed necessary within another eight months and (Article 8) decision within one year thereafter. The Swiss Federal Council accepted the office of arbiter on September 8, 1898, and the original cases were submitted by the Baron of Rio Branco for Brazil [24] and by France,[25] with a second presentation for Brazil, December 5, 1899, and an answer by France; and there was much discussion by unofficial jurists.[26] The Swiss Federal Council [27] handed down its award on December 1, 1900,[28] deciding that the Treaty of Utrecht in Article 8 by the Japoc or Vicente Pinzón meant the Oyapock emptying into the Atlantic at 4°10′ N. immediately west of Cape d'Orange, and adopting for the inland boundary the intermediate line suggested in Article 2 of the arbitration convention, from the principal source of the Oyapock to the Dutch frontier, the watershed of the Amazon basin, which in that region is constituted almost wholly by the crest of the Tumuc Humac mountains. An area of some 31,000 square miles with a population of 18,000, mostly Indians, negroes, and half-breeds, was involved; and by the award thus largely favorable to Brazil she obtained 30,000 square miles and France about 1,000 square miles of the disputed territory.

Early European treaties named various rivers as the boundary, and the identification on the ground of the one of these called for by the Treaty of Utrecht of 1713 constituted the arbiter's problem. The decision was accepted at once by both countries,[29] the line has since been partly marked, and this boundary seems definitely settled.

[24] *Mémoire* (Paris, 1899), 3 vols. and atlas. Second *Mémoire* (Berne, 1899), 5 vols. and atlas.

[25] *Mémoire* (Paris, 1899), 2 vols. and atlas. *Réponse* (Paris, 1899).

[26] Albert Burckhardt-Finsler, *Historisches Gutachten über den französisch-brasilianischen Grenzstreit* (1900). J. Fruh, *Gutachten über den geographischen teil des dem schweizerischen Bundesrate . . . in Guyana* (Zurich, 1900). J. Fruh, *Tabellen* (1900). P. Schweizer, *Gutachten über den Grenzstreit zwischen Frankreich & Brasilien* (1900). Stoll, *Franko-Brasilianischer Grenzstreit* (Zurich, 1900).

[27] Of seven members; Walther Hauser, President, and G. Ringier, Chancellor.

[28] *Sentence du Conseil Fédéral Suisse* (Berne, 1900), 846 pp. and maps. *Urteil des Bundesrates* (Bern, 1900), 841 pp. and maps. Martens, *Nouv. Rec. Gén. de Traités,* 3e Sér., X, 153–179. *Rev. Gén. de dr. int. pub.,* VIII (1901), 48–53. José Manoel Cardoso de Oliveira, *Actos Dipl. do Brasil* (Rio de Janeiro, 1912), II, 287–288.

[29] Rafael Torres Campos, "Explicación histórico-geográfica," *Bol. de la Real Soc. Geog.,* XLIV, 604–606. Fernando Antonio Raja Gablagia, *As Fronteiras do Brasil* (Rio de Janeiro, 1916), 305–311. João Ribeiro, *As Nossas Fronteiras* (Rio de Janeiro, 1930), 139–142.

17. BRAZIL–GREAT BRITAIN. PIRARA

(See map, p. 145, *supra*.)

The Treaty of San Ildefonso of October 1, 1777,[1] described the northern and eastern end of the boundary between the Spanish and Portuguese possessions only as running by the mountains which form the divide between the Orinoco and the Amazon, directing the line wherever possible to the north. After the British had acquired from the Dutch permanently in 1814 the three colonies of Berbice, Demerara, and Essequibo, attention was primarily devoted to encouraging and strengthening the settlements on the coast and navigable parts of the rivers, and little attention was paid to the inland region. In 1828 the Church Missionary Society sent to Essequibo to convert the Indians a Lutheran minister named Armstrong, and in 1832 he was joined by a Methodist missionary, Thomas Youd, and they explored and established missions as far up the Rupununi as Pirara, among the Macuchi Indians. In 1835 the Royal Geographical Society of London sent an expedition under Sir Robert Hermann Schomburgk, a German traveler, to study the physical and astronomical geography of the interior. He made numerous journeys inland, observing and mapping, and in May 1838 met Youd at Pirara, which both thought it would be desirable for England to possess, for its desirable position on the line of communication between the Essequibo and the Amazon. Brazil heard of their talk and in August 1838 established at Pirara a military post, under Captain Leal, ordered the British missionaries to withdraw to their own territory, and sent a Carmelite priest, José dos Santos Innocentes, to keep the Indians from following them. Schomburgk on July 1, 1839, proposed to Colonel Henry Light, Governor[2] of British Guiana, that he should make a demarcation of the frontiers of the colony, suggesting alternative lines north of the Tacutú. Governor Light transmitted the proposition officially to the Marquess of Nomanby in London on July 15, 1839,[3] where it was approved by the colonial and foreign offices. The British government adopted as the boundary the westernmost line indicated, so notified Light on April 23, 1840, and in November 1840[4] officially designated Schomburgk to make a preliminary reconnaissance of the whole of the southern and western frontiers of the colony. On February 20, 1841, William George Ouseley, British minister at Rio de Janeiro, following instructions of November 28, 1840, notified Aureliano de Souza e Oliveira Coutinho, Brazilian minister of foreign

---

[1] Article 12. See §2, this chap., *supra*.
[2] 1838–1848.

[3] *Venezuela-British Guiana Arbitration, Case of Venezuela* (New York, 1898), III, 70–75. [4] *Ibid.*, pp. 76–135.

relations, of Schomburgk's appointment and of instructions given to Governor Light to oppose any resistance in Pirara or neighboring frontier regions which until then had been occupied by independent tribes. On March 24 Coutinho replied, asserting, with diplomatic arguments and maps, Brazil's right to the territory. Governor Light in February 1841 sent William Crichton, inspector-general of police, and Lieutenant Hackett of the British army to Pirara to oblige Captain Leal and Father José to evacuate the village, and to inform them that, if they did not leave, England would send troops from Demerara or would blockade the ports of Brazil. The two Brazilians replied that they could only transmit the demand to their chiefs and await orders, and the Englishmen agreed to give them four months to decide. On January 8, 1842, in a note to the British legation Coutinho proposed negotiations for fixing the boundary, Pirara to be declared neutral until the decision, both missionaries but no military forces to be allowed to remain meanwhile; and this proposition was fully accepted by the British cabinet on August 29. Meanwhile Lieutenant Bingham and another officer with forty soldiers sent by Governor Light arrived at Pirara and obliged Captain Leal, Father José, and the one soldier they had to leave; but the Brazilian government remained cool, assumed that Governor Light had misinterpreted his orders from London, and refused to allow to start for Pirara the troops which the vice-president of the state of Pará had raised to expel the invaders. On March 5, 1842, the English detachment retired to east of the river Pirara, a mile from the village; on June 15 they received orders to come back, and they reached Demerara on September 1. Schomburgk, who had proceeded to follow the frontier and raise monuments against protests of the Brazilian authorities in various places, was in November 1842[5] definitely ordered from London to withdraw. Araujo Ribeiro, Brazilian minister in Paris, went to London toward the end of 1843 and had with Lord Aberdeen a series of conferences which elicited various propositions, but no common line could be agreed on and the negotiations were finally broken off on November 24, 1843.[6] By the Treaty of Caracas of May 5, 1859,[7] Brazil and Venezuela agreed in running the line between them along the highest summits of the Pacaraima ridge as far as the territories of the two states extended eastward, so that the question of where the Brazil-British Guiana boundary began was left unaffected.

In 1888 there was a tentative suggestion by the Baron of Penedo, Brazilian minister in London, to Lord Salisbury for a treaty establishing a mixed

[5] *Ibid.*, pp. 136–140.
[6] J. M. N. d'Azambuja, *Limites do Brazil com as*

Guayanas Franceza e Ingleza (Rio de Janeiro, 1892), II, 137–206. [7] See §15, this chap., *supra.*

commission to survey the frontier for a definite line, but Great Britain thought certain other difficulties ought to be adjusted first. On September 12, 1891, Sir Thomas Sanderson informed Souza Corrêa, Brazilian minister in London, that Lord Salisbury was ready to open discussions on the Mahú-Tacutú line at Rio de Janeiro, but political events in Brazil prevented action. On March 15, 1897, Corrêa presented a treaty, with a memoir discussing the matter, offering to negotiate on the line of the *divortium aquarum,* but Lord Salisbury on April 22, 1897, made a counter proposal of the Mahú-Tacutú line, which Corrêa refused on December 20, 1897. On May 24, 1898, Salisbury made a new proposition for a line entirely along the rivers, to which Corrêa on November 30, 1898, made a counter proposition for a Mahu-Rupununi line, which England rejected, but suggested arbitration by a third power. Brazil received this suggestion favorably on January 17, 1899, but before embodying the agreement in a treaty for arbitration, England on August 23, 1900, made a final attempt at direct settlement on a still different line which Brazil would not accept.[8] The last two British proposals would, as it turned out, have given Brazil respectively 21 per cent or 69 per cent more territory than she received under the arbitral award.

In the arbitration under the Treaty of 1897 between Venezuela and Great Britain, the commission at Paris on October 3, 1899,[9] awarded most of the disputed territory to Great Britain, but declared that the boundary fixed by that decision should not prejudice any existing question between Brazil and Great Britain or between Brazil and Venezuela. By this award, the boundary between Venezuela and Great Britain south of Mount Roraima should be the Cotinga or Surumu and the Tacutú into which it flows and which lower joins the Branco; but by the Treaty of Caracas of May 5, 1859,[10] Brazil and Venezuela had agreed that their boundary was to run along the highest summits of the Pacaraima ridge so that the waters which flowed into the Branco should belong to Brazil. Accordingly, it was Brazil and not Venezuela which was adjoining British Guiana south of Mount Roraima, and Brazil cautioned the Paris commission at its first meeting against any decision which might affect the rights of a third party not represented and protested to both nations against the award when announced. It was ineffective against Brazil, as she maintained thereafter in her negotiations and claims concerning her boundary with British Guiana, and as the arbiter of that line declared.

Joaquim Aurelio Nabuco de Araujo, Brazilian minister, and Henry

[8] José Manoel Cardoso de Oliveira, *Actos Dipl. do Brasil* (Rio de Janeiro, 1912), II, 293, 294.

[9] See §24, this chap., *infra.*
[10] See §15, this chap., *supra.*

Charles Keith Petty Fitz-Maurice, Marquess of Lansdowne, British secretary
of state for foreign affairs, signed at London on November 6, 1901,[11] a treaty
for an amicable settlement of the boundary between Brazil and the colony
of British Guiana in which the two nations agreed (Article 1) to invite the
king of Italy to decide as arbitrator the question of that boundary; (Article 2) the territory in dispute to be taken to be the territory lying between
the Tacutú and the Cotinga and a line drawn from the source of the Cotinga
eastward following the watershed to a point near Mount Ayangcanna, thence
in a southeasterly direction still following the general direction of the watershed as far as the hill called Annai, thence by the nearest tributary to the
Rupununi, up that river to its source and from that point crossing to the
source of the Tacutú; (Article 3) the arbitrator to be requested to investigate and ascertain the extent of the territory which, whether the whole or a
part of the zone described, might lawfully be claimed by either party and to
determine the boundary line; (Article 4) the arbitrator to ascertain all facts
he deemed necessary and be governed by such principles of international law
as he should determine to be applicable; (Article 5) printed cases to be delivered in duplicate and exchanged within twelve months from the exchange
of ratifications; (Article 6) within six months thereafter counter cases; (Article 7) within four months thereafter printed arguments, and (Article 9) the
arbitrator to be requested to make his written decision within six months
thereafter if possible. On signing this treaty the parties annexed a declaration that they adopted as the frontier (east of the Rupununi) the watershed
line between the basins of the Amazon and of the Corentyn and the Essequibo from the source of the Corentyn to that of the Rupununi or of the
Tacutú or to a point between them according to the decision of the arbitrator.
Brazil thus conceded to Great Britain at the outset and kept out of the arbitration an area of 17,700 square miles on the southern border of British
Guiana north of the watershed along the Arary and the Acarahy mountains;
for the reason, Brazil explained in her case, that she had always meant to
claim only as much as Portugal had always said belonged to her and not all
the territory that the Dutch said was Portuguese. Whether the Cutari or
the New River is to be considered the main stream, so that the source of the
Corentyn thus indicated should be in the Acarahy range or in the Arary range
100 miles farther west, does not appear from the declaration; but the settle-

[11] Coll. das Leis do Brazil de 1902, I (Parte 2), 47-52. 94 British and Foreign State Papers 23-29. U. S. For. Rel., 1902, pp. 103-105. Martens, Nouv. Rec. Gén. de Traités, 2ᵉ Sér., XXXII, 413-416. Arch. Dipl., 3ᵉ Sér., IV, 90-95. Sanctioned by Brazil, Decree #824, Dec. 27, 1901; ratified by Great Britain, Dec. 23, 1901; ratifications exchanged at Rio de Janeiro, Jan. 28, 1902; promulgated by Brazil, Decree #4329, Jan. 28, 1902.

ment of that question with Great Britain affects not so much Brazil as the Netherlands.[12]

King Victor Emmanuel III accepted the office of arbiter and the Brazilian case [13] was submitted at Rome on February 27, 1903, by Joaquim Nabuco, who had been aided in its preparation by the Baron of Rio Branco, the counter case on September 26, 1903, and the argument on February 25, 1904. The award given at Rome on June 6, 1904,[14] decided that the frontier should be a line from Mount Yakontipú eastward along the watershed to the source of the Ireng (Mahú), thence down that river to its confluence with the Tacutú; up the Tacutú to its source or where it joins the line agreed upon in the declaration annexed to the treaty of arbitration; all of the contested zone east of this frontier line to belong to Great Britain, all to the west, to Brazil; the frontier along the rivers Ireng-Mahú and Tacutú to follow the thalweg of those rivers and they to be open to the free navigation of the two adjoining states; if the rivers divide into several branches, the frontier to follow the thalweg of the easternmost branch. The preliminary recital reasoned that to acquire sovereignty in new regions occupation was indispensable; there must be effective, uninterrupted, and permanent possession in the name of the state, a simple affirmation of rights or a manifest intention to render occupation effective not being sufficient; Portugal first and Brazil subsequently had not taken effective possession of all the territory in dispute; the award of October 3, 1899, in the arbitration between Great Britain and Venezuela was ineffective against Brazil; the British rights, in succession to those of Holland, were based on the exercise of rights of jurisdiction by the Dutch West India Company, with sovereign powers from the Dutch government, and like acts of authority and jurisdiction were afterwards continued in the name of Great Britain, resulting in the gradual development and acquisition of sovereignty over a part of the territory in dispute; historical and legal claims did not fix with precision the limit of the zone over which the right of sovereignty of either party was established, and the contested territory should be divided in accordance with the lines traced by nature. The line fixed by this award followed exactly the British proposals of 1891 and 1897 and, except for thirty miles at the southern end, that of 1843; and divided the

[12] See §26, this chap., *infra*.

[13] *First Mémoire, Annexes* (Paris, 1903), 5 vols. and atlas. *Second Mémoire* (Paris, 1903), 3 vols., *Annexes*, 3 vols. *Troisième Mémoire* (Paris, 1904), 4 vols.

[14] José Manoel Cardoso de Oliveira, *Actos Dipl. do. Brasil* (Rio de Janeiro, 1912), II, 322-323. 99 *British and*

Foreign State Papers 930–932. Arch. Dipl., 3ᵉ Sér., XCII, 1283–1287. Martens, *Nouv. Rec. Gén. de Traités*, 2ᵉ Sér., XXXII, 485–489. Fernando Antonio Raja Gabaglia, *As Fronteiras do Brasil* (Rio de Janeiro, 1916), 289–304. João Ribeiro, *As Nossas Fronteiras* (Rio de Janeiro, 1930), 125–128.

territory of about 13,000 square miles submitted to arbitration, giving 5,400 square miles to Brazil and 7,600 square miles to Great Britain.[15]

There was signed by Austen Chamberlain, British secretary of state for foreign affairs, and Raul Regis de Oliveira, Brazilian minister, at London on April 22, 1926,[16] a special complementary convention to rectify certain inaccuracies in the award and a general boundary treaty to describe clearly and demarcate properly the frontier. The convention provided that (Article 1) from Mount Yakontipú westwards as far as the Roraima chain the frontier should follow the watershed between the Cotingo (Kwating) in Brazilian territory and the Paikwa in British territory; ascending the Roraima mountains between the Paikwa fall to the north and the Cotingo falls to the south, and leaving the sources of the Cotingo on the Brazilian side, to end where Venezuelan territory commences, between the sources of the Cotingo and those of the Arapopo (Arabopo) on the Roraima mountains, so far as the nature of the ground or the locality permits of these sources being explored or located; and (Article 2) declared that the source of the Tacutú at the end of the boundary line fixed by the arbitral decision was situated on Mount Wamuriaktawa and not on Mount Vindaua (Wintawa) as was supposed. The treaty provided that (Article 1) the frontier should be finally fixed as (Sec. 1) commencing on the heights of the Roraima mountains between the headwaters of the Cotingo (Kwating) and those of the Arapopo (Arabopo) at the point of convergence of the frontier of the two countries with that of Venezuela; thence down by the northeastern part of such mountains between the Paikwa fall to the north and the Cotingo falls to the south; thence as far as Mount Yakontipú along the watershed between the Cotingo in Brazilian territory and the Paikwa in British territory; (Sec. 2) from Mount Yakontipú eastward along the watershed as far as the source of the Mahú or Ireng; thence down that river to its confluence with the Tacutú; thence up the Tacutú to its source, situated not on Mount Vindaua as was supposed but on Mount Wamuriaktawa about three miles above toward the northeast in the same chain; (Sec. 3) from the source of the Tacutú on Mount Wamuriaktawa along the watershed between the Amazon basin and the Essequibo and Corentyn basins

[15] Paul Fauchille, "Le Conflit de Limites entre le Brésil et la Grande-Bretagne," Rev. gén. de dr. int. pub., XII (1905), 25–142. Albert Geouffre de Lapradelle et Nicolas Socrate Politis, L'Arbitrage anglo-brésilien de 1904 (Paris, 1905).

[16] Coll. de Actos Int., Min. das Rel. Ext. (Rio de Janeiro, 1929), No. 11. Treaty Series (London, 1929), No. 14 (Cmd. 3341). 123 British and Foreign State Papers 468–471. League of Nations Treaty Series, No. 2097, XCII, 312–319. Martens, Nouv. Rec. Gén. de Traités, 3e Sér., XXIII, 268–274. Sanctioned by Brazil, Decree #5646, Jan. 8, 1929; ratified by Brazil, Feb. 5, 1929; ratified by Great Britain, Mar. 15, 1929; ratifications exchanged at London, Apr. 16, 1929; promulgated by Brazil, Decree #18722, Apr. 30, 1929.

as far as the point of junction of the frontier of the two countries with that of Dutch Guiana (Surinam); (Article 2) special commissioners appointed by each government to constitute a mixed commission to meet within six months from the exchange of ratifications should make a reconnaissance of the various frontier lines thus specified, draw up plans of each section, and set up marks where they appeared necessary; and (Article 3) differences between the commissioners which were not settled amicably by the two governments should be submitted to the arbitral decision of three members of the Academy of Sciences of the Institute of France chosen by the president of that academy.

The second protocol of December 9, 1905,[17] between Brazil and Venezuela ran their boundary to the point on Mount Roraima where the three frontiers of Brazil, Venezuela, and British Guiana meet, thus adopting not the terminus of the arbitral award of 1904, Mount Yakontipú, but resting on the Roraima range thirty miles farther westward, a difference to Venezuela's disadvantage of which Brazil and Great Britain took the benefits in this convention and treaty of 1926. A protocol of instructions for the demarcation commission, to finish its work within five years, was signed at London, March 18, 1930,[18] and the demarcation has since been carried out.

Early negotiations agreed that the frontier in this unsettled river-beset region should be a watershed but differed as to the rivers involved, and, after a large area had been conceded as never really Portuguese, an arbitral award fixed a compromise boundary close to some of the voluntary offers. From the friendly and pacific relations of the two countries, it is altogether probable that no further difficulty will ever arise upon the boundary thus settled and marked.

18. Brazil–Netherlands. Tumuc–Humac

(See map, p. 145, *supra*.)

The Treaty of San Ildefonso of October 1, 1777,[1] described the northern and eastern end of the boundary between the Spanish and Portuguese possessions only as running along the mountains which form the divide between the Orinoco and the Amazon, directing the line wherever possible to the north. The permanent loss of Berbice, Demerara, and Essequibo to the British in 1814 cut off the Dutch in Surinam from any conflict with the successors to the Spanish territory, and with a colony of a European nation on either side

---

17 See §15, this chap., *supra*.
18 *Coll. de Actos Int., Min. das Rel. Ext.* (Rio de Janeiro, 1930), No. 28. 132 *British and Foreign State Papers* 219–222. *League of Nations Treaty Series*, No.

2339, CI, 401–407. Martens, *Nouv. Rec. Gén. de Traités*, 3e Sér., XXIII, 274–278.

1 Article 12. See §2, this chap., *supra*.

left only the southern boundary to be settled with an American state. Nothing had been agreed upon regarding the frontier between Brazil and Dutch Guiana when in 1852 [2] Joaquim Caetano da Silva, Brazilian chargé d'affaires at The Hague, proposed to the Dutch government a consideration of principles for an agreement as to the boundary; but apparently neither side then thought the line should be the watershed of the Tumuc-Humac ridge, and the negotiations lapsed. In 1891 [3] the award by Czar Alexander III in the arbitration between France and the Netherlands decided that the frontier of French Guiana and Surinam should be the Awa, as the upper course of the Maroni; and in 1905 the two countries agreed that above the Awa the Itany should be the boundary; in 1900 [4] the award by the Swiss Federal Council in the arbitration between Brazil and France decided that the frontier of Brazil and French Guiana should be the Oyapock and the watershed of the Amazon basin, on the crest of the Tumuc-Humac Mountains, from the principal source of the Oyapock to the Dutch frontier; in 1901 [5] the declaration annexed to the treaty of arbitration between Brazil and Great Britain fixed the southern frontier of Brazil and British Guiana as the watershed between the basins of the Amazon and of the Corentyn and the Essequibo from the source of the Corentyn; and from 1831 [6] Great Britain and the Netherlands have tacitly agreed on the river Corentyn as the boundary of their possessions. These determinations fixed the adjoining corners pretty clearly on the watershed in the Tumuc-Humac range, and it presumably seemed better to both sides to follow these suggestions for the line between them than for either to prolong a doubtful struggle to secure a salient projecting into the territory of the other with a boundary which would not be in line with the frontiers of the countries on either side.

Frédéric Palm, minister of the Netherlands, and the Baron of Rio Branco signed a treaty at Rio de Janeiro, May 5, 1906,[7] which provided that (Article 1) the frontier between Brazil and Surinam should be, from the French to the British frontier, the watershed between the basin of the Amazon on the south and the basins of the streams which flow toward the north to the Atlantic; (Article 2) demarcation commissioners to be named by both governments as soon as thought desirable; and (Article 3) any differences which might

[2] Fernando Antonio Raja Gablagia, *As Fronteiras do Brasil* (Rio de Janeiro, 1916), 304. João Ribeiro, *As Nossas Fronteiras* (Rio de Janeiro, 1930), 133-134.
[3] See §25, this chap., *infra*.
[4] See §16, this chap., *supra*.
[5] See §17, this chap., *supra*.
[6] See §26, this chap., *infra*.

[7] *Coll. das Leis do Brazil de 1908*, II, 1102-1104. 99 *British and Foreign State Papers* 932-933. *U. S. For. Rel.*, 1908, pp. 54-56. Martens, *Nouv. Rec. Gén. de Traités*, 3e Sér., III, 70-71. Sanctioned by Brazil, Decree #1659, June 25, 1907; ratified by the Netherlands, Sept. 12, 1908; ratifications exchanged at The Hague, Sept. 15, 1908; promulgated by Brazil, Decree #7133, Sept. 24, 1908.

arise between the parties as to the application or interpretation of the treaty to be submitted to the Hague Permanent Court of Arbitration, under a special agreement in each case determining clearly the subject of the litigation and the extent of the powers of the arbiter or arbitral tribunal. It will be observed that running the boundary on the watershed to the British frontier leaves unaffected the question of where on that watershed is the source of the Corentyn, which by the declaration of 1901 is the end of the Brazil-Great Britain boundary, whether at the head of the Cutari or of the New River; but the settlement of that question with the Netherlands affects not so much Brazil as Great Britain.[8]

A protocol of instructions for the mixed commission for the demarcation of the frontier, to commence work not later than October 10, 1932, was signed at Rio de Janeiro, April 27, 1931,[9] accepted by notes exchanged at Rio de Janeiro, September 22, 1931, and the demarcation is understood to be nearly or quite completed.

After the corners of adjacent territories had been formally adjusted, it was obvious that this boundary should run along the plain watershed between the established points, and fair and amicable neighbors so agreed. This frontier may be quite definitely assumed to be fully and finally settled.

19. CHILE–PERU. TACNA–ARICA

On September 24, 1865,[1] the Spanish fleet which had begun war with Peru in April 1864 by seizing the Chincha Islands[2] blockaded Valparaiso, and soon after declared a blockade of Caldera, Coquimbo, Herradura (Guyacan), Talcahuano, and Tomé, reduced on December 21, 1865,[3] to Valparaiso and Caldera only. Spain broke off diplomatic relations with Chile, and after attempts at mediation by the United States,[4] England,[5] and France[6] had failed, Chile joined Peru in the war. On December 5, 1865,[7] a treaty of alliance was signed at Lima under which the naval forces of the two republics were to act in combination against the Spaniards. On March 31, 1866, the Spanish fleet under Admiral Casto Méndez Núñez after notice, notwith-

[8] See §26, this chap., *infra*.
[9] *Coll. de Actos Int.* (Rio de Janeiro, 1932), No. 40. *League of Nations Treaty Series*, No. 2986, CXXX, 114–126.

[1] *U. S. Dipl. Corr.*, 1864, IV, 189–190. 55 *British and Foreign State Papers* 296–297; 58 *ibid.*, 583–589. *Arch. Dipl.*, 1866, II, 39–95.
[2] See chap. II, §3, *infra*.

[3] 56 *British and Foreign State Papers* 646.
[4] *U. S. Dipl. Corr.*, 1865, II, 536–537, 545–553, 555–562, 564–565, 579–584; *ibid.*, 1866–67, I, 565–574, 583–615, 619–625, II, 334–429.
[5] 56 *British and Foreign State Papers* 720–787, 792–896, 897–945, 949–952.
[6] *Arch. Dipl.*, 1866, I, 259–269.
[7] *U. S. Dipl. Corr.*, 1866–67, II, 658–660. *U. S. For. Rel.*, 1875, I, 188–189. 56 *British and Foreign State Papers* 707–709. Ratifications exchanged at Lima, Jan. 14, 1866.

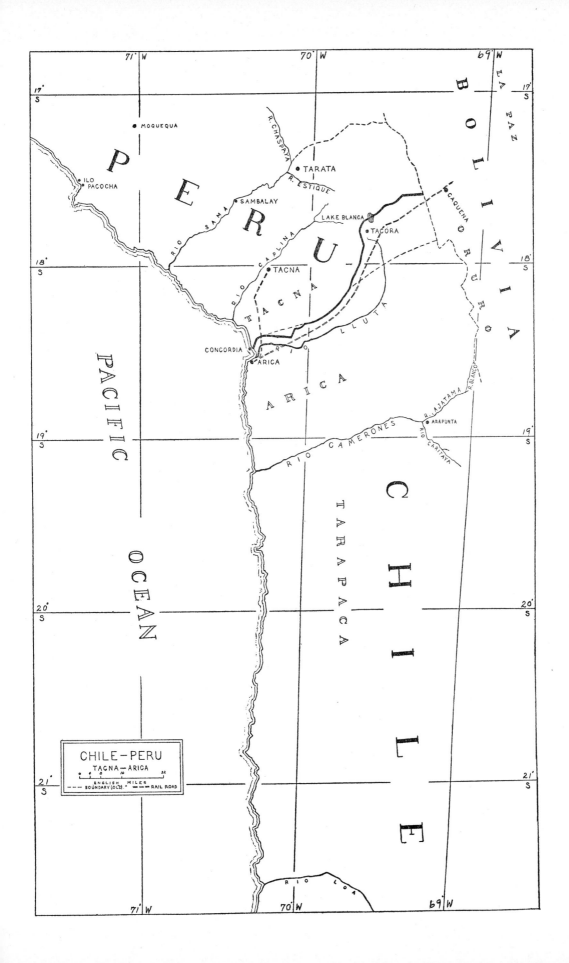

BOLIVIA

LA PAZ

PERU

MOQUEQUA

ILO
PACOCHA

R. CHASPAYA

TARATA

R. ESTIQUE

SAMBALAY

CAQUENA

LAKE BLANCA

TACORA

ORURO

RIO SAMA

RIO CAPLINA

TACNA

TACNA

LLUTA

CONCORDIA

RIO

RIO

ARICA

R. AJATAMA

R. BLANCO

ARICA

PACIFIC

ARAPUNTA

RIO CAMERONES

RIO CARITAYA

C

OCEAN

TARAPACA

H

I

L

E

CHILE — PERU

TACNA — ARICA

ENGLISH   MILES
BOUNDARY (OLD)   RAIL ROAD

RIO LOA

standing protest from the diplomatic corps,[8] bombarded Valparaiso for three hours, causing the destruction by fire of numerous buildings, including customs warehouses. The Spanish fleet raised the blockade of Caldera on January 16, 1866,[9] and of Valparaiso on April 14, 1866,[10] and after bombarding Callao on May 2, wholly suspended hostilities on the Pacific coast and on May 9, 1866, sailed away,[11] but the technical state of war continued until April 11, 1871,[12] when through the mediation of the United States a general armistice was signed at Washington between Spain and the allied republics of Bolivia, Chile, Ecuador, and Peru. In the course of this conflict the United States declared a policy of non-intervention in cases of war between the Spanish-American states, even with a European power, when, to reassure Chile of the friendship of the United States, Secretary of State William H. Seward wrote Judson Kilpatrick, United States minister to Chile:

> We maintain and insist, with all the decision and energy which is compatible with our existing neutrality, that the republican system which is accepted by the people in any one of those (Spanish-American) states shall not be wantonly assailed, and that it shall not be subverted as an end of a lawful war by European powers. . . . We therefore concede to every nation the right to make peace or war for such causes other than political or ambitious as it thinks right and wise. In such wars as are waged between nations which are in friendship with ourselves, if they are not pushed, like the French war in Mexico, to the political point before mentioned, we do not intervene, but remain neutral. . . . We obtained assurances from Spain at the beginning, and at other stages of the present war, that, in any event, her hostilities against Chile should not be prosecuted beyond the limits which I have before described. We understand ourselves now and henceforth ready to hold Spain to this agreement, if, contrary to our present expectations, it should be found necessary. . . . We used our good offices . . . to secure an agreement for peace without dishonor, or even damage, to Chile. Those who think that the United States could enter as an ally into every war in which a friendly republican state on this continent becomes involved, forget that peace is the constant interest and the unwavering policy of the United States. . . . The United States . . . have from the time of Washington adhered to the principle of non-intervention.[13]

Prior to 1866 Peru owned from Tacna to the river Loa 235 miles of the nitrate regional strip along the narrow desert coast, and Bolivia claimed the next 240 miles, from the river Loa to 25° S. Peru signed with Bolivia at Lima on February 6, 1875,[14] a secret treaty of defensive alliance against all foreign aggression; and when Chile occupied Antofagasta on February 14,

---

[8] 56 *British and Foreign State Papers* 787–791, 946–948, 953–987. *U. S. Dipl. Corr.*, 1866–67, II, 282; *ibid.*, 1867, II, 260–276. Clunet, *J. de Dr. Int.*, XLV (1918), 811–813.

[9] 56 *British and Foreign State Papers* 896.

[10] *Ibid.*, 646–647.

[11] *U. S. Dipl. Corr.*, 1868, II, 311–326.

[12] *Col. de Trat. de Chile* (Santiago, 1875), II, 69–75.

U. S. For. Rel., 1872, 592–593. *Arch. Dipl.*, 1869, II, 594–600; *ibid.*, 1875, II, 8–9. Ratifications exchanged at Washington, Jan. 24, 1872.

[13] Letter of June 2, 1866. *U. S. Dipl. Corr.*, 1866–67, II, 413–414. *Arch. Dipl.*, 1866, IV, 139–141.

[14] Ricardo Aranda, *Col. de Trat. del Peru*, II, 440–445. 70 *British and Foreign State Papers* 214–216. Ratifications exchanged at La Paz, June 16, 1873.

1879, and on March 17 [15] asked Peru to proclaim neutrality in Chile's resulting war with Bolivia, Peru on March 21,[16] declined. On April 5, 1879,[17] Chile declared war on Peru and Bolivia and blockaded Iquique.[18] On April 6 [19] President Mariano I. Prado proclaimed the existence of the *casus foederis* and the coming into effect of the Treaty of 1873, and Peruvian troops joined the Bolivians in the field against Chile. The Chileans defeated a combined Peruvian-Bolivian army at Tarapacá on November 27, 1879, and the Peruvians retreated to Tacna province, losing thus the whole Tarapacá nitrate area. In February 1880, 12,000 Chileans landed at Pacocha near Ilo, eighty miles north of Arica, and on March 20 they occupied Moquegua and drove the Peruvians out of Tarata, which commands the southwestern passes into the Titicacan upland. In April the Chileans marched south across the desert to Tacna, where on May 26 they met and defeated the allied army on the crest of the sand dunes above the city, now called the Campo de la Alianza. Two thousand Peruvians fell back upon Arica, where for a month they held out in the Morro, a fortified rocky headland 400 feet high, against land attacks and naval bombardment, the place being finally carried by assault with no quarter on June 7, 1880. On January 17, 1881, the Chilean army took possession of Lima,[20] and Callao surrendered on January 18, 1881. The conquerors remained in occupation of Lima until General Miguel Iglesias, who with Chilean support had been elected president, approved the Treaty of Ancón. On October 25, 1883, the Peruvian flag was hoisted once more in Lima, and the army of occupation was reduced to 4,000 men. On March 8, 1884,[21] a constituent assembly at Lima, reciting the inescapable necessity, ratified the Treaty of Ancón. In May the last Chilean forces were withdrawn from Lima and on August 3, 1884, from Chorrillos.

The War of the Pacific which had for its objective possession of the mineral coastal zone from Tacna to Antofagasta thus ended with Chile completely victorious and she imposed her will on the loser Peru. The Treaty of Ancón, signed by José Antonio de Lavalle, Peruvian minister of foreign relations, Mariano Castro Saldívar, Peruvian minister, and Jovino Novoa, Chilean minister, at Lima on October 20, 1883,[22] provided that (Article 2) Peru

[15] Ricardo Aranda, *Col. de Trat. del Peru*, IV, 171–173.

[16] *Ibid.*, 173–174.

[17] *Ibid.*, 191. 70 *British and Foreign State Papers* 184–185, 341–360.

[18] *Ibid.*, 1195.

[19] Ricardo Aranda, *Col. de Trat. del Peru*, IV, 208–209. 70 *British and Foreign State Papers* 692. *Arch. Dipl.*, 1878–79, III, 332–348, 363–365.

[20] Ricardo Aranda, *Col. de Trat. del Peru*, IV, 325–329.

[21] *Ibid.*, 660, n.

[22] A. Bascuñán Montes, *Recop. de Trat. de Chile* (Santiago, 1894), II, 158–166. Ricardo Aranda, *Col. de Trat. del Peru*, IV, 655–661. *Actos Int. del Peru* (Lima, 1915), No. 25. *U. S. For. Rel.*, 1883, pp. 731–732. 74 *British and Foreign State Papers* 349–353; 77 *ibid.*, 1016. Martens, *Nouv. Rec. Gén. de Traités*, 2e Sér., X, 191–195. Victor Andres Belaunde, *The Treay of Ancón in the Light of International Law* (Washington, 1923). Ratified by Peru, Mar. 28, 1884; ratifications exchanged at Lima, Mar. 28, 1884; promulgated by Chile, May 21, 1884.

ceded to Chile in perpetuity and unconditionally the territory of the littoral province of Tarapacá,[23] bounded north by Camarones ravine and river, south by Loa ravine and river, east by Bolivia, and west by the Pacific; (Article 3) the territory of Tacna and Arica provinces, bounded north by the Sama river from its source in the cordilleras adjoining Bolivia to its mouth at the sea, south by Camarones ravine and river, east by Bolivia and west by the Pacific, should continue in the possession of Chile and subject to Chilean legislation and authorities for ten years from the ratification of the treaty; and after (or at the end of) that period a plebiscite by popular vote should decide if the territory of those provinces would remain permanently under the dominion and sovereignty of Chile or if it would continue to be part of Peruvian territory, the country to which the two provinces should be annexed to pay to the other 10,000,000 pesos; a special protocol, to be considered an integral part of the treaty, to establish the form in which the plebiscite should be held and the terms and instalments for payment of the ten millions.

Chile in the exercise of administrative authority [24] imposed certain taxes in the region she was holding, and on January 20, 1885,[25] decreed the division of the department of Tacna, in the province of the same name, into eight administrative districts, of which (5th) Tarata was bounded north by Chaspaya river and ravine, declared to be the main tributary of the river Sama, and east by Bolivia and the department of Puno, Peru, and (6th) Sama was bounded north and west by the frontiers of the territory and east by the narrows of Sambalai which separated it from Tarata. Peru protested on February 16, 1885,[26] that according to the Treaty of Ancón Tarata formed no part of the territory which Chile should occupy, but Chile replied that it was all south of the Sama, which was the northern boundary of her possession under the treaty, and offered to have a commission of two experts, one named by each country, meet, study the matter, and inspect the course of the Sama from its sources to its mouth. Peru declined the commission and declared that the only question was the boundary of the province of Tarata, and that it was the Estique and not the Chaspaya which flowed down to become the Sama; but on November 9, 1885,[27] when Chile made a new division of the department of Tacna into nine districts, she included (8th) Tarata and (9th) Sama with the same boundaries as before. British pressure induced Chile to

[23] As to criminal jurisdiction in Tarapacá after the cession, see Clunet, *J. de dr. int. privé*, XVII (1890), 586–605.

[24] As to inheritance rights in Tacna during the possession by Chile, see Clunet, *J. de dr. int. privé*, XXXV (1908), 226–229.

[25] *Bol. de las Leyes* (Santiago, 1885), LIV, 15–18.

[26] Ricardo Aranda, *Col. de Trat. del Peru*, IV, 690–698.

[27] *Bol. de las Leyes*, LIV, 1123–1129.

make a supplementary agreement on January 8, 1890,[28] giving up a considerable part of further proceeds from the guano islands which she had exacted in payment of her expenses for the war.

On April 4, 1893,[29] Peru asked Chile to proceed to the preparation of the protocol which should govern the form of the plebiscite and the terms for the payments. A protocol signed by José Mariano Jiménez, Peruvian minister of foreign relations, and Javier Vial Solar, Chilean minister at Lima, on January 26, 1894,[30] called simply for the plebiscite to be held under such conditions of reciprocity as should assure an honest vote, to be the faithful expression of the popular will; but a change of government in Chile prevented this from being ratified. Differences of opinion over who should be allowed to vote and other details protracted the negotiations until on March 28, 1894, the end of the ten years stipulated for Chile's possession under the treaty, Peru proposed to put the provinces into the hands of a third power which should hold the plebiscite and deliver the territory according to the result. Chile rejected this proposal, as she did all others made by Peru as to the qualifications of voters or time and security for payment of the ten millions, and meanwhile made with Bolivia the unexecuted secret treaty of May 18, 1895,[31] by which (Article 1) if Chile acquired permanent dominion and sovereignty over Tacna and Arica she was to transfer them to Bolivia, and (Article 3) Chile was to use all her efforts to obtain complete property over those territories.

After the expiration of the treaty period Chile remained in possession of the two provinces, and negotiations continued until there was signed by Juan José Latorre, Chilean minister of foreign relations, and Guillermo E. Billinghurst, Peruvian vice-president and special minister, at Santiago on April 16, 1898,[32] when Chile appeared to be on the verge of war with Argentina, a protocol submitting the questions of electoral qualifications and payment of the ten millions to the arbitration of the Queen Regent, Maria Cristina, of Spain.[33] The Peruvian Congress ratified and the Chilean Senate on August 1, 1898, approved this protocol, but the Chilean Chamber of Deputies refused to accept it, and negotiations were resumed. Diplomatic relations were broken off from March 1901 until October 21, 1905. On September 23,

[28] A. Bascuñán Montes, *Recop. de Trat. de Chile* (Santiago, 1894), II, 345-349, 380-381. Ratifications exchanged, Feb. 14, 1890.

[29] *Mem. del Min. de Rel. Ext. del Peru, 1896* (Lima, 1896), pp. 83-94. *Rev. de dr. int. et de lég. comp.*, XXIX (1897), 660-665.

[30] *Mem. del Min. de Rel. Ext. del Peru, 1896* (Lima, 1896), pp. 95-146.

[31] See §7, this chap., *supra.*

[32] *Circular sobre la Cuestión Tacna y Arica, Min. de Rel. Ext. del Peru* (Lima, 1901), 302-310. *Algunas Reflecciones acerca del Protocolo Billinghurst-Latorre* (Lima, 1898).

[33] Carlos Wiesse, *Apuntaciones sobre el Plebiscito* (Lausana, 1898).

1902,[34] Peru made the boundary treaty with Bolivia which provided for demarcation of the frontier between the Peruvian provinces of Tacna and Arica and the Bolivian province of Carangas; and on October 20, 1904,[35] Chile made with Bolivia the boundary treaty which provided that Chile should pay the expense of constructing a railroad from Arica to La Paz with free transit to Bolivian commerce forever by ports on the Pacific, against which treaty Peru protested. In private litigation before Chilean courts in Arica over the title to borax deposits in Chilcaya, it appeared that Chile following a decree of May 4, 1904, held that from Arapunta, where the Ajatama from the northeast and the Caritaya from the southeast join to form the Camarones, the boundary between Tarapacá [36] and Arica provinces ran up the Ajatama to the Blanco and thence to the Bolivian frontier, while Peru apparently maintained that the Caritaya was the true boundary to its source on the Bolivian frontier.

The United States continued its efforts at mediation begun during the war and carried on intermittently since 1880 without success, and in 1909 [37] was exchanging views on proposals for a plebiscite agreement when the Vatican, which had kept the parishes of Belén, Cedfa, Estique, Tacna, Tarapa, and Tarata within the Peruvian See of Arequipa,[38] refused to submit new appointments of priests in those parishes by the Bishop of Arequipa to the formality of approval by Chile, and Chilean authorities under an order of February 17, 1910, expelled the Peruvian priests and closed the churches. On March 19, 1910, Peru withdrew her legation in Santiago, and the United States on an intimation from Chile declined to take over the representation of Peruvian interests.

On November 20, 1912,[39] Wenceslao Valera, Peruvian minister of foreign relations, proposed by telegram to Antonio Huneeus, Chilean minister of foreign relations, that the plebiscite should take place in 1933 under the direction of boards appointed by a commission of five, two Chileans appointed by Chile, two Peruvians appointed by Peru, and the president of the Supreme Court of Chile, to preside; all persons able to read and write born in Tacna and Arica or resident there for three years to be entitled to vote. Chile accepted by telegram the same day, and President Guillermo E. Billinghurst in November 1912 sent the protocol with a secret message to the Peru-

[34] See §9, this chap., *supra*.

[35] See §7, this chap., *supra*.

[36] Carlos Paz Soldán, *Límites entre Arica y Tarapacá* (Lima, 1904).

[37] Victor M. Maúrtua, *La Cuestión del Pacífico* (Lima, 1901; Philadelphia, 1901; New York, 1902; Lima, 1919). *Comunicaciones cambiadas entre Chile y el Peru, 1905 á 1908* (Santiago, 1908). *"Rose Book" of Chile, Confiden-* *tial* (Washington, 1913). José Maria Barreto, *El problema peruano-chileno* (3ª ed., Lima, 1919). *U. S. For. Rel.*, 1913, pp. 1164–1239.

[38] Juan José Julio y Elizalde, *Los Chilenizadores de Tacna y Arica* (Callao, 1908). J. Perez Canto, *El Conflicto después de la Victoria* (Lima, 1921).

[39] Victor Andrés Belaunde, *Nuestra Cuestión con Chile* (Lima, 1919), p. 245.

vian Senate, but popular opinion thought the arrangement conceded too much, Congress refused to approve it, and the issue became one of the moving causes for President Billinghurst's deposition on February 4, 1914. The Chilean government supported the agreement, but after it became evident that Peru would not ratify the Chilean Congress failed to act on it.

There were suggestions of mediation by the United States while President Woodrow Wilson was in Paris in December 1918.[40] On November 1, 1920,[41] Peru, as she had notified France in January 1919 [42] she proposed to do, presented to the League of Nations a request [43] that the Assembly to meet for the first time at Geneva, November 15, 1920, reconsider and revise the Treaty of Ancón, invoking Articles 15 and 19 of the Covenant, on the grounds that that treaty was imposed and maintained by force, had not been carried out by Chile in essential provisions and involved a serious danger of war. On December 2, 1920, probably because of pressure from Washington, Peru withdrew her request, reserving the right to submit her difference with Chile to the League at a later date. On December 12, 1921, Chile invited Peru to agree on arrangements for a plebiscite on the basis of the Huneeus-Valera plan, but Peru refused on December 17 on the ground that a plebiscite under Chilean auspices after so many years would only tend to increase the differences; and proposed arbitration under the auspices of the United States. On January 17, 1922, President Warren G. Harding invited the governments of Chile and Peru to send delegates to Washington to devise means of reaching an agreement regarding the unfulfilled provisions of the Treaty of Ancón, either by direct negotiations or through recourse to arbitration. Bolivia by telegram of President Bautista Saavedra on January 21, 1922, to President Harding asked to be included in the negotiations, but both Chile and Peru, who had accepted, refused to admit her, and President Harding, although he had invited the others, answered Bolivia that he could not take the initiative.

Carlos Aldunate S. and Luis Izquierdo for Chile and Melitón F. Porras and Hernán Velarde for Peru met in the Pan American Union building in Washington on May 15, 1922, were welcomed by Secretary of State Hughes, and held a series of conferences which finally adjourned July 21, 1922.[44] After a month's discussion between the special missions, no agreement being in sight, Secretary Hughes suggested a formula which became the basis of the

[40] David Hunter Miller, *My Diary at the Conference of Paris* (New York, 1924-26), II, 512-518; *ibid.*, III, 1-3, 184-187, 214-215. Francisco Enrique Malaga Grenet, *Una Carta á Wilson* (Arequipa, 1919; Lima, 1919).

[41] *League of Nations, Records of First Assembly, Plenary Meetings* (Geneva, 1920), pp. 580-581, 596-597. *Amer. J. Int. Law*, XV (1921), 70-73. *U. S. For. Rel.*, 1920, I, 349-350.

[42] David Hunter Miller, *My Diary at the Conference of Paris* (New York, 1924-26), IV, 200-201; *ibid.*, XVII, 55-56.

[43] *Cf.* Bolivia's petition, 1920. §7, this chap., *supra*.

[44] *Las Conferencias de Washington, Min. de Rel. Ext. de Chile* (Santiago, 1922). Luis Arteaga G., *Las Negociaciones de Washington* (Santiago, 1922).

solution finally adopted. On July 17 the delegates informally asked President Harding to act as arbitrator. On July 20, 1922,[45] there was signed a protocol of arbitration and a complementary act defining the scope of the arbitration. The protocol recited (Article 1) that it was established that the only difficulties arising from the Treaty of Ancón on which the two countries were not in accord were the questions concerning the unexecuted provisions of Article 3 of that treaty and provided (Article 2) that those difficulties should be submitted to the arbitration of the president of the United States, who should decide them without right of appeal, after hearing both parties and their allegations and proofs, and should settle times and procedure; and the complementary act agreed that the arbitrator should, (Sec. 1) in order to determine the manner in which Article 3 of the Treaty of Ancón ought to be executed, decide whether or not the plebiscite should be held under existing circumstances; (Sec. 2) in case he should find for a plebiscite, determine its conditions; (Sec. 3) if he should decide against a plebiscite, the parties should discuss the situation so created, the administrative organization of the provinces to be maintained meanwhile; (Sec. 4) if they could not agree, the two governments should seek the good offices of the United States; and (Sec. 5) the pending claims concerning Tarata and Chilcaya should be included according to the determination of the final disposition of the territory referred to in Article 3 of the Treaty of Ancón. President Harding, being formally invited on January 16, 1923, accepted the office of arbitrator on January 29, and on March 13 approved a special convention concerning procedure made by the parties on March 2. The printed cases were presented in Washington in November 1923 by Carlos Aldunate S. and Ernesto Barros, agents [46] for Chile,[47] and Melitón F. Porras and Solón Polo, representatives [48] for Peru,[49] and the counter cases in April 1924.

On March 4, 1925,[50] President Calvin Coolidge [51] handed down his opinion and award, deciding that the plebiscite should be held under a plebiscitary

[45] League of Nations Treaty Series, No. 537; XXI, 142–146. 116 British and Foreign State Papers 673–675. Martens, Nouv. Rec. Gén. de Traités, 3ᵉ Sér., XX, 30–31. Amer. J. Int. Law, XVII (1923), 82–89. Clunet, J. de dr. int., XLIX (1922), 780–781. Rec. des Cours, VIII (1925), 297–300. Bull., Pan-Amer. Union, LV (1922), 217–228. Ratified by Chile, Decree #1577, Nov. 30, 1922; ratified by Peru, Res. Leg. #4522, Sept. 13, 1922; ratifications exchanged at Washington, Jan. 15, 1923.

[46] Counsel: Robert Lansing, Lester H. Woolsey.

[47] Case and Appendix (Washington, 1923). Counter Case, Appendix and Notes on Peruvian Case (Washington, 1924). Alegato y Anexos (Washington, 1923; Santiago, 1924). Contra Alegato y Anexos (Washington, 1924; Santiago, 1924).

[48] Counsel: Edwin M. Borchard, Joseph E. Davies, Wade H. Ellis, Hoke Smith, José Salvador Cavero.

[49] Case and Appendix (Washington, 1923). Counter Case and Appendix (Washington, 1924). Replica del Peru (Washington, 1924). Alegato del Peru (Lima, 1925).

[50] Opinion and Award of the Arbitrator (Washington, 1925). Fallo Arbitral (Santiago, 1925). El Fallo Arbitral, Alberto Ulloa (Lima, 1925). Rev. Universitaria, Año XIX, Vol. I, pp. 3–110. Samuel A. Maginnis, "Our Government Blunders in Tacna-Arica," Curr. Hist., XXV, 47–52, Amer. J. Int. Law, XIX (1925), 393–432. 122 British and Foreign State Papers 219–262. Rev. gén. de dr. int. pub., XXXII (1925), 422–424, 443–470. Rev. de dr. int. et de lég. comp., 3ᵉ Sér., VI (1925), 295–309. Rev. de Der. Int. (Havana), VIII (1925), 78–129. H. Lauterpacht, Private Law Sources and Analogies of International Law (London, 1927), pp. 290–293.

[51] Vice-president until President Harding died, Aug. 2, 1923.

commission of three, with appeal from their decisions to the arbitrator;[52] (Par. 1) the territory to which Article 3 of the Treaty of Ancón related, whose disposition was to be determined by the plebiscite, was the territory of the Peruvian provinces of Tacna and Arica as they stood on October 20, 1883, that is, so much of Tacna province as was bounded north by the river Sama, and the whole of Arica province (bounded south by the line between the old provinces of Arica and Tarapacá); and (Par. 2) the arbitrator reserved the power and right to appoint a special commission of three [53] to draw the boundary lines (as to Tarata and Chilcoya) of the territory covered by Article 3 of the Treaty of Ancón in accordance with the foregoing determination. Money claims of both parties arising during the occupation were dismissed, and the ten million pesos were to be paid after the proclamation by the arbitrator of the result of the plebiscite, one million within ten days, one million within a year, and two millions annually thereafter for four years. Voters were to be males over twenty-one able to read and write or owning real property, born in Tacna and Arica, and Chileans and Peruvians who had on July 20, 1922, resided two years continuously in the territory and continued so to reside until the day of registration.

The usual United States ignorance or inappreciation of South American realities and reactions, which in 1922 in a legalistic gesture to Bolivia closed the door to such broadening of the discussion as might have alleviated or even averted the Chaco War, thus went on in 1925 with continued disregard of human nature to refuse to Peru the neutralization which alone after forty years of partisan control could have made free voting possible.

The award was immediately accepted by Chile, but Peru was perceptibly disheartened by it, and on April 2, 1925, asked [54] of President Coolidge, and was refused by him on April 9, the concession of certain special guarantees for the plebiscite, which would have been equivalent to modification of the award as rendered. For the plebiscitary commission, President Coolidge named General John J. Pershing as president, Chile named Augustín Edwards, former minister of foreign relations, and Peru, finally persuaded to accept the award, on June 18, 1925,[55] named Manuel de Freyre y Santander, her minister to Argentina. Chile on May 14 and Peru on July 25, 1925, en-

[52] On Dec. 16, 1925, Chile made an appeal concerning the commission's decision on conditional dates to the arbitrator, who on Jan. 15, 1926, dismissed the appeal and upheld the commission. On Feb. 8 both countries appealed against certain provisions of the regulations as to qualifications of voters and the arbitrator on Feb. 25 affirmed the findings and decisions of the commission. *Amer. J. Int. Law*, XX (1926), 605-625.

[53] President Coolidge on Mar. 26, 1925, named Gen.

Jay J. Morrow, former governor of the Panama Canal Zone, as the United States member of this commission. Chile named Ernesto Greve, engineer, and Peru on June 25, 1925, named Lt.-Col. Oscar H. Ordóñez. They first met at Tacna, Aug. 4, 1925.

[54] *Rev. de Der. Int.* (Havana), VIII (1925), 130-142.

[55] *Bol. del Min. de Rel. Ext. del Peru* (Lima, 1925), 2ª Época, Num. 6, pp. 9-15.

acted laws giving the plebiscitary commission complete control over the plebiscite, with authority to settle all questions concerning registration and voting. General Pershing arrived at Arica on August 2 on the United States cruiser *Rochester,* and the commission met at Arica on August 5 to inaugurate its work and had forty sessions thereafter.

On September 1, 1925, in the presence of the plebiscitary commission the province of Tarata [56] north of Estique was delivered over by Chile to Peru, in accordance with the arbitral decision. Peru insisted upon complete neutralization of the territory, before the voting, alleging intimidation by officials, expulsion of Peruvian sympathizers, and other acts of violence, some of which seemed to be substantiated by the observations of the commission's president and eight observers chosen from United States employees in the Panama Canal Zone. It was announced from Washington on December 28, 1925, that General Pershing might have to give up his post on account of his health, and on December 29 that he was about to return to the United States. On January 12, 1926, it was announced that Pershing had resigned and that Major-General William Lassiter, commander of the United States forces in the Canal Zone, had been appointed to succeed him, permanently, since there was no provision for a temporary appointment, though Pershing might go back. Immediately after the commission meeting of January 27 at which were adopted the registration and election regulations, General Pershing sailed for the United States on the cruiser *Denver.* Major-General Lassiter sailed from Panama on January 13 and arrived at Arica in time to preside at the meeting of the commission on January 30. The regulations were published on February 15, and on February 23 sixty-one United States army officers, mostly captains and lieutenants, arrived in Arica to serve on the registration and election boards. On March 25 Peru demanded an indefinite postponement of the plebiscite on the ground that Peruvian voters would not be sufficiently protected, but this was denied by the commission, and registration began on March 27, with Peruvian board members absent and most of the Peruvian voters not registering. By the twenty-sixth of April 5,721 had registered, claimed to be all Chileans, and registration was prolonged to May 21. Violence continued, although Peru had began to ship back to Callao the voters she had been bringing in. On June 9 General Lassiter proposed a delay in the time for voting to see if the direct negotiations which had been going on in Washington since April 6 between special representatives of the two countries meeting with Secretary of State Frank B. Kellogg would result in a settlement which should make the plebiscite unnecessary; and after stating

[56] *Cuestión Tarata, Circula de 20 set., 1921,* Min. de Rel. Ext. (Lima, 1921).

his own views as to the existing state of terrorism which made impossible a free and fair plebiscite, General Lassiter presented a resolution to terminate the plebiscitary proceedings. At the request of the Chilean commissioner, who asserted that the commission was not competent to declare the plebiscite impracticable and read a long statement in support of his motion to fix June 21 for the voting, action on the resolution was postponed. At the next meeting, on June 14, after the reading of a long statement by General Lassiter with argument and instances tending to show fatally bad plebiscitary conditions, the resolution for termination of the proceedings was carried by the vote of the president and the Peruvian commissioner, the Chilean commissioner not voting. The commission, to wind up its affairs, held four further sessions from which the Chilean commissioner absented himself and on June 21 declared itself adjourned,[57] to meet at the call of its president. On June 18 Chile withdrew from the direct negotiations in Washington because of the ending of the plebiscitary arrangements. General Lassiter left for Panama on the U.S.S. *Denver* on June 21, and the Peruvian delegation and many sympathizers sailed on June 23 for Callao.

On November 30, 1926,[58] Secretary of State Kellogg renewed his proposal for settlement by transfer of the disputed territory to Bolivia, which was refused by both Chile and Peru, the latter declaring that as Chile had prevented the carrying out of the plebiscite required by Article 3 of the Treaty of Ancón, she had lost all her rights under that article and Peru was now fully entitled to possession of Tacna and Arica,[59] a claim which, however logical and lawful, was obviously impossible of realization in fact. On July 9, 1928, Secretary of State Kellogg suggested the reëstablishment of direct intercourse, to which both countries agreed, and diplomatic relations, broken off since March 19, 1910, were renewed on October 3, 1928. On October 17, 1928, it was agreed to suspend for four months, and in February 1929 for three months more, the operation of the boundary commission called for by Paragraph 2 of the arbitral decision; on May 17, 1929,[60] President Herbert C. Hoover as arbitrator (in succession to President Coolidge) ordered the indefinite suspension of its labors, and on August 2, 1929, their termination. Direct negotiations between the two governments, urged, smoothed, and forwarded

[57] Domingo Arturo Garfias, *El Proceso Plebiscitario* (Santiago, 1926). *Documentos relativos al Plebiscito* (Lima, 1927), 6 vols. William J. Dennis, *Documentary History of the Tacna-Arica Dispute* (University of Iowa Studies in the Social Sciences, Iowa City, 1927), vol. 8, No. 3. Sarah Wambaugh, *Plebiscites since the World War* (Washington, 1933), I, 331-410; *ibid.*, II, 281-491.

[58] *El Proceso de Tacna y Arica, 1925-1927* (Lima, 1927). Juan Angulo Puente Amao, *Historia de los Límites del Perú* (Lima, 1927), pp. 167-312. *Amer. J. Int. Law,*

XXI (1927), Supp., 11-15.

[59] Edwin M. Borchard, *Opinion on the Controversy between Peru and Chile* (Washington, 1920).

[60] *Documentos de la Comisión Especial de Límites* (Lima, 1926), 4 vols. Enrique Brieba, *Memoria sobre los Límites entre Chile y Perú* (Santiago, 1931), 3 vols. *Mem. del Min. de Rel. Ext. de Chile, 1929* (Santiago, 1930), pp. 25-29. *Mem. del Min. de Rel. Ext. del Perú, 1929* (Lima, 1929), Anexos, pp. 30-32.

by the two United States ministers, William S. Culbertson [61] at Santiago and Alexander P. Moore [62] at Lima, with some minor difficulties removed by a proposal of final bases for a settlement by President Hoover in the exercise of good offices on May 14, 1929, resulted at last in adjustment of the long dispute by a division of the territory.[63] Emiliano Figueroa Larraín, Chilean minister, and Pedro José Rada y Gamio, Peruvian minister of foreign relations, signed at Lima on June 3, 1929,[64] a treaty providing that (Article 1) the controversy arising from Article 3 of the treaty of October 20, 1883, was finally settled; (Article 2) the territory of Tacna and Arica should be divided into two parts by a line from a point on the coast to be called "Concordia" ten kilometers (6.21 miles) north of the bridge over the Lluta; thence eastward parallel to the Chilean section of the railroad from Arica to La Paz and distant ten kilometers from it,[65] with such deflections as might be necessary to utilize in the demarcation the near-by geographic features, so as to leave in Chilean territory the Tacora sulphur beds and their appurtenances; thence through the center of Lake Blanca so that one of its parts should remain in Chile and the other in Peru; Chile ceded forever to Peru all rights over Uchusuma and Mauri (Azucarero) canals, without prejudice to her sovereignty over such parts of those aqueducts as remained in Chilean territory after the laying down of the boundary line just described; and as to both canals Chile established in the parts which cross her territory the fullest rights of perpetual servitude in favor of Peru, to include the right to widen the existing canals, modify their course, and collect all the water available in their course through Chilean territory, except the waters which then flowed into the Lluta and those which supply the Tacora sulphur beds; (Article 3) the frontier thus described to be fixed and marked on the ground by posts by a mixed commission of one member named by each government, and disagreement to be resolved by the inappealable vote of a third member designated by the President of the United States; (Article 4) Chile should deliver to Peru thirty days after the exchange of ratifications the territory which thus ought to belong to Peru; (Article 5) for the use of Peru, Chile should construct at her own expense within 1,575 meters of Arica bay a landing wharf for steam vessels, a building for the Peruvian customs and a terminal station for the rail-

[61] Decorated by Chile on Dec. 18, 1929, with the Grand Cross of the Order of Merit and by Peru in 1929 with the Grand Cross of the Order of the Sun.

[62] Died, Feb. 17, 1930.

[63] Mem. del Min. de Rel. Ext. de Chile, 1929 (Santiago, 1930), pp. 9-24. Mem. del Min. de Rel. Ext. del Peru, 1929 (Lima, 1929), pp. xxxii-cviii, cxxxiii-cxlvii.

[64] League of Nations Treaty Series, No. 2157, XCIV,

402-411; ibid., C, 467. 130 British and Foreign State Papers 463-466. Amer. J. of Int. Law, XXIII (1929), 605-610. British Year Book of International Law, XI (1930), 187-193. Ratified by Chile (113 to 14 and 3 abstentions), July 4, 1929; ratified by Peru (144 to 1), July 2, 1929; ratifications exchanged and check delivered at Santiago, July 28, 1929; promulgated by Chile, July 28, 1929.

[65] Except at Lake Blanca.

road to Tacna, in which establishments and zone commerce in transit for Peru should enjoy the independence of a most ample free port; (Article 6) Chile to deliver to Peru simultaneously with the exchange of ratifications six million dollars and without any cost to Peru all the public works completed or in construction and all the public real property situated in the territories which were to remain under Peruvian sovereignty; (Article 7) both governments should respect private rights legally acquired in their respective territories, including the concession granted by Peru to the Arica-Tacna Railroad Company in 1852 [66] according to which that railroad at the end of its contract should become the property of Peru, and without prejudice to her sovereignty Chile constituted in favor of Peru the fullest perpetual servitude over that part of the line which crossed Chilean territory; (Article 8) all money claims between the parties should be reciprocally canceled, whether or not arising from the Treaty of Ancón; (Article 9) the parties would make a convention as to frontier police for public security in the territories adjoining the division line; (Article 11) to commemorate the consolidation of their friendly relations the countries should erect on the Morro at Arica a symbolic monument of a design to be agreed upon; and (Article 12) in case of any disagreement as to the interpretation of any of the provisions of this treaty, in which in spite of their good will no agreement could be reached, the president of the United States should decide the controversy. A complementary protocol of the same date, June 3, 1929, provided that (Article 1) neither government might without previous agreement with the other cede to any third power all or any part of the territory which, in accordance with the treaty, remained under their respective sovereignties, nor might without such agreement construct across such territories new international railroad lines; (Article 2) the port facilities granted to Peru under Article 5 of the treaty should consist of the most absolutely free transit of persons, merchandise, and armaments to Peruvian territory and from such across Chilean territory; and (Article 3) the fortifications on the Morro at Arica should be dismantled and Chile should construct at her expense the monument provided for in Article 11 of the treaty. The thirty-nine mile railroad to Tacna, begun in 1851 [67] and completed in 1856, the second railroad in South America, already had a sufficient, if small, terminal station in Arica, with customs rooms at one end.

The province of Tacna was handed back by Chile to Peru at a private

---

[66] As to the railroad's acquired right to tax exemption, see Clunet, *J. de dr. int. privé*, XL (1913), 1331.

[67] Law of Dec. 18, 1851. *Col. de Leyes del Peru* (Huaraz, 1853), XII, 346. *El Peruano* (Lima), July 26, 1856, XXXI, 25–26; *ibid.*, May 27, 1857, XXXII, 485; *ibid.*, Sept. 16, 1857, XXXIII, 113; *ibid.*, July 9, 1859, XXXVII, 3–4; *ibid.*, Jan. 12, 1861, XL, 15; *ibid.*, June 6, 1863, XLIV, 251–252.

ceremony in Tacna on August 28, 1929.[68] The demarcation mixed commission [69] was promptly appointed and the delegates met at Arica on September 2, 1929, and again on October 6, proceeding then to set up posts of iron or stone within sight of each other along the boundary from Concordia on the shore north of Arica to the Bolivian line. Artillery, wire entanglements, and barracks on the Morro at Arica have been removed, trenches filled in, and bomb-proofs destroyed, and the whole top left as an open public area. A convention as to frontier police, permitting hot pursuit across the boundary but requiring local imprisonment and extradition, signed at Santiago, April 29, 1930,[70] came into force November 25, 1930. On April 30, 1930,[71] the department of Arica was incorporated by Chile in the province of Tarapacá, with its northern boundary the frontier with Peru as marked by the mixed commission under Article 3 of the Treaty of June 3, 1929. By a treaty signed at Lima, March 17, 1934,[72] it was agreed that in lieu of the wharf, customs office, and railroad terminal station which the government of Chile was to construct in Arica for the use of Peru, Chile should deliver materials up to the value of 2,500,000 pesos which Peru might use in Tacna or elsewhere for public works; and erection of the commemorative monument on the Morro of Arica should be postponed until 1935.

The port of Arica is in the peculiar position of having two railroad terminals and custom houses alien to the flag of its own sovereign, facilities for free transit with La Paz being guaranteed to Bolivia and with Tacna to Peru. Merchandise for La Paz and the northwestern portion of Bolivia in peace time is, on account of the preferential tariffs, shipped for the most part through the former Bolivian port of Antofagasta, even though the rail haul is 711 miles, more than two and a half times as long as the 273 miles from Arica to La Paz; and naturally munitions and supplies for use in the Chaco were landed at the more southern port and sent up to Uyuni to turn south. Traffic with Tacna is slowly growing less. The desert can be made green and inhabitable only in narrow strips lying along the mountain-fed watercourses, and even the Caplina, the largest stream, on which Tacna is situated, disappears in the gray sands before reaching the ocean. The population according to the Chilean census of 1920 of 19,016 for the department, of whom 14,376 were in the town of Tacna, has since been steadily diminishing and was

[68] Chile, Decree #904, June 20, 1929. *Mem. del Min. de Rel. Ext. de Chile, 1929* (Santiago, 1930), pp. 30–41.

[69] Chile, Decrees #1270, Aug. 24, 1929; #1492, Oct. 4, 1929; #1689, Nov. 14, 1929; #1724, Nov. 19, 1929. *Mem. del Min. de Rel. Ext. de Chile, 1929* (Santiago, 1930), pp. 42–45.

[70] *League of Nations Treaty Series*, No. 2612, CXII, 134–138.

[71] Decree #760. *Bol. de Leyes y Decretos* (Santiago, 1930), XCIX, 1231–1236.

[72] *Bulletin, Pan American Union*, LXVIII (1934), 530–531.

probably well under 15,000 in 1934. Moquegua is seventy-five miles to the northwest across the desert, with three principal valleys to cross and no fixed road; and the cordillera prevents easy access to any fertile territory to the northeast. In 1920 Arica had 15,348 inhabitants in the department, of whom 9,015 were in the town, and both are now much smaller (the town had about 4,000 in 1933) and still losing population.

After the will of the conqueror to make permanently her own two provinces taken in war had long postponed final determination and broken down a stipulated plebiscite, an arbitral award as to a minor portion having been carried out, voluntary adjustment by treaty divided the territory. The forty-six year contention over this drear 9,000 square miles seems now to have been definitely settled in a way reasonably satisfactory to both parties.[73] It is not beyond possibility that in an act of continental friendship Chile with the consent of Peru may some day bestow fresh rights and presumed benefits on Bolivia, with generosity similar to that with which Brazil favored Uruguay in 1909.[74]

20. COLOMBIA–ECUADOR. ORIENTE–AGUARICO

The territory of the audiencia of Quito, which defined the later boundary claims of Ecuador, as created November 29, 1563, and added to the viceroyalty of Santa Fé del Nuevo Reino de Granada, May 27, 1717, was by the fundamental law enacted at Santo Tomás de Angostura, December 17, 1817, included as part of the viceroyalty of New Granada in the republic of Colombia. The Colombian territorial division law of June 25, 1824,[1] provided that (Article 9) the department of Cauca should include the four provinces of Popayán, Chocó, Pasto, and Buenaventura; (Article 11) the department of Ecuador should include the three provinces of Pichincha, Imbabura, and Chimborazo; (Article 12) the department of Azuay should include the three provinces of Cuenca, Loja, and Jaen de Bracamoros y Mainas; (Article 13) the department of Guayaquil should include the two provinces of Guayaquil and Manabí; (Article 20) the department of Ecuador should have in the interior the boundaries which divided it from the departments of Azuay and of Guayaquil, and on the shore from the port of Atacames near the mouth of the Esmeraldas to the mouth of the Ancón, the southern boundary of the province of Buenaventura on the coast of the South Sea; (Article 21) the

[73] Cecil Jane, "The Question of Tacna-Arica," Trans., Grotius Soc., XV (1930), 93-119. William J. Dennis, Tacna and Arica (New Haven, 1931).
[74] See §14, this chap., supra.

[1] Col. de las Leyes de Colombia, 1823 y 1824 (Bogotá, 1826), pp. 150-158.

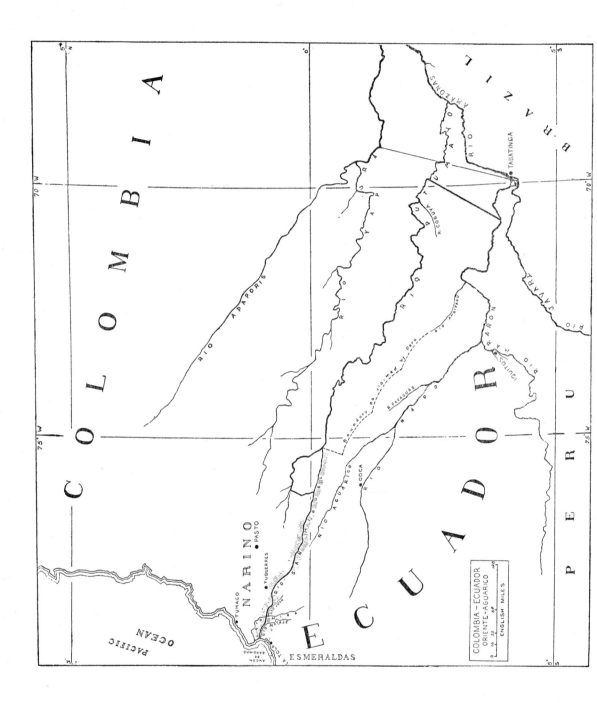

new province of Manabí in the department of Guayaquil should occupy that part of the territory of Esmeraldas which extended along the coast from the Colenche to Atacames, inclusive, and in the interior should have the boundaries which had separated the province of Quito from that part of the territory of Esmeraldas; and (Article 22) the department of Cauca should be divided from the department of Ecuador by the boundaries which had separated the latter from the province of Popayán at the Carchi, which served as boundary of the province of Pasto. In 1830 the three departments of the South proclaimed their autonomy and in the constitution adopted by the national convention at Riobamba in August 1830 declared that (Article 1) the departments of Azuay, Guayas, and Quito formed the independent state of Ecuador, and (Article 6) the territory of the state included the three departments of Ecuador within the boundaries of the ancient kingdom of Quito. Soon after there were local uprisings in various towns of the department of Cauca against the authorities in central Colombia and on December 20, 1830, General Juan José Flores, president of Ecuador, issued at Quito a decree declaring those towns incorporated with Ecuador. The government at Bogotá protested as soon as it learned of this decree and demanded that General Flores abandon the occupied provinces of Pasto and Buenaventura. General Flores replied that the provinces of Chocó and Popayán were at liberty to decide their own future, but that the province of Pasto and a part of Buenaventura were not, as they were definitely annexed to Ecuador. The New Granadan convention on November 8, 1831, decreed that the executive should take the necessary steps for the reincorporation in New Granada of the department of Cauca, and on November 17, 1831, adopted a law providing that (Article 2) the boundaries of the state of New Granada should be those which in 1810 divided the territory of New Granada from the captaincies-general of Venezuela and Guatemala and from the Portuguese possessions of Brazil; to the south, the boundaries should be definitely fixed on the south of the province of Pasto, as soon as there should have been determined what was suitable with respect to the departments of Ecuador, Azuay, and Guayaquil, for which there would be prescribed separately the lines to be adopted. On February 10, 1832, the New Granadan convention by decree authorized (Article 1) the executive to recognize by a treaty Ecuador as a new state composed of the departments of Ecuador, Azuay, and Guayaquil, by the boundaries which they had in 1830, fixed by the territorial division law of June 25, 1824, and (Article 2, Sec. 2) subject to assumption of a proportionate part of the domestic and foreign debts of the republic of Colombia. The con-

vention on February 29, 1832, adopted a constitution for the state of New
Granada which provided that (Article 2) the boundaries of the state to the
south should be definitely fixed on the south of the province of Pasto. Negotiations for the treaty proceeded in Bogotá from February 18 to March 2,
in Ibarra from May 21 to June 9, and in Quito from July 12 to August 16,
1832, when they were broken off because Ecuador would not recede from her
claim to the whole of the ancient kingdom of Quito, including the department of Cauca as far as Cartago, and New Granada insisted on retaining
the whole of the department of Cauca, including the provinces of Pasto and
Buenaventura. War broke out, Colombia was successful in sharp, brief en-
counters, an armistice was agreed upon on October 9, and conferences commencing on December 3 resulted in the signature at Pasto on December 8,
1832,[2] of a treaty of peace and friendship which provided that (Article 2)
the boundaries between New Granada and Ecuador should be those which
according to the Colombian law of June 25, 1824, separated the provinces of
the old department of Cauca from that of Ecuador, the provinces of Pasto[3]
and Buenaventura consequently remaining incorporated in New Granada and
in Ecuador the towns south of the Carchi, the line fixed by Article 22 of such
law of 1824 between the provinces of Pasto and Imbabura; (Article 7)
Ecuador to assume a proportionate part of the domestic and foreign debts of
the republic of Colombia. By an additional pact on the same day it was
agreed that (Article 1) as Ecuador claimed that the ports of Tola and Tu-
maco, included in the province of Buenaventura by the Colombian law of
June 25, 1824, ought to belong to Ecuador, since before 1810 they were incorporated in the territory of the presidency and gobernación of Quito, and as
the commissioners of New Granada did not feel themselves authorized to
come to any agreement on this point, the government of Ecuador should negotiate directly with that of New Granada to resolve and determine the
question by special pacts or stipulations.

Taking advantage of the internal disturbances in New Granada in 1839–
40, General Flores, again president of Ecuador, after local uprisings probably instigated by him, proclaimed the immediate and perpetual annexation
to Ecuador of the province of Túquerres and the temporary and conditional
annexation of the province of Pasto, until the restoration of the central government of New Granada. The chargé d'affaires of New Granada at Quito

[2] Lino de Pombo, *Recop. de Leyes de la Nueva Gra-
nada* (Bogotá, 1845), pp. 442-444. 20 *British and Foreign
State Papers* 1206-1211; 23 *ibid.*, 242-243. Martens, *Nouv.
Rec. de Traités*, XIII, 58-63. Ratified (first 9 articles) by
New Granada Executive, Dec. 29, 1832; by New Granada
Congress, May 30, 1833; ratifications exchanged at Quito,
Sept. 15, 1835.

[3] 25 *British and Foreign State Papers* 1051.

protested vigorously, and finally to avoid a rupture Ecuador consented to rescind the annexation. Negotiations in September 1841 at Túquerres and in November 1841 at Pasto came to nothing. An agreement at Santa Rosa del Carchi, May 29, 1846, provided for the negotiation of a treaty to determine the boundary, and the treaty of peace signed at Bogotá, June 29, 1846,[4] (Article 2) reaffirmed the existence and promised observance of the treaty of December 8, 1832, and (Article 3) agreed to open negotiations as soon as possible, within one year, for a new treaty of friendship, commerce, navigation, and boundaries or for the exchange of ratifications of a commercial treaty concluded at Bogotá, January 20, 1845, and already approved by the Congress of New Granada. There was signed at Bogotá, July 9, 1856,[5] a treaty of friendship, commerce, and navigation which provided that (Article 26) until the territorial boundaries between the two republics should be settled by a special convention in the manner which might seem best, there should continue to be mutually recognized the boundaries which according to the Colombian law of June 25, 1824, separated the old departments of Cauca and Ecuador; and (Article 27) the treaties of Pasto of December 8, 1832, were annulled and canceled.

In 1858 Ecuadorian troops invaded Aguarico and on complaint and demand for reparation by New Granada it was agreed in general terms by diplomatic notes that pending questions between the two republics, including the boundaries in the eastern region, should be submitted to the arbitral decision of Chile; but as there was no treaty or formal agreement which defined exactly the questions to be submitted to the arbiter or settled its jurisdiction. and internal disturbances intervened again in both countries, nothing came of this proposal. In 1871 and in 1876 mixed commissions to fix the frontier line were agreed on by notes, but the agreements were never executed.

Ecuador and Peru [6] signed at Quito, May 2, 1890,[7] the Garcia-Herrera treaty which provided that the northern part of the boundary between them should run from the southernmost source of the Cobuya down the Cobuya to its confluence with the Putumayo and down the Putumayo to the point of intersection and meeting with the first mark on the straight line stipulated (in 1851) as boundary between Peru and Brazil,[8] drawn from Tabatinga to

[4] Martens et Cussy, *Rec. Man. et Prat. de Traités* (Leipzig, 1849), V, 670–672.

[5] *Leyes i Decr. de la Nueva Granada en 1857*, Ed. Ofic. (Bogotá, 1858), pp. 91–98. 47 *British and Foreign State Papers* 1270–1277. Pedro Moncayo, *Colombia i el Brasil* (Valparaiso, 1862), 3ª parte, pp. 103–125. Ratifications exchanged at Quito, May 26, 1857; promulgated by New Granada, July 10, 1857.

[6] See §23, this chap., *infra.*

[7] Ecuador approved with additional protocols of June 5 by legislative decree, June 19, 1890; revoked by legislative decree, July 27, 1894; Peru approved with modifications by legislative resolution, Oct. 25, 1891, reconsidered and recalled, Oct. 28, 1893. *Mem. del Min. de Rel. Ext. del Peru,* 1894 (Lima, 1894), pp. 96–98.

[8] See §13, this chap., *supra.*

the mouth of the Apaporis on the Yapurá. Colombia as soon as she learned of this treaty protested [9] against those clauses of it which directly or indirectly affected her rights in the territories and rivers referred to. Colombia authorized on December 22, 1890,[10] the purchase and equipment of a steam gunboat for police service in the Putumayo, the Caquetá, and their affluents, and the organization, in concert with the ecclesiastical authority, of missions to reduce to civilized life the savage tribes which lived in the Colombian territory drained by the Putumayo, Caquetá, Amazon, and their affluents. Peru protested against this law as injurious to her territorial rights. Because of the reciprocal protests and to treat generally of the frontier situation between Colombia and Peru a series of conferences in which Ecuador was invited to and did take part was held at Lima from October 11 to December 15, 1894.[11] A tripartite convention signed at Lima, December 15, 1894,[12] purported to modify the convention for arbitration between Ecuador and Peru signed at Quito, August 1, 1887,[13] by admitting Colombia to the arbitration by the king of Spain therein provided for, and extending correspondingly the jurisdiction of the arbiter; but although this convention was approved by the Congresses of Colombia and Peru, it failed to obtain the approval of Ecuador, and accordingly never went into effect.

Colombia and Ecuador continued to discuss the question, with occasional frontier clashes, and on June 15, 1900,[14] signed at Bogotá a protocol to suppress violation of neutrality along the boundary by rebels and revolutionaries, agreeing to submit any disagreement which might arise in their mutual relations to the arbitration of a friendly nation, extended by an additional protocol signed at Quito, August 21, 1900,[15] to promise the immediate disarmament of fleeing revolutionaries and to condemn all policy of intervention. Ecuador in 1901 [16] divided the territories of Napo and Zamora, forming the Oriental Region, into four departments, of Napo first and second and Aguarico first and second, established customs houses in Aguarico and in La Coca, organized temporary police and regulated public administration from Archidona and Aguarico or Curaray, reciting that by reason of the unbounded nature of the territory it was not possible to establish exactly the limits of departments

[9] Notes of Sept. 27, 1890, Oct. 19, 1891, and Mar. 2, 1892. *Mem. del Min. de Rel. Ext. del Peru*, 1896 (Lima, 1896), pp. 153–161.

[10] Law #103. *Leyes Nacionales de 1890* (Bogotá, 1891), p. 245.

[11] Aurelio Noboa, *Col. de Trat. del Ecuador* (Guayaquil, 1902), II, 357–446. *Anales Dipl. y Consul. de Colombia* (Bogotá, 1901), II, 681–796.

[12] Aurelio Noboa, *Col. de Trat. del Ecuador* (Guayaquil, 1902), II, 201–204. *Leyes y Res. del Peru de 1895*, Ed. Ofic. (Lima, 1897), pp. 99–100. Demetrio Salamanca

T., *Fronteras Amazonicas de Colombia* (Bogotá, 1905), pp. 148–152. *U. S. For. Rel.*, 1895, I, 250. Ratified by Colombia, Law #52, Oct. 27, 1896; approved by Peru, Dec. 2, 1895; revoked and disapproved, Feb. 4, 1904.

[13] See §23, this chap., *infra*.

[14] Aurelio Noboa, *Col. de Trat. del Ecuador* (Guayaquil, 1902), II, 205–208.

[15] *Ibid.*, 209–211.

[16] Decree of Jan. 1, 1901, Decrees of Feb. 23, 1901, and Decree of April 18, 1901. *Anuario de Leg. Ecuat.*, 1901 (Quito, 1902), pp. 86, 96, 98, 181.

and sections as the law required. Colombia protested on February 20, 1902,[17] that these decrees affected her territorial rights, as placing under Ecuadorian jurisdiction districts which Colombia believed and claimed to be hers. Ecuador signed with Brazil at Rio de Janeiro on May 6, 1904,[18] a treaty providing that the boundary line between them should be the geodesic line from the mouth of the Santo Antonio on the left (north) bank of the Amazon between Tabatinga and Leticia to the confluence of the Apaporis with the Yapurá or Caquetá, but to follow the bed of the Iça or Putumayo between two points where it intersected such geodesic line; without prejudice to any boundary questions pending between Ecuador, Colombia, and Peru. Ecuador thus released to Brazil all possible claims by Ecuador in the area between the Yapurá and the Amazon east of the indicated line and definitely restricted her further discussions with Colombia and Peru to the west of that line. Conferences begun October 26, 1904, between General Julio Andrade, Ecuadorian minister, and Julio Betancourt, Colombian special minister, resulted in the signature at Bogotá, November 5, 1904,[19] of a boundary arbitration convention providing that (Article 1) the two governments submitted to the absolutely unappealable judgment of the emperor of Germany the question of the boundary between the two republics; (Article 3) within fifteen months from his acceptance the cases and documents should be presented, and (Article 4) thereafter only such further expositions or documents as the arbiter might judge necessary; (Article 6) the principal bases for the derivation of rights in the arbitration should be (a) the Colombian law of territorial division of June 25, 1824, (b) the treaty of peace between Colombia and Peru of September 22, 1829, and (c) the part still in force of the treaty between New Granada and Ecuador of July 9, 1856, without excluding other historic-juridical antecedents thought opportune so far as not contrary to these three; (Article 7) Ecuador declared that the territories of the Oriental Region from the course of the Napo to the course of the Caquetá or Yapurá were not included in the arbitration which Ecuador and Peru submitted to the king of Spain under the treaty of August 1, 1887; and (Article 9) if the emperor of Germany should not accept, the president of Mexico should be the arbiter.

General Alfredo Vásquez Cobo, Colombian minister of foreign relations, and General Andrade, Ecuadorian minister, signed at Bogotá, June 5, 1907,[20] an additional convention substituting an arbitral tribunal of six, three named

[17] Aurelio Noboa, *Col. de Trat. del Ecuador* (Guayaquil, 1902), II, 448–455.

[18] See §11, this chap., *supra*.

[19] *Tratados Púb. de Colombia*, Ed. Ofic. (Bogotá, 1913), Segundo Apen., pp. 38–40. Ratified by Colombia, Law #55, Dec. 2, 1904; ratified by Ecuador, Oct. 17, 1905; ratifications not exchanged.

[20] *Leyes de 1907 de Colombia* (2ª Ed. Ofic., Bogotá, 1910), pp. 130–134. Approved by Colombia, Law #38, July 15, 1907; not approved by Ecuador.

by each country, aided by a technical commission of two engineers for each party, to sit at Quito and determine the dividing line according to existing treaties and the present modifications, with departure from the strict right to adopt an equitable line where necessary and convenient for both countries. Neither the 1904 treaty nor its 1907 modification was ever carried into effect, and the same ministers, Andrade and Betancourt, as the result of conferences begun March 25, signed at Bogotá May 24, 1908,[21] a new boundary treaty which provided that (Article 1) the boundary line should run from the mouth of the Mataje at Ancón de Sardinas on the Pacific Ocean up the Mataje to its sources on the ridge of a great branch of the Andes which separates the tributary waters of the Santiago from those which flow to the Mira; thence along that ridge to the headwaters of the Canumbí, and down the Canumbí to its mouth in the Mira; thence up the Mira to its confluence with the San Juan; thence up the San Juan to the mouth of the Agua Hedeonda stream or ravine and by it to its origin on Chiles volcano; thence by the summit of that volcano to the principal source of the Carchi; thence down the Carchi to the bridge of Rumichaca; thence by the watercourse of the Carchi to the mouth of the Tejes or Teques ravine and by that ravine to La Quinta hill, thence to Troya hill; from this hill to the mouth of the Pun stream or ravine on the river which Codazzi and Wolf call the Chúnquer, the demarcation commission should fix the frontier in accordance with the rights which the parties might have respectively in that region; from the mouth of the Pun ravine on such river to the mouth of the Ambiyacú on the Amazon, which are the two ends of the frontier in the Oriental Region, the line should run in the middle of the high lands which form the *divortium aquarum* between the Putumayo and the Napo, so that the latter and the waters which compose it should belong to Ecuador, and the waters which flow to the Putumayo, as well as that river, should continue to belong to Colombia; the demarcation commission might fix the frontier, where there are no heights which determine clearly the *divortium aquarum,* by dividing in equal parts the territorial area which separates the Putumayo and the Napo, so that a perfectly perceptible frontier should remain well established to avoid conflicts of jurisdiction between the authorities of the two countries, and to this end the commission might adopt as frontier the currents of water which might be found on the median line between the Putumayo and the Napo, with regard to the foregoing conditions, until reaching the headwaters of the Ambiyacú; thence down that river to its mouth in the Amazon, which was where the frontier between

[21] Colombia approved by Law #3, Aug. 10, 1908;   Ecuador.
repealed by Law #63, Dec. 13, 1909; not approved by

Colombia and Ecuador ended as had been stated. General Andrade, Ecuadorian minister, and Francisco José Urrutia, Colombian minister of foreign relations, signed at Bogotá, July 21, 1908,[22] an additional convention fixing the boundary in Pianguapí Bay, on the Pacific coast, but this and the treaty of 1908 both failed of ratification.

Conferences at Bogotá from November 4, 1915, to July 13, 1916, resulted in the signature by Alberto Muñoz Vernaza, Ecuadorian minister, and Marco Fidel Suárez, Colombian minister of foreign relations, and Nicolás Esguerra, José Maria González Valencia, Hernando Holguín y Caro, Antonio José Uribe, and Carlos Adolfo Urueta, members of the foreign relations committee of the Colombian Congress, at Bogotá on July 15, 1916,[23] of a boundary treaty which provided that (Article 1) the frontier should be agreed upon and fixed as running from the mouth of the Mataje on the Pacific Ocean up that river to its sources on the ridge of the great branch of the Andes which separates the tributary waters of the Santiago from those which flow to the Mira; thence along that ridge to the headwaters of the Canumbí, and down the Canumbí to its mouth in the Mira; thence up the Mira to its confluence with the San Juan; thence up the San Juan to the mouth of the Agua-Hedeonda stream or ravine and by it to its origin on Chiles volcano; by the summit of that volcano to the principal source of the Carchi; thence down the Carchi to the mouth of the Tejes or Teques ravine and by that ravine to La Quinta hill, thence to Troya hill; and from the peaks of that hill to the Ricos plain; thence by the Pun ravine from its origin to its mouth on the Chingual (or Chúnquer, according to some geographers); thence to the peak whence flows the principal source of the San Miguel; down that river to the Sucumbios and down that river to its mouth in the Putumayo; from that mouth southwestward to the *divortium aquarum* between the Putumayo and the Napo; by that *divortium aquarum* to the principal source of the Ambiyacú, and by the course of that river to its mouth in the Amazon; it being understood that the territories situated on the north bank of the Amazon and included between this frontier line and the boundary with Brazil belonged to Colombia, who for her part left in reserve the possible rights of third parties; (Article 2) the islands in the Bay of Pianguapí in the mouth of the Mataje should belong to the state then actually possessing them; (Article 3) a mixed commission of six persons, three named by each party within two

[22] Approved by Colombia, Law #8, Aug. 14, 1908; not approved by Ecuador.

[23] *Anales Dipl. y Consul. de Colombia* (Bogotá, 1918), V, 1038-1064. *Leyes de Colombia de 1916* (Bogotá, 1917), pp. 102-106. 110 *British and Foreign State Papers* 826-829. Martens, *Nouv. Rec. Gén. de Traités*, 3ᵉ Sér., XXI, 193-195. Antonio José Uribe, *Colombia-Ecuador* (Bogotá, 1931), pp. 197-274, 604-608. Ratified by Colombia, Law #59, Dec. 6, 1916; ratified by Ecuador, Sept. 23, 1916; ratifications exchanged at Bogotá, Jan. 26, 1917.

months after the exchange of ratifications, should fix and mark on the land the frontier thus agreed; (Article 4) such commission should be authorized to clear up points and to make slight modifications and compensations in the frontier line if such should be indispensable for the dividing line to be established with certainty and clearness; (Article 5) if differences should arise in the commission which could not be settled amicably by the two governments, they should be determined unappealably by an arbiter named by the parties; (Article 6) there should be reciprocal right of free navigation forever in the common rivers, subject to fiscal and police regulations; and (Article 7) the two states submitted themselves expressly to the principle of obligatory arbitration. The demarcation mixed commission thus provided for was duly appointed,[24] met at Quito, July 16, 1917, and finished its work in Cartagena, July 9, 1919.

By a treaty of March 24, 1922,[25] Colombia and Peru made a new adjustment of their boundary to give Peru a strip on the right (south) bank of the Putumayo which had in the 1916 settlement between Colombia and Ecuador been ceded to Colombia; so that from the San Miguel eastward Ecuador is now shut in north, east and south by Peruvian soil. Following ratification by Colombia of this treaty in 1925, Ecuador broke off diplomatic relations, alleging that the settlement of 1916 included an agreement that Colombia should never dispose of the territory she gained except by recession to Ecuador,[26] and relations were not renewed until August 18, 1931.

Reluctance of the smaller nation to abondon its claim to include all the lands of the incompletely bounded audiencia of Quito and even of the still vaguer territory of the ancient Cara kingdom of Quito, complicated by postrevolutionary annexations, caused the rejection or nonexecution of various compromises, but a treaty agreement was finally reached and carried out. The boundary between Colombia and Ecuador from the Pacific Ocean to the San Miguel appears to be definitely and finally settled. From that point eastward Ecuador bounds no longer with Colombia but with Peru; but if Colombia's 1922 adjustment with Peru should prove not to be final and be set aside, so that Colombia resumed possession of the northern parcel south of the Putumayo and northeast of the Ambiyacú, the eastern portion of their boundary would remain again to be settled between Ecuador and Colombia. Ecuador may be presumed protectively to prefer that her exposed eastern territory be bordered on the north by a different nation from the one adjoining on the

[24] *Anales Dipl. y Consul. de Colombia* (Bogotá, 1918), V, 1050. *Anuario de Leg. Ecuat.*, 1917, Pub. Ofic. (Quito, 1918), XVI, 2ª Parte, 92–93.

[25] See §21B, this chap., *infra.*
[26] *Revista Universitaria* (Guayaquil, 1932), III, 455.

south; but as the price of holding onto that strip Colombia might demand agreement on a line farther south than Ecuador's previous claims. In that event Ecuador would probably argue that the treaty of July 15, 1916, was in effect upon the full length of the territory owned by Colombia, so that the line should again run down the San Miguel to the Putumayo, thence south-westward to the *divortium aquarum* between the Putumayo and the Napo, by that *divortium aquarum* to the principal source of the Ambiyacú and down that river to its mouth in the Amazon.

21A. COLOMBIA–PERU. LORETO

The territory of the republic of Colombia which became independent in 1819 purported to include everything within the boundaries of the old cap-taincies-general of Granada and Venezuela in the viceroyalty of the New Kingdom of Granada; and Peru in 1821 proclaimed the independence of all the intendencies which had formed the viceroyalty of Peru. The treaty of perpetual union, league, and confederation between Colombia and Peru signed by Joaquín Mosquera, senator and special envoy of Colombia, and Bernardo Monteaguado, Peruvian minister of foreign relations, at Lima July 6, 1822,[1] provided that (Article 9) the demarcation of the exact boundaries which should divide their territories should be arranged by a special convention, after the next constituent Congress of Peru should have authorized the ex-ecutive of that state to settle the point, and differences which might arise in the matter should be ended by conciliatory and peaceful means, appropriate to the two sister allied nations. Peru had just previously included in the call to elect deputies to her Congress the towns of Quijos and Mainas provinces north of the Marañón, to which Colombia protested on June 20, 1822,[2] that these places had since 1718 formed part of the territory of New Granada; and it may have been an unwillingness to meet at once that issue that led Peru to put off dealing with the boundary line by the reference to authority from the next Congress, which strictly seems unnecessary since Article 12 of the treaty pro-vided for its ratification by the Congresses of both countries. Mosquera and José Maria Galdiano, Peruvian minister, signed at Lima on December 18, 1823,[3] a convention which recited that (Article 1) both parties recognized as

[1] Ricardo Aranda, *Col. de Trat. del Peru*, III, 140–145. Aurelio Noboa, *Col. de Trat. del Ecuador* (Guayaquil, 1901), I, 89–95. 11 *British and Foreign State Papers* 105–114. Martens, *Nouv. Rec. de Traités*, VI, 58–63. Approved, with modifications in Arts. 2, 10, and 11, by Colombia, July 12, 1823; approved by Peru, Oct. 11, 1823.

[2] Ricardo Aranda, *Col. de Trat. del Peru*, III, 423–441.
[3] *Ibid.*, 444–446. Aurelio Noboa, *Col. de Trat. del Ecuador* (Guayaquil, 1901), I, 127–128, 359–394. Ap-proved by Peru, Leg. Dec., Dec. 19, 1823; disapproved by Colombian Congress, June 10, 1824.

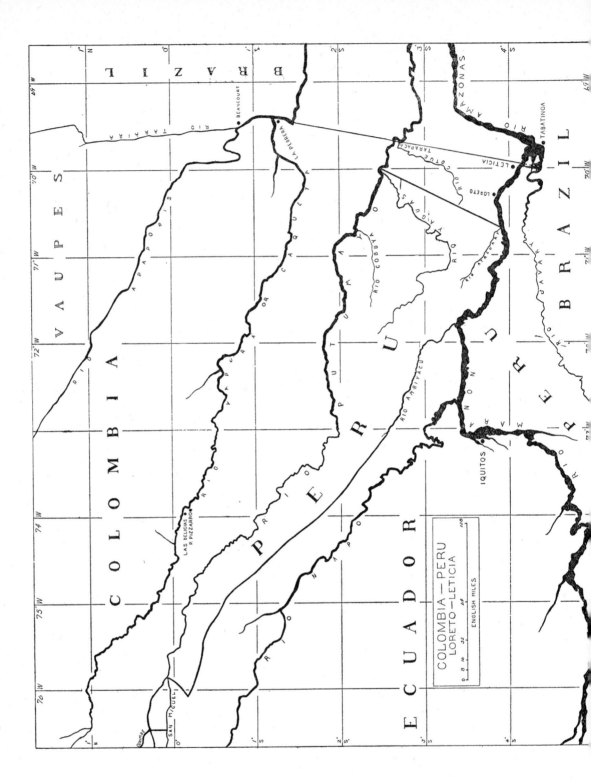

boundaries of their respective territories those which the former viceroyalties of Peru and New Granada had in 1809; but this convention was not ratified by Colombia.

The Colombian territorial division law of June 25, 1824,[4] provided that (Article 12) the department of Azuay included the three provinces of Cuenca, Loja, and Jaen de Bracamoros y Mainas, with the capital Jaen and (Sec. 3) the cantons of the province of Jaen y Mainas, and their headquarters, were (1) Jaen, (2) Borja, and (3) Jeveros. No protest was made by Peru, but it does not appear when or how she first learned of this law. In 1826 Peru included in a call to vote for deputies the province of Jaen de Bracamoros, but to Colombia's protest Peru replied that the call was limited to the towns in the strip on the south bank of the Marañón. Discussions of the boundary question, repayment of debts and other complaints in Bogotá in 1828 grew warm and bitter until diplomatic relations were broken and Bolivar for Colombia declared war on Peru on July 3, 1828,[5] including as one of the reasons the retention of the province of Jaen and part of Mainas which Peru had usurped. A Peruvian naval expedition captured Guayaquil on January 19, 1829,[6] and La Mar's main army of 4,000 men occupied the Colombian province of Loja, but was defeated and retired. General Sucre won a complete victory for Colombia at Tarqui on February 27, 1829, and the preliminary convention of peace signed at Jirón, February 28, 1829,[7] provided that (Article 2) the parties should name a commission to settle the boundaries of the two states, using as a basis the political division of the viceroyalties of New Granada and Peru in August 1809, when the Quito revolution occurred; and they promised to cede reciprocally such small pieces of territory as by the defects in an inexact demarcation had been prejudicial to the inhabitants. Peru refused to be bound by this convention of Jirón, and General José de la Mar, who approved it as president in camp on March 1, was deposed on June 7, 1829. General Agustín Gamarra, who succeeded him, continued the war until an armistice was signed at Piura, July 10, 1829,[8] providing that (Article 5) a diplomatic commission should assemble with all possible speed to conclude within sixty days the negotiations for peace. The treaty of peace signed at Guayaquil, September 22, 1829,[9] provided that

[4] Col. de las Leyes de Colombia, 1823 y 1824 (Bogotá, 1826), pp. 150-158.

[5] Ricardo Aranda, Col. de Trat. del Peru, III, 150-185. Aurelio Noboa, Col. de Trat. del Ecuador (Guayaquil, 1901), I, 395-444.

[6] Ricardo Aranda, Col. de Trat. del Peru, III, 185-190.

[7] Ibid., 198-202. Aurelio Noboa, Col. de Trat. del Ecuador (Guayaquil, 1901), I, 444-449. 16 British and Foreign State Papers 1237-1239.

[8] Ricardo Aranda, Col. de Trat. del Peru, III, 213-216. 16 British and Foreign State Papers 1239-1241.

[9] Ricardo Aranda, Col. de Trat. del Peru, III, 230-238. 16 British and Foreign State Papers 1242-1248; 18 ibid., 1274-1275. Pedro Moncayo, Colombia i el Brasil (Valparaiso, 1862), 2ª parte, pp. 41-102. Ratified by Peru, Oct. 16, 1829, and by Bolivar.

(Article 5) the parties acknowledged as the boundaries of their respective territories those which the old viceroyalties of New Granada and Peru had before their independence, with only the variations which they should find it suitable to agree upon, to which end they then promised to make reciprocally such cessions of small pieces of territory as should contribute to fix the dividing line in a more natural and exact manner to avoid strife and incidents between the frontier authorities and inhabitants; (Article 6) to obtain this result as soon as possible, a commission of four, two named by each republic, should survey, rectify, and fix the dividing line thus agreed on, and should put each party in possession of the area which belonged to it, as fast as they traced the line, beginning at Túmbez on the Pacific Ocean; (Article 7) the boundary commission to begin its work within forty days from ratification of the treaty and finish within six months thereafter, any disagreement among its members to be reported to the respective governments, who should settle the question amicably in the most suitable way; and (Article 19) any difference of opinion as to the meaning of any article or failure to settle any disagreement between the commissioners should be submitted to a friendly government, whose decision should be absolutely obligatory upon both parties; and in a declaration on signing Colombia named Chile as her choice for arbiter. Following ratification of this treaty, two boundary demarcation commissioners were named by each country and a protocol of bases for their work was signed by Carlos Pedemonte, Peruvian minister of foreign relations, and Tomás C. de Mosquera, Colombian minister, at Lima, August 11, 1830;[10] but Colombia was dissolved, Ecuador intervened in the boundary problem, and the demarcation under the Treaty of 1829 was not undertaken.

With the new disputes between Ecuador and Colombia[11] on one hand and Ecuador and Peru[12] on the other, the argument between Colombia and Peru lapsed into a stage of occasional protests. The treaty of October 23, 1851,[13] between Brazil and Peru evoked a complaint from New Granada on July 9, 1853, to the Brazilian chargé d'affaires in Santiago de Chile that the agreed boundary between the parties by the straight line from Tabatinga to the Yapurá opposite the confluence of the Apaporis injured her territorial rights. On March 10, 1853,[14] Peru created provisionally on the Loreto frontiers a political and military government independent of the Amazon prefecture; to

[10] *Arbitraje de Límites entre el Peru y el Ecuador; Documentos Anexos a la Memoria del Peru* (Madrid, 1905), I (Num. 26), 192-196. Ricardo Aranda, *Col. de Trat. del Peru*, III, 464-477. Aurelio Noboa, *Col. de Trat. del Ecuador* (Guayaquil, 1901), I, 463-495.
[11] See §20, this chap., *supra*.
[12] See §23, this chap., *infra*.
[13] See §13, this chap., *supra*.
[14] Ricardo Aranda, *Col. de Trat. del Peru*, III, 248. *Col. de Doc. Ofic. referentes á Loreto*, Ed. Ofic. (Lima, 1905), I, 19-20.

include the banks of the Amazon and the Marañón from the Brazilian boundary, all the territories and missions to the north and south of those rivers,
according to the principle of *uti possidetis* adopted in the American republics
and furthermore in this case to the rule of the Royal Cédula of July 15,
1802, and the rivers which empty into the Marañón, especially the Huallaga, Santiago, Morona, Pastaza, Putumayo, Yapurá, Ucayali, Napo, Javary,
and others, and their banks, all according to the contents of such Royal
Cédula. New Granada protested at Lima that this resolution damaged her
by including lands and rivers which belonged to her, and subjected them to
Peru. The Royal Cédula of July 15, 1802,[15] separated the gobierno and commandancy-general of Mainas, with the towns of the gobierno of Quijos except
Papallacta, from the viceroyalty of Santa Fé and province of Quito and attached it to the viceroyalty and gobierno of Peru, the commandancy-general
to extend not only down the Marañón to the frontiers of the Portuguese colonies but also on all the other rivers which enter the Marañón on its north and
south banks, such as the Morona, Huallaga, Pastaza, Ucayali, Napo, Javary,
Putumayo, Yapurá, and others smaller, up to the place where these by their
falls and insurmountable rapids ceased to be navigable. Colombian statesmen
had not known of this cédula, and professed to think it queer that it had not
been mentioned before, but Peru thereafter relied on it most strongly in support of her claims. On June 25, 1853,[16] Peru signed at Bogotá a convention
with New Granada agreeing to pay to that nation and Ecuador 2,860,000 pesos
or 71½ units of the debt which Peru contracted with the former Colombia for
expenses of the war for independence. Colombia protested to Peru in 1866
and again in 1869 [17] against acts of the Brazil-Peru demarcation commission
under the convention of October 22, 1858,[18] alleging that the commission had
invaded Colombian territory and presumed to exercise acts of sovereignty in
it, to which Peru answered that her commissioners had withdrawn on May
9, 1867, and that she would never assume to take possession of territories
which did not belong to her; and Peru invited Colombia, Brazil, and Ecuador to join her in a general conference and demarcation of her northern boundaries. In 1875 and 1876 [19] Colombia protested to Brazil against the fixing of
a mark on the bank of the Putumayo for the Brazil-Peru boundary and the
exchange of small areas on either side of the Putumayo under the convention

[15] Aurelio Noboa, *Col. de Trat. del Ecuador* (Guayaquil,
1901), I, 15-21. *Col. de Doc. Ofic. referentes á Loreto*,
Ed. Ofic. (Lima, 1905), I, 3-10. Federico González Suárez,
Estudio Historico sobre la Cédula del 15 julio 1802 (Quito,
1905).
[16] Ricardo Aranda, *Col. de Trat. del Peru*, III, 251-253.

60 *British and Foreign State Papers* 1130-1131.
[17] Demetrio Salamanca T., *Fronteras Amazonicas de
Colombia* (Bogotá, 1905), pp. 67-135.
[18] See §13, this chap., *supra*.
[19] Ricardo Aranda, *Col. de Trat. del Peru*, III, 484-487.

of February 11, 1874.[20] Ecuador refused to approve the tripartite convention of December 15, 1894,[21] which would have permitted Colombia to join in the arbitration by the king of Spain of the boundary between Ecuador and Peru under the Treaty of August 1, 1887.[22]

Luis Tanco Argáez, Colombian minister, and José Pardo y Barreda, Peruvian minister of foreign relations, signed at Lima, May 6, 1904,[23] an arbitration treaty which provided that (Article 1) the parties submitted to the unappealable decision of the king of Spain the boundary question pending between them, to be decided with reference not only to the legal titles [24] and arguments presented but also to the conveniences of the parties, adjusting them so that the frontier line should be founded on law and equity; (Article 3) within six months after the arbiter's acceptance both cases to be presented, (Article 4) with replies a reasonable time thereafter fixed beforehand by the arbiter; and (Article 6) in case of refusal of the king of Spain to act, to request in order the president of France, the king of the Belgians, or the Swiss Federal Council. The same ministers signed also at Lima, May 6, 1904,[25] a convention of *modus vivendi* which stipulated that (Article 1) the governments should maintain the authorities which they had then established on the Napo and Yapurá or Caquetá, respectively, and withdraw all those which they had in the rest of the disputed territories; and (Article 2) if later circumstances should require the establishment on the Putumayo or in any other part of such disputed territories of fiscal and police authorities, it should be done by common agreement between the two governments, either by fixing zones of respective provisional occupation or by establishing mixed authorities; (Article 4) the agreement not to be invoked against either country in the arbitration. By a note of August 6, 1904, Francisco de P. Matéus, Colombian minister of foreign relations, informed Tanco Argáez that the government after mature reflection had found both the arbitration treaty and the convention of *modus vivendi* inacceptable for Colombia, adding that they had been signed by him without express instructions for the purpose and without the necessary special full powers. Tanco Argáez and Clímaco Calderón, Colombian minister of foreign relations, signed with Hernán Velarde, Peruvian minister, at Bogotá, September 12, 1905,[26] a boundary arbitration treaty

[20] See §13, this chap., *supra*.
[21] See §20, this chap., *supra*.
[22] See §23, this chap., *infra*.
[23] *Bol. del Min. de Rel. Ext. del Peru*, Lima, Num. 9. *U. S. For. Rel.*, 1904, pp. 694-696.
[24] Carlos Larrabure i Correa, *Col. de Documentos Oficiales referentes á Loreto*, Ed. Ofic. (Lima, 1905-1909), 18 vols.
[25] Vicente Olarte Camacho, *Los Convenios con el Peru*

(Bogotá, 1911), pp. 259-261. *Bol. del Min. de Rel. Ext.* (Lima, 1906), Año III, Num. 9.
[26] Rep. de Colombia, *Leyes de 1907* (2ª ed. ofic., Bogotá, 1910), pp. 19-22; *ibid.*, 1909 (Bogotá, 1910), pp. 405-407. *Bol. del Min. de Rel. Ext.* (Lima, 1906), Año III, Num. 9, pp. 24-26. Pablo Antonio Rada, *Estudio de Límites entre el Peru y Colombia* (Lima, 1907). Colombia approved by Law #6, Apr. 24, 1907; repealed by Law #61, Dec. 13, 1909; not approved by Peru.

which provided that (Article 1) the governments submitted to the unappealable decision of His Holiness the Supreme Roman Pontiff the boundary question pending between them, to be decided with reference not only to the legal
titles and arguments presented but also to the conveniences of the parties,
adjusting them so that the frontier line should be founded on law and equity;
(Article 2) this agreement to be expressly subordinate to the arbitration between Peru and Ecuador agreed upon by the treaty of August 1, 1887, then
under way before the king of Spain, and taking effect only in case the royal
arbiter should adjudge to Peru territories claimed by Colombia as hers, and
Colombia declared that the stipulations of this agreement did not affect the
treaty of similar nature between Colombia and Ecuador signed November 5,
1904, which should take effect as soon as the Peru-Ecuador arbitration of
1887 should be terminated. The same three ministers signed also at Bogotá,
September 12, 1905,[27] a convention of *modus vivendi* by which the two governments agreed to maintain the *status quo* in the disputed territory until
the final solution of the controversy under the arbitration treaty signed the
same day; and in order to avoid all difficulty and dangerous conflicts in the Putumayo region, to establish there during the transient situation two zones of
provisional occupation, the North and the South, separated by the waters of
that river; the zone pertaining to Colombia to include the territories situated
to the north or on the left bank and that to Peru the territories situated to
the south or on the right bank, between the Cobuya and the Cotué. The same
ministers signed a complementary act at Bogotá, September 23, 1905,[28] reciting the desirability of making clear Colombia's declaration in Article 2 of the
treaty, and agreeing that it did not mean that Peru accepted the legitimacy
of the treaty referred to, especially in its Article 7, which excluded from the
Peru-Ecuador arbitration then under way before the king of Spain a territorial zone which Peru considered included in that arbitration.

Luis Tanco Argáez, Colombian minister, Javier Prado y Ugarteche, Peruvian minister of foreign relations, and Hernán Velarde, Peruvian minister to
Colombia, signed at Lima, July 6, 1906,[29] a new convention of *modus vivendi*
by which the two governments agreed (Article 1) to maintain the *status quo*
in the disputed territory until the final solution of the controversy under the

[27] *Bol. del Min. de Rel. Ext.* (Lima, 1906), Año III,
Num. 9, pp. 28-30. Vicente Olarte Camacho, *Los Convenios
con el Peru* (Bogotá, 1911), pp. 263-265.

[28] *Bol. del Min. de Rel. Ext.* (Lima, 1906), Año III,
Num. 9, p. 27. Vicente Olarte Camacho, *Los Convenios
con el Peru* (Bogotá, 1911), p. 266.

[29] *Bol. del Min. de Rel. Ext.* (Lima, 1906), Año III,

Num. 11, pp. 204-207. *Mem. del Min. de Rel. Ext. del
Peru* (Lima, 1906), pp. 27-30. 99 *British and Foreign
State Papers* 1019-1020. *U. S. For. Rel.,* 1906, Part 2,
pp. 1219-1220. Martens, *Nouv. Rec. Gén. de Traités,* 3ᵉ
Sér., VI, 635-636. In effect without legislative ratification;
denounced by Colombia in December 1907.

arbitration agreed on at Bogotá, September 12, 1905, and (Article 2) in order to avoid all difficulty and dangerous conflicts in the Putumayo region both to withdraw from that river and its affluents during the transient situation all the garrisons, civil and military authorities, and customs houses which they had established there, (Article 5) the stipulations to imply no renunciation or recognition of territorial rights in favor of either party, this agreement entirely to supersede the one of September 12, 1905.

The Putumayo territory of from 10,000 to 12,000 square miles between the Caquetá and the Amazon west of the Brazilian frontier was the source of an extensive though not inexhaustible supply of raw rubber. It was exploited for some years by the Peruvian firm of Julio C. Arana Hermanos, whose deliberate policy was to supersede by purchase or force all Colombian rivals on the river and to employ in a system closely approaching slavery, with company indebtedness, fear, flogging, torture, and murder, such Indians as could be captured and held of the tribes of Boras and Huitotos and the smaller groups of Andoques and Ocainas who inhabited the region. One hundred and ninety-six negro laborers had been recruited in Barbados in 1904–1905 and taken into the Putumayo to Abisinia and other stations to work the local managers' will on the Indians. Following the withdrawal of the Colombian authorities in accordance with the convention of 1906, the Arana company by its managers, Augusto Jiménez, Miguel Loaiza, Victor Macedo, Bartolomé Zumaeta, and others began to push farther and farther, even into territory indisputably Colombian, in their search for rubber gatherers, and armed groups of raiders or bandits from south of the Putumayo in 1907 and 1908 killed numerous Huitoto Indians and some white Colombians, causing intense resentment when known in Bogotá, and some striking back by the Colombians when occasion offered. The Arana firm on June 30, 1907, turned over its business, posts, and employees to the Peruvian Amazon Rubber Company, Ltd., a corporation registered in London in September 1907 with a capital of £1,000,000 floated in England, with four British directors under the active management of Julio César Arana. Stories of cruelties practiced on the Indians were published in two newspapers in Iquitos, *La Sanción* and *La Felpa*, in 1907; and December 3, 1907,[30] Charles C. Eberhardt, United States consul at Iquitos, wrote to Secretary of State Elihu Root concerning the alleged mistreatment. Nothing was done, however, until Walter E. Hardenburg,[31] a United States engineer who

---

[30] Slavery in Peru; transmitted to Congress with message of President William H. Taft and printed, Feb. 7, 1913. House Doc., 62nd Congress, 3rd Session, No. 1366.

[31] Walter E. Hardenburg, *The Putumayo, the Devil's Paradise* (London, 1912).

had been at work for fifteen months in Colombia, heard there was work in Brazil and proceeded across the country on foot and by river from February to May 1909. He heard tales of violence from one of his guides and becoming interested began to make inquiries from others until he was so convinced of improper conditions that on reaching Iquitos he reported to Consul Eberhardt something of what he had found. Hardenburg proceeded to London and told his story to such effect that *Truth* on September 22, 1909, September 29, and in following issues drew a vivid picture of alleged conditions and demanded an inquiry. William C. Farabee,[32] who had been in the Putumayo region on a scientific expedition, told stories of some of the things he had seen to Leslie Combs, United States minister at Lima, who wrote of them to Secretary of State Philander C. Knox on November 4, 1909; but the United States Department of State was apparently still uninterested. The British public was aroused, however, and Roger Casement, who had investigated the Belgian atrocities in the Congo, was appointed consul general of Great Britain in Brazil and sent out to investigate. The Peruvian Congress protested against Casement's mission, as it seemed to them to threaten intervention; and on November 22, 1909, the Peruvian Senate passed a resolution demanding an inquiry.

Melitón F. Porras, Peruvian minister of foreign relations, and Tanco Argáez, Colombian minister, signed at Lima, April 21, 1909,[33] a convention to put a cordial end to the disagreements between the two governments which (Article 1) recited the deep regret of both governments for the events which occurred in the Putumayo region last year, and agreed to establish, by a special convention within three months, an international commission to investigate and clarify the occurrences and report; and if after such report the two governments could not agree on the resulting responsibilities, the matter should be submitted to an arbitral decision; (Article 2) the two governments agreed to renew their negotiations as to settling their frontiers immediately after the decision in the arbitration under way in Madrid by virtue of the 1887 treaty between Peru and Ecuador, and to have recourse to arbitration if they could not reach directly a solution of their differences; and (Article 3) if the king of Spain should not make his award in the Peru-Ecuador arbitration within three months, the two governments would make an agreement of *modus vivendi* for the disputed territory. This agreement was amended by a convention

[32] Ph.D. (Harvard), 1903; Instructor in Anthropology (Harvard), 1903–1913; died, 1925.
[33] Vicente Olarte Camacho, *Los Convenios con el Peru* (Bogotá, 1911), pp. 277–278. 102 *British and Foreign State Papers* 400–402. *U. S. For. Rel.,* 1909, pp. 507–508. Martens, *Nouv. Rec. Gén. de Traités,* 3ᵉ Sér., VI, 16–17, 339–340. *Arch. Dipl.,* 3ᵉ Sér., CXII, 116–117.

signed by Carlos Calderón, Colombian minister of foreign relations, and Ernesto de Tezanos Pinto, Peruvian minister, at Bogotá, April 13, 1910,[34] which provided that (Article 2) the mixed commission should meet at Rio de Janeiro and be composed of one delegate named by Colombia, another named by Peru, and the third, to preside with a deciding vote, Baron of Rio Branco, Brazilian minister of foreign relations, if he would accept, and (Article 3) if he would not, in order, the minister of Great Britain at Rio de Janeiro, the minister of Germany at Rio de Janeiro, or a third to be named by agreement between the other two delegates when they met. Neither the Baron of Rio Branco nor the ministers of Great Britain or Germany would accept, and Colombia notified Brazil by note of March 6, 1911, that she considered herself at liberty to proceed in the matter in such way as should best serve her interests.

Casement left England July 23, 1910, and arrived at Iquitos on August 31; leaving there on September 14 with the company's own commission of inquiry of four Englishmen, he traveled through the district from September 22 to November 16 and reached Iquitos again on November 25. Via Pará and Cherbourg he returned to London and on January 7, 1911, presented a preliminary report that in his opinion the worst charges were true.[35] He had interviewed chiefly the Barbadian negroes, as British subjects, and kept the British share of responsibility the main theme of his final report of March 17, 1911. The British minister in Lima notified the Peruvian government of Casement's conclusions, and in July 1911 Great Britain secured the diplomatic support of the United States minister at Lima. Judge Rómulo Paredes was sent by Peru as a judicial commissioner to the district, arrived at La Chorrera on March 27, 1911, and made his report on September 30. He issued warrants of arrest against 215 persons, few of whom were apprehended and apparently none ever brought to trial. President Leguía on April 22, 1912,[36] issued a decree appointing a commission of five to recommend reforms and by a further decree of May 30, 1912,[37] appointed an auxiliary commission of two with residence at Iquitos, and sent Dr. Parades back for further study and recommendations before January 1, 1913. When Peru took no apparent further steps

[34] *Convenio entre Colombia y el Peru reform. del de 21 de abril de 1909, Documentos, Min. de Rel. Ext.* (Bogotá, 1910). Vicente Olarte Camacho, *Los Convenios con el Peru* (Bogotá, 1911), pp. 280-283. 103 *British and Foreign State Papers* 401-404. Martens, *Nouv. Rec. Gén. de Traités*, 3e Sér., VI, 17-20, 340-344.

[35] *H. C. Papers and Reports, 1912-13*, IX (354), (509); 1913, XIV (148). *Command Papers*, 1912-13, vol. 68 [6266], Bluebook; Misc. No. 8 of 1912. Vicente Olarte

Camacho, *Las Crueldades en el Putumayo y en el Caquetá* (Bogotá, 1910). Cornelio Hispano, *De París al Amazonas* (Paris, n.d.), William S. Robertson, *Hispanic-American Relations with the United States* (New York, 1923), pp. 368-371.

[36] *El Peruano, Diario Ofic.* (Lima, Apr. 24, 1912), Año 72, I, 727.

[37] *Ibid.* (June 7, 1912), Año 72, I, 1015.

to correct the abuses, in July, 1912, although the United States Department of State advised delay, Casement's reports were transmitted to Parliament. The House of Commons on October 23, 1912, appointed a select committee of fifteen members to inquire into the responsibility of the British directors of the company, then in liquidation. The committee held thirty-one public and five closed sessions between October 29, 1912, and February 6, 1913, and heard twenty-seven witnesses, including Hardenburg, who came over from Canada, and Arana. The four British directors, among whose counsel was Raymond Asquith, were found by the committee to have been culpably negligent; and a discussion of the applicability of British penal laws for offenses committed in the territory of another nation was included in the report.

On July 10, 1911, a considerable Peruvian force from Loreto under Major Oscar Benavides attacked some seventy Colombian guards under General Isaias Gamboa at La Pedrera, and on July 12 the Colombians surrendered. On July 15, 1911, the consuls of Colombia and Peru at Manaos signed an act according to which the Colombian forces were ordered not to advance and to suspend hostilities, and the Peruvians were ordered to withdraw from the Caquetá.

Enrique Olaya Herrera, Colombian minister of foreign relations, and Tezanos Pinto, Peruvian minister, signed at Bogotá, July 19, 1911,[38] a convention which provided that (Article 1) Colombia should maintain only at Puerto Córdoba or La Pedrera a garrison which in no case should exceed 110 men, including the Colombian customs personnel and guards, would not permit this garrison to advance beyond the place named, and would stop at Manaos, or where it then was, the last expedition sent to the Caquetá, which left Puerto Colombia on June 8, 1911; and (Article 2) Peru undertook that its forces and the Peruvian colonists in those regions should refrain from any act of hostility against the Colombian guards or colonists of Puerto Córdoba or La Pedrera and would turn aside towards the Putumayo any expedition then in progress toward the Caquetá; (Article 4) such situation to last while negotiations continued between the two countries to reach a *modus vivendi*; (Article 5) Colombia declared that the presence of Peruvian authorities and forces in the disputed region did not signify any recognition of right on the part of Peru over that zone, and Peru declared that the presence of Colombian authorities and forces in Puerto Córdoba or La Pedrera did not signify any recognition of right on the part of Colombia over the zone on the right (south) bank of the

[38] *Actos Int. del Peru* (Lima, 1916), No. 102. Vicente Olarte Camacho, *Los Convenios con el Peru* (Bogotá, 1911). Plicarpo Bustillo P., *Reseña Histórica de la Cuestión de Limites* (Cartagena, 1916). Cayetano Rengifo, "Colombia y el Peru," *Rev. Juridica* (Bogotá), XVIII (1926), 573-588. Approved by Peru, Sept. 28, 1911.

Caquetá. In April 1912 Colombia complained of the presence of Peruvian troops at Puerto Pizarro and Las Delicias on the Caquetá. George B. Michell, British consul at Iquitos, and Stuart J. Fuller, United States consul at Iquitos, traveled in the Putumayo district from August 7 to October 6, 1912, and reported [39] that the company's policy had been partially modified under the new manager, Juan A. Tizón, the condition of the Indians was apparently somewhat better, and British interests had been largely eliminated.[40] Here as in other tropical jungles competition of the Far Eastern cultivated plantations has made hunting the wild rubber unprofitable, and white traders are gradually withdrawing. Attempts in Lima from May to July 1912 [41] to settle the bases for a new *modus vivendi* came to nothing; and subsequent negotiations for ten years intermittently discussed arbitration and a direct settlement; but no agreement could be reached, and the dispute continued to disturb the relations between the countries. A century of substantially fruitless negotiations ended with the boundary very nearly as unsettled as it had been at the beginning.

21B.   COLOMBIA–PERU.   LETICIA

(See map, p. 186, *supra.*)

The hundred years of diplomatic arguments, unexecuted agreements, and short-lived *modus vivendi* entered upon a new phase in negotiations carried on by wire between Bogotá and Lima from February 5 to March 20, 1922.[1] Alberto Salomón, Peruvian minister of foreign relations, and Fabio Lozano T., Colombian minister, signed at Lima, March 24, 1922,[2] a treaty of boundaries and free river navigation which provided that (Article 1) the frontier line should run from the point at which the meridian of the mouth of the Cuhimbé on the Putumayo cuts the San Miguel or Sucumbios; thence up that meridian to such mouth of the Cuhimbé; thence by the thalweg of the Putumayo to the confluence of the Yaguas; thence by a straight line from that confluence to the confluence of the Atacuari on the Amazon, and thence by the thalweg of

[39] *Command Papers*, 1913, LI, 6678. Carlos Larraburé y Correa, *Peru y Colombia en el Putumayo* (Barcelona, 1913). Carlos Rey de Castro, *Los Escandalos del Putumayo* (Barcelona, 1913). Pablo Zumaeta, *Las Cuestiones del Putumayo* (Barcelona, 1913), Folletos Nos. 1 and 2. Julio C. Arana, *ibid.*, Folleto No. 3.

[40] *Inf. del Min. de Rel. Ext. de Colombia*, 1924, pp. 52–53.

[41] Juan Ignacio Gálvez, *Conflictos Internacionales* (Buenos Aires, 1919; 3a ed. corr. y aum., Santiago, 1919; in English, Santiago, 1920).

[1] Antonio José Uribe, *Colombia y el Peru* (Bogotá, 1931).

[2] *League of Nations Treaty Series*, No. 1726, LXXIV, 10–17. 122 *British and Foreign State Papers* 275–278. Martens, *Nouv. Rec. Gén. de Traités*, 3° Sér., XXV, 669–672. Approved by Colombian Legislature, Law #55, Oct. 5, 1925; ratified by Colombian executive, Mar. 17, 1928; ratified by Peruvian Legislature (102 to 7). Resolution #5940, Dec. 20, 1927, ratified by Peruvian executive, Jan. 23, 1928; ratifications exchanged at Bogotá, Mar. 19, 1928.

the Amazon to the boundary between Peru and Brazil established by their treaty of October 23, 1851; Colombia declaring that there belonged to Peru by this treaty the territories included between the right (south) bank of the Putumayo, eastward from the mouth of the Cuhimbé, and the line established and marked as the frontier between Colombia and Ecuador, in the basins of the Putumayo and the Napo, by virtue of their boundary treaty of July 15, 1916, and that she reserved as regards Brazil her rights to territories situated eastward of the Tabatinga-Apaporis line agreed on between Peru and Brazil by the treaty of October 23, 1851; and both parties declaring that there remained definitely and irrevocably ended all of the differences which by reason of their boundaries had arisen between them up to date and that no difference could arise in the future which should alter in any way the line of frontier fixed by this treaty; (Article 2) the two governments should name within two months from the exchange of ratifications a mixed commission, of three persons for each party, to fix and mark the agreed frontier line, to meet at Iquitos within six months and immediately begin their work; (Article 3) with authority to clarify and make slight modifications and compensations in the frontier line if indispensable to establish the dividing line with all certainty and clarity; (Article 4) differences in the demarcation commission to be referred to the two governments, and if they could not reach an amicable solution, to be determined by the Hague Permanent Court of Arbitration, whose decision should be unappealable and executed without delay; (Article 6) if either government should not nominate its commissioners within the indicated time, those of the other government might proceed alone to fix and mark the line, with that scrupulous probity and rectitude which becomes the loyalty and good name of nations; (Article 8) both nations recognized reciprocally forever in the fullest manner the liberty of land transit and the right of navigation of their common rivers and their affluents and confluents, subject to fiscal and river police laws and regulations; and (Article 9) each party would maintain and respect concessions of land and other rights acquired by nationals and foreigners in lands which according to this treaty belonged respectively to each nation.

The firm of Julio C. Arana Hermanos, interested in a rubber concession in an area of 5,000,000 hectares (19,300 sq. miles) obtained from Peru in August, 1921,[3] tried to prevent Peru from agreeing to any pact which did not require Colombia to pay the syndicate for loss of the concession, £2,000,000 being one figure mentioned; but Colombia roundly refused to allow any mat-

---

[3] *Cf.* §21A, this chap., *supra.*

ters of private ownership to enter into the diplomatic discussion or to treat of any indemnities to private persons, and finally Peru accepted as sufficient the provision in Article 9. A more serious obstacle appeared before either of the parties had ratified the treaty when Brazil in November 1924 presented to Peru a memorandum attacking the treaty as injurious to her interests in the region. At Colombia's request, United States Secretary of State Charles E. Hughes took the matter up with Brazil, sending his opinion to Peru by Leo S. Rowe, director of the Pan American Union, who arrived in Lima early in December 1924; and after further negotiations all around, there was signed at Washington at 5 P.M. on Secretary Hughes' last day in office, March 4, 1925,[4] an act [5] in which Brazil agreed to withdraw her observations as to the treaty, Colombia and Peru agreed to ratify the treaty, and Colombia agreed to sign with Brazil a convention which should recognize as boundary between them the Apaporis-Tabatinga line, and Brazil should establish forever in favor of Colombia liberty of navigation of the Amazon and other rivers common to the two countries. There was more delay, and opposition [6] to be overcome in both Congresses, but the treaty was finally ratified by both countries and ratifications were exchanged March 19, 1928. The demarcation mixed commission, promptly appointed, met at Iquitos, November 11, 1929, and finished its work at the same place March 14, 1930.[7] Possession of the new trapezium, from the Putumayo down to the Amazon, formerly claimed by Peru as part of the Department of Loreto, was delivered to Colombia on August 17, 1930. The territory of about 4,000 square miles with less than 500 white inhabitants and 1,500 Indians includes at its northeast corner on the Putumayo the town of Tarapacá, and at its southeast corner on the Amazon 2,500 miles from the Atlantic Ocean the town of Leticia, eighty-two feet above mean river level, with a normal population of about 300. Colombia made no formal delivery of the small parcel at the west end of the boundary line between the San Miguel or Sucumbios and the Putumayo, but notified Peru, whose territory touched it only in the water at the point of confluence of the San Miguel and the Putumayo, that she might thereafter exercise sovereignty over it. Negotiation and execution of this treaty played a considerable part in the

[4] João Ribeiro, *As Nossas Fronteiras* (Rio de Janeiro, 1930), pp. 91–105. *Informe del Min. de Rel. Ext. de Colombia*, 1925 (Bogotá, 1925), pp. 60–62. *Bol. del Min. de Rel. Ext. del Peru* (Lima, 1925), 2ª Epoca, Num. 4, pp. 19–21. Juan Angulo Puente Arnao, *Historia de los límites del Peru* (Lima, 1927), pp. 50–78, 112–126. *U. S. Treaty Inf. Bull.*, IV (1930), 4. Martens, *Nouv. Rec. Gén. de Traités*, 3ᵉ Sér., XXV, 672–674. *Amer. J. Int. Law*, XXV (1931), 331.

[5] See §10, this chap., *supra*.
[6] J. C. Arana, *El Protocolo Salomón-Lozano* (Lima, 1927). Carlos A. Valverde, *Por la Paz de América* (Lima, 1928). Evaristo San Cristóval, *Los desastres internacionales de la Dictadura* (Lima, 1928). Carlos A. Valcarcel, *Crítica del Tratado Salomón-Lozano* (Lima, 1931). Evaristo San Cristóval, *Páginas internacionales* (2ª ed., Lima, 1932).
[7] *League of Nations Treaty Series*, C, 230–246.

downfall of the Peruvian president, Augusto B. Leguía y Salcedo, who was forced to resign August 24, 1930.

Local feeling in Loreto, whether genuine or accelerated, appeared to be opposed to the 1922 treaty settlement and to the transfer of any part of the area to Colombia. On September 1, 1932, an armed band of some 300 Peruvian civilians entered Leticia, seized the public buildings and town offices, expelled the Colombian officials and raised the Peruvian flag The Peruvian government in Lima promptly disavowed the action, but local Peruvian authorities in Loreto furnished military support, and on November 26, 1932, Peruvian regular troops under General Oscar H. Ordóñez were said to have occupied Leticia. The Colombian government prepared to send 1,500 men in six vessels under General Alfredo Vásquez Cobo around the Atlantic coast and up the Amazon as a police expedition to restore law and order in Colombian territory; but Peruvian public opinion regarded the expedition as punitive and aggressive against Peru and called on the government in Lima to protect their fellow citizens. Peru in a note of September 16 told Colombia that to facilitate a peaceful solution it was necessary that Colombia should avoid any measures of force. War spirit rose rapidly in both countries, with enlistments and patriotic loans. Peru on October 3, 1932, in accordance with Article 1 of the conciliation convention of January 5, 1929, asked the Permanent Commission on Inter-American Conciliation, consisting of the ministers in Washington of Guatemala, Uruguay, and Venezuela, to do what was necessary under Article 5 of the Treaty of Santiago of May 3, 1923, to examine into the difficulty. The request was forwarded to Colombia, but she replied on October 12 that the question of her sovereignty over Leticia was a domestic and not an international matter, and definitely rejected recourse to the Permanent Conciliation Commission. Eduardo Santos, special minister of Colombia, from Paris on January 2, 1933,[8] sent a long note concerning the situation to the Secretary of the League of Nations.

The Colombian expedition reached Manaos on January 9 and remained there until January 23, when it sailed for Teffé. On January 14 the acting president of the Council of the League requested information from both nations, expressing confidence that they would refrain from action contrary to the League Covenant. On January 20 [9] Peru replied to the Colombian note

[8] *League of Nations Documents*, 1933, VII; C 20, M 5. *League of Nations Official Journal*, 1933, 14th Year, pp. 543–547. Guillermo Valencia, *Informe del Presidente de la Comisión Asesora* (Bogotá, 1932).

[9] *League of Nations Documents*, 1933, VII; C 58,

M 23; C 134, M 59. *League of Nations Official Journal*, 1933, 14th Year, pp. 566–572. Manley O. Hudson, *The Permanent Court of International Justice* (New York, 1934), p. 409.

calling the attention of the League to the Colombian expedition, and expressing her desire to complete, soften, and give a new force to the 1922 treaty forced on her by a dictatorial regime. On January 23 Colombia asked the United States and other signatories of the Briand-Kellogg treaty of August 27, 1928, to remind Peru of her obligations under that treaty to renounce war as an instrument of national policy. The League Council at its session on January 24, 1933, appointed a committee of three [10] to study the matter. Brazil offered to both governments her mediation on the basis that Peru should use her moral support and influence to induce the invaders to turn the disputed territory over to the possession of the Brazilian government for provisional administration, Brazil to reëstablish in their posts as soon as possible the Colombian officials deposed by the insurgents, Colombia to agree that the delegates of both countries should meet immediately thereafter at Rio de Janeiro with experts to examine the 1922 treaty in a broad spirit of conciliation, to find a formula acceptable to both parties. These bases were accepted in full by Colombia but Peru proposed certain amendments which Colombia rejected, and Brazil on February 3 declared her mediation efforts closed.

United States Secretary of State Henry L. Stimson, after a diplomatic conference with ministers of the signatories in Washington, on January 25 [11] sent a note to Peru reminding her of her adherence to the nonaggression resolution voted at the Sixth International Conference of American States at Havana, February 20, 1928, and to the declaration of the American republics denouncing resort to arms, signed at Washington August 3, 1932, and supporting the Brazilian proposal. On January 26 the Council of the League called the attention of Peru to her duty as a League member not to hinder Colombian authorities from the exercise of full sovereignty and jurisdiction in territory recognized by treaty to belong to Colombia, and warned Colombia to avoid any violation of Peruvian territory. Peru replied on January 28 professing loyalty to the Briand-Kellogg treaty and other international nonaggression agreements but refused to desist from protecting her citizens who seized Leticia. On January 31 President Luis M. Sánchez Cerro of Peru stated that the best way for Colombia and Peru to reach an agreement in the controversy was by direct negotiation. On February 14 Peruvian planes dropped bombs at the Colombian gunboat *Córdoba* in the Putumayo close to or in Brazilian waters, without doing any damage, and were driven off by Colombian planes under Major Boy; and on February 15 the Colombians took, with small casu-

[10] Sean Lester of the Irish Free State, Chairman; José Matos of Guatemala; and Salvador de Madariaga of Spain, the same as the Council's committee on the Chaco Boreal.

See §8, note 43, *supra*.
[11] U. S. Dept. of State, *Press Releases*, Jan. 28, 1933, No. 426, pp. 66-70.

alties, Tarapacá on the south bank of the Putumayo. The countries broke off diplomatic relations on February 15. On February 17 Colombia appealed to the League Council under Article 15 of the Covenant and asked that an extraordinary session be held to deal with the matter, upon which Peru declared that South American legal doctrine had established that such conflicts must be settled by American commissions or mediators. Peruvian Minister Enrique Carrillo and his secretary, González Ulloa, left Bogotá February 18 by special train and sailed from Buenaventura February 19. On February 18 a street mob attacked and set fire to the Colombian legation at the Balneario de Barranca, seven and a half miles from Lima; the minister, Fabio Lozano y Lozano, son of the Colombian minister who signed the 1922 treaty, escaped with his wife and daughter to the Chilean legation, and on February 20 he flew to Guayaquil. On February 25 the League committee of three proposed that a League commission should take charge of the territory, using Colombian forces as international during the negotiations, the Peruvian forces to be withdrawn. The League Council approved the plan on March 1 and asked the United States to support the suggestion.

On March 1, 1933, Francisco Garcia Calderón, Peru's representative before the League of Nations, made such strong remarks in the public meeting of the League Council about injurious and unconstitutional treaties imposed by a dictatorship that Chile, who had also made territorial arrangements with the Leguía government of Peru by the Tacna-Arica treaties of July 20, 1922, and June 3, 1929, pointedly instructed her representative in Lima to inquire just what was meant. Peru, not seeking simultaneous contests on two fronts, offered to send a special delegate to Geneva to clarify her position, and evidently sent adequate word to Garcia Calderón, for on March 4 [12] he explained to the Council that, in referring to the treaty of 1929 as a judgment of Solomon, he meant it was an equitable division.

Colombia accepted the League plan on February 27, but Peru on March 6 made counter suggestions which the Committee of Three and the Council on March 8 found unacceptable and so notified Peru. On March 18 [13] the Council of the League adopted and broadcast a report condemning Peru as supporting invaders, declaring the situation resulting from the presence of Peruvian forces in Colombian territory to be incompatible with the principles of international law, and recommending complete evacuation of the trapezium by Peruvian forces and thereafter the opening of negotiations between the

[12] *League of Nations Official Journal,* 1933, 14th Year, pp. 504-505, 514.
[13] *League of Nations Documents,* 1933, VII, 3; C 194,

M 91. *League of Nations Official Journal,* 1933, 14th Year, pp. 492-614, 944-979.

parties upon all their existing problems. The Council set up an advisory committee of thirteen [14] to watch the situation and to report to the Council within
three months. The advisory committee met on March 18 and invited Brazil
and the United States to collaborate in its work. The United States accepted
on March 18, with a reservation against being bound in advance by any action of the committee, and named Hugh R. Wilson, United States Minister
to Switzerland, as its representative, without vote. Brazil accepted on March
24. The League committee's broadcast report, though prompt and informa-
tive and suggesting a possible means of settlement, was of course no verdict by
any authoritative body [15] and as usual no sanctioned judgment was entered
upon it.[16]

On March 26 the Colombians reported that they had captured Güepi, on
the south bank of the Putumayo, from 500 soldiers of Peru's regular army.
President Sánchez Cerro of Peru was assassinated April 30,[17] and the former
friendship in London of President Oscar R. Benavides, elected by Congress
in special session the same day to succeed him, with Alfonso López, prominent Colombian diplomat, made itself evident almost at once in relaxed tension and less show of bitterness between the countries. López flew to Bogotá
and conferred with President Enrique Olaya Herrera and then flew south,
reaching Lima on May 15 and remaining until May 20. On May 3 the Peruvian cruiser *Almirante Grau* and two submarines passed through the Panama
Canal into the Caribbean Sea, Peru replying on May 7 to an inquiry of the
League advisory committee that they were bound for the upper Amazon, and
on May 8 they reached Willemstad, Curaçao, took on supplies and left for
Port of Spain, Trinidad, and Pará, Brazil. On May 10 the League of Nations
advisory committee proposed the evacuation of Leticia by Peru, a League
commission in the name of Colombia and at her expense to take over and administer for not over one year the trapezium and enforce order by international forces it should select, and direct negotiations for a settlement of the
territorial question. Colombia accepted these proposals on May 12 and Peru
on May 24. Eduardo Santos, Colombian delegate to the League, Francisco

[14] Representatives of China, Czechoslovakia, France,
Germany, Great Britain, Guatemala, Irish Free State, Italy,
Mexico, Norway, Panama, Poland, and Spain.

[15] Manley O. Hudson, *The Verdict of the League* (Boston, 1933).

[16] Luis Anderson, "El Incidente entre Colombia y el
Peru," *Rev. Der. Int.* (Havana), XXIII (1933), 5–23.
Maurice Lachin, *Le conflit entre la Colombie et le Pérou*
(Paris, 1933), 3e Année, pp. 209–217. Louis Le Fur,
"L'Affaire de Leticia," *Rev. gén. de dr. int. pub.*, 3e Sér.,
VIII (1934), 129–147. *La Opinión Internacional y el Con-*

flicto de Leticia (Legación de Colombia, Washington, 1933;
in English, Washington, 1933). *Exposición de la Soc. Geog.
y el Inst. Hist. del Peru* (Lima, 1932). Pedro Ugarteche,
Documentos que Acusan (Lima, 1933). Alberto Ulloa, "La
Cuestión de Leticia," *Rev. de Der. Int.* (Havana), XXIII
(1933), 24–46. Jesús María Yepes and others, "L'Affaire
de Leticia entre la Colombia et le Pérou," *Rev. de dr. int.*
(Paris), XI (1933), 133–209, 235–371, 740–742. *Documents Politiques*, 1933–34, 14e Année, pp. 37–43, 108–113,
151–156, 348–340; *ibid.*, 15e Année, pp. 324–325.

[17] *Current History*, XXXVIII, pp. 345–347.

García Calderón, Peruvian delegate to the League, and Francisco Castillo Nájera of Mexico, new president of the League Council, signed at Geneva May 25, 1933 [18] an agreement embodying the plan, after a statement broadcast [19] by Chairman Lester of the League advisory committee. The League appointed to the commission Colonel Arthur W. Brown [20] of the United States army, judge advocate general's department, first president; Captain Alberto de Lemos Basto of the Brazilian navy; Captain Francisco Iglesias, [21] Spanish aviator; and Armando Mencía of Cuba, secretary. [22] They held their first plenary meeting at Teffé, Brazil, on June 19, on board the Colombian S.S. *Mosquera*, adopted a distinctive flag, [23] and chose fifty Colombian troops [24] for their service. On June 23, 1933, the commission took charge of Leticia, then inhabited by sixty Peruvians, Tarapacá, Güepi, and the entire trapezium. Thus the League of Nations successfully accomplished, in the manner originally suggested by Brazil, the withdrawal of the Peruvians from the area and its eventual redelivery to Colombia without further hostilities. This was the first instance of assumption of direct control over territory by a League of Nations commission and the first actual operation by the League in the western hemisphere. [25] On September 28, 1933, the Colombian Senate passed a resolution declaring that Colombia had no boundary dispute since Peru had officially stated that she recognized the juridical force of the 1922 treaty. On January 24, 1934, the population of Leticia was 142 Colombians and 121 Peruvians, and on May 22, 1934, 253 in all, with 999 in the rest of the territory. A wireless station built by Marconi's Wireless Telegraph Company, Ltd., for and under contract with the Colombian government was delivered to the commission on February 14 and officially opened on February 16 under a Colombian staff. On May 16 the commission discovered a secret service for espionage and agitation in Leticia, communicating with Loreto, and on May 17 expelled from the territory the persons implicated, without further incident.

Peru on September 8, 1933, and Colombia a little later appointed delegates for direct negotiations. Conferences under the presidency of Afranio de Mello Franco, Brazilian minister of foreign relations, as neutral commissioner, to which Peru declined to permit Ecuador to send an observer, began

[18] *U. S. Treaty Inf. Bull.*, 1934, No. 57, pp. 23–31.

[19] *Bull. Pan American Union*, LXVII (1933), 595–597.

[20] Major General from Dec. 1, 1933; left Leticia for Washington, Feb. 6, 1934; succeeded by General Edwin B. Winans, United States Army, Feb. 5, 1934.

[21] Resigned, Dec. 13, withdrew resignation, Dec. 18, 1933; resigned, Mar. 10, 1934; succeeded, May 10, by Guillermo Giraldez y Martínez de Espinosa, Spanish consul at Bordeaux.

[22] Suspended, Sept. 18, 1933, removed, Sept. 19; succeeded by Carlos Garcia Palacios, Nov. 26, 1933.

[23] A white rectangle with inscription in dark blue, "League of Nations Commission, Leticia."

[24] Increased to seventy-five, Feb. 15, 1934, and to 150, May 25, 1934. *League of Nations Official Journal*, 1934, 15th Year, pp. 283–284, 874–949.

[25] *League of Nations, 15th Assembly, 5th Plenary Meeting, Verbatim Record*, 1934, p. 5.

at Rio de Janeiro on October 26, 1933, and continued until November 24 without appreciable progress; they were resumed on February 9, 1934, and dragged along until April 2, when Dr. de Mello returned from a vacation in Minas Geraes with a new formula on which complete and final agreement was reached on May 18, 1934. On May 22 two Colombian transports with 1,650 troops called at Port of Spain, Trinidad, en route to Leticia. The agreement for temporary control by the League commission was to expire on June 19 or 23. Roberto Urdaneta Arbeláez, minister of foreign relations, Guillermo Valencia and Luis Cano for Colombia, and Victor M. Máurtua, Victor Andrés Belaunde, and Alberto Ulloa for Peru, meeting under the presidency of Dr. de Mello, signed at Rio de Janeiro May 24, 1934,[26] a protocol reciting that (Article 1) Peru deplored sincerely the events since September 1, 1932, which had disturbed her relations with Colombia, and both desiring to restore past friendship and cordiality had agreed to renew diplomatic relations; (Article 2) the boundary treaty of March 24, 1922, ratified January 23, 1928, constituted one of the juridical ties which bound Colombia and Peru and could not be modified or affected except by common consent of the parties or by a decision of International Justice in the terms established by Article 7 below; (Article 3) negotiations between the two countries should continue by normal diplomatic means to give a just, lasting, and satisfactory solution to all pending problems; (Article 4) the two nations should adopt special agreements as to customs, commerce, free river navigation, protection of the inhabitants, transit, and frontier police; (Article 5) the two states should study by a technical commission of four, two named by each party, a means of demilitarization of the frontier according to the normal needs of security; (Article 6) to protect the agreements of Article 4 and to stimulate their execution there should be a commission of three, one each named by the governments of Peru, Colombia, and Brazil, if the latter would coöperate, her nominee to be president, sitting within the region, to collaborate most efficiently with the local authorities of both states for the maintenance of a permanent regime of peace and neighborliness on a common frontier, for four years, extendable at the will of the two governments, such mixed commission to have no judicial competence in the territories subject to the full jurisdiction of the parties, and its decisions to be appealable by either nation to the Permanent Court of International Justice; and (Article 7) both nations agreed solemnly not to make war nor

[26] *Rev. de Der. Int.* (Havana), XXV (1934), 280–291. Russell M. Cooper, *American Consultation in World Affairs* (New York, 1934), pp. 285–342. *Am. J. Int. Law,* XXIX (1935), 94–99. *Bull., Pan Amer. Union,* LXVIII (1934), 546–555. Approved by Peru (61 to 11), Nov. 3, 1934.

employ force directly or indirectly as a means of solution of their existing problems or of any others which might arise in the future; and if in any case they could not come to an agreement by direct diplomatic negotiations either of the parties might have recourse to the procedure established by Article 36 of the Statute [27] of the Permanent Court of International Justice, without reservations. The same seven delegates signed also at Rio de Janeiro on May 24, 1934, an additional act of eighteen articles concerning free river navigation and transit in the Amazon and Putumayo basins, customs and port regulations and charges, and individual guarantees and protection of the inhabitants, civilized or savage, under a mixed commission of six and technical services.

The 1922 treaty is thus specifically recognized, and Peru is remitted to normal diplomatic means to change it to any solution more satisfactory to her. It was unofficially reported from Rio de Janeiro that Colombia might be willing to give up the trapezium in exchange for the south bank of the Putumayo and all the territory between the Putumayo and the Napo, which would give Colombia its desired access to the Amazon, but would involve some of the territory agreed to be Ecuadorian by Colombia in 1916.

The League commission transferred Leticia to General Ignacio Moreno, intendant of the Amazonas, republic of Colombia, in a brief ceremony on June 19, 1934, without disturbance. The commission was dissolved, and all the members left Leticia the same day. The protocol submitted August 10, 1934, to the Peruvian Congress was ardently discussed but finally approved November 3, 1934. It had even harder going in the Colombian Congress, which began to debate it on December 17, 1934, and adjourned on February 7, 1935, without having approved it. The two governments agreed at Bogotá, February 23, on an extension of the time for ratification to November 30, 1935, and so notified Brazil and the League of Nations.[28] The Colombian oppositionist Conservatives, with strength almost equal to the government Liberals, appeared to object chiefly to the provisions in Articles 2 and 7 concerning action before the Permanent Court of International Justice and to desire amendments limiting the scope and nature of questions to be submitted. Fabio Lozano T., the former minister who signed the 1922 treaty, was president of the Senate, and with former Supreme Court Justice José Miguel Arango led the opposition, while Roberto Urdaneta Arbeláez, one of the signers, resigned as minister of foreign relations in December 1934 to become a senator, and ex-President

[27] La Cour Permanente de Justice International, Statut et Règlement (Leyde, 1922), pp. 55–58.

[28] League of Nations Official Journal, Mar. 1935, 16th Year, pp. 443–446.

Olaya Herrera became minister of foreign relations in February 1935 to work for ratification. After much bitter criticism, and at least one challenge to a duel, the Colombian House of Deputies ratified the protocol on September 17, 1935.

Lack of precision either in documents, marks, occupation and control, or knowledge of the terrain on the boundary between two of the earliest viceroyalties, of New Granada and Peru, with subsequent varying assertions of right and the appearance of a third nation part way between the original contestants, created a situation so difficult that attempts at arbitration were thwarted, and finally a treaty on a surprisingly fresh basis of settlement incited resistance leading to armed conflict in a part of the ceded territory, and was executed only under the auspices of the League of Nations subject to a simultaneous promise of consideration of revision. Under the protocol of 1934 the boundary as fixed by the 1922 treaty became once more legally and officially recognized, but the two countries are still to continue diplomatic negotiations as to their frontier; and whether by a new treaty revising or superseding the 1922 treaty, a proceeding before the Permanent Court of International Justice, independent arbitration or otherwise, the time and manner of final settlement of this boundary must be considered highly problematical.

22A. COLOMBIA–VENEZUELA. GOAJIRÁ–GUAINÍA

Following the dissolution of Bolívar's great Colombia in 1830, the constitution of Venezuela adopted at Valencia, September 24, 1830, provided that (Article 5) the territory of Venezuela should include all that which before the political transformation of 1810 was called the captaincy-general of Venezuela, and the fundamental law of the state of New Granada enacted at Bogotá, November 17, 1831, provided that (Article 2) the boundaries of the state should be the same as those which in 1810 divided the territory of New Granada from the captaincies-general of Venezuela and Guatemala and the Portuguese possessions of Brazil. As the result of conferences, begun September 9, 1833, in the course of which New Granada agreed to Venezuela's proposal for a line rather of convenience than of strict right, Santos Michelena, Venezuelan minister, and Lino de Pombo, New Granadan minister of foreign relations, signed at Bogotá, December 14, 1833,[1] a treaty of friendship, alliance, commerce, navigation, and boundaries, which provided that (Article 27) the

---

[1] *Cuerpo de Leyes de Venezuela en 1834-35-36* (Caracas, 1836), pp. 139-140. 24 *British and Foreign State Papers* 1405; 25 *ibid.*, 1049. Approved by New Granada, 1834; approved by Venezuelan Congress, Mar. 7, 1836, except Articles 6, 27, 28, and parts of 30 and 31.

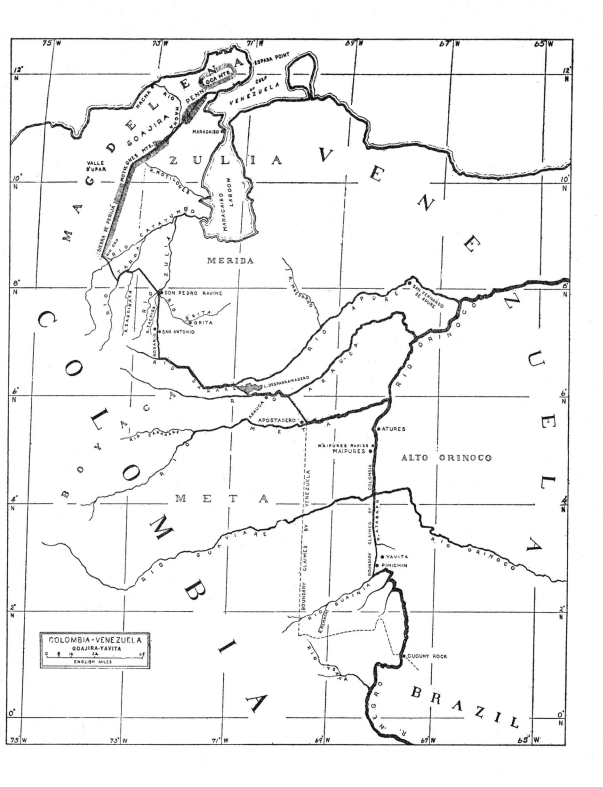

COLOMBIA-VENEZUELA
GOAJIRA-YAVITA
ENGLISH MILES

boundary line between the two republics should begin at Cape Chichivacoa
on the Atlantic coast, and run toward the hill called Las Tetas; then to the
Aceite ridge and thence to Teta Goajirá ridge; thence by a straight line toward
the heights of the Oca mountains and thence by their peaks and those of Perijá
until meeting the origin of the Oro, tributary of that which runs between the
parish of the same name and the city of Ocana; thence down by its waters to
the confluence of the Catatumbo, thence by the eastern foothills of the mountains and passing by the Tarra and Sardinata rivers by the points theretofore
known as boundaries by a straight line toward the mouth of the Grita in the
Zulia; thence by the curve then recognized as frontier to the Don Pedro ravine
and down that ravine to the Táchira; up that river to its headwaters; thence
by the crest of the mountains whence spring the tributary rivers of the Torbes
and the Uribante to the slopes of the Nula, thence by its waters to (lake) Desparramadero on the Sarare; thence southward to Lake Sarare and around it
by its eastern shore to its overflow into the Arauquita; by that stream to the
Arauca and by its waters to Viento pass; thence by a straight line to pass the
most western part of Término lake; thence to Apostadero on the Meta and
thence due south to the Brazilian frontier; and (Article 28) to fix this frontier with more precision and to place marks to designate exactly the boundary, there should be a mixed commission of one person named by each country,
whose acts and operations in agreement should be taken as part of the treaty
and have the same force and effect as if inserted in it. A supplementary convention signed at Bogotá, January 25, 1834,[2] concerned the manner of carrying into effect the military alliance agreed on in the foregoing treaty, and was
dependent upon it. Notwithstanding successive postponements of the time
for ratification and a favorable committee report in 1838, the Venezuelan Congress definitely refused to approve the treaty's boundary articles. The same
New Granadan minister, Lino de Pombo, and Juan J. Romero, Venezuelan
minister, signed at Caracas, July 23, 1842,[3] a treaty of friendship, commerce,
and navigation in which (Article 2) the two governments promised to open as
soon as possible within four years a new negotiation for the exact determination and recognition of the territorial boundaries between the two republics
and their demarcation on the ground by special commissioners. Conferences
especially upon four disputed points of the line began at Bogotá, April 19,
1844, between Colonel Joaquín Acosta, New Granadan minister of foreign

[2] *Recop. de Leyes de Venezuela*, Ed. Ofic. (Caracas, 1874), I, 251–253.
[3] *Recop. de Leyes de la Nueva Granada* (Bogotá, 1845), pp. 449–453. *Actos Leg. de Venezuela en 1844* (Caracas, 1844), pp. 10–18. 33 *British and Foreign State Papers* 819–827. Ratified by Venezuela, May 1, 1843; ratifications exchanged at Bogotá, Nov. 7, 1844.

relations, and Fermin Toro, Venezuelan minister, in which they came to substantial agreement upon the boundary in La Goajirá, San Faustino, and the former province of Barinas, but could reach no settlement of the line on the upper Orinoco, Casiquiare, and Negro, and the sessions ended on January 20, 1845, with a protocol in which New Granada proposed arbitration. Venezuela would not agree then nor in 1872 when arbitration was again proposed by Colombia, nor, after various border incidents, at the close of further conferences from October 2, 1874, to April 19, 1875.[4] Diplomatic relations were broken off in 1873 and again in 1875 until 1880.

Justo Arosemena, Colombian minister, and Antonio Leocadio Guzmán, adviser to the Venezuelan minister of foreign relations, signed at Caracas, September 14, 1881,[5] an arbitration *juris* treaty for the purpose of reaching a true legal territorial delimitation, such as existed by the decrees of the former common sovereign, and claimed by both parties for a long period without their having come to an agreement as to their respective rights or the *uti possidetis juris* of 1810, providing that (Article 1) the parties submitted to the judgment and decision of the government of the king of Spain as arbiter and legal judge the points of difference on such boundary question, to obtain a final unappealable decision according to which all the territory which belonged to the jurisdiction of the ancient captaincy-general of Caracas by royal acts of the former sovereign till 1810 should remain jurisdictional territory of Venezuela and all which by similar acts to the same date belonged to the jurisdiction of the viceroyalty of Santa Fé should remain territory of Colombia; (Article 2) both parties should request the king of Spain to accept the office, and eight months thereafter they should present cases with their claims and supporting documents. The "convenient" demarcation was in this treaty rejected by Venezuela in favor of the line of strict right because the government said that the former would involve the alienation of territory, which was prohibited by the federal constitution.

King Alfonso XII accepted the office of arbiter and on November 19,

[4] *Negociación de Límites en 1874 y 1875,* Ed. Ofic., (Caracas, 1875). *Títulos de Venezuela en sus Límites con Colombia,* Ed. Ofic. (Caracas, 1876), 3 vols. Antonio Leocadio Guzmán, *Límites entre Venezuela y Nueva Colombia,* Ed. Ofic. (Caracas, 1880). *Apen. a la Mem. del Sec. de 10 Int. i Rel. Est.* (Bogotá 1881). Justo Arosemena, *Límites entre los E. U. de Colombia y los E. U. de Venezuela, Estudio Crítico* (Bogotá, 1881). Anibal Galindo, *Límites entre Colombia y Venezuela, Respuesta al . . . Guzmán,* Ed. Ofic. (Bogotá, 1881). Antonio Guzmán Blanco, *Refutación del Folleto del Sr. Dr. Arosemena* (Madrid, 1883). 34 *British and Foreign State Papers* 1227, 1250; 50 *ibid.* 1044;

58 *ibid.,* 233. *U. S. For. Rel.,* 1874, pp. 362–363; *ibid.,* 1876, p. 85; *ibid.,* 1880, p. 311.

[5] Pedro Ignacio Cadena, *Col. de Trat. Pub. de Colombia,* Ed. Ofic. (Bogotá, 1883), I, 83–84. *Trat. Pub. de Venezuela* (Caracas, 1924), I, 360–361. *Recop. de Leyes de Venezuela* (Caracas, 1887), X, 7–8, 168–169. 73 *British and Foreign State Papers* 1107–1108. Approved by Colombian executive, Nov. 7, 1881; approved by Colombian Congress, Law #3, Mar. 28, 1882; approved by Venezuela, Law #2404, Apr. 17, 1882; ratifications exchanged at Caracas, June 9, 1882; promulgated by Venezuela, Decree #2451, June 14, 1882.

1883,[6] appointed a technical commission of five to study the matter attentively and propose the conclusions which they thought proper. Colombia's case [7] was prepared by Aníbal Galindo, submitted November 17, 1883, and Venezuela's case [8] by Julian Viso, submitted October 20, 1883, and reply October 20, 1884. The King died [9] without having rendered any decision, and Carlos Holguín, Colombian minister to Spain, and General Antonio Guzmán Blanco, Venezuelan minister to Spain, Great Britain and other countries, signed at Paris, February 15, 1886,[10] a declaration which recited that both the spirit and the letter of the treaty of 1881 conferred on the existing government of Spain jurisdiction to continue to hear the boundary question until an award should be handed down, and agreed that the arbiter might fix the line in the manner thought most to approximate existing documents, in any point on which all the desirable clarity was not shed. The government of Queen Maria Cristina accordingly continued to consider the case.

The award signed by the Queen Regent in the name of Alfonso XIII was handed down March 16, 1891,[11] and after reciting the uncertainty or indefiniteness of various royal cédulas and other early authorities so that in places an approximate line should be fixed, determined the frontier to be (Sec. 1) from the hillocks called the Frailes, at the point nearest Juyachi in a straight line in continuation of that which divides the Upar valley from the province of Maracaibo; the Hacha on the side above the Oca mountains, the boundaries of those mountains serving as the exact lines; along Valle Dupar ridge and Juyachi hill and the seashores; (Sec. 2) from the line which separates the Upar valley from the province of Maracaibo and the Hacha by the peaks of Perijá and Motilones ridges to the source of the Oro; thence to the mouth of the Grita in the Zulia, by the line of the *statu quo* across the Catatumbo, Sardinata and Tarra; (Sec. 3) from the mouth of the Grita in the Zulia by the curve then recognized as frontier to the Don Pedro ravine and down that ravine to the Táchira; (Sec. 4) from the Don Pedro ravine on the Táchira up that river to its source and thence by the Tamá ridge and páramo to the course of the Oirá; (Sec. 5) by the course of the Oirá to its confluence

[6] Real Decreto #569. *El Libro Amarillo* (Caracas, 1884), pp. 315–316. *Bol. de Rev. Gen. de Leg. y Jur.*, LXXI (1883), 611–613. *Col. Leg. de España*, CXXXI (1884), 748–752. *Rev. de dr. int. et de lég. comp.*, XVII (1885), 163.

[7] *Alegato*, Ed. Ofic. (Bogotá, 1882).

[8] *Alegato* (Madrid, 1883). *Contestación de Venezuela al Alegato de Colombia* (Madrid, 1884).

[9] On Nov. 24, 1885. Alfonso XIII was born May 17, 1886.

[10] *Trat. Pub. de Venezuela*, Ed. Conmem. (Caracas, 1924), I, 443–446. 77 *British and Foreign State Papers* 1012–1013. *Rev. de dr. int. et de lég. comp.*, XIX (1887),

198–199. Approved by Colombian National Legislative Council, Law #9, Aug. 30, 1886; approved by Venezuela, May 10, 1886; ratifications exchanged at Bogotá, Mar. 23, 1887.

[11] *La Nueva Frontera Oriental, Min. de Rel. Ext.*, Ed. Ofic. (Bogotá, 1891). *Trat. Pub. de Ven.* (Caracas, 1924), I, 456–462. 83 *British and Foreign State Papers* 387–391. Martens, *Nouv. Rec. Gén. de Traités*, 2° Sér., XXIV, 110–114. Moore, *Int. Arbitrations* (Washington, 1898), V, 4858–4862. Paul Fauchille, "Le Conflit de Limites," *Rev. Gén. de dr. int. pub.*, XXVII (1920), 181–216. *Rec. des Cours*, XXXI (1930), 766. Published in the official *Gaceta de Madrid*, Mar. 17, 1891.

with the Sarare, by the waters of the Sarare crossing in the middle Lake Desparramadero to the place at which they enter the Arauca, down the waters of the Arauca to a point equidistant from the town of Arauca and the point at which the meridian of the confluence of the Masparro and the Apure also cuts the Arauca; thence in a straight line to Apostadero on the Meta and by the waters of the Meta to its mouth in the Orinoco; (Section 6, 1st portion) from the mouth of the Meta in the Orinoco by the watercourse of the Orinoco to the Maipures rapids, but, taking into account that from the time of its foundation the settlement of Atures had made use of a road on the left (west) bank of the Orinoco to avoid the rapids from opposite such settlement of Atures to the landing place to the north of Maipures, opposite Macuriana hill and northward from the mouth of the Vichada, there was expressly appointed in favor of Venezuela the right of passage over such road for twenty-five years from the date of publication of the award, or until there should be constructed a road in Venezuelan territory which should make unnecessary passage over Colombian soil, reserving meanwhile to the parties the right to regulate by common agreement the exercise of this easement; (Sec. 6, 2nd portion) from the Maipures rapids by the watercourse of the Orinoco to its confluence with the Guaviare; by the course of the Guaviare to the confluence of the Atabapo; up the Atabapo to thirty-six kilometers (22 1/3 miles) north of the settlement of Yávita, thence by a straight line to the Guainía thirty-six kilometers west of the settlement of Pimichín and by the bed of the Guainía, which farther along takes the name of the Negro, to Cucuhy rock. The award thus followed a considerable portion of the line claimed by Colombia but traced in three places a compromise line, giving Colombia the whole Goajirá peninsula and a small parcel at San Faustino, and Venezuela the valley of the Totoli northwest of Maracaibo, a triangle north of Apostadero on the Meta and at the southern end the large parcel enclosed by the Casiquiare, Orinoco, Atabapo, and Guainía. The award upset about 100 miles of the west end of the Brazil-Venezuela boundary as fixed between them by the treaty of May 5, 1859,[12] by giving to Colombia the area bounded north by the Guainía from thirty-six kilometers west of Pimichín down the Guainía and the Negro to Cucuhy rock and south by the watershed between the Guainía and the Isana from the sources of the Memachí to Cucuhy rock. Venezuela asked for a delay in the time of execution, to permit obtaining from her Congress authority and appropriations to send a mixed commission to fix and mark the frontier and Colombia agreed to postponement until May 1894.

Conferences at Bogotá resulted in the signing there by Marco Fidel

[12] See §15, this chap., *supra*.

Suarez, Colombian minister of foreign relations, and José Antonio Unda, Venezuela minister, on April 4, 1894,[13] of an act declaring that (Article 1) Venezuela accepted the award; (Article 2) there were many questions between the two republics whose relations were intimately connected with the frontier, which would be greatly favored by an act of noble generosity on the part of Colombia in rectifying certain points; (Article 3) the controversy being ended by virtue of the arbitral decision, nothing prevented the governments from adopting modifications, preserving the validity and unappealable character of the award and having in mind their mutual convenience and the development of their common interests, with reciprocal compensations; and (Article 4) Colombia found the considerations just and, preserving the effectiveness of the award, considering international cordiality and common interests, accepted in principle the proposition of Venezuela for some modifications in the frontier line. The same ministers signed at Bogotá, April 24, 1894,[14] a treaty of frontier navigation and commerce which provided that (Article 41) inasmuch as Venezuela possessed establishments and settlements on the east coast of La Goajirá and in the Atabapo and Negro territories, which she greatly wished to preserve, Colombia ceded to Venezuela forever dominion over those territories and agreed that the frontier line should be from Espada Point on the Goajirá peninsula toward Teta Goajirá, passing by Yuripiche and Masape hills; from Teta Goajirá by a straight line to the Oca mountains; thence by the boundary line traced in the award to the mouth of the Guaviare in the Orinoco; by the watercourse of the Guaviare to the mouth of the Inírida, thence up that river to the meridian which passes through the ancient Apostadero on the Meta, and down by that meridian to near the headwaters of the Memachí at the high ground which divides into two systems the affluents of the Guainía and the Negro, some of which flow to the northeast to empty into the upper part of that river and others flowing to the southeast empty into the lower part of the same river; thence by the line indicated by this hydrographic division to Cordero hill and thence to Cucuhy rock; (Article 42) immediately after the exchange of ratifications the parties should proceed to take possession of the respective portions of the territory separated by this frontier, and (Article 43) immediately after the exchange of ratifications the governments should name and send out a mixed commission, of one engineer for each party and necessary assistants, to fix upon the ground and mark the dividing line in those portions in which it is artificial, that is to

[13] Antonio José Uribe, *Anales Dipl. y Consul. de Colombia* (Bogotá, 1901), I, 121–122. *U. S. For. Rel.*, 1894, 200–201.

[14] Antonio José Uribe, *Anales Dipl. y Consul. de Colombia* (Bogotá, 1901), I, 122–147.

say, in the Goajirá peninsula from Espada point to the Oca mountains; in Arauca from that river to the Apostadero on the Meta; and in the section of the meridian which passes through such Apostadero included between the Inírida and the headwaters of the Memachí. The government of Venezuela did not accept this treaty but proposed twenty-four modifications, for further territorial and commercial concessions and regulations, offering in exchange the free navigation of the Orinoco. Colombia in turn proposed modifications, among others the making perpetual of the easement over the Atures road; but Venezuela would not accept, and on August 24, 1894,[15] the Venezuelan Congress authorized the president to take the necessary steps to carry out the arbitral award. The Colombian Congress on November 16, 1894,[16] authorized the government to name the demarcation commission.

General Jorge Holguín, Colombian minister of foreign relations, Marco Fidel Suárez, Colombian ex-minister of foreign relations, and General Marco Antonio Silva Gandolphi, minister of Venezuela, signed at Bogotá, November 21, 1896,[17] a treaty of frontier navigation and commerce which reproduced in Articles 36, 37, and 38 the provisions of Articles 41, 42, and 43 of the Treaty of 1894, adding at the end of Article 36 the provision that Colombia accepted in favor of Venezuela the perpetual easement of transit over the road from Atures to Maipures. The same ministers signed also at Bogotá, November 21, 1896, a declaration that (1) if either Congress should not approve this treaty, negotiations should be broken off and left without effect; (2) each republic should proceed to take possession of the territories adjudicated to it by the arbitral award, (3) nominate the mixed commission and make the other necessary provisions for the demarcation and for the formal delivery of the places and regions which under the award should pass to the other country, and (4) if for any reason except war either nation should be unable to execute the award immediately, the other might with six months' notice proceed to mark the frontier, subject to necessary precautions not to injure any right of the adjoining nation. The Colombian Congress attacked vigorously the provisions of the treaty for cessions of territory, and it was not approved.

Luis Carlos Rico, Colombian minister, and Santiago Briceño, Venezuelan special minister, signed at Caracas, December 30, 1898,[18] a convention for ex-

[15] Law #6054. *Recop. de Leyes de Venezuela* (Caracas, 1896), XVII, 457-458.

[16] Law #59. *Leyes Colombianas de 1894* (Bogotá, 1894), pp. 56-57. Antonio José Uribe, *Anales Dipl. y Consul. de Colombia* (Bogotá, 1901), I, 148-165.

[17] *Ibid.*, 165-190.

[18] *Ibid.*, 191-194. *Col. de Trat. Pub. de Colombia* (Bogotá, 1906), Apen. pp. 19-21. *Recop. de Leyes de Venezuela* (Caracas, 1903), XXII, 3-5. *Trat. Pub. de Venezuela* (Caracas, 1924), I, 478-481. Ratified by Colombia on or before Mar. 2, 1899; ratified by Venezuela, Jan. 4, 1899; ratifications exchanged at Caracas, Apr. 21, 1899.

ecution of the arbitral award of 1891 providing that (Article 1) the parties should give practical execution to the award and in consequence should proceed to the demarcation and marking of the boundaries traced by it, where they were not rivers or peaks of a ridge or chain; (Article 2) the line should be divided into two great portions, the first composed of Sections 1, 2, 3, and 4 established by the award, and the second by Section 5 and the two parts of Section 6; (Article 3) the two governments should name a mixed commission of one engineer and one lawyer for each party for each of the two great portions, (Article 4) within four months; (Article 8) doubts or differences which might arise should be submitted by the commissioners to their respective governments, (Article 9) who should resolve them amicably; and (Article 11) if either of the governments should not make its nominations, or if the commissioners should fail to meet within the indicated periods, the commissioners of the other might proceed alone to the marking and tracing of the line, with that scrupulous probity and rectitude which becomes the loyalty and good name of nations; and the line so traced should be the definite boundary between the two nations. The commissioners were appointed by Colombia on May 31, 1899,[19] and by Venezuela on August 16, 1899,[20] and proceeded in 1900 to their work, but suspended operations in 1901[21] because of disagreements in the commission, civil war in Colombia, and internal disturbances in Venezuela. On September 17, 1900,[22] Colombia created a special Oriental intendancy, bounded by the third meridian (71°20′ W.) east of the meridian of Bogotá to its intersection with the Meta, down the Meta to its mouth in the Orinoco; thence by the Orinoco following the frontier with Venezuela to Cucuhy rock, the boundary of Colombia with Brazil, and thence by the boundaries with Brazil and Peru to the third meridian east of Bogotá. On October 13, 1900,[23] Colombia established a customs house at Rio Negro. On account of Venezuela's alleged interference with Colombia's internal affairs, Vice-President José Manuel Marroquín of Colombia broke off diplomatic relations with Venezuela on November 16, 1901,[24] and when Colombia was ready to send a minister, in July 1904, December 1905, and February 1906, Venezuela declined to receive him until the two countries could agree on bases for a treaty of navigation, boundaries, and commerce.[25] Negotiations

[19] Decree #265. Antonio José Uribe, *Anales Dipl. y Consul. de Colombia* (Bogotá, 1901), I, 195–248.

[20] Executive Decree #7423 and Resolution #7562. *Recop. de Leyes de Venezuela* (Caracas, 1903), XXII, 60–61, 595–596.

[21] *Trat. Pub. de Venezuela* (Caracas, 1927), III, 363–381.

[22] Decree #97. Antonio José Uribe, *Anales Dipl. y*

Consul. de Colombia (Bogotá, 1901), I, 248–249.

[23] Decree #155. Antonio José Uribe, *Anales Dipl. y Consul. de Colombia* (Bogotá, 1901), I, 249–250.

[24] Ricardo Aranda, *Col. de Trat. del Peru*, XII, 669–675. 94 *British and Foreign State Papers* 553–554.

[25] *U. S. For. Rel.*, 1906, Part 2, pp. 1438–1440. *Doc. Dipl. Fran.*, 2e Sér., I, 525, 680.

begun in June 1907 ended in February 1908 [26] without result, and bases agreed on in Caracas, June 2, 1909,[27] were disapproved by the Colombian government, as were others proposed by Venezuela, July 7, 1912, and March 4 and July 1913.[28] Venezuela in 1913 definitely opposed further occupation by Colombia, averring that the award of 1891 must be carried out as a whole after demarcation of the entire frontier, and not partially, by portions, as Colombia maintained.[29]

The negotiations upon this boundary thus lasted for fifty years before even arbitration could be agreed upon, it was ten years more before the arbiter decided the case, and the disappointed party postponed execution of the award for another twenty-five years, leaving the actual boundary on the ground nearly as far from settlement after eighty-five years as it had been at the creation of the two republics.

22B. Colombia–Venezuela. Arauca–Yávita

(See map, p. 207, *supra*.)

The nonexecution of the 1891 arbitral award began to be increasingly embarrassing in various ways, locally and internationally. General Ignacio V. Andrade, Venezuelan minister of foreign relations, in a note of December 27, 1915, repeated to the Colombian government Venezuela's view that Colombia could not properly enter into possession of any of the territory given her by the award until the whole frontier line as described should have been marked on the ground, and asked Colombia to choose definitely between the integral execution of the award or an agreement with mutual compensations. Colombia answered on February 2, 1916, that although it seemed to her proper to execute the award as to those portions of the line already determined, she would approve the designation by a friendly government of an arbitral commission to settle any differences between the members of the demarcation mixed commission. There ensued negotiations between the two governments which resulted in the signature by Marco Fidel Suárez, Colombian minister of foreign relations, Nicolás Esguerra, José Maria González Valencia, Hernando Holguín y Caro, Antonio José Uribe, and Carlos Adolfo Urueta, members of the Colombian committee on foreign relations, and Demetrio Lossada

[26] *Cuestión Venezolano-Colombiana* (Caracas, 1908).
[27] 102 *British and Foreign State Papers* 402–403.
[28] *Tratados de Colombia de 1913*, Ed. Ofic. (Bogotá, 1914), pp. 336–343.

[29] Albert Geouffre de Lapradelle and Nicolas Socrate Politis, "L'Indivisibilité de la Frontière et le Conflit Colombo-Vénézuélien," *Rev. gén. de dr. int. pub.*, XXVIII (1921), 107–121.

Dias, Venezuelan minister, at Bogotá, November 3, 1916,[1] of a convention which recited that (Article 1) as pursuant to the arbitral award of March 16, 1891, and the convention of December 30, 1898, Colombia considered that she had the right to enter into possession of the territories which the award recognized as hers and which were clearly bounded by nature or by the work of the demarcation commissions and Venezuela considered that this could not be done until the common frontier line had been wholly marked on the ground, the parties had agreed to submit to the decision of a legal arbiter the question whether the award could be executed partially, as Colombia alleged or had to be executed integrally as Venezuela alleged, as to the occupation of territories assigned to each nation and not occupied by them before the award of 1891, and agreed that the arbiter should decide also the further points set forth in the convention; (Article 2) pending decision, the existing occupation of both states should be maintained without change; (Article 3) the parties entrusted to the arbiter the complete termination of the tracing and marking of the frontier fixed by the award, by means of experts of the same nationality as the arbiter, freely named by the arbiter immediately after the decision; (Article 4) the parties designated as arbiter the president of the Swiss Confederation; and if he would not accept or for any reason had to be replaced, the two executives might name the substitute; (Article 5) the arbiter should give his decision on the question in Article 1 within one year after the presentation of the cases, which the parties should present within six months from the exchange of ratifications; and (Article 6) immediately after ratification, the parties would proceed to negotiate a treaty of navigation of common rivers and frontier commerce and transit on the basis of equity and mutual convenience. It was agreed at Caracas, July 20, 1917, on the exchange of ratifications that Article 4 of the treaty should be interpreted to mean that the arbiter should be the Swiss Federal Council.

The Council accepted the office, and as representatives Colombia appointed José Maria Quijano Wallis, later replaced by Francisco J. Urrutia, and Antonio José Restrepo, and Venezuela appointed José Gil Fortoul and Vicente Arroyo Parejo. The Colombian printed case was submitted January 19, 1918,[2] an answer May 16, 1919, a reply June 30, 1920, and additional indications requested of both parties on October 20, 1920, by the arbiter were submitted April 30, 1921; the Venezuelan printed case was submitted in 1918,

[1] *Trat. Pub. de Venezuela* (Caracas, 1925), II, 560–563. 110 *British and Foreign State Papers* 829–831. Martens, *Nouv. Rec. Gén. de Traités*, 3e Sér., XX, 371–374. Ratified by Colombia, Law #64, Dec. 13, 1916; ratified by Venezuela, May 29, 1917; ratifications exchanged at Caracas, July 20, 1917.

[2] *Premier Mémoire* (Neuchatel, 1918). *Mémoire Responsif* (Neuchatel, 1919). *Réplique* (Neuchatel, 1920). *Documents* (Neuchatel, 1918), 2 vols. *Renseignements Complémentaires* (Neuchatel, 1921).

a reply June 30, 1920,[3] and the additional indications April 30, 1921. A preliminary decision issued June 24, 1918,[4] established rules as to procedure, and on July 10, 1921, the arbiter declared the process closed. The award handed down by the Council [5] at Berne on March 24, 1922,[6] in six chapters set forth the history of the dispute, explained the conclusions, and decided that (1) the execution of the arbitral award of March 16, 1891, could be carried out by parts; (2) consequently, each of the parties might proceed to definite occupation of the territories bounded by natural frontiers which were indicated in the 1891 award and by artificial frontiers which had been fixed by common agreement in 1900 and 1901 by the mixed commission constituted under the convention of December 30, 1898; namely (a) all of the first sector of the Spanish award (Goajirá), (b) the second sector except territory claimed by either party in the present arbitration, between the confluence of the Oro with the Catatumbo and the confluence of the Zulia with the Grita, (c) the third sector except territory claimed by either party in the present arbitration, between the springs of La China and the course of the Don Pedro stream, (d) the whole of the fourth sector, (e) the fifth sector except territory claimed by either party in the present arbitration, included in the triangle formed by joining (i) the mark placed on the Arauca equidistant from the town of Arauca and the meridian of the confluence of the Masparro with the Apure, (ii) the confluence of the Casanare and the Meta, and (iii) the confluence of the Meta with the Apostadero outlet, (f) all the sixth sector except the territory included between the two lines traced September 21, 1900, by the mixed commission to show the claims of the two parties in the Yávita and Pimichín region; (3) for the work of tracing and marking, which was left to the arbiter, there should be appointed a technical commission with an arbitral character, having power to decide by delegation from the (Swiss) Federal Council, to be designated by the Federal Council on nomination of the (Swiss) Department of Foreign Affairs, and to be responsible for their acts on the same conditions as Swiss diplomatic representatives abroad; (4) to complete their work before December 31, 1924, or in case of exceptional difficulties or absolute necessity, within a further period granted by the Federal Council. The award [7] thus answered the legal question as to integral or piecemeal ex-

[3] *Premier Mémoire* (Neuchatel, 1918). *Documents* (Neuchatel, 1919). *Réplique* (Neuchatel, 1920). *Renseignements Complémentaires* (Neuchatel, 1921). *Replica* (Caracas, 1921).

[4] *Sentence préparatoire* (Neuchatel, 1918).

[5] Robert Haab, president; Charles Scheurer, vice-president; Steiger, chancellor.

[6] *Sentence arbitrale* (Neuchatel, 1922). *Documents Techniques* (Neuchatel, 1924). *Trat. Pub. de Venezuela* (Caracas, 1927), III, 33-37.

[7] Antonio José Uribe, *Colombia-Venezuela* (Bogotá, 1931), pp. 1-85, 561-591. James Brown Scott, "The Swiss Decision in the Boundary Dispute," *Amer. J. Int. Law*, XVI (1922), 428-431. *Rev. de Der. Int.* (Havana), II (1922), 339-343. Fernand de Visscher, "Le Litige Colombo-Vénézuélien," *Rev. de dr. int. et de lég. comp.*, 3ᵉ Sér., III (1922), 463-479. Carlos Alamo Ybarra, *Nuestras Fronteras Occidentales* (Caracas, 1927).

ecution of the former award in accordance with Colombia's contention; and left the location of the line in the four disputed sectors to be settled by engineer experts.

The Swiss Federal Council on May 29, 1922,[8] decreed the organization of the commission of Swiss expert-arbiters with a chief and two sections of six members each, and issued regulations and general instructions for them. The commission organized on July 14, 1922, and in October arrived on the ground and proceeded to work on the specified portions of the second, third, fifth, and sixth sectors. They returned to Switzerland at the end of 1923 and prepared a report with maps, and on July 30, 1924, the Swiss Federal Council notified the two countries of the final decisions on demarcation made by the commission. By notes exchanged at Caracas July 20, 1925,[9] the two governments agreed to build at equal joint expense an international bridge over the Táchira between San Antonio, Venezuela, and Rosario de Cúcuta, Columbia, with a boundary column half-way across, the bridge to be neutral in case of international or civil war, and construction to be by Venezuela in accordance with the plans of a Venezuelan engineer superintending the work with a Colombian engineer assistant.

As some of the marks placed by the mixed commissions in 1900 and 1901 had disappeared and it was necessary to assign certain river islands, trace some of the straight lines between the rivers, and determine the principal source of the Oro, the two governments agreed by notes exchanged at Caracas, December 17, 1928,[10] that the line should be marked in a conspicuous and permanent manner, the main channel of the Arauca and other frontier rivers should be determined and maintained, and two sectional mixed commissions, each of one nominee of each government with the necessary assistants, should carry out the technical work, with power to determine facts only and not to modify any of the decided lines. The commissioners were named in 1930 and in entire agreement finished their work in 1932.

The two countries, though agreeing that their boundary should be that which in 1810 divided the captaincy-general of Venezuela from the captaincy-general of Granada, both in the viceroyalty of the New Kingdom of Granada, could not satisfactorily locate that line on the ground, and a protracted arbitration resulted in a compromise award which both nations soon agreed to modify and one still put off carrying out until another arbitral award declared it must be executed, and further determined the correct line. The boundary

[8] *Trat. Pub. de Venezuela* (Caracas, 1927), III, 38–42.
[9] *League of Nations Treaty Series*, No. 993; XXXIX, 16–24. 125 *British and Foreign State Papers* 299–301. *Rev.*
gen. de dr. int. pub., XXXIII (1926), 559–561.
[10] 129 *British and Foreign State Papers* 284–287.

partly fixed by the arbitral award of 1891, partly adjusted by the convention of 1898, executed according to the further award of 1922, and marked for most of its length by mixed commissions may be supposed to be finally settled, with any question of detail that may yet arise capable of being settled amicably by direct negotiations.

23. ECUADOR–PERU. ORIENTE–MAINAS

With the creation of Ecuador as an independent state in 1830, Peru's boundary dispute with Colombia [1] shifted to Ecuador as to the western part of the line, from the Pacific over the mountains to the Marañón. A treaty of friendship and alliance signed by José Maria de Pando, Peruvian minister of foreign relations, and Diego Novoa, Ecuadorian minister, at Lima, July 12, 1832,[2] provided that (Article 14) until a boundary convention was signed between the two states, the existing boundaries should be recognized. Negotiations for a boundary treaty between Matias León, Peruvian minister, and José Felix Valdivieso, Ecuadorian chancellor, at Quito in 1841 proved fruitless and were broken off January 12, 1842. New negotiations in Quito in 1842 between Agustín G. Charún, Peruvian minister, and Ecuadorian Minister Daste got nowhere in four conferences, and the Ecuadorian representative withdrew April 23, 1842, leaving a long note demanding of Peru the return of Mainas and Jaén. The Ecuadorian law of November 26, 1853,[3] establishing free navigation on the Chinchipe, Santiago, Morona, Pastaza, Tigre, Curaray, Naucana, Napo, Putumayo, and other tributaries of the Amazon, and the part of the Amazon belonging to Ecuador evoked a protest from Peru that those rivers were within the limits of the Royal Cédula of 1802 [4] and therefore part of Peru, to which Ecuador replied, denying the legal force of that cédula. In 1857 [5] Ecuador attempted to wipe out some of her external debt, consolidated by contracts of 1854, by adjudicating vacant lands in Atacames and Canelos to the English company of holders of Ecuadorian (formerly Colombian) bonds. The treaty of peace, friendship, and alliance authorized by General Guillermo Franco, temporarily dictator at Guayaquil, after the blockade of that port by Peruvian war vessels, and signed there January 25, 1860,[6] provided that

[1] See §21A, this chap., *supra*.

[2] *Col. de Leyes del Peru* (Lima, 1837), IV, 232–234.

[3] *Constitución, Leyes, Decretos y Resoluciones de 1853* (Quito, 1854), II, 23–24.

[4] See §21A, this chap., *supra*.

[5] *Leyes de 1854* (Quito, 1855), pp. 53–59. 28 *British and Foreign State Papers* 999. *El Peruano: Boletín Oficial* (Oct., 1887), Año 46, XI, 66–67.

[6] Ricardo Aranda, *Col. de Trat. del Peru*, V, 295–307.

El Peruano (Feb. 11, 1860), Año 19, XXXVIII, 45–47. 50 *British and Foreign State Papers* 1086–1092. *Arch. Dipl.*, 1863, III, 278–284. Ratified by Ecuador, Jan. 27, 1860; ratified by General Ramon Castilla, president of Peru, Jan. 26, 1860; ratifications exchanged at Guayaquil, Jan. 28, 1860. "Mapasingue" treaty disapproved by Ecuadorian National Convention, Apr. 8, 1861, clarified June 7, 1861; disapproved by Peru, Jan. 28, 1863.

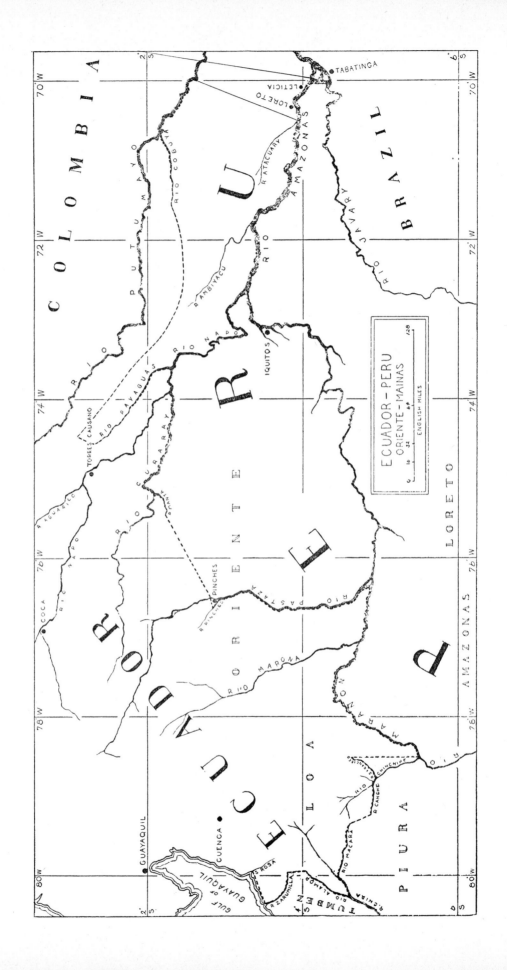

(Article 5) Ecuador, considering the force of the Royal Cédula of July 15, 1802, and other documents [7] presented by Peru substantiating Peru's right to the territories of Quijos and Canelos, declared void and of no effect the adjudication of any part of those territories to the British creditors of Ecuador; (Article 6) the two governments agreed to rectify the boundaries of their territories and to appoint within two years from the exchange of ratifications a mixed commission to fix such boundaries, in the meantime both to accept those arising from the *uti possidetis* acknowledged in Article 5 of the Colombia-Peru treaty of September 22, 1829,[8] which were those of the ancient viceroyalties of Peru and Santa Fé according to the Royal Cédula of July 15, 1802;[9] (Article 7) notwithstanding the two preceding articles, Ecuador reserved the right to prove her title to the territories of Quijos and Canelos within two years, after which, unless proved, the right of Ecuador should expire and that of Peru over those territories should be confirmed; and (Article 23) neither nation should employ its arms against the other without having previously demanded justice and without the difference being submitted to the decision of a neutral power. Throughout the discussion Peru relied on the Royal Cédula of July 15, 1802, and later occupation, and Ecuador relied on the treaty of 1829, claiming, with some support from the Roman Catholic clergy, to succeed to the alleged rights of Colombia.[10] Difficulties arose again in 1875 over the navigation of the Morona and the Pastaza, and in 1881 Ecuador took advantage of Peru's disability after her defeats by Chile and occupied some of the disputed territory, as far as the confluence of the Coca and the Napo. Peru protested in 1882 and continued sending notes until 1887, when Ecuador again tried to cancel some of her external debt with lands in the disputed territories.

After conferences, J. Modesto Espinosa, Ecuadorian minister of foreign relations, and Emilio Bonifaz, Peruvian minister, signed at Quito August 1, 1887,[11] a convention providing that to settle amicably the question of boundary pending between the two nations (Article 1) they submitted such questions to the king of Spain, to settle them as arbiter in a final way without appeal; (Article 2) both governments to request his acceptance within eight

[7] *Documentos encontrados ultimamente en el Archivo Oficial de la Sub-prefectura de Moyobamba* (Lima, 1860).

[8] See §21A, this chap., *supra*.

[9] See §21A, this chap., *supra*.

[10] Pedro Moncayo, *Cuestión de Límites entre el Ecuador i el Peru* (Santiago, 1860). Segundo Alvarez Arteta, *La Cuestión de Límites* (Sevilla, 1901). Pedro Cornejo M., *El Ecuador y el Peru* (Quito, 1905). Marqués de Olivart, *Sucesion Territorial en los Cambios de Soberania* (Madrid,

1906). Marqués de Olivart, *La Frontera de la Antigua Colombia con el Peru* (Madrid, 1906). Pedro Cornejo M., *La Defensa Peruana* (Quito, 1909).

[11] Ricardo Aranda, *Col. de Trat. del Peru*, V, 803-806. Aurelio Noboa, *Col. de Trat. del Ecuador* (Guayaquil, 1902), II, 202 n.(1)-203. *78 British and Foreign State Papers* 47-48. Ratified by Ecuador, Aug. 9, 1887; ratified by Peru, Sept. 28, 1887; ratifications exchanged at Lima, Apr. 14, 1888.

months from the exchange of ratifications; (Article 3) one year after his acceptance cases to be submitted; (Article 4) both nations to reply thereafter to any communications the arbiter might address to them; (Article 5) the decision to be obligatory on both parties as soon as officially published; (Article 6) before the decision and as soon as possible, the parties by direct negotiations should do their utmost to settle all or some of the points at issue and if such agreements were completed in the form of treaties, they should be brought to the knowledge of the arbiter, and the arbitration should be terminated or limited to the points not agreed on; and (Article 7) if the king of Spain should not accept, the arbiter should be the president of France, the king of the Belgians, or the Swiss Federal Council, in that order.

Alfonso XIII of Spain was less than fifteen months old when this treaty was signed, but Queen Regent Maria Cristina accepted for him on December 12, 1887, the office of arbiter. The Spanish government announced to both countries on December 24, 1888, that the study of the case would have to be deferred until after the handing down of the decisions in the Colombia-Venezuela and Colombia-Costa Rica arbitrations then before His Majesty; whereupon both Ecuador and Peru expressed the hope that such delay might be eliminated, to avoid long expectation and uneasiness in their countries. The Peruvian representative, José Pardo y Barreda, presented Peru's statement in Madrid, December 10, 1889. Ecuador at first took the position [12] that the arbiter should require Peru to name with Ecuador the demarcation mixed commission required by Article 6 of the Treaty of September 22, 1829; [13] but shortly abandoned that theory, and her statement [14] prepared by Pablo Herrera, after being mislaid following its delivery to a lady to be carried from Paris to Madrid, was finally found and presented. No decision had been rendered [15] when after twelve conferences in Quito beginning October 28, 1889, [16] Arturo Garcia, Peruvian minister, and Pablo Herrera, Ecuadorian special minister, signed at Quito, May 2, 1890, [17] a treaty to put a friendly termination to the boundary dispute between the two republics, in accordance with Article 6 of the arbitration convention of August 1, 1887, providing that (Article 1) the republics recognized for the future as the definite frontier of their territories a line which beginning at the west at the Capones mouth of the great estuary of Santa Rosa enters the mouth of the Zarumilla

[12] N. Clemente Ponce, *Límites entre el Ecuador y el Peru* (3a ed., Washington, 1921).

[13] See §21A, this chap., *supra.*

[14] *Alegato* (Quito, 1892).

[15] Ricardo Aranda, *Col. de Trat. del Peru*, V, 806-825.

Rev. de dr. int. et de lég. comp., XX (1888), 511. *Arch. Dipl.*, 2e Sér., XXXVI, 358.

[16] Ricardo Aranda, *Col. de Trat. del Peru*, V, 834-867.

[17] *Ibid.*, 867-872. Approved by Ecuador, June 19, 1890; later revoked and disapproved.

and runs up the course of that river to its most remote source; (Article 2) from the source of the Zarumilla to the Alamor or La Lamor crossing the Túmbez and following in every case the line which separated the existing possessions of the two countries, so that there should remain to Peru the towns, villages, farms, and fields which she then possessed, and to Ecuador those which were then in her possession; (Article 3) down the Alamor to its confluence with the Chira and thence up the Chira to the mouth of the Macará; thence up the Macará Calvas or Espindola its full length to its most distant source; (Article 4) from the source of the Macará along the ridge of the cordillera to the first northernmost source of the Canche or Canchis, and thence by the course of that river to its confluence with the Chinchipe, and thence by the Chinchipe to the confluence on its left (east) bank of the San Francisco ravine or river; (Article 5) by the San Francisco ravine to its beginning, and thence to the confluence of the Chinchipe with the Marañón in such way that there should remain to Peru the towns, villages, farms, fields, and lands which she then possessed north of the Chinchipe; (Article 6) from the confluence of the Chinchipe and the Marañón down the Marañón to the confluence from the left (north) of the Pastaza, and thence up the Pastaza to its union with the Pinches; (Article 7) from the confluence of the Pinches with the Pastaza up the Pinches to three leagues (nine miles) from its mouth, and thence by an imaginary straight line to the Pastaza one league (three miles) north of the town of Pinches, thence by an imaginary straight line to the cordillera south of the Curaray Grande at the point in that cordillera whence springs the Manta; (Article 8) thence down the Manta to its confluence with the Curaray Grande, and thence by that river to its mouth in the Napo; (Article 9) from the mouth of the Curaray Grande in the Napo down the course of the Napo to the confluence on its left (north) bank of the Payaguas; (Article 10) thence up the Payaguas to its northernmost source, thence northward (in fact, southeastward) by the ridge of the Payaguas or Putumayo cordillera to the first southernmost source of the Cobuya; (Article 11) thence down the course of the Cobuya to its union with the Putumayo, and thence by the course of the Putumayo to the point of meeting the first post placed on the boundary of Peru and Brazil, where ended the demarcation or frontier line of Peru and Ecuador; (Article 12) each republic renounced perpetually and irrevocably the territories and rights and titles over them, which by this line thenceforward belonged to the other; (Article 13) each country recognized reciprocally the right of free navigation in the common rivers; (Article 14) consequently Peru agreed that Ecuadorian vessels might pass in the Marañón or Amazon and other common rivers to Peruvian territory or other countries, subject to Peruvian fiscal and river police regulations; (Article 15) Ecuador in reciprocity and compensation agreed that Peruvian vessels might pass in the Marañón or Amazon and other common rivers to Ecuadorian territory or other countries, subject to Ecuadorian fiscal and river police regulations. A complementary protocol signed by the same ministers at Quito June 5, 1890,[18] provided that (Article 1) within eight months from the exchange of ratifications of the treaty a mixed commission should survey the frontier from the Capones mouth of the estuary of Santa Rosa to the confluence of the Chinchipe with the Marañón and erect marks at the points they considered necessary; (Article 2) to be composed of one commissioner for each republic, with engineers as the respective governments think desirable; (Article 3) in places where there were no natural boundaries, the commission should follow the course of the line of actual possession of both countries; (Article 4) in places not marked by natural lines nor the line of actual possession, the commissioners should fix the frontier according to the features of the ground which best lend themselves to the demarcation, considering always equity between the parties; (Article 5) to fix the line or section from the beginning of the San Francisco ravine to the confluence of the Chinchipe with the Marañón, the commissioners should follow the natural boundaries nearest the line of actual possession of Peru for the whole distance; (Article 10) the governments of the two countries on giving their instructions to the commissioners might modify the irregular, imaginary, or approximate lines which had been adopted in the treaty, making reciprocal compensations, so long as it was a question of details which would not alter substantially the general base of the treaty, and with the object of making a regular frontier, marked where possible by natural bounds.

The Garcia-Herrera treaty of 1890 failed of approval by Peru when Congress tried to introduce modifications in the line and President Remijio Morales Bermúdez declared that under the Constitution Congress had no power to modify treaties. There followed international recriminations and discussions in which feeling ran so high that legations and consulates in both countries were attacked by mobs and the nations were on the point of war.[19] The arbitration under the convention of 1887 accordingly remained unaffected and theoretically proceeded, but was in fact suspended and the arbiter still delayed, perhaps from fear of war between the countries if an award were made.[20]

[18] Ricardo Aranda, *Col. de Trat. del Peru*, V, 872–875.

[19] *Memorias y Doc. Dipl.*, Min. de Rel. Ext. (Lima, 1892). Luciano Coral, *Conflicto Internacional* (Guayaquil, 1894).

[20] *Mem. del Min. de Rel. Ext. de 1891* (Lima, 1891), 155–161.

Bolivia made an unsuccessful attempt to be admitted to the arbitration. Ecuador refused to approve the tripartite supplementary convention of December 15, 1894,[21] by which Colombia was to be admitted to the arbitration with a corresponding enlargement of the arbiter's jurisdiction; further negotiations between Ecuador and Peru were suspended, and numerous frontier incidents occurred, irritating to both countries. José Pardo y Barreda, Peruvian minister of foreign relations, and Augusto Aguirre Aparicio, Ecuadorian chargé d'affaires, signed at Lima, January 21, 1904,[22] a protocol which recited regret for the lamentable conflict at Angotera (on the Napo) July 26, 1903,[23] and agreed to submit Ecuador's claim for that event and its results to the final unappealable decision of an agent of a friendly nation accredited to the governments of Peru and Ecuador or to another nation friendly to both, cases to be presented within six months and the arbiter to have power to form a mixed commission with one delegate from each government if he required to investigate the facts at the place where they occurred. A protocol signed by Miguel Valverde, Ecuadorian minister of foreign relations, and Mariano H. Cornejo, Peruvian minister, at Quito, February 19, 1904,[24] provided that, direct negotiations on the boundary controversy not having had success, and Peru having disapproved (on February 4, 1904, after previous approval) the treaty of tripartite arbitration, both countries agreed to ask the king of Spain to send a royal commissioner at the expense of the parties to study in Quito and in Lima documents in the archives, collect exact information, and weigh the serious interests involved in the controversy, so that the arbiter's decision should not err for lack of full information.

On July 28, 1904, an Ecuadorian detachment of seventy men under Carlos A. Rivadeneira attacked the Peruvian garrison of forty men under Sergeant-Major José Chaves Valdivia at Torres Causano at the confluence of the Aguarico and the Napo, but was driven off with twenty casualties and five for the defenders. By a pact signed by Ministers Cornejo and Valverde at Quito, October 23, 1904, the question of responsibility for this clash also was to be submitted to the royal commissioner requested to be sent by the king of Spain in the protocol of February 19, 1904. Ramón Menéndez Pidal was appointed, and he, Miguel Valverde, Ecuadorian minister of foreign relations, Honorato Vásquez, Ecuadorian special minister, and Mariano H.

[21] See §20, and §21A, this chap., *supra.*

[22] *Bol. del Min. de Rel. Ext.* (Lima, 1904), Año 1, Num. 1, pp. 78-79.

[23] *Correspondencia Diplomática desde 23 ago. 1902 hasta oct. 1903* (Quito, 1903). *Bol. del Min. de Rel. Ext.*, Año 1, Num. 1, pp. 1-77. Enrique Vacas Galindo, *Límites Ecua-*

toriano Peruanos (Quito, 1903), 3 vols. Enrique Vacas Galindo, *La Integridad Territorial de la República del Ecuador* (Quito, 1905). *U. S. For. Rel.,* 1904, pp. 680-683.

[24] *Bol. del Min. de Rel. Ext.* (Lima, 1904), Año 1, Num. 2, pp. 198-207.

Cornejo, Peruvian minister, signed at Quito, January 29, 1905, a protocol in which Ecuador agreed to withdraw to Quito the military garrison which she had in Aguarico and Peru to Iquitos that which she had in Torres Causano; and Menéndez answered the parties' inquiry as to the time needed for his sovereign's decision by saying that he hoped that it might in no event be more than six months. Menéndez reached Callao March 12 and on April 13, 1905, left for Spain. Lengthy new cases with documents and opinions were presented by Honorato Vásquez for Ecuador [25] and José Pardo y Barreda, Mariano H. Cornejo, and Felipe de Osma for Peru,[26] and the king of Spain named a technical commission to study carefully all the documents presented by both parties and make a report to be submitted for the consideration of the Spanish council of state.[27] Peru in 1905 protested to both Colombia and Ecuador against the declaration by Ecuador in Article 7 of the arbitration treaty of November 5, 1904,[28] between those two countries that the territories of the Oriental region from the course of the Napo to the course of the Caquetá or Yapurá were not included in the Ecuador-Peru arbitration under the treaty of August 1, 1887, but got no satisfaction.

In 1910 the arbiter was supposed to be near a decision, and Ecuador understood that the line fixed was unfavorable to her.[29] An outcry in the press aroused public excitement, the Peruvian legation in Quito and some Peruvian consuls were attacked, Peruvian properties raided, and their owners injured and insulted. The populace in Lima and Callao undertook reprisals against Ecuadorians there, and the Peruvian government ordered a general mobilization, getting out 22,000 men in thirty days. On May 22, 1910, Garcia Mansilla of Argentina, C. de Rostaing Lisboa of Brazil, and Leslie Combs of the United States, ministers of their countries, respectively, in Lima, by notes to Melitón F. Porras, Peruvian minister of foreign relations, offered the mediation of their nations,[30] considering that it was not possible that a war in America should break out over a question already submitted to arbitration. Peru accepted the mediation unconditionally on May 23, and

[25] *Memoria Histórico-Jurídica* (Quito, 1904). *Memorandum* (Madrid, 1905); *Segundo Memorandum* (Madrid, 1905). *Exposición* (Madrid, 1906). *Dictámenes en Derecho* (Madrid, 1906), 2 vols. *Itinerario del Litigio con un Apendice* (Madrid, 1908). *El Epílogo Peruano* (Madrid, 1907). *Contra-memorandum* (Madrid, 1909). Marqués de Olivart, *Algo Mas, Cartas* (Madrid, 1908).

[26] *Alegato* (Madrid, 1905). *Documentos Anexos al Alegato* (Madrid, 1905), 2 vols. *Memoria* (Madrid, 1905–06), 4 vols. *Documentos Anexos a la Memoria* (Madrid, 1905–06), 7 vols. *Dictamenes* (Madrid, 1906), 3 vols. *Indices* (Madrid, 1907). *Memorandum Final* (Madrid, 1909).

[27] Councilor Felipe Sánchez Román registered two dissents in June 1909. *Votos Particulares* (Madrid, 1909). *Litigio de Limites entre el Ecuador y el Peru* (Madrid, 1910), 2 vols.

[28] See §§20–21A, this chap., *supra*.

[29] Enrique Vacas Galindo, *Resumen de la Cuestión de Limites* (Madrid, 1909).

[30] *Americo Latino, La Cuestión de Limites entre el Peru y el Ecuador* (Buenos Aires, 1910). José Manoel Cardoso de Oliveira, *Actos Diplomaticos do Brasil* (Rio de Janeiro, 1912), II, 381–382. *U. S. For. Rel.*, 1910, pp. 438–507; *ibid.*, 1911, 177–186, 687–688; *ibid.*, 1913, 1147–1164.

Ecuador urged by Chile also accepted on May 24, 1910, but used phrases which hinted at an intention to reject the award and indicated that her questions with Peru could be settled only by direct agreement.[31] The Spanish government noted Ecuador's apparent feeling and intention, and by cable of November 24, 1910, twenty-three years after acceptance, the king of Spain withdrew from the arbitration and declined to issue a decision. The military forces were demobilized and slow direct diplomatic negotiations were again begun. The neutral mediation got nowhere and was finally abandoned in 1913.

N. Clemente Ponce, Ecuadorian minister of foreign relations, and Enrique Castro Oyanguren, Peruvian minister, signed at Quito, June 21, 1924,[32] a protocol which embodied a so-called mixed formula and provided that (Article 1) the two governments, with leave of the United States, should send to Washington their respective delegations to treat there in a friendly manner of the question of boundaries, in order that even if they did not succeed in fixing a definite line, they might agree upon the zones which each party recognized reciprocally and which would have to be submitted to the arbitral decision of the president of the United States; (Article 2) either of the foregoing ends when reached to be embodied in a protocol to be submitted for the approval of the Congresses of both nations; (Article 3) the delegations to meet in Washington immediately after the decision of the question which the governments of Peru and Chile had submitted to the arbitration of the president of the United States; and (Article 4) without prejudice to the foregoing, the two governments by their respective ministers to try to advance the solution of the dispute. Peru in August 1926 named Alberto Bresciani, formerly minister to Ecuador and to Japan, to prepare her case. The Chile-Peru arbitral award was handed down March 4, 1925, and those countries finally adjusted their difficulty by treaty June 3, 1929, but it was not until 1933 that there was any move toward carrying forward the stipulated conference in Washington.[33] A clash of patrols on October 10, 1932, near Huaquillas was smoothed over when the prefect of the Peruvian civil guard apologized to the Ecuadorian governor of Machala. In February 1933 [34] Ecuador attempted to correct before the League of Nations a statement by Peru as to Ecuador's attitude to events in Leticia. Peru refused to permit Ecuador to send an observer to

[31] *Documentos Diplomáticos referentes al Conflicto Ecuatoriano-Peruano* (2a Ser., Quito, 1910). *Manifesto de la Junta Patriotica Nacional* (2a ed., Quito, 1910). *U. S. For. Rel.*, 1910, pp. 430-436. Juan Ignacio Gálvez, *Conflictos Int.* (Buenos Aires, 1919; 3a ed. corr. y aum., Santiago, 1919; in English, Santiago, 1920).

[32] *Protocole, Discursos* (Quito, 1935). *League of Nations Treaty Series*, No. 694, XXVII, 346-348. 122 *British* and *Foreign State Papers* 421-422. Martens, *Nouv. Rec. Gén. de Traités*, 3e Sér., XX, 616-617.

[33] Juan Angulo Puente Arnao, *Historia de los Límites del Peru* (2a ed., Lima, 1927), 79-112. *Amer. J. Int. Law*, XXV (1931), 330.

[34] *League of Nations Official Journal*, 1933, 14th Year, 593-598.

the Colombia-Peru conferences concerning Leticia which began at Rio de Janeiro, October 26, 1933;[35] and thereupon the Ecuadorian Congress passed a resolution declaring that Ecuador would not recognize any agreements reached at Rio de Janeiro without her participation. On October 18, 1933,[36] Peru assured Ecuador that the conferences would not go beyond the treaty of March 24, 1922, and therefore would not affect territories over which Ecuador possessed or claimed rights, and invited Ecuador to open direct negotiations at Lima for a solution of the boundary problem between them in accordance with the protocol of June 21, 1924. On November 21 Ecuador accepted the invitation, while reserving full liberty of action with regard to the Rio de Janeiro conference. On February 6, 1934,[37] President Franklin D. Roosevelt announced to the ministers of both countries in Washington the consent of the United States to the sending of delegates by Ecuador and Peru to Washington to discuss the adjustment of their common frontier as requested by them in identic notes on January 31, 1934.

In November 1935 tension was reported along the frontier because of an alleged invasion by Ecuadorian cavalry and police of the Peruvian province of Túmbez. Peru admitted reinforcing the garrison of Túmbez, as a precaution in view of the Ecuadorian authorities having expelled Peruvian citizens from the district along the Zarumilla River and forbidden the free passage of trucks and automobiles. Somewhat later, Ecuador replied that Peruvian tobacco planters in Zarumilla had driven defenseless Ecuadorian planters from their lands, seized their plantations and tools, and destroyed their homes, which the Peruvian Foreign Office denied in a long statement on March 8, 1936. On November 30, 1935, Peruvian Foreign Minister Carlos Concha announced that Peru had invited Ecuador to submit arbitration of the question of disputed territory between the old and new beds of the Zarumilla River and the Túmbez frontier to the Permanent Court of International Justice at The Hague. Peru alleged that the Zarumilla River in the Túmbez area had changed its channel since 1890; which Ecuador officially denied on April 28, 1936, and renewed a suggestion made in December that three engineers to be named by the president of the United States survey and designate the real channel of the river. The rich bottom lands are coveted by squatters for tobacco crops.

On July 8, 1936, it was announced from Washington, D. C., that a proto-

[35] See §21B, this chap., *supra*.

[36] Manuel Cabeza de Vaca, *La Posición del Ecuador en el Conflicto Colombo-Peruano* (Quito, 1934). Nicolás F. López, *Estudios Int. sobre el Conflicto Colombo-Peruano*

(Quito, 1934). *League of Nations Official Journal*, 1934, 15th Year, pp. 284–286.

[37] *Bull., Pan Amer. Union*, LXVIII (1934), 257.

col had been signed in Lima on July 6 providing for arbitration of the dispute by President Franklin D. Roosevelt [38] according to the terms of the Ponce-Castro protocol of June 21, 1924, if direct negotiations should fail. The delegates [39] began their conferences in Washington on September 30, 1936, after being received and addressed by President Roosevelt. Meetings have been intermittent during thirteen months, and nothing official has been given out, but it is understood that both delegations appear to be animated by a conciliatory spirit. It is said that on the basis largely of prior settlement and occupation Ecuador has recognized Peru's right to all territory east of a meridian through the head of navigation on the Aguarico and the Coca and running west of the town of Coca, about 75°45′ W., and Peru has withdrawn all claim to any land west of the meridian of Carrelos, Sarayacú, and Puerto Pardo, about 77°15′ W.; but that it has so far been found impossible to agree on a division or assignment of the intervening zone of 150 miles, which is to be left to the arbitral decision of the president of the United States in accordance with the 1924 protocol. If the whole arbitration does not break down over some foolish pride or politician's selfishness the formal case will doubtless be presented and argued before some United States lawyer or judge appointed by President Roosevelt, with the assistance of the State Department; and after solemn deliberation he will recommend and the president will announce a compromise award splitting the remaining disputed area. Demarcation commissions may be expected to be arranged for, before the conferees finally adjourn. The Ecuadorian legation in Buenos Aires on May 14, 1937, gave out a pessimistic statement reciting that the commissions in Washington had been unable to agree upon the zone to be submitted to President Roosevelt's arbitration and that Ecuador had therefore proposed the appointment of Dr. Afranio Melo Franco, ex-foreign minister of Brazil, as a neutral statesman probably capable of helping the negotiators to compromise their differences.

Irreconcilable claims based on ambiguous and inconsistent early Spanish administrative acts were submitted to a Spanish arbiter whose decision after a delay of many years was finally withheld altogether and subsequent direct negotiations for twenty-five years failed to bring an agreement. The eastern portion of the boundary was especially doubtful and subject to a wide range

---

[38] Notification to President Roosevelt by ministers of both countries in Washington, July 9, 1936. U. S. Dept. of State, *Press Releases*, XV, 17-18, 283-288; Washington, 1936.

[39] For Ecuador: Dr. Homero Viteri Lafronte, minister to Peru, president; Drs. Alejandro Ponce Borja, and José Vicente Trujillo. For Peru, Dr. Francisco Tudala y Varela, president; Drs. Arturo Garcia Salazar, minister to Ecuador, and Victor Andrés Belauarde.

of claims. The dispute involved some 120,000 square miles of territory east of the Andes drained by many rivers running in three principal systems to the Amazon, and final success of the full claims of Peru would reduce Ecuador to a comparatively narrow strip of coastal plain and mountain plateau. In area and importance to the countries concerned and their neighbors the controversy was second, in South America, only to that over the Chaco Boreal.

24. VENEZUELA–GREAT BRITAIN. GUAYANA

(See map, p. 145, *supra.*)

Although the Guiana coast had probably been seen by Columbus in 1498 and by Ojeda and Vespucci in 1499, Vicente Yáñez de Pinzón in 1500 was the first to sail close along the shore. He entered some of the rivers, and the Oyapock was at first called by the Dutch the Yáñez Pinzón and later by the French the Vincent Pinzón.[1] Both Spanish and Portuguese explorers from the first kept away from the coast between the Orinoco and the Oyapock. In 1597–1598 a Dutch expedition examined the river mouths from the Amazon to the Orinoco[2] and started the series of Dutch, English and French attempts at settlement, fighting the climate, the jungle, and the Indians. The French in 1604 sent a reconnoitering expedition to the neighborhood of Cayenne, and the English under Captain Leigh made on the Oyapock a settlement which failed. The Dutch had by 1613 three or four settlements on the coast near the Demerara and the Essequibo,[3] and by 1616 they had erected a fortified depot at Fort Kijkoveral, on an island at the junction of the Essequibo and the Mazaruni, and penetrated inland. The English in 1613 under Robert Harcourt and in 1627 made further unsuccessful attempts to found colonies on the Oyapock. The Dutch West India Company was formed in 1621 and took over the ownership of Essequibo. In 1624 the company sent out an expedition under Admiral Jacob Willekens which captured the fortress at São Salvador (Bahia) and sacked the town, but after a siege it was recaptured on January 27, 1625, by the Portuguese, aided by a Spanish fleet. Traders from Rouen in 1626 made the first settlement on the Sinnamary. In 1627 the Dutch under Abraham van Peere, a Flushing merchant, with forty men and twenty youths made the second permanent settlement, at Fort

[1] See §16, this chap., *supra.*
[2] L. F. Viala, *Les Trois Guyanes* (1893). British Foreign Office, "Introduction to the Guiana Colonies," *Peace Handbooks* (London, 1920), vol. XXI, Nos. 134–137. James

Rodway, *Guiana, British, Dutch and French* (rev. ed., London, 1924).
[3] River of the Fire Stones, supposed to have been named by the Arawaks from a legend of upset canoes.

Nassau on the Berbice, independent of the other Dutch colonies. Captain Marshall with sixty settlers from Barbados, St. Kitts, and other British West Indian islands in 1630 founded Tararica, up the Surinam, and planted tobacco, but the settlement was abandoned in 1645.

In 1635 the last Portuguese posts, Dom Jesus and São Augustino, surrendered to the Dutch. In 1637 the directorate of the company sent out as governor-general of all their territory Count John Maurice of Nassau-Siegen, an excellent administrator. He reduced to Dutch possession about 472,000 square miles, comprising all the country north of the São Francisco, capturing Ceará, and destroying the Brazilian base of supplies in Sergipe, and occupying the region in 1640. In 1641 he seized Maranhão, and the whole of Brazil from 3° to 12° S. seemed lost to the Portuguese, who retained only Bahia and isolated settlements in Pará and a few in the more southern provinces. In 1644 Count Maurice demanded of his company more troops to govern properly the large territory he had mastered for them; and on being refused, he resigned. Maranhão immediately revolted, and the Dutch had to abandon that captaincy. In 1646 General Sigismundus von Schoppe arrived with a fine army from the Netherlands, but on August 18, 1648, the Brazilians defeated him at Guararapes and shut the Dutch up in Pernambuco.

All Brazil south of the Amazon was finally lost to the Dutch in 1654, and non-Catholics were given four months within which to leave Bahia. In May 1654 there was a great exodus of Dutch and Jews: sixteen emigrant ships sailed, of which one, the *Saint Charles*, arrived at New Amsterdam in September 1654, bringing the first Jewish settlers to North America. On January 26, 1655, after thirteen years of war, von Schoppe surrendered Pernambuco and all other places held by his forces in Brazil to General João Fernandes Vieira. Colonies of Zeelanders and refugees from Brazil settled on the Pomeroon, establishing in 1658 a settlement at New Middelburg, near the mouth, with Fort Zeelandia for protection a little way up the river; while the English were building up substantial interests on the Surinam. A settlement under David Nassy was made in Cayenne in 1659. By a treaty of peace signed at The Hague on August 6, 1661,[4] the Dutch renounced all claims on Brazil in return for certain trade concessions.

Charles II of England in 1663 granted to Lord Willoughby and Lawrence Hyde 120 miles of coast land, excellent for sugar cane, from the Coppenham or the Saramacca east to the Maroni. Many Jews from England, Holland, Italy, and Brazil came to settle in Surinam, and on August 17, 1665,

---

[4] José Justino de Andrade e Silva, *Coll. Chron. de Leg. Portugueza, 1657-1674* (2ª Sér., Lisboa, 1856), pp. 64–71.

a group of Nassy colonists driven from Cayenne by the French obtained from Lord Willoughby a special grant, which was the first ever made by an English government to Jews. An English expedition from St. Kitts in 1665 under Major John Scott raided and destroyed the Dutch settlements on the Essequibo and the Pomeroon, but was repulsed from Berbice, whence a relieving force soon retook the other places. On February 27, 1667, Admiral Crynssen with a fleet of seven vessels captured Willoughbyland, Paramaribo, and Surinam [5] from Governor William Byam for the states of Zeeland. The British retook the colony on October 6, 1667, but Crynssen at once recaptured it. The English Admiral Harmon on August 19, 1667, captured Cayenne from the French, Governor De Lezy fleeing to Surinam; and soon after Harmon took Surinam from the Dutch. By the Treaty of Breda, July 21, 1667, providing that all places captured in the war should be retained, the land of the Willoughby grant was left with the Netherlands, while the English kept, in partial exchange, the Dutch settlement of New Amsterdam on Manhattan Island in North America. The Dutch possessions then extended unbroken from the Maroni to the Orinoco, and the English remained without possessions or claims in Guiana. A new Dutch West India Company was formed in 1674 to succeed the original company, which had failed. The Treaty of Westminster, February 14, 1674, which ended the third English-Dutch war and provided that all conquests should be restored, left Surinam to the Dutch. In 1682, at the height of the slave traffic, the States of Zeeland sold their entire colony for 260,000 florins to the new Dutch West India Company and the States General gave their sanction by granting to the company a charter for Guiana from the Maroni to the Orinoco. The next year the company sold an undivided third of its Guiana holdings to the city of Amsterdam and another third to Cornelius van Aessens, Lord of Sommelsdijk. A chartered Society of Surinam was formed by the three owners, and Sommelsdijk went out in September 1683 to be governor, at his own expense. In 1686 he repelled a military expedition from French Guiana with great loss to the French; but he was killed on June 17, 1688, in a mutiny of his soldiers. His heirs tried to sell his one-third share to William II of England, but the city of Amsterdam finally bought it in 1770 for 700,000 florins. Berbice was raided by the French corsair Du Casse in 1689 and again on November 8, 1712, by a French squadron under Baron de Mouans. In 1732 the Dutch gave Berbice a charter and status as an independent colony; in 1740 there were ninety-three plantations on the Berbice and twenty on the Canje.

[5] *The Conduct of the Dutch; Case of Jeronimy Clifford* (London, 1760).

The Spaniards from the Venezuelan coast had been pushing southward, and explored somewhat on and south of the Orinoco, leaving an occasional settlement or mission. Although Diego de Ordaz, who had received the early grant of 200 leagues from the Orellana (Amazon) toward Maracapana, made no settlement and except for his brief explorations in 1531 took no possession, the Spanish still theoretically claimed the whole country west of the Tordesillas line, at the mouth of the Amazon, and it pleased the king officially to ignore the actual existence of French and Dutch settlements on the coast between the Amazon and the Orinoco. The province of Guiana was one of those included in the viceroyalty of New Granada from its creation on April 29, 1717,[6] until it became again a part of the viceroyalty of Peru on November 5, 1723.[7] The province originally depended on the government of the island of Trinidad, but on June 30, 1731,[8] it was transferred to the governor of the fort which had been erected on the island of Fajardo in the Orinoco, province of Cumaná. It became again a part of the viceroyalty of New Granada when that was reëstablished on August 20, 1739.[9] The commandant of Guiana was on May 5, 1768,[10] given charge of the new settlements of the Lower and Upper Orinoco and the Negro, and at that time the boundaries of Guiana were said to be: north, the Orinoco, southern boundary of the provinces of Cumaná and Venezuela; west, the upper Orinoco, the Casiquiare, and the Negro; south, the Amazon; and east, the Atlantic Ocean. Governor Miguel Marmion in a more realistic description of the province written on July 10, 1788,[11] bounds it on the east by the Dutch colonies of Essequibo, Demerara, Berbice, and Surinam and the French colony of Cayenne. So much of Guiana as actually remained to the Spaniards became the province of Guiana in the captaincy-general of Venezuela. The Dutch in 1773 made Demerara, which had been administered as a part of Essequibo, an independent colony, under Paulus van Schuylenberg as first commander. In March 1781 British privateers seized Essequibo, Demerara, and Berbice, and Lord Rodney placed them under the governor of Barbados; but in March 1782 a squadron of French, then supposed to be allies of the Dutch, captured the three colonies. By the terms of the Peace Treaty of Paris, September 2, 1783,[12] they were restored to the Netherlands, and they were evacuated by the French on March 6, 1874. The Dutch united Essequibo and Demerara under one governor again, with the capital at Stabroek, a town built on piles, begun by the

[6] Ricardo S. Pereira, *Doc. sobre Límites de los E. U. de Colombia* (Bogotá, 1883), pp. 5-10, 72-74.

[7] *Ibid.*, pp. 9-10.

[8] Ricardo S. Pereira, *Cédula, Doc. sobre Límites de los E. U. de Colombia* (Bogotá, 1883), pp. 72-74.

[9] Ricardo S. Pereira, *Doc. sobre Límites de los E. U.* de Colombia (Bogotá, 1883), pp. 11-14. *Recop. de las Indias*, Libro II, Tit. 15, Ley 8, Note 3.

[10] Ricardo S. Pereira, *Cédula, Doc. sobre Límites de los E. U. de Colombia* (Bogotá, 1883), pp. 75-76.

[11] *Ibid.*, p. 77.

[12] Martens, *Rec. de Traités*, III, 514-518.

French in 1782 as Fort Dauphin (Georgetown since 1812). A British expedition [13] of three warships with 1,200 troops under Major-General Whyte from Barbados captured Demerara and Essequibo from Governor Beaujon on April 22, 1796, Berbice on May 3, 1796, and Surinam in 1799, and held them until the Peace Treaty of Amiens, March 25/27, 1802,[14] by which they were returned to the Netherlands. They were taken again by the British in September 1803. By the treaties at the end of the Napoleonic Wars, Surinam was returned to the Dutch and the other three Dutch colonies were ceded to England.[15] From 1828 until 1848 the governor of Surinam, at Paramaribo, administered also the islands of the Dutch West Indies: Aruba, Bonaire, Curaçao, Saba, St. Eustatia, and the southern part of St. Martin. On March 4, 1831,[16] the three former Dutch colonies were consolidated by the British into the single colony of British Guiana, divided into three counties; and later the British brought in East Indian coolies to work on the sugar plantations.

Surinam is administered by a governor and advisory council of four members nominated by the queen of Holland, and the colonial states of thirteen elected members.[17] On July 18, 1928, a new constitution [18] and legislative council came into force for British Guiana, succeeding the constitution of August 1, 1891, and the Court of Policy, a form of government which had been retained since Dutch times. In 1934 it was proposed by Great Britain to the League of Nations, after the breakdown of a scheme for the settlement in Brazil of 50,000 Assyrians from Iraq, that they should be settled in the Rupununi district between 5° N. and 2° N. in the western part of British Guiana; but it was announced on April 18, 1935, that the plan had been abandoned.

When Great Britain by the treaty of August 13, 1814,[19] obtained definite title to Berbice, Demerara, and Essequibo from the Netherlands, and Venezuela in 1830 [20] finally gained her independence, the new neighbors carried on the old boundary dispute which had long been argued between the Dutch and the Spaniards. Venezuela maintained that the Essequibo was the true

---

[13] John G. Stedman, *Narrative of a Five Years' Expedition* (London, 1796).

[14] Article 3. Martens, *Rec. des Prin. Traités*, VII, 404–413.

[15] At first, commerce was restricted: 28 George III, cap. 6, Mar. 20, 1788, trade with British West Indies; 54 George III, cap. 72, June 17, 1814, permitting trade with United Provinces; 56 George III, cap. 91, June 26, 1816, applying rules for British West Indies and repealing preceding; 1 George IV, cap. 34, July 8, 1820, continuing preceding to Jan. 1, 1826. 3 *British and Foreign State Papers* 382–385; 7 *ibid.*, 865–866. Decree of William, King of the Netherlands, Dec. 21, 1815; 3 *British and Foreign State Papers* 770–772.

[16] Commission to Major-General Sir Benjamin D'Urban as governor.

[17] *Staatsblad*, 1902, No. 37; as amended.

[18] 18 George V, cap. 5, British Guiana Act, Mar. 28, 1928. British Guiana (Constitution) Order in Council, July 13, 1928.

[19] Conventions between Great Britain and Netherlands: Treaty of London, Aug. 13, 1814; 2 *British and Foreign State Papers* 370–378. Martens, *Nouv. Rec. de Traités*, II, 57–62. Aug. 12, 1815; 3 *British and Foreign State Papers* 386–400.

[20] *Const. de Venezuela* (4a ed., Caracas, 1842). 18 *British and Foreign State Papers* 1119–1152. Promulgated by Pres. José A. Paez, Sept. 22, 1830.

western boundary of British Guiana, but English pioneers had been pushing
ever farther westward and establishing trading posts and settlements in regions never actually occupied by either Spaniards or Venezuelans. In 1841
Sir Robert Hermann Schomburgk, who had explored, plotted and in part
marked the southern and southwestern boundaries of British Guiana with
Brazil,[21] carried his line on north from Mount Roraima through to the Atlantic. Negotiations for a boundary treaty failed in 1844 [22] because Venezuela
was not willing to agree to the line approximating the Schomburgk position
as proposed by Lord Aberdeen. In 1850 there was a somewhat indefinite
agreement that neither nation should make new settlements in the disputed
territory. Little progress toward permanent adjustment was made, and in 1881
serious proposals by José M. de Rojas, Venezuelan minister in Europe, and
Lord Granville, British minister of foreign affairs, came to nothing. On October 21, 1886,[23] the British Colonial Office gave public notice that no title to
or any right in or over any land within the territory claimed by Great Britain
as forming part of the colony of British Guiana purporting to be derived from
or through Venezuela would be admitted or recognized by Queen Victoria or
by the government of British Guiana; and on December 31, 1887 [24] Charles
Bruce, governor of British Guiana, gave similar warning against any rights
claimed under concessions by Venezuela for constructing a railway from Guayana Vieja on the Orinoco eighty miles south to Guacipati and in and over
territories claimed to form part of the colony. In 1886 Great Britain proclaimed the Schomburgk line as the minimum limit of her territorial claim and
established outposts at points on that line as the provisional boundary; and
Guiana police and Venezuelan soldiers watched each other from opposite
banks of Amacuro inlet at the mouth of the Orinoco and at Yuruan on the
upper Cuyuni. Venezuela gave up hope of reaching any agreement through
direct negotiations, broke off diplomatic relations February 21, 1887,[25] and a
little later President Joaquín Crespo appealed to the United States, on the
ground that Great Britain's repeated encroachments on Venezuela's territory
fell within the scope of the Monroe Doctrine.[26] In 1893 [27] Brazil and Peru at

[21] See §17, this chap., *supra*.

[22] 34 *British and Foreign State Papers* 1251.

[23] 77 *British and Foreign State Papers* 980.

[24] *Ibid.*, 660-661.

[25] *Correspendencia entre el Gobierno de Venezuela y el Gobierno del S. M. B.* (Caracas, 1887), 3 parts. *Ultima Correspondencia sobre la Cuestión de Límites de Guayana* (Caracas, 1887; in English, Caracas, 1887). Rafael Fernando Seijas, *El Derecho Internacional Venezolano, Límites Británicos de Guayana* (Caracas, 1888). *Arch. Dipl.*, 2e Sér., XXIII, 249-281; *ibid.*, XXIV, 19-106; *ibid.*, XXXVII, 234-235; *ibid.*, XLI, 376-377. *Rev. de dr. int. et de lég. comp.*, XIX (1887), 199-201; *ibid.*, XX (1888), 512-514.

Martens, *Nouv. Rec. Gén. de Traités*, 2e Sér., XIV, 469-471.

[26] Edward R. Johnes, *The Anglo-Venezuelan Contro-versy and the Monroe Doctrine* (New York, 1888). William L. Scruggs, *British Aggressions in Venezuela or the Monroe Doctrine on Trial* (Atlanta, 1894). William L. Scruggs, *The Venezuelan Question* (Atlanta, 1896). William S. Robertson, *Hispanic American Relations with the United States* (New York, 1923), pp. 105-113. Moore, *Dig. Int. Law* (Washington, 1906), VI, 533-583.

[27] José Manoel Cardoso de Oliveira, *Actos Dipl. do Brasil* (Rio de Janeiro, 1912), II, 198. Ricardo Aranda, *Col. de Trat. del Peru*, XII, 649-660.

the request of Venezuela asked the British government to submit the question to arbitration and received polite declinations. On March 31, 1894, José Andrade, Venezuelan minister in Washington, sent a lengthy memorandum on the situation to Walter Quinton Gresham, United States secretary of state. In June 1894 Venezuela asked the Pope to try to get the British government to consent to arbitration, but the move had no success.

President Grover Cleveland in 1895 [28] took up Venezuela's cause, and a strongly worded correspondence ensued between United States Secretary of State Richard Olney and the Marquess of Salisbury, the British foreign minister, from February to November 1895.[29] In the course of a long statement sent Thomas F. Bayard, the United States ambassador at London, on July 20, 1895, to be read to Lord Salisbury, Secretary Olney said:

> That distance and three thousand miles of intervening ocean make any permanent political union between an European and an American state unnatural and inexpedient will hardly be denied. . . . Is it true, then, that the safety and welfare of the United States are so concerned with the maintenance of the independence of every American state as against any European power as to justify and require the interposition of the United States whenever that independence is endangered? The question can be candidly answered in but one way. . . . There is, then, a doctrine of American public law, well founded in principle and abundantly sanctioned by precedent, which entitles and requires the United States to treat as an injury to itself the forcible assumption by an European power of political control over an American state. . . . The declaration of the Monroe message — that existing colonies or dependencies of an European power would not be interfered with by the United States — means colonies or dependencies then existing, with their limits as then existing.[30]

Lord Salisbury replied on November 26, 1895, refusing to agree to unrestricted arbitration,[31] whereupon President Cleveland in a special message to Congress on December 17, 1895,[32] submitted the whole correspondence and recommended the appointment of a commission to make a thorough investiga-

[28] Grover Cleveland, *Presidential Problems* (London and New York, 1904), pp. 173-281. Grover Cleveland, *The Venezuelan Boundary Controversy* (Princeton and London, 1913).

[29] 87 *British and Foreign State Papers* 741, 1061-1107.

[30] *U. S. For. Rel.*, 1895, Part I, pp. 545-562. Moore, *Dig. Int. Law* (Washington, 1906), VI, 535-559. *Rev. de dr. int. et de lég. comp.*, XXVIII (1896), 502-524.

[31] 88 *British and Foreign State Papers* 1242-1327. *U. S. For. Rel.*, 1888, Part I, pp. 698-702; *ibid.*, 1890, pp. 322, 337-342, 776-788; *ibid.*, 1894, pp. 250-252, 803-846; *ibid.*, 1895, Part I, pp. 545-576; *ibid.*, 1895, Part II. pp. 1480-1491; *ibid.*, 1896, pp. 240-255. *Venezuela y la Gran Bretaña*, Pub. Ofic. (Caracas, 1890). José M. de Rojas, *Las Fronteras de Venezuela* (Paris, 1891). *La Misión Diplomática de Michelena en la Gran Bretaña* (Caracas, 1894). *Límites de Guayana, Arts. del Diario de Caracas* (Caracas, 1896). *Correspondence between Great Britain and the United States with respect to Proposals for Arbitration*; U. S. No. 2 (1896), C-8105. *Correspondencia entre los E. U. y la Gran Bretaña* (Caracas, 1896). Martens, *Nouv. Rec. Gén. de Traités*, 2e Sér., XXIII, 316-355. *Mem. del Min. de Rel. Ext. acerca de la Nota de Lord Salisbury al Señor Olney fechada a 26 nov. 1895* (Caracas, 1896). Joseph Strickland, *Documents and Maps on the Boundary Question* (Rome, 1896). *Arch. Dipl.*, 2e Sér., LVII, 125-126, 169-190, 248, 277-291; *ibid.*, LIX, 209-210. Moore, *Dig. Int. Law* (Washington, 1906), VI, 559-575. *Amer. Law Rev.*, XXX (1896), 916-920.

[32] *Messages and Papers of the Presidents* (New York, 1897), XIII, 6087-6090. *U. S. For. Rel.*, 1895, Part I, pp. 75-76, 204, 542-545. Henry James, *Richard Olney and his Public Service* (Boston and New York, 1923), pp. 95-142, 221-253. Moore, *Dig. Int. Law* (Washington, 1906), VI, 576-579. 87 *British and Foreign State Papers* 1210-1214. *Amer. J. Int. Law*, VIII (1914), 430. *Arch. Dipl.*, 2e Sér., LVI, 310-313.

tion of the merits of the controversy. There was strong feeling and intense excitement for a time in both England and the United States, and Congress on December 21, 1895,[33] voted $100,000 for the expenses of an investigating commission. Before the commission of jurists with Justice David J. Brewer as president had made its report, Great Britain in January 1896 indicated her willingness to submit the controversy to arbitration if settled districts should be excluded. The United States refused to consider this condition, and it took further months of negotiation to obtain agreement in October 1896 upon the rule that possession of land for fifty years should be judged to constitute good and sufficient title. With this outcome, the United States gained practical recognition from the most important European maritime power for the Monroe Doctrine as it was then interpreted and gave it an international standing it had never previously enjoyed. After winning this point, United States officials and most of the public appeared to lose interest in the outcome of the fundamental territorial question. The United States investigating commission was appointed by President Cleveland on January 1, 1896,[34] and sat in Washington at intervals from January 4, 1896, to May 26, 1897. It asked and received the assistance of both governments [35] and examined maps and other historical evidence, but on November 10, 1896, was notified of the conclusion of negotiations for arbitration, and in a report of February 27, 1897,[36] merely published historical summaries, documents and maps.

The treaty signed by Sir Julian Paunceforte, British minister, and José Andrade, Venezuelan minister, at Washington, February 2, 1897,[37] provided that (Article 1) an arbitral tribunal should immediately be appointed to determine the boundary line between the colony of British Guiana and the United States of Venezuela, (Article 2) to consist of five jurists: Farrer Baron Herschell (who died before the commission met and was replaced by Charles Baron Russell of Killowen, lord chief justice of England) and Sir Richard Henn Collins, lord justice, nominated by the judicial committee of the British

[33] Chap. I; 29 *U. S. Stat. L.* 1, *Cong. Rec.*, XXVIII, Part I, 204-212, 249-250, 253-262, 271-281. *Acuerdo del Congreso de Venezuela dictado el 9 marzo 1896* (Caracas, 1896). See also J. Res. No. 17 of Feb. 20, 1895; 28 *U. S. Stat. L.* 971.

[34] David Josiah Brewer, justice of the United States Supreme Court, president; Richard Henry Alvey, Frederic R. Coudert, Daniel C. Gilman, Andrew D. White; Severo Mallet-Prevost, secretary.

[35] James J. Storrow, Sr., of Boston represented Venezuela as counsel. Great Britain never directly recognized the commission, but at the United States State Department's request furnished copies of documents for it.

[36] *The Case of Venezuela* (Atlanta, 1896). *Alegato de*

Venezuela, Ed. Ofic. (Caracas, 1896). *Historia Oficial de la Discusión entre Venezuela y la Gran Bretaña* (Nueva York, 1896). William L. Scruggs, *Fallacies of the British Blue Book* (Washington, 1896). *Cuestión de Límites de Guayana* (Caracas, 1897). *Senate Doc. No. 106, 55th Congress, 1st Session* (Washington, 1897), 4 vols. *Senate Doc. No. 91, 55th Congress, 2nd Session* (Washington, 1898), 2 vols.

[37] 89 *British and Foreign State Papers* 57-65. *Recop. de Leyes de Venezuela* (Caracas, 1899), XX, 484-488. Moore, *Int. Arbitrations* (Washington, 1898), V, 5017-5018. Martens, *Nouv. Rec. Gén. de Traités*, 2ᵉ Sér., XXVIII, 328-332. Ratified by Venezuela, Apr. 17, 1897; ratifications exchanged at Washington, June 14, 1897; promulgated by Venezuela, Decr. Ejec. #6901, July 23, 1897.

Privy Council; Melville Weston Fuller, chief justice of the United States, nominated by the president of Venezuela; David Josiah Brewer, justice of the United States Supreme Court, nominated by the justices of the United States Supreme Court; and a fifth, to be president of the tribunal, to be selected by these four or if they failed to agree within three months from the exchange of ratifications by the king (Oscar II) of Sweden and Norway, substitutes if necessary to be appointed by the judicial committee of the Privy Council, by a majority of the justices of the United States Supreme Court, or by the other four arbitrators, respectively; (Article 3) the tribunal should investigate and ascertain the extent of territories belonging to or that might be lawfully claimed by the Netherlands or Spain at the time of the acquisition by Great Britain of the colony of British Guiana and should determine the boundary line between British Guiana and Venezuela; (Article 4, Rules) (*a*) adverse holding or prescription by exclusive political control or actual settlement during a period of fifty years to make a good title, (*b*) rights and claims resting on any other ground whatever valid according to international law and on any principles of international law the arbitrators deem applicable to be recognized; (Article 5) the arbitrators to meet at Paris within sixty days after delivery of the printed arguments, or in any other place they may determine, questions to be decided by a majority; (Article 6) printed cases with documents to be delivered and exchanged within eight months from the exchange of ratifications; (Article 7) counter cases within four months thereafter; (Article 8) printed arguments within three months thereafter; (Article 9) such periods to be extended for thirty days by the arbitrators if they thought fit; (Article 10) decision to be made if possible within three months from the close of the argument, and (Article 13) to be considered by the parties a full, perfect, and final settlement of all the questions referred to the arbitrators. Professor Frederic de Martens, Russian privy councilor, was named by the four as the fifth arbitrator, and after the cases,[38] counter cases and arguments had been exchanged and the preliminaries closed, three of the commission met at Paris, January 25, 1899 [39] to arrange procedure,[40] and the full

[38] Great Britain, *British Guiana Boundary Case, Appendix, Atlas, Counter Case, Appendix, Argument* (London, 1898), 7 vols. *Misc. Papers, Index* (London, 1899). Venezuela, *British Guiana Boundary Case* (3 vols.), *Atlas, Counter Case* (3 vols.), *Atlas, Argument* (New York, 1898) (2 vols.). *British Case,* "Venezuela No. 1 (1899), C–9336"; *Counter Case,* "Venezuela No. 2 (1899), C–9337"; *Argument,* "Venezuela No. 3 (1899), C–9338" (London, 1899). *Case of Venezuela,* Official Ed. (Washington, 1897–98), 2 Parts. *Case of Venezuela,* "Venezuela No. 4 (1899), C–9499"; *Counter Case,* "Venezuela No. 5 (1899), C–9500";

Printed Argument, "Venezuela No. 6 (1899), C–9501" (London, 1899).

[39] Chief secretary, Martin; undersecretaries, L. D'Oyly Carte and Perry Allen. First meeting only: secretary, Paul Vieugué of France, assistant secretary, Tatischeff of Russia. British agent, George W. Buchanan; Venezuelan agent, José M. de Rojas.

[40] 92 *British and Foreign State Papers* 466–469. *Amer. Law Rev.,* XXXI (1897), 481–503. *Rev. de dr. int. et de lég. comp.,* XXIX (1897), 671–672; *ibid.,* XXX (1898), 117–118.

commission sat at Paris in a hall of the foreign ministry for fifty-four days from June 15 to September 27, 1899 [41] and heard oral argument by seven counsel.[42] After deliberation behind closed doors the commission met in final open session and handed down its unanimous award on October 3, 1899,[43] determining that the boundary line between the colony of British Guiana and the United States of Venezuela should be as follows:

> Starting from the coast at Point Playa, the line of boundary shall run in a straight line to the River Barima at its junction with the River Mururuma, and thence along the mid-stream of the latter river to its source, and from that point to the junction of the River Haiowa with the Amakuru, and thence along the mid-stream of the Amakuru to its source in the Imataca Ridge, and thence in a southwesterly direction along the highest ridge of the spur of the Imataca Mountains to the highest point of the main range of such Imataca Mountains opposite to the source of the Barima, and thence along the summit of the main ridge in a southeasterly direction of the Imataca Mountains to the source of the Acarabisi, and thence along the mid-stream of the Acarabisi to the Cuyuni, and thence along the northern bank of the River Cuyuni westward to its junction with the Wenamu, and thence following the mid-stream of the Wenamu to its westernmost source, and thence in a direct line to the summit of Mount Roraima, and from Mount Roraima to the source of the Cotinga, and along the mid-stream of that river to its junction with the Takutu, and thence along the mid-stream of the Takutu to its source, thence in a straight line to the westernmost point of the Akarai Mountains, and thence along the ridge of the Akarai Mountains to the source of the Corentin called the Cutari River,

provided that the line should be subject and without prejudice to any questions then existing or which might arise between Great Britain and Brazil or between Brazil and Venezuela; the Amakaru and Barima to be open to navigation by the merchant ships of all nations, subject to just regulations and dues, and goods in transit not to be charged duties.

By this award, although neither country gained its entire claim,[44] the boundary fixed followed most of the tentative Schomburgk line, giving to Great Britain the greater part of the disputed 42,000 square miles of territory but leaving to Venezuela a protective area on the south side of the mouth of

---

[41] Proceedings, 11 vols., 3241 pp. More than 2,650 documents were submitted.

[42] In order of speaking: Sir Richard Everard Webster, British attorney general, for Great Britain; Severo Mallet-Prevost and James Russell Soley for Venezuela; Sir Robert Reid and G. R. Askwith for Great Britain; Benjamin F. Tracy for Venezuela; Webster again for Great Britain; and Benjamin Harrison for Venezuela.

[43] 92 British and Foreign State Papers 160-162. Award, Venezuela No. 7 (1899), C-9533 (London, 1899). Recop. de Leyes y Decr. de Venezuela (Caracas, 1903), XXII, 609-614. Trat. Pub. de Venezuela (Caracas, 1924), I, 491-498. Rev. gén. de dr. int. pub., VIII (1901), 71-80. Mar-

tens, Nouv. Rec. Gén. de Traités, 2e Sér., XXIX, 581-587.

[44] H. D. Hoskold, Cuestiones de Límites (Buenos Aires, 1897), pp. 59-135. Georges Pariset, Historique Sommaire du Conflit Anglo-Vénézuélien en Guyane (Paris, 1898). Everard F. im Thurn, "British Guiana and its Boundary," Proc. Royal Colonial Institute (London, 1900), XXXI, 133-161. Georges Pariset, L'Arbitrage Anglo-Vénézuélien de Guyane (Paris, 1900). H. Lauterpacht, Private Law Sources and Analogies of International Law (London, 1927), pp. 227-233, 275-276. Geoffrey Butler and Simon Maccoby, The Development of International Law (London, 1928), pp. 396-397.

the Orinoco and a parcel in the Yuruari territory west of the Wenamu. Brazil on July 25, 1899,[45] and again on December 7, 1899, after the award, protested to the tribunal against a decision prejudicial to Brazil's rights, and the saving clause was probably a result of the earlier of these representations. In execution of the award, commissions were named by each country to mark the line. The Venezuelan commission [46] on November 5, 1900, left La Guaira for Trinidad and proceeded to Georgetown, whence they returned to Mururuma to meet the four British commissioners and started work on November 24, 1900; [47] they reached the headwaters of the Barima on October 31, 1901; and after the difficulties referred to below a second commission carried the line on south and finished its labors and closed its records at Caracas, August 2, 1905.[48] Minor deviations from the exact line of the award, suggested by the commissioners owing to the impassability of the country, to follow the watersheds of the Caroni, Cuyuni, and Mazaruni, were agreed to by both governments.

In 1901 [49] Belgium, France, Germany, Great Britain, Italy, Mexico, the Netherlands, Spain, Sweden, and Norway, and the United States had pending against Venezuela a large number of money claims for personal injuries and damages to nationals during the civil wars since 1898, seizure and plundering of vessels, and breaches of contract in connection with the building of railways and other large undertakings; and the government under President Castro showed itself particularly intractable to foreigners and unwilling to make settlements through diplomatic negotiations. Germany, Great Britain, and Italy came to an understanding for joint action, and after explaining to the United States that there was no purpose or intention of making even the smallest acquisition or permanent occupation of Venezuelan territory on the South American continent or the islands adjacent, England and Germany presented ultimatums on December 7, 1902, but failed to obtain a satisfactory response within the forty-eight hours specified. In the next few days the entire Venezuela fleet of twelve small vessels except the steamer *Miranda*, whose where-

[45] José Manoel Cardoso de Oliveira, *Actos Dipl. do Brasil* (Rio de Janeiro, 1912), II, 274–275.

[46] An engineer in chief, four engineers, a lawyer, a doctor, and an interpreter-secretary.

[47] Marks were erected at Punta Playa at 8°33′22″ N. 59°59′48″ W. and Mururuma at 8°18′13″ N. 59°48′28.7″ W.

[48] Elias Toro, *Por las selvas de Guayana* (Caracas, 1905). Domingo A. Sifontes, *Límites Guayaneses* (Caracas, 1909). *Trat. Pub. de Venezuela* (Caracas, 1927), III, 356–363.

[49] 95 *British and Foreign State Papers* 1054–1135; 96

ibid., 439–506. Moore, *Dig. Int. Law* (Washington, 1906), VI, 586–594. *Int. Conciliation* (New York, 1928), No. 242, pp. 435–438. William S. Robertson, *Hispanic-American Relations with the United States* (New York, 1923), pp. 114–121. *Arch. Dipl.*, 3e Sér., LXXXV, 168–172, 293–342; *ibid.*, LXXXVI, (II), 103–140, 215–216; *ibid.*, LXXXVII, 43–62; *ibid.*, LXXXIX, 47–58, 165–178, 281–306; *ibid.*, XC, 437–442, 567–574, 699–710; *ibid.*, XCI, 972–995; *ibid.*, XCIII, 68–96; *ibid.*, XCIV, 423–449; *ibid.*, XCV, 71–119. *Doc. Dipl. Fran.*, 2e Sér., I, 525–526; *ibid.*, III, 43–45, 61–63, 67–68, 161–164.

abouts were not known, were captured or destroyed by five British war vessels [50] under Vice-Admiral Sir A. L. Douglas, and four German ships [51] under Commodore Scheder, without resistance or opposition anywhere except a few rifle shots fired at the *Charybdis* from Puerto Cabello on December 13. On December 9 at La Guaira four boats from the *Retribution* seized the leased steamer *Ossun* belonging to a French company and disabled the hauled-up destroyer *Margarita* by carrying off her machinery, while six boats from the *Panther* and the *Vineta* captured the revenue cutter *Totumo* and the *General Crespo.* On December 9, at Port-of-Spain, Trinidad, the *Charybdis* and *Alert* seized the gunboat *Bolívar;* the *Alert* captured on December 11 at Güiria the *Zamora,* near Güiria the gunboat *Zumbador* and near Irapa the *Veinte Tres de Mayo,* on December 14 at Cumaná the government schooner *Coqueta,* and on December 15 at Carúpano the sailing-cutter *Britania,* all five of which were sent into Port-of-Spain. On December 11 at sea the *Gazelle,* which had been patrolling the coast with the *Falke* to prevent any vessel's escaping, captured the *Restaurador.* The British restored the *Ossun* to its French owners before December 19, but the Germans sank the *Totumo* and the *General Crespo.* On December 13 the *Charybdis* and the *Vineta* bombarded Forts Libertador and Vigia at Puerto Cabello and the next day landed demolition parties which destroyed the walls and all the modern and mounted iron guns of Fort Libertador, the British commander, Commodore R. A. J. Montgomerie, bringing off four small brass guns and a flag but sending no party against Fort Vigia, as he had heard they might be fired on from the hills back of the town. Germany explained that she was at first inclined to a pacific blockade, but yielded to the wishes of Great Britain in the establishment of a war-like blockade with no declaration of war or any hostile step beyond the blockade. After United States Secretary of State John Hay on December 16, 1902,[52] directed Charlemagne Tower, United States ambassador at Berlin, to ascertain discreetly what was intended by war-like blockade without war, Arthur J. Balfour, the British prime minister, stated in the House of Commons that he agreed in thinking that there could be no such thing as a pacific blockade. On December 20, 1902,[53] Great Britain blockaded the ports of La Guaira, Carenero, Guanta, Cumaná, Carúpano, and the mouths of the Orinoco; Germany blockaded Puerto Cabello and Maracaibo; and Italy announced that her naval forces would take part in the blockade. On December 21 the *Pan-*

[50] The *Alert, Charybdis, Indefatigable, Quail,* and *Retribution.*

[51] The *Falke, Gazelle, Panther,* and *Vineta.*

[52] *U. S. For. Rel.,* 1903, p. 421.

[53] *Ibid.,* pp. 788–803. 95 *British and Foreign State Papers* 425–428. *Rev. gén. de dr. int. privé,* XI (1904), 362–458. *Bull., Arg. de Dr. Int. Privé* (Buenos Aires, 1903), 1re Année, pp. 145–177.

ther and the *Vineta* bombarded Fort San Carlos at Maracaibo without prior consultation with the British naval commander. A protest of December 29, 1902,[54] by Foreign Minister Luis M. Drago of Argentina to the United States, first formulating the Drago Doctrine, was severely criticized in Brazil. As early as December 15, 1902, Venezuela asked the United States to convey a proposal of arbitration to Germany and Great Britain, and on December 18 conferred on Herbert W. Bowen, United States minister at Caracas, full powers to enter into negotiations. After acceptance in principle but reservation of certain specified demands, and declination by President Theodore Roosevelt to act as arbitrator, all the nations interested accepted a reference to the Permanent Court of Arbitration at The Hague. Finally, by protocols signed at Washington on February 13, 1903,[55] by the three blockading powers and soon after by the seven others,[56] the substance of the various claims was submitted to several mixed commissions at Caracas, and by protocols signed at Washington on May 7, 1903,[57] the question only of preferential rights by the blockading powers was submitted to The Hague. The blockade by the three allies was raised on February 15, 1903.[58] The claim of Germany, Great Britain, and Italy for preferential payment was allowed by a unanimous award of February 22, 1904,[59] in which the action of the blockading powers was termed war-like operations and war. On May 27, 1903,[60] President Castro, to assist in carrying out the payments of awards for which customs dues were pledged, suppressed temporarily the custom houses at Caño Colorado, Ciudad Bolívar, Guanta, Güiria, La Vela de Coro, and Puerto Sucre, leaving open those at Carúpano, La Guaira, Porlamar, and Puerto Cabello.

[54] *Arch. Dipl.,* 3e Sér., LXXXVIII, 54–58.

[55] *Col. de Trat. Pub. de Venezuela* (Caracas, 1910), pp. 289–296. 96 *British and Foreign State Papers* 99–101, 803–805. *Arch. Dipl.,* 3e Sér., LXXXV, 72–73; *ibid.,* LXXXVII, 257–272, 285–286; *ibid., XCIII,* 138–139. Martens, *Nouv. Rec. Gén. de Traités,* 3e Sér., I, 46–53. *Rev. de dr. int. privé,* V (1909), 41–63.

[56] Belgium, Mar. 7, 1903. *Col. de Trat. Pub. de Venezuela* (Caracas, 1910), pp. 306–307. 96 *British and Foreign State Papers* 806–808. *Rec. Int. des Traités du XXe Siècle* (Paris, 1903), pp. 571–574.

France, Feb. 27, 1903. *Col. de Trat. Pub. de Venezuela* (Caracas, 1910), pp. 302–303. *Arch. Dipl.,* LXXXVII, 285–286. *Rec. Int. des Traités du XXe Siècle* (Paris, 1903), pp. 563–565.

Mexico, Feb. 26, 1903. *Col. de Trat. Pub. de Venezuela* (Caracas, 1910), pp. 300–301. *Rec. Int. des Traités du XXe Siècle* (Paris, 1903), pp. 558–562.

The Netherlands, Feb. 28, 1903. *Col. de Trat. Pub. de Venezuela* (Caracas, 1910), pp. 304–305. 96 *British and Foreign State Papers* 818–820. *Rec. Int. des Traités du XXe Siècle* (Paris, 1903), pp. 566–570.

Spain, Apr. 2, 1903. *Col. de Trat. Pub. de Venezuela* (Caracas, 1910), pp. 310–311. *Rec. Int. des Traités du*

XXe Siècle (Paris, 1903), pp. 578–582.

Sweden and Norway, Mar. 10, 1903. *Col. de Trat. Pub. de Venezuela* (Caracas, 1910), pp. 308–309. *Rec. Int. des Traités du XXe Siècle* (Paris, 1903), pp. 574–578.

The United States, Feb. 17, 1903. *Col. de Trat. Pub. de Venezuela* (Caracas, 1910), pp. 298–299. *U. S. For. Rel.,* 1903, pp. 804–805. *Rev. Int. des Traités du XXe Siècle* (Paris, 1903), pp. 554–558.

[57] *Col. de Trat. Pub. de Venezuela* (Caracas, 1910), pp. 312–316. 96 *British and Foreign State Papers* 99–105, 801–803. *Arch. Dipl.,* 3e Sér., LXXXVII, 273–284. Martens, *Nouv. Rec. Gén. de Traités,* 3e Sér., I, 54–57. William L. Penfield, *The Venezuelan Arbitration before the Hague Tribunal, 1903* (Washington, 1905), pp. 195–198, 482–487, 496–499, 504–506, 512, 773–775, 778–779.

[58] 96 *British and Foreign State Papers* 795–797.

[59] *Arch. Dipl.,* 3e Sér., LXXXVIII, 89–105, 241–293; *ibid.,* LXXXIX, 191–201. Martens, *Nouv. Rec. Gén. de Traités,* 3e Sér., I (1909), 57–64. Clunet, *J. dr. int. privé,* XL (1913), 735. H. Lauterpacht, *Private Law Sources and Analogies of Int. Law* (London, 1927), pp. 250–255.

[60] 96 *British and Foreign State Papers* 805–806. Clunet, *J. dr. int. privé,* XL (1913), 735.

The original boundary conflict between documentary title and actual occupation, possession, and control could not be adjusted by direct negotiations, but was submitted to arbitration after outside pressure on the larger nation, whom the subsequent award mainly favored. This boundary as determined by the decision and fully marked on the ground may be considered entirely settled, beyond probability of any trouble over details or incidents which cannot be settled by direct diplomatic means.

25. France–Netherlands. Maroni

(See map, p. 145, *supra*.)

The issue on the east boundary of Surinam was as to which of two tributaries formed the main stream of a named river. The Maroni was always agreed to be the proper dividing line, and no dispute arose as to the location of that river from its mouth southward about 100 miles to where the Awa from the south and the Tapanahoni from the southwest join to form the lower stream; but above that confluence it was uncertain which stream was properly to be considered the Maroni. In carrying out the award of the Congress of Vienna, Portugal,[1] without the participation of the Netherlands, undertook to restore French Guiana from the Oyapock, whose mouth lies between 4° and 5° N., up to 322° east of the Island of Ferro (55°40′ W.) at 2°24′ N., which would carry the southwest line near the Tapanahoni. On November 9, 1836, the governors of Cayenne and Surinam agreed that the territory on the right (east) bank of the Maroni from its source belonged to France, but neither mother country paid much attention to this agreement, which, indeed, left unsettled the real question as to which stream was in fact to be considered the Maroni above the confluence. In 1849 the Dutch government expressly declared that this agreement could not be regarded as settling the boundary between the colonies. In 1861, following an arrangement between the governors, a mixed commission was appointed to determine which upper river was the Maroni, but they reported that the name Maroni was only applied to the lower part of the river and could not justly be given to either of the principal affluents; of which the more important, to the east, bore the name of Awa below and Itany above, while the other, from the southwest, was known only as the Tapanahoni. The report was thus inconclusive, and discussions continued without any definite outcome until 1876[2] when the matter lapsed. As the

---

[1] Article 1 of Treaty of Aug. 28, 1817. See §16, note 18, this chap., *supra*.

[2] *Archives Dipl.*, 2ᵉ Sér., XXV, 316; *ibid.*, XXXII, 6–7.

result of fresh negotiations France and the Netherlands signed at Paris on November 29, 1888,[3] a convention agreeing to submit the question of the boundary above the crucial junction to an arbitrator to be selected. Czar Alexander III of Russia was chosen, and after preliminary objections by him, that under the submission his power would be limited to determining one of the two rivers mentioned to be the boundary, had been obviated over some Dutch opposition by widening the submission on April 28, 1890,[4] so as to authorize the selection of any intermediate line, the Czar consented to act. The case was promptly submitted and after deliberation the Czar found on May 13/25, 1891,[5] that the Dutch government had since 1700 had military posts on the Awa, that the French government had several times recognized that negroes settled in the disputed territory were under Dutch jurisdiction, that both parties had always admitted that the Maroni from its source ought to be the boundary, and that the mixed commission of 1861 had found the Awa to be the upper course of the Maroni; and accordingly declared that the Awa ought to be considered the boundary river and frontier, the territory west of the Awa above its confluence with the Tapanahoni to belong henceforth to Holland. On August 23, 1891, the respective governors had a conference at St. Laurent in French Guiana near the mouth of the Maroni and agreed, subject to approval by their home governments, subsequently granted, that exploitation permits issued by the French government for lands and mines in the Awa region should be recognized by the Dutch government for forty years.[6]

With the increase of settlements and commerce on the Maroni there arose a similar question higher up as to which affluent formed the main stream,[7] and difficulties over the use of the broad estuary extending twenty-five miles up from the sea. A joint conference at The Hague, April 25 to May 13, 1905, drew up the project of a treaty which fixed the boundary more precisely as the Itany, which from the southwest joins the Marouini from the south to form the Awa sixty-five miles up from the Tapanahoni, and in the lower river agreed on the thalweg; but this project did not give satisfaction, and no settlement was reached. Ten years later an accord was arrived at, and France and the Netherlands signed, by M. Théophile Delcassé and A. de Stuers, at

---

[3] *Ibid.*, 5–6. Clunet, *J. dr. int. privé*, XVII (1890), 761. 79 *British and Foreign State Papers* 795–796. Ratifications exchanged at Paris, July 17, 1889.

[4] Louis Renault, *Archives Dipl.*, 2ᵉ Sér., XXXIII, 371; *ibid.*, XXXIV, 239. Clunet, *J. dr. int. privé*, XVII (1890), 991–992. *Rev. dr. int. lég. comp.*, XXIII, 83–86. 82 *British and Foreign State Papers* 1018. Jackson H. Ralston, *International Arbitration from Athens to Locarno* (Stanford University, 1929), p. 23.

[5] Louis Renault, *Archives Dipl.*, 2ᵉ Sér., XXXIX, 5–6. Martens, *Nouv. Rec. Gén. de Traités*, 2ᵉ Sér., XVIII, 100–

101; *ibid.*, XXVII, 136–137. 83 *British and Foreign State Papers* 426–427. Moore, *Int. Arbitrations* (Washington, 1898), V, 4869–4870.

[6] Louis Renault, *Archives Dipl.*, 2ᵉ Sér., XL, 207–208. *Rev. gén. de dr. int. pub.*, X (1903), 662n. (1).

[7] British For. Office, "Dutch Guiana," *Peace Handbooks* (London, 1920), vol. XXI, No. 136, Appendix, p. 68. Melville Jean and Frances S. Herskovits, *Rebel Destiny among the Bush Negroes of Dutch Guiana* (New York, 1934).

Paris on September 30, 1915,[8] a convention by which the parties agreed that from the north end of the Dutch island of Stoelman to the south end of the French island of Portal the boundary should be the median line of the stream at ordinary height of water, with islands following the nationality of that side of such line in which they were wholly or for their greater part situated;[9] provided for free navigation in the part of the river between the two islands named, previous joint agreement on any constructions capable of modifying the course of the stream or affecting navigation and on dredging concessions, and assignment of any minerals taken out of this part of the river in equal halves to each country; and any question arising from the application and interpretation of the convention which could not be settled by diplomatic means was to be submitted to the Permanent Court of Arbitration at The Hague. No question appears yet to have arisen and been so referred.

26. GREAT BRITAIN–NETHERLANDS. CORENTYN

(See map, p. 145, *supra*.)

Since 1831 British Guiana has by common consent been separated on the east from Surinam by the river Corentyn from its mouth southward about 200 miles. There was occasional discussion between the British and the Dutch as to whether the rest of the way to the Brazilian line the boundary should run ninety miles up the Cutari to its source in the Serra Acarahy or 140 miles up the New River, farther to the southwest, to the Serra Arahy. Brazil and Great Britain annexed to their arbitration treaty of November 6, 1900,[1] a declaration that the southern boundary of Brazil and British Guiana ended on the watershed at the source of the Corentyn, and Brazil and the Netherlands in their treaty of May 5, 1906,[2] agreed that the frontier between Brazil and Surinam should be the watershed from which streams flow north to the Atlantic. A boundary commission has been at work on the line for several years but has not yet announced its conclusions. In April 1936 a preliminary decision was said to have required Dr. Otto Vogt von Sickengen of Austria to register in British Guiana a claim to a rich radium field he asserted he found in 1934 in a location then thought to lie in Surinam. There would appear to be open still between Great Britain and the Netherlands the question as to whether the source of the Corentyn is in fact at the head of the Cutari or of the New River.

[8] Martens, *Nouv. Rec. Gén. de Traités*, 3ᵉ Sér., XII, 269-271. 110 *British and Foreign State Papers* 872-874. *Staatsblad, 1916,* Nos. 304 and 481. Ratifications exchanged at Paris, Sept. 16, 1916.

[9] So, Langa-Tabiti, and Pacearebo or Blakkerebo are wholly Dutch, and Guidala is wholly French.

[1] See §17, this chap., *supra*.
[2] See §18, this chap., *supra*.

CHAPTER II

ISLAND POSSESSIONS

1. AVES ISLAND

AVES is an uninhabited island in the Caribbean Sea about 700 yards long by 125 yards broad, with a maximum height of 36 feet, at 15°40′ N. 63°35′ W., 125 miles a little south of west of Guadeloupe and 350 miles north of the Venezuelan coast. It is 140 miles a little west of south of Saba, to which it may formerly have been connected by a sand bank. It is to be distinguished from the small group called Aves Islands, belonging to the state of Nueva Esparta, Venezuela, fifty miles southeast of Bonaire and eighty miles from the coast. Its specific discovery and actual possession by Spain were doubtful, except as one of the Windward group. If it was included in the ancient audiencia of Santo Domingo, it was transferred by Spanish Royal Ordinance of June 13, 1786, to the audiencia of Caracas. It was visited in May 1835 by the British ship *Race Horse,* and for many years the inhabitants of the Dutch West Indian islands of Saba and St. Eustatia were accustomed to visit Aves annually to take turtles and birds' eggs. In March 1854 [1] and thereafter the brigantine *John R. Dow,* Captain N. P. Gibbs, and other vessels belonging to Lang & Delano and Shelton & Company of Boston went to the island to load guano.[2] Venezuela heard of the landings and sent out an armed schooner with twenty-seven men under Colonel Domingo Diaz, which arrived at the island on December 12, 1854, and found three United States vessels at anchor, with a complement of eighty armed men. On December 13 Colonel Diaz landed and, after negotiations with the ships' agents, signed with them a written agreement by which the loading of guano was to be completed and further exploration permitted until the arrival of the holders of the Venezuelan contract or the approval or disapproval of the government, the ships to furnish such aid as the garrison might require and to put their pieces of artillery and armament under the Venezuelan flag, to which they acknowledged the island belonged. The government at Caracas later disavowed this arrangement. On December 21 the government granted a concession for fifteen years

---

[1] Mariano de Briceño, *Memoir on the Isla de Aves Question* (Washington, 1858). Rafael F. Seijas, *Derecho Internacional Hispano-Americano* (Caracas, 1884), IV, 150–216, 523–537.

[2] U. S. Act of Aug. 18, 1856, c. 164; 11 *U. S. Stat. L.* 119–120. Moore, *Dig. Int. Law* (Washington, 1906), I, 556–569.

of all the guano on Aves and other islands of the republic to J. D. Wallace
of Philadelphia, a United States citizen, for certain money payments; and on
December 30 the Boston vessels left, with the guano they had loaded, on order
of the Venezuelan representative. On January 15, 1855, the two firms applied to the United States government for damages from Venezuela for their
expulsion and expected future profits. On April 30 Wallace assigned his contract to the American Guano Company of Philadelphia, a Pennsylvania corporation; but, his drafts being unpaid, on May 22 the government annulled
the Wallace concession. On July 28, 1855, by presidential decree the exportation of guano from Aves and other islands was opened to foreign commerce.
In September the American Guano Company asked and obtained the aid of
the United States in sustaining the Wallace concession and sent John Pickrell
in the schooner *White Swan* to the island. On being prohibited from loading
there, he proceeded to Caracas, where with the help of Charles Eames, the
United States minister, he demanded restitution of the Wallace concession,
which the government on September 29 granted. As soon as the Venezuelan
occupation in 1854 was known, the Dutch consul general at Caracas and the
Dutch governor of Curaçao protested that it was a violation of Dutch territory, but got no satisfactory reply. In March 1856 Dutch vessels of war arrived at La Guaira and presented an ultimatum demanding adjustment of
another claim, recognition of the Dutch right to Aves Island, and the withdrawal of the Venezuelan troops stationed there. On December 20, 1856, Minister Eames demanded indemnity for the United States citizens expelled, but on
February 27, 1857, the government rejected the claim. On further communications from Minister Eames, President José Tadeo Monagas submitted the
claim to the government council, which ordered proof to be taken. On June 11
Minister Eames demanded his passports, as the result of the pending question, and received them on June 12. On August 5, 1857,[3] Venezuela signed
with the Netherlands a convention agreeing to submit the question of the dominion and sovereignty of Aves Island to the arbitration of a friendly power.
William L. Marcy, the United States secretary of state, in pressing the claims [4]
at first maintained that Aves Island up to July 1854 had no owner and being
uninhabitable had never been taken possession of by any government. On
January 14, 1859,[5] Venezuela and the United States signed at Valencia a con-

[3] *Trat. Pub. de Ven.* (Caracas, 1924), I, 207–209.
Martens, *Nouv. Rec. Gén. de Traités*, XVII, 222–229.
Ratifications exchanged at Valencia, Oct. 13, 1858.
[4] *Messages and Papers of the Presidents* (New York, 1897), VII, 2952.
[5] *Trat. Pub. de Ven.* (Caracas, 1924), I, 231–232. 59

British and Foreign State Papers 274–276. *U. S. Treaty Series*, No. 368. 17 *U. S. Stat. L.* 803–805; 18 *ibid.*, II, 796. Moore, *Dig. Int. Law* (Washington, 1906), I, 266, 571–572; *ibid.*, V, 211–212; *ibid.*, VII, 122–123. *Amer. J. Int. Law*, XII (1918), 521. Ratified by Venezuela with modifications, Feb. 3, 1859; not submitted to U. S. Senate.

vention by which Venezuela agreed to pay $105,000 for Shelton & Company and $25,000 for Lang & Delano in full settlement of their claims, and the United States agreed to desist from all further claims respecting Aves Island. Although the issue obviously involved early Spanish administrative acts, Queen Isabella II of Spain was chosen arbitrator under the Convention of 1857 and the cases were submitted in 1860. On June 30, 1865,[6] the Queen, in accord with her council of ministers and after having heard the advice of the entire council of state, decided that the property of Aves Island belonged to Venezuela, under obligation however to indemnify Dutch subjects if they should be prohibited from fishing there. The reasoning in support of the award was very vague; from the discovery the island belonged to Spain as part of the West Indies, over which some of the basic decrees of the Recopilación de Indias affirmed Spain's sovereignty, notwithstanding failure actually ever to occupy the island and lack of proof of intention to appropriate it. Both countries in May 1866 indicated their intention to accept the award. Aves Island, formerly included in the federal territory of Colón, is now administered as one of the federal dependencies of Venezuela.

2. CHILOÉ ARCHIPELAGO

This is a group of islands in the Pacific consisting of Chiloé, 110 miles long by 40 miles wide, and numerous small interior islets at 42°30′ S. 74° W. separated from the mainland and Puerto Montt by Chacao Channel and enclosing Ancud and Corcovado Gulfs, thirty miles wide. Garcia Hurtado de Mendoza discovered the archipelago on February 24, 1558, and called it Cananea; and in February 1567 Ruiz de Gamboa, with sixty men, explored and subdued the island and founded the town of Castro. In 1599 the island was made part of the captaincy-general of Chile. In 1600 the Dutch Admiral Van Noort with five ships killed the garrison in the fort at Ancud and plundered the town. Charles Darwin with the *Beagle* explored the group from November 1, 1834, to January 1, and from January 18 to February 4, 1835. In April 1936, in connection with the revival of her campaign for the Falkland Islands, Argentina issued a map stamp on which, probably by inadvertence or inaccuracy in the printing, a strip along the southern coast of Chile seemed to be of the Argentine color. Chilean newspapers urged the Chilean minister of foreign relations to demand of Argentina the withdrawal of the stamp; but,

---

[6] Moore, *Int. Arbitrations* (Washington, 1898), V, 5037–5041. Lapradelle et Politis, *Rec. des Arbitrages Int.* (Paris, 1924), II, 404–421. *Rec. de Cours*, XXXV (1931), 391– 392. *Rev. de dr. int. et de lég. comp.*, 2ᵉ Sér., IV (1902), 365.

very likely from some degree of sympathy with Argentine's claim against England, nothing official was done. Chiloé and Chonos Archipelagoes now form Chiloé province of Chile.

3. Chincha Islands

These are fourteen or more small guano islands in the Pacific at 13°38′ S. 76°28′ W. in the bay formed by Point Huacas northwest of Pisco and some twelve miles distant from the coast. The largest, Isla del Norte, is about four-fifths of a mile in length, one-third of a mile in breadth, and 113 feet in altitude at its highest point; and others are Chincha, Ballestas, and San Gallán. The digging and export of guano was begun by Peru in 1840[1] but at first with little care and danger of speedy exhaustion of the supply. On December 8, 1841,[2] Peru granted an exclusive privilege of exporting guano to Europe for five years to Francisco Quiros and Achilles Allier, and on March 21, 1842,[3] issued a decree for the prevention of illicit extraction and sale, leaving only the island north of Chincha and the Pabellón de Pica open to national vessels. The islands were the chief prize of the so-called Guano War in 1853–1854 between President José Rufino Echenique and General Ramón Castilla, who defeated Echenique, January 5, 1855.

On May 13, 1857,[4] the National Convention authorized a convention with Great Britain and France by which those nations agreed for ten years, and thereafter until denunciation of the agreement, to coöperate in protecting from usurpation, fraud, or adulteration the legal exportation of Peruvian guano from the Chincha, Lobos, and other islands or deposits, so that the national credit of Peru should be sustained abroad and the proceeds should be assured for the external public debt to which they were pledged[5] for payment of English and French creditors; but such coöperation was in no case to extend to any protectorate over the islands or deposits nor to taking possession of nor occupying them, nor to interfering in their government or administration or in the contracts concerning them, and it was not to be understood that Peru ceded, renounced, or diminished her right of sovereignty, dominion, possession, government, and free administration of the deposits. This convention failed of ratification.

[1] 45 *British and Foreign State Papers* 1209-1210. Cf. Law #3069 of Jan. 27, 1919, *Anuario de la Leg. Peruana*, Ed. Ofic. (Lima, 1919), XIII, 248-253. *National Geographic Magazine*, XXXVII, 537-566; *ibid.*, XLVI, 278-302.
[2] 31 *British and Foreign State Papers* 1094-1097. The contracts were signed Feb. 19, 1842.
[3] 31 *British and Foreign State Papers* 1097-1102.
[4] Ricardo Aranda, *Col. de Trat. del Peru*, VII, 558-563. Signed by the Council of Ministers May 21, 1857.
[5] 31 *British and Foreign State Papers* 1368-1372; 45 *ibid.*, 1244-1268.

On January 24, 1858,[6] the Peruvian steamer *Tumbes* seized while loading guano at Pabellón de Pica the bark *Lizzie Thompson,* of Kennebec, Maine, Captain H. A. Wilson; and at Punta de Lobos the bark *Georgiana,* of Boston, Massachusetts, Captain Stephen Reynolds. They were taken into Callao charged with infraction of the guano laws and ordered for trial before the Collector of Callao. J. Randolph Clay, minister of the United States at Lima, at once protested and demanded indemnities of $109,632.82 for the *Lizzie Thompson* and $46,353.53 for the *Georgiana.* In May both vessels were condemned, and on November 6 they were sold at public auction on the order of the collector, as judge of confiscations. United States Secretary of State Lewis Cass argued that the civil war raging at the time in Peru made it proper for the captains to enter any port and obey the regulations of any authorities they found there, regardless of national laws in existence elsewhere. After a protracted interchange of notes, the United States submitted an ultimatum in September 1859, and on October 9 Mr. Clay demanded his passports. President Lincoln restored diplomatic relations, and a convention was signed at Lima on December 20, 1862,[7] by which the question was agreed to be submitted to the king of Belgium as arbitrator. Leopold I, after examining what had been published concerning the controversy, declined in January 1864 to act as arbitrator; and on confidential information that he did not think the United States had the stronger side of the case, the United States decided to treat the claims as finally disposed of. On July 9, 1864, Secretary of State William H. Seward notified Peru that there was no intention on the part of the United States to refer the subject to the arbitrament of any other power or to pursue the matter further.

On April 14, 1864, the Spanish fleet under Rear Admiral Luis H. Pinzón began the war with Peru by seizing the Chincha Islands, and for a time Spain asserted that, as she had never recognized the independence of Peru, the seizure was only a lawful retaking of her original possession. The islands were abandoned by Spain early in 1865, and the Spanish squadron left the Peruvian coast on May 9, 1866. The islands now form part of the department of Lima of Peru.

4. Chonos Archipelago

This is a group of numerous small islands, of which Melchor is the largest, in the Pacific at 45° S. 74° W. between Chiloé Island and Corcovado Gulf

---

[6] Moore, *Int. Arbitrations* (Washington, 1898), II, 1593–1613. Moore, *Dig. Int. Law* (Washington, 1906), I, 43–44; *ibid.,* V, 840. Lapradelle et Politis, *Rec. des Arbitrages Int.* (Paris, 1924), II, 387–403.

[7] William M. Malloy, *Treaties of the U. S.* (Washington, 1910), II, 1406–1407. 54 *British and Foreign State Papers* 1123–1124. Ratifications exchanged at Lima, Apr. 21, 1863.

to the north and Taito Peninsula to the south, enclosing Moraleda Channel
and Darwin Bay. They were discovered by José de Moraleda y Montero, First
Pilot of Spain, in 1793–94. Charles Darwin with the *Beagle* explored the group
from January 7 to January 15, 1835.

Despite Chile's proclaimed neutrality in the World War, the British
cruisers *Monmouth* and *Glasgow* operated in the South Pacific from a secret
base in these islands at 45°24' S. 74°18' W. until they were defeated by the
German squadron under Vice-Admiral Graf von Spee at the battle of Coronel
on November 1, 1914. Chonos Archipelago, including all the islands to
47° S., now forms, with the Chiloé Archipelago, Chiloé province of Chile.

5. Curaçao

Curaçao is the principal island of the Dutch West Indies in the Caribbean Sea at 12° N. 69° W., about fifty miles from the Venezuelan coast, 210
square miles in area, forty miles long and from three to seven miles wide,
with hills along the southwest side rising in places to 1,200 feet. The chief
harbor is St. Anna on the southwest coast, with Willemstad, the capital, on
the inner harbor of Schottegat, separated from the western suburb of Over-
zijde by the narrow channel of the Waigat, crossed by a pontoon toll bridge.
The other islands of the Dutch group are Aruba, with an area of sixty-nine
square miles, fifty miles west of Curaçao; Bonaire (Buen Ayre) of ninety-five
square miles, forty miles east of Curaçao; and, 500 miles to the north between
the Virgin Islands and Guadeloupe, Gustavia or St. Bartholomew, ten square
miles, Saba, five square miles, St. Eustatia, seven square miles, and the
southern part of St. Martin, seventeen square miles. The chief industry of
Curaçao is refining crude petroleum brought out from the Lake Maracaibo
basin.

Curaçao was discovered by Hojeda in 1499 and occupied by Spain in
1527. It was taken by the Dutch in 1634 and immediately became an important post, trading with Coro, Puerto Cabello, and La Guaira. In 1798 and
again from 1806 to 1814 it was held by Great Britain as a consequence of
Anglo-Dutch wars in Europe. In 1804 Curaçao was besieged and blockaded
by a British squadron from Jamaica under Rear Admiral Sir John Duckworth.
The British governor, J. Hodgson, on September 4, 1813,[1] made a suggestion
to General Simón Bolívar at Valencia that European Spaniards in Venezuelan
prisons be allowed to depart instead of being executed, but Bolívar replied on
October 2 and 9 that the War to the Death was unfortunately necessary and
that the Spanish General Monteverde refused an exchange of prisoners.

[1] *British and Foreign State Papers*, II, 1247–1254.

In August 1868 [2] the Venezuelan government in Caracas complained to the Netherlands that the defeated rebel Yellow party of General Falcón and President Bruzual was obtaining supplies and shelter in Curaçao. In November 1874 an expedition from Curaçao under Luis Maria Díaz started an uprising at Coro, which caused President Antonio Guzmán Blanco to break off diplomatic relations with the Netherlands on October 19, 1875,[3] and after the rebels had been defeated to present substantial claims for damages. The Netherlands, having insisted on the reopening of the ports of Coro and Maracaibo as a condition precedent even to examining the claims, finally wholly rejected them on July 6, 1889, and relations were not resumed until August 20, 1894.[4]

Only one political incident has excited Curaçao in recent years. In the evening of June 8, 1929, two truck loads of exiled Venezuelan revolutionists under General Rafael Simón Urbina rode armed into Willemstad from the near-by settlement of Rio Canario. They proceeded to seize the waterfront, attacking and wounding several policemen and civilians, and captured Governor Frutier in the governor's palace and Captain Borren, commandant, when he came to the scene. They seized the 1,000-ton United States steamer *Maracaibo,* Captain H. E. Morris, which had just arrived from Maracaibo, loaded her with arms and ammunition from the fort, forced the governor to sign an order for the sailing of the *Maracaibo* to an unnamed destination and for the opening of the pontoon bridge, took the governor, commandant, and six soldiers along as hostages, and sailed on June 9 to La Vela, in the state of Falcón, 200 miles west of Caracas. There about 250 rebels landed, but were defeated and dispersed in their attack on Coro, whose garrison had been warned of their coming by telegraph from General Gómez. The *Maracaibo* returned unharmed to Willemstad on June 10 with all hostages and crew uninjured. There was an outcry in the Netherlands against the government but Foreign Minister Bellaerts van Blokland announced that Venezuela was not to be held responsible for the attack. The Dutch destroyer *Kortenaer* and the battleship *Hertog Hendrik* were sent to Curaçao, but the incident was closed when the Venezuelan government expressed regrets. Many Gomistas fled to Curaçao after the death of the old general, December 17, 1935.

Curaçao is administered by a governor and council of four members and a colonial council of thirteen crown nominees,[5] as a colony of the Netherlands.

---

[2] *U. S. Dipl. Corr.*, 1868, Part II, pp. 968–970.

[3] *Venezuela y Holanda* (Caracas, 1875). *Venezuela et les Pays-Bas, Documents* (Paris, 1875). *Holanda y Venezuela, Refutación* (Curazao, 1876).

[4] Martens, *Nouv. Rec. Gén. de Traités*, 2ᵉ Sér., XXII, 606–607.

[5] *Staatsblad, 1902,* No. 38, as amended.

6. EASTER ISLAND

Easter or Pascua is a triangular island, 102 square miles in area, more recently called Rapanuí, or, erroneously, Waihu, in the Pacific at 27°10′ S. 109°26′ W., about 2,000 miles west of Caldera, Chile. Near it to the northeast are Sala y Gómez Island at 26°27′ S. 105°28′ W. and Minnehaha Rock. It was first reported in 1687 by the pirate Captain Edward Davis, but the Dutch Admiral Roggeveen was the first European to land on it, on April 5, 1722, Easter Sunday (Pascua), from which he named it. It was inhabited by Polynesians who probably arrived in or before the fourteenth century, under a legendary chief named Hotu Matua, first in a list of fifty-seven kings. It was visited in 1774 by Commander James Cook in the *Resolution* on his second voyage. The island is chiefly famous for numerous symbolic inscriptions cut on rocks and over six hundred monolithic images,[1] from three to thirty feet high, some weighing six tons, quarried on the island and transported, inscribed, and set up facing the sea each at the head of an *ahu* or village common grave, thirty feet wide by two hundred feet long, by an early race whose history appears now to be entirely lost. Both in design (some wear top hats) and execution, the figures are quite different from the smaller monoliths at Tiahuanaco on the Bolivian plain south of Lake Titicaca, but some of the inscriptions are said to resemble those at Mohenjodaro in the Indus Valley, India. A Franco-Belgian scientific expedition started for the island in March 1934, and after the death in Chile of the original leader, Professor Louis Watelin, went on under Professor Alfred Metraux, and M. Henri Lavachery, landed on July 29, 1934, and remained until January 3, 1935. Dr. Metraux, continuing his study at the Bishop Museum in Honolulu, announced that he thought the statues were much more recent than had been supposed, and might have been erected about 1800. Knowledge of how the statues were moved and ability to read the inscriptions had been lost by 1886. Templeton Crocker of San Francisco in his yacht *Zaca* took some American Museum of Natural History scientists to the island in September 1934. In December 1935 a Chilean government commission of scientific experts reported in Santiago that they believed the island was of volcanic origin, not part of "Lemuria" or any other submerged continent. The island has now about 450 residents and is in part a penal colony, in part a national monument and park, and belongs to and is administered as a part of the maritime territory of Chile.

[1] *National Geographic Magazine*, XL, 628–646.

7. FALKLAND ISLANDS

This is a group of two large islands and over a hundred small islets in the South Atlantic between 51°7' and 52°31' S. and 57°45' and 61°3' W., about 250 miles northeast of Tierra del Fuego, and 300 miles from Cape Vírgenes and the east coast of Argentine Patagonia, with a population of 2,290. East Falkland (Port Louis or Soledad), with an area of 2,580 square miles, has the capital and chief town of Stanley on the east coast, and is separated by Falkland Sound from West Falkland (Port Egmont), with an area of 2,038 square miles. In 1592 the islands were first reported by Captain John Davis, who sailed from Plymouth in the *Desire* on August 26, 1591; on February 2, 1594, Sir Richard Hawkins probably sighted and sailed along their north shore; and on January 24, 1600, the Dutch captain, Sebald de Weert, sighted them and called them the Sebaldes. Captain Cook's buccaneering expedition in the *Bachelor's Delight* visited the islands on January 8, 1684. On January 28, 1690, Captain John Strong in the *Welfare* sailed through the dividing passage and called it Falkland Sound, probably in honor of Anthony, Viscount Falkland, from which the islands came to bear the name by which they are known in English. In January 1764 the French captain, Antoine Louis de Bougainville, founded St. Louis on Berkeley Sound and on April 5, 1764, took formal possession for Louis XV of all the islands, under the name of Les Malouines, given by sailors from St. Malo. Charles III for the Crown of Castile claimed Las Malvinas, and, after negotiations approved by France, Bougainville agreed to turn over his rights for 680,000 livres. On April 1, 1767, in the presence of a joint French and Spanish fleet possession was delivered, and the new colony was placed by Spain under the captain-general of Buenos Aires. In January 1765 the British Commodore John Byron on the *Dolphin* took possession of the islands for King George III, on the ground of prior discovery, and located on Saunders Island the site of Port Egmont, which was settled by a second British expedition on January 8, 1766. The French and English settlers either did not know of or purposely ignored each other's presence until December 2, 1766, when the English discovered Port Louis and warned the French to leave. During complicated and crafty negotiations in Europe,[1] Spain on February 25, 1768, ordered Francisco P. Bucareli, intendent at Buenos Aires, to permit no English settlements in his jurisdiction and to expel by force any already set up, if they did not leave

---

[1] Isaac P. Areco, *Títulos de la Rep. Arg. a la Soberania y Posesión de las Islas Malvinas* (Buenos Aires, 1885). V. F. Boyson, *The Falkland Islands* (Oxford, 1924). *Rev. de dr. int. et de lég. comp.*, XX (1888), 163–173. Julius Goebel, Jr., *The Struggle for the Falkland Islands* (New Haven and London, 1927). Juan G. Beltrán, *El Zarpazo Inglés a las Islas Malvinas* (Buenos Aires, 1934).

on being warned. In November 1769 an expedition consisting of the frigates *Santa Catalina* and *Santa Rosa* and the xebec *Andalusia* left Buenos Aires and on reaching Puerto de la Soledad (East Falkland) met there on November 28, 1769, the English Captain Anthony Hunt in the frigate *Tamar* and warned him to leave. A lively exchange of letters ensued in the course of which Hunt on December 10 ordered the Spaniards to evacuate; and in March 1770 Hunt sailed for England, and the Spanish returned to Buenos Aires. A second expedition of the three frigates *Industria*, *Santa Barbara*, and *Santa Catalina* and the xebec *Andalusia*, with 1,400 troops under Juan Ignacio de Madariaga, reached Port Egmont on June 4, 1770, and on June 8 demanded of the English Captains William Maltby of the frigate *Favorite* and George Farmer that the English quit the islands. They refused and prepared to defend the port, but Madariaga landed his troops, fired on the blockhouse, and on June 10 [2] the English surrendered. Further diplomatic negotiations between the European capitals resulted on January 22, 1771, [3] in the signing by England and Spain of reciprocal declarations by which Port Egmont was to be returned to the British in the state in which it was on June 10, 1770, its possession not in any wise to affect the question of the prior right of sovereignty of the islands; and Lord North, apparently supported by William, Earl of Rochford, and the other ministers, secretly agreed orally to evacuate the island and the port as soon as the opposition party at home could be overcome. Port Egmont was restored on September 15, 1771, to British forces landing from a squadron under Captain Stott. After the discussion in Parliament had died down, Spain began to press for the promised abandonment, whereupon England insisted that Spain was to abandon her establishment also. Though the British garrison was reduced on the ground of expense, the matter of total evacuation dragged on until on May 20, 1774, the British commanding officer, Lieutenant S. W. Clayton, with his garrison, formally departed, leaving on the blockhouse a leaden plaque which bore an inscription stating that

the Falkland Islands, with this fort, the storehouses, wharfs, harbors, bays, and creeks thereunto belonging are the sole right and property of His Most Sacred Majesty George the Third, King of Great Britain, France and Ireland, Defender of the Faith, etc. In witness whereof this plate is set up, and his Britannic Majesty's colors left flying as a mark of possession.

The Spanish continued their own colony on Soledad under Governor Felipe Ruiz Puente and his eight successors, but no steps were taken to

[2] *Papers Relating to the Taking of Port Egmont and Falkland's Island from the English* (London, 1777); Parts I and II.
[3] Martens, *Rec. de Traités*, II, 1–4.

occupy the Gran Malvina (West Falkland), and in 1777 the buildings still standing at Port Egmont were destroyed by order of the viceroy of Buenos Aires. On January 8, 1811, one of the governments at Buenos Aires decided that the colony at Soledad should be discontinued on account of expense, and the governor of Montevideo ordered the removal of the remaining inhabitants. In 1820 the frigate *Heroina,* under Colonel Daniel Jewitt, was sent to the islands and on November 6, 1820, he took formal possession of the group for Buenos Aires, so notifying the fifty-odd sealers and whalers he found in the various harbors. In 1823 Pablo Aregusti was appointed governor, and the Argentine Confederation granted to Jorge Pacheco and Louis Vernet a concession of land on Soledad and use of fisheries and wild cattle. Vernet, a Frenchman who had long lived in Hamburg, organized an expedition which in January 1826 founded a settlement, and on January 28, 1828, he obtained a further grant of the island of Staatenland and all the lands off the island of Soledad except those previously granted to Pacheco, and a strip of ten square leagues on the Bay of San Carlos reserved by the government, on condition that a colony should be established within three years. The colony was successful, and on June 10, 1829, Vernet was appointed military and political governor, and charged to enforce the law and the seal fishery regulations. Vernet soon after bought out Pacheco. On August 30, 1829, Vernet notified masters of fishing and sealing vessels to cease operations under penalty of being arrested and sent to Buenos Aires for trial, but few of them paid any attention. On July 30, 1831,[4] Vernet seized the schooner *Harriet* of Stonington, Connecticut, Captain Gilbert R. Davison, which had been warned in 1829, and two other United States vessels, the schooner *Superior* of New York, Captain Stephen Congar, and the schooner *Breakwater,* Captain Carew. The *Breakwater* escaped a few days later, and after some discussion, under a contract signed on September 8, 1831,[5] the *Superior* was allowed to give security for her reappearance and proceed to a new sealing ground. The *Harriet* was to go for trial to Buenos Aires, whither she proceeded with Vernet on board and arrived on November 19, 1831. Her arrival was promptly reported by United States Consul George W. Slacum at Buenos Aires to Secretary of State Edward Livingston, and Slacum wrote Tomás Manuel de Anchorena, the minister of foreign affairs, denying the right of the Buenos Aires government to regulate seal fishing and claiming for citizens of the United States right to the freest use of the fisheries. In Decem-

[4] William R. Manning, *Dipl. Corr. of the U. S., Inter-American Affairs, 1831–1860* (Washington, 1932), I, 3–228. 19 *British and Foreign State Papers* 1192–1193; 20 *ibid.,* 311–441, 1153; 22 *ibid.,* 1130; 23 *ibid.,* 193; 25 *ibid.,* 645. [5] 20 *ibid.,* 373–376.

ber 1831 the United States sloop of war *Lexington* under Commander Silas Duncan arrived at Buenos Aires, and, after conferences and correspondence with Slacum, Duncan declared that he regarded it his duty to proceed to the Falklands to protect American citizens. Slacum on December 6 wrote to Anchorena that Duncan's departure would be postponed until December 9 to await a reply having reference to the immediate suspension of the right of capture of vessels of the United States and ordering the restoration of the schooner *Harriet* and all the property taken. Duncan also demanded the instant surrender of Vernet for trial as a pirate and robber or that he be tried and punished by the laws of Buenos Aires. On December 9 after Duncan had sailed Anchorena requested Slacum not to interfere in a matter which the government regarded as a private litigation, and notified him that if the commander of the *Lexington* or any other person dependent on the United States government should commit any acts tending to set at naught the rights of Buenos Aires to the Falklands, a formal protest would be addressed to the United States government, and every means would be used to assert those rights and cause them to be respected. The *Lexington* entered the harbor of Puerto Soledad on December 28, under the French flag; and Duncan after inviting on board the governor's two representatives, Matthew Brisbane and Henry Metcalf, held the former a prisoner and released the latter. Duncan landed on December 31, 1831, with an armed party, spiked the guns of the fort, seized all the small arms, burned the powder magazine, plundered some of the houses, seized some sealskins from the store of William Dickson, a Dutch merchant, declared the island free of all government, and sailed away with Brisbane and six Argentinians in irons. He anchored off Montevideo and notified Slacum that he would liberate the prisoners if the government would give its assurance that they had been acting under its authority. The assurance was given on February 15, 1832, and the prisoners were released a few days later. President Andrew Jackson in his third annual message of December 6, 1831,[6] referred to the seizure of the *Harriet,* and in January 1832 he appointed Francis Baylies, a Massachusetts lawyer, chargé d'affaires at Buenos Aires. Baylies was instructed by Secretary of State Livingston [7] to demand of the Buenos Aires government disavowal of Vernet, restoration of property, and payment of an indemnity, on the grounds that the United States had been in actual use of the islands as a fishery for over fifty years and that Spain had exercised no sovereignty over the Patagonian and Fuegian coasts to which

[6] *Messages and Papers of the Presidents* (New York, 1897), III, 1116.

[7] Moore, *Dig. Int. Law* (Washington, 1906), I, 876–888.

Buenos Aires was heir. Baylies reached Buenos Aires in June 1832 on the United States sloop of war *Peacock*, and as soon as he was accredited began a correspondence with Manuel V. de Maza, acting minister of foreign affairs. After some violent verbal exchanges, which included a demand by de Maza for prompt and ample satisfaction, reparation, and indemnity for Duncan's acts, Baylies on August 18 demanded his passports, which after an interview with de Maza on August 27 he insisted upon and received, and sailed for the United States in the U.S.S. *Warren* on September 25, 1832. Slacum, who was being sought by the police, was on September 6 made private secretary to Baylies and returned to the United States with him.

On December 20, 1832,[8] the British warships *Clio* and *Tyne* arrived at Port Egmont, where Commander J. J. Onslow put up a notice of possession and attempted to repair the ruins of the old fort. On January 2, 1833, Onslow went to Port Louis, where he found the Argentine armed schooner *Sarandí* under José Maria de Pinedo, who had brought the new governor Juan Esteban Mestivier and put down a revolt of the colonists in which the former governor had been killed. Onslow told Pinedo that he had come to take possession in the name of his Britannic majesty and requested Pinedo to lower the Argentine flag and depart. Pinedo refusing, on January 3, 1833, Onslow landed a force, raised the British flag, lowered the Argentine flag and delivered it on board the *Sarandí*. The Argentine republic at once protested to Great Britain, but to an inquiry on April 24 by Manuel Moreno, Argentine minister in London, as to whether orders had been given by the British government to expel the Buenos Aires garrison and whether Onslow's declaration of possession had been authorized, Lord Palmerston replied on April 27 that they had. Formal protests were renewed in 1834, and in 1841 Moreno attempted to get the British to restore at least Soledad on the ground that that island had never belonged to Great Britain but had been in the undisputed possession of Spain since 1767. Great Britain refused to discuss the question further, and resting on her "incontestable rights" proceeded to effect permanent colonization of the islands,[9] founding Stanley as capital in 1844. Charles Darwin in the *Beagle* visited the islands on March 1, 1833, and May 16, 1834.

General Carlos M. Alvear, Argentine minister to the United States, in 1839 presented a claim for Vernet's losses sustained by the acts of Duncan in

[8] 20 *British and Foreign State Papers* 1153-1154, 1194-1199; 22 *ibid.*, 1130, 1366-1394; 23 *ibid.*, 193; 25 *ibid.*, 645-646; 27 *ibid.*, 853; 31 *ibid.*, 1003-1005, 1140.

[9] 31 *ibid.*, 1211-1212; 50 *ibid.*, 689-690; 69 *ibid.*, 359-360; 78 *ibid.*, 74-75; 84 *ibid.*, 262-266, 1162-1163; 85 *ibid.*, 137-140; 94 *ibid.*, 123-127. *Arch. Dipl.*, 2ᵉ Sér., XLII, 103.

1831, but Secretary of State Daniel Webster advised him on December 4, 1841, that as the right of the Argentine government over the Falklands was contested by another power under a claim long antecedent to the acts of Duncan, the United States ought not to give a final answer until that controversy was settled.[10] The claim was renewed by Luis L. Domínguez, Argentine minister to the United States, in 1884 and again put off on the same grounds. President Grover Cleveland in his first annual message of December 8, 1885,[11] characterized the action of Duncan as "breaking up a piratical colony" and declared that the government considered the claim as wholly groundless. On December 8, 1914, in a battle to the southeastward of the islands, a British squadron of seven ships under Vice-Admiral Sir Doveton Sturdee destroyed a German squadron of five ships under Vice-Admiral Graf von Spee, only the *Dresden* escaping.

Argentina has continued to regard the British possession of the Falklands as unlawful,[12] and makes periodical formal demands for them on Great Britain. Lately Argentina is evidently seeking more vigorously to reopen the question. On August 17, 1934, Congress appropriated 30,000 pesos ($9,000) to translate and publish a French book supporting the Argentine claims;[13] and on February 22, 1935, the minister of the interior ordered that police certificates issued about 1920 to two persons born in the islands stating that they were British subjects be canceled and that thereafter any one born in the Falklands who solicited identification papers or a safe conduct from Argentine police or diplomatic representatives should be given an Argentine passport. In January 1936 Argentina issued a map postage stamp (of 1 peso value) which showed the Malvinas colored as Argentine territory. On February 10 Anthony Eden, British foreign secretary, in a written answer to a question in the House of Commons revealed that Great Britain had warned Argentina that the issuance of such stamps could "only be detrimental to the good relations of the two countries," and said he welcomed the opportunity to state that His Majesty's Government could not admit any such claim to the islands, "which are British territory." There is no international convention to prevent the issue of "misleading stamps of this kind." Carlos Saavedra Lamas, Argentine foreign minister, said Argentina hoped that one day her claims would be fulfilled, but at present there was no reason for the republic "to vary the momentary solution" of the problem, and Ar-

[10] Moore, *Dig. Int. Law* (Washington, 1906), I, 889–890.
[11] *Messages and Papers of the Presidents* (New York, 1897), XI, 4910.
[12] Martens, *Nouv. Rec. Gén. de Traités*, XI, 381.
[13] Paul Groussac, *Les Iles Malouines. Cf. United Empire* (London, 1933), N.S., XXIV, 58, 63–64, 71–76, 158–161, 235–236, 388.

gentine would continue to claim, in a friendly way, that the Malvinas were rightly hers. In other words, Argentina would wait and watch and do nothing rash at present but seize the first favorable opportunity for putting on the pressure for recognition of her claims when next she should have Great Britain in a tight spot for bargaining, over some diplomatic slip or desired trade concession. The islands now have little economic value but are of strategic importance as controlling the eastern entrance to the Strait of Magellan, and of potential value as a naval base.

Included as administrative dependencies since July 21, 1908,[14] are South Georgia, with an area estimated at 1,000 square miles, the South Orkneys, the South Shetlands, the Sandwich Islands, Graham's Land, and all islands and territories south of 50° S. between 20° and 50° W. and south of 58° S. between 50° and 80° W. The Falkland Islands have a governor, with an executive council of three officials and one other member, and a legislative council of four officials and two other members, and are administered as a crown colony of Great Britain.

8. GALÁPAGOS ARCHIPELAGO

This is a group of thirteen large and about forty small islands, formerly called Las Encantadas, in the Pacific between 0°38′ N. and 1°27′ S. and 89°16′ to 91°40′ W., 580 miles west of Ecuador, with a total land area of about 2,870 square miles.[1] The largest, Isabela (Albemarle), really two islands with a sand bar, "Istmo de Perry," between, is about seventy-five miles long, with an area of 1,650 square miles; others are Santa Cruz (Chaves, Indefatigable), 390 square miles; Fernandina (Narborough), 250 square miles; San Salvador (Santiago, James), 180 square miles; San Cristóbal (Chatham), 174 square miles; Albany, Bartolomé, Cowley, Crossman, Culpepper, Daphne, Eden, Española (Hood), Gardner, Genovesa (Tower), Marchena (Bindloe), Pinta (Abington), Pinzón (Duncan), Rábida (Jervis), Santa Fé (Barrington), Santa Maria (Floreana, Charles), Sin Nombre (Nameless), Tortuga (Brattle), and Wenman. There are craters of 2,000 volcanoes, the highest 4,700 feet, but, except for two said by Dr. William Beebe to have been in eruption in April 1925, none has been active since 1813. The islands formerly were the home of sea lions and of fifteen species of giant tortoises (*galápagos*), but they were unrestrainedly killed by sailors

[14] 101 *British and Foreign State Papers* 76–77; 111 *ibid.*, 16–17. Gustav Smedal, *Acquisition of Sovereignty over Polar Areas* (Oslo, 1931), pp. 9, 37–38, 74–75; in French (Paris, 1932), pp. 56, 87, 112–114.

[1] *National Geographic Magazine*, XXIX, 17–30. *Bol. de la Soc. Geog. de Madrid*, XXXI (1891), 153–199, 351–402.

and are now on the verge of extinction. Running wild are the descendants of cattle, asses, goats, pigs, dogs, and cats from wrecks or intentionally put ashore. San Cristóbal, owned by the Cobos family, raising sugar and coffee and producing alcohol, formerly worked by convict labor from a settlement called El Progreso, and Isabela, owned by the Gil family, with sulphur mines and cattle, are the only islands privately claimed.

The group was uninhabited when discovered in 1535 by the Spaniard, Tomás de Borlanga. They were visited by Captain David Porter in the United States frigate *Essex* in 1812. In 1831 General José de Villamil made an attempt to plant a colony on the islands. The scheme failed, but interest in the islands was aroused and they were formally taken possession of for Ecuador on February 12, 1832, by Colonel Ignacio Hernández. From September 15 to October 20, 1835, they were explored by the *Beagle* and Charles Darwin who landed on Chatham Island on September 17, 1835, found a population of 200 or 300 people. A treaty signed on November 20, 1854,[2] between the United States and Ecuador provided for a loan of $3,000,000 which was to be repaid by exploitation of the guano on the islands by United States citizens who should be protected by the United States against any invasion or depredation by any other nation; but the arrangement was not approved in Washington. There was talk in 1866[3] of their being sold to the British holders of Ecuadorian bonds; and in 1869 it was thought that Ecuador might convey the islands to the United States. Chile and Peru[4] made inquiries which resulted in the express declaration by Ecuador that such alienation was not intended. Secretary of State William H. Seward wrote W. T. Coggeshall, United States minister at Quito, on December 5, 1866: "The United States lay no claim to those islands. I do not understand that the fact of their ownership by Ecuador is established."[5]

A contract for a colonization project was made with the Compañía Suiza-Escandinava on August 8, 1884; but the plan did not succeed. A law of August 20, 1885,[6] providing for the government of the archipelago as part of the province of Guayas exempted the colonists for five years from all taxes and military service and permitted free importation of goods for local use. A law of June 22, 1892,[7] changed the official name of the archipelago to Colón, in honor of Columbus, and substituted Spanish for the former English names of the principal islands.

[2] Rafael F. Seijas, *Der. Int. Hisp.-Amer.* (Caracas, 1884), IV, 520–521.

[3] *U. S. Dipl. Corr.*, 1866–67, Part II, pp. 480–483.

[4] Ricardo Aranda, *Col. de Trat. del Peru*, V, 406–418. *Amer. J. Int. Law*, XI (1917), 721–722.

[5] *U. S. Dipl. Corr.*, 1866–67, Part II, p. 483.

[6] *Leyes y Decretos del Ecuador*, 1885–86 (Quito, 1887), pp. 17–22.

[7] *Reg. Ofic. del Ecuador* (Quito, 1892), pp. 9–11.

In 1912 there was a rumor that Ecuador intended to lease the islands to European interests, and in the United States Senate the Galápagos were mentioned in the debate upon the resolution proposed by Senator Henry Cabot Lodge on the occasion of a proposed sale to Japanese subjects of a large concession owned by United States citizens on Magdalena Bay, Lower California, Mexico. The resolution as passed by the Senate on August 2, 1912, recited that:

> When any harbor or other place in the American continent is so situated that the occupation thereof for naval or military purposes might threaten the communications or the safety of the United States, the Government of the United States could not see without grave concern the possession of such harbor or other place by any corporation or association which has such a relation to another Government, not American, as to give that Government practical power of control for naval or military purposes.[8]

A law of October 30, 1913,[9] to promote colonization permitted settlers, of whom three-fourths must be Ecuadorians, exemption for fifteen years from military duty and revenue taxes and authorized the establishment of free ports.

Certain individual experiments in free living, chiefly by German individuals, on Santa Maria (Floreana) Island from July 1929 to December 1934, interested the world, as romantically reported from time to time,[10] and in 1932 an Ecuadorian representative went out to investigate a rumor that one of the residents was calling herself empress. It was announced that on threat of deportation she reduced her claims and was allowed to remain; but the experiments ended with the death of several of the principals.

In 1934 Dr. Wolfgang von Hagen organized in Guayaquil with official approval the Corporación Cientifica Nacional para el Estudio y Protección de las Riquezas Naturales del Archipiélago de Colón, of which he is the only foreign member, of professors of the University of Guayas and others to act as intermediary between the government and any accredited scientist or institution that wishes to establish facilities for study on the islands. Dr. von Hagen erected on Chatham Island a monument to commemorate Darwin's landing on September 17, 1835. In April 1936 the Ecuadorian government denied that there had been any negotiations toward the sale of the islands, and reaffirmed the determination to maintain territorial integrity. The archi-

---

[8] S. Res. #371. *Cong. Rec.*, XLVIII, Part X, 10045–10047. *Amer. J. Int. Law*, VI (1912), 937–939; *ibid.*, IX (1915), 816; *ibid.*, XI (1917), 676–677, 687; *ibid.*, XII (1918), 536–537.

[9] *Anuario de Leg. Ecuat.*, 1913, pp. 159–160.

[10] Charles F. Ritter in the *Atlantic Monthly*, CXLVIII (1931), 409–418, 565–575, 733–743. Dora Strauch, *Satan Came to Eden as told to Walter Brockmann* (New York, 1936).

pelago, now under the ministry of war, with a major as governor and a small garrison with headquarters on San Cristóbal Island, is administered directly by the executive as a territory of Ecuador.

9. JUAN FERNÁNDEZ ISLANDS

These are two islands in the South Pacific at about 33°40′ S.: Mas-a-Tierra (Santa Clara), at 78°52′ W., thirteen by four miles, 415 miles a little south of west of Valparaiso, and Mas-a-Fuera, at 80°45′ W., 140 miles further west. The only fair anchorage is in Cumberland Bay, on the north side of Mas-a-Tierra. The islands were perhaps seen by Sarmiento de Gamboa in 1565; and were sighted and named by the Spanish pilot, Juan Fernández, in 1580. He obtained a grant of them from the Spanish government and stocked them with goats and pigs, but soon abandoned them. In 1616 they were visited by the Dutch sailors Jacob le Maire and Willem Cornelis Schouten. In February 1700 the French captain, Dampier, touched at the islands, and five seamen remained. In September 1704 Alexander Selkirk was landed on Mas-a-Tierra from the *Cinque Ports,* of which he was sailing master, after a quarrel with Captain Thomas Stradling, and maintained himself alone until February 1709, when he was taken off on the *Duke.* In June 1741 the British Commodore Anson visited the islands in the *Centurion*, and when he got to England proposed that a British settlement be established. In 1750 the Spanish from Lima garrisoned the islands; and in 1753 a settlement was established by Governor Domingo Ortiz de Rosas on Mas-a-Tierra. In May 1767 Philip Carteret visited Mas-a-Tierra. In 1788 the United States vessel *Columbia* from Boston for Alaska, battered by storms, put into Cumberland Bay and repaired her rudder and mast, and obtained water and firewood. The governor, Blas González, was reprimanded, deposed, and tried for having furnished aid to the distressed vessel; and the viceroy of Peru issued instructions that every strange ship which appeared in the South Sea was to be treated as an enemy, even though her flag be that of an ally of Spain.

Vice-Admiral Graf von Spee's German squadron of seven vessels remained at Mas-a-Fuera for seven days coaling and provisioning in November 1914,[1] which action occasioned a protest by Chile to Germany. On March 9, 1915, the German cruiser *Dresden,* escaped from the Falkland Islands battle, anchored in Cumberland Bay 500 meters (547 yards) from the shore,

---

[1] *Mem. del Min. de Rel. Ext. de Chile, 1914–1915* (Santiago, 1918), pp. 170–171.

and her commander asked the Chilean governor, Natalio Sanchez, for permission to remain eight days to repair her engines, which he said were out of order. The governor refused to grant the request, as he considered it unfounded and believed that in reality coal was lacking, and ordered the *Dresden* to leave the bay within twenty-four hours, threatening to intern her if she stayed beyond that period. At the end of the time she had not gone, and the governor notified the captain that the *Dresden* was interned, and reported the situation to the Chilean authorities in Santiago. On March 14 three British ships, the cruisers *Kent* and *Glasgow* and the armed transport *Orama*, arrived at Cumberland Bay and immediately opened fire on the *Dresden* as she lay at anchor, whereupon most of her crew jumped overboard and swam ashore. The *Dresden* fired fourteen shots in reply and then hoisted a flag of truce and sent an officer to notify the *Glasgow* that she was in neutral waters, to which the British commander replied with a summons to surrender, warning the German that if he refused he would be destroyed. The captain of the *Dresden* then gave orders to blow up the powder magazine, and the ship sank with her flag flying. The English ships left the bay twenty-three hours after their arrival. Chile at once protested vigorously to Great Britain,[2] which offered a full apology, but added that they were aiding in maintaining Chilean neutrality.

Mas-a-Tierra has been used as a place of detention, especially for political prisoners, and a wireless station has recently been erected. Tourist visits from Valparaiso are being encouraged, and the colony of San Juan Bautista is successfully developing lobster fisheries. The islands are now a national park and administered as a part of the maritime territory of Chile.

10. LOBOS ISLANDS

This is a group of one large and three small guano islands and several adjacent rocks in the Pacific south of Punta de Aguja and from ten to thirty-five miles from the coast of Peru; the largest are Lobos de Tierra (Solavento) at 6°35′ S. 80° 45′ W. and Lobos de Afuera (Barlovento) at 6°59′ S. 80°42′ W. The islands were apparently discovered by Francisco Pizarro in 1526, and guano from them seems to have been used in Lambayeque in 1590 and 1612. They are spoken of by the travelers Colnett in 1793 and Captain Amasa Delano in 1806, and they were visited by Captain Benjamin

² *Ibid.*, 172–190, 207–225. 109 *British and Foreign* *tions*, 1931, pp. 104–107. *State Papers* 668–671. Naval War College, *Int. Law Situa-*

Morrell, a sealer from the United States, in September 1823. In 1834 [1] there was a controversy over seal fishing on the islands by the British schooner *Campeadora*. On May 10, 1851,[2] Henry John Temple, Viscount Palmerston, British foreign minister, suggested that the proximity of the islands to Peru would give her a prima facie claim to them, and he and his successors consistently declined to oppose Peruvian jurisdiction there, when English merchants wished to work the guano on them.[3] The United States entered into a discussion with Peru as to the title to them in 1852,[4] in the course of which Daniel Webster, United States secretary of state, declared that as the right of jurisdiction of any sea-coast nation extends to the distance of a cannon shot or three marine miles from the shore as a limit, the question as to title to the Lobos Islands must turn upon whether Peru had "exercised such unequivocal acts of absolute sovereignty and ownership over them as to give her a right to their exclusive possession, as against the United States and their citizens, by the law of undisputed possession." The Peruvian government showed that as early as 1590 the people on the adjoining mainland were in the habit of taking guano from the islands off the coast, and traced a long-continued exercise of jurisdiction by Peru. An order which had been given to United States naval forces to protect vessels taking cargoes from the islands was countermanded, and afterwards the United States withdrew "unreservedly" all objections to Peru's title.

In the War of the Pacific, the Chilean corvette *Chacabuco* under Captain Oscar Viel and the transport *Loa* landed at Lobos de Afuera on March 10, 1880,[5] burned and destroyed wharves, cars, and launches, and embarked horses, mules, livestock, and provisions, leaving food for eight days only for the inhabitants, who were taken to the mainland as rapidly as possible. The United States protested to Chile against the injuries thus caused its citizens. By the Treaty of Ancón of October 20, 1883,[6] (Article 9) the Lobos Islands were to continue to be administered by the government of Chile until the extraction of 1,000,000 tons of guano from the existing beds had been completed, and they were then to be restored to Peru; and meanwhile 50 per cent of the proceeds of the guano extracted from the Lobos Islands was to be ceded by Chile to Peru. The islands now form part of the department of Lambayeque of Peru.

[1] 26 *British and Foreign State Papers* 1218–1222; 28 *ibid.*, 1054–1059.

[2] 45 *ibid.*, 1180.

[3] 31 *ibid.*, 1094–1097; 35 *ibid.*, 1278–1301; 45 *ibid.*, 1178–1244. *Amer. J. Int. Law,* XII (1918), 521.

[4] Rafael F. Seijas, *Derecho Internacional Hispano-* *Americano* (Caracas, 1884), IV, 516–520. Moore, *Dig. Int. Law* (Washington, 1906), I, 265–266, 575–576.

[5] *U. S. For. Rel.,* 1880, pp. 840–841, 845.

[6] Ricardo Aranda, *Col. de Trat. del Peru,* IV, 655–661. A. Bascuñán Montes, *Recop. de Trat.* (Santiago, 1894), II, 158–166. 74 *British and Foreign State Papers* 349–352.

11. Los Roques

These are a group of 365 small uninhabited islands and keys at about 11°45′ N. 66°45′ W. eighty miles north of La Guaira, of which the largest is Cayo de Sal and others are Cayo Grande and Gran Roque. Before 1860 [1] Dutch subjects from Bonaire and Curaçao were accustomed to land and cut wood, and the Netherlands made some claim to title to the islands on the ground of such use, but Venezuela protested and asserted her continuous jurisdiction and sovereignty, and the Dutch pretension was dropped. For seventy years after April 28, 1856,[2] they formed part of the island state of Nueva Esparta (the old province of Margarita, later in part the territory of Colón), but they are now one of the federal dependencies of Venezuela.

12. Malpelo Archipelago

This is a group of small islands including Los Cocos [1] in the Pacific southwest of Buenaventura. Mail service is maintained from the neighboring Colombian ports.[2]

A law of September 15, 1919,[3] provided for a detailed study of the archipelago, to reorganize its public administration, and to see if it should depend directly on the national government or continue to form an integral part of the department of Valle del Cauca of Colombia.

13. Roncador Island

Roncador and Quitasueño are two small islands in the Caribbean Sea on the great undersea bank between Nicaragua and Jamaica, 225 miles east of Nicaragua, 285 miles north of Colón, and 350 miles northwest of Cartagena. J. W. Jennett claimed to have discovered them in 1869, and the United States issued a certificate under the Guano Act on November 22, 1869.[1] Colombia inquired on December 8, 1890, whether the United States had authorized Jennett to remove guano from them, as they were notoriously the property of Colombia; and James G. Blaine, secretary of state, answered on January 19, 1891, that the United States had given Jennett such per-

[1] Lapradelle et Politis, *Rec. des Arbitrages Int.* (Paris, 1924), II, 411, 419.
[2] Law of Territorial Division, Art. 4; *Actos Leg. de Ven. de 1856* (Caracas, 1856), pp. 36–44. Law of the State of Nueva Esparta, Jan. 4, 1926, Arts. 10, 11.
[1] *Inf. del Min. de Rel. Ext. de Col.*, 1922, pp. 15–16.

[2] Law #32 of July 18, 1923. *Leyes de Col.*, Ed. Ofic. (Bogotá, 1923), p. 204.
[3] Law #23. *Leyes de Col.*, 1919 (Bogotá, 1920), p. 29.
[1] Moore, *Dig. Int. Law* (Washington, 1906), I, 568, 578.

mission and questioned Colombia's title. Colombia declared that they were part of the San Andrés y Providencia Archipelago [2] and continued to maintain her claim to them.[3] Roncador, Quitasueño, and Serrana keys, "whose dominion is in dispute between Colombia and the United States" were expressly excepted from the Treaty of March 24, 1928,[4] between Colombia and Nicaragua. On April 10, 1928,[5] there was an exchange of notes between the Colombian minister at Washington and Secretary of State Frank B. Kellogg, which recited that both governments had claimed the right to sovereignty over these islands and Serrana Bank, that the principal interest of the United States lay in the maintenance of aids to navigation and of Colombia that her nationals should uninterruptedly possess the opportunity of fishing in the waters adjacent to the islands, and agreed that the *status quo* should be maintained, the United States to continue its establishment of aids for navigation and Colombian nationals to continue to use the waters appurtenant to the islands for the purpose of fishing. Honduras, which had disputed with Nicaragua the title to the islands, protested to Colombia and to the United States, but both countries refused to concede Honduras any rights in the matter. The islands may originally have been considered part of the San Andrés y Providencia group which was ceded on September 26, 1866, by the state of Bolívar to the United States of Colombia; they are now administered by Colombia as part of the archipelago forming the intendency of San Andrés y Providencia.

14. San Ambrosia and San Félix Islands

These are two small islands, with Isla González and Roca Catedral, in the Pacific at 26°15′ S. 80° W., 570 miles west of Chañaral. They are administered as part of the maritime territories of Chile.

15. San Andrés y Providencia Archipelago

This is a group of three islands and numerous keys and banks in the Caribbean Sea about 135 miles east of Nicaragua and 435 miles northwest of Cartagena. San Andrés, at 12°31′40″ N. 81°43′6″ W., is about seven miles long and three miles wide; San Luis de Providencia, at 13°22′54″ N. 81°21′26″ W.,

---

[2] See §15, *infra*.

[3] *Anales Dipl. y Cons. de Col.* (Bogotá, 1914), IV, 650. *Trat. de Col., 1913* (Bogotá, 1914), pp. 343-344.

[4] *League of Nations Treaty Series*, No. 2426, CV, 338-342. 129 *British and Foreign State Papers*, Part II, 277-278.

[5] *U. S. Treaty Series*, No. 760½. *Amer. J. Int. Law*, XXV (1931), 328.

is five miles long by four wide and lies fifty miles north of San Andrés; Santa Catalina is smaller. The canton of San Andrés in the province of Cartagena was erected into a territory by a law of April 28, 1847;[1] and passed later under the jurisdiction of the state of Bolívar. From about 1852 that state exercised little or no jurisdiction over the islands, and on September 26, 1866,[2] ceded them to the United States of Colombia, which also bestowed little government upon them. In 1914,[3] Colombia asked Great Britain and the Netherlands to require their nationals to obey the Colombian fishing laws and to refrain from fishing at the archipelago and adjacent keys.

Since 1890 Colombia had disputed with Nicaragua as to which nation inherited from Spain the Mosquito Coast and these islands and others in the Caribbean Sea;[4] but by a treaty signed at Managua on March 24, 1928,[5] Nicaragua recognized the sovereignty and full dominion of Colombia over the islands of San Andrés, Providencia, Santa Catalina, and all the other islets and keys which form part of the archipelago of San Andrés. Mail service is maintained from Cartagena[6] and the government has by grants of special privileges[7] endeavored to encourage settlers. A law of April 11, 1931,[8] authorized the executive to send a scientific expedition to the archipelago to prepare maps and study its population (5,988 in 1928), administration, and economic possibilities. The archipelago with Roncador and Quitasueño is administered as an intendency of Colombia.

16. Tierra del Fuego

The land south of the Strait of Magellan from 65°7' to 74°44' W. called Tierra del Fuego is an archipelago comprising the great island of Tierra del Fuego proper (Onisia) and many smaller ones, including Cape Horn at 55°59' S. 67° 16' W.[1] The highest peak is Mt. Sarmiento, 6,910 feet, at the west end of the Cordillera Darwin on the Chilean part of the great island. Since the

[1] *Codif. Nac., Ano de 1847* (Bogotá, 1928), XII, 47.
[2] Accepted by Law of June 4, 1868. *Actos Leg. del Congreso de Col. de 1868* (Bogotá), pp. 71–78. *U. S. Dipl. Corr.*, 1868, Part II, pp. 1061, 1074–1075.
[3] *Informe del Min. de Rel. Ext.*, 1915, p. 145. *Trat. de Col., 1913* (Bogotá, 1914), pp. 343–344.
[4] Antonio José Uribe, *Colombia, Venezuela, etc., Las Cuestiones de Limites* (Bogotá, 1931), pp. 361–383, 396–407, 443–448, 452–469.
[5] *League of Nations Treaty Series*, No. 2426, CV, 338–342. Antonio José Uribe, *Colombia, Venezuela, etc., Las Cuestiones de Limites* (Bogotá, 1931), pp. 618–619. 129 *British and Foreign State Papers*, Part II, pp. 277–278. Ratifications exchanged at Managua, May 5, 1930.

[6] Law #32 of July 18, 1923. *Leyes de Col.*, Ed. Ofic. (Bogotá, 1923), p. 204.
[7] Law #17 of Sept. 15, 1927. *Leyes de Col.*, Ed. Ofic. (Bogotá, 1927), pp. 58–59.
[8] Law #47 of 1931. *Leyes de Col.*, 1931; Sesiones Extra., Ed. Ofic. (Bogotá, 1931), pp. 160–161.

[1] Others are: Banner, Barnevelt, Basket, Bayly, Beauclerk, Camden, Carlos, Clarence, Dawson, Desolation, Enderby, Evans, Fincham, Gordon, Grafton, Graves, Grévy, Henderson, Hermite, Hoste, Isabella, Jacque, Kempe, Landfall, Lennox, London, Londonderry, Lort, Magill, Navarino, Noir, Nueva, O'Brien, Picton, Santa Inés, Stanley, Staten, Steward, Thomas, Waterman, and Wollaston.

discovery the aboriginal Alakaluf, Yagan, and Ona Indians have rapidly died out. There are Chilean settlements and a Roman Catholic mission on Dawson Island. Alluvial gold was discovered in the southern part in 1880, but most of the great island is given to cattle and sheep grazing.

After the voyage of Magalhães in 1520 it was of course known that the strait was a passage from ocean to ocean which left land to the south, and barren and desolate as the area beyond the strait must have appeared, it seemed worth controlling. The grant on the South Sea (west coast of South America) of July 26, 1529,[2] to Simon de Alcazaba ran from the Strait of Magellan, and the four grants of May 4 and 21, 1534, all ran toward the Strait of Magellan, but in 1539 the grant to Francisco de Camargo ran to the strait, and on January 24, 1539,[3] there was granted to Pedro Sancho de Hoz the land on the other side of the strait not given to any other persons. Joseph de Herrera y Sotomayor, governor of the province of Buenos Aires, on January 23, 1683,[4] sent to Charles II a project for an expedition to the strait, and various permissive orders were issued, but little seems to have been done. From December 17, 1832, to February 28, 1834, Charles Darwin and others on the *Beagle* under Captain Robert Fitz Roy explored the land and many of the channels of the region, and in June 1834 they visited some of the Antartic islands. Picton, Nueva, and Lennox islands, at the easterly entrance of Beagle Channel, are claimed by Argentina as adjacent to her part of Tierra del Fuego and by Chile[5] as south of Beagle Channel, but the dispute is at present not being pressed.

Following the arbitral award of King Edward VII on November 20, 1902,[6] the eastern portion of Tierra del Fuego Island with capital at Ushuaia, the island of Los Estados (Staten), and the small islands to the east in the Atlantic form the Tierra del Fuego territory of Argentina; and the western portion of the great island, the numerous other islands south of Beagle Channel to Cape Horn, west of Tierra del Fuego, and north to 47° S., and an area on the barren mainland, with capital at Magallanes (formerly a convict settlement, called Punta Arenas)[7] form the territory of Magallanes of Chile.

[2] Ricardo Aranda, *Col. de Trat. del Peru,* I, 32–38.

[3] Miguel Luis Amunátegui, *La Cuestión de Limites entre Chile i la República Arjentina* (Santiago, 1879), I, 128–129.

[4] Pedro de Angelis, *Memoria Histórica sobre los Derechos de Soberania y Dominio de la Confederación Argentina a la parte austral del Continente Americano* (Buenos Aires, 1852). Dalmacio Velez Sarsfield, *Discusión de los Títulos del Gobierno de Chile a las Tierras del Estrecho de Maga-*llanes (Buenos Aires, 1853). Miguel Luis Amunátegui, *Títulos de la República de Chile a la Soberania i Dominio de la estremidad austral del Continente Americano* (Santiago, 1853).

[5] J. Guillermo Guerra, *La Soberania Chilena en las Islas al Sur del Canal Beagle* (Santiago, 1917).

[6] See chap. 1, §3, *supra.*

[7] See "The Magellan Pirates" (Great Britain, Admiralty, 1853), 1 Spink's *Eccl. and Adm. Rep.* 81.

17. TRINDADE ISLAND

Trindade is a small island in the South Atlantic at 20° 31′ S. 29° 20′ W., 651 miles east of Victoria on the Brazilian coast. It was discovered by the Portuguese in 1501 and visited on April 15, 1700, by the English Captain Edmund Halley and on May 31, 1775, by Commander James Cook in the *Resolution* on his second voyage. The British at war with Spain in 1781 occupied it as a base for operations against the commerce with the Plata colonies, at which Spain protested to Portugal and the viceroy of Brazil was directed to retake the island. The British had withdrawn by admiralty orders of August 22, 1782, before the expedition arrived from Brazil, but a Portuguese military post was established and maintained until February 6, 1795. The Portuguese abandoned the island after Brazil became independent in 1822, and in 1825 the Brazilians sent their corvette *Itaparica* to examine into its usefulness. On November 29, 1884,[1] Pedro II granted to João Alves Guerra permission to explore mines for two years, extract natural products for ten years, and establish salt pits for thirty years on the island. It was visited from Brazil in 1856 by the corvette *Doña Isabel*, in 1871 by the corvette *Bahiana*, in 1871 and 1884 by the corvette *Nictheroy*, and in 1894 by the transport *Penedo* under First Lieutenant Joaquin Sarmanho. In 1891 Brazil had some intention of making use of the island for penitentiary purposes, and after the suppression of the revolt of November 1935 it was proposed to send most of the captured rebels to detention there.

In January 1895[2] the British cruiser *Baracuta* landed a small force on the island and raised the British flag. As soon as the news of this action was received, in July 1895, Brazil protested to Great Britain; but the British prime minister, Robert Arthur Talbot Cecil, Marquis of Salisbury, replied that possession was first taken by the British in 1700, when there was no evidence of Portuguese possession and no protest by Portugal; when England resumed possession of Trindade and of Martin Vaz islands, in January 1895, no trace of foreign occupation was found; and as Trindade was required as a cable telegraph station, England would not waive her rights to it. Brazil refused arbitration, but, on mediation by Portugal, Great Britain finally consented to restore the island,[3] and it now forms part of the territory of the state of Espirito Santo of Brazil.

[1] *Actos do Poder Exec. 1884*, pp. 627–629.
[2] *U. S. For. Rel.*, 1895, I, 63–70. Martens, *Nouv. Rec. Gén. de Traités*, 2ᵉ Sér., XXI, 633–639. *Arch. Dipl.*, 2ᵉ Sér., LV, 192–197.
[3] *Arch Dipl.*, 2ᵉ Sér., LIX, 163.

18. TRINIDAD ISLAND

This island between 10°3′ and 10°50′ N. and 60°39′ and 62° W., forty-eight miles long and thirty-five miles broad, with an area of 1,862 square miles, six miles north and east of the coast of Venezuela, enclosing the Gulf of Paria, is the southernmost and next to Jamaica the largest of the British West Indian islands. Tucuche, the highest peak, rises to 3,100 feet; the capital is Port-of-Spain, on the inside harbor; and the chief product is asphalt from a pitch lake, thirty-eight miles southeast of Port-of-Spain, in the ward of La Brea, of 114 acres in extent and three miles in circumference, under lease to a private company since 1888. Oil fields have been developed, and the colony was in 1933 the largest producer of petroleum within the British empire. Tobago, twenty-six miles northeast of Trinidad, with an area of 114 square miles, governed at first with St. Vincent, was joined administratively with the Windward Islands until 1889.

Trinidad was discovered by Columbus, probably on his third voyage, on July 31, 1498, and soon settled by the Spaniards. Antonio Sedeno was named the first governor, in 1528; Juan Ponce in 1540; and Antonio de Berrio y Oruna on April 23, 1593. It was under the jurisdiction of Cumaná in Nueva Andalusia from 1622 to 1640 and thereafter under Caracas in the captaincy-general of Venezuela. In 1595 Sir Walter Raleigh on his first expedition to the Orinoco burned the capital, San José de Oruna. The Catholic Church established missions for Indians on the island, and quarrelled with the municipal authorities from 1743 to 1783. The island was taken from the Spaniards by the British general, Sir Ralph Abercromby, on February 16, 1797, at which time the Spanish ship *Apodacas* laden with gold bullion is supposed to have been burned and sunk in Chaguaramas Bay. By the Treaty of Amiens on March 27, 1802,[1] Spain ceded Trinidad permanently to England.

Eastward of the southern channel, called the Serpent's Mouth, between Trinidad and the mainland, are three small islands, Patos, Huevos, and Monos, of which the principal one, Patos, is about three miles from the coast of Guiria and ten miles from the nearest point of Trinidad. On September 15, 1791, the last Spanish governor of Trinidad, Colonel José Maria Chacón, being at odds with the governor of the province of Cumaná, made a grant of the three islands in perpetuity to the municipality of Puerto España, to be leased for revenue; but it does not appear in the Archives of the Indies that the concession was ever confirmed by any royal decree. On December 26,

[1] Martens, *Rec. des Prin. Traités*, VII, 404–413.

1839, the minutes of the Cabildo show a report by Attorney-General Fuller against the claim of George Deher to certain lands on Monos alleged to have been granted to his father by the Spanish governor in 1785, finding a tenancy only and rent paid. In 1859 a Venezuelan skiff captured two contraband boats on Patos Island, and when the British colonial authorities objected that this was a violation of British territory, Lovera, the agent in Trinidad of the governor of Caracas, on May 31, 1859, wrote the governor of Trinidad that the island belonged to Venezuela. On August 8, 1866, the municipality of Port-of-Spain granted to Felix O'Connor a ten years' lease of Patos Island, and Dr. Domingo Montbrun, the Venezuelan consul at Trinidad, protested on August 9, 1866, and February 15, 1867, that the island belonged to Venezuela. Great Britain replied that it was and always had been a dependency of Trinidad, and the correspondence was maintained without result, with proposals by Venezuela for arbitration of the question, until in 1883 Lord Granville told Venezuela that if a satisfactory adjustment could be made as to the disputed boundary with British Guiana and other pending questions, the wishes of Venezuela as to the "cession" of Patos Island would obtain favorable consideration. The question was included in a memorandum of Archibald Primrose, Lord Rosebery, to Venezuela on July 20, 1886, concerning the settlement of various pending matters but was not disposed of, and Venezuela reiterated to Great Britain on February 14, 1887, that she considered Patos part of her territory. In 1891 Patos was forfeited by the municipality of Port-of-Spain to the colonial government for nonpayment of taxes.

On January 22, 1901,[2] the Venezuelan gunboat *Augusto* found at Patos and carried off four cargo boats and about twenty-five persons, including some British subjects, suspected of being engaged in smuggling; on February 27, 1901, a Venezuelan coast guard pirogue under Captain Agripino Lairet seized the *Sea Horse* belonging to John Craig, a Trinidad fisherman who had landed on Patos; and on August 31, 1901, the Venezuelan revenue cutter *Totumo* seized some goods from Port-of-Spain which the Venezuelan sloop *Pastor*, owned by Numa Audry, had landed on Patos, captured some of her men, and fired on the boat in what the Trinidad authorities alleged to be British waters. These incidents formed part of the British claims against Venezuela which brought on the joint blockade of December 20, 1902,[3] and were included in the first class of claims to be paid in cash without submission to a mixed commission by the protocol of February 13, 1903,[4] and the agreement of May 7,

---

[2] *Expt. del Min. de Rel. Ext. de Venezuela*, 1902, Ed. Ofic. (Caracas, 1902), pp. 27–49. 95 *British and Foreign State Papers* 1064–1066.

[3] See chap. I, §24.
[4] See chap. I, §24.

1903.[5] This apparently left the question of the ownership of Patos still unsettled. On May 27, 1904,[6] the island of Patos was nominally included by Venezuela in the federal territory of Cristóbal Colón. The British minister, Outram Bax-Ironside, protested on August 8, 1904,[7] that Patos was British. Gustavo J. Sanabria, the Venezuela minister of foreign relations, replied on August 24 that it belonged to Venezuela, which Bax-Ironside wrote on August 26, 1904, would be reported to the Marquis of Lansdowne, the British prime minister. In 1907 the islands of Huevos and Monos were transferred by the municipality of Port-of-Spain to the government in exchange for lands in the city. In November 1911 an island of hot mud about two and a half acres in extent, accompanied by bluish flames, rose from the sea in Erin Bay, between Erin and Chatham, on the south coast of Trinidad, and entirely disappeared from erosion a few years later. In November 1934 an upheaval on shore near Erin rocked and cracked the earth and formed a new beach 800 feet long, probably from the slipping of a fault in the earth's crust, but perhaps from the rejuvenation of a large mud volcano near the coastline.

Venezuela still purports to include the three islands among her federal dependencies, but they are actually managed by the government of the British colony of Trinidad. The islands of Trinidad and Tobago were politically united from January 1, 1889;[8] and they are now administered[9] by a governor, an executive council of such persons as the king may direct, and a legislative council of twelve officials and thirteen other members, six nominated and seven elected, as a colony of Great Britain.

19. Tristán da Cunha Islands

This is a group of small islands in the South Atlantic at 37° 6′ S. 12° 16′ W. a little south of a line between Buenos Aires and the Cape of Good Hope, 1,500 miles west of Capetown, consisting of Tristán da Cunha, an extinct volcano with its 8,000-foot peak at 37° 5′ 50″ S., 12° 16′ 40″ W. and a base circumference of twenty-one miles, Inaccessible, two miles long (on which the *Blenden Hall* was wrecked, July 23, 1821), Nightingale, one mile long, and two islets. They were discovered by the Portuguese in 1506. On August 14, 1816, the group was taken possession of by Great Britain, annexed to the Cape

---

[5] See chap. I, §24.

[6] Decree #9526. *Recop. de Leyes y Decr. de Venezuela* (Caracas, 1905), XXVII, II, 239–240.

[7] *Expt. del Min. de Rel. Ext. de Venezuela*, 1905 (Caracas, 1905), pp. 8–10.

[8] Authorized, Statute of Sept. 16, 1887, 51 Vict. c. 44;

Order in Council, Nov. 17, 1888; Letters Patent, June 6, 1924. *S. R. & O.* (1924), 1907–1913. 78 *British and Foreign State Papers* 828.

[9] 119 *ibid.*, 105–121; 128 *ibid.*, 86–88. *Rev. d'Hist. Dipl.* (Paris, 1933), 47e Année, pp. 175–188.

Colony and garrisoned by a relief regiment for St. Helena. Thomas Currie, an Englishman, who had landed in 1810, was found living alone on the island when the British troops arrived but died before they left. When the troops were withdrawn, William Glass, a Royal Artillery driver, and two companions were on November 7, 1817, given official permission to remain. An equality agreement was made on June 12, 1820, among eleven inhabitants. The islands were visited annually by a British warship until 1900, one of the Empress ships now usually calls on an annual tourist cruise and a London newspaper correspondent went over from Rio de Janeiro in 1936. Diego Alvarez, or Gough's Island, at 40°20′ S. 11°30′ W., 250 miles south-southeast of Tristán da Cunha, is eight miles long by four miles broad and has one peak of 4,380 feet. It was visited by Captain Gough in 1731, when it had no permanent population, and since 1816 it has been claimed by Great Britain. The only even moderately successful crop is potatoes, and there is constant warfare with the hordes of rats, descendants of the survivors of an 1882 shipwreck, which overrun the islands, but all attempts to induce the inhabitants of the group to leave have so far been fruitless.[1] The Rev. A. G. Partridge from England visited Tristán da Cunha in 1932 at the request of the Colonial Office, and set up one Repetto, since died, as chief of the islanders, with three officers to work under him. The Rev. Harold Wilde, an Anglican priest, is schoolmaster, magistrate, doctor, and dentist. The population is 187, with but seven surnames,[2] and in the last three years there have been one death, from an accident, and twelve births. Mrs. Repetto, now sixty-one, is chief woman of the islands. The group is a dependency of the former Colony of the Cape of Good Hope, since 1909 a province of the Union of South Africa, a self-governing unit of the British Empire, and is proposed as a refueling station for a Buenos Aires-Capetown airway.

[1] Clunet, *J. du dr. int.*, XLIX (1922), 255.
[2] Glass, Green, Hodges, Rogers, Swain, Lavarello, and Repetto, the last two borne by descendants of two shipwrecked Italian sailors.

CHAPTER III

EXISTING TREATY RELATIONS

[Treaties in brackets are not in force.]

A. GENERAL CONSIDERATIONS

BOUNDARY disputes involve the possibility of eventually losing some portion, however insignificant, of territory which has been considered or at any rate claimed for a time as national property; and such potential loss [1] always appears to threaten in some degree the national sovereignty and to affect the national honor, and arouses immediate and vociferous popular indignation. A government, therefore, which yields in the slightest once a boundary question has arisen, or takes any steps toward submitting the issue to an impartial or arbitral decision, invites unified opposition and its own downfall. This ardent defense of the national area is one of the perhaps rare points of view shared by all the Latin-American republics and, in combination with the geographical vagueness of the Spanish regime and the approximately equal arguments, seldom squarely joining issue, as to the status in 1810, has in the past made the arbitration of South American boundary disputes a difficult and precarious matter. Despite the so-far successful Colombia-Peru accord,[2] there is little reason to expect better results in the future when a territorial conflict suddenly arises. The government in power on either side will push its claims to the utmost, to gain domestic support, and diplomatic correspondence, strategy, and maneuvers will postpone as long as possible facing the critical choice between an expensive appeal to force and the public-pride-wounding resort to arbitration. It is to be noted that in the thirty years covered by the current treaties, there have been a war, several near-wars, armed clashes, diplomatic incidents, and severing of relations over frontier questions, with but one reference in a special treaty [3] and one reference during negotiations [4] to existing general arbitration treaties. Not too much faith, therefore, should be placed in the power of arbitration treaties to avert or adjust boundary disputes when they appear; but such treaties may fairly be listed as one of the factors to be considered by foreign ministries sincerely desirous of keeping the peace.

[1] As in Peru's (eleventh) Constitution of 1933. *Revista del Foro* (Lima, 1933), XX, 39–62. Promulgated by President Luis M. Sanchez Cerro, Apr. 9, 1933.

[2] See chap. I, §21B, *supra.*
[3] See chap. I, §9, *supra.*
[4] See chap. I, §21B, *supra.*

Of the forty-five possible pairs of the ten nations, twenty-five have general arbitration treaties (§§ 1, 2, 3, 4, 5, 6, 8, 9, 10, 12, 15, 16, 17, 18, 20, 21, 22, 23, 24, 25, 29, 39, 43, 44, 45, *infra*). Two of such treaties (§§ 15 and 18) make no exceptions, ten (§§ 1, 2, 3, 4, 5, 6, 8, 9, 25, and 29) except questions affecting constitutional provisions, eight (§§ 10, 20, 21, 24, 25, 29, 39, and 44) except questions affecting vital interests, territory, independence, sovereignty, or honor,[5] and nine (§§ 9, 12, 16, 17, 22, 23, 24, 43, and 45) except questions within the jurisdiction of domestic courts. There are four peace and friendship treaties (§§ 13, 31, 33, and 41) providing for arbitration in a general way; and (exclusive of any treaties which may be ratified as a result of the Buenos Aires Conference of December 1936) in the twenty cases with no bipartite arbitration treaties three pairs of nations (§§ 7, 13, and 34) have signed or adhered to four multipartite treaties, seven pairs (§§ 11, 19, 26, 31, 36, 37, and 38) to five treaties, nine pairs (§§ 14, 27, 28, 30, 32, 33, 35, 41, and 42) to six treaties, and one pair (§ 40) to seven treaties. Experience indicates that boundary disputes will usually be asserted by one or both parties, especially the one which fears that it has the weaker legal position, to fall within the expressly exempted class and to require a special treaty, in which certain phases of the original dispute would be withheld from the tribunal. The excepting clauses are hereinafter indicated in each case, but the interpretation to be placed on them by the party nations when a conflict arises cannot be determined in advance.[6] Finland on May 13, 1929,[7] presented to the tenth Assembly of the League of Nations a proposal to permit arbitral decisions in cases of alleged lack of jurisdiction or exceeding of powers by the arbitral tribunal to be reviewed by the Permanent Court of International Justice; but no other nation actively supported the idea and except perhaps for the provision in Article 10 of Accord II of April 28, 1930,[8] concerning Hungary, nothing has come of it.

For the sake of completeness and comparison there are listed existing arbitration treaties between any two South American nations,[9] whether or not they are now actual neighbors or possess remote islands so that a land dispute would be possible between them. The multipartite [10] treaties are in-

[5] *Rel. do Min. das Rel. Ext. do Brazil* (Rio de Janeiro, 1928), I, 212.

[6] Gaspar Toro, *Notas sobre Arbitraje Internacional en las Repúblicas Latino-Americanas* (Santiago de Chile, 1898).

[7] *League of Nations Official Journal*, 1929, Special Supp. No. 76, pp. 82–86. *Rev. de Der. Int.* (Havana), XXII (1932), 50–70.

[8] Manley O. Hudson, *The Permanent Court of International Justice* (New York, 1934), pp. 373–375. *League of Nations Treaty Series*, CXXI, 80–91. Cf. Sidney B. Jacoby, *Virginia Law Review*, XXII (1936), 404–415.

[9] Gonzalo de Quesada, *Arbitration in Latin America* (Rotterdam, 1907), Chap. V, pp. 125–135.

[10] "Multipartite" is here used to denote an international agreement signed by the representatives of more than two nations, not, as sometimes, to mean an agreement of which more than two original copies are signed. E.g., *Amer. J. Int. Law*, XXIX (1935), 120.

cluded to complete the picture and supply some links for which there is as yet no stronger and more definite bipartite substitute. Such treaties are in international practice no more multiple than bipartite agreements, because experience shows that in any dispute the principals will hold the issue to themselves and not permit intervention by strangers to the question at bar from the mere fact that they also have signed the pact; nor are multipartite any more than bipartite treaties "legislation," notwithstanding the perhaps wish-fulfilling use of that convenient but inaccurate term by a recent writer.[11] They are mutual promises by nations to refrain from or, less often, to perform, some act by their executive or legislative departments; they contain no sanctions; and no individual, apart from domestic law, is punished for infraction of them.[12]

Japan in China and in the mandated islands, Italy in Ethiopia, Bolivia and Paraguay in the Chaco Boreal, are proof enough that no existing agency is able or willing to prevent the resort to force over border or dominion disputes when there is the will to aggress. Within the next score of years, however, some of the Latin-American nations [13] are going to be forced by their necessities into economic pacts with their neighbors; and when the resulting benefits have sufficiently demonstrated that coöperation does not necessarily injure national honor, affront national dignity, or lower national prestige, it is possible that thoughts may be turned to the advantages of friendly agreement in other departments. It is not inconceivable that within a half-century there should be set up an American international tribunal empowered to hear and determine boundary questions that arise anywhere in Latin America. With the favorable support of Argentina, Brazil, Chile, Mexico, and Peru it might make a start with a provisional trial period of ten years. A complete league or permanent court with general jurisdiction, the Central American failures seem to postpone to a more distant date; but the calming effect of the constant availability of an impartial peaceful tribunal for boundary disputes only may be really welcomed by the more enlightened governments.

Thirteen bilateral arbitrations [14] were sanctioned by special treaties from 1878 to 1925 to determine eleven boundaries, among all of the South American jurisdictions except Uruguay. Two were unfinished;[15] seven [16] adopted

[11] Manley O. Hudson, "International Legislation," *Amer. Soc. Int. Law, Proc.*, 1923, pp. 52–54. Manley O. Hudson, *International Legislation* (Washington, 1931), Introduction, I, xiii–xvii. See book reviews: Clyde Eagleton, *Pol. Sci. Q.*, XLVIII (1933), 142. James W. Garner, *Amer. J. Int. Law*, XXVI (1932), 435. Philip C. Jessup, *Col. Law Rev.*, XXXII (1932), 1271. Henry A. Rolin, *Harv. Law Rev.*, XLVI (1933), 1039. E. G. Trimble, *Yale Law Journal*, XLI (1932), 1263.

[12] Joseph H. Beale, *Treatise on Conflict of Laws* (New York, 1935), I, Sec. 5.1, p. 51.

[13] Agustin Edwards, "Latin America and the League of Nations," *Journal Royal Inst. of Int. Affairs*, VIII (1929), 134–153.

[14] Chap. I, §§2, 3A, 3B, 4, 9, 16, 17, 19, 22A, 22B, 23, 24, 25, *supra*.

[15] By resignation of the arbiter, chap. I, §23; by majority vote before execution, §19, *supra*.

[16] Chap. I, §§2, 4, 16, 22A, 22B, 24, 25, *supra*.

nearly or wholly the line of one of the disputants and four [17] drew mainly a compromise line. The arbiters were in three cases plural tribunals [18] and in ten cases nominally individuals,[19] changed after the original arbitration treaty was signed, four times unexpectedly by the death of the arbiter originally chosen [20] and three times foreseeably by the succession of an elective president.[21] Twice [22] the losing party protested that the compromise award as made exceeded the arbiter's jurisdiction according to the terms of the submission, and once [23] the decision resulted in a temporary severance of relations between the arbiter's country and one of the litigants. In two cases [24] disputed territory was transferred after the arbitration treaty was signed; and twice [25] after a demarcation commission had started work on the awarded boundary more of the line was entrusted to it. In five instances [26] the cases were submitted directly nearly or quite simultaneously and not exchanged, but in eight instances [27] successive pleadings were allowed. Three foreign demarcation commissions were English,[28] and one was Swiss.[29]

B. BIPARTITE TREATIES

1. ARGENTINA–BOLIVIA

Treaty [1] of general arbitration of all controversies of whatever nature which for any cause may arise between the parties so far as they do not affect the precepts of the constitution of either country and provided they cannot be solved by direct negotiations; by a tribunal to be constituted for each case, of three judges if not otherwise agreed; the points at issue to be fixed and the scope of the arbiter's powers determined by the parties; with no appeal except to the same tribunal before the period set for execution, or within three months, for forgery of a document or error of fact; the treaty to remain in force for ten years and be successively renewed for ten-year periods if not denounced six months before the end of any such period.

Signed at Buenos Aires, February 3, 1902; ratified with an addition by

---

[17] Chap. I, §§3A, 3B, 9, 17, *supra*.

[18] Swiss Federal Council, chap. I, §§16, 22B; Special Tribunal, §24, *supra*.

[19] Argentina, chap. I, §9; Great Britain, §3B; Italy, §17; Russia, §25; Spain, §§22A, 23; United States, §§2, 3A, 4, 19, *supra*.

[20] Chap. I, §§3B, 9, 19, 22A, *supra*.

[21] Chap. I, §§2, 4, 19, *supra*.

[22] Chap. I, §§3B, 9, *supra*.

[23] Chap. I, §9, *supra*.

[24] Chap. I, §§9, 23, *supra*.

[25] Chap. I, §§3A, 9, *supra*.

[26] Chap. I, §§2, 3A, 3B, 4, 25, *supra*.

[27] Chap. I, §§9, 16, 17, 19, 22A, 22B, 23, 24, *supra*.

[28] Chap. I, §§3A, 3B, 9, *supra*.

[29] Chap. I, §22B, *supra*.

---

[1] *Tratados de Argentina*, Pub. Ofic. (Buenos Aires, 1911), II, 195–204. *Tratados Vigentes* (Bolivia, 1925), I, 68–79. 95 *British and Foreign State Papers* 399–402. *Rev. de Der. Int.* (Havana), II (1922), 353–356. Martens, *Nouv. Rec. Gén. de Traités*, 2e Sér., XXXI, 264–267. *Archives Dipl.*, 3e Sér., XCVIII, 294–299.

Argentina, Law #4090, July 26, 1902; ratified by Bolivia, December 23, 1902; ratifications exchanged at Buenos Aires, January 27, 1903.

Argentina signed and Bolivia signed and ratified the Convention of October 18, 1907 (§ 48, *infra*); and Argentina signed and Bolivia adhered to the Treaty of May 3, 1923 (§ 50, *infra*), and the Treaty of October 10, 1933 (§ 55, *infra*).

2. ARGENTINA–BRAZIL

Treaty [2] of general arbitration of controversies between the parties which it has not been possible to solve by direct negotiations or by any of the other means for amicable solution of international differences, provided such controversies do not turn upon questions which affect constitutional precepts of either party; the points at issue to be fixed with due clarity by the parties, who should also determine the scope of the powers of the arbiters; by a tribunal of three to be created by a special agreement or separate instrument; with no appeal except to the same tribunal before the completion of execution for forgery of a document or error of fact; the treaty to remain in force for ten years and be successively renewed for ten-year periods if not denounced six months before the end of any such period.

Signed at Rio de Janeiro, September 7, 1905; ratified by Argentina, Law #6281, November 4, 1908; sanctioned by Brazil, Decree #1971, October 1, 1908; ratified by Brazil, November 9, 1908; ratifications exchanged at Buenos Aires, December 5, 1908; promulgated by Brazil, Degree #7277, January 7, 1909.

Argentina signed and Brazil signed and ratified the Convention of October 18, 1907 (§ 48, *infra*), the ABC Pact of May 25, 1915 (§ 49, *infra*), and the Treaty of May 3, 1923 (§ 50, *infra*); and both nations signed the Treaty of October 10, 1933 (§ 55, *infra*).

3. ARGENTINA–CHILE

Treaty [3] of general arbitration of all controversies of whatever nature which for any cause may arise between the parties, so far as they do not affect the precepts of the constitution of either country and provided they

---

[2] *Trat. de Argentina* (Buenos Aires, 1911), II, 703–710. *Col. das Leis do Brazil*, 1909, I, 2ª Parte, 2–9. *Rev. de Der. Int.* (Havana), II (1922), 356–359. 100 *British and Foreign State Papers* 605–608. *U. S. For. Rel.*, 1908; pp. 51–54. Martens, *Nouv. Rec. Gén. de Traités*, 3ᵉ Sér., II, 274–277. *Arch. Dipl.*, 3ᵉ Sér., CXIII, 162–165. *Rev. gén. de dr. int. pub.*, XVI (1909), 86–94.

[3] *Trat. de Argentina* (Buenos Aires, 1911), VII, 267–276. *Recop. de Trat. de Chile*, Ed. Ofic. (Santiago, 1913), VI, 10–19. 95 *British and Foreign State Papers* 758–761. *Rev. de Der. Int.* (Havana), II (1922), 359–363. Martens, *Nouv. Rec. Gén. de Traités*, 2ᵉ Sér., XXXV, 297–300. *Arch. Dipl.*, XCI, 1202–1206; *ibid.*, XCVIII, 5–9.

cannot be solved by direct negotiations; by the government of his Britannic majesty, or if either party severs friendly relations with that government, by the government of the Swiss Confederation; the points, questions, or differences at issue to be fixed and the scope of the arbiter's powers determined by the parties; with no appeal except to the same arbiter before the period set for execution for forgery of a document or error of fact; the treaty to remain in force for ten years and be successively renewed for ten-year periods if not denounced six months before the end of any such period.

Signed at Santiago, May 28, 1902; ratified by Argentina, Law #4092, July 30, 1902; ratified by Chile, 1902; ratifications exchanged at Santiago, September 22, 1902; promulgated by Argentina, August 25, 1902; promulgated by Chile, September 22, 1902.

These two nations signed the Convention of October 18, 1907 (§ 48, *infra*), and the ABC Pact of May 25, 1915 (§ 49, *infra*); and Argentina signed and Chile signed and ratified the Treaty of May 3, 1923 (§ 50, *infra*), and the Treaty of October 10, 1933 (§ 55, *infra*).

4. ARGENTINA–COLOMBIA

Treaty [4] of general arbitration of all controversies which for any cause may arise between the parties, provided they do not affect the precepts of the constitution of either country, and have not been able to be solved by direct negotiations; the parties to sign a special agreement which shall determine the object of the litigation; by a tribunal to be constituted for each case, of three members if not otherwise agreed; with no appeal except to the same tribunal before execution if the decision was based on false or erroneous documents or vitiated in whole or in part by an error of fact resulting from the proceedings or documents in the cause; the treaty to remain in force for ten years, and thereafter until one year after either party shall have denounced it.

Signed at Washington, January 20, 1912; ratified by Argentina, Law #11031, August 27, 1920; ratified by Colombia, Law #64, November 6, 1912; ratifications exchanged at Buenos Aires, August 12, 1921.

Argentina signed, and Colombia signed and ratified the Treaty of May 3, 1923 (§ 50, *infra*); and Argentina signed and Colombia adhered to the Treaty of October 10, 1933 (§ 55, *infra*).

[4] *Leyes de Colombia de 1912* (Bogotá, 1912), pp. 172–176. Martens, *Nouv. Rec. Gén. de Traités*, 3e Sér., XX, 360–362. 113 *British and Foreign State Papers* 876–878.

5. ARGENTINA–ECUADOR

Treaty [5] of general arbitration of all differences of whatever nature which may arise between the parties and which cannot be solved by diplomatic means, except those relative to constitutional dispositions in force in either state; the parties to sign a special agreement which shall determine the object of the litigation; by a tribunal to be constituted for each case, of three members if not otherwise agreed, with no appeal except to the same tribunal before execution if the decision was based on false or erroneous documents or vitiated in whole or in part by an error of fact resulting from the proceedings or documents in the cause; the treaty to remain in force for ten years and be successively renewed for ten-year periods if not denounced six months before the end of any such period.

Signed at Caracas, July 12, 1911; ratified by Argentina, Law #11029, August 27, 1920; Exec., October 9, 1922; ratified by Ecuador, Decr. Leg., September 13, 1922; ratifications exchanged at Quito, January 22, 1923.

Argentina signed and Ecuador signed and ratified the Treaty of May 3, 1923 (§ 50, *infra*); and Argentina signed and Ecuador adhered to the Treaty of October 10, 1933 (§ 55, *infra*).

6. ARGENTINA–PARAGUAY

Treaty [6] of general arbitration of all controversies of whatever nature which for any cause may arise between the parties, so far as they do not affect the precepts of the constitution of either country, and provided they cannot be solved by direct negotiations; by a tribunal to be constituted for each case, of three judges if not otherwise agreed; the points at issue to be fixed and the scope of the arbiters' powers determined by the parties; with no appeal except to the same tribunal before the period set for execution for forgery of a document or error of fact resulting from the proceedings or documents in the cause; the treaty to remain in force for ten years and be successively renewed for ten-year periods if not denounced six months before the end of any such period.

Signed at Asunción, November 6, 1899, with additional protocol as to manner of selecting the third arbiter signed at Asunción, January 25, 1902; ratified by Argentina, Law #4045, December 18, 1901, and the modification

[5] *Trat. y Conv. Vig. de Argentina* (Buenos Aires, 1925), I, 381–384.

[6] *Trat. de Argentina* (Buenos Aires, 1912), IX, 268–279. 92 *British and Foreign State Papers* 485–488. Rev.

de Der. Int. (Havana), V (1924), 404–409. Martens, *Nouv. Rec. Gén. de Traités,* 2e Sér., XXXI, 17–19; *ibid.,* XXXII, 404–407. *Arch. Dipl.,* XCII, 1198–1202; *ibid.,* XCVIII, 16–20.

on May 8, 1902; ratified by Paraguay, December 31, 1901; ratifications exchanged at Asunción, June 5, 1902; promulgated by Argentina, May 15, 1902.

These two nations signed the Treaty of January 29, 1902 (§ 46, *infra*); Argentina signed and Paraguay signed and ratified the Convention of October 18, 1907 (§ 48, *infra*), and the Treaty of May 3, 1923 (§ 50, *infra*); and both signed the Treaty of October 10, 1933 (§ 55, *infra*).

7. ARGENTINA–PERU

Treaty [7] of friendship, commerce, and navigation, declaring that (Article 1) the peace and friendship happily maintained and cultivated without the least interruption between the parties shall be perpetually firm and inviolable, relying upon the liveliest interest of the governments of both republics to maintain between themselves and their respective territories, towns, and citizens, without distinctions of persons or places, the most cordial relationship. [Article 33 provided for recourse to arbitration and not to war after failure of diplomatic negotiations.]

Signed at Buenos Aires, March 9, 1874; ratified with modifications by Argentina, Law #687, September 28, 1874; approved with same modifications by Peru, May 31, 1875; ratified with modifications by Peru, October 29, 1875; ratifications exchanged at Buenos Aires, December 20, 1875; promulgated by Argentina, December 15, 1875; denounced, except Article 1, by Peru, 1885.

Argentina signed and Peru signed and ratified the Treaty of January 29, 1902 (§ 46, *infra*); both signed the Convention of October 18, 1907 (§ 48, *infra*); Argentina signed and Peru adhered to and ratified the Treaty of May 3, 1923 (§ 50, *infra*); and Argentina signed and Peru adhered to the Treaty of October 10, 1933 (§ 55, *infra*).

8. ARGENTINA–URUGUAY

Treaty [8] of general arbitration of all controversies of whatever nature which for any cause may arise between the parties, so far as they do not affect the precepts of the constitution of either country and provided they cannot be solved by direct negotiations; by a tribunal to be constituted for each case, of three judges if not otherwise agreed; the points at issue to be

---

[7] *Trat. de Argentina* (Buenos Aires, 1912), IX, 316–336. William R. Manning, *Arbitration Treaties among the American Nations* (New York, 1924), No. 66, pp. 99–100.

[8] *Trat. de Argentina* (Buenos Aires, 1912), IX, 596– 606. 94 *British and Foreign State Papers* 525–528. *U. S. For. Rel.*, 1899, pp. 9–10. Martens, *Nouv. Rec. Gén. de Traités*, 2ᵉ Sér., XXX, 237–240. *Arch. Dipl.*, LXXXVIII, 161–164; *ibid.*, XCVIII, 306–313.

fixed and the scope of the arbiters' powers determined by the parties; with
no appeal except to the same tribunal before the period set for execution for
forgery of a document or error of fact resulting from the proceedings or documents in the cause; the treaty to remain in force for ten years and be successively renewed for ten-year periods if not denounced six months before
the end of any such period.

Signed at Buenos Aires, June 8, 1899; with additional protocol as to
manner of selecting the third arbiter, signed at Buenos Aires, December 21,
1901; ratified with the modification by Argentina, Law #4044, December
18, 1901; ratified by Uruguay, Law #2624, March 17, 1900; protocol ratified
by Uruguay, Law #2728, December 28, 1901; ratifications exchanged at
Buenos Aires, January 18, 1902; promulgated by Argentina, January 12, 1902.

Argentina signed and Uruguay signed and ratified the Treaty of January 29, 1902 (§ 46, *infra*); both signed the Convention of October 18, 1907
(§ 48, *infra*); Argentina signed and Uruguay signed and ratified the Treaty
of May 3, 1923 (§ 50, *infra*); and both signed the Treaty of October 10, 1933
(§ 55, *infra*).

9. ARGENTINA–VENEZUELA

Treaty [9] of general arbitration of all controversies of whatever nature
which may arise between the parties and have not been able to be solved
by diplomatic means, except those relative to constitutional dispositions in
force in either state and those which in conformity with domestic laws ought
to be decided by the judges and tribunals which such laws provide; the parties to sign a special agreement which shall determine the object of the litigation; by a tribunal to be constituted for each case, of three members if
not otherwise agreed; with no appeal except to the same tribunal before execution if the decision was based on false or erroneous documents or vitiated in
whole or in part by an error of fact resulting from the proceedings or documents in the cause; the treaty to remain in force for five years and be successively renewed for one year at a time if not denounced six months before
the end of any period.

Signed at Caracas, July 22, 1911; ratified by Argentina, Law #11030,
August 27, 1920; ratified by Venezuelan legislature, May 27, 1912; ratified
by Venezuelan executive, Decree #14598, April 4, 1924; ratifications exchanged at Caracas, May 24, 1924.

[9] *Trat. y Conv. Vig. de Argentina* (Buenos Aires, 1925), I, 817–819. *Trat. Pub. de Venezuela* (Caracas, 1925), II, 454–457. *League of Nations Treaty Series*, No. 715, XXVIII, 288–295. 118 *British and Foreign State Papers* 12–14. Martens, *Nouv. Rec. Gén. de Traités*, 3e Sér., XIV, 426–428.

Argentina signed and Venezuela signed and ratified the Treaty of May 3, 1923 (§ 50, *infra*); and Argentina signed and Venezuela adhered to the Treaty of October 10, 1933 (§ 55, *infra*).

BOLIVIA–ARGENTINA

Treaty of February 3, 1902. See § 1, this chap., *supra*.

10. BOLIVIA–BRAZIL

Treaty [10] of general arbitration of controversies which may arise between the parties which it has not been possible to solve by direct negotiations or by any of the other means for amicable solution of international differences, provided such controversies do not turn upon questions which affect the vital interests, the territorial integrity, the independence or the sovereignty and the honor of either of the states; the points at issue to be fixed with due clarity by the parties, who should also determine the scope of the powers of the arbiters; by a tribunal of three to be created by a special agreement; before execution a party which has knowledge of forgery of any document or that the sentence in whole or in part was based on an error of fact may ask revision by the same tribunal; the treaty to remain in force for ten years and be successively renewed for ten-year periods if not denounced six months before the end of any such period.

Signed at Petropolis, June 25, 1909; ratified by Bolivia, November 12, 1910; sanctioned by Brazil, Decree #2396, December 31, 1910; ratified by Brazil, February 3, 1911; ratifications exchanged at La Paz, May 10, 1912; promulgated by Brazil, Decree #10371, July 30, 1913.

Bolivia adhered to and Brazil signed and ratified the Treaty of May 3, 1923 (§ 50, *infra*); Bolivia signed and Brazil signed and ratified the Treaty of January 5, 1929 (§ 53, *infra*), and the Convention of January 5, 1929 (§ 54, *infra*); and Bolivia adhered to and Brazil signed the Treaty of October 10, 1933 (§ 55, *infra*).

11. BOLIVIA–CHILE

There appears to be no treaty of arbitration in existence between these countries.

Bolivia signed and ratified and Chile signed the Convention of October 10, 1907 (§ 48, *infra*); Bolivia adhered to and Chile signed and ratified

[10] *Trat. Vig.* (Bolivia, 1925), I, 171–180. 104 *British and Foreign State Papers* 824–827. Martens, *Nouv. Rec.*   *Gén. de Traités*, 3e Sér., XV, 479–482.

the Treaty of May 3, 1923 (§ 50, *infra*); Bolivia signed and Chile signed and ratified the Treaty of January 5, 1929 (§ 53, *infra*), and the Convention of January 5, 1929 (§ 54, *infra*); and Bolivia adhered to and Chile signed and ratified the Treaty of October 10, 1933 (§ 55, *infra*).

12. BOLIVIA–COLOMBIA

Treaty [11] of full general arbitration of all controversies of whatever nature which shall and may arise between the parties, provided that they shall not be solved by direct diplomatic means, except only such questions as may arise whose decision may be within the ordinary jurisdiction of the Bolivian or Colombian tribunals of justice; the tribunal to be selected from the chiefs of state of the American republics or when thought necessary American judges or experts or, in case of inability to agree, to be the Hague Permanent Court of Arbitration; the parties to make a special agreement in each case to determine the nature of the litigation and the constitution of the tribunal; the treaty to remain in force for ten years and be successively renewed for ten-year periods if not denounced six months before the end of any such period.

Signed at Bogotá, November 13, 1918; ratified by Bolivia, June 28, 1921; ratified by Colombia, Law #61, November 14, 1919; ratifications exchanged at La Paz, February 19, 1923.

Bolivia adhered to and Colombia signed and ratified the Treaty of May 3, 1923 (§ 50, *infra*); and both nations signed the Treaty of January 5, 1929 (§ 53, *infra*), and the Convention of January 5, 1929 (§ 54, *infra*), and adhered to the Treaty of October 10, 1933 (§ 55, *infra*).

13. BOLIVIA–ECUADOR

Treaty [12] of friendship providing that (Article 15) neither party shall lend direct support to the segregation of any portion of the territories of the other, and (Article 18) in case any question or conflict shall arise between the parties, they shall exhaust the means which circumstances suggest to solve them directly through diplomatic agents, and if this is not possible shall submit the controversy to the decision of an arbiter named by them, so that in no event shall they resort to the disastrous recourse of war.

Signed at La Paz, April 17, 1911; ratified by Bolivia, November 4, 1911;

---

[11] *Trat. Vig.* (Bolivia, 1925), I, 257–262. 125 *British and Foreign State Papers* 252–253. Martens, *Nouv. Rec. Gén. de Traités*, 3e Sér., XV, 483–484.

[12] *Trat. Vig.* (Bolivia, 1925), I, 373–382. Martens, *Nouv. Rec. Gén de Traités*, 3e Sér., VIII, 431–434.

ratified by Ecuador, Decr. Leg., October 19, 1912; ratifications exchanged at Quito, May 23, 1913.

Bolivia adhered to and Ecuador signed and ratified the Treaty of May 3, 1923 (§ 50, *infra*); both nations signed the Treaty of January 5, 1929 (§ 53, *infra*); Bolivia signed and Ecuador signed and ratified the Convention of January 5, 1929 (§ 54, *infra*); and both adhered to the Treaty of October 10, 1933 (§ 55, *infra*).

14.   BOLIVIA–PARAGUAY

There appears never to have been any treaty of arbitration between these countries. The boundary protocol [13] signed at Asunción on April 5, 1913, provided in Article 3 that if it should not be possible to make a treaty by direct agreement, the parties should submit the question of boundaries to legal arbitration.

These two nations signed the Treaty of January 29, 1902 (§ 46, *infra*); both signed and ratified the Convention of October 18, 1907 (§ 48, *infra*); Bolivia adhered to and Paraguay signed and ratified the Treaty of May 3, 1923 (§ 50, *infra*); both signed the Treaty of January 5, 1929 (§ 53, *infra*), and the Convention of January 5, 1929 (§ 54, *infra*); and Bolivia adhered to and Paraguay signed the Treaty of October 10, 1933 (§ 55, *infra*).

15.   BOLIVIA–PERU

Treaty [14] of general arbitration of all controversies then pending and which may arise during the existence of the treaty between the parties, whatever may be their nature and causes, provided that it has not been possible to solve them by direct negotiations; the parties to make a special agreement for each case to determine the subject matter of the controversy and fix the points which should be decided and the scope of the powers of the arbiter; the arbiter to be the Permanent Arbitration Tribunal to be established by virtue of the resolutions of the Pan-American Conference then meeting in Mexico, or, before such tribunal is established, the governments of Argentina, Spain, and Mexico, successively; the decision in boundary questions to be in accord with the American principle of the *uti possedetis* of 1810, in the absence of agreement on special rules; with no appeal except to the same tribunal before the period set for execution and within six months of notice of the decision

---

[13] See chap. I, §8, note 10, *supra*.
[14] *Trat. Vig.* (Bolivia, 1925), II, 59–67. *Col. de Actos Int. del Peru* (Lima, 1916), No. 55. 95 *British and For-* *eign State Papers* 1018–1020. *U. S. For. Rel.*, 1902, pp. 891–893. Martens, *Nouv. Rec. Gén de Traités*, 3ᵉ Sér., III, 47–49. *Arch. Dipl.*, 3ᵉ Sér., XCVIII, 34–38.

for forgery of a document or an error of fact resulting from the proceedings or documents in the cause; the treaty to remain in force for ten years and be successively renewed for ten-year periods if not denounced six months before the end of any such period.

Signed at La Paz, November 21, 1901; ratified by Bolivia, December 28, 1903; ratified by Peru, October 10, 1903; ratifications exchanged at La Paz, December 29, 1903.

Bolivia signed and Peru signed and ratified the Treaty of January 29, 1902 (§ 46, *infra*); Bolivia signed and ratified and Peru signed the Convention of October 18, 1907 (§ 48, *infra*); Bolivia adhered to and Peru adhered to and ratified the Treaty of May 3, 1923 (§ 50, *infra*); Bolivia signed and Peru signed and ratified the Treaty of January 5, 1929 (§ 53, *infra*), and the Convention of January 5, 1929 (§ 54, *infra*); and both adhered to the Treaty of October 10, 1933 (§ 55, *infra*).

16. BOLIVIA–URUGUAY

Treaty [15] of obligatory general arbitration of all controversies of whatever nature which for any cause may arise between the parties and which it has not been possible to solve by diplomatic means and, except for a denial of justice, not including questions between a citizen of one party and the other state when the judges or courts of the latter have by its legislation jurisdiction to decide the question; by a chief of state or president of a court or superior tribunal of justice or person notably skilled in the subject matter of the litigation; the parties to sign a special agreement for each case, to determine the arbiter, the extent of his powers, and the subject matter of the litigation; the treaty to remain in force for five years and be successively renewed for five-year periods if not denounced up to one month before the end of any period, and then to remain in force for one year from such denunciation.

Signed at Montevideo, April 27, 1917; ratified by Bolivia, June 9, 1917; ratified by Uruguay, Law #5876, June 25, 1918; ratifications exchanged at La Paz, October 23, 1918.

Bolivia adhered to and Uruguay signed and ratified the Treaty of May 3, 1923 (§ 50, *infra*); both signed the Treaty of January 5, 1929 (§ 53, *infra*); Bolivia signed and Uruguay signed and ratified the Convention of January 5, 1929 (§ 54, *infra*); and Bolivia adhered to and Uruguay signed the Treaty of October 10, 1933 (§ 55, *infra*).

[15] *Trat. Vig.* (Bolivia, 1925), II, 186–192. *Bol. del Min. de Rel. Ext.* (Montevideo), VI (1918), 811–815.   Martens, *Nouv. Rec. Gén. de Traités*, 3e Sér., XX, 20–22.

17. BOLIVIA–VENEZUELA

Treaty [16] of full general arbitration of all controversies of whatever nature which shall and may arise between the parties, provided that they shall not be solved by direct diplomatic means; except only such questions as may arise whose decision may be within the ordinary jurisdiction of the Bolivian or Venezuelan tribunals of justice; the tribunal to be selected from the chiefs of state of the American republics or when thought necessary from American jurists, or, in case of inability to agree, to be the Hague Permanent Court of Arbitration; the parties to make a special agreement in each case to determine the nature of the litigation and the constitution of the tribunal; the treaty to remain in force for ten years and be successively renewed for ten-year periods if not denounced six months before the end of any such period.

Signed at Caracas, April 12, 1919; ratified by Bolivia, June 28, 1921; ratified by Venezuelan legislature, June 9, 1919; ratified by Venezuelan executive, Decree #14290, January 10, 1923; ratifications exchanged at La Paz, April 14, 1923.

Bolivia adhered to and Venezuela signed and ratified the Treaty of May 3, 1923 (§ 50, *infra*); Bolivia signed and Venezuela signed and ratified the Treaty of January 5, 1929 (§ 53, *infra*); both signed the Convention of January 5, 1929 (§ 54, *infra*); and both adhered to the Treaty of October 10, 1933 (§ 55, *infra*).

BRAZIL–ARGENTINA

Treaty of September 7, 1905. See § 2, this chap., *supra*.

BRAZIL–BOLIVIA

Treaty of June 25, 1909. See § 10, this chap., *supra*.

18. BRAZIL–CHILE

Treaty [17] of arbitration of controversies which arise between the parties during the present treaty in which the opposing contentions can be formulated juridically and with respect to which it has not been possible to obtain a friendly solution by direct negotiations; the parties to make in each case a

---

[16] *Trat. Vig.* (Bolivia, 1925), II, 219–222. *Trat. Pub. de Ven.* (Caracas, 1925), II, 580–582. 125 *British and Foreign State Papers* 254–255. Martens, *Nouv. Rec. Gén. de Traités*, 3e Sér., XX, 381–382.

[17] *Recop. de Trat. de Chile* (Santiago, 1908), V, 71–77. 99 *British and Foreign State Papers* 880–882. Martens, *Nouv. Rec. Gén de Traités*, 3e Sér., I, 21–24.

special convention which shall fix the precise object of the litigation and the duration of the power of the arbiter; by one arbiter selected by a friendly power agreed on by the parties; before execution a party which has knowledge of forgery of any document or that the sentence in whole or in part was based on an error of fact may ask revision by the same arbiter; the treaty to remain in force for ten years and thereafter until one year after either party denounces it.

Signed at Rio de Janeiro, May 18, 1899; sanctioned by Brazil, Decree #601, September 6, 1899; ratified by Chile; ratifications exchanged at Santiago, March 7, 1906; promulgated by Brazil, Decree #5965, April 14, 1906; promulgated by Chile, March 7, 1906.

Brazil signed and ratified and Chile signed the Convention of October 18, 1907 (§ 48, *infra*), and the ABC Pact of May 25, 1915 (§ 49, *infra*); both signed and ratified the Treaty of May 3, 1923 (§ 50, *infra*), the Treaty of January 5, 1929 (§ 53, *infra*), and the Convention of January 5, 1929 (§ 54, *infra*); and Brazil signed and Chile signed and ratified the Treaty of October 10, 1933 (§ 55, *infra*).

19. BRAZIL–COLOMBIA

[Treaty of general arbitration.]

Signed at Bogotá, July 7, 1910; ratified by Brazil, February 21, 1911; not ratified by Colombia.

Brazil signed and ratified and Colombia signed the Convention of October 18, 1907 (§ 48, *infra*); both signed and ratified the Treaty of May 3, 1923 (§ 50, *infra*); Brazil signed and ratified and Colombia signed the Treaty of January 5, 1929 (§ 53, *infra*), and the Convention of January 5, 1929 (§ 54, *infra*); and Brazil signed and Colombia adhered to the Treaty of October 10, 1933 (§ 55, *infra*).

20. BRAZIL–ECUADOR

Convention [18] of arbitration of controversies of legal character or relating to the interpretation of existing treaties which may arise between the parties and which it has not been possible to solve by diplomatic means, provided they do not affect the vital interests, the independence or the honor of the parties or put in question the interests of third parties; by the Hague Permanent Court of Arbitration or, if either of the parties prefer, by the chief

---

[18] 103 *British and Foreign State Papers* 386–388. Martens, *Nouv. Rec. Gén. de Traités*, 3ᵉ Sér., VI, 352–355.　　*Arch. Dipl.*, 3ᵉ Sér., CXXV, 8–11.

of a friendly state or by chosen arbiters; the parties to make in each case a special agreement determining clearly the subject matter of the litigation and the scope of the powers of the arbiter or arbiters; the convention to remain in force for five-year periods if not denounced six months before the end of any such period.

Signed at Washington, May 13, 1909; sanctioned by Brazil, Decree #2396, December 31, 1910; ratified by Brazil, March 9, 1911; ratified by Ecuador, Decr. Leg., November 4, 1909; ratifications exchanged at Quito, February 12, 1912; promulgated by Brazil, Decree #9516, April 10, 1912.

These two nations signed and ratified the Treaty of May 3, 1923 (§ 50, *infra*); Brazil signed and ratified and Ecuador signed the Treaty of January 5, 1929 (§ 53, *infra*); both signed and ratified the Convention of January 5, 1929 (§ 54, *infra*); and Brazil signed and Ecuador adhered to the Treaty of October 10, 1933 (§ 55, *infra*).

21. Brazil–Paraguay

Convention [19] of arbitration of controversies which may arise between the parties and which it has not been possible to solve by direct negotiations or by any of the other means of solving amicably international litigations, provided such questions do not affect the vital interests, the territorial integrity, the independence, or the honor of either party; by the Hague Permanent Court of Arbitration, or if agreed by a chief of state or a friendly government or by one or more arbiters; the parties to make in each case a special agreement determining clearly the subject matter of the litigation and the scope of the powers of the arbiter or arbiters; the convention to remain in force for ten years and be successively renewed for one year at a time if not denounced six months before the end of any period.

Signed at Asunción, February 24, 1911; sanctioned by Brazil, Decree #2581, June 17, 1912; ratified by Brazil, August 31, 1914; ratified by Paraguay, Law #43, August 26, 1913; ratifications exchanged at Rio de Janeiro, September 7, 1914; promulgated by Brazil, Decree #11142, September 16, 1914.

These two nations signed and ratified the Treaty of May 3, 1923 (§ 50, *infra*); Brazil signed and ratified and Paraguay signed the Treaty of January 5, 1929 (§ 53, *infra*), and the Convention of January 5, 1929 (§ 54, *infra*); and both signed the Treaty of October 10, 1933 (§ 55, *infra*).

---

[19] 110 *British and Foreign State Papers* 779–781. Martens, *Nouv. Rec. Gén. de Traités*, 3e Sér., IX, 48–51.

22. BRAZIL–PERU

Convention [20] of obligatory general arbitration of all controversies of whatever nature and for whatever cause which may arise between the parties, provided that a direct solution cannot be reached by diplomatic means and, except for a denial of justice, not including cases between a citizen of one party and the other state when the cause is within the ordinary jurisdiction of Peruvian or Brazilian courts; by the Hague Permanent Court of Arbitration or the international court that may be established in the future with the consent or adhesion of Peru and Brazil; with no appeal; the convention to remain in force for five years and be successively renewed for five-year periods if not denounced six months before the end of any such period.

Signed at Rio de Janeiro, July 11, 1918; sanctioned by Brazil, Decree #3619, December 23, 1918; ratified by Brazil, April 26, 1927; approved by Peru Leg., Res. Leg. #4085, May 5, 1920, and March 21, 1927; ratified by Peru Exec., May 30, 1927; ratifications exchanged at Rio de Janeiro, July 28, 1927; promulgated by Brazil, Decree #17870, August 2, 1927.

The prior general arbitration treaty of December 7, 1909,[21] was expressly abrogated by a protocol signed at Rio de Janeiro, July 28, 1927.

Brazil signed and ratified and Peru adhered to and ratified the Treaty of May 3, 1923 (§ 50, *infra*); both signed and ratified the Treaty of January 5, 1929 (§ 53, *infra*), and the Convention of January 5, 1929 (§ 54, *infra*); and Brazil signed and Peru adhered to the Treaty of October 10, 1933 (§ 55, *infra*).

23. BRAZIL–URUGUAY

Convention [22] of obligatory general arbitration of all controversies of whatever nature which may arise between the parties and which it has not been possible to solve by diplomatic means and, except for a denial of justice, not including cases between a citizen of one party and the other state when the judges and courts of the latter are by law competent to try the case; by the chief of a state, the president of a superior court of justice or a person of recognized competence in the matter, or if the parties are unable to agree, by the Hague Permanent Court of Arbitration; a special agreement to be signed

[20] *Mem. del Min. de Rel. Ext. del Peru* (Lima, 1928), Anexos, pp. 11-14. 125 *British and Foreign State Papers* 255-256. Martens, *Nouv. Rec. Gén. de Traités*, 3ᵉ Sér., XX, 378-381. Clunet, *J. du dr. int.*, XLV (1918), 1527.

[21] 127 *British and Foreign State Papers* 147. *Rel. do Min. das Rel. Ext. do Brazil* (Rio de Janeiro, 1928), Annexo A, pp. 144-145. William R. Manning, *Arbitration Treaties among the American Nations* (New York, 1924), No. 221, pp. 450-454.

[22] *Coll. das Leis do Brazil de 1918* (Rio de Janeiro, 1919), II, 642-647. 111 *British and Foreign State Papers* 672-674. Martens, *Nouv. Rec. Gén. de Traités*, 3ᵉ Sér., XX, 374-376.

in each case naming the arbiter and determining the scope of his powers and the object of the litigation; the convention to remain in force for five years and be successively renewed for five-year periods if not denounced one month before the end of any such period.

Signed at Rio de Janeiro, December 27, 1916; sanctioned by Brazil, Decree #3447, December 31, 1917; ratified by Brazil, June 10, 1918; ratified by Uruguay, Law #5624, January 8, 1918; ratifications exchanged at Rio de Janeiro, June 10, 1918; promulgated by Brazil, Decree #13084A, June 27, 1918.

[Treaty of conciliation and obligatory arbitration.]

Signed at Rio de Janeiro, August 22, 1934; not ratified.

These two nations signed and ratified the Treaty of May 3, 1923 (§ 50, *infra*); Brazil signed and ratified and Uruguay signed the Treaty of January 5, 1929 (§ 53, *infra*); both signed and ratified the Convention of January 5, 1929 (§ 54, *infra*); and both signed the Treaty of October 10, 1933 (§ 55, *infra*).

24. BRAZIL–VENEZUELA

Convention [23] of arbitration of controversies of juridical character or relating to the interpretation of existing treaties which may arise between the parties and which it has not been possible to solve by diplomatic means, provided they do not affect the vital interests, the independence, or the honor of the parties, and do not prejudice the interests of a third party, and excluding, by notes exchanged, questions which according to domestic law should be decided by national tribunals; by the Hague Permanent Court of Arbitration or if either of the parties prefer by the chief of a friendly state or by chosen arbiters; the parties to make in each case a special agreement determining clearly the subject matter in litigation and the scope of the powers of the arbiter or arbiters; the convention to remain in force for five years and be successively renewed for one year at a time if not denounced six months before the end of any period.

Signed with exchange of notes at Caracas, April 30, 1909; sanctioned by Brazil, Decree #2396, December 31, 1910; ratified by Brazil, March 6, 1911; ratified by Venezuelan legislature, July 28, 1909; ratified by Venezuelan executive, August 5, 1909; ratifications exchanged at Caracas, January 8, 1912; promulgated by Brazil, Decree #9390, February 28, 1912; promulgated by Venezuela, Decree #11184, January 8, 1912.

[23] *Trat. Pub. de Ven.* (Caracas, 1925), II, 397–399.   *Nouv. Rec. Gén. de Traités*, 3ᵉ Sér., VI, 20–22.
102 *British and Foreign State Papers* 190–193. Martens,

These two nations signed and ratified the Treaty of May 3, 1923 (§ 50, *infra*), and the Treaty of January 5, 1929 (§ 53, *infra*); Brazil signed and ratified and Venezuela signed the Convention of January 5, 1929 (§ 54, *infra*); and Brazil signed and Venezuela adhered to the Treaty of October 10, 1933 (§ 55, *infra*).

CHILE–ARGENTINA

Treaty of May 28, 1902. See § 3, this chap., *supra*.

CHILE–BOLIVIA

No bipartite treaty of arbitration. See § 11, this chap., *supra*.

CHILE–BRAZIL

Treaty of May 18, 1899. See § 18, this chap., *supra*.

25. CHILE–COLOMBIA

Convention [24] of arbitration of controversies which may arise between the parties and which it has not been possible to solve by diplomatic means, excepting those which may affect national sovereignty, honor, or security, the constitutional dispositions of either state, or the interests of another power; by a friendly government, the Hague Permanent Court of Arbitration, or one or more chosen arbiters; the parties to sign in each case a special agreement determining the object of the litigation and the scope of the powers of the arbiter or tribunal; the convention to remain in force for five years, and if not denounced six months before the end of such period to continue in force for one year from the date of any denunciation.

Signed at Bogotá, November 16, 1914; ratified by Chile; ratified by Colombia, Law #14, October 13, 1930; ratifications exchanged at Bogotá, February 14, 1931.

These two nations signed and ratified the Treaty of May 3, 1923 (§ 50, *infra*); both adhered to and ratified the Treaty of August 27, 1928 (§ 52, *infra*); Chile signed and ratified and Colombia signed the Treaty of January 5, 1929 (§ 53, *infra*), and the Convention of January 5, 1929 (§ 54, *infra*); and Chile signed and ratified and Colombia adhered to the Treaty of October 10, 1933 (§ 55, *infra*).

---

[24] *Leyes de Colombia de 1930*, Ed. Ofic. (Bogotá, 1931), pp. 61–63. *League of Nations Treaty Series*, No. 2659, CXIV, 112–116. Martens, *Nouv. Rec. Gén. de Traités*, 3ᵉ Sér., XXV, 491–492.

26.　CHILE–ECUADOR

[Treaty of arbitration.]

Signed at Santiago, July 11, 1908; ratified by Ecuador, Decr. Leg., December 4, 1908; not ratified by Chile.

Chile signed and Ecuador signed and ratified the Convention of October 18, 1907 (§ 48, *infra*); both signed and ratified the Treaty of May 3, 1923 (§ 50, *infra*); Chile signed and ratified and Ecuador signed the Treaty of January 5, 1929 (§ 53, *infra*); both signed and ratified the Convention of January 5, 1929 (§ 54, *infra*); and Chile signed and ratified and Ecuador adhered to the Treaty of October 10, 1933 (§ 55, *infra*).

27.　CHILE–PARAGUAY

There appears to be no treaty of arbitration in existence between these countries.

Chile signed and Paraguay signed and ratified the Convention of October 18, 1907 (§ 48, *infra*); both signed and ratified the Treaty of May 3, 1923 (§ 50, *infra*); both adhered to and ratified the Treaty of August 27, 1928 (§ 52, *infra*); and Chile signed and ratified and Paraguay signed the Treaty of January 5, 1929 (§ 53, *infra*), the Convention of January 5, 1929 (§ 54, *infra*), and the Treaty of October 10, 1933 (§ 55, *infra*).

28.　CHILE–PERU

[Treaty [25] of friendship, commerce, and navigation for reciprocal enjoyment and advantages provides that (Article 17) if any unfortunate differences should cause an interruption in friendly relations, and after having exhausted all means of reaching an amicable and satisfactory settlement, the parties should not be able to reach an agreement for their common good, they shall submit such differences by common agreement to the arbitration of a third power to avoid a final break.]

Signed at Lima, December 22, 1876; ratified by Peru, February 6, 1877; not ratified by Chile.

There appears to be no treaty of arbitration in existence between these countries.

These two nations signed the Convention of October 18, 1907 (§ 48, *infra*); Chile signed and ratified and Peru adhered to and ratified the Treaty of

---

[25] Ricardo Aranda, *Col. de Trat. del Peru*, IV, 116–124. William R. Manning, *Arbitration Treaties among the Amer-* ican Nations (New York, 1924), No. 75, p. 113.

May 3, 1923 (§ 50, *infra*); both adhered to and ratified the Treaty of August 27, 1928 (§ 52, *infra*); both signed and ratified the Treaty of January 5, 1929 (§ 53, *infra*), and the Convention of January 5, 1929 (§ 54, *infra*); and Chile signed and ratified and Peru adhered to the Treaty of October 10, 1933 (§ 55, *infra*).

29.   CHILE–URUGUAY

Treaty [26] for settlement of disputes; all questions which in the future may arise between the parties and which it has not been possible to solve by diplomatic means, except any question which might affect the sovereignty, honor, or vital interests of either party, the dispositions of their fundamental charters, or the interest of a third power, to be submitted for investigation and report to an international commission of five members, the parties not to declare war or initiate hostilities during the period of investigation and before exhausting all the resources provided in the treaty; if within six months after the report the two governments cannot arrive at an amicable solution, the question to be submitted to the Hague Permanent Court of Arbitration; the treaty to remain in force for five years and be successively renewed for five-year periods so long as neither party has communicated to the other its denunciation.

Signed at Montevideo, February 27, 1915; ratified by Chile, 1915; ratified by Uruguay Law #5355, December 13, 1915; ratifications exchanged at Montevideo, December 31, 1915; promulgated by Chile, Law #3054, January 14, 1916.

These two nations signed and ratified the Treaty of May 3, 1923 (§ 50, *infra*); Chile signed and ratified and Uruguay signed the Treaty of January 5, 1929 (§ 53, *infra*); both signed and ratified the Convention of January 5, 1929 (§ 54, *infra*); and Chile signed and ratified and Uruguay signed the Treaty of October 10, 1933 (§ 55, *infra*).

30.   CHILE–VENEZUELA

There appears to be no treaty of arbitration in existence between these countries.

Chile signed and Venezuela signed and ratified the Convention of October 18, 1907 (§ 48, *infra*); both signed and ratified the Treaty of May 3, 1923 (§ 50, *infra*); both adhered to and ratified the Treaty of August 27, 1928 (§ 52,

---

[26] *Recop. de Trat. de Chile* (Santiago, 1916), VII, 182–188; 109 *British and Foreign State Papers* 885–887.

infra); both signed and ratified the Treaty of January 5, 1929 (§ 53, *infra*); Chile signed and ratified and Venezuela signed the Convention of January 5, 1929 (§ 54, *infra*); and Chile signed and ratified and Venezuela adhered to the Treaty of October 10, 1933 (§ 55, *infra*).

COLOMBIA–ARGENTINA

Treaty of January 20, 1912. See § 4, this chap., *supra*.

COLOMBIA–BOLIVIA

Treaty of November 13, 1918. See § 12, this chap., *supra*.

COLOMBIA–BRAZIL

No bipartite treaty of arbitration. See § 19, this chap., *supra*.

COLOMBIA–CHILE

Treaty of November 16, 1914. See § 25, this chap., *supra*.

31. COLOMBIA–ECUADOR

Treaty [27] of friendship, commerce, and navigation, declaring that (Article 1) there shall be peace and perpetual friendship between the parties in the whole extent of their territories and possessions; and (Article 3) the parties solemnly promise not ever to appeal to the sad recourse of arms before exhausting that of negotiation nor until due satisfaction is expressly denied after a friendly and neutral power chosen as arbiter shall have decided as to the justice of the demand; the treaty to be perpetual as to Articles 1 and 3.

Signed at Quito, August 10, 1905; ratified by Colombia, Law #9, April 9, 1907; Exec., June 21, 1907; ratified by Ecuador, Decr. Leg., October 3, 1905; ratifications exchanged at Quito, October 24, 1907; Article 11 denounced by Colombia, October 16, 1929.

Colombia signed and Ecuador signed and ratified the Convention of October 18, 1907 (§ 48, *infra*); both signed and ratified the Treaty of May 3, 1923 (§ 50, *infra*); both signed the Treaty of January 5, 1929 (§ 53, *infra*);

[27] *Trat. Pub. de Col.* (Bogotá, 1913), 2ᵉ Apen., pp. 30–36. *Leyes de Colombia de 1907* (Bogotá, 1910), pp. 30–41. 99 *British and Foreign State Papers* 1012–1019.

Martens, *Nouv. Rec. Gén. de Traités*, 3ᵉ Sér., II, 265–272; *ibid.*, V, 856–863.

Colombia signed and Ecuador signed and ratified the Convention of January 5, 1929 (§ 54, *infra*); and both adhered to the Treaty of October 10, 1933 (§ 55, *infra*).

32. COLOMBIA–PARAGUAY

There appears to be no treaty of arbitration in existence between these countries.

These two nations signed the Convention of October 18, 1907 (§ 48, *infra*); both signed and ratified the Treaty of May 3, 1923 (§ 50, *infra*); both adhered to and ratified the Treaty of August 27, 1928 (§ 52, *infra*); both signed the Treaty of January 5, 1929 (§ 53, *infra*), and the Convention of January 5, 1929 (§ 54, *infra*); and Colombia adhered to and Paraguay signed the Treaty of October 10, 1933 (§ 55, *infra*).

33. COLOMBIA–PERU

[Treaty [28] of friendship, commerce, and navigation declaring that (Article 1) the peace and friendship happily maintained and cultivated for a long time between the parties shall be perpetually firm and inviolable; and (Article 30) the parties agree not to appeal to arms before exhausting the means of negotiation nor so long as there is hope of obtaining thereby due satisfaction; the government which thinks itself aggrieved to call on the other to join in submitting the question to the decision of a third chosen as arbiter from five governments previously designated; the treaty to be perpetual as to Article 1, and as to the rest to remain in force for ten years and if not denounced one year before the end of such period to continue in force for one year from the date of any denunciation.]

Signed at Bogotá, August 6, 1898; ratified by Colombia, Law #45, December 11, 1898; approved by Peru, October 26, 1903; approval repealed by Colombia, Law #61, December 13, 1909.

[Treaty [29] of general arbitration of all controversies of whatever nature which for any cause may arise between the parties and which it has not been possible to solve by diplomatic means, excepting on questions which affect national independence and honor; by His Holiness the Supreme Roman Pontiff, or in case of his declination, the president of Argentina; the parties to make a special agreement in each case to determine the precise object of the contro-

---

[28] *Leyes Colombianas, 1898*, Ed. Ofic. (Bogotá, 1899), pp. 49–60. *Leyes de 1909* (Bogotá, 1910), pp. 389–399.

[29] Signed at Bogotá, Sept. 12, 1905; ratified by Colombia, Law #8, Apr. 25, 1907; not approved by Peru. *Leyes de Colombia de 1907* (Bogotá, 1910), pp. 26–29.

versy and relative points and circumstances which they think it desirable to note; the sentence to be inappealable except that before execution revision may be asked of the same arbiter if the sentence resulted from a false document or in whole or in part was based on an error of fact, positive or negative; the treaty to remain in force for ten years and if not denounced six months before its expiration to be considered renewed for another period of ten years and so successively.]

These two nations signed the Convention of October 18, 1907 (§ 48, *infra*); Colombia signed and ratified and Peru adhered to and ratified the Treaty of May 3, 1923 (§ 50, *infra*); both adhered to and ratified the Treaty of August 27, 1928 (§ 52, *infra*); Colombia signed and Peru signed and ratified the Treaty of January 5, 1929 (§ 53, *infra*), and the Convention of January 5, 1929 (§ 54, *infra*); and both adhered to the Treaty of October 10, 1933 (§ 55, *infra*).

34.   COLOMBIA–URUGUAY

[Treaty [30] of general arbitration of all controversies of whatever nature which for any cause may arise between the parties and which it has not been possible to solve by diplomatic means, and, except for a denial of justice, not including questions between a citizen of one party and the other state when the judicial authorities of the latter have by its laws jurisdiction to decide the question; by the chief of state of one of the American republics or a tribunal of American judges or experts or, in case of inability to agree, to the Hague Permanent Court of Arbitration; the parties to make a special agreement in each case to designate the arbiter and to determine the extent of his mandate and the subject matter of the litigation; the treaty to remain in force for five years and if not denounced one month before the end of that period to be successively renewed for five-year periods and remain in force for one year from any denunciation.]

Signed at Bogotá, August 25, 1918; ratified by Colombia, Law #21, September 25, 1918; not ratified by Uruguay.

These two nations signed and ratified the Treaty of May 3, 1923 (§ 50, *infra*); both signed the Treaty of January 5, 1929 (§ 53, *infra*); Colombia signed and Uruguay signed and ratified the Convention of January 5, 1929 (§ 54, *infra*); and Colombia adhered to and Uruguay signed the Treaty of October 10, 1933 (§ 55, *infra*).

[30] *Leyes de Colombia, 1918* (Bogotá, 1919), pp. 33–34.

35. Colombia–Venezuela

[Treaty [31] of peace, friendship, and defensive alliance providing (Article 1) for an inalterable peace and a perpetual friendship between the parties as well as between their citizens; (Article 6) the parties uphold as invariable rules of their public law the principle of the *uti possidetis*, which excludes conquest, and the principle of arbitration which is the safeguard of international peace; and (Article 9) the parties agree to resolve every controversy whatever which might arise between them by the means of conciliation, and if that should not be possible, to submit the question to the decision of an arbiter power; the treaty to remain in force for twenty years and be renewable.]

Signed at Bogotá, November 21, 1896; not ratified.

Colombia signed and Venezuela signed and ratified the Convention of October 18, 1907 (§ 48, *infra*); both signed and ratified the Treaty of May 3, 1923 (§ 50, *infra*); both adhered to and ratified the Treaty of Aug. 27, 1928 (§ 52, *infra*); Colombia signed and Venezuela signed and ratified the Treaty of January 5, 1929 (§ 53, *infra*); both signed the Convention of January 5, 1929 (§ 54, *infra*); and both adhered to the Treaty of October 10, 1933 (§ 55, *infra*).

Ecuador–Argentina

Treaty of July 12, 1911. See § 5, this chap., *supra*.

Ecuador–Bolivia

Treaty of April 17, 1911. See § 13, this chap., *supra*.

Ecuador–Brazil

Treaty of May 13, 1909. See § 20, this chap., *supra*.

Ecuador–Chile

No bipartite treaty of arbitration. See § 26, this chap., *supra*.

Ecuador–Colombia

Treaty of August 10, 1905. See § 31, this chap., *supra*.

[31] *Rev. de dr. int. et de lég. comp.*, XXIX (1897), 669-671.

36. ECUADOR–PARAGUAY

There appears to be no treaty of arbitration in existence between these countries.

These two nations signed and ratified the Convention of October 18, 1907 (§ 48, *infra*), and the Treaty of May 3, 1923 (§ 50, *infra*); both signed the Treaty of January 5, 1929 (§ 53, *infra*); Ecuador signed and ratified and Paraguay signed the Convention of January 5, 1929 (§ 54, *infra*); and Ecuador adhered to and Paraguay signed the Treaty of October 10, 1933 (§ 55, *infra*).

37. ECUADOR–PERU

There appears to be no treaty of arbitration in existence between these countries.

Ecuador signed and ratified and Peru signed the Convention of October 18, 1907 (§ 48, *infra*); Ecuador signed and ratified and Peru adhered to and ratified the Treaty of May 3, 1923 (§ 50, *infra*); Ecuador signed and Peru signed and ratified the Treaty of January 5, 1929 (§ 53, *infra*); both signed and ratified the Convention of January 5, 1929 (§ 54, *infra*); and both adhered to the Treaty of October 10, 1933 (§ 55, *infra*).

38. ECUADOR–URUGUAY

There appears to be no treaty of arbitration in existence between these countries.

Ecuador signed and ratified and Uruguay signed the Convention of October 18, 1907 (§ 48, *infra*); both signed and ratified the Treaty of May 3, 1923 (§ 50, *infra*); both signed the Treaty of January 5, 1929 (§ 53, *infra*); both signed and ratified the Convention of January 5, 1929 (§ 54, *infra*); and Ecuador adhered to and Uruguay signed the Treaty of October 10, 1933 (§ 55, *infra*).

39. ECUADOR–VENEZUELA

Treaty [32] of arbitration of any question which may arise between the parties, after exhaustion of the means which the circumstances suggest for solving directly through their diplomatic agents; if this should not be possible,

---

[32] *Anuario de Leg. Ecuat.*, Pub. Ofic. (Quito, 1922), I, 143-145. *Trat. Pub. de Ven.* (Caracas, 1927), III, 7-8. 118 *British and Foreign State Papers* 196-197. *Rev. de Der. Int.* (Havana), IV (1923), 471-472. Martens, *Nouv. Rec. Gén. de Traités*, 3e Sér., XX, 382-384.

by one arbiter to be named or, if the parties cannot agree, by three, the third to be named by the president of Brazil; arbitration not to be obligatory for questions which affect the independence, the national honor, or the vital interests of the parties or of either of them, but such exception in no case to include pecuniary claims, controversies relating to the interpretation and application of pacts referring to matters of a class exclusively juridical, administrative, economic, commercial, or of navigation, and those originating in a denial of justice; the parties to make a special agreement in each case to name the arbiter or arbiters and to determine the subject matter of the litigation; no period for duration of the treaty stated.

Signed at Quito, May 24, 1921; ratified by Ecuador, Decr. Leg. September 24, 1921; ratified by Venezuelan legislature, June 29, 1922; ratified by Venezuelan executive, Decree #14272, December 9, 1922; ratifications exchanged at Quito, March 16, 1923.

These two nations signed and ratified the Treaty of May 3, 1923 (§ 50, *infra*); Ecuador signed and Venezuela signed and ratified the Treaty of January 5, 1929 (§ 53, *infra*); Ecuador signed and ratified and Venezuela signed the Convention of January 5, 1929 (§ 54, *infra*); and both adhered to the Treaty of October 10, 1933 (§ 55, *infra*).

PARAGUAY–ARGENTINA

Treaty of November 6, 1899. See § 6, this chap., *supra*.

PARAGUAY–BOLIVIA

No bipartite treaty of arbitration. See § 14, this chap., *supra*.

PARAGUAY–BRAZIL

Treaty of February 24, 1911. See § 21, this chap., *supra*.

PARAGUAY–CHILE

No bipartite treaty of arbitration. See § 27, this chap., *supra*.

PARAGUAY–COLOMBIA

No bipartite treaty of arbitration. See § 32, this chap., *supra*.

PARAGUAY–ECUADOR

No bipartite treaty of arbitration. See § 36, this chap., *supra*.

40. PARAGUAY–PERU

[Treaty [33] of friendship and commerce, declaring that (Article 1) the peace and friendship which have always existed between the parties shall be perpetually firm and inviolable; and providing that (Article 2) any controversy which may arise between the parties over the interpretation of existing or future treaties or points not foreseen in such pacts shall be submitted to an arbiter agreed upon; with no appeal; the provision of Article 1 to be perpetual, and the rest of the treaty to remain in force for ten years and if not denounced one year before the end of such period to continue in force for one year from the date of any denunciation.]

Signed at Lima, May 18, 1903; not ratified.

[Treaty of friendship and arbitration.]

Signed July 24, 1904; not ratified.

Paraguay signed and Peru signed and ratified the Treaty of January 29, 1902 (§ 46, *infra*); Paraguay signed and ratified and Peru signed the Convention of October 18, 1907 (§ 48, *infra*); Paraguay signed and ratified and Peru adhered to and ratified the Treaty of May 3, 1923 (§ 50, *infra*); both adhered to and ratified the Treaty of August 27, 1928 (§ 52, *infra*); Paraguay signed and Peru signed and ratified the Treaty of January 5, 1929 (§ 53, *infra*), and the Convention of January 5, 1929 (§ 54, *infra*); and Paraguay signed and Peru adhered to the Treaty of October 10, 1933 (§ 55, *infra*).

41. PARAGUAY–URUGUAY

Treaty [34] of peace, friendship, and recognition of debt declaring that (Article 1) there shall be perpetual peace between the parties and providing that (Article 8) any questions of a grave character and of a nature to affect friendly relations before resort to extreme means shall be submitted to the arbitral judgment of one or more friendly powers; no period for duration of the treaty stated.

Signed at Asunción, April 20, 1883; ratified by Paraguay, September 25,

---

[33] *Col. de Trat. del Peru* (Lima, 1907), X, 631–635.
[34] *Col. de Trat. del Uruguay* (Montevideo, 1925), III, 249–252. 74 *British and Foreign State Papers* 696–698. Martens, *Nouv. Rec. Gén. de Traités*, 2ᵉ Sér., IX, 751–752.

Arch. Dipl., 2ᵉ Sér., XIII, 159–160. William R. Manning, *Arbitration Treaties among the American Nations* (New York, 1924), No. 89, pp. 132–133.

1883; ratified by Uruguay, Law #1659, September 21, 1883; ratifications exchanged at Montevideo, November 24, 1883.

[Treaty of general obligatory arbitration.]

Ratified by Uruguay, Law #7376, June 17, 1921; not ratified by Paraguay.

Paraguay signed and Uruguay signed and ratified the Treaty of January 29, 1902 (§ 46, *infra*); Paraguay signed and ratified and Uruguay signed the Convention of October 18, 1907 (§ 48, *infra*); both signed and ratified the Treaty of May 3, 1923 (§ 50, *infra*); both signed the Treaty of January 5, 1929 (§ 53, *infra*); Paraguay signed and Uruguay signed and ratified the Convention of January 5, 1929 (§ 54, *infra*); and both signed the Treaty of October 10, 1933 (§ 55, *infra*).

42. PARAGUAY–VENEZUELA

There appears to be no treaty of arbitration in existence between these countries.

These two nations signed and ratified the Convention of October 18, 1907 (§ 48, *infra*), and the Treaty of May 3, 1923 (§ 50, *infra*); both adhered to and ratified the Treaty of August 27, 1928 (§ 52, *infra*); Paraguay signed and Venezuela signed and ratified the Treaty of January 5, 1929 (§ 53, *infra*); both signed the Convention of January 5, 1929 (§ 54, *infra*); and Paraguay signed and Venezuela adhered to the Treaty of October 10, 1933 (§ 55, *infra*).

PERU–ARGENTINA

Treaty of March 9, 1874, Article 1 only. See § 7, this chap., *supra*.

PERU–BOLIVIA

Treaty of November 21, 1901. See § 15, this chap., *supra*.

PERU–BRAZIL

Treaty of July 11, 1918. See § 22, this chap., *supra*.

PERU–CHILE

No bipartite treaty of arbitration. See § 28, this chap., *supra*.

PERU–COLOMBIA

Treaty of August 6, 1908. See § 33, this chap., *supra*.

PERU–ECUADOR

No bipartite treaty of arbitration. See § 37, this chap., *supra*.

PERU–PARAGUAY

No bipartite treaty of arbitration. See § 40, this chap., *supra*.

43.   PERU–URUGUAY

Treaty [35] of obligatory general arbitration of all controversies of whatever nature which for any cause may arise between the parties and which it has not been possible to solve amicably by direct diplomatic negotiations, and, except for a denial of justice, not including questions between a citizen of one party and the other state when the judges and courts of the latter have by its legislation jurisdiction to decide the questions; by a chief of state or president of a court of justice or of an institution officially recognized or person notably skilled in the subject matter of the litigation; the parties to sign a special agreement for each case, to determine the arbiter, the extent of his powers, and the subject matter of the litigation; the treaty to remain in force for five years and be successively renewed for five-year periods if not denounced up to one month before the end of any period, and then to remain in force for one year from such denunciation.

Signed at Lima, July 18, 1917; approved by Peru, Res. Leg. #4089, May 5, 1920; ratified by Peru Exec. October 23, 1921; approved by Uruguay, Leg. Law #5874, June 25, 1918; ratified by Uruguay Exec. December 26, 1921; ratifications exchanged at Lima, February 15, 1922; promulgated by Uruguay, March 7, 1922.

Peru adhered to and ratified and Uruguay signed and ratified the Treaty of May 3, 1923 (§ 50, *infra*); Peru signed and ratified and Uruguay signed the Treaty of January 5, 1929 (§ 53, *infra*); both signed and ratified the Convention of January 5, 1929 (§ 54, *infra*); and Peru adhered to and Uruguay signed the Treaty of October 10, 1933 (§ 55, *infra*).

[35] *League of Nations Treaty Series*, No. 384, XIV, 359–365. 114 *British and Foreign State Papers* 912–913. Martens, *Nouv. Rec. Gén. de Traités*, 3e Sér., XX, 22–24.

44. Peru–Venezuela

Treaty [36] of general arbitration of any international disagreement between the parties, after exhaustion of all efforts to solve it peacefully and directly; if this should not be attainable, by one or more arbiters named by the parties; excluding questions which affect the independence, the national honor, or the vital interests of the parties, or of either of them, but such exceptions not to include pecuniary claims, whatever their origin, controversies relating to the interpretation and application of pacts referring to matters of a class exclusively juridical, administrative, economic, commercial, or of navigation, and those originating in a denial of justice; the parties to make a special agreement in each case to determine the arbiter or arbiters and the subject matter of the litigation; no period for duration of the treaty stated.

Signed at Lima, March 14, 1923; ratified by Peru, Res. Leg. #4934, January 28, 1924; ratified by Venezuela, Leg., July 3, 1923; ratified by Venezuela, Exec., Decree #14587, February 20, 1924; ratifications exchanged at Lima, August 9, 1924.

Peru adhered to and ratified and Venezuela signed and ratified the Treaty of May 3, 1923 (§ 50, *infra*); both adhered to and ratified the Treaty of August 27, 1928 (§ 52, *infra*); both signed and ratified the Treaty of January 5, 1929 (§ 53, *infra*); Peru signed and ratified and Venezuela signed the Convention of January 5, 1929 (§ 54, *infra*); and both adhered to the Treaty of October 10, 1933 (§ 55, *infra*).

Uruguay–Argentina

Treaty of June 8, 1899. See § 8, this chap., *supra*.

Uruguay–Bolivia

Treaty of April 27, 1917. See § 16, this chap., *supra*.

Uruguay–Brazil

Treaty of December 27, 1916. See § 23, this chap., *supra*.

Uruguay–Chile

Treaty of February 27, 1915. See § 29, this chap., *supra*.

---

[36] *Trat. Pub. de Ven.* (Caracas, 1927), III, 50–51. 122 *British and Foreign State Papers* 1020–1021. Martens, *Nouv.* *Rec. Gén. de Traités*, 3e Sér., XX, 384–385.

Uruguay–Colombia

No bipartite treaty of arbitration. See § 34, this chap., *supra*.

Uruguay–Ecuador

No bipartite treaty of arbitration. See § 38, this chap., *supra*.

Uruguay–Paraguay

Treaty of April 20, 1883. See § 41, this chap., *supra*.

Uruguay–Peru

Treaty of July 18, 1917. See § 43, this chap., *supra*.

45. Uruguay–Venezuela

Treaty [37] of obligatory general arbitration of all controversies of whatever nature which for any cause may arise between the parties, including those relating to the interpretation or execution of the present treaty, provided they cannot be solved by direct negotiation, and, except for a denial of justice, not including questions between a citizen of one party and the other state when the judges or courts of the latter have by its legislation jurisdiction to decide the question; by a chief of state of one of the Spanish-American republics or a president of a Spanish-American court or tribunal of justice, or a tribunal of Uruguayan, Venezuelan, or Spanish-American judges and experts, or if unable to agree, by the Permanent Court of International Justice; the parties to make a special agreement in each case to determine the arbiter, the scope of his powers, and the subject matter of the litigation; the treaty to remain in force for ten years and if not denounced twelve months before the end of such period to continue in force for one year from the date of any denunciation.

Signed at Montevideo, February 28, 1923; ratified by Uruguay, Law #7815, January 23, 1925; ratified by Venezuela, Leg., July 4, 1923; ratified by Venezuela, Exec., Decree #14867, January 27, 1925; ratifications exchanged at Montevideo, June 16, 1925; promulgated by Uruguay June 18, 1925.

[37] *Comp. de Leyes y Decr. del Uruguay* (Montevideo, 1930), LII, 224–226. *Trat. Pub. de Ven.* (Caracas, 1927), III, 48–50. *League of Nations Treaty Series*, No. 942, XXXVI, 452–456; *ibid.*, LXIII, 431. 120 *British and Foreign State Papers* 983–984. Martens, *Nouv. Rec. Gén. de Traités*, 3e Sér., XIV, 675–676.

These two nations signed and ratified the Treaty of May 3, 1923 (§ 50, *infra*); Uruguay signed and Venezuela signed and ratified the Treaty of January 5, 1929 (§ 53, *infra*); Uruguay signed and ratified and Venezuela signed the Convention of January 5, 1929 (§ 54, *infra*); and Uruguay signed and Venezuela adhered to the Treaty of October 10, 1933 (§ 55, *infra*).

Venezuela–Argentina

Treaty of July 22, 1911. See § 9, this chap., *supra*.

Venezuela–Bolivia

Treaty of April 12, 1919. See § 17, this chap., *supra*.

Venezuela–Brazil

Treaty of April 30, 1909. See § 24, this chap., *supra*.

Venezuela–Chile

No bipartite treaty of arbitration. See § 30, this chap., *supra*.

Venezuela–Colombia

No bipartite treaty of arbitration. See § 35, this chap., *supra*.

Venezuela–Ecuador

Treaty of May 24, 1921. See § 39, this chap., *supra*.

Venezuela–Paraguay

No bipartite treaty of arbitration. See § 42, this chap., *supra*.

Venezuela–Peru

Treaty of March 14, 1923. See § 44, this chap., *supra*.

Venezuela–Uruguay

Treaty of February 28, 1923. See § 45, this chap., *supra*.

C. MULTIPARTITE TREATIES

46. SECOND INTERNATIONAL CONFERENCE OF AMERICAN STATES

Treaty of arbitration of all controversies which exist or may exist between the parties and which cannot be solved by diplomatic means, provided that in the exclusive judgment of the interested nations such controversies do not affect either independence or national honor; controversies as to boundaries not to be considered as affecting independence or national honor; by the Hague Permanent Court of Arbitration unless any of the parties prefers a specially organized tribunal; in force when three signatory states notify Mexico of their approval; no period for duration of the treaty stated; denunciation to affect only nation denouncing and after one year.

Signed at Mexico City, January 29, 1902, among others by Argentina, Bolivia, Paraguay, Peru, and Uruguay; in force, April 1903.

	RATIFIED
Argentina	Signed, not ratified
Bolivia	May 12, 1904
Paraguay	Signed, not ratified
Peru	Oct. 10, 1903
Uruguay	Law #2777, Oct. 2, 1902
	Exec. April 15, 1903

Col. de Trat. del Uruguay (Montevideo, 1926), IV, 465–474. *Comp. de Leyes y Decr. del Uruguay* (Montevideo, 1930), XXIV, 355–360. 95 *British and Foreign State Papers* 1009–1014. Martens, *Nouv. Rec. Gén. de Traités*, 2e Sér., XXXI, 253–257; *ibid.*, 3e Sér., VI, 149–157. *Arch. Dipl.*, XCVIII, 285–293.

47. THIRD INTERNATIONAL CONFERENCE OF AMERICAN STATES

Resolution ratifying adherence to the principle of arbitration and recommending to the nations at the Conference that their delegates to the Second Peace Conference at The Hague be instructed to endeavor to secure by the said assembly, of world-wide character, the celebration of a general arbitration convention, so effective and definite that, meriting the approval of the civilized world, it shall be accepted and put in force by every nation.

Signed at Rio de Janeiro, August 7, 1906, by Argentina, Bolivia, Brazil, Chile, Colombia, Ecuador, Paraguay, Peru, and Uruguay. (Venezuela was not represented at the Conference.)

Martens, *Nouv. Rec. Gén. de Traités*, 3e Sér., VI, 230–232.

48.   Second Hague Peace Conference

Convention for the pacific settlement of international disputes by good offices, mediation, inquiry commissions, and arbitration in questions of a juridical nature, with general or special agreements, and creation of the Permanent Court of Arbitration; ratifications to be deposited at The Hague; no period for duration of the convention stated; denunciation to affect only nation denouncing and after one year.

Signed (No. 1) at The Hague October 18, 1907, among others by Argentina, Bolivia, Brazil, Chile, Colombia, Ecuador, Paraguay, Peru, Uruguay, and Venezuela; in force, January 25, 1908.

	RATIFIED	DEPOSITED	PROMULGATED
Argentina	Signed, not ratified		
Bolivia	Nov. 24, 1908	Nov. 27, 1909	
Brazil	Decr. #2395, Dec. 31, 1910 (Jan. 5, 1914, with reservation)		Decr. #10719 Feb. 4, 1914
Chile	Signed with reservation, not ratified		
Colombia	Signed, not ratified		
Ecuador	Signed; approved, Decr. Leg., Oct. 10, 1914		
Paraguay	Law #1299, Jan. 16, 1933; Exec., Apr. 25, 1933		
Peru	Signed, not ratified		
Uruguay	Signed, not ratified (1928)		
Venezuela	Approved, May 23, 1911, with reservation; ratified, June 13, 1911		

Col. de Trat. Int. del Uruguay (Montevideo, 1928), V, 197–235. 100 *British and Foreign State Papers* 298–314. *U. S. For. Rel.*, 1907, Part 2, pp. 1181–1199. *Hague Peace Conf., Proc.* (New York, 1920), I, 599–615, 698. Martens, *Nouv. Rec. Gén. de Traités*, 3ᵉ Sér., III, 360–413. *Arch. Dipl.*, 3ᵉ Sér., CV, 53–68.

49.   ABC Pact

[Treaty of general arbitration of controversies on whatever questions which may arise between the three parties or any two of them and which recourse to diplomacy or arbitration in accordance with existing treaties has not been able to solve; by a permanent commission of three, one to be named by each state; the treaty to remain in force for one year after denunciation by any party.]

Signed at Buenos Aires, May 25, 1915, by Argentina, Brazil, and Chile; approved by Brazil, Decr. #3019, November 10, 1915; not ratified by Argentina or Chile.

Alejandro Alvarez, *La Grande Guerre Europeenne et la Neutralité du Chili* (Paris, 1915), pp. 67–74. Clunet, *J. du dr. int.*, XLII (1915), 950–951; *ibid.*, XLV (1918), 1606–1608. *Rev. gen. de dr. int. pub.*, XXII (1915), 475–479.

50. Fifth International Conference of American States

Treaty (Gondra) to avoid or prevent conflicts between the American states; all controversies which for any cause whatsoever may arise between two or more of the parties and which it has been impossible to settle through diplomatic channels or to submit to arbitration in accordance with existing treaties; to be submitted to a commission of inquiry of five American members; ratifications to be deposited with Chile; the treaty to remain in force indefinitely; a denunciation to take effect as regards the party denouncing only, one year after notification thereof.

Signed at Santiago, May 3, 1923, among others by Argentina, Brazil, Chile, Colombia, Ecuador, Paraguay (by Manuel Gondra, minister of foreign relations, ex-president), Uruguay, and Venezuela; and Bolivia and Peru later acceded; in force according to ratifications.

	RATIFIED	DEPOSITED	PROMULGATED
Bolivia, adhered	Aug. 31, 1927 (not ratified)		
Brazil	Decree #4807, Jan. 12, 1924	Oct. 8, 1924	Decr. #16685, Nov. 26, 1924
Chile	Decr. Leg. #547, Sept. 22, 1925	Sept. 23, 1925	
Colombia	Leg. Law #13, Oct. 13, 1930; Exec., Nov. 5, 1931		
Ecuador	Decr. Leg., Jan. 19, 1929	Mar. 6, 1929	
Paraguay	Law #639, July 26, 1924; Exec., May 20, 1925	June 23, 1925	
Peru, adhered	July 30, 1928	Dec. 26, 1928	
Uruguay	Law #8163, Dec. 23, 1927	Apr. 18, 1928	
Venezuela	Leg., June 4, 1924; Exec., Decree #15246, Oct. 28, 1924	July 17, 1925	

League of Nations Treaty Series, No. 831, XXXIII, 26–45; *ibid.*, LXXXVIII, 323. 122 *British and Foreign State Papers* 53–57. *Trat. Pub. de Ven.* (Caracas, 1927), II, 68–74. 44 *U. S. Stat. L.* III, 2527–2546. *U. S. Treaty Series*, No. 752. Manley O. Hudson, *Int. Legislation* (Washington, 1931), II, 1006–1014. *Amer. J. of Int. Law*, XXI (1927), Supp., 107–113. *Rev. de Der. Int.* (Havana), V (1924), 108–113. V. B. Galeano, "The Gondra Treaty," *Trans. Grotius Soc.*, XV (1930), 1–15. Manley O. Hudson, *By Pacific Means* (New Haven, 1935), pp. 147–152.

51.   Sixth International Conference of American States

Resolution declaring that the American republics adopt obligatory arbitration as the means to be employed for the pacific solution of their international differences of juridical character; and that they should meet at Washington within one year in a conference of conciliation and arbitration.

Adopted at Habana, February 18, 1928, and signed February 20, 1928, among others by Argentina, Bolivia, Brazil, Chile, Colombia, Ecuador, Paraguay, Peru, Uruguay, and Venezuela.

Rev. de Der. Int. (Havana), XIII (1928), 159.

52.   Briand–Kellogg Pact

Treaty for the renunciation of war as an instrument of national policy except in self-defense; the settlement or solution of all disputes or conflicts of whatever nature or of whatever origin which may arise among the parties never to be sought except by pacific means; ratifications to be deposited at Washington.

Signed at Paris, August 27, 1928; in force, July 25, 1929.

	Adhered	Deposited
Brazil	Feb. 20, 1934	
Chile	Jan. 11, 1929	Aug. 12, 1929
Colombia		May 28, 1931
Paraguay		Dec. 4, 1929
Peru		July 23, 1929
Venezuela		Oct. 24, 1929

League of Nations Treaty Series, No. 2137, LXXXIX, 374–379; *ibid.*, XCIV, 58–64. *U. S. Treaty Series*, No. 796. Manley O. Hudson, *Int. Legislation* (Washington, 1931), IV, 2522–2526. *Amer. J. Int. Law*, XXII (1928), 253–261; *ibid.*, Supp., 171–173. Martens, *Nouv. Rec. Gén. de Traités*, 3ᵉ Sér., XXI, 3–8. *L'Europe Nouvelle*, 1928, pp. 1142–1143, 1153–1158, 1162–1171. *Bull. Int. News* (London, 1928), IV, 537–546, 617–624; *ibid.*, V, 23–34, 69–74. *British Year Book of Int. Law*, X (1929), 208–210. Manley O. Hudson, *By Pacific Means* (New Haven, 1935), pp. 153–156.

53. Conference on Conciliation and Arbitration

Treaty of general inter-American arbitration of all differences of an international character which have arisen or may arise between the parties by virtue of a claim of right made by one against the other under treaty or otherwise, which it has not been possible to adjust by diplomacy and which are juridical in their nature by reason of being susceptible of decision by the application of the principles of law; excepting controversies which are within the domestic jurisdiction of any of the parties to the dispute and are not controlled by international law; exceptions and reservations withdrawable as provided in a separate protocol; by an arbiter to be designated by agreement of the parties, or in the absence of agreement by a court of five American members; a special agreement to be made in each case to define clearly the particular subject matter of the controversy; ratifications to be deposited with the United States; the treaty to remain in force indefinitely; a denunciation to take effect as regards the party denouncing only, one year after notification thereof.

Signed at Washington, January 5, 1929, among others by Bolivia, Brazil, Chile, Colombia, Ecuador, Paraguay, Peru, Uruguay, and Venezuela; in force, October 28, 1929. Suppression of word "nao" in the Portuguese text, November 1929: *Bol. del Min. de Rel. Ext. del Ecuador* (Quito, 1929), Num. 88, pp. 77–78.

	Ratified	Deposited	Promulgated
Bolivia	Signed with reservations		
Brazil	Dec. 15, 1931	Jan. 25, 1932	Decr. #21158, Mar. 15, 1932
Chile	Dec. 13, 1929, with reservations	Feb. 27, 1930	
Colombia	Signed with reservations		
Ecuador	Signed with reservations; not ratified		
Paraguay	Signed with reservation		
Peru	Res. Leg. #6768, Feb. 10, 1930	May 23, 1934	
Uruguay	Signed with reservation		
Venezuela	Leg., June 20, 1932; Exec., Decree #17948, July 21, 1932, with reservations	Sept. 1, 1932	

League of Nations Treaty Series, No. 2988, CXXX, 136–160. Manley O. Hudson, *Int. Legislation* (Washington, 1931), IV, 2625–2633. *Amer. J. of Int. Law*, XXII (1928),

642; *ibid.*, XXIII (1929), 143–152, 273–291; *ibid.*, XXIII (1929), Supp., 82–89. *Cong. Rec.*, LXXV, Part 2, 2240–2248. *Rev. de Der. Int.* (Havana), XIV (1928), 330–337; *ibid.*, XV (1929), 102–130; *ibid.*, XVI, 85–102; *ibid.*, XXI (1932), 327–380. Manley O. Hudson, *By Pacific Means* (New Haven, 1935), pp. 169–174.

54. Conference on Conciliation and Arbitration

Convention of general inter-American conciliation, to maintain the achievement of the (Gondra) Treaty of May 3, 1923, by giving additional prestige and strength to the action of the commissions established by it; ratifications to be deposited with Chile; the convention to remain in force indefinitely; a denunciation to take effect as regards the party denouncing only, one year after notification thereof.

Signed at Washington, January 5, 1929, among others by Bolivia, Brazil, Chile (with a reservation), Colombia, Ecuador, Paraguay, Peru, Uruguay, and Venezuela; in force, November 15, 1929; with an additional protocol as to members of the commissions signed at Montevideo, December 26, 1933, among others by Chile, Ecuador, and Uruguay.

	RATIFIED	DEPOSITED	PROMULGATED
Brazil	Dec. 15, 1931	Jan. 22, 1932	Decr. #21017, Feb. 2, 1932
Chile	Dec. 13, 1929	Dec. 28, 1929	
Colombia	(without reservation) Law #55, Nov. 26, 1930		
Ecuador	Decr. Leg., Dec. 10, 1932	Feb. 22, 1933	
Peru	Feb. 6, 1930	May 11, 1934	
Uruguay	Law #9160–2, Dec. 8, 1933	Oct. 15, 1934	
Venezuela	July 15, 1929	Not deposited	

Leyes Exped. de Colombia de 1930 (Bogotá, 1931), pp. 198–204. *League of Nations Treaty Series*, No. 2309, C, 400–415. 46 *U. S. Stat. L.* II, 2209–2225. *U. S. Treaty Series*, No. 780. 131 *British and Foreign State Papers*, II, 131–134. Manley O. Hudson, *Int. Legislation* (Washington, 1931), IV, 2635–2642. *Amer. J. of Int. Law*, XXIII (1929), Supp., 76–82. *Cong. Rec.*, LXXVIII, Part 11, 11571–11572. Manley O. Hudson, *By Pacific Means* (New Haven, 1935), pp. 175–181.

55. South American Anti–War Pact

Treaty proposed by Foreign Minister Carlos Saavedra Lamas of Argentina and first published November 17, 1932, declaring in Article 1 that the parties solemnly condemn wars of aggression in their mutual relations and that the solution of conflicts or differences of whatever class which may arise between them ought to be obtained only by the pacific means established by international law, and in Article 2 that territorial questions ought not to be settled by violence, and that the parties will not recognize any territorial arrangement whatever which has not been procured by pacific means, nor the validity of the occupation or acquisition of territories which has been obtained by force of arms; conflicts to be submitted to conciliation by a commission of five members; ratifications to be deposited with Argentina; the treaty to remain in force indefinitely; a denunciation to take effect as regards the party denouncing only, one year after notification thereof.

Signed at Rio de Janeiro, October 10, 1933, with Mexico by Argentina, Brazil, Chile, Paraguay, Uruguay; and Bolivia, Colombia, Ecuador, Peru, and Venezuela later acceded; in force, October 14, 1935.

	RATIFIED	DEPOSITED
Argentina		Oct. 14, 1935
Bolivia, adhered	Apr. 26, 1934	Apr. 27, 1934
Brazil, adhered		
Chile	Aug. 3, 1934, with reservations	Aug. 22, 1934
Colombia, adhered	Apr. 27, 1934	Feb. 19, 1936
Ecuador, adhered	Decr. Ejec. Feb. 7, 1934, with reservations as to Art. 5, a, b, c, and d	Mar. 6, 1936
Paraguay, adhered		
Peru, adhered 1934	Feb. 19, 1936	Feb. 21, 1936
Uruguay, adhered		
Venezuela, adhered	Apr. 27, 1934	Dec. 27, 1935

Rev. de Der. Int. (Havana), XXIII (1933), 283–316; *ibid.*, XXVII (1935), 94–101. *Amer. J. Int. Law*, XXVIII (1934), Supp., 79–84. *U. S. Treaty Series*, No. 906. *Bull. Pan. Amer. Union*, LXVII (1933), 320–350. Cong. Rec., LXXVIII, Part 11, pp. 11569–11571. *League of Nations Off. Journal*, 1934, 15th Year, pp. 133–136, 208–212. Manley O. Hudson, *By Pacific Means* (New Haven, 1935), pp. 182–187.

56. SEVENTH INTERNATIONAL CONFERENCE OF AMERICAN STATES

Resolution inviting countries to adhere to and ratify five peace instruments: the Gondra Treaty of May 3, 1923 (§ 50, *supra*), the Briand-Kellogg Treaty of August 27, 1928 (§ 52, *supra*), the Arbitration Treaty of January 5, 1929 (§ 53, *supra*), the Conciliation Convention of January 5, 1929 (§ 54, *supra*), and the Saavedra-Lamas Treaty of October 10, 1933 (§ 55, *supra*).

Signed at Montevideo, December 16, 1933, among others by Argentina, Bolivia, Brazil, Chile, Colombia, Ecuador, Paraguay, Peru, Uruguay, and Venezuela.

U. S. Treaty Inf. Bull. (1934), 52, 2–3. *Rev. de Der. Int.* (Havana), XXV (1934), 9–10. *Amer. J. Int. Law*, XXVIII (1934), 316.

57. Inter–American Conference for the Maintenance of Peace

This conference, at which all twenty-one American republics were represented, with ninety-three voting delegates, met at Buenos Aires from December 1 to December 23, 1936, on the original suggestion of President Franklin D. Roosevelt in personal letters sent February 11, 1936, to the heads of all Latin-American governments, and on the subsequent invitation of President Agustin P. Justo to meet in his capital. President Roosevelt made the trip from Charleston, South Carolina, on the United States heavy cruiser *Indianapolis*, and with President Justo attended and addressed the opening session, on December 1. Eleven of the delegations were headed by the national minister of foreign affairs. Numerous agenda proposals had been considered by a preparatory commission of the ambassadors and ministers of the Latin-American diplomatic corps in Washington, with Secretary of State Cordell Hull as chairman, and the program was limited to the six general topics of organization of peace, neutrality, limitation of armaments, juridical problems, economic problems, and intellectual coöperation. A bloc of ten nations agreed to keep out of the conference all subjects not included in the official program; especially the Chaco stalemate before the committee of six neutrals, which Bolivia announced she did not wish and Paraguay declared she would not permit to be discussed. In the background of the conference were two political theories as to the best method of peace organization: Argentina and Mexico led a group which favored coöperation with European nations, presumably through Geneva, while the United States, Brazil, and Colombia were opposed to any European combination, and the latter two at least preferred an American regional system.

The conference adopted 73 projects,[1] in the form of 2 treaties, 8 conventions, 40 resolutions, 22 recommendations, and 1 declaration, which the delegation leaders enthusiastically declared set up efficient machinery for preserving permanent peace in the western hemisphere. Many were general affirmances of the principles of amity, solidarity, coöperation, consultation, collective action, and common defense; but some bore more directly on the proposed solution of conflicts. One resolution called upon the countries that have not already done so to ratify the same five pacts described in the Montevideo Resolution of December 16, 1933 (§ 56, *supra*). A declaration of inter-American solidarity and coöperation asserted four principles to have been accepted by the American community: (1) no acquisition of territory by force will be recognized; (2) intervention of one state in the internal or external

[1] Only unofficial texts are yet available. Full official forms may be expected in the publication of proceedings of the conference, and parts separately in other special sources.

affairs of another has been condemned; (3) compulsory collection of pecuniary obligations is illegal, and (4) every difference or dispute among American nations, no matter what its nature or origin, shall be solved by conciliation, by arbitration, or by international justice. A nonintervention convention was hailed by the Latin-Americans as ending forever the Monroe Doctrine, and a collective security convention was held by the United States to have made the Monroe Doctrine an inter-American policy. Action on a proposed inter-American court of international justice was referred to the Eighth International Conference of American States to be held at Lima, Peru, in 1938; the Pan American Union in the meantime to make a thorough study of the nine projects [2] submitted at the present conference and to prepare a report and recommendations. The subjects of an American League of Nations [3] and woman suffrage were kept out of the plenary sessions of the conference, and Mexico's proposed code of peace, Bolivia's requested definition of an aggressor, and various projects for coördinating existing American treaties on conciliation and arbitration were referred to a committee of experts to report at Lima. Eight treaties and conventions and the protocol relative to nonintervention, having been approved by the United States Senate, were signed by President Roosevelt on July 15, 1937.

[2] By Colombia, Costa Rica, Dominican Republic, Guatemala, Mexico, Nicaragua, Panama, Peru, and Salvador.

[3] *Cf.* chap. III, A, *supra.*

APPENDICES

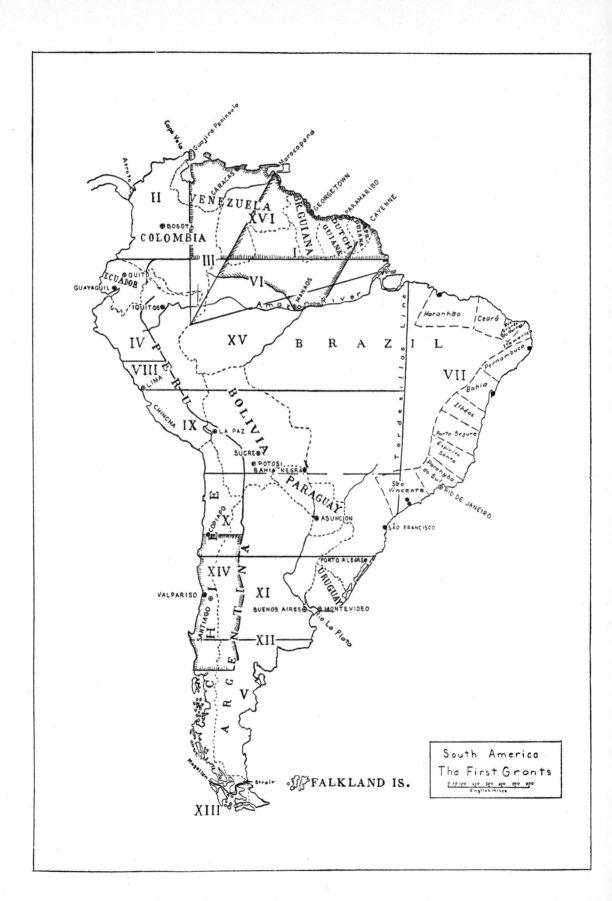

II

CARACAS

VENEZUELA

XVI

BR. GUIANA

GEORGETOWN

PARAMARIBO

CAYENNE

DUTCH GUIANA

FR. GUIANA

Cape Vela

Guajira Peninsula

Maracaopana

Atroto

BOGOTA

COLOMBIA

III

I

ECUADOR

QUITO

VI

GUAYAQUIL

IQUITOS

MANAOS

Amazon River

Maranhão

Ceará

Rio Grande do Norte

Parahyba

Pernambuco

IV

XV

B R A Z I L

VIII

P E R U

VII

Bahia

LIMA

Ilhéos

CHINCHA

IX

La Paz

BOLIVIA

Porto Seguro

Espirito Santo

SUCRE

POTOSI

BAHIA NEGRA

Parahyba do Sul

Tordesillas Line

São Vincente

RIO DE JANEIRO

PARAGUAY

COPIAPO

X

ASUNCION

São Francisco

PORTO ALEGRE

URUGUAY

XIV

C H I L E

XI

VALPARISO

BUENOS AIRES

MONTEVIDEO

SANTIAGO

XII

Rio La Plata

A R G E N T I N A

V

Magellan Strait

FALKLAND IS.

XIII

South America
The First Grants

0 50 100 200 300 400 500 600
English Miles

APPENDIX A

THE FIRST GRANTS

Date	Name	Grantee	Miles (approx.)		Boundaries
I Sept. 5, 1501		Vicente Yáñez Pinzón		E	Santa Maria de la Concepción (Point)
				W	Cape San Vicente
II 1508	New Granada	Alonso de Ojeda	(500)	E	Goajirá
				W	Atrato
III Mar. 27, 1528	(New Granada)	A. and B. Welser, assignees	(1,100)	E	Maracapana
				W	Cape Vela
IV July 26, 1529	New Castile	Francisco Pizarro	600	N	Tenumpuela (Santiago) (about 1°20′ N)
				S	Chincha
V July 26, 1529		Simon de Alcazaba	(1,200)	S	Strait of Magellan
				N	Toward Chincha
VI c. 1530	New Andalucia	Diego de Ordaz	600	E	Amazon, mouth
				W	Maracapana
VII Sept. 1532	Brazil	Donatories (See below)	(3,000)	N	Amazon, mouth
				S	Porto Alegre
VIII May 4, 1534	New Castile	Francisco Pizarro	210	N	Chincha
				S	Toward Strait of Magellan
IX May 21, 1534	New Toledo	Diego de Almagro	600	N	Pizarro's boundary
				E	Toward Strait of Magellan
X May 21, 1534	New Extremadura	Pedro de Mendoza	600	N	The Plata, Almagro's boundary
				S	Toward Strait of Magellan
XI May 21, 1534	New Leon	Simon de Alcazaba	600	N	Mendoza's boundary
				S	Toward Strait of Magellan
XII Dec. 8, 1536	New Leon	Francisco de Camargo	(700)	N	Mendoza's boundary
				S	Strait of Magellan (52°42′15″ S)
XIII Jan. 24, 1539	(Tierra del Fuego)	Pedro Sancho de Hoz	(200)	N	Strait of Magellan
				S	All land on the other side of the Strait
XIV Apr. 23, 1548	New Extremadura	Pedro de Valdivia	(900)	N	Copiapó (27° S)
				S	Lat. 41° width of 300 miles from coast
XV 1567	(Amazonas)	Juan Alvares Maldonado	(1,700)	W	Lake Opotari
				E	Amazon, mouth
XVI May 15, 1568	New Andalucia	Diego Hernández de Zerpa	(900)	N	Vriapari (river)
				S	Marañón

THE BRAZILIAN CAPTAINCIES

In September 1532 King John III of Portugal authorized and soon thereafter created twelve captaincies, resembling feudal fiefs, to run fifty leagues each on the coast, east of the shore ends of the Tordesillas line, from the mouth of the Amazon to the island of Santa Catharina. The donatory (capitãomor), as in Madeira and the Azores, could found cities, issue land grants, levy taxes, and appoint local and municipal officers and judges. These grants were, from north to south:

NAME	DONATORY	DATE OF CHARTER	REMARKS
Maranhão	Fernão Alvares de Andrade	Mar. 11, 1535	French settlement, 1612
Ceará	Antonio Cardoso de Barros	Nov. 20, 1535	Coast settlement, 1603
Rio Grande (do Norte)	João de Barros and Ayres da Cunha	Mar. 11, 1535	Natal founded, 1597
Itamaracá	Pero Lopes (brother of M. A. da Souza)	Oct. 6, 1534	Settled, 1536
Pernambuco	Duarte Coelho Pereira	Oct. 24, 1534	Settled, 1535. Soon absorbed Itamaracá
Bahia	Francisco Pereira Coutinho	Aug. 26, 1534	First town was destroyed by Indians
Ilhéos	Jorge de Figueiredo Correa	Apr. 1, 1535	Absorbed by Bahia
Porto Seguro	Pero de Campo Tourinho	May 27, 1534	Absorbed by Bahia
Espirito Santo	Vasco Fernandes Courtinho	Oct. 7, 1534	Victoria, nucleus of present state of Espirito Santo
Parahyba do Sul	Pero de Goes da Silveira	Feb. 29, 1536	Rio de Janeiro founded 1567
São Vicente and São Thomé	Martim Affonso da Souza	Oct. 6, 1534	Settled, January 1532; near Santos and São Paulo
Santo Amaro	Pero Lopes (brother of M. A. da Souza)	Oct. 6, 1534	Settled, 1536; within few miles of São Vicente

"From here (Itamaracá) northward the coast was less known and three parcels of the captaincy of Maranhão were granted by charter of March 11, 1535, to João de Barros, Ayres da Cunha, and Fernão Alvares de Andrade. Out of these were created the captaincy of Rio Grande and the captaincy of Maranhão. The tenth captaincy was, therefore, the captaincy of Rio Grande, assigned jointly to João de Barros and Ayres da Cunha, extending northward from Itamaracá. . . . And finally the twelfth captaincy was that of Maranhão, which included the stretch granted to Fernão Alvares de Andrade, seventy-five leagues to the westward . . . and fifty leagues farther along the coast, granted jointly to João de Barros and Ayres de Cunha." [1]

Only ten of the twelve captaincies were ever occupied by or on behalf of their owners, and in December 1548 the system was changed so that although the donatories might remain in possession of their grants, they lost some of their political and judicial rights and the whole country was put under a governor-general appointed by the king, and corregidores who had both military and judicial power. The donatories' remaining rights were finally taken away by Joseph I in 1755 on advice of the Marquis of Pombal.

---

[1] Herman G. James, *Brazil After a Century of Independence* (New York, 1925), pp. 63–67.

APPENDIX B

UTI POSSIDETIS

The territories of the several Indian families who shared South America at the end of the fifteenth century were bounded by the physical features of the continent: mountain ranges and river valleys. These, in the absence of extreme pressure, sufficed in the main to keep the separate stocks from wandering outside of the areas in which by their tradition they had been settled for many years before their existence became known to the Conquistadores and the world.

Columbus appears to have sighted the mainland of South America on his third voyage, on August 1, 1498, and to have sailed westward along the coast some 330 leagues from about the delta of the Orinoco or the Island of Trinidad and Paria Peninsula to Cape de la Vela. In June 1499 Alonso de Ojeda, a Spanish navigator, claimed to have made the coast of the mainland not far from Cape São Roque; and in January 1500 Vicente Yáñez Pinzón, a navigator from Palos in Andalusia, and in February or March Diego de Lepe, also Spanish, saw land in the neighborhood of Cape São Roque and sailed away northwest, Yáñez later obtaining a grant for his discoveries;[1] but these Spanish voyages produced no permanent results. In 1499 Ojeda, accompanied by Amerigo Vespucci, sailed along the shore for 400 miles to near Goajira on Cape de la Vela, just west of the Gulf of Maracaibo, where he saw an Indian village built on piles, and called the place Venezuela (Little Venice); and in 1500 Rodrigo de Bastidas doubled the Goajirá peninsula and continued westward, sighting the mountains of Santa Marta, discovering and naming on St. Mary Magdalen's day, July 22, the Magdalena River, and finding the Atrato River in the Gulf of Urabá at the south end of the Gulf of Darien. On March 9, 1500, Pedro Alvarez Cabral, a Portuguese noble, sailed from Lisbon for the East Indies, and forty-two days later, on April 21, he saw signs of land at about Carravellas in the southern part of the state of Bahia; on April 22, in Easter week, he sighted a mountain which he called Paschoal, some 400 miles northeast of Rio de Janeiro; and on April 24, 1500, he founded Porto Seguro in territory he called La Isla de la Vera Cruz, believing it an island from the fact that he saw no quadrupeds. On January 1, 1501, Vespucci saw and named the Bay of São Sebastião do Rio de Janeiro, then continued south to about 32° S., turned back, and on St. Francis' day, October 4, 1501, found and named the São Francisco River, between Bahia and Pernambuco. Yáñez and Solis made further explorations to the west of the boundary line with Portgual, pursuant to leave they obtained March 23, 1508.[2] In 1508 the Crown granted to Ojeda the territory from Goajirá to the Atrato and in 1510 one of his lieutenants founded Sebastién on the eastern shore of the Gulf of Darien, but it was soon destroyed by the Indians. Santo Domingo on the Island of Española, founded in 1496 and a focus of Spanish population almost from Columbus' first discovery, was the starting point for many of the early expeditions, including the one which in 1510 under Martín Fernández de Enciso founded Santa María del Antigua,[3] the

[1] Capitulation, Sept. 5, 1501; Ricardo Aranda, *Col. de Trat. del Peru*, I, 18–21.

[2] Capitulation, Ricardo Aranda, *Col. de Trat. del Peru*, I, 21–25.

[3] Named in memory of the Antigua of Seville.

first settlement on the mainland, at Urabá, on the west shore of the gulf of the same name. In 1515 Juan Díaz de Solís, Grand Pilot of Spain, touched the coast of Brazil near Rio de Janeiro, sailed south and around Punta del Este, and in February 1516 reached the estuary of the Plata, where he appears to have tasted the water far from land and named it the Mar Dulce. He sailed up the river and discovered the island of Martín García, which he named after his pilot. He and eight of his men were on landing killed by the Indians, but Alejo García, one of the landing party, survived and in 1525 was sent by Martim da Souza, governor of Brazil, across Brazil and Paraguay to Bolivia near Chuquisaca, and was killed by the Indians on the return journey. Fernando Magalhães, a Portuguese in Spanish service, sailed from San Lucar on September 20, 1519, and on January 15, 1520, sighted and named Montevideo Bay. He spent the winter from March 31 to August 24, 1520, at San Julián Bay in Patagonia, and on St. Ursula's day, October 21, 1520, he sighted and named in honor of her and her companions Cape Vírgenes and entered the strait, which he called Todos los Santos, coming out into the Pacific thirty-eight days later. He was killed in the Philippines on April 27, 1521, but his captain, Juan Sebastián del Cano, kept on with the *Victoria* and on September 6, 1522, reached San Lucar to complete the first circumnavigation of the globe.

In 1523 a cavalier, Pascual de Andagoya, returned sick to Panama from an expedition beyond the Gulf of San Miguel with glowing reports of a land called Birú. Francisco Pizarro, born out of wedlock in 1470 in Trujillo, Estremadura, a soldier-adventurer in Santo Domingo in 1510, formed a partnership to explore the west coast by contract of March 10, 1526, in Panama with Diego de Almagro, who came to America in 1514, and a priest, Fernando de Luque, agent or borrower of Gaspar de Espinosa, a lawyer of Santo Domingo then in Panama, who according to a contract of August 6, 1531, furnished the whole sum of 20,000 pesos advanced for the expedition. Pizarro set out from the Isthmus on November 15, 1524, with 200 men in one small vessel, but got only as far south as the San Juan River. On his second voyage, in 1526, after waiting on the Island of Gallo near the northern boundary of Ecuador seven months for provisions, and probably touching at Atacames, Pizarro reached Túmbez, on the south side of the Gulf of Guayaquil, 900 miles south from the Isthmus. He returned to Panama and in 1528 went from Nombre de Dios to Spain, where he had audience with Charles I, was legitimatized (later made Marquis de los Atavillos or Charcas) and named Adelantado of Peru, with formal authorization to conquer and settle Peru in the name of the king of Castile. He secured from Queen Isabel at Toledo in Charles I's absence on July 26, 1529,[4] a grant of New Castile to run 200 leagues along the coast south from Tempula (Zemuquella) or Santiago to the town of Chincha, and in January 1530 he left San Lucar to return to Panama. On December 28, 1530, Pizarro sailed from Panama with three small ships, landed in Ecuador, marched down the coast to the Gulf of Guayaquil, crossed to the Island of Puna, slaughtered its inhabitants, and was there joined by Hernando de Soto with adventurers from Nicaragua and horses. Crossing to Túmbez, Pizarro marched south to Paita, where he established his base, and in 1532 founded San Miguel de Piura in the Paita valley. On September 24, 1532, he left San Miguel and marched 200 miles south along the coast to a point opposite Cajamarca, to which place he ascended by the Quichuan military road, being supplied with provisions along the way by order of Atahualpa, the thirteenth Inca. On November 15, 1532, Pizarro entered Caja-

[4] Capitulation, Ricardo Aranda, *Col. de Trat. del Peru*, I, 25-32.

marca with the Dominican friar, Vicente Valverde, treacherously seized Atahualpa at a conference the next day, and held him hostage in Cajamarca. His subjects delivered gold, said to have been piled nine feet high in a room seventeen by twenty-two feet, and silver which filled twice a smaller adjoining room, to a value altogether of some $15,500,000, for his ransom; but instead of being released he was "tried" by Pizarro and Almagro as judges, sentenced to death, and strangled with a bow string in the plaza on August 29, 1533. The sentence was changed from burning in consideration of his having consented to become a Christian, after he had been bound to the stake, and being baptized by Valverde. Pizarro then divided the ransom, a part of which Fernando Pizarro in May had gone to Pachacamac to collect, evacuated Cajamarca, marched along the northern plateau over the Cerro de Pasco into the fertile Jauja valley and up the central plateau toward Cuzco, defeating the Quichuan general, Quizquiz, and entering Cuzco on November 15, 1533, with Manco Capac, whom Pizarro crowned as the fifteenth Inca. In December 1533 Sebastian Moyano de Benalcazar,[5] who had been with Columbus on his third voyage, under Pizarro's authority entered San Francisco de Quito, and in December 1534 he took formal possession of it for the king of Spain. Fernando Pizarro, having carried to Charles I the king's share of Atahualpa's ransom, obtained for Francisco Pizarro on May 4, 1534,[6] an extension of his grant of New Castile in the land of the caciques Coli and Chipi, not over seventy leagues further along the coast to the southward, and for Almagro on May 21, 1534,[7] a grant of New Toledo, to run 200 leagues from Francisco Pizarro's southern boundary to the east toward the Strait of Magellan.

The territorial rivalry between Spain and Portugal reached tentative adjustment with the signing at Madrid on January 13, 1750,[8] of a treaty which, abandoning the imaginary lines of Pope Alexander VI and the inapplicable theories of the Treaty of Tordesillas, virtually recognized the *uti possidetis*. Spain acknowledged Portugal's title by settlement to large sections of the Amazon and Paraná basins, while Spain's title to the Philippine archipelago was admitted by Portugal. The Portuguese agreed to give up Colonia and the Spanish to abandon the Seven Missions of the Jesuits in the Ibicuhy region, 350 miles to the north. Navigation of the parts of the rivers along which the frontier passed should be common to both nations without fortification or any impediment, but where both banks belonged to one, the navigation should be exclusively that nation's. Instructions for a proposed demarcation commission were agreed upon [9] but the work was not carried out. When the provisions of the Treaty of Madrid became known in Spain the Jesuits and public opinion generally made such violent and bitter protests against the abandonment of this territory that the Spanish government did not dare to carry it out, and by a convention signed at Pardo February 12, 1761,[10] the treaty was annulled, and matters reverted in theory to their previous status. The boundary remained thus unsettled until a new treaty, negotiated by the Count of Florida Blanca, was signed at San Ildefonso on October 1, 1777.[11] This agreement followed the general form and in many places the exact lines of the failed

[5] From Belalcazar, for euphony.
[6] Ricardo Aranda, *Col. de Trat. del Peru*, XIII, 5-6.
[7] Capitulation, Ricardo Aranda, *Col. de Trat. del Peru*, I, 39-44.
[8] Cantillo, *Tratados de Espana* (Madrid, 1843), pp. 400-408.
[9] *Questao de Limites Brazileira-Argentina, Exposicao do Brazil* (New York, 1894), IV, 25-67.

[10] Cantillo, *Tratados de Espana* (Madrid, 1843), pp. 467-468.
[11] *Ibid.*, 537-544. Meliton Gonzalez, *El Limite Oriental del Territorio de Misiones* (Montevideo, 1883), I. Ricardo Aranda, *Col. de Trat. del Peru*, II, 637-652. Martens, *Recueil de Traités* (2e ed., Gottingue, 1817), II, 545-558. *Cf.* Report of Theodorick Bland, Nov. 2, 1818; 6 *British and Foreign State Papers* 706.

Treaty of Madrid: the Seven Missions (Ibicuhy) and Colonia del Sacramento remained Spanish, but southern Rio Grande do Sul and Santa Catharina Island were restored to the Portuguese; and the river navigation proposition was repeated. To determine more exactly the boundary described in the treaty and in order that there "might not be the least doubt about it in the future," a commission of experts was to survey and mark the line. Although the survey was never completed, the 5,000-mile line as described in this treaty was accepted for a century and a half as the true boundary between Brazil and her neighbors and the later difficulties arose over the identification of the rivers, the selection of the principal upper stream or chief source, the location of some of the points designated by name or otherwise, and the determination of the correct watershed or crest of the mountains. By the Treaty of San Ildefonso Portugal obtained clear title to territory in South America more than twice as large as the area confirmed to her by the Treaty of Tordesillas. The new line ran (Article 3) from the Atlantic [12] at Chuy creek and San Miguel Fort near the south end of Lake Mirim, which remained all Portuguese, around the west shore of that lake and across to the sources of the Negro, then (Article 4) northward, leaving all the rivers emptying into the Plata and the Uruguay, and the Piratini and the Ibimini to the west, Spanish, and Lagoa dos Patos, the Grande de San Pedro, the Yacuy, Tahim creek, Lake Manguera, San Gonzalo fort, the Ararica, and the Coyacuy to the east Portuguese, to the Uruguay [13] where the Piquiry or Pepiri-guazu enters it on the west (north) bank, (Article 8) up the Piquiry to its chief source, across by the highest land to the source of the San Antonio, down the San Antonio to the Curituba or Iguazu, down the Curituba to the Paraná, up the Paraná [14] to the Igurey, (Article 9) up the Igurey to its chief source, then by a straight line to the head of the nearest river ("perhaps that called the Corrientes") that empties into the Paraguay, down that river to its main channel in dry weather to the Paraguay, up the Paraguay [15] to the Lake of Xarayes, across the lake to the mouth of the Jauru, (Article 10) then in a straight line to the south bank of the Guapore or Itenes, opposite the mouth of the Sarare, or other river near if found more easy and certain, down the Guapore to its junction with the Mamoré, (Article 11) down the Mamoré and the Madeira to a point equidistant from the Marañon or Amazon and the mouth of the Mamoré, thence by an east-west line [16] to the east bank of the Javary,[17] down the Javary to the Marañon or Amazon, down the Amazon (Orellana or Guiana) to the westernmost mouth of the Yapurá, (Article 12) up the Yapurá [18] far enough to include the Portuguese establishments on its banks and those of the Negro and the channel between and thence by the mountains [19] which form the divide between the Orinoco and the Marañon or Amazon, directing the line wherever possible toward the north. This differed from the 1750 line in leaving the Ibicuhy region and the northwest quarter of Rio Grande do Sul to Spain, and in running the north boundary along the dividing mountains more to the northeast than due east, so leaving it later to Brazil rather than to Venezuela to make the principal stand against the pressure of England, the Netherlands, and France from their Guiana colonies.

Throughout the dependency period Spanish settlement proceeded on substantially the same principles all around the continent: coast towns built near good ports or principal in-

[12] See chap. I, §14, *supra*.
[13] See chap. I, §2, *supra*.
[14] See chap. I, §12, *supra*.
[15] See chap. I, §6, *supra*.

[16] See chap. I, §13, *supra*.
[17] See chap. I, §§10, 11, *supra*.
[18] See chap. I, §15, *supra*.
[19] See chap. I, §§16, 17, 18, *supra*.

terior capitals taken as centers after overthrow of the previous governments; new towns founded by expeditions of soldiers to regions of particular interest, first for mining, later for agriculture and grazing. Forts or strong places thus planted supported gradually increasing rings of villages and estates dependent upon them, but the great size of the terrain permitted until comparatively late the continuance of unsettled wastes or regions of slight value between the occupied areas, crossed only by connecting roads or trails. Growth in this manner had two marked effects upon boundary problems: it postponed them for the most part until the settlements eventually spread enough to come into actual contact with each other, and it left great bonds of interstitial country wholly uninhabited or dwelt in only by unassigned Indians or temporary missionaries, so that any legally helpful actual possession often could not be found at all when some incident of unexpected importance or flash of national pride stirred up the dispute for sovereignty. Another cause of conflict, especially potent in the earlier years, was the ignorance in Madrid of the real geographic and physical conditions in the overseas kingdoms, so that many of the decrees and ordinances based on the partisan representation of a petitioner or the fragmentary or hearsay report of an untutored explorer could not in fact be applied on the ground at all by the ambitious but harassed governors.[20]

Nevertheless, the Spanish administrative divisions did determine in a general way the outlines of many of the later republics. The treaties of Madrid (1750) and of San Ildefonso (1777) drew the whole line between the Spanish and Portuguese dominions, except perhaps from the Atlantic to the Uruguay, virtually where actual possession required, especially on the Portuguese side, though in the interior the line crossed long stretches of vacant or unknown land with but the vaguest of courses. Charles III in his extensive governmental changes marked still more closely the political lines of the later independent parts; and it is of interest to note, on the other hand, that he and his successor rejected a scheme that would most certainly have given the separatist struggles very different aspects. When Spain had accepted from England East and West Florida in exchange for Gibraltar, the Conde de Aranda[21] after profound study submitted to Charles III a remarkably prophetic secret memorial, in which he said he was convinced that Spain could not long successfully defend her lands in the New World, that the United States would first take by force the Floridas and then proceed to further conquests, and that to meet the peril Spain should give up direct control of her overseas possessions except only the strategic military and commercial points of Cuba, Puerto Rico, and one port to be selected in South America, erecting three substantially independent kingdoms of Mexico, Peru, and Tierra Firme (New Granada), to be ruled by kings chosen from princes of the Spanish royal family, in perpetual offensive and defensive alliance with Spain, and paying to the king of Spain as emperor a

[20] The following, among many volumes of varying merit, give good general views: John M. Niles, *History of South America . . . revolutions* (Hartford, 1837), 2 vols.; Clements R. Markham, "Colonial History of South America," *Narrative and Critical History of America* (New York, 1889), VIII, Chap. 5, pp. 295-368; José Coroleu, *America, Historia de su Colonización, Dominación é Independencia* (Barcelona, 1894-1896), 4 vols.; Alfred Déberlé, *Historie de l'Amerique du Sud depuis la conquète jusdu'a nos jours* (3ᵉ ed., Paris, 1897); Bernard Moses, *South America on the Eve of Emancipation* (New York, 1908); Thomas C. Dawson, *The South American Republics* (New York, 1910), 2 vols.; Herman G. James and Percy A. Martin, *The Republics of Latin America* (New York, 1923); William S. Robertson, *History of the Latin-American Nations* (rev. ed., New York, 1929); William W. Sweet, *A History of Latin America* (rev. and enl. ed., New York, 1929); M. W. Williams, *The People and Politics of Latin America* (Boston & New York, 1930); Charles E. Chapman, *Colonial Hispanic America* (New York, 1933).

[21] Pedro Pablo Abarca de Bolea, soldier, diplomat, president of the Council of Castille, ambassador to France from 1773 to 1787.

moderate tribute of mineral or farm products. Unfortunately for his successors, Charles III, though the greatest, was still a Bourbon, who could comprehend no future gain that justified present yielding, and he rejected the entire proposal. When the advantages of his administrative and accounting reforms began to be lost in the recrudescence of incompetence and graft under Charles IV, Aranda's project came up again and was even approved by Félix Amat, archbishop of Palmira, the king's confessor, but was vetoed by Manuel Godoy, Príncipe de la Paz y de Basano, the king's councilor, minister, and favorite.

Spanish America, from the first interference of Napoleon in Spain, rejected the French and would have none of Joseph Bonaparte as king; the uprisings of 1810 began as municipal outbreaks, in the name of Ferdinand VII, against the party of the Cortes, and continued as struggles of the creoles against the European-born Spaniards for control of the local governments, without any announced pretensions of independence except in Paraguay and Venezuela until after 1814. England was of course the ally of Spain against Napoleon, but it irked her to support the absolutist Ferdinand VII, whose restoration of the restricted trade system would have injured British commerce. She gave the revolutionists quiet aid, although she did not come out in the open with any direct assistance until Canning in 1823, presumably not forgetting France's help to the British North American colonies, initiated his policy of speedy recognition, determined that if France was to have Spain it should be without Spanish America. After the restoration of Ferdinand VII, Madrid grew increasingly anxious over affairs in America, but seemed still unable or unwilling to comprehend the extent to which government there had got out of hand. After the Spanish revolution of 1820, the Cortes, in which deputies from Mexico were present, appointed on May 3, 1821, a special committee to propose, jointly with the executive, measures to put a stop to the disputes and dissensions which unfortunately prevailed in the provinces of America; but the committee reported on June 24, 1821,[22] after the king had vetoed a plan at first approved by his ministers, that public opinion was not yet prepared for a definite solution. The American deputies, deeply disappointed, presented an address and the plan which the ministers had approved, calling for three sections of Cortes with limited powers in America: one in Mexico City for all of New Spain (Mexico) and Guatemala, one in Bogotá for New Granada and Tierra Firme, and one in Lima for Peru, Buenos Aires, and Chile; each of the three divisions to be governed by a delegate, who might be of the royal family, appointed by the king to exercise in his name the executive power, responsible only to the Crown and the General Cortes, with commerce to be considered internal within the monarchy, and large contributions by America to Spain's foreign debt. No action was taken on any plan, though on June 27, 1821, the Cortes passed a law [23] for the encouragement of colonization by Spaniards and foreigners in the provinces of Spain beyond the seas. On February 12, 1822, a committee of the Cortes reported [24] that all propositions for settlement should be transmitted to the legislative power and all treaties between Spanish leaders and American governments (such as that of O'Donojú with Iturbide in Mexico) should be null, as respects the acknowledgment of independence; and an amendment, proposed during discussion, that the Cortes declare the independence of all those provinces of both Americas that actually were independent, on condition of the payment by each of an annual subsidy, was required to be withdrawn. On

[22] 9 *British and Foreign State Papers* 400-405. *American State Papers* (Class I, For. Rel., 1834), IV, 827-831.
[23] Approved by the king, Mar. 12, 1822. 8 *British and Foreign State Papers* 1303-1309.
[24] 9 *ibid.*, 756-759.

December 25, 1823,[25] the king abolished forever in his dominions in America the Constitution of March 7, 1820, reëstablishing their governments conformably to the laws and ordinances existing before that date; on February 9, 1824, he issued a decree [26] permitting foreigners to trade with the provinces overseas as before 1820; and on February 26, 1824,[27] he annulled the powers and acts of all commissioners sent by the constitutional government to treat with the revolutionists for the pacification of those provinces. By January 1826 even Callao had surrendered, and Ferdinand VII's reactionary gestures had little overseas effect outside of Cuba, Puerto Rico, and the Philippines.

The doctrine that the boundaries of the American republics should ordinarily coincide [28] with the boundaries of the preceding Spanish administrative divisions and subdivisions was not embodied in any of the early treaties among the new nations, and of course not in any between them and Spain; but rather it came gradually to be accepted as a general guiding principle, in South America known as the doctrine of the *Uti Possidetis* [29] of 1810, and proclaimed in the Congress of Lima in 1848.[30] The first juntas seemed to recognize the general frontiers [31] of their jurisdiction at the boundaries of the former governments in whose capitals they were functioning, and tacitly to recognize the mutual advantages [32] of such limitations, which the vacant and usually non-vital border territory made it easy to observe. Interesting confirmation of this attitude is seen in the proclamations and manifestos of leaders of armies who crossed the line from another province: that they came to fight for the independence of the sister, i.e., separate, nation. As early as 1821 [33] the Congress at Montevideo rejected both the *uti possidetis* and the Treaty of San Ildefonso in their act declaring that the Banda Oriental belonged to Portuguese America; but except as to Uruguay Brazil regularly asserted that her lands extended to the bounds sketched by the Treaty of San Ildefonso, while her neighbors usually maintained that their limits should be determined by the possession of 1810.

Bolívar's decrees in 1825 establishing the new state of Bolivia followed in general the ancient limits of the audiencia of Charcas. Here and in his broader consideration of the principles of division for the great territory he had liberated, it seems likely that Bolívar accepted the Spanish administrative divisions as furnishing temporarily lines of practical convention with which the new governments might make a start; and, knowing that such lines were unsatisfactory because of the inexact state of knowledge of the country when they were traced, meant to have them rectified when the necessary exploration had been

[25] 11 *ibid.*, 862–864.

[26] *Ibid.*, 864–865.

[27] *Ibid.*, 865.

[28] *Uti possidetis* defined as narrower than *statu quo*: Roland E. L. Vaughan Williams, "Les Méthodes de Travail de la Diplomatie." *Rec. des Cours*, IV (1924), 229 at 257.

[29] Gaspar Toro, *Notas sobre Arbitraje Int.* (Santiago de Chile, 1898), pp. 134–136. Vicente G. Quesada, *Historia Diplomática Latino-Americana* (Buenos Aires, 1918), I, "Derecho Int. Latino-Americano, 41–114. Gustavo Augusto da Frota Braga, *Posse e Usocapião* (Ceara, 1922). James Brown Scott, "The Swiss Decision," *Amer. J. Int. Law*, XVI (1922), 428–429. Albert Guani, "La Solidarité Internationale dans L'Amérique Latine," [Chap. VI, Les Questions de Frontières en Amérique du Sud], *Rec. des Cours*, VIII (1925), 293–297. Jackson H. Ralston, *Law and Procedure of Int. Tribunals* (Stanford University, 1926), pp. 322–323. Eusebio Ayala, "El Uti-Posidetis en América,"

Rev. de Der. y Cien. Soc. (Asunción, 1933), VI, Nums. 20, 21 y 22, pp. 5–35.

[30] Alejandro Alvarez, "Latin America and International Law," *Amer. J. Int. Law*, III (1909), 269 at 290. Daniel Antokoletz, *Tratado de Der. Int. Pub.* (2ª ed., Buenos Aires, 1928), II (Sec. 344), 287–288.

[31] Frontiers may be natural or artificial, and the latter visible or invisible. Walther Schoenborn, "La Nature Juridique du Territoire," *Rec. des Cours*, XXX (1929), 131. Robert Redslob, "Le Principe des Nationalités," *Rec. des Cours*, XXXVII (1931), 26–27.

[32] Geographic and economic frontiers do not always coincide. John Fischer Williams, "Quelques Aspects Juridiques des Transferts Contractuels de Richesse entre États," *Rec. des Cours*, XVI (1927), 580. Jacques Ancel, "Une théorie française sur la geographie des frontières," *Affaires Étrangères*, I (1931), 287.

[33] See chap. I, §14, *supra*.

completed, to make the interior divisions natural and stable, and to bind the entire northern country into a homogeneous whole. He preferred republics to a monarchy [34] and apparently at one time envisioned the organization of Spanish South America around three principal geographic factors: the Isthmus of Panama for Great Colombia, the Bolivian tableland for a Confederation of the Pacific, and the Plata valley and estuary for Argentina. When Bolívar's unification efforts came to nought, his policies were abandoned, and even greater Colombia fell apart, the interior lines were transformed into important and vexatious frontiers from which sprang many later conflicts.

Later geographers have suggested interesting natural unities. Malagrida [35] proposes to group (1) the Plata country on the axis of the Paraná with the estuary as functional center, bounded by lines from Porto Alegre (Rio Grande do Sul) and Cape Horn meeting in the main cordillera on the western edge of Matto Grosso, to include all of Argentina, Paraguay, and Uruguay, the southeastern part of Bolivia, and a small piece of southernmost Brazil; (2) the countries of the Pacific as a high mountain ridge with a narrow strip of fertile land on either side in an arc from the Gulf of Guayaquil to Patagonia, centering about southern Peru or the Bolivian plateau, to include Chile, Peru, western Bolivia, and the southern part of Ecuador; (3) the north-Andean countries from Guayaquil to the Guianas, controlled somewhat by the Magdalena and Orinoco valleys, to include Colombia, Venezuela, and the northern part of Ecuador; and (4) the tremendous Brazilian terirtory plus northeastern Bolivia, eastern Ecuador, southern Venezuela, and the Guianas, with the three great socio-geographically important river systems of the Amazon, the Araguaya, and the Paraguay. Kirkpatrick [36] regroups for the future (1) Bolivia, Colombia, Ecuador, and Peru, and (2) Argentina, Chile, Paraguay, and Uruguay; apparently respecting Brazil's political and racial unity and being uncertain what to do with Venezuela.

The *Uti Possidetis* of 1810 was to be the determining principle with respect to the boundaries betwen New Granada and Venezuela in the Treaty of 1883 [37] which failed of approval by the Venezuelan Congress. As early as 1818 a doctrine of *uti possidetis* was proposed by Spain, as to the boundaries of Louisiana when held by France in 1764, in a controversy with the United States.[38] The United States [39] supported the theory for all of America in the Bulwer Treaty correspondence in 1856: "The United States regard it as an established principle of public law and of international right that when a European Colony in America becomes independent, it succeeds to the territorial limits of the Colony as it stood in the hands of the parent country." [40] The development and application of the doctrine

[34] Bolívar's "Letter from Jamaica," Kingston, Sept. 6, 1815. José Félix Blanco, *Documentos para la historia de la vida pública del Libertador* (Caracas, 1876), V, 331–342. Felipe Larrazábal, *Vida del Libertador Simón Bolivar* (Nueva Ed. Mod., Madrid, 1918), I, 386–403.

[35] Carlos Badia Malagrida, *El factor geográfico en la política sub-americana* (Madrid, 1919), pp. 128–130, 134.

[36] Frederick A. Kirkpatrick, *South America and the War* (Cambridge, Eng., 1918).

[37] See chap. I, §22A, *supra*.

[38] *American State Papers* (Class I, For. Rel., 1834), IV, 481.

[39] Frontiers as American problems do not come within

the Monroe Doctrine. Alejandro Alvarez, "Latin America and International Law," *Amer. J. Int. Law*, III (1909), 269 at 314–317. Charles Evans Hughes, *The Centenary of the Monroe Doctrine* (Washington, 1923), pp. 10–11. Paul Heilborn, "Les Sources du Droit International," *Rec. des Cours*, XI (1926), 45.

[40] Instruction from Secretary of State William L. Marcy to George M. Dallas, minister to Great Britain, July 26, 1856; No. 23, Instructions, Great Britain, 17, 1–26. To appear in William R. Manning's "Diplomatic Correspondence of the United States: Inter-American Affairs, 1831–1860" (Washington), volume on Great Britain.

have been discussed in Chapter I in connection with the various boundary disputes,[41] but it may be pointed out here that merely to invoke the *uti possidetis* at a given time does not of itself determine the solution of conflicting claims, since the boundaries as set down on paper of an administrative, judicial, or even ecclesiastical division often differ materially from the lines to which permanent occupation or occasional jurisdictional authority has actually been carried.[42] Hence properly to settle a controversy by this doctrine it is commonly necessary first to know to which greater weight is to be given, possession *de jure* or possession *de facto*.

[41] Raye R. Platt, "Present Status of International Boundaries in South America," *Geog. Rev.* XIV, 622–638. Lester H. Woolsey, "Boundary Disputes," *Amer. J. Int. Law,* XXV (1931), 324–333.

[42] Alejandro Alvarez, *Le Droit Int. Américain* (Paris, 1910), pp. 65–68. Ernest Nys, *Le Droit International* (nouv. ed., Paris, 1912), I, 542.

APPENDIX C

MARINE BOUNDARIES

With the general European emphasis on real property rights and preoccupation with land wars from the Middle Ages through the Napoleonic era, ocean boundaries attracted less analytical attention and in the South American possessions seem to have raised no controversies. In an ordinance of October 1565 Philip II fixed the visual horizon as the limit of Spain's jurisdiction. The theory of the cannon-shot distance of one marine league (three nautical miles) suggested by Cornelius van Bynkershoek in 1702 gradually grew up in the eighteenth century, with the waning of the notion of particular sovereignty in portions of the high seas, and was widely accepted without serious question until the invention and general installation of long-range guns in coastal fortifications gave the theorists opportunity to discuss whether or not the limit should be extended,[1] as some nations have asserted and particular treaties have provided. Spain's[2] claim to a six-mile limit was challenged by France, Great Britain,[3] and the United States,[4] and eventually practically withdrawn. Portugal has long held the three-mile doctrine, and presumably the same law was extended over the kingdom of Brazil and continued in the empire. In the case of the American brig *Aurora*, seized four or five leagues from Cape Baxos but within Pará Bay, Marshall, chief justice, for the United States Supreme Court[5] did not decide the point as to whether or not the whole of the bay, which is some fifty miles between headlands, was within the jurisdiction of Portugal.

The Civil Code of Argentina (1869) declares in Article 2340[6] that the public property of the general state or of the individual states includes: the seas adjacent to the territory of the republic to the distance of one marine league, measured from the lowest tide line, but the right of police as to matters concerning the security of the country and the observance of the revenue laws extends to the distance of four marine leagues, measured in the same manner; inland seas, bays, inlets, ports and anchorages, rivers and their beds and all

[1] Robert Phillimore, *Comm. upon International Law* (3rd ed., London, 1879), I (Secs. 197-198), 274-275. Charles Calvo, *Le Droit International* (5e ed., Paris, 1896), I (Secs. 353-356), 477-480. John B. Moore, *Digest of International Law* (Washington, 1906), Sec. 144, I, 698-699. John Westlake, *International Law* (Cambridge, 1910), I, 187-190. "De l'étendue de la Mer Territoriale," Clunet, *J. dr. int. privé*, XLI (1914), 131-136. L. Oppenheim, *International Law* (3rd ed., London, 1920), I (Secs. 185-186), 333-336. Paul Fauchille, *Traité de Droit Int. Pub.* (Paris, 1925), I (2e Partie, Secs. 493-493⁴), 173-194. George G. Wilson, *Handbook of International Law* (2nd ed., St. Paul, 1927), pp. 74-76. Thomas Baty, "The Three-Mile Limit," *Amer. J. Int. Law*, XXII (1928), 503-537. *Wheaton's Elements of International Law*, ed. by A. Berriedale Keith (6th Eng. ed., London, 1929), I, 361-369. Antonio S. de Bustamante y Sirvén, *El Mar Territorial* (Habana, 1930), Bk. I, Chap. 4. Ellery C. Stowell, *International Law* (New York, 1931), p. 57. Arnold Paestad, "La Portée du Canon comme Limite de la Mer Territoriale," *Rev. gén. de dr. int. pub.*, XIX (1912), 598-623.

[2] Art. 1. There belong to the national domain and public use . . . Sec. 2. The littoral sea, or rather the maritime zone, which surrounds the coast or frontiers of the lands of Spain, to the full width determined by international law, with its inlets, roadsteads, bays, ports and other openings utilizable for fishing and navigation. Ley de Puertos, May 7, 1880. 124 *Col. Leg.* II, 787. *Bol. Rev. Gen. Leg. Jr.*, LXI, 55. *Rev. gén. de dr. int. pub.*, XXI, 409-419. *Cf.* Partida III, Title 28, Laws 3 and 4. Civil Code of Spain (1889), Art. 339.

[3] Thomas W. Fulton, *Sovereignty of the Sea* (Edinburgh and London, 1911), pp. 569, 664-665. 70 *British and Foreign State Papers* 185-188.

[4] *Cf.* United States v. Canillo (1935) 13 *F. Supp.* 121.

[5] Church v. Hubbart (1804), 2 *Cranch* 187-239. Moore, *Dig. Int. Law* (Washington, 1906), I, 728.

[6] José O. Machado, *Exp. y Com. del Codigo Civil Argentino* (Buenos Aires, 1922), VI, 212-219. Philip C. Jessup, *Law of Territorial Waters* (New York, 1927), pp. 46-47, 104.

water which runs in natural channels; shores of the sea and of navigable rivers, so far as necessary to navigation to highest tide mark; lakes navigable by vessels of over 100 tons and their shores; and islands formed or which may be formed in the territorial sea, in all rivers or in navigable lakes. The Montevideo treaty concerning international penal law, to which Argentina was a party,[7] provides in Article 12 that for the purposes of penal jurisdiction territorial waters include an extent of five miles from the coast of terra firma and the islands which form part of the territory of each state. In the regulations for enforcing her proclamation of neutrality of August 5, 1914,[8] Argentina declared that the neutral zone around her coasts should be five miles in width, but the British refused to be bound to respect more than a three-mile belt. Argentina claims to control fisheries in the territorial sea to a width of 18,520 meters (11.5 miles) from the line of high water around the mainland, and including San Matias, Nuevo, and San Jorge Gulfs.[9] In the North Atlantic Coast Fisheries Arbitration[10] at The Hague in 1910 Dr. Luis M. Drago in the course of his dissenting opinion mentioned the Plata estuary as one of a class of historical bays which belong to the littoral nation whatever their depth or width at the entrance, when such country has asserted its sovereignty over them and particular circumstances such as geographical configuration, immemorial usage, and, above all, the requirements of self-defense, justify such a pretension.

The Montevideo treaty concerning international penal law to which Bolivia was a party[11] provides in Article 12 that for the purposes of penal jurisdiction territorial waters include an extent of five miles from the coast of terra firma and the islands which form part of the territory of each state.

Brazil appears to have supported the three-mile rule for the limit of territorial jurisdiction over marginal waters,[12] and expressly adopted it as the width of the zone for neutrality purposes during the World War.[13] In 1914 Brazil, supported by Ecuador and Peru, declared that any belligerent warship receiving hospitality from one American state should not receive it from any other American state within a period of three months; but this novel principle of collective neutrality for the continent did not obtain general support, and no instance is known in which the question of its application was raised.

The Chilean Civil Code (1855) provides in Article 593 that: the adjacent sea to the distance of one marine league measured from the lowest tide line is territorial sea and part of the national domain; but the right of police for matters concerning the security of the country and the observance of the fiscal laws extends to a distance of four marine leagues measured in the same manner. On March 7, 1874, the English steamer *Tacna* sailed from Valparaiso and was wrecked the next day a little north of Pichidangui from seven to nine miles off the coast. In a proceeding brought against the master, Captain John Hyde, the crim-

[7] Signed by Argentina, Jan. 23, 1889; approved by Argentina, Law #3192, Dec. 11, 1894. *Actas y Trat. del Congreso Sud-Americano* (Buenos Aires, 1928), pp. 611–612, 877–890. *Leyes y Res. del Peru, 1888 y 1889*, Ed. Ofic. (Lima, 1891), pp. 266–272. *Comp. de Leyes y Decr. del Uruguay* (Montevideo, 1930), XVIII, 279–287. Martens, *Nouv. Rec. Gén. de Traités*, 2e Sér., XVIII, 432–441.
[8] Jan H. W. Verzijl, *Le Droit des Prises de la Grande Guerre* (Leyde, 1924), p. 274. *Rev. gén. de dr. int. pub.*, XXII (1915), doc. 180–181. Clunet, *J. dr. int.*, XLII (1915), 87–88, 234; *ibid.*, XLIII (1916), 370–371, 1448.
[9] Fishing and Hunting Regulations, Secretary of Agriculture, Sept. 18, 1907. *Reg. Nac. 1907* (Buenos Aires,

1915), III, Trim. 188–190. Thomas W. Fulton, *Sovereignty of the Seas* (Edinburgh and London, 1911), pp. 661–663.
[10] Elihu Root, *North Atlantic Coast Fisheries Arbitration* (Cambridge, 1917), p. xcviii. Philip C. Jessup, *Law of Territorial Waters* (New York, 1927), p. 379.
[11] Signed by Bolivia, Jan. 23, 1889; approved by Bolivia by Law of Nov. 17, 1903. See n. 7, *supra*.
[12] Philip C. Jessup, *Law of Territorial Waters* (New York, 1927), pp. 47, 63, 104.
[13] Note on Aug. 25, 1914. *British Year Book of Int. Law*, 1920–21, p. 131.

inal court at Valparaiso took jurisdiction; but on appeal the Supreme Court held [14] that the jurisdiction of the republic in criminal matters did not extend to waters from seven to nine miles distant from the coast, and accordingly the Valparaiso criminal court was incompetent in the case. On November 5, 1914,[15] Chile declared that the adjacent sea up to three marine miles from the line of lowest tides was considered as her jurisdictional sea for purposes of neutrality; and on December 15, 1914,[16] declared further that the interior waters of the Strait of Magellan and of the southern channels, even where more than three miles distant from either shore, were to be considered part of her territory and jurisdictional sea. On March 14, 1915, the Norwegian steamer *Bangor,* Captain Hansen, was captured by the British man of war *Bristol* about opposite Port Tamar anchorage in the middle of the Strait of Magellan where it is seven miles wide, put in charge of a prize crew, and taken to the Falkland Islands. To the objection of the owners that she was immune from capture because she was in the territorial waters of a neutral state, the British Prize Court said: "The assumption that the capture took place within the territorial waters of the Republic of Chile . . . of course, does not imply any expression of opinion on the character of the Strait of Magellan as between Chile and other nations. . . . There is a right of free passage through the strait for commercial purposes. It is not inconsistent with this . . . that during war between any nations entitled to use it for commerce the strait should be regarded, in whole or in part, as the territorial waters of Chile, whose lands bound it on both sides. . . . It is only by the neutral State concerned that the legal validity of the capture can be questioned." [17]

A Colombian decree of November 6, 1866,[18] declared that there belonged to national territory and was subject to its jurisdiction all the sea which bathed its coasts from the highest tides to a distance of one marine league from the coast; but wharves, dikes, landings, railways, etc., might be constructed, with the permission of the government. A law of January 31, 1923,[19] provided that, for the purposes of the laws relating to deposits of hydrocarbons and to fishing, there should be understood by territorial sea a zone of twelve nautical miles around the continental and insular domain of the republic.

The Ecuadorian Civil Code (1887) provides in Article 582 that the adjacent sea to the distance of one marine league, measured from the lowest tide line, is territorial sea and national domain; but the right of police for matters concerning the security of the nation and observance of the customs laws extends to the distance of four marine leagues measured in the same way. In a circular of the Ministry of Foreign Relations of November 19, 1914,[20] it was stated that Ecuador's territorial waters for purposes of neutrality were to be understood as determined by Article 582 of the Civil Code, up to four marine leagues (13.8 miles) of 5,555 meters each.

[14] Santiago, Apr. 21, 1874. Clunet, *J. dr. int. privé,* II (1875), 36–38.

[15] Decree #1857. *Bol. de las Leyes* (Santiago, 1914), LXXXIII, 1531–1532. Philip C. Jessup, *Law of Territorial Waters* (New York, 1927), pp. 47–48, 104–105.

[16] Decree #1996. *Bol. de las Leyes* (Santiago, 1914), LXXXIII, 1660–1661. *Amer. J. Int. Law,* XIV (1920), 32. *Rev. de Der. Int.* (Havana), XVI (1929), 185–187.

[17] *Law Journal Reports* (London, 1916), N.S. LXXXV, 218–220. Lloyd's *Prize Cases* (1919), V, 308–316. Naval War College, *Int. Law Situations,* 1931, pp. 56–57, 102–103. Fauchille et Basdevant, *Jurispr. Brit. en matière de Prises Maritimes* (Paris, 1927), II, 166–169.

[18] *Codif. Nac. de Colombia* (Bogotá, 1932), XXII, 601.

[19] Article 17, Law #14 of Jan. 31, 1923. *Leyes,* Ed. Ofic. (Bogotá, 1923), 138–145. *Rev. de Dr. Int. Privé* (Paris), XVIII (1923), 499.

[20] 108 *British and Foreign State Papers* 818–821. Philip C. Jessup, *Law of Territorial Waters* (New York, 1927), pp. 48, 91, 105.

Paraguay has adopted the Civil Code of Argentina as her own,[21] and Article 2340 [22] is therefore in effect, so far as applicable; but the republic has no sea coast, and although the rivers which form her boundaries open out into shallow lakes more than three miles wide in places, ownership and jurisdiction over them are matters to be settled with the nations on the opposite shores, and cannot involve questions with other nations as on the high seas. The Montevideo treaty concerning international penal law to which Paraguay was a party [23] provides in Article 12 that for the purposes of penal jurisdiction territorial waters include an extent of five miles from the coast of terra firma and the islands which form part of the territory of each state.

The Montevideo treaty concerning international penal law to which Peru was a party [24] provides in Article 12 that for the purposes of penal jurisdiction territorial waters include an extent of five miles from the coast of terra firma and the islands which form part of the territory of each state.

In her regulations for the observance of neutrality of August 7, 1914,[25] Uruguay decreed that, in accordance with the principle consecrated in Article 12 of the Treaty of Montevideo of January 23, 1889,[26] concerning international penal law and with the principles generally accepted in such matters, waters should be considered territorial to a distance of five miles from the coast of the mainland and islands, measured from the visible adjoining shoals and fixed beacons marking invisible shoals, and from a straight line at the point nearest the entrance across bays and places on the coast with the form of bays and an opening of not over ten miles. The British objected to recognizing jurisdiction for more than three miles from shore.[27] Uruguay claims as state property and capable of being granted by municipal concession [28] the seal fisheries [29] off the coasts of the departments of Maldonado and Rocha and the islands of Lobos, Castillos, Polonio, and Coronilla. On November 11, 1904,[30] the Canadian sealer *Agnes G. Donahoe* was captured about 500 meters (547 yards) from Marco island, with boats down taking seals; and the captain, Matthew Ryan, two mates, and sixteen crew were taken into Montevideo and tried for larceny or robbery and violation of the customs laws. The trial court on May 16, 1905, found them guilty, but on appeal the upper court on August 11, 1905, reversed the judgment as to larceny or robbery, on the ground that seals were wild animals, *res nullius,* not the subject of property until taken into possession, and so there had been no fraudulent deprivation of property of the concessionaire; but the conviction for customs violation was affirmed, as there were acts and intention to carry the skins taken in jurisdictional waters out of the country without paying the duty imposed by law. Captain Ryan was sentenced to ten months' imprisonment,

[21] Law of Aug. 19, 1876; *Reg. Ofic. del Paraguay*, 1876–1885 (Asunción, 1887), p. 122. Law of July 27, 1889; *ibid.*, 1889 (Asunción, 1896), pp. 89–90.

[22] See n. 6, *supra.*

[23] Signed by Paraguay, Jan. 23, 1889, approved by Paraguay by Law of Sept. 3, 1889. See n. 7, *supra.*

[24] Signed by Peru, Jan. 23, 1889, approved by Peru by Law of Nov. 4, 1889. See n. 7, *supra.*

[25] *Registro Nacional de Leyes del Uruguay*, 1914 (Montevideo, 1915), pp. 392–395, 408, 540–541. 108 *British and Foreign State Papers* 856–858. Philip C. Jessup, *Law of Territorial Waters* (New York, 1927), pp. 48–49, 362. Naval War College, *Int. Law Topics*, 1916, pp. 106–109.

[26] Signed by Uruguay, Jan. 23, 1889, approved by Uruguay by Law #2207 of Oct. 3, 1892. See n. 7, *supra.*

[27] Jan H. W. Verzijl, *Le Droit de Prises de la Grande Guerre* (Leyde, 1924), p. 274.

[28] Uruguayan Laws of July 11, 1895, July 20, 1900, and Dec. 12, 1906; *Col. Leg. del Uruguay*, XVIII (1896), 194–197; *ibid.*, XXIII (1901), 360–361; *ibid.*, XXIX (1907), 819–821.

[29] See chap. I, §5, *supra.*

[30] *Rev. de Der. Juris. y Admin.* (Montevideo, 1905), Año XI, 299–301; Año XII, 13–16, 23–24.

and the seizure of the ship and cargo was confirmed. Later, on protests by the British government, the vessel is said [31] to have been released.

The Civil Code of Venezuela (1922) contains no express mention of the extent of sea coast claimed as national domain, only providing (Article 517) that lakes and rivers belong to the public domain, except that the bed of non-navigable rivers belong to the riparian proprietors according to a line supposed to be drawn down the middle of the watercourse, and (Article 520) that all lands within the territorial limits which have no other owner belong to the private domain of the nation, if within the federal territory or district, of the states if within them. Thus the extent of Venezuela's claim to the marginal sea is left to be stated as occasion may arise.

[31] Thomas W. Fulton, *Sovereignty of the Sea* (Edinburgh and London, 1911), p. 663. Philip C. Jessup, *Law of Territorial Waters* (New York, 1927), p. 48.

INDEX

INDEX